T0319024

TRANSPORT ECONOMICS

TRANSPORT ECONOMICS
Selected Readings

Edited by

Tae Hoon Oum
John S. Dodgson
David A. Hensher
Steven A. Morrison
Christopher A. Nash
Kenneth A. Small
W.G. Waters II

 Routledge
Taylor & Francis Group

LONDON AND NEW YORK

First Published 1997
by Harwood Academic Publishers.
Reprinted 2004
by Routledge,
2 Park Square, Milton Park, Abingdon, Oxon, OX14 4RN

Transferred to Digital Printing 2004

Copyright © 1997 OPA (Overseas Publishers Association) Amsterdam B.V.
Published in The Netherlands by Harwood Academic Publishers.

British Library Cataloguing in Publication Data
A catalogue record for this book is available from the British Library.

ISBN 90-5702-186-2

TABLE OF CONTENTS

v

Notes on the Editors

Tae Hoon Oum is Van Dusen Foundation Professor of Transport Economics at the University of British Columbia. His research has focused on regulatory and industry policy, demand modelling, cost and productivity analysis, pricing and infrastructure issues in the transportation and telecommunications industries. Recently, he has researched extensively on public policy and corporate strategy in the air transport industry. He has advised various government agencies and major corporations in Canada, the US, Europe and Asia.

John S. Dodgson is Reader in Economics at the University of Liverpool. He specialises in transport economics, and has particular interests in deregulation and privatization of air bus and rail services, railways policy, competition policy and the global warming implications of the transport sector.

David A. Hensher is Professor of Management, and Director of the Institute of Transport Studies: A Commonwealth Key Centre of Teaching and Research in Transport Management in the Graduate School of Business at the University of Sydney. David is President of the International Association of Travel Behaviour Research and Chair of the Local Scientific Committee of the 7th World Conference of Transport Research.

Steven A. Morrison is a Professor of Economics at Northeastern University. He has also held positions at the University of British Columbia, the London School of Economics, the Brookings Institution and MIT. His work focuses on the economics of the airline industry. Morrison earned a BA in economics from the University of Florida and a Ph.D. in economics from the University of California, Berkeley.

Christopher A. Nash is Professor of Transport Economics and Director of the Institute for Transport Studies, University of Leeds, UK. He has researched extensively on various topics in rail transport including privatization of rail systems in Europe and cost-benefit analysis. He has advised various UK and European government agencies including the Transport Committee of the House of Commons and the House of Lords Select Committee on European Affairs. He is Joint Editor of the *Journal of Transport Economics and Policy*.

Kenneth A. Small, Professor of Economics at the University of California at Irvine, is the author of *Urban Transportation Economics*, coauthor of *Road Work*, and co-editor of the journal *Urban Studies*. He has advised governmental organizations in the US, Canada and the European Union, and has served his university as Chair of Economics and Associate Dean of Social Sciences.

W.G. Waters II is an Associate Professor of Transportation and Logistics, in the Faculty of Commerce and Business Administration, the University of British Columbia in Vancouver. He is also the Editor of the *Logistics and Transportation Review* published there. He has been a teacher or visiting scholar at the Universities of Oxford, Sydney, Tasmania and Wisconsin.

PREFACE

This book came about because of a desire to collect a set of readings which convey clearly the fundamental concepts, theory and methodologies essential for the study of transport economics. Most of the transport economics textbooks in the market differ in their coverage and emphasis. Therefore, most instructors supplement or replace textbooks with readings on specific topics. The purpose of this book is to publish a selected set of readings in one volume which will appeal to many teachers and students in transport economics courses as well as to transport researchers and policy makers who wish to learn about formal treatment of their topics of interest.

Since there are significant variations among instructors in the way transport economics is taught, it was necessary for the seven editors (and teachers) to pool their efforts to decide on the topics to be included. Our hope is that the resulting articles will appeal to a variety of instructors who, inevitably, will have some different points they wish to emphasize. The collection was more of a challenge than we expected: it took seven iterations for the editors to decide on the final list of papers. An important constraint was the total size of the volume; many excellent articles had to be deleted. Although every instructor of transport economics courses is likely to be disappointed at some omissions, we hope this volume will contribute to efficient teaching and learning of transport economics.

We emphasize that this is not a collection of 'classic' articles on the subject. The articles were selected by the editors because they are useful in teaching various aspects of transport economics. Some articles are fairly basic; others are more challenging. Even the more technical articles generally provide an overview of the subject they address. The articles include economic concepts and principles, analytical and empirical methods, empirical studies, and some recent public policy developments.

The editors thank one another for their patience in wrangling over which articles to include, and we are grateful for the suggestions advanced by others whom we contacted. Of course, we must thank the generations of students who have read and provided feedback on the usefulness of many of these articles. Six of the co-editors especially thank Tae Oum who provided the leadership and decisiveness necessary to bring closure to the selections. Finally, we are indebted to Dr Yangho Cho, Chairman & CEO of the Korea Research Foundation for the 21st Century for the financial support for this project, and Harwood Academic Publishers for publishing this volume. We hope they share our enthusiasm for the end result.

Tae Hoon Oum,
John S. Dodgson,
David A. Hensher,
Steven A. Morrison,
Christopher A. Nash,
Kenneth A. Small,
W.G. Waters II

INTRODUCTION

Tae Hoon Oum, John S. Dodgson, David A. Hensher,
Steven A. Morrison, Christopher A. Nash,
Kenneth A. Small and W.G. Waters II

This volume came about because of our desire to collect a set of readings which convey clearly the basic concepts, theory and methodologies essential for the study of transport economics. In selecting the papers we paid particular attention to ease of reading and the effectiveness of the article as a teaching tool. The papers are also chosen carefully to cover most of the core dimensions in transport economics and to include a collection of methodological, empirical and applied policy analysis papers on each topic. Therefore, this volume is ideal to adopt as a textbook for a transport economics course where the instructor would wish to provide pertinent references to supplement his or her own lecture notes. The volume is also organized so that researchers, practitioners and policy analysts who have not taken a transport economics course can teach themselves about the subject.

The volume is organized into six parts:

    I.   Transport Demand and Forecasting
    II. Transport Costs and Cost Analysis
   III. Pricing of Transport Services
   IV. Infrastructure Pricing and Investment
    V. Market Structure, Regulation and Deregulation
   VI. Project Evaluation

Transport Demand and Forecasting

Except for joy rides and cruises, the demand for transport is a derived demand: goods and people move not for the sake of travelling, but because of an increase in value which can be obtained by relocating in space. The study of transport demand forms a basic input for formulating management strategies, policy analysis and project planning and evaluation. The demand section must cover (1) the overall framework for demand forecasting; (2) demand and choice modelling which allows one to identify the variables which affect demand and the user's choice; and (3) estimates of how responsive user choices are to changes in these variables.

Meyer and Straszheim (1971) provide a concise introduction to the demand forecasting framework for urban transportation. They present the four traditional stages of demand forecasting: generation (forecasts of total trips); distribution (predicting patterns of trips among origins and destinations); mode split (choice of travel mode); and route assignment (specific routes used). With the inclusion of feedbacks and linkages between the components, this basic framework persists to this day and has been applied to inter-city and international transport demand studies as well. However, Small (1992) illustrates the importance of recognizing other aspects of behaviour in studying urban transport demands. The traditional sequential urban forecasting models are limited in their ability to represent the complexity of individuals' travel decisions. Urban trips often reflect complex scheduling of activities and multiple trip purposes. This points the way for future investigations of transport demands in many transport markets.

Oum, Waters and Yong (1992) explain different concepts of price elasticities of demand for transport, summarize empirical estimates, and review a number of the problems encountered in measuring price elasticities. This article emphasizes price as an influence on transport demands. In many transport markets price is not as important as quality of service variables such as travel time, frequency of service, on-time performance, comfort and safety. These influences on transport demand can be studied analogously to measuring responsiveness to price. In Part VI Hensher (1989) reports on the value people place on saving time in making travel decisions, and how this is relevant for evaluation of transport infrastructure investment.

Studies of transport demand often focus on the choice of mode rather than volume of traffic for a given mode. McFadden (1978) explains the theory and practice of these disaggregate choice models. For example, observing people's choices between automobiles and public transit, in relation to differences in their costs, travel times and other variables can be used to predict the probability of choosing a mode as its service characteristics are changed. In recent years, researchers have relied more on questionnaire data for estimating mode choice models. Hensher (1994) explains step-by-step the methodology of these 'stated preference' methods, and provides an up-to-date survey of applications.

Transportation Costs and Cost Analysis

The analysis of costs is a major theme in transport economics. There are several reasons for the focus on costs: (1) to examine how costs change as output expands or contracts (i.e., the absence or extent of economies of scale); (2) to examine how costs change as the mix of outputs change (i.e., absence or extent of economies of scope); and (3) to measure the costs of specific traffic or outputs in multiproduct transport firms.

The presence of economies of scale means that unit costs decline as firms grow. Such industries are prone to monopoly because of the inherent advantages of size in such markets. Where competition is attempted, it might be 'destructive' because firms could reduce prices to cover only marginal costs to drive out rivals while weakening themselves in the process (referred to as the 'empty core' problem in recent literature). Thus if economies of scale are important, government ownership or regulation may be required. This was a rationale for government controls over the railroad, telecommunications and electrical power industries for many decades. The presence of economies of scope means that the cost of producing multiple products by a single firm (for example, both scheduled and charter passenger services) is less than the total cost of producing each product separately by different firms. The first paper by Keeler (1983) provides an overview of economies of scale and economies of scope and their implications for multiproduct industries. An important distinction to make is between economies of scale (increasing returns when all inputs are increased) and economies of density. The latter refer to reductions in average costs due to the more intense use of a given route network. The implications for market structure (monopoly versus competition) and public policy are quite different, as explained by Keeler. It is now widely accepted that scale economies in the conventional sense are not a significant factor in most transportation industries, whereas economies of density are important. Caves, Christensen and Tretheway (CCT, 1984) show that the lower average costs of large airlines was not explained by their larger size per se (scale), but by the nature of the markets served which make economies of density very important. The CCT paper is also useful because it uses a translog cost function, the most widely used form of so-called 'flexible' functions which are capable of providing a second-order approximation to an unknown function.

Another emphasis on costs concerns the difficulty of measuring the costs of specific traffic carried. Transportation enterprises typically supply an immense number of different markets using shared facilities and operations. It is difficult and may be impossible to identify specific portions of total shared costs with specific outputs provided. But if we are unable to measure marginal and average costs accurately, firms or public policy makers cannot make use of the tools of economics. Hence the transport economics literature has emphasized procedures and tools for improved cost measurement. The article by Waters (1976) provides an overview of the use of statistical analysis to help understand the relationship between costs and different output categories. The paper by Beesley and Kettle (1986) illustrates the steps necessary to identify the costs of different activities and how these are crucial for improving planning and decision-making in a transportation enterprise. Later in Part III (Pricing of Transport Services), Baumol, *et al.* (1962) and Glaister and Lewis (1978) emphasize the importance of identifying the costs of specific services for setting prices and making output decisions.

Pricing of Transport Services

The knowledge of demand and cost is used for pricing transport services. Although transport economists often focus on optimal pricing from society's point of view and how unregulated equilibrium prices compare with the socially optimal prices, the knowledge gained here can also be used to investigate firm's profit maximizing prices.

Although it was written during the regulated era, Baumol *et al.*'s (1962) discussion of the role of costs in the pricing of rail services remains a very clear exposition of the importance of being guided by marginal cost principles. Baumol and Bradford (1970) provide a succinct analytical and geometric treatment of optimal departures from marginal cost pricing in four alternative versions for easy understanding and application.

The excellent paper by Glaister and Lewis (1978) shows the theory and framework for optimal pricing of urban transport in a multimodal context: bus, rail and private cars in London, both peak and off-peak. In particular, it considers the second-best situation where prices cannot be set equal to marginal costs for car users because of the absence of road congestion charging (see Newbery's paper below). Turvey and Mohring (1975) provide a concise and very thought-provoking treatment of optimal bus fares when travellers' waiting time is taken into consideration, and shows how it affects marginal cost pricing guidelines.

Finally, Oum, Zhang and Zhang (1993) show how to measure and test a firm's pricing conduct in oligopoly airline markets, and apply the methodology to American Airlines—United Airlines duopoly markets in order to measure price elasticities faced by each firm.

Infrastructure Pricing and Investment

Transport infrastructure is a major component of social overhead capital and plays an important role in economic development, especially for less developed countries. In the advanced and industrialized economies it is important for the government to make sure that transport infrastructure is optimally placed and priced in order to maximize the efficiency of transport industries and other sectors of its economy.

Newbery (1990) presents the economic principles relevant to road pricing including the effect of congestion externalities. This paper therefore considers the first-best pricing solution, and sets out the standard graphical analysis of road congestion charging. Small and Gomez-Ibanez (1995) review road pricing cases covering a wide range of sites, objectives and details of implementation. The cases reviewed include Singapore's area license scheme, Hong Kong's experiment with electronic road pricing technology, a proposed congestion charging scheme in Cambridge, England, urban toll rings operating in Norway and planned for Stockholm, the weekend peak spreading on an expressway in Northern France, time-of-day pricing on private toll lanes in California, and various proposals for the Randstad in The Netherlands and for

Greater London.

Winston (1991) gives an excellent summary of his work with Steven Morrison on airport infrastructure, and his work with Kenneth Small on highway durability and pricing. He reports the cost savings anticipated under the efficient investment and pricing of airport and road infrastructure. Keeler and Small (1977) construct a peak-load pricing model for highways, estimate a highway capacity cost function, estimate the tradeoff between travel time and capacity utilization, and calculate the optimal long run tolls for San Francisco Bay Area Freeway services.

Market Structure, Regulation and Deregulation

Drawing on the concepts of economies of scale, density and scope covered in Part II, this part presents papers on market structure, regulation and deregulation of several transport industries.

Douglas and Miller (1974) is a classical paper showing how price and entry regulation distorts market equilibrium in quality attributes and thus introduces inefficiency. It does so by creating a vicious cycle of artificially high prices, excess quality competition and consequent financial losses due to increased costs. Although this paper analyzes and measures the cost of economic regulation of the US airlines as it existed until 1978, it has spurred applications to many other regulated sectors.

The concept of contestable markets had an important influence on transport deregulation. Morrison and Winston (1987) develop a way to test the contestability hypothesis and apply it to measure the extent of contestability in the deregulated airline markets in the US. They do this by comparing actual welfare on airline routes with the optimal welfare on the route which would result from perfect contestability. Borenstein (1992) provides a valuable account of US airline deregulation and what happened in the industry as a result, including the failure of many low cost entrants, the mergers between carriers and the development of strategic entry barriers.

Competition policy has been a relevant issue in many deregulated transport markets. Dodgson, Katsoulacos and Newton (1993) consider the issue of allegations of predatory behaviour which have been made in deregulated British bus markets. They use an economic modelling approach to analyze the competition which occurred in the town of Inverness to see whether the actions of the two competing firms indicate whether either was involved in predation. Nash and Preston (1995) describe the recent effort to introduce competition into the railway industry in Britain and other parts of Europe and attempt to analyze its impacts on rail business. Chow (1995) describes the regulatory changes in trucking in the US, Canada and Mexico, and summarizes the effects of deregulation.

Project Evaluation

Transport is among the first fields in which cost-benefit analysis (CBA) came into regular application as a part of government decision making. The papers in this section illustrate its range of applicability.

Nash (1993) describes the basic methods and the value of cost-benefit analysis of transport projects. He also provides a critique of British Department of Transport practice of CBA as well as presenting alternative approaches to project appraisal, including objectives-based and multicriteria techniques. Hensher (1989) provides a comprehensive review of the literature and empirical estimates of the values of travel time savings, the major user benefit in transport project evaluation. Kay, Manning and Szymanski (1989) report on their study for estimating the potential profitability and overall social benefits of the Channel Tunnel project between Britain and France. This study is particularly interesting in the way it uses a game theoretic approach to determine the equilibrium prices (which in turn determine usage of the Tunnel and both financial and social rates of return) in the competitive cross-Channel market where the Tunnel with its high sunk costs faces competition from the ferry services.

PART I

TRANSPORT DEMAND
AND FORECASTING

CHAPTER 1

TRANSPORT DEMAND: THE BASIC FRAMEWORK*

John R. Meyer** and Mahlon R. Straszheim[†]

In a market economy, transportation demand presumably arises as a result of utility or profit maximization decisions by households and firms. Consumption of transportation services also tends to be highly complementary to the use of other commodities. The demand for transportation is therefore commonly labeled "a derived demand," in the sense that transport is not normally demanded for itself but as a derivative of buying or seeking some other service or commodity.

Early efforts to estimate transport demand relationships have been in large part what an economist would call neoclassic, Marshallian, and single equation in orientation: origins or flows of transportation demands are determined by relating output to price, income, and other variables. In practice, this approach has tended to conceal many of the important structural dimensions of trip makers' behavior. An alternative, multiple-equation format that attempts a more accurate representation of the underlying structure has therefore evolved slowly over time. This approach customarily begins with land-use or spatial-location characteristics and derives trip demands and trip destinations and then follows this with an assignment or allocation of these trips to a network. The

---

 * Reprinted from *Techniques of Transport Planning*: Vol. I (Pricing and Project Evaluation), Brookings Institution, Ch. 7, pp. 99-109.
 **Harvard University.
 †University of Maryland.

*Figure 1. Schematic Model for Forecasting Passenger and
Freight Transportation Demand*

Passenger

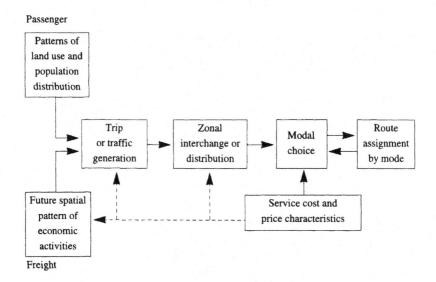

Freight

procedure is portrayed schematically in the flow chart of Figure 7-1. Such multiequation systems are well suited to modeling the spatial location and macroeconomic determinants of travel. They are also especially useful for representing trip demands over complex networks with many substitute destinations, modes, and routings, as in urban areas.

A basic determinant of transport demand is obviously location choice. However, location theory for households and firms is not well developed empirically. The location facing a firm is complex, involving evaluation of the cost of various inputs (in delivered prices) and the location of markets in which the firm sells. Classical location theory has concerned itself with the spatial location of input and product markets and cost minimization problems.[1] Generally, this abstraction provides little

---

1. For a discussion and bibliography of this literature, see Walter Isard (1960) and Edgar M.Hoover (1948). The classic location problem formulated by Alfred Weber (1929) illustrates the nature of much of this literature. The problem is to locate a factory selling its product in one city, produced by two inputs bought in two other cities, so as to minimize transport costs. William Alonso (1967) has recently discussed this problem, indicating the difficulties of finding an analytic solution.

that is empirically useful in forecasting location choices.

The interrelationship between location choices and transport demands, especially the location or land-use feedbacks over time arising from transport system performance, might be modeled, for example, by using a large-scale behavioral simulation model. The simpler demand estimation procedures described in this volume are first approximations at best.

As will be seen in the review in succeeding chapters of specific attempts to model transport demands, many unsettled questions remain. In particular, too little empirical information exists about the influence on demand of price, scheduling, and service characteristics.[2]

In the remainder of this chapter, the general structure of transport forecasting procedures will be discussed. Succeeding chapters will consider particular forecasting methods as applied to urban and interurban passenger and freight demands, with substantial emphasis on the statistical methodology appropriate in view of the sample date normally available. Considerable attention is also given to developing those generalizations about transport choices that seem most justifiable in light of the limited evidence available.

Land-Use or Economic Location Patterns

All transport demand forecasts must begin with some knowledge of the geographic or spatial distribution of economic activities. This entails analyzing the present and the potential economy of the area affected by the proposed development, given the transportation system that serves it.

---

2. The modeling of a transport system in Volume 2 of this study includes a demand model for shipment that shows a subjective weighting scheme which reflects these sorts of considerations. A measure of the transport service offered by a single transport link is represented as a linear combination of a set of performance factors, p_i and the corresponding valuation v_i, assigned to each factor by the shipper. Each element in the performance vector corresponds to the quantity of a particular attribute experienced as a result of traveling over the link under consideration—transport charge, travel time, probability of loss, waiting time. The weights in the valuation vector are those of the shipper. The product of the two vectors gives a measure of overall link rating. The transport services chosen by a shipper are then estimated by finding the route through the network from point of origin to point of destination which minimizes this overall rating, using standard minimum path algorithms.

The basic spatial or location element in most passenger demand studies has been a land-use model of some sort. Essentially, land-use models are attempts to forecast the spatial distribution of people and their activities. The underlying behavioral assumption is that stable empirical relationships exist between patterns of land use and need or demands for transportation services. In urban transportation studies, the primary emphasis has been on estimating residential and work-place locations and the relationship between them. In intercity studies, by contrast, the focus is shifted slightly to the estimation of what makes people interact with one another. Thus, government and holiday centers are expected to interact with manufacturing cities or commercial centers in different ways than commercial centers are expected to interact with one another or with manufacturing cities.

To estimate the demand for freight transportation, the forecast of the future spatial pattern of economic activity is conventionally labeled an economic base study. These studies perform for freight transportation essentially the same function as land-use studies do in urban or intercity passenger forecasts: they provide a basis for predicting major needs for transport at specific geographic points. Ordinarily, an economic base study includes an appraisal of natural resources, the population and labor force, and the existing industry of the economy under consideration. It may also include some analysis of the social structure, attitudes, and incentives of the people involved. It attempts to identify those industries which are the primary users of transport facilities and to specify their present and potential future location and level of output.

To be satisfactory for long-range transport demand demand forecasting, the economic base study should also incorporate regional growth characteristics-to explain migrations of labor and capital among regions, changes in the composition of output, and so on. Satisfactory regional models, however, are not readily available.[3] Circumstances will govern the choice of an appropriate model. It will differ, for example, for underdeveloped and developed economies, and for imperfect or highly regulated and relatively free or competitive market economies. For a context of perfect markets, Borts and Stein have conducted by far the most comprehensive analysis of regional growth. They suggest that differences in growth rates are best explained by modeling the market's

---

3. For a survey of regional models in the literature, see John R. Meyer (1963), pp. 19-54.

response to regional differences in the rates of return on capital and labor, and the induced migrations in labor and capital that result.[4] There have been other empirical studies made of United States growth patterns, though the models implicit in the findings are not always obvious.[5] The task of modeling regional development is probably easier in simpler, less developed economies (though, again, little progress has been made to date). The crucial variables in these circumstances are probably the location of natural resources, entrepreneurship, and capital, and the accessibility of various areas.

Most location models or analyses focus on the decisions of producers, apparently on the premise that capital is usually more mobile than labor. Considerable differences exist among industries in their responsiveness to the availability of particular inputs, the costs of their transport, and the location of product markets. An interview study by the University of Michigan revealed, for example, that, in addition to purely economic considerations, many qualitative and subjective dimensions affect industrial location choices—personal ties of the management with its markets and financial sources or personal tastes for a region as a result of being raised and started in business there.[6] In a project context, ad hoc heuristic procedures and sampling and survey techniques are probably sufficient to yield a reasonable estimate of basic industrial locations. However, in large-scale planning (for example, an intercity road network to be built during the next several decades) a systematic model of regional growth, incorporating the feedbacks of the transport system on that growth, can be imperative.[7]

Trip Generation

To be useful for transport planning, estimates of the future location of population and industry must be converted into physical estimates of the transportation requirements generated and terminated at different points in geographic space. The conventional nomenclature for this exercise is

---

4. George H. Borts and Jerome L. Stein (1964): also George H. Borts (1964).
5. Daniel Creamer (1963); Harvey S. Perloff and others (1960); Victor R. Fuchs (1962).
6. Eva Mueller. Arnold Wilken, and Margaret Wood (1961).
7. The Northeast Corridor Project in the United States is one example. The second is the system study in volume 2.

"trip generation." In the case of passenger trip generation, the usual unit of analysis will be the household. The forecasting exercise will seek to estimate how many trips the members of the household will make to work, school, place of recreation, retailing establishments, and so forth. Roughly similar models, with only slight modification, are used to estimate passenger trip demands for business firms or other basic behavioral units. When forecasting freight, this means estimating how many tons of freight must be transported into a plant or area in order to manufacture certain commodities, and how much transport away from the area is required to remove these final goods or commodities from their production sites to their markets.

No attempt is usually made when modeling trip generation to derive or estimate the directional flow of the actual travel demands (see Figure 7-1). Rather, the emphasis is on the estimated travel requirements for specific points of the system. In essence, trip generation provides a picture of the origins and destinations of different trip and travel demands but not of the flows or interchanges between different points within the system.

Zonal Interchange or Distribution

Given the number of trips originating in and destined to each area, zonal interchange models provide a description or forecast of travel between areas. The most familiar technique used for this purpose is the gravity, or inverse impedance, model.

The gravity model is based on the premise that the volume of transport between two areas, i and j, depends directly on the number of tons of freight or passenger trips originating in i, needed at or destined for j, and is inversely related to the distance, elapsed time, cost, or some other measure of separation between i and j. The customary statement of models of this sort assumes that flows between regions i and j can be statistically represented by one or more attraction parameters, such as population or income levels, and impedance parameters representing costs or other such effects.[8] Interzonal trips are normally stratified by commodity

---

8. For an excellent summary of gravity models, see Walter Isard (1960), Chap. 11. The gravity model is of the form:

$$x_{ij} = \frac{f(P_i P_j)}{d_{ij}}$$

trips, trip purpose, land use, and other variables to obtain greater homogeneity and behavioral regularity.

Gravity models have a considerable history. In simplest form, they are used to represent pairs of zonal interchanges independently of each other.

Urban transportation planners, however, have developed techniques for simultaneously determining interchanges: the model is calibrated (parameterized) so that travel from any one node is affected by service to, and the attractions of, all other nodes. Such simultaneous determination is especially important in urban demand forecasting since the network is more complex and the options to travelers more numerous. This allows more substitution between alternative destinations and routings. Basically, the objective in urban application of interchange models has been to distribute a fixed set of trip requirements; internal consistency requires the inclusion of a variety of constraints in order that the demands and supplies of all nodes are met.

Another popular model for forecasting zonal interchanges is the intervening opportunity model. This model is based on the premise that total travel time from a point is minimized, subject to the condition that every destination point considered has a stated probability of being acceptable. The fundamental notion is that a trip is made to the closest acceptable location, regardless of time, distance, or cost. Acceptability is defined in a behavioral sense by varying the parameters of the model to achieve some sort of "best fit." The intervening opportunity model thus has considerable flexibility, much the same as the gravity model. Its use has generally been confined to urban transportation demand modeling, as will be described in Chapter 8.

A third approach to determining zonal interchanges is by linear pro-

---

where x_{ij} is travel between cities i and j, P is a measure of trip generation or activity level, for example, population, and d is distance of some representation of travel cost. The pioneers were John Q. Stewart (1948) and George K. Zipf (1946).

Usually function forms that can be transformed to linear equations are chosen to make estimation easy, though there is only mixed evidence as to whether the distance variable or a suitable proxy can be represented linearly. Income has often been used as a measure of trip attraction. Thus this form

$$x_{ij} = k \frac{y_i^{\alpha} y_j^{\beta}}{d_{ij}^{\gamma}}$$

where y is income and k, α, β, and γ are parameters has become popular in practical applications, linear in logs.

gramming. In this approach, though behavioral rationality is assumed, known, and sought, specifically, the zonal interchanges are distributed so as to minimize costs, subject to the constraints on system capacity.[9] Lack of data has often restricted the application of linear programming models. The model has important behavioral implications which may or may not be realistic. As one might suppose, it has proved to be most useful as an empirical description of behavior in fully competitive industries under conditions of spatial price equilibrium.[10]

Modal Choice

The choice of a particular mode and routing for meeting a transport demand between two points, as specified by the trip generation and zonal interchange forecast, requires an investigation of the basic economic and service characteristics of the available transportation modes and routes. Model choice introduces major considerations on the supply side of the transport market; that is, an assessment of the capacity, cost, and performance of the existing or proposed transport system. Shippers and travelers can be presumed to select that particular mode or combination of modes which will minimize total cost or maximize utility. Nevertheless, these choices may be difficult to model.

In particular, a mode may have higher directly assignable costs for

---

9. The mathematics of the linear programming can be stated quite simply. Flows between regions i and j are determined so that they minimize

$$\sum_{i=1}^{m} \sum_{j=1}^{m} C_{ij} F_{ij},$$

subject to the constraints;

$$\sum_{j=1}^{m} F_{ij} \leq S_i \qquad\qquad (i = 1,2,\ldots,n)$$

$$\sum_{i=1}^{m} F_{ij} \leq D_j \qquad\qquad (j = 1,2,\ldots,m)$$

$$\sum_{i=1}^{m} S_i = \sum_{j=1}^{m} D_j \qquad\qquad (F_{ij} \geq 0)$$

where S_i, is the supply of that subcommodity produced at node i, D_j is the demand for the subcommodity at node j, and C_{ij} is the cost of transporting the subcommodity from i to j. Finally F_{ij} is the flow.

10. See William W. Cooper and Alexander Henderson (1953), James M. Henderson (1958), and Frank L. Hitchcock (1941), pp. 224-33.

performing a transport service, but the savings on handling, packaging, inventory, and other distribution costs may more than compensate. Similar comments apply to choice of passenger modes; in any good analysis, time savings and comfort must be recognized as having value to the traveler choosing a particular mode.

The question of modal choice can be further complicated by the fact that services offered by each mode may in some instances be both complementary and competitive. This sort of complication is introduced by network topology. For example, a combination of modes may be needed in order to complete a trip between two given points. At the same time, modal interchange can introduce considerable costs. Consequently, the choice of mode by a shipper is not typically a simple choice of rail, truck, air, or water but is a complicated selection over a mix of possible modes, routes, and schedules. The choice is very much a function of the network and performance conditions that exist at any given time. Indeed, modal choice and routing are often considered problems to the solved simultaneously by the shipper. This simultaneity may exist, moreover, even if the freight shipper does not really determine routing directly. Thus, in many circumstances, shippers may be picking a bundle of services that produces a certain transport result without knowing how this bundle of services is created in terms of modes. Though institutional and regulatory constraints often retard multimodal shipment, there are more and more such shipments, and more entry into the freight forwarding business, which uses all modes.

Route Assignment

Closely allied to the problem of determining modal choice is that of making route assignments by mode. Route assignment essentially maps zonal interchanges for a particular mode. Assignment provides specific estimates of demand placed on different links within a rail, highway, waterway, or air transport system and thereby details modal utilization.

Assignment is also closely related to network specification and coding.[11] Since route assignment involves specifying the particular patterns

---

11. Coding is the process of describing link characteristics in a quantitative scheme suitable for analysis and quantitative manipulation.

of flow on each transport system or mode, each modal network must be described in considerable detail, that is, in all of its relevant linkages. Once a description of interzonal travel and modal choices has been outlined, the assignment problem is that of allocating trips to the coded network.

Most assignment programs use some kind of minimum path algorithm. When a network is being modeled, there may be a large number of alternative paths that can be used for each interzonal trip, even within a specified mode. Minimum path algorithms select the shortest route (least time, distance, or cost) for each trip.

If link capacities were infinite, the assignment problem would be relatively simple and, in fact, largely irrelevant. However, as flows on a transportation network change, the cost-performance characteristics on the network also change. This is most evident on urban facilities during rush hours. But performance characteristics of freight and intercity passenger transport networks also react to changes in flow. Real world users adapt their behavior to local capacity shortages. If a shorter, faster route becomes congested (and thereby slower), users will shift to a less congested and formerly slower alternative. The result is a complex equilibrating process of travel demands, travel speeds, and link volumes. Analysts have found the description of this equilibrating behavior difficult but often essential.

The response of shippers to capacity-performance relationships on the system may be confined to shifts in routes within a single mode, but it may include changes among modes as well. This response, of course, suggests simultaneity between modal choice and route assignment decisions. In some cases, therefore, much can be said for performing the modal choice and route assignment simultaneously, for example, by using mathematical programming techniques. An adequate simultaneous formulation can, however, sometimes be difficult. Recognition must be made of the cost of transferring from one mode to another so as to avoid an unrealistically large number of intermodal transfers. Similarly, the underlying linearity (that is constant cost) assumptions of conventional linear programming formats may also be questionable in a multimodal context since the cost-performance relationship of many facilities appears to be nonlinear. Proliferation of the network, and therefore of the number of possible linkages, can also greatly expand the computational burden of solving programming problems. These difficulties need not necessarily be insurmountable, however, so long as large electronic computers are available.

Summary

The demand forecasting procedure outlined in this chapter is essentially sequential. In particular, zonal interchanges are estimated before modal choices, After the modal choices have been identified, route assignments to specific modal networks or systems are made. Such organization adheres closely to conventional practice.

This procedure, however, clearly abstracts from much simultaneity or behavioral feedbacks observed in reality. For example, the performance of a transport system will affect modal choice and routing. It should also have some effect on how many trips are made and to what destination. Ultimately, too, transport system performance should affect location or land use, with firms' and households' choices responsive in some degree to the system performance.

Thus, while the flow chart portrayed in Figure 7-1 has some intuitive appeal, the rationale for this particular demand model, a recursive structure, is not compelling. Much of its popularity lies in the advantages it affords in conceptualizing and programming for the computer. As with any recursive model used as an approximation to a system with important simultaneous relationships, it will probably yield only rough approximations on initial application. Improvement can be expected in the quality of the forecasts if repeated loops, or iterations of the analysis, are used, both to improve the internal consistency and accuracy of the traffic forecasting and flows and to simulate better the reaction of the future economy to possible (hypothetical) changes in the transportation system.

To the extent the resources permit, a particular improvement in the quality of the demand forecast might be achieved if, after one iteration, the land-use or economic base studies were reassessed and the whole process repeated. Unfortunately, this feedback, though often discussed, is seldom incorporated into transportation demand analyses. Indeed, the greatest failure of individual project evaluation techniques is typically that these macroeconomic or location feedbacks or loops are rarely analyzed in depth. Even in many purported systems analyses, the transportation land-use feedback is not one of the system effects well treated.

One fascinating aspect of the development of transport demand models is the extent to which similar methods are increasingly being employed for estimating different types of transportation requirements. The underlying logical flow of the procedures used for estimating intercity freight and passenger transportation needs is becoming more and more akin to that employed (and usually pioneered) in urban passenger demand studies. The only major differences tend to be in the underlying economic analyses: passenger models are concerned, quite naturally, with land-use and population migration patterns while freight models are almost invariably founded on some kind of economic base study. These differences, of course, merely reflect the fact that passenger and freight systems serve different needs. A question still to be answered is whether this emerging consensus on technique provides a sufficient basis for adequate project evaluation.

References

Alonso, William. "A Reformulation of Classical Location Theory and Its Relation to Rent Theory," in Morgan D. Thomas, ed., *Papers, The St. Louis Meeting, November, 1966*, Vol. 19, Regional Science Association, 1967.

Borts, George H. "A Theory of Long-Run International Capital Movements," *Journal of Political Economy*, Vol. 72 (August 1964).

Borts, George H., and Jerome L. Stein. *Economic Growth in a Free Market*. New York: Columbia University Press, 1964.

Charnes, Abraham, *Introduction to Linear Programming*, Part 2: *Lectures on the Mathematical Theory of Linear Programming*, New York, Wiley, 1953.

Cooper, William W., and Alexander Henderson. *Introduction to Linear Programming*, Part 1: *An Economic Introduction to Linear Programming*. New York: Wiley, 1953.

Creamer, Daniel. *Changing Location of Manufacturing Employment*, Pt. 1: *Changes by Type of Location, 1947-1961*. New York: National Industrial Conference Board, 1963.

Fuchs, Victor R. *Changes in the Location of Manufacturing in the United States since 1929*. New Haven: Yale University Press, 1962.

Henderson, James M. *The Efficiency of the Coal Industry: An Application of Linear Programming.* Cambridge: Harvard University Press, 1958.

Hitchcock, Frank L. "The Distribution of a Product from Several Sources to Numerous Localities," *Journal of Mathematics and Physics*, Vol. 20 (1941).

Hoover, Edgar M. *The Location of Economic Activity.* New York: McGraw-Hill, 1948.

Isard, Walter. *Location and Space-Economy; A General Theory Relating to Industrial Location, Market Areas, Land Use, Trade, and Urban Structure.* Cambridge: M.I.T. Press, 1956.

Isard, Walter. *Methods of Regional Analysis: An Introduction to Regional Science.* Cambridge: M.I.T. Press, 1960.

Meyer, John R. "Regional Economics: A Survey," *American Economic Review*, Vol. 53 (March 1963).

Mueller, Eva, Arnold Wilken, and Margaret Wood. *Location Decisions and Industrial Mobility in Michigan, 1961.* Ann Arbor: University of Michigan, Survey Research Center, 1961.

Perloff, Harvey S., Edgar S. Dunn, Jr., Eric E. Lampard, and Richard F. Muth. *Regions, Resources, and Economic Growth.* Baltimore: Johns Hopkins Press for Resources for the Future, 1960.

Stewart, John Q. "Demographic Gravitation: Evidence and Applications," *Sociometry*, Vol. 2 (February and May 1948).

Weber, Alfred. *Theory of the Location of Industries.* Chicago: University of Chicago Press, 1929.

Zipf, George K. "The P_1P_2/D Hypothesis: On the Intercity Movement of Persons," *American Sociological Review*, Vol. 11 (December 1946).

CHAPTER 2

CONCEPTS OF PRICE ELASTICITIES OF TRANSPORT DEMAND AND RECENT EMPIRICAL ESTIMATES* AN INTERPRETATIVE SURVEY

Tae Hoon Oum, W.G. Waters II and Jong-Say Yong**

I. Introduction

The past two decades have seen several refinements to the theory and empirical estimation of transport demand. Among major developments are the advancements in discrete choice modelling and the associated computational algorithms, the increasing popularity of flexible functional forms, and a better linkage between empirical demand models and the theory of consumer or firm behaviour. In recognition of these and other advances in transport demand research, this paper surveys the major

*Reprinted with the permission of *Journal of Transport Economics and Policy*, Vol. XXVI, No. 2 (May, 1992), 139-154 and 164-169.

**University of British Columbia. Tae Hoon Oum and W.G. Waters II are in the Faculty of Commerce and Business Administration, and Jong-Say Yong is a Ph.D. student in the Department of Economics. The authors gratefully acknowledge the financial support of the World Bank for their earlier research on this topic. Tae H. Oum gratefully acknowledges the research grant support from the Social Science and Humanities Research Council of Canada (SSHRC).

empirical studies of own-price elasticities of demand for transport that emerged in the last ten years or so. In the process, various concepts of and linkages between demand elasticities are outlined. Some shortcomings of existing empirical studies are also discussed.

The literature review began with the collection of articles from economics journals in Waters (1984, 1989), supplemented by a search of most major journals in transport. With emphasis on recent studies, we concentrated on studies which appeared in the 1970s and 1980s. Our emphasis on journal articles meant we generally excluded empirical studies appearing in books and technical reports. In view of the vast literature related to transport demand, some omissions are inevitable. Nonetheless, the articles reviewed should provide an adequate sample for reviewing the concepts and methods of estimating transport demand elasticities.[1]

The plan of this paper is as follows. The next section acknowledges some previous survey articles concerning the demand for transport. Section 3 discusses various concepts of elasticities used in empirical demand studies, and Section 4 reviews the results of many recent empirical studies. Our observations on common shortcomings of existing studies and priorities for future research appear in Section 5. Some concluding remarks follow in Section 6.

II. Previous Surveys of Transport Demand

There is an extensive literature on the characteristics of and factors affecting transport demand, but few reviews have concentrated on empirical estimates of transport demand elasticities. Authors of specific demand studies often discuss previous empirical estimates (for example, Frankena, 1978), but these reviews are incidental rather than the primary purpose of their papers. Wilson (1980) attempted to identify "typical" values of freight transport demand elasticities. He discussed various ways of deriving freight transport demand elasticities from the elasticities of individual commodities, and included a list of elasticity estimates

---

1. An earlier review of demand studies covering all modes of transport was compiled as a World Bank Working Paper (Oum, Waters and Yong, 1990). The present paper is based on a subset of those studies and includes some references not in the working paper.

of freight transport demand for 127 commodities compiled by the United States Interstate Commerce Commission.

Other recent surveys of the demand for freight transport include Winston (1983) and Zlatoper and Austrian (1989). Both these surveys place major emphasis on methodological issues. Winston provides an overview of various models of freight transport demand and discusses various applications of these models. The emphasis is on the theoretical foundations of these models, although many econometric issues are also discussed. The paper by Zlatoper and Austrian contains detailed discussion of more than a dozen econometric studies on freight transport demand published since the mid-1979s. It describes the variables, data sources and estimation procedures of these studies as well as their empirical results.

More recently, Goodwin (1991) summarizes studies which report empirical estimates of elasticities of demand for car and public transport. Interestingly, there are few studies which overlap between his paper and this survey. The main reason for the difference is that Goodwin's survey includes a number of government and consulting reports, conference and working papers, as well as papers published in academic and professional journals. We concentrate on studies published in academic journals. Further, Goodwin's survey is confined to the demand for car and public transport while we include both passenger and freight, and other modes of transport. Our wide coverage made searching for unpublished studies and technical reports a time-consuming and costly venture which is beyond our resources. Goodwin's survey is a valuable complement to our review since he uses a larger sample and is able to discuss demand elasticities of car and public transport in greater detail.

This review summarizes empirical results from both passenger and freight demand studies. We pay particular attention to the methodological issues behind these empirical results. We discuss theoretical considerations and review a rich array of empirical estimates of transport demand elasticities. Our reliance on refereed journals serves as a screen to help to ensure that studies are methodologically sound. Further, academic journals are also the expected outlet for methodological advances. We must, however, admit that this review is more narrowly focused than many discussions of transport demand since we concentrate solely on the *own-price* elasticities of demand for transport. In many markets, particularly for higher valued freight and passenger travel, quality variables may be more important than price. Indeed, the thriving air, motor freight and container markets are testimony to the importance of service quality relative to price. This review has not looked into these "quality elasticities," but this is in no way suggesting that they are unimportant.

III. Concepts of Elasticities

A price elasticity of demand measures the responsiveness of demand to a change in price. Within this general notion are a number of different concepts which are important for understanding transport demand elasticities. These concepts are discussed below and the linkages between them are summarized at the end of this section.

1. Ordinary and Compensated Demand Elasticities

The ordinary or Marshallian demand is derived by maximising a representative consumer's utility function subject to a budget constraint. Formally, the ordinary demand is

$$d\,(p,y,s,\varepsilon) = \underset{x}{\text{Argmax}}\ [U\,(x,s,\varepsilon)\ \text{s.t.}\ x \in B\,(p,y)], \qquad (1)$$

where x is a vector of goods and services, s is a vector of observed socio-economic characteristics of the consumer, ε is a vector of unobserved variables and $B\,(p,y)$ is the consumer's budget constraint, which is a function of prices (p) and income (y).[2]

The compensated or Hicksian demand, on the other hand, is derived by minimizing the consumer's expenditure for achieving a given utility level. Formally, the compensated demand is

$$h\,(p,u,s,\varepsilon) = \underset{x}{\text{Argmax}}\ [px\ \text{s.t.}\ U(x,s,\varepsilon) \geq u]. \qquad (2)$$

The price elasticity derived from each type of demand is sometimes

---

2. Alternatively, applying Roy's identity to a well-behaved indirect utility function (or its reciprocal) will also yield an ordinary demand system. See Diewert (1974) for a theoretical discussion and Oum and Gillen (1983) for an application to transport demand modelling.

referred to as, respectively, the ordinary and compensated elasticity. Since utility level is held constant in the case of compensated demand, the compensated price elasticity measures only the substitution effect of a price change. In contrast, the ordinary price elasticity measures both the substitution and income effects of a price change.

In practice, however, the compensated demand function is not estimable because it is a function of utility, which is not directly observable. Hence, virtually all passenger travel demand studies estimate an ordinary demand function and report the associated elasticities. The situation is different for the case of freight demand.

The same interpretation of demand functions and elasticities apply to the case of freight transport demand although the terminology and the units of measurement differ. Typically, a representative firm's production technology is represented by a production function $q=q \ (x,c,\varepsilon)$ where x is a vector of inputs, c is a vector of observed characteristics of the firm and ε is a vector of unobserved variables. The firm is assumed to maximise profit, taking both input and output price as given. The optimal values of q and x that solve the firm's maximization problem are, respectively, the firm's supply and input demand functions.[3] They are of the form:

$$q^* = s \ (p,w,c,\varepsilon), \tag{3}$$
$$x^* = z \ (p,w,c,\varepsilon), \tag{4}$$

where p is the output price and w is a vector of input prices. It is important to note that the firm's output does not appear as an argument in the input demand system. This is in contrast to the case where the firm is assumed to minimize cost for a given output level. In this case, the conditional input demand is[4]

$$x \ (q,w,c,\varepsilon) = \underset{x}{\text{Argmax}} \ [wx \ \text{s.t.} \ q(x,c,\varepsilon) \geq q] \tag{5}$$

---

3. Alternatively, the firm's supply and input demand functions can be derived by applying Hotelling's lemma to a well-behaved profit function.
4. It is worth noting that, mathematically, (5) is of the same form as (2). Thus, conditional input demand can also be derived by applying Shephard's lemma to a well-behaved cost function.

Since output is being held constant in (5), the associated demand elasticity measures only the substitution effect of a price change. On the other hand, the ordinary input demand elasticity associated with (4) measures the combined substitution and scale or output effects of a price change.

In measuring ordinary price elasticities of freight demand, (3) and (4) indicate that the demand system must be estimated simultaneously with the shippers' output decisions, that is, treating shippers' output as endogenous. Ignoring the endogeneity of shippers' output decisions is equivalent to assuming that changes in freight rates do not affect output levels. This, in turn, is equivalent to ignoring the scale or output effect of a change in input prices. Our survey reveals that many freight demand models do not treat the output effect properly, thus the reported elasticity values may be biased.

Furthermore, in most *ad hoc* demand specifications, it is unclear whether the resulting estimates are ordinary or conditional input demand elasticities. Nonetheless, by virtue of (4) and (5), we think the following may serve as a guide: in the case of a time-series study, if shippers' output is not included in the demand equation, it is more appropriate to regard the resulting estimates as ordinary demand elasticities. On the other hand, if shippers' output is included in the demand equation, the resulting estimates may be treated as conditional or compensated elasticities. Similar interpretation applies to cross-section studies, except it should be noted that information on shippers' output is rarely available in cross-section data. A further difficulty arises when some freight demand studies include an indicator for market size in the models. Although this may be interpreted as a proxy for the aggregate output of shippers, its accuracy is questionable.

Since the mid-1970s, many economists have estimated neoclassical input demand systems by deriving them from the firm's or industry's cost function, often specified as a translog or other flexible functional form. Examples are Spady and Friedlaender (1978), Oum (1979a, 1979b) and Friedlaender and Spady (1980). Most of these models are derived by minimizing the input costs (including freight transport costs) for transporting a given (exogenously determined) output, which corresponds to (5). Because most of these studies use cross-section data, which typically do not contain information about shippers' output, the resulting elasticity measures are thus conditional rather than ordinary input demand elasticities. The freight demand study by Oum (1979b) is an exception in that ordinary elasticities were derived by adding the output effects to the conditional elasticities computed from the neoclassical freight demand system.

2. Aggregate Market, Mode-Specific and Mode-Choice Elasticities

The concepts of demand elasticity discussed above can be applied to the study of the aggregate demand for transport as well as the demand for individual modes of transport. The market demand refers to the demand for transport relative to other (non-transport) sectors of the economy. Under the usual aggregation condition (that is, conditions for the existence of a consistent aggregate), the linkage between mode-specific elasticities (own-price elasticity F_{ii} and cross-price elasticities F_{ij}) and the own-price elasticity for aggregate transport demand, F, is:

$$F = \sum_i S_i \left(\sum_j F_{ij} \right), \tag{6}$$

where S_i denotes the volume share of mode i. In the two-mode case, the relationship becomes $F = S_1 (F_{11} + F_{12}) + (F_{21} + F_{22})$. Since the cross-price elasticities generally are positive because of competition among modes, (6) indicates that the aggregate elasticity is lower, in absolute value, than the weighted average of the mode-specific own-price elasticities.

In examining mode-specific demand studies, it is important to distinguish between mode-choice (also known as mode-split and volume share) elasticities and regular demand elasticities. Mode-choice studies are studies which examine shares of a fixed volume of traffic among modes. In many early studies on mode choice, logit models were applied to aggregate route or regional market share data, which not only leads to a loss of important information about changing market size in response to a price change, but is also theoretically inconsistent, as pointed out by Oum (1979c). More recently, disaggregate discrete choice models have been used to investigate users' mode choice decisions. It is, however, important to note that not all discrete choice models produce mode-choice elasticities; this and other aspects of discrete choice models are discussed below. Aggregate mode-choice studies produce elasticities between modes but they differ from the demand elasticities discussed earlier in that they do not take into account the effect of a price change on the *aggregate volume* of traffic. It is possible to derive mode-choice elasticities from regular demand elasticities but this entails a loss of information, and thus would rarely be a useful exercise (Taplin, 1982). Since ordinary demand elasticities generally are more useful than mode-choice elasticities, it is desirable to be able to convert mode-choice elasticities to ordinary demand elasticities.

The relationship between mode-choice and ordinary demand elasticities can be summarized by the following formula (see Taplin, 1982, and Quandt, 1968).

$$F_{ij} = M_{ij} + \delta_j \quad \text{for all } i \text{ and } j, \tag{7}$$

where F_{ij} is the price elasticity of the ordinary demand for mode i with respect to price of mode j, M_{ij} is the mode-choice elasticity of choosing mode i with respect to the price of mode j, and δ_j is the elasticity of demand for the aggregate traffic, denoted Q, with respect to the price of mode j. Because information on δ_j's is not usually available, the following formula may be useful in computing them.

$$\begin{aligned} \delta_j &= (\partial Q/\partial P_j)\,(P_j/Q) \\ &= F(\partial P/\partial P_j)\,(P_j/P) < 0, \end{aligned} \tag{8}$$

where F is the price elasticity of aggregate market demand for transport (that is, $(\partial Q/\partial P)\,(P/Q)$), and $(\partial P/\partial P_j)\,(P_j/P)$ is the elasticity of aggregate price P with respect to the price of mode j. Therefore, an explicit conversion of a mode-choice elasticity to an ordinary demand elasticity for a particular mode requires information about either the elasticity of aggregate transport demand with respect to price of each mode (δ_j) or the price elasticity of aggregate transport demand (F) and the second term in (8). Unfortunately, this information is not available in the studies reviewed here. Consequently, it is virtually impossible to draw on the extensive mode-choice literature to help establish values of ordinary demand elasticities. However, a special case of (7) for the expression of own-price elasticity, $F_{ii} = M_{ii} + \delta_i$, indicates that, in terms of absolute value, the own-price mode-choice elasticity (M_{ii}) understates the ordinary own-price elasticity (F_{ii}) because δ_i is negative. The size of the difference, $\delta_i = F_{ii} - M_{ii}$, cannot be determined without further information.[5] However, it shows that the own-price elasticities of mode-choice may serve as lower bounds for ordinary elasticities in terms of absolute values. Taplin (1982) suggests that estimates of ordinary elasticities could be constructed from mode-choice elasticities using equation (7) in conjunction with an assumed value for one ordinary demand elasticity, and various constraints on elasticity values based on theoretical considerations. Of course, the accuracy of the elasticities computed depends heavily upon the validity of the assumed value of the elasticity chosen to initiate the computation. An illustration of this can be found in Taplin (1982) (see also Oum, Waters and Yong, 1990).

3. Disaggregate Discrete Choice Models

Another important development in transport demand research is the introduction of disaggregate discrete choice models. (For more general discussions of discrete choice models, see Amemiya, 1981, and Maddala, 1983, among others.) These models investigate users' travel-choice behaviour based on attributes of various modes of transport and individuals' socio-economic characteristics. Unlike conventional demand models, which assume that consumers make marginal adjustments in response to changes in the environment, discrete choice models assume that consumption is an all or-nothing decision—one either takes the transit or uses the car. (A more detailed discussion of discrete choice models can be found in Domencich and McFadden, 1975, Hensher and Johnson, 1981, and Ben-Akiva and Lerman, 1985, among others.)

It is important to note that various demand elasticity measures can be computed from discrete choice models. For example, it is possible to compute an elasticity which measures the percentage change in the *probability* of a representative individual choosing to travel by bus given a change in transit fare.[6] It is important to note that this is *not* the same as the regular demand elasticity *nor* mode-choice elasticity discussed earlier. Based on their empirical experience, Domencich and

---

5. Taplin notes that the sum of these "second stage elasticities," Âj,dj, is the price elasticity of the aggregate market demand in (6).

6. In most cases, the representative individual is the one with characteristic variables equal to the sample means (see, for example, Richards and Ben-Akiva, 1975). Its accuracy as an approximation to the aggregate elasticity is questioned by Dunne (1984).

McFadden report that the derived regular demand elasticity is likely to
be one-half to three-quarters lower than the corresponding representative individual elasticity of choice probability. In order to derive the regular demand elasticity, it is necessary to aggregate across individuals in
the *population*. Conceptually, a consistent and unbiased estimate of the
fraction of population choosing a particular mode is the expected value
of the sample probability. In practice, various aggregation procedures
are used to approximate the population demand. A comprehensive
review of various aggregation procedures can be found in Ben-Akiva
and Lerman (1985), chapter 6. Many studies use the sample aggregate
as an approximation. The accuracy of this approach clearly depends on
the sampling procedure used. Obviously, different procedures will be
likely to produce numerically different elasticity estimates. It is therefore important for researchers to state explicitly the aggregation procedure used to derive the aggregate demand and associated elasticities.

Some discrete choice models are concerned solely with users' mode-
choice decisions given a fixed volume of traffic. Many studies of urban
work trips fall into this category. The demand elasticities computed
from these models are more appropriately interpreted as mode-choice
elasticities rather than regular demand elasticities since the effect of a
price change on *aggregate traffic* is not taken into account. This is illustrated in the lower right of Figure 1. Clearly, discrete choice models that
produce regular demand elasticities must include in the users' choice set
the option of not making the trip. This will require socio-economic characteristics and other data on non-travellers. Therefore, an easy way to
identify the types of demand elasticities reported by a discrete choice
study is to examine whether the sample contains non-travellers.
Although some authors recognise the importance of data on non-travellers, none of the studies reviewed here collects such data. This is
rather unsatisfactory, particularly for long-run policy planning, since the
planner not only needs to know how existing travellers will respond but
also how overall traffic will grow given a change in transport policy.

4. Firm-Specific Demand Elasticities

In addition to mode-choice and market demand elasticities, one could
focus on demand elasticities of individual firms. Firm-specific elasticities vary considerably depending upon the extent and nature of competi-

Figure 1. A Schematic of Concepts and Empirical Approaches
to Estimation of Transport Demand Elasticities

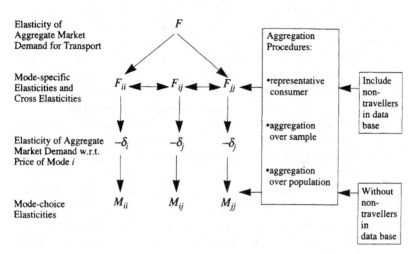

tion between firms. For example, firms operating in a competitive environment will in general face very different demand elasticities than those in a collusive oligopoly market. Not surprisingly, demand elasticities of firms in an oligopolistic market depend greatly on the nature of competition, for example Cournot quantity competition, Bertrand price competition, and so on. A growing number of economists have examined the price sensitivity of demand facing a firm within the framework of conjectural variations (see, for examples, Appelbaum, 1982, and Slade, 1984). As far as we are aware, the only application in transport pricing is Brander and Zhang (1990), which is a study of inter-firm competition between duopoly airlines in the United States. Empirical estimates of transport demand rarely focus on demand elasticities facing individual firms, hence we do not consider them further in this review.

5. Short-Run and Long-Run Elasticities

There is also an important distinction between short-run and long-run elasticities of demand. In the long run, consumers or firms are better able to adjust to price signals than in the short run. Hence long-run demand tends to be more elastic than short-run demand. Unfortunately, few studies are explicit about the time horizon of their elasticity estimates.

Theoretically, consumers and firms are able to vary their location choice and asset holding (for example, vehicle ownership) in the long run, whereas in the short run these are not possible. Viewed in this light, a long-run demand model should ideally model consumers' or firms' location choice and asset ownership together with their transport demand. These are particularly important for long-run policy planning since major changes in transport policy are likely to affect consumers' and firms' asset ownership and location choice. These decisions, in turn, will have significant impacts on transport demand. However, because of the enormous data requirement and the complexity involved in explicitly modelling transport decisions, asset ownership and location choice jointly, estimation of a full long-run model is, to the best of our knowledge, non-existent. Examples of studies which model households' vehicle ownership together with transport demand are Thobani (1984), and Mannering and Winston (1985). However, we are not aware of any transport demand model that includes both location choice and asset ownership. Goodwin's survey (1991) is probably the best attempt thus far to compile short- and long-run transport demand elasticities. However, he is often forced to rely on the original authors' interpretation of their results, rather than compiling elasticity estimates from studies which explicitly model short- and long-run effects.

It is common to use distributed lag models with time-series data in practice in an attempt to capture the long-run effect of price changes. In this case, the direct impact of a price change is used to compute the short-run elasticities, while the long-run elasticities are computed by allowing for the full impact of a price change (for example, Oum, 1979b). The distributed lag model is a theoretically sound and convenient procedure which, if properly executed, will capture the long-run effect of a price change. It is, however, unable to identify the different components that constitute the total effect of a price change.

6. Linkages between Concepts of Demand Elasticities

Figure 1 is a schematic summary of concepts of transport demand elasticities and relationships between them. On the left side of the figure, the elasticity of aggregate market demand (denoted F) is decomposed into mode-specific demand elasticities, F_{i}, F_{ij} and F_{jj}. The right side of Figure 1 depicts the disaggregate discrete choice models. Subject to potential sampling and aggregation errors, the aggregated elasticities derived from discrete choice models can be regarded as estimates of the corresponding aggregate elasticities. It is worth noting that a discrete choice model using trip diaries as the data base can capture the stimulation effect on total demand of a lower price if those who participated in the survey represent a true random sample of the population and the researcher incorporates the trip frequency information explicitly in the model. The resulting elasticity estimates (properly aggregated) should then approximate the regular demand elasticity. On the other hand, discrete choice studies which do not include information on non-travellers produce elasticity estimates which approximate aggregate mode-choice elasticity. In sum, although it is possible conceptually to link aggregate and disaggregate transport demand elasticities, the two approaches continue to evolve empirically with few comparisons between the two.

IV. Summary of Elasticity Estimates

The major survey results are summarized in the tables below. The results are divided into two categories: Tables 1 to 5 report the elasticity estimates of passenger travel demand whereas Tables 6 and 7 report the elasticity estimates of freight demand. The tables show the specific elasticities (or ranges) reported by authors. We do not compute means or standard deviations by mode since our sample sizes are small and there is heterogeneity among studies. Our World Bank working paper presents subjective "most likely" ranges of elasticity values for various transport demand categories. The sources of these estimates are included at the end of each table.

Table 1 reports the elasticity estimates of automobile usage by countries and time horizons. We rely on the original authors' judgement to distinguish between long-run and short-run estimates. All estimates are from single-mode studies. All these studies use household survey data, except one which uses observations on ridership changes before and after a fare change. The elasticity estimates range from –0.09 to –0.52. Although long-run elasticity estimates are in general higher, the difference does not appear to be significant, although this may reflect the fact that few studies develop true long-run models which take into account

Table 1. Demand Elasticities of Automobile Usage
(all elasticity estimates are in negative values)

	Short Run	Long Run	Unspecified
United States	0.23	0.28	0.13–0.26, 0.15–0.45
Australia	0.09–0.24	0.22–0.31	0.22–0.52, 0.25–0.34
United Kingdom	n.a.	n.a.	0.14–0.36

Sources: From 7 single-mode studies. They are: Hensher (1985); Hensher, Milthorpe and
Smith (1990); Hensher (1986); Mannering (1986); Mannering and Winston (1985);
McCarthy (1986); and White (1984).

Table 2. Demand Elasticities of Urban Transit
(all elasticity estimates are in negative values)

Data Types	Elasticity Estimates
Time Series	0.01–0.62, 0.17–0.59, 0.18–0.22, 0.23–0.25, 0.23–0.27,
	0.27–0.78, 0.29–0.34, 0.36–1.32
Cross-section	0.05–0.34
Pooled data	0.06–0.44
Before/after data	0.10–0.60, 0.70

Sources: From 12 studies. They are: Anas and Lee (1982); Benham (1982); Cummings,
Fairhurst, Labelle and Stuart (1989); De Rus (1990); Doi and Allen (1986);
Gaudry (1980); Gilbert and Jalilian (1991); Goodwin and Williams (1985); Hamberger and Chatterjee (1987); Kyte, Stoner and Cryer (1988), Wang and Skinner
(1984); and White (1981).

changes in vehicle ownership and location choice. Despite the fact that
these studies were conducted in different countries, the estimates produced are remarkably similar. All the estimates show that the demand
for automobile usage is fairly inelastic. From the perspective of policymaking, the low elasticity estimates in Table 1 indicate that monetary
disincentives may not be very effective in controlling automobile usage
in urban cities.

Table 2 reports the elasticity estimates of the demand for urban transit
by data types. Eight of the ten studies are single-mode studies. Ideally,
the elasticity estimates should be classified according to peak and off-

peak hours since urban travel demand is expected to differ substantially in these two periods. Unfortunately, most studies do not report their results in this manner. The range of elasticity estimates varies from –0.01 to –0.78, with most of the values falling between –0.1 to –0.6. These recent figures indicate that the demand for urban transit continues to be rather inelastic, which is consistent with other surveys of demand for public transit, such as Frankena (1978) and Goodwin (1991).

Table 3 contains estimates of demand elasticities of air passenger travel. The classification is by data types and nature of travel. The elasticity estimates range from –0.4 to –4.51, with the majority of the figures falling within –0.8 and –2.0. Unlike the demand for automobile usage and urban transit, the demand elasticities of air travel exhibits far greater variability. Results from a few studies (for example, Oum, Gillen and Noble, 1986: Straszheim, 1978) suggest that demand elasticities differ significantly among different fare classes (for example, first class, standard economy, and discount fares) and distance (for example, long haul versus short haul). This is hardly surprising because price-sensitive holiday-makers form the majority of travellers on long-distance routes whereas less price-sensitive short-distance travellers are mostly business travellers. Unfortunately, classification by fare class or distance is not possible here because most studies reviewed do not maintain these distinctions in their empirical estimates. Nonetheless, Table 3 shows that the demand for business travel is less elastic than that for leisure travel and elasticity estimates from cross-section data generally are higher than

Table 3. Demand Elasticities of Air Passenger Travel
(all elasticity estimates are in negative values)

	Time Series	Cross-section	Others*
Leisure travel	0.40-1.98, 1.92	1.52	1.40-3.30, 2.20-4.60
Business travel	0.65	1.15	0.90
Mixed or unknown	0.82, 0.91, 0.36-1.81	0.76-0.84, 1.39, 1.63	0.53-1.00, 1.80-1.90
	1.12-1.28, 1.48	1.85, 2.83-4.51	

*Included in this column are studies with unknown data sources.
Sources: From 13 studies. They are: Abrahams (1983); Agarwal and Talley (1985); Andrikopoulos and Terovitis (1983); Doganis (1985); Fridstroöm and Thune-Larsen (1989); Haitovsky, Solomon and Silman (1987); Ippolito (1981); Oum and Gillen (1983); Oum, Gillen and Noble (1986); Straszheim (1978); Talley and Eckroade (1984); Talley and Schwarz-Miller (1988); and Taplin (1980).

those from time-series data. However, it should be noted that data problems are likely to account for part of the differences. In particular, many researchers use regular full fare class as an approximation for business travel. This may have caused the demand elasticity of business travel to be over-estimated, since some holiday-makers travel by the regular fare class, particularly in the regulated markets (for example, in the 1970s in the United States). Like most transport analysts, we believe that the demand elasticity of business air travel is less than unity while that of holiday travel is greater than unity, although the empirical estimate is not unambiguous.

The elasticity estimates for intercity rail travel are presented in Table 4. Similar to the case of air travel, the classification is by data types and nature of travel. The elasticity estimates range from –0.12 to –1.54, with business travel showing elasticity estimates generally below unity while considerable variation exists in the non-business and mixed travel category. It is again difficult to generalize about the demand for intercity rail travel as a whole. However, it is likely that the presence of competing modes such as air or bus may significantly affect the elasticity values. This is likely to account for the substantial differences among elasticity estimates obtained from different cities.

Table 5 presents elasticity estimates from disaggregate discrete choice models, by mode and type of travel. With a few exceptions, these elasticity estimates are somewhat lower than those obtained from direct

Table 4. Demand Elasticities of Intercity Rail Travel
(all elasticity estimates are in negative values)

	Time Series	Cross-section	Others*
Business travel	0.67-1.00	0.70	0.15
Non-business and mixed travel	0.37-0.40, 0.74-0.90, 0.81-1.17, 0.14-1.18, 1.08-1.54	1.40	1.19-1.50, 1.00, 0.12-0.49

*Included in this column are studies with unknown data sources.
Sources: From 9 studies. They are: Glaister (1983); Goodwin and Williams (1985); Jones and Nichols (1983); Kroes and Sheldon (1985); Kroes and Sheldon (1988); McGeehan (1984); Owen and Phillips (1987); Oum and Gillen (1983); and White (1981).

Table 5. Travel Demand Elasticities from Discrete Choice Models
(all elasticity estimates are in negative values)

	Urban Travel	Intercity Travel
Automobile	0.01-0.02, 0.04, 0.06-0.08, 0.16-0.62, 0.32-0.47, 0.46-2.03, 0.02-0.88[†] 0.16-0.97[†], 0.12-1.26[†]	0.08, 0.70-0.96, 0.83
Bus	0.01-0.03, 0.04, 0.06, 0.03-0.14, 0.10, 0.12-0.24, 0.37-0.56, 0.45-0.58	0.32, 0.32-0.69, 0.45-0.60
Rail	0.22-0.25, 0.57, 0.08-0.75[†]	0.32, 0.57-1.20, 0.86-1.14
Air	n.a.	0.18-0.38, 0.26-0.38, 0.62

†Denotes elasticity of choice probability of the representative individual

Sources: From 16 studies. They are: Anas and Moses (1984); Bajic (1984); Dunne (1984); Geltner and Barros 91984); Gillen and Cox (1979); Grayson 91981); Johnson and Hensher (1982); Madan and Groenhout (1987); Hensher and Bullock (1979); McCarthy 91982); McFadden (1974); Morrison and Winston (1983); Morrison and Winston (1985); Southworth (1981); Swait and Ben-Akiva (1987); and Thobani (1984).

demand models using aggregate data. As noted earlier, discrete choice models can produce either mode-choice or regular demand elasticities, depending on the data set used. However, because all the studies reviewed here use data sets that do not contain information about non-travellers, the elasticity estimates reported probably are more appropriately interpreted as mode-choice elasticities.[7] It should be noted that some studies report the elasticity estimates of the representative individual's choice probability. These estimates are identified † in the table. As expected, these elasticity estimates are in general higher in absolute values. A more difficult problem arises when some studies do not state explicitly the types of elasticities they report. Furthermore, most studies do not outline the aggregation procedure used to derive the regular demand elasticity estimates. As a consequence, it is difficult to ensure that these estimates are comparable with each other or with the elasticity

7. Many discrete choice studies do allow for growth in the aggregate traffic volume among existing users in response to a price or service change. However, since they do not contain information of non-travellers in their data, the resulting elasticity estimate will be between the mode choice and regular price elasticity, as discussed above and shown on the right-hand side of Figure 1.

estimates reported in other tables.

Tables 6 and 7 report, respectively, elasticity estimates of demand for rail and truck freight by commodity groups and functional forms. A notable feature of these elasticity estimates is the wide range of values, not only across different commodity groups, but also for the same group of commodities estimated using different functional forms.

In summary, our survey results show that only the demand for automobile usage and urban transit are unambiguously inelastic; less can be said about intercity rail and air travel, and still less about freight transport. We believe that many factors may have contributed to the diversity of these empirical results. The following section identifies a number of the important factors, together with some priority areas for future research.

Table 6. Demand Elasticities of Rail Freight: Selected Commodities and Functional Forms

(all elasticity estimates are in negative values)

Commodities	Log-linear	Aggregate Logit	Translog	Discrete Choice Model*
Aggregate commodities	1.52	0.25-0.35, 0.83, 0.34-1.06	0.09-0.29, 0.60	n.a.
Chemicals	n.a.	0.66	0.69	2.25
Fabricated metal products	n.a.	1.57	2.16	n.a.
Food products	0.02, 1.18	1.36	2.58, 1.04	n.a.
Iron & steel products	n.a.	n.a.	2.54, 1.20	0.02
Machinery	n.a.	0.16-1.73	2.27-3.50	0.61
Paper, plastic & rubber products	0.67	0.87	1.85	0.17-1.09
Petroleum products	n.a.	n.a.	0.99	0.53
Stone, clay & glass products	n.a.	0.69	1.68	0.82
Textiles	n.a.	2.03	n.a.	0.56
Transport equipment	n.a.	n.a.	0.92-1.08	2.68
Wood & wood products	0.05	0.76	1.97, 0.58	0.08

* The estimates in this column are mode-choice elasticities.

Sources: From 11 studies. They are: Babcock and German (1983); Boyer (1977); Friedlaender and Spady (1980); Guria (1988); Levin (1978); Lewis and Widup (1982); Oum (1979a); Oum (1979b); Oum (1989); Wilson, Wilson and Koo (1988); and Winston (1981).

Table 7. Demands Elasticities of Truck Freight: Selected Commodities
and Functional Forms
(all elasticity estimates are in negative values)

Commodities	Log-linear	Aggregate Logit	Translog	Discrete Choice Model*
Aggregate commodities	1.34	0.93	0.69	n.a.
Chemicals	n.a.	n.a.	0.98	2.31
Fabricated metal products	n.a.	n.a.	1.36	0.18
Food products	1.18, 1.54	0.97	0.52, 0.65, 1.00	0.99
Machinery	n.a.	n.a.	1.08-1.23	0.78
Paper, plastic & rubber products	n.a.	n.a.	1.05	0.29
Petroleum products	n.a.	n.a.	0.52	0.66
Stone, clay & glass products	n.a.	n.a.	1.03	2.04
Transport equipment	n.a.	n.a.	0.52-0.67	2.96
Wood & wood products	n.a.	n.a.	0.56, 1.55	0.14

* The estimates in this column are mode-choice elasticities.
Sources: From 6 studies. They are: Friedlaender and Spady (1980); Lewis and Widup
(1982); Oum (1979b); Oum (1989); Wilson, Wilson and Koo (1988); and Winston
(1981).

V. Pitfalls and Suggested Priorities for Future Research

After reviewing over sixty empirical studies of transport demand, we
identify a number of issues which warrant attention in existing studies.
In addition, we also identify some areas where future research is needed.

1. The Presence or Absence of Intermodal Competition

Some studies do not take into account the presence of intermodel
competition. As a result, the own-price elasticity estimates reflect in part
the intensity of intermodal competition. In particular, the own-price
elasticity may be under-estimated if the prices of competing modes have
changed in the same direction as that of the mode under study. Therefore, it is important to include in a mode's demand specification the

prices and service quality variables of competing modes.

2. The Use of Different Functional Forms

Different functional forms can result in widely different elasticity estimates, even with the same set of data. This point is demonstrated by Oum (1989) and is evident from Tables 6 and 7. The problem is long neglected by researchers and transport practitioners. Typically, an *ad hoc* demand specification is used and little attention is directed towards testing the specification against an alternative. With the advances in econometric theory and computing technology, we think that specification testing should become an integral part of empirical transport demand research in the future.

3. Differences in Time Horizons and Locations

It is well known that demand becomes more elastic in the long run because users are better able to adjust to price changes. The distinction between long-run and short-run, however, is quite arbitrary in most transport demand studies. More carefully structured long-run studies are needed to integrate location choice and asset ownership decisions with transport demand. In addition to long-run and short-run distinctions, data drawn from different cities or countries often show markedly different elasticity estimates. This may be due, in part, to specification problems and different degrees of competition between modes in different cities or countries.

4. The Degree of Aggregation

As more disaggregated markets are investigated, the range of elasticity estimates tends to widen because each estimate reflects unique market conditions. For example, suppose the freight demand elasticity of steel is –0.5 and that of fresh fruits is –1.2. The aggregated elasticity will lie somewhere between –0.5 and –1.2. Aggregation "averages out" some of the underlying variabilities of price sensitivity in different markets. The appropriate degree of aggregation is important if elasticity estimates are to be of practical use to decision makers.

5. The Identification Problem in Empirical Estimation

In practice, the data observed by researchers are the result of interactions between forces of demand and supply. It is well known in econometrics that the parameter estimates will be biased if such interactions are not recognised. This was not a serious problem in the past because prices and service conditions were tightly controlled by regulatory agencies in many transport industries. Supply decisions were made in response to regulated price and service conditions, thus variations in observed data primarily reflect changes in demand. However, the situation has changed drastically since the early 1980s, when many countries deregulated their transport industries. Now, firms have discretion over price and service conditions and it is more difficult to sort out supply and demand effects in the data. Unfortunately, most empirical studies of transport demand have failed to take this into consideration. Greater effort needs to be directed towards modelling the interactive forces of demand and supply in future studies.

6. The Problem of Aggregation in Discrete Choice Models

As noted earlier, it is necessary to aggregate across individuals in order to derive the regular demand elasticity estimates from discrete choice models. This will, however, widen the confidence intervals of the resulting elasticity estimates since, in addition to the standard errors associated with the parameter estimates, there is also an error of aggregation. More importantly, the statistical distribution of the demand elasticity estimates will be difficult, if not impossible to determine, since there are two sources of errors. This problem clearly deserves further investigation in future studies.

V. Concluding Remarks

In the preparation of this paper, we surveyed over sixty studies from academic journals which report estimates of own-price elasticities of transport demand. They include both passenger and freight demand studies, using different data bases and covering many countries and cities. We have attempted to clarify the different concepts of demand elasticities used in these studies. In addition, various problems in interpreting the empirical estimates are discussed. While some generalisations, particularly on demand elasticities of automobile usage and public transit are possible, across-the-board generalisations about transport demand are impossible. This is in contrast to "conventional wisdom," which states that the demand for transport is inelastic because it is a derived demand. This is particularly the case in freight demand, which is believed to be inelastic because freight charges generally are only a fraction of the prices of commodities transported, which usually have inelastic demand themselves. In reality, competition between modes, routes or firms gives rise to a wide range of price elasticities, generally much more elastic than conventional wisdom would suggest. Furthermore, factors such as the time horizon, the degree of aggregation, the functional specification, and so on, have a significant bearing on the elasticity estimates. They also suggest that there is no short-cut to obtaining reliable demand estimates for a specific transport market without a detailed study of that market.

References
(by Philip Goodwin, Tae Hoon Oum, W.G. Waters II and Jong-Say Yong)

Abraham, M. (1983): "A Service Quality Model of Air Travel Demand: An Empirical Study." *Transportation Research*, 17A (5), 385-93.

Agarwal, V. and W. Talley (1985): "The Demand for International Air Passenger Service Provided by U.S. Air Carriers." *International Journal of Transport Economics*, 12 (1), 63-70.

Amemiya, T. (1981): "Qualitative Response Models: A Survey." *Journal of Economic Literature*, 19, 1483-536.

Anas, A. and G.Y. Lee (1982): "The Potential for a Value Capture Policy to Finance Rapid Transit Projects in Chicago's Southwest Side: An Empirical Simulation Analysis." *Research in Urban Economics*, 2, 171-202.

Anas, A. and L.N. Moses. (1984): "Qualitative Choice and the Blending of Discrete Alternatives." *Review of Economics and Statistics*, 66 (4), 547-55.

Andrikopoulos, A.A. and T. Terovitis (1983): "An Abstract Mode Model: A Cross-Section and Time Series Investigation. *Interna-*

tional Journal of Transport Economics, 10 (3), 563-76.

Appelbaum, E. (1982): "The Estimation of the Degree of Oligopoly Power." *Journal of Econometrics,* 19, 287-99.

Babcock, M.W. and W. German (1983): "1985 Forecast: Rail Share of Intercity Manufacturers Freight Markets." *Transportation Research Forum,* 24 (1), 614-20.

Bajic, B. 91984): Choice of Travel Mode for Work Trips: Some Findings for Metropolitan Toronto." *International Journal of Transport Economics,* 11 (1), 78-96.

Bamford, J. (1984): *Rail Elasticities.* Oxford University Transport Studies Unit, Working Paper 246, April.

Bates, J.J. and M. Roberts (1979): *The Interrelationship of Car Ownership and Public Transport.* Paper MI. PTRC 1979, July.

Bates, J.J. and M. Roberts (1981): *Forecasts for the Ownership and Use of a Car.* Round Table 55, European Conference of Ministers of Transport, Paris.

Ben-Akiva, M. and S.R. Lerman (1985): *Discrete Choice Analysis: Theory and Application to Travel Demand.* Camb. Mass.: MIT Press.

Ben-Akiva, M., S.R. Lerman, and M.L. Manheim (1986): *Disaggregate Models: an Overview of Some Recent Research Results and Practical Applications.* Paper N25, PTRC, July.

Benham, J.L. (1982): "Analysis of a Fare Increase by Use of Time-Series and Before-and-After Data." *Transportation Research Record,* 877, 84-90.

Berkovek, J. (1985): "Forecasting Automobile Demand." *Transportation Research* 19B (4), August.

Berkovek, J. and J. Rust (1985): "Nested Logit Model of Automobile Holdings." *Transportation Research* 19B (4), August.

Bland, B.H. (1984): *Effect of Fuel Price on Final Use and Travel Patterns.* LR1114, Transport and Road Research Laboratory, Crowthorne, Berks.

Blase, J.H. (1985): *The Effect of Doubling LT Fares.* GLTS81 Analysis Report 3, TS 146, Greater London Council, April.

Bonsall, P.W. and A.F. Champernowne (1976): "Some Finding on Elasticity of Demand for Petrol." *Traffic Engineering and Control,* October.

Boyer, K.D. (1977): "Minimum Rate Regulation, Modal Split Sensitivities, and the Railroad Problem." *Journal of Political Economy,* 85

(3), 493-512.

Brander, J.A. and Z. Zhang (1990): "Market Conduct in the Airline Industry: An Empirical Investigation." *Rand Journal of Economics,* 21, pp. 567-84.

Button, K.J., A.D. Pearman and A.S. Fowkes (1980): "Car Availability and Public Transport." *International Journal of Transport Economics* VII (3) December.

Cervero, R. (1985): "Examining Recent Transit Fare Innovations in the U.S." *Transport Policy and Decision Making* 3 (1).

Commission of the European Communities (1980): *Interim Report of the Special Group on the Influence of Taxation on Car Fuel Consumption,* 150/VII/80-EN, April.

Copley, G. and S. Lowe (1981): *The Temporal Stability of Trip Rates.* Paper N19, PTRC July.

Cummings, C.P., M. Fairhurst, S. Labelle, and D. Stuart, (1989): "Market Segmentation of Transit Fare Elasticities." *Transportation Quarterly,* 43 (3), 407-20.

Daly, A.J. and S. Zachary (1977): *The Effect of Free Public Transport on the Journey to Work.* Supplementary Report 338, Transport and Road Research Laboratory, Crowthorne, Berks.

Daor, E. and P.J. Hathaway (1973): *The Influence of Bus and Rail Accessibility on Car Ownership.* Research Memorandum 390, Greater London Council, January.

De Rus, G. (1990): "Public Transport Demand Elasticities in Spain." *Journal of Transport Economics and Policy,* 24, 189-201.

Diewert, W.E. (1974): "Applications of Duality Theory." In M.D. Intriligator and D.A. Kendrick (eds.) *Frontiers of Quantitative Economics.* Vol. II. North-Holland, Amsterdam.

Dix, M.C. and P.B. Goodwin (1982): "Petrol Prices and Car Use; a Synthesis of Conflicting Evidence." *Transport Policy and Decision Making* 2 (2).

Doi, M. and W.B. Allen (1986): "A Time Series Analysis of Monthly Ridership for an Urban Rail Rapid Transit Line." *Transportation* 13 (3), 257-69.

Domencich, T.A. and D. McFadden (1975): *Urban Travel Demand: A Behavioral Analysis.* North-Holland, Amsterdam.

Donelly, K.A. (1985): "A State-Level Variable Elasticity of Demand for Gasoline Model." *International Journal of Transport Economics,*

XII, 2.

Doganis, R. (1985): *Flying Off Course: The Economics of International Airlines.* George Allen & Unwin, U.K.

Drollas, L.P. (1984): "The Demand for Gasoline." *Energy Economics,* January.

Drollas, L.P. (1987): "The Demand for Gasoline—a Reply." *Energy Economics,* October.

Dunne, J.P. (1984): "Elasticity Measures and Disaggregate Choice Models." *Journal of Transport Economics and Policy,* 18, 189-97.

Fairhurst, M.H. (1975): "Influence of Public Transport on Car Ownership." *Journal of Transport Economics and Policy,* 9 (3), September.

Fairhurst, M.H., J.F. Lindsay and M. Singha (1987): *Traffic Trends Since 1970.* Economic Research Report R266, London Regional Transport, April.

Fowkes, A.S., C.A. Nash and A.F. Whiteing (1985): "Understanding Trends in Inter-City Rail Traffic in Great Britain." *Transport Planning and Technology,* 10, 65-80.

Frankena, M.W. (1978): "The Demand for Urban Bus Transport in Canada." *Journal of Transport Economics and Policy,* 12, 280-303.

Fridstroöm, L. and H. Thune-Larsen (1989): "An Econometric Air Travel Demand Model for the Entire Conventional Domestic Network: The Case of Norway." *Transportation Research,* 23B (3), 213-24.

Friedlaender, A.F. and R.H. Spady (1980): "A Derived Demand Function for Freight Transportation." *Review of Economics and Statistics,* 62, 432-41.

Gaudry, M.J.I. (1980): "A Study of Aggregate Bi-Modal Urban Travel Supply, Demand and Network Behavior Using Simultaneous Equation with Autoregressive Residuals." *Transportation Research,* 14B (1-2), 29-58.

Geltner, D. and R.C. Barros (1984): "Travel Behavior and Policy Analysis in a Medium-size Bazilian City." *Transport Policy and Decision Making,* 2, 425-505.

Gilbert, C.L. and H. Jalilian (1991): "The Demand for Travel and for Travelcards on London Regional Transport." *Journal of Transport Economics and Policy,* 25, 3-29.

Gillen, D.W. and D.J. Cox (1979): "Assumed versus Estimated Functional Form in Disaggregate Mode Choice Models." *Regional Science and Urban Economics,* 9, 185-95.

Glaister, S. (1983): "Some Characteristics of Rail Commuter Demand." *Journal of Transport Economics and Policy,* 17 (2) May, 115-32.

Godward E. (1984): *Some Evidence on Elasticities of Demand for Rail Services in West Midlands.* West Midlands Passenger Transport Executive, working note.

Goodwin, P.B. (1973): *Some Causes and Effects of Variations in the Structure of Demand for Urban Passenger Transport.* Ph.D thesis, University of London.

Goodwin, P.B. (1975): *A Method for Calculating the Effects of Flat Fares.* PTD Note 14, Greater London Council.

Goodwin, P.B. (1987a): "Dynamic Car Ownership Modelling." In G. Rhys and G. Harbour (eds.) *Modelling Vehicle Demand, Alternative Views,* University of Wales.

Goodwin, P.B. (1987b): "Long Term Effects of Public Transport Subsidy." In S. Glaister (ed.) *Transport Subsidy, Policy Journals.*

Goodwin, P.B. (1988): "Circumstances in which People Reduce Car Ownership; a Comparative Analysis of Three Panel Data Sets." *Journal of International Association of Traffic and Safety Sciences,* 12, 2, Tokyo.

Goodwin, P.B. (1991): *Evidence on Car and Public Transport Demand Elasticities.* Transport Studies Unit Working Paper 427 (reserved) University of Oxford.

Goodwin, P.B. and H.C.W.L. Williams (1985): "Public Transport Demand Models and Elasticity Measures: An Overview of Recent British Experience." *Transportation Research,* 19B (3), 253-8.

Goulcher, A. (1990): *Fares Elasticities for Underground Travel.* Research Note U13, Strategic Planning Unit, London Underground Ltd.

Grayson, A. (1981): "Disaggregate Model of Mode Choice in Intercity Travel." *Transportation Research Record,* 835, 36-42.

Greater London Council (1977): *Fares and Petrol Price Tests in the GLTS Model.* paper AC/T40, Transportation Branch, August.

Grimshaw, F. (1984): *Public Transport Fare Elasticities: Evidence from West Yorkshire.* Seminar paper, Oxford University Transport Studies Unit Report 246, April.

Guria, J.C. (1988): "Effects of the Recent Road Transport Deregulation on Rail Freight Demands in New Zealand." *International Journal of Transport Economics,* 15 (2), 169-87.

Haitovsky, Y., I. Salomon and A. Silman (1987): "The Economic Impact of Charter Flights on Tourism to Israel: An Econometric Approach." *Journal of Transport Economics and Policy,* 21 (2), 111-34.

Hallam, P. (1978): *London Travel Survey 1976.* Department of Transport, April.

Hamberger, C.G. and A. Chatterjee (1987): "Effects of Fare and Other Factors on Express Bus Ridership in a Medium-sized Urban Area." *Transportation Research Record,* 1108, 53-9.

Harbour, G. (1987): "An Overview of Academic Research on Vehicle Demand Modelling." In G. Rhys and G. Harbour (eds.) *Modelling Vehicle Demand: Alternative Views,* University of Wales.

Hensher, D.A. (1985): "An Econometric Model of Vehicle Use in the Household Sector." *Transportation Research,* 19B (4), 303-14.

Hensher, D.A. and R.G. Bullock (1979): "Price Elasticity of Commuter Mode Choice." *Transportation Research* 13A, (3), 193-202.

Hensher, D.A. and L.W. Johnson (1981): *Applied Discrete Choice Modelling.* John Wiley and Sons, N.Y.

Hensher, D.A. and N.C. Smith (1986a): "A Structural Model of the Use of Automobiles by Households: a Case Study of Urban Australia." *Transport Reviews* 6 (1), Jan.-March.

Hensher, D.A. and N.C. Smith (1986b): *Very Fast Train Project Elasticities.* Unpublished working paper, Mcquarie University.

Hensher, D.A. (1986): "Sequential and Full Information Maximum Likelihood Estimation of a Nested Logit Model." *Review of Economics and Statistics,* LXVIII (4), November.

Hensher, D.A., P.O. Barnard, N.C. Smith and F.W. Milthorpe (1992): *Dimensions of Automobile Demand,* North-Holland, Amsterdam.

Hensher, D.A., F.W. Milthorpe and N.C. Smith (1990): "The Demand for Vehicle Use in the Urban Household Sector. *Journal of Transport Economics and Policy,* 24, 119-37.

Hensher, D.A., and J.L. Young (1991): *Demand Forecasts and Demand Elasticities for Australian Transport Fuel.* Occasional Paper 103, Bureau of Transport and Communications Economics, Canberra.

Horowitz, J. (1982) "Modelling Traveller Responses to Alternative Gasoline Allocation Plans." *Transportation Research* 16A (2).

Hughes, P. (1980): *Fares Elasticity of Suburban Rail Travel.* Supplementary Report 614, Transport and Road Research Laboratory, Crowthorne, Berks.

Ippolito, R.A. (1981): "Estimating Airline Demand with Quality of Service Variables." *Journal of Transport Economics and Policy,* 15 (1), 7-16.

Johnson L. and D. Hensher (1982): "Application of Multinomial Probit to a Two-period Panel Data Set." *Transportation Research,* 16A (5-6), 457-64.

Jones, I.S. and A.J. Nichols (1983): "Demand for Intercity Rail Travel." *Journal of Transport Economics and Policy* 17 (2), May, 133-53.

Jones, P.M. (ed.) (1990): *Developments in Dynamic and Activity-Based Approaches to Travel Demand.* Avebury, Aldershot.

Jones, S.R. and J.C. Tanner (1979): *Car Ownership and Public Transport.* Supplementary Report 464, Transport and Road Research Laboratory, Crowthorne, Berks.

Koenig, J.G. (1980): "Indicators of Urban Accessibility, Theory and Applications." *Transportation,* 9 (2), June.

Kroes, E.P. and R.J. Sheldon (1985): "Stated Preference Techniques in Measuring Travel Elasticities." In Jansen *et al.* (eds.) *Transportation and Mobility in an Era of Transition,* Elsevier, North Holland.

Kroes, E.P. and R.J. Sheldon (1988): "Stated Preference Methods: An Introduction." *Journal of Transport Economics and Policy,* 22 (1), 11-25.

Kyte, M., J. Stoner and J. Cryer (1988): "A Time-Series Analysis of Public Transit Ridership in Portland, Oregon, 1971-82." *Transportation Research,* 22A (5), 345-59.

Levin, R.C. (1978): "Allocation in Surface Freight Transportation: Does Rate Regulation Matter?." *Bell Journal of Economics,* 9 (1), 18-45.

Lewis, D. (1978): "Public Policy and Road Traffic Levels, a Rejoinder." *Journal of Transport Economics and Policy,* 12 (1), January.

Lewis, K.A. and D.P. Widup (1982): "Deregulation and Rail-Truck Competition: Evidence from a Translog Transport Demand Model for Assembled Automobiles." *Journal of Transport Economics and Policy,* 16 (2), 139-49.

McCarthy, P.S. (1982): "Further Evidence on the Temporal Stability of Disaggregate Travel Demand Models." *Transportation Research,* 16B (4), 263-78.

McCarthy, P.S., (1985): "An Econometric Analysis of Automobile Transactions." *International Journal of Transport Economics,* XII (1), February.

McCarthy, P.S., (1986): "Shared Fleet Arrangements: Implications for

Vehicle Demand Using a Simultaneous Equation Approach." *International Journal of Transport Economics,* 13 (1), 87-103.

McFadden, D. (1974): "The Measurement of Urban Travel Demand." *Journal of Public Economics,* 3, 303-28.

McGeehan, H. (1984): "Forecasting the Demand for Inter-Urban Railway Demand Travel in the Republic of Ireland." *Journal of Transport Economics and Policy,* 18 (3), 275-91.

McKenzie, R.P. and P.B. Goodwin (1986): "Dynamic Estimation of Public Transport Demand Elasticities: Some New Evidence." *Traffic Engineering and Control* 27 (2) February.

Mackett, R.L. (1984): *The Impact of Transport Policy on the City.* Supplementary Report 821, Transport and Road Research Laboratory, Crowthorne, Berks.

Mackett, R.L., (1985): "Modelling the Impact of Rail Fare Increases." *Transportation,* 12 (4), May, 293-312.

Madan, D.B. and R. Groenhout (1987): "Modelling Travel Mode Choices for the Sydney Work Trip." *Journal of Transport Economics and Policy,* 21 (2), 135-49.

Maddala, G.S. (1983): *Limited-Dependent and Qualitative Variables in Econometrics.* Camb. Univ. Press, N.Y.

Mannering, F.L. (1986): "A Note on Endogenous Variables in Household Vehicle Utilisation Equations." *Transportation Research,* 20B (1), 1-6.

Mannering, F.L. and C. Winston (1985): "A Dynamic Empirical Analysis of Household Vehicle Ownership and Utilization." *Rand Journal of Economics,* 16 (2), 215-36.

Meurs, H., T. van Eijk and P.B. Goodwin (1990): "Dynamic Estimation of Public Transport Demand Elasticities." In P. Jones (ed.) *Developments in Dynamic and Activity-Based Approaches to Travel Analysis,* Avebury, Aldershot.

Mogridge, M.J.H. (1983): *The Car Market.* Pion, London.

Morrison, S.A. and C. Winston (1983): "The Demand for Intercity Passenger Transportation: The Impact on the Bus Industry in a Changing Environment." *Transportation Research Forum,* 24 (1), 526-34.

Morrison, S.A. and C. Winston (1985): "An Econometric Analysis of the Demand for Intercity Passenger Transportation. *Research in Transportation Economics,* 2, 213-37.

National Bus Company (1984): *Public Transport Demand Elasticities.* Seminar paper, Oxford University Transport Studies Unit Report 246, April.

Oldfield, R. (1979): *Effect of Car Ownership on Bus Patronage.* Laboratory Report 872, Transport and Road Research Laboratory, Crowthorne, Berks.

Oldfield, R.H. and E. Taylor (1981): *The Elasticity for Medium Distance Rail Travel.* LR 993, Transport and Road Research Laboratory, Crowthorne, Berks.

Oum, T.H. (1979a): "Derived Demand for Freight Transport and Intermodal Competition in Canada." *Journal of Transport Economics and Policy,* 13 (2), 149-68.

Oum, T.H. (1979b): "A Cross-Sectional Study of Freight Transport Demand and Rail-Truck Competition in Canada." *Bell Journal of Economics,* 10, 463-82.

Oum, T.H. (1979c): "A Warning on the Use of Linear Logit Models in Transport Mode Choice Studies." *Bell Journal of Economics,* 10, 374-88.

Oum, T.H. (1989): "A Alternative Demand Models and Their Elasticity Estimates." *Journal of Transport Economics and Policy,* 23 (2), 163-87.

Oum, T.H. and D.W. Gillen (1983): "The Structure of Intercity Travel Demand in Canada: Theory, Tests and Empirical Results." *Transportation Research,* 17B (3), 175-91.

Oum, T.H., D.W. Gillen and S.E. Noble (1986): "Demand for Fareclasses and Pricing in Airline Markets." *Logistics and Transportation Review,* 22 (3), 195-222.

Oum, T.H., W.G. Waters II and J.S. Yong (1990): *A Survey of Recent Estimates of Price Elasticities of Demand for Transport.* World Bank Working Paper, WPS359, Washington D.C.

Owen, A.D. and G.D.A. Phillips (1987): "The Characteristics of Railway Passenger Demand." *Journal of Transport Economics and Policy,* 21 (3), September, 231-53.

Quandt, R.E. (1968): "Estimation of Modal Splits." *Transportation Research,* 2, 41-50.

Richards, M.G. and M.E. Ben-Akiva (1975): *A Disaggregate Travel Demand Model.* Saxon House.

Ryder, P. (1982): *Estimated Effects of Petrol Price and LT Fare Changes*

Using the GLTS Model. TS Note 113, Greater London Council, January.

Slade, M.E. (1984): *Conjectures, Firm Characteristics and Market Structure: An Analysis of Vancouver s Gasoline Price Wars*. Discussion Paper, No. 84-25, Department of Economics, the University of British Columbia, Vancouver.

Smith, J.E.R. (1982): *The Effects of the LT Fares Reduction*. Revised version, Transportation Branch, Greater London Council, September.

Southworth, F. (1981): "Calibration of a Multinomial Logit Model of Mode and Destination Choice." *Transportation Research*, 15A (4), 315-26.

Spady, R.H. and A. Friedlaender (1978): "Hedonic Cost Functions for the Regulated Trucking Industry." *Bell Journal of Economics*, 9, 154-79.

Straszheim, M.R. (1978): "Airline Demand Functions in the North Atlantic and Their Pricing Implications." *Journal of Transport Economics and Policy*, 12, 179-95.

Studemund, A.H. and D. Connor (1982): "The Free Fare Transit Experiments." *Transportation Research* 16A (4).

Swait, J. and M. Ben-Akiva (1987): "Empirical Test of a Constrained Discrete Choice Model: Mode Choice in Sao Paulo, Brazil." *Transportation Research*, 21B (2), 103-16.

Talley, W.K. and W.R. Eckroade (1984): "Airline Passenger Demand in Monopoly Flight Segments of a Single Airline." *Transportation Journal*, 24 (2), 73-9.

Talley, W.K. and Schwarz-Miller (1988): "The Demand for Air Services Provided by Air Passenger-Cargo Carriers in a Deregulated Environment." *International Journal of Transport Economics*, 15 (2), 159-68.

Tanner, J.C. (1981): *Methods of Forecasting Kilometres per Car*. Laboratory Report LR 968, Transport and Road Research Laboratory, Crowthorne, Berks.

Tanner, J.C. (1983): *A Lagged Model for Car Ownership Forecasting*. LR1072, Transport and Road Research Laboratory, Crowthorne, Berks.

Taplin, J.H.E. (1980): "A Coherence Approach to Estimates of Price Elasticities in the Vacation Travel Market." *Journal of Transport Economics and Policy*, 14 (1), 19-35.

Taplin, J.H.E. (1982): "Inferring Ordinary Elasticities from Choice or Mode-Split Elasticities." *Journal of Transport Economics and Policy,* 16, 55-63.

Thobani, M. (1984): "A Nested Logit Model of Travel Mode to Work and Auto Ownership." *Journal of Urban Economics,* 15, 287-301.

Thomson, J.M. (1972): *Methods of Traffic Limitation in Urban Areas.* WP3, Environment Directorate, OECD Paris.

Tyson, W.J. (1984): *Evidence on Elasticities.* Seminar paper, Oxford University Transport Studies Unit, Report 246, April.

Uri, N.D. (1982): "Demand for Energy in the US Transport Sector." *Journal of Transport Economics and Policy,* 16 (1), January.

Vaes, T. (1982): *Forecasting Petrol Consumption.* Paper Q3, PTRC, July.

Wabe, J.S. (1987): "The Demand for Gasoline: A Comment on the Cross Section Analysis by Drollas." *Energy Economics,* October.

Wang, G.K.H. and D. Skinner (1984): "The Impact of Fare and Gasoline Price Changes on Monthly Transit Ridership." *Transportation Research* (B) 18, 1, 29-41.

Waters II, W.G. (1984): *A Bibliography of Articles Relevant to Transportation Appearing in Major Economics Journals: 1960-1981.* Centre for Transportation Studies, University of British Columbia.

Waters II, W.G. (1989): *A Bibliography of Articles Relevant to Transportation Appearing in Major Economics Journals: Update 1982-1987.* Centre for Transportation Studies, University of British Columbia.

Webster, F.V. and P.H. Bly (eds.) (1980): *The Demand for Public Transport.* Report of an International Collaborative Study, Transport and Road Research Laboratory, Crowthorne, Berks.

White, P.R. (1981): "Recent Developments in the Pricing of Local Public Transportation Services." *Transport Reviews,* 1 (2), 127-50.

White, P.R. (1984): "Man and His Transport Behavior: Part 4a: User Response to Price Changes: Application of the 'threshold concept." *Transport Reviews,* 4(4), 367-86.

Wilson, W.W., and W. Koo (1988): "Modal Competition in Grain Transport." *Journal of Transport Economics and Policy,* 23 (3), 319-37.

Wilson, G.W. (1980): *Economic Analysis of Intercity Freight Transportation.* Bloomington: Indiana University Press.

Winston, C. (1983): "The Demand for Freight Transportation: Models and Application." *Transportation Research A,* 17A, 419-27.

Winston, C. (1985): "Conceptual Developments in the Economics of Transportation: An Interpretive Survey." *Journal of Economic Literature,* 23, 57-94.

Winston, C. (1981): "A Disaggregate Model of the Demand for Intercity Freight Transportation." *Econometrica,* 49 (4), 981-1006.

Zahavi, Y. (1982): *The UMOT Travel Model II.* Mobility Systems Inc. Bethesda, M.D.

Zahavi, Y., and J.M. McLynn (1983): *Travel Choices under Changing Constraints as Predicted by the UMOT Model.* 10th Transportation Planning Research Colloquium, Zandfoort, December.

Zlatoper, T.J. and Z. Austrian (1989): "Freight Transportation Demand: A Survey of Recent Econometric Studies." *Transportation,* 16, 27-46.

Zudak, L.S. and R.K. Koshal (1982): "Demand for Gasoline and Automobile Characteristics." *International Journal of Transport Economics* IX (3), December.

CHAPTER 3

THE THEORY AND PRACTICE OF DISAGGREGATE DEMAND FORECASTING FOR VARIOUS MODES OF URBAN TRANSPORTATION*

*Daniel L. McFadden***

A major responsibility of transportation planners is to forecast those changes in travel demand induced by alternative transportation policies. In recent years, the range of analyzed policy alternatives and the range of considered policy questions have greatly expanded. Emphasis has shifted from long-run planning of highway networks to short-run planning and to management of integrated multimodal transportation systems. These shifts have placed considerable strain on conventional forecasting tools, which were originally designed to address problems of highway network design.

Flexible demand forecasting methods have consequently been sought, particularly those capable of incorporating the behavioral forces linking individual transportation decisions. The resulting behavioral disaggregate methods expand the policy sensitivity of forecasts. Tests and practical experience with these methods indicate that they are comparable or superior to conventional forecasting techniques in terms of data gathering and computational requirements and forecast accuracy. They provide, in short, a useful way of tackling the expanded list of contempo-

* Reprinted from *Emerging Transportation Planning Methods*, U.S. Department of Transportation, Washington, D.C., 1978, pp. 1-27.
** Professor of Economics, Massachusetts Institute of Technology.

rary planning questions.

Most conventional forecasting models were originally developed to address problems of highway design, and were conceived using analogies with physical systems-with traffic flows described in terms of hydraulic or gravity flow models. Different model components in conventional modeling are not developed from a unified framework. For example, a trip generation model may be developed quite independently of a model of modal split. Another deficiency of conventional models is that they often involve costly and time consuming data gathering and computational requirements, and they are not easily adapted to short-run planning and transportation system management. In particular, they are poorly adapted to pencil-and paper or quick-response policy analyses planners need.

In contrast to conventional methods, disaggregate behavioral forecasting methods are based on a unified conceptual framework. They start from the idea that all travel demand is generated by individual choice behavior, and more specifically (in the current generation of disaggregate behavior models) generated by maximization of preferences or utility. An advantage of disaggregate forecasting is that it is not based on one model; it is an approach or system for building models, and as such it can provide the planner with a method of dealing with a variety of problems as they occur. It is possible to build complex disaggregate behavioral model systems on a scale approaching or exceeding that of conventional models. On the other hand, it is possible to use these techniques to do "quick-and dirty" planning, using "back of-the envelope" calculation, without extensive data collection requirements. In general, the use of behavioral models greatly conserves data collection costs relative to conventional models in both the calibration phase and the forecasting phase. A major advantage of disaggregate models is that they allow the planner to address questions, such as the demand for a new mode, which are difficult to answer in a conventional framework. The current generation of disaggregate models have accuracies comparable to or better than that of conventional models. Disaggregate models have proved practical and successful in a number of applications. I emphasize that the state-of-the-art of disaggregate modelling is evolving rapidly; current models are not the final answer, and have some undesirable features. There are many unexpected characteristics of disaggregate models, and many uncharted pitfalls for the user. Disaggregate models are valuable now for solving some planning problems. In the future, as better disaggregate models evolve, the list of effective applications will grow.

The rich, poor, healthy, and handicapped are rarely homogenous and the aggregate forecasting methods which treat them as such make a specification error. More importantly, these methods preclude the possibility of answering questions such as who benefits and who pays for policy changes. These shortcomings are frequently corrected in part by segmenting the zone population by income class in conventional models. Further segmentation by those socioeconomic characteristics other than income that influence travel patterns would be useful. Conventional calibration of an aggregate model for numerous market segments requires an often unobtainable quantity of data. Pursued to a logical conclusion, each segmented market in an aggregate model should contain a sub-population with identical socioeconomic characteristics and identical transportation environments. This segmentation would amount in practice to distinguishing *each individual* as a "market segment." Aggregate forecasts would then be regarded as the sum of the travel demand of *individuals*, which is a disaggregate forecasting procedure. Disaggregate demand modelling is, then, essentially market segmentation carried to an extreme and is one end of a continuum, with aggregate demand forecasting at the opposite extreme. Consider for example, the mode split for work trips from an origin zone to a destination zone. The aggregate share of a mode is by definition the sum over market segments of the share of the mode in each market segment, weighted by the proportion of the total origin-zone population contained in this market segment. If the segmentation is complete, then one has the formula shown below, with each homogenous market segment having a share for the particular mode. The aggregate share is the weighted average of the shares in the homogenous market segments.

$$
\begin{bmatrix} \text{Aggregate} \\ \text{Share of} \\ \text{A mode} \end{bmatrix} = \begin{bmatrix} \text{Share of mode} \\ \text{in First Market} \\ \text{Segment} \end{bmatrix} \times \begin{bmatrix} \text{Proportion of first} \\ \text{Market Segment in} \\ \text{Population} \end{bmatrix}
$$

$$
+ \begin{bmatrix} \text{Share of Mode} \\ \text{in Second} \\ \text{Market Segment} \end{bmatrix} \times \begin{bmatrix} \text{Proportion of Second} \\ \text{Market Segment in} \\ \text{Population} \end{bmatrix} \quad (1)
$$

$$
+ \cdots + \begin{bmatrix} \text{Share of Mode} \\ \text{in Last Market} \\ \text{Segment} \end{bmatrix} \times \begin{bmatrix} \text{Proportion of Last} \\ \text{Market Segment in} \\ \text{Population} \end{bmatrix}
$$

This formula is one that will recur many times.

An axiom of behavioral disaggregate, choice theory is that the individual is the basic decisionmaking unit, choosing from available alternatives the most desirable. The desirability—or *utility*—of a choice depends upon its attributes and upon the characteristics of the individual. Suitably modified to take account of the psychological phenomena of learning and perception errors, this theory has been used widely and successfully in analyzing and forecasting economic consumer behavior, of which transportation behavior can be viewed as a part.

Let us first clarify what transportation behavior is. A complete definition of a transportation alternative for an individual includes the total pattern of travel: location of residence and job; purchases of vehicles; frequency of work, shopping, personal business, recreation and other trips; destination of trips; scheduling of trips; mode choice; and route choice. In practice, travel demand models concentrate on certain dimensions of travel behavior such as mode choice, taking as given other aspects such as scheduling of trips or location of residence. (A great deal of the *behavioral* theory of disaggregate modelling which will not be presented explicity here deals with how these decisions can be broken apart.)

An alternative's attributes include the transportation level of service variables associated with its pattern of travel. The individual's utility of an alternative is a function of level-of-service variables for the alternative. Utility also depends on the individual's tastes and background-or socioeconomic characteristics. Examples of level-of-service variables are travel time and travel cost. Examples of socioeconomic characteristics are income and family size. An individual chooses among the available alternatives the one which maximizes utility.

Some socioeconomic characteristics and level-of-service variables are observed by the transportation planner. Others are unobserved. For example, income and in-vehicle travel time are usually observed or calculated, while attitudes towards privacy or vehicle noise level are usually not observed.

Consider a group of individuals with similar observed backgrounds and decision environments, characteristics, and observed level-of-service variables for the alternatives. This could be called a *homogeneous market segment*. The frequency of choice for an alternative within a homogeneous market segment is determined by the number of members of this group whose unobserved level-of-service and socioeconomic variables, operating in tandem with the observed variables, give this alternative the highest utility. For example, if an individual's observed travel times on alternative modes, in combination with unobserved attitudes towards privacy, lead him to a higher utility for bus than for auto, then he will choose the bus. Other people with the same observed travel time, and therefore in the same homogeneous market segment, may have different attitudes towards privacy, and as a result may take the auto.

A disaggregate choice model is defined by specifying a probability distribution of the unobserved variables affecting utility, given the values of observed variables in a homogeneous market segment. This probability distribution then determines the *choice probabilities*-the proportions of the group with maximun utility for each alternative.

In summary, a disaggregate behavioral model is specified by forming a concrete individual utility function, a probability distribution of the unobserved variables, and a share of each market segment in the population. Examples of specific utility functions and probability distributions are given below. Using the formula in equation (1), once a concrete utility function is formed and the distribution of unobserved variables specified, each of the shares in a homogeneous market segment is specified. Knowing the proportions of the population in the various market segments, one can then compute the average share.

I will define the mean utility of a homogeneous market segment to be the average of the utilities of all the individuals in this segment. Mean utility depends on the observed level-of-service and socioeconomic variables, and on other determinants of the *distribution* of unobserved variables.

Assuming a concrete probability distribution for the unobserved components of utility leads to a concrete formula for the choice probability. Unfortunately, most distributions of unobserved components yield computationally forbidding choice probability *formulae*, making them difficult to use in practical calibrations and forecasting. One exception is the multinomial logit model, which has choice probabilities of the form shown below. ("Exp" denotes exponentiation.)

The multinomial logit model has the following characteristics: first, it can be interpreted as a disaggregate behavioral model with special assumptions on the probability distribution of the unobserved variables

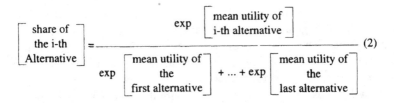

$$\begin{bmatrix} \text{share of} \\ \text{the i-th} \\ \text{Alternative} \end{bmatrix} = \cfrac{\exp \begin{bmatrix} \text{mean utility of} \\ \text{i-th alternative} \end{bmatrix}}{\exp \begin{bmatrix} \text{mean utility of} \\ \text{the} \\ \text{first alternative} \end{bmatrix} + ... + \exp \begin{bmatrix} \text{mean utility of} \\ \text{the} \\ \text{last alternative} \end{bmatrix}} \qquad (2)$$

which will not be detailed here. Second, a multitude of possible disaggregate travel demand models can be formulated in the multinomial logit framework, with the form of the mean utility function depending on the application. Third, the multinomial logit model has the mathematical form of share models used in conventional travel demand forecasting systems, such as the gravity or intervening opportunity models. For example, consider a singly constrained aggregate gravity model for distribution,

$$N_{kj} = O_k A_j / T_{kj}^h \qquad (3)$$

Where N_{kj} = number trips from zone k to zone j;
      A_j = attraction of zone j;
      T_{kj} = impedance between k and j;
      O_k = scale factor to equate trips distributed from zone k to trips originating in zone k.

Then, the *share* of trips from zone k to zone i satisfies

$$P(i \mid T_{k1}, ..., T_{kJ}, A_j) = \cfrac{A_i / T_{ki}^h}{\sum_{j=1}^{J} A_j / T_{kj}^h} \qquad (4)$$

This is a multinomial logit functional form in equation (2) with mean utility = $\log A_i - h \log T_{ki}$. Hence, the multinomial logit form is not new to planners, but has been widely used in one form or the other, although perhaps not widely recognized. As the example makes clear, the multinomial logit form can be used in ways which are quite different in motivation than the principles of disaggregate behavioral theory. In the special case of two alternative modes, the multinomial logit model is termed the (binomial) logit mode split model. This case gives a response curve to a type familiar to every planner in which the share of a particular mode is plotted against the relative desirability of the mode, as in Figure 1. If desirability is measured in terms of relative impedance or

Figure 1. - Binary logit response curve.

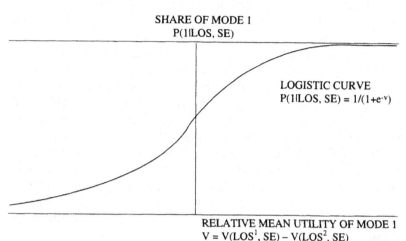

SHARE OF MODE 1
P(1|LOS, SE)

LOGISTIC CURVE
$P(1|LOS, SE) = 1/(1+e^{-v})$

RELATIVE MEAN UTILITY OF MODE 1
$V = V(LOS^1, SE) - V(LOS^2, SE)$

more generally relative disutility, standard mode split models can be interpreted as behavioral models.

What then are the primary differences between traditional aggregate share models and the multinomial logit disaggregate models? First, the structure of the mean utility function in the multinomial logit model is based on economic and psychological regularities in individual behavior. As a consequence it will have a similar form in models of different aspects of transportation choice such as generation, scheduling, distribution, and mode split. For example, if one can determine the variables that matter in mode split, it should be the case that similar variables matter in trip distribution. Second, the calibration and utilization of the model are carried out at the disaggregate level for homogeneous market segments rather than applied to aggregate data.

A successful forecasting model, behavioral disaggregate or otherwise, must assess correctly the impact of level-of-service changes on demand. This requires in calibration that the effects on demand of variations in level-of-service be sorted out from the effects of nontransportation variables. For example, suppose large families with small children locate disproportionately in the suburbs where walk time to transit is high, and workers in large families are disposed to transit because of competing needs of household automobiles. Then a mode split model which fails to control family size and attributes the pattern of transit usage to variations in walk time will understate the onerousness of walk time and yield faulty predictions of the impact on transit patronage of policies influencing transit walk time. The problem is corrected by including family size as an explanatory variable in the model.

Disaggregate calibration methods allow inclusion of a more extensive list of level-of-service and socioeconomic variables than do most aggregate methods, improving the possibility of untangling the effects of level-of-service and other variables. It should be noted, however, that it is possible to develop simple disaggregate models using only conventional variables familiar to planners, such as travel time and travel cost. Empirical tests suggest that the introduction of variables other than conventional components of impedance in a disaggregate mode choice model may improve only marginally the ability of the model to "explain" observed choices in a calibration data base, but may significantly improve forecasting accuracy.

It should be emphasized that the disaggregate behavioral approach is a systems approach to modelling, not a specific model. Disaggregate models can be developed to meet the specific needs of the individual planner. In particular, one can build disaggregate models which are completely analogous to conventional models in terms of data used and types of variables employed, such as travel time and cost. Alternately, one can expand on these models by expanding the description of level-of-service attributes, thereby increasing the ability of the models to be responsive to expanded policy questions. Or, one can expand the socioeconomic description of these models to take into account correlations between level-of-service variables and socioeconomic variables which may have been leading planners to spuriously impute impacts to level-of-service variables. Finally, even though when one thinks of forecasting models, one usually thinks in terms of concrete and well defined variables such as travel time and travel cost which can themselves be forecast from networks under alternative policy scenarios, it is also possible to develop models which depend on survey data on perceptions or attitudes. Although a distinction is sometimes made between attitudinal models and behavioral models, the disaggregate systems approach to building models incorporates both.

Disaggregate models are relatively parsimonious in terms of data requirements. A typical mode choice model, for example, can be calibrated on a sample size of 300 to 3,000 individuals with quite tolerable levels of accuracy. Socioeconomic variables are normally available at an individual level from household surveys. Transportation level-of-service variables are much harder to provide at the level of the individual traveler. Typically these data are obtained from transportation networks, which can provide data only at a traffic analysis zone level. Studies have shown that it is usually reasonable to approximate level-of-service variables for the individual by zonal averages. One exception is walk time to transit, where significant improvements in forecast accuracy can be obtained by segmenting zones geographically and recording individual walking distances. A final point is that the accuracy of any model, conventional or disaggregate, which uses network data is limited in forecasting accuracy by the accuracy of the network. There are many subjective elements and assumptions that go into coding of networks, and one has to be careful in applying forecasting models to understand how these assumptions interact with model calibration.

In principle, the mean utility function in a disaggregate behavioral multinomial logit model can be a very complex function of personal characteristics and level-of-service variables. In existing practical models, however, these variables have appeared in a simple form, usually linearly, with an "importance weight" attached to each variable. For example, mean utility might equal the negative of the sum of travel time and travel cost deflated by wage, each weighted by an importance weight. It may be useful to describe how such a specification can be related to an underlying theory of individual behavior. I will outline a very simple model which provides this special structure. Let us assume that the utility or desirability of an alternative depends on the amount of goods an individual consumes; the amount of leisure he has available; the hours spent traveling (a "bad" rather than a "good" for most people); amenities of various travel destinations; and unobserved factors. The alternatives available to the individual in this model are destination and mode choice, so this is a joint destination and mode choice model. The option of no trip is included as an alternative, so that the model includes trip generation as well.

Each individual is assumed to be constrained by a budget which requires his total expenditures, equal to expenditure on goods plus expenditure on travel, be equal to his total income, which in turn equals wage income plus other income. Time is allocated between leisure, labor, and travel in a way to maximize utility. First, for any travel alternative a mix of labor and leisure is chosen to maximize utility. If the individual considers the alternative of taking the bus to a particular shopping destination, then the optimal amount of time worked, adjusted to take into account the choice of this alternative, will be determined. At this optimal mix, the marginal utility of goods (defined to be the amount of additional utility obtained from one additional unit of goods) multiplied by the wage rate equals the marginal utility of leisure. Second, the travel alternative actually chosen is the one maximizing utility, taking into account the labor-leisure adjustment above for each alternative. The features of this model are summarized in Table 1.

The preceding argument provides a justification-from the economic theory of utility maximizing behavior-for the entry of travel time and travel cost divided by wage as linear variables in the mean utility function. Generalization of this model is possible in several directions.

Time, cost, and other attributes of alternatives may have subcomponents. Time, for example, can be partitioned into in-vehicle time under congested or non-congested conditions, walk time, and wait time. Costs can be divided into overheads, indirectly charged per-trip costs such as fuel and maintenance, and daily out-of-pocket costs such as tolls. These components can be given separate coefficients in equation(*) of the preceding table; the relative weights of components can then be determined as part of the calibration of the model, which is preferable to assigning traditional weights.

The coefficients b_T, b_C, and b_A may depend on observed socioeconomic variables. For example, the weight b_T associated with the walk time component of travel time may be a function of an individual's age and health status, or of those neighborhood characteristics correlated with safety. If this association is expressed in a linear-in parameters form, then the mean utility function (*) is linear in these parameters, and the calibrated model will describe both the importance weight attached to walk time and the variation of this weight with socioeconomic factors.

There are a number of methods available to calibrate disaggregated behavioral multinomial logit models.The technique which is most commonly used is maximum likelihood estimation. From the user's point of view, this method is comparable to regression analysis-the inputs and outputs of computer programs which carry out this calibration resemble

Table 1. A Simple Behavioral Utility Model

- Utility depends on goods, leisure, hours spent traveling, amenities at various travel destinations, unobserved factors
- Alternatives describe destination and mode choice, including the no trip option
- Each individual is constrained by a budget:

$$\begin{array}{c} \text{Expenditure} \\ \text{On Goods} \end{array} + \begin{array}{c} \text{Travel} \\ \text{Cost} \end{array} = \begin{array}{c} \text{Wage} \\ \text{Income} \end{array} + \begin{array}{c} \text{Other} \\ \text{Income} \end{array} \qquad (5)$$

- Time is allocated between leisure, labor, and travel
- For any travel alternative, the mix of labor and leisure is chosen to maximize utility. At this mix, the marginal utility of goods, multiplied by the wage rate, equals the marginal utility of leisure
- The chosen alternative maximizes utility

$$\begin{bmatrix} \text{UTILITY} \\ \text{OF } i^{th} \\ \text{ALTERNATIVE} \end{bmatrix} = \left(\begin{bmatrix} \text{TRAVEL} \\ \text{TIME} \end{bmatrix} + \frac{[\text{TRAVEL COST}]}{[\text{WAGE}]} \right) \times \begin{bmatrix} \text{MARGINAL} \\ \text{UTILITY} \\ \text{OF LEISURE} \end{bmatrix}$$

$$+ \begin{bmatrix} \text{TRAVEL} \\ \text{TIME} \end{bmatrix} \times \begin{bmatrix} \text{MARGINAL UTILITY} \\ \text{OF TRAVEL TIME} \end{bmatrix}$$

$$+ [\text{AMENITIES}] \times \begin{bmatrix} \text{MARGINAL UTILITY} \\ \text{OF AMENITIES} \end{bmatrix}$$

$$+ \begin{bmatrix} \text{UNOBSERVED} \\ \text{ATTRIBUTES} \end{bmatrix} \times \begin{bmatrix} \text{MARGINAL UTILITY OF} \\ \text{UNOBSERVED ATTRIBUTES} \end{bmatrix}$$

$$\begin{bmatrix} \text{MEAN UTILITY} \\ \text{OF THE } i^{th} \\ \text{ALTERNATIVE} \end{bmatrix} = -b_T \times \begin{bmatrix} \text{TRAVEL} \\ \text{TIME} \end{bmatrix} - b_c \times \frac{[\text{TRAVEL COST}]}{[\text{WAGE}]}$$

$$+ b_A \times [\text{AMENITIES}] \qquad (*)$$

b_T, b_C, AND b_A ARE PARAMETERS

closely the inputs and outputs of regression programs, and require the same skills from the user as do regression analyses. Therefore, any planning organization which currently has the capacity to do regression analyses also has the potential ability to calibrate multinomial logit models.

There are good statistical computer programs available for multinomial logit analyses using the maximum likelihood method. One available to many planners is the ULOGIT programs in the UTPS package.

There are several other stand alone logit programs available with options not included in ULOGIT. QUAIL, a flexible data management and multinomial program developed by McFadden and his colleagues, is available in versions suitable for use on CDC or IBM machines. Multinomial logit programs for IBM machines are also available from Cambridge Systematics, Inc. and from Charles Manski at Hebrew University. All these programs are available at the cost of reproducing tapes and manuals.

In addition to maximum likelihood estimation, there are several other techniques for fitting multinomial logit models. One technique, currently available only on QUAIL, is non-linear least squares. This method has an advantage relative to maximum likelihood estimation in that it is less sensitive to data measurement errors, an important consideration given the nature of transportation data. Finally, there is an estimation technique called the Berkson-Theil method which requires grouped data rather than individual observations. If data is collected by individual, it must be grouped to use this method. On the other hand, the method requires only a standard regression program, and hence is readily available to most planners. When data can be grouped easily, the Berkson-Theil procedure is recommended. It has good statistical properties, and is considerably less expensive than maximum likelihood estimation.

Let us next consider a simple calibrated disaggregate multinomial logit model with work trip mode choice. The model in Table 2 was calibrated by the maximum likelihood technique on a sample of 771 commuters in the San Francisco Bay Area in 1973, before the inauguration of BART Trans-Bay service. The explanatory variables in this model are the level-of-sevice attributes commonly used to define impedance in conventional models, in-vehicle travel time, excess or out-of-vehicle time, and cost divided by wage. The model contains four alternatives: auto drive alone, auto shared with someone else (either family or non-family carpool), and bus, subdivided by access mode. Auto access to bus includes "kiss-n-ride" and "park-n-ride." Alternative-specific dummy variables are introduced to capture the average influence of unobserved attributes of each mode. The number of dummy variables is one less than the number of alternatives, as the coefficient of the bus-with-walk-access dummy is normalized to zero. One such arbitrary normalization is necessary.

A negative coefficient for a variable indicates that an increase in this

Table 2. A Simple Work Trip Mode Choice Model, Estimated Pre-BART

(Mode 1–Auto Alone; Mode 2–Bus, Walk Access;
Mode 3–Bus, Auto Access; Mode 4–Carpool)
Model: Multinomial Logit, Fitted by the Maximum
Likelihood Method

(The Variable takes the described value in the
alternatives listed in parentheses and zero in
non-listed alternatives)

Independent Variable	Estimated Coefficient	T-Statistic
Generic		
Cost divided by post-tax wage, in cents		
divided by cents per minute(1-4) · · · · · · · · · · · · · ·	– .0412	7.63
In-vehicle time, in minutes(1-4) · · · · · · · · · · · · · ·	– .0201	2.78
Excess time, in minutes(1-4) · · · · · · · · · · · · · · · ·	– .0531	7.54
Specific		
Auto alone dummy(1) ·	– 0.892	3.38
Bus with auto access dummy(3) · · · · · · · · · · · · ·	–1.78	7.52
Carpool alternative dummy(4) · · · · · · · · · · · · · ·	–2.15	8.56

Likelihood ratio index	0.1499
Log likelihood at zero	– 1069.0
Log likelihood at convergence	– 717.7
Percent correctly predicted	
(by maximum probability)	58.50(compared with 39.42 by chance)

Value of time saved as a percent of wage(t-statistics in parentheses):

In vehicle time	49 (2.68)
Excess time	129 (5.16)

All cost and time variables are calculated round-trip. Excess time is defined as the sum of walk time, transfer time, wait time, and half of initial headways. Dependent variable is alternative choice (one for chosen alternative, zero otherwise).

Number of people in sample who chose

Auto alone	429
Bus with walk access	134
Bus with auto access	30
Carpool	178
Total sample size	771

variable for a mode will lower the mode's choice probability. For example, the coefficient of excess time is negative. If excess time rises for a particular mode—say, bus-with-walk-access—then the mean utility of this mode will fall, and as a consequence the choice probability for this mode in a homogeneous market segment will fall. The T-statistics on the right-hand-side are indicators of the precision of the parameters. Values less than two indicate that the parameters cannot be reliably distinguished between zero. This particular model indicates that individuals react strongly to transportation level-of-service variables. The average effects of unobserved variables, reflected in the coefficients of the alternative-specific dummy variables, are important.

I will expand further on the nature of the variables entering this model, and specifically on the alternative-specific dummy variables. Socioeconomic variables which influence the mean utility of every alternative in exactly the same way have no influence on choice probabilities. They change both the numerator and the denominator of the multinomial logit formulae by a factor which cancels out. Hence, there is interest only in those socioeconomic variables which interact with level-of-service variables to affect the mean utility of different alternatives differently. For example, income can matter only if, when income changes, it increases the attractiveness of one of the alternatives relative to a second. Travel cost divided by wage is one example of interaction. A second example is a variable which takes the value of one for an alternative which requires driving a vehicle when the individual has a driver's license, and is zero otherwise. The variable in this example is the product of a socioeconomic variable which is one if the individual can drive and zero otherwise, and a level-of-service variable which is one if the alternative requires driving and zero otherwise. In the model in Table 2, an alternative-specific dummy variable for an alternative is one for this alternative and zero for all other alternatives. Mean utility may be included in alternative-specific dummy variables appearing alone, or in interaction with other variables. The coefficient of an alternative-specific dummy variable can be interpreted as reflecting the impacts of an alternative's unmeasured level-of-service attributes that are not captured in the remaining variables. For example, the auto-alone dummy variable is one for the auto-alone mode and zero otherwise. (The number following the name of the variable indicates for which alternatives it is non-zero.) The coefficient -.892 can be interpreted as representing the average impact of unmeasured characteristics of the auto alternative relative to the bus-with-walk access alternative.

A variable which is the result of interaction between an alternative-specific dummy variable and another variable is termed an alternative-specific variable. An example of an alternative-specific variable would be one which gives the value of out-of-vehicle travel time for the bus with auto access alternative and zero for all other alternatives. The coefficient of this variable compared with the coefficients of other alternative-specific travel times would reflect the impact of specific attributes of auto-accessed transit on the onerousness of transit travel time. A generic, or homogeneous-effect, variable is one which does not incorporate interaction with alternative-specific dummy variables. An example is a variable which gives out-of-vehicle travel time for each alternative, uninfluenced by the name of the alternative; i,e., an out-of-vehicle time of fifteen minutes is treated the same whether it is auto access time or transit wait time. In this model the level-of-service variable—cost, in-vehicle travel time, and access time—were all generic or homogeneous-effects. Each of these variables has values for each of the four alternatives. For example, travel time in auto has the same importance weight as travel time in transit.

Individual utility, expressed as a function of observed and unobserved variables, should depend on only generic variables. The reason for this is behavioral—individual utility depends on the constellation of physical experience associated with an alternative, and cannot depend on labels such as "auto," "transit," or "CBD"—attached to alternatives by the planner. Mean utility on the other hand may depend on alternative-specific variables which mimic or act as proxies for the influence of unobserved generic variables. For example, suppose individual utility depends on generic in-vehicle travel time weighted by a generic index of comfort. Suppose the comfort index is unobserved, but varies between alternatives. Then the mean utility for an alternative will have a coefficient of in-vehicle time which reflects the average comfort index on this alternative. It will then appear to the planner that mean utility depends on alternative-specific travel times. Alternative-specific variables in a multinomial logit model are evidence of failure to observe generic variables which are influencing behavior. A long-run objective of behavioral demand analyses is to improve model specification and data collection to the point where alternative-specific variables are not needed.

Models based solely on generic variables are also desirable from the point of view of forecasting. Coefficients of alternative-specific variables do not isolate behavioral sources of variation across alternatives, or establish that alternative-specific effects will be stable or extendable to new situations when forecasting. In the current state-of-the-art of disaggregate demand analyses, alternative-specific effects do capture the impacts of variables not observed in standard transportation data sets; their omission would bias the importance weights associated with other variables.

In the lower half of Table 2 are several summary statistics which give some notion of the goodness-of-fit of this model to the calibration data base. The likelihood ratio index in an analog of the multiple correlation coefficient in regression analysis. Empirically, its values run lower than typical values for a multiple correlation coefficient. A value of .2 to .3 indicates a good fit. A second measure of goodness-of-fit is the ability of the model to forecast accurately. In this particular sample, 39% of the choices of individuals would be predicted correctly by change, whereas the model predicts 58% correctly. A third method commonly used to assess the merit of models is to compute the implicit values of time implied by the model. This is a potentially misleading measure of goodness-of-fit, both because these statistics tend to be very unreliable and because there is some tendency to accept or reject models on the basis of consistency with earlier result in the literature, which could perpetuate errors in the assessment of time evaluations. On the other hand, the critical role of value of time tradeoffs in policy applications makes it necessary to compute these values. Value of time calculations in the multinomial logit model are determined from the ratio of time and cost coefficients. These calculations assume that within a homogeneous market segment, the value of time is uniform. Note that this is not necessarily a good assumption. For the model in Table 2, in-vehicle time is valued at half the wage rate and access time at 130% of the wage rate. Table 3 describes a more complex multinomial logit modal split model.

One way of judging the effectiveness or the accuracy of a disaggregate demand model is to compute what is called a prediction success table. Table 4 is a prediction success table for the model in Table 3. Each column corresponds to a predicted alternative and each row corresponds to an actual choice. The number 296.6, for example, is the number of persons who were predicted to take auto alone who did in fact

Table 3. Work Trip Mode Choice Model, Estimated Pre-BART

(Mode 1–Auto Alone; Mode 2–Bus, Walk Access;
Mode 3–Bus, Auto Access; Mode 4–Carpool)
Model: Multinomial Logit, Fitted by the Maximum
Likelihood Method

(The Variable takes the described value in the
alternatives listed in parentheses and zero in
non-listed alternatives)

Independent Variable	Estimated Coefficient	T-Statistic
Cost divided by post-tax wage, in cents divided by cents per minute(1-4)	− .0284	4.31
Auto-in-vehicle time, in minutes(1, 3, 4)	− .0644	5.65
Transit in-vehicle time, in minutes(2,3)	− .0259	2.94
Walk time, in minutes(2,3)	− .0689	5.28
Transfer wait time, in minutes(2,3)	− .0538	2.30
Number of transfers(2,3)	− .105	0.776
Headway of first bus, in minutes(2,3)	− .0318	3.18
Family income with ceiling of $7,500, in $ per year(1)	− .00000454	0.0511
Family income minus $7,500 with floor of $0 and ceiling of $3,000, in $ per year(1)	− .0000572	0.430
Family income minus $10,500 with floor of $0 and ceiling of $5,000, in $ per year(1)	− .0000543	0.907
Number of persons in household who can drive(1)	− .102	4.81
Number of persons in household who can drive(3)	− .990	3.29
Number of persons in household who can drive(4)	− .872	4.25
Dummy if person is head of household(1)	− .627	3.37
Employment density at work location(1)	− .00160	2.27
Home location in or near CBD (2=in CBD, 1=near CBD, 0 otherwise)(1)	− .502	4.18
Autos per driver with a ceiling of one(1)	5.00	9.65
Autos per driver with a ceiling of one(3)	2.33	2.74
Autos per driver with a ceiling of one(4)	2.38	5.28
Auto alone alternative dummy(1)	−5.26	5.93
Bus with auto access dummy(3)	−5.49	5.33
Carpool alternative dummy(4)	−3.84	6.36

Likelihood ratio index	.294
Log likelihood at zero	− 1069.0
Log likelihood at convergence	− 595.8

Table 3. Work Trip Mode choice Model, Estimated Pre-BART (Continued)

Percent correctly predicted
  (by maximum probability)   67.83 (compared with 39.42 by chance)
Value of time saved as a percent of wage (t-statistics in parentheses):
  Auto in-vehicle time   227 (3.20)
  Transit in-vehicle time   91 (2.43)
  Walk time   243 (3.10)
  Transfer wait time   190 (2.01)
Value of initial headways as a percent of wage: 112 (2.49)

All cost and time variables are calculated round-trip. Dependent variable is alternative choice (one for chosen alternative, zero otherwise).

Number of people in sample who chose
  Auto alone   429
  Bus with walk access   134
  Bus with auto access   30
  Carpool   178

  Total sample size   771

choose this alternative, and 29.0—the next number below it—is the number predicted to take auto alone who in fact took bus with walk access. Predictions in this table are based on the choice probabilities of individuals. For example, the entry 29.0 is the sum of the predicted choice probabilities of auto alone, taken over the set of all individuals who actually chose bus-with-walk-access. This prediction success table summarizes goodness-of-fit of the model to its calibration data base. This table has the property that the average observed shares (56% auto, 17% bus/walk, 4% bus/auto, and 23% carpool in this sample) coincide with the predicted values. This is a consequence of calibration, and says nothing about the accuracy of the model. A notion of how well the model fits is obtained by looking at the percent correctly predicted in aggregate for each alternative. For auto alone, 69% of our predictions are correct, while for the bus with auto alternative, only 22% are predicted correctly. These figures illustrate that it is much easier to be successful when you are predicting demand for a highly used mode than when you are predicting demand for a little used mode. This observation applies throughout travel demand modeling, including conventional models. An index of prediction accuracy for an alternative can be

Table 4. Prediction Success Table for Pre-BART
Model and Calibration Data Base

Actual Alternatives	Predicted Alternatives					
	(1) Auto Alone	(2) Bus/ Walk	(3) Bus/ Auto	(4) Carpool	Row Total	Observed Share (%)
(1) Auto alone	296.6	29.4	10.0	93.1	429.0	56
(2) Bus/Walk	29.0	75.1	6.6	23.3	134.0	17
(3) Bus/Auto	9.8	5.9	6.7	7.6	30.0	4
(4) Carpool	93.6	23.7	6.7	54.0	178.0	23
Column Total	429.0	134.0	30.0	178.0	771	100
Predicted Share(%)	56	17	4	23	100	
Percent Correct	69.1	56.1	22.3	30.4	56.0	
Success Index	1.23	3.30	5.58	1.32		

The equality of predicted and observed shares is a consequence of the calibration process.

obtained by dividing the percent correctly predicted by the percent correct you could achieve by chance. The higher this prediction success index, the better the model. In terms of the prediction success index, the model in Table 3 has the most difficulty distinguishing between auto alone and carpool, and does reasonably well in predicting transit usage.

A more interesting test of the accuracy or validity of a disaggregate model is to examine its ability to predict on a data set different than the calibration data set. Recall that the model in Table 3 was fitted to 1973 data, prior to the inauguration of Trans-Bay BART service. To test the validity of the model, we used it to forecast mode split in 1975, including full BART service. This was done by comparing the actual mode choices of a 1975 sample with the choices predicted by the model in Table 3 when the 1975 set of alternatives and level of explanatory variables were substituted for each individual. The prediction success table for these forecasts is given in Table 5. The columns correspond to predictions using the 1973 calibrated model. Recall that the 1973 model has no BART alternatives, only auto-alone or shared-or bus-with-walk or auto access. From these alternative we wish to predict the patronage on two new models, BART with auto access and BART with walk access.

Transport Demand and Forecasting

Table 5. *Prediction Success Table for Pre-BART*
Model and Post-BART Data

Actual Alternatives	Predicted Alternatives					
	(1) Auto Alone	(2) Bus/ Walk	(3) Bus/ Auto	(4) BART/ Bus	(5) BART/ Auto	(6) Carpool
(1) Auto alone	255.1	22.21	6.362	1.513	13.72	79.07
(2) Bus/Walk	11.56	36.43	2.988	1.679	1.421	13.92
(3) Bus/Auto	1.249	2.811	.687	.0066	1.625	2.622
(4) BART/Bus	.858	1.934	.120	1.391	.258	1.440
(5) BART/Auto	8.898	3.149	1.756	.695	8.828	9.674
(6) BART/Bus	74.68	12.43	3.305	1.357	7.497	37.73
Column Total	352.4	78.97	15.22	6.642	35.35	144.4
Predicted Share(%)	55.8	12.5	2.4	1.0	5.3	22.9
(Standard error)	(11.4)	(3.4)	(1.4)	(.5)	(2.4)	(10.7)
Percent Correct	72.4	46.1	4.5	21.0	26.5	26.1
Success Index	1.30	3.69	1.88	21.0	5.0	1.14
Predicted Share less observed share	-4.1	1.7	1.0	0.05	0.1	1.2
Actual Share(%)	59.9	10.8	1.4	.95	5.2	21.7

Totals
Sample Size   631
Percent Correct   53.9 (42.0 by chance)
Success Index   1.28

The model in Table 3 contains some alternative-specific variables, and it was necessary to make judgments about what form those alternative-specific variables would have in the post-BART situation. We assumed that BART with auto access has the same unobserved characteristics as bus with auto access, so that their alternative-specific variables would enter with the same coefficients. Analogously, we assumed that BART with bus access has the same characteristics as bus-with-walk-access, with alternative-specific variables entering with the same coefficient. An overall judgment from Table 5 is the disaggregate model in Table 3 which is relatively successful in predicting demand for a major new transportation mode. The model forecasts a BART mode share of 6.3

percent, compaed with an observed share of 6.2 percent. A caveat is necessary, however. The statistical imprecision of the calibrated coefficient of the pre-Bart model would lead one to expect forecasts for modes with low aggregate shares, such as BART, to have relatively large percentage errors. The actual prediction accuracy here is better than one could expect by chance, given the size of these standard errors of the forecasts. Further, disaggregate models in the form in Table 3 tend to be quite sensitive to the selection of variables entering the mean utility function, and to the definition and measurement of explanatory variables. For example, one of the problems which appears in this table is an overforecast of bus usage. An explanation can be found in the network calculation of bus access time. To construct these times, we used a 1980 Bay Area network which was constructed assuming 1980 bus service levels. The network was scaled back to 1975 by dropping bus links which did not exist in 1975, but the 1980 walk times were shortened because the assumed 1980 transit service remained at the 1980 levels. As a result, walk time from our network calculations under-estimate true bus access time. This data measurement problem seems to be the major source of prediction error in Table 5. However, Disaggregate models such as the one in Table 3 exhibit some anomalies when calibration samples are partitioned by location, family composition, or choice alternative definition, suggesting that there are factors influencing travel demand which the current models do not capture adequately.

A statistical test of whether the post-BART data was in fact explained by the pre-BART model failed. That is to say, from a statistical point of view there are post-BART factors which are not explained adequately by the 1973 model despite the fact that it does a reasonably good job of forecasting aggregate BART patronage. In short, disaggregate demand forecasting has the flexibility and the potential accuracy to meet current planning needs, but the field of disaggregate demand forecasting is relatively uncharted, offering many potential pitfalls to the planner.

One property of the multinomial logit model which has gained some noteriety is called the *independence from irrelevant alternatives*(IIA) condition. This is a feature of the model which occurs when the mean utility of an alternative depends only on the attributes of that alternative and on the characteristics of the decisionmaker, and not on the attributes of other alternatives. In this case, the IIA property requires that the relative share of any two alternatives is independent of the attributes of the remaining alternatives. The terminology is due to the psychologist Duncan Luce, who first proposed the IIA property as an axiom for behavior in psychological choice.

The IIA property is a blessing and a curse for the multinomial logit model. It has some significant advantages. First, it allows calibration without having to consider all possible alternatives. For example, if one wants to carry out a study of destination choice, it is possible to calibrate the model with data on a selected number of destinations rather than having to consider the full set of destinations. This can substantially reduce data collection requirements. Second, IIA permits quick determination of the effects of introducing a new alternative, because the forecast of mode share for a new alternative mode can be obtained by including one additional term in the denominator of the multinomial logit formula.

The IIA property also has some major disadvantages. It fails to allow for different degrees of competition of similarity between alternatives. Consider the following example. Suppose that individuals initially have a shopping choice between the central business district (CBD) and a shopping mall—call it East Mall; and suppose that they initially split 50–50 between these two destinations. For simplicity, assume all individuals have exactly the same observed explanatory variables; i,e., they represent a homogeneous market segment. Suppose now that a new situation is introduced in which a North Mall is constructed. Suppose the North Mall and East Mall are equally far away for these individuals, with equal amenities. Then one would expect individuals who previously chose to shop in the CBD to continue to do so, and individuals who previously went to the East Mall to now split evenly between the East and North Malls. Hence, one would expect in this situation to observe a split of 50% CBD, and 25% for each of the two Malls. On the other hand, a multinomial logit model will predict a one-third split for each of the alternatives. The reason it does so is that it assumes that the relative odds of choosing between CBD and East Mall will be unchanged when an additional alternative is introduced—the North Mall. In other words, the multinomial logit model is unable to take account of the fact that the new North Mall will be more competitive with the East Mall than it will be with CBD shopping.

Let us pursue this example one step further. Suppose that we could break down the "homogeneous" market segment further, into, say, males and femles, and that there were very strong differentials in shopping characteristics for these two socioeconomic groups. Suppose before the construction of North Mall the female segment divides 95-5 in favor of shopping at East Mall, while the male segment divides 95-5 in favor of CBD destinations. The aggregate share for the two segments is 50-50. Suppose now one applies the multinomial logit model to forecast destinations after North Mall is built, with separate forecasts for males and females. Then, the predicted splits for the female segment will be 48.7% for each Mall and 2.6% for CBD destinations; for the male segment, 4.8% for each Mall and 90.5% for CBD destinations; and finally an aggregate mode split of 46.5% for CBD destinations and 27% for each of the two Malls. Compare this to the observed split which is 50% for CBD destinations and 25% for each Mall. Then, the error introduced by the failure of IIA is small when market segmentation is effective in dividing the market.

In summary, the IIA property is extremely useful for practical planning. Its limitations are a more serious problem in aggregate modelling than in disaggregate modelling, where refining market segments can minimize errors. Although much of the discussion of the IIA property in the literature is concentrated on its logical possibility, a much more important consideration for the practising planner is its empirical validity. If the disaggregate multinomial logit model having the IIA property can be shown to fit a calibration data set well and to forecast accurately in a particular application, then it is a useful tool for the planner.

Specific statistical tests for the IIA property applicable to transportation data sets have been developed by McFadden, Tye, and Train. These tests can be used to investigate various specific sources of failure of IIA. Tests of IIA have been applied to a seven-alternative work trip data set for the San Francisco Bay Area. Because of the Multiple Transit alternatives (we have three BART, two bus, auto alone, and carpool alternatives) with common main-mode characteristics for alternative access modes, one would expect this data set to provide a rather stringent test of the IIA property. The multinomial logit model tested was of the same general form as the model in Table 3. The hypothesis that the model satisfied the IIA property was accepted for all the tests performed, with two exceptions which tended to point to data specification problems rather than IIA problems. Hence, this empirical study suggests that although IIA is an unpalatable logical restriction from the standpoint of the general theorist, it may be inconsequential from the standpoint of practical planning. At the very least, satisfaction of IIA is an empirical question, not a question of doctrine.

What should a planner do about the IIA property, given that its validity is a matter of concern in the profession? First, carry out diagnostic tests of the validity of the property for the specific data set you are using. If you reject the IIA property, try to refine the specification of your model by a more detailed market segmentation, improving data definition, or by adding variables to the model. If necessary, replace the multinomial logit model with one allowing patterns of substitution between alternatives.

The multinomial logit model is a special case of a disaggregate model, and not in any sense the end of the line in terms of realism and accuracy. However, it is the only disaggregate model which I believe is of current widespread practical useability.

I have described the process of defining and calibrating disaggregate behavioral models. Now I will discuss how these models are applied in forecasting. First, one must translate policy questions into specific technological features of the proposed transportation service. For example, suppose the policy question posed is "How much more transit service can we provide with a $1,000,000 block grant?" The question must be first translated into specific operating proposals for headways, route density, and so forth. Then, network or manual calculations, or an idealized supply model, must be used to provide the level-of-service variables resulting from a proposal. These variables must be provided for each homogeneous market segment for the level of segmentation at which the analysis is being carried out. Next, the size of each homogeneous market segment must be determined. In the short-run, one can normally assume population demographics continue to hold. For long-run forecasting, one must make projections of land use and demographic trends, and factor these forecasts into the segmentation. Finally, one must use the basic aggregation formula in equation (1) to predict changes in aggregate shares. Information on homogeneous market segments can be used to calculate the distributional consequence of proposals if this information is needed. Patronage and revenue calculations for the homogeneous market segments can be carried out, and aggregated to give totals. These figures, along with the capital and operating costs of alternative proposals, determine their feasibility. Among those proposals forecast to be feasible, a selection can be made using the evaluation criterion employed by the planning agency.

Consider the following example of the use of this procedure. Assume in Figure 2 that the square box at the top represents a traffic zone. Assume that the traffic zone is bisected by an express busway, and that one busway station denoted by the black dot serves the zone. The population densities within the zone are such that 75% of the people live north of the busway, and the remaining 25% live south of it. Suppose there is no parking provided at the busway station; hence, the people either walk, take feeder bus, or are driven to the station. Suppose current feeder-bus headways are twenty minutes on both the north and the south side and that the modal shares to the busway station are as follows: on the north side 52% walked; 18% take the bus; 30% are driven. On the south side 10% walk; 10% take the bus; 80% are driven and in total in this zone 41% walk; 16% take the feeder bus; 43% are driven.

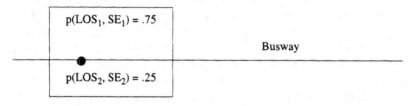

Current Modal Shares

	Walk	Bus	Driven	Proportion in Population
North	52	.18	.30	.75
South	.10	.10	80	.25
Total	.41	.16	43	1.0

Figure 2.—An example:The impact of improved feeder bus service.

The Planning commission is contemplating improving the feeder bus service on the north side by reducing the headway from twenty minutes to five minutes, but leaving it unchanged in the low density area south of the busway. The consequences of this policy are calculated using a multinomial logit model with mean utility function at the bottom of

Table 6. The mean utility is 3.11 times a variable which is 1 if the person walks and 0 otherwise, plus .495 times a variable which is 1 if the individual takes the bus, zero otherwise, minus .11 times travel times, minus .08 times headway, minus .2 time cost, plus .672 times the number of drivers (if the person is driven) and 0 otherwise. Here are the changes in mode shares calculated from the multinomial logit model when north-side feeder bus headways are reduced: North of the segment, the walk share goes down by .15, the bus share rises by .24, the number driven goes down by .90. Summed over the zone, the impact then is a .18 increase in the feeder bus share, a .11 decrease in the walk share, and a .07 decrease in the share of persons driven.

So far I have discussed the calculation of the effects of policy change on a homogeneous market segment. It is necessary to in general combine results for homogeneous market segments into an aggregate prediction for the population as a whole. If the segmentation is extremely detailed, then it may not be practical to carry through the aggregation by summing over all homogeneous market segments. There are a number of short-cuts or approximations to the aggregation process which can be used. I will mention four. First, one can approximate the empirical distribution of homogeneous market segments in the population with a mathematical distribution for which the expectation, or average, can be calculated analytically, possibly after a transformation of variables. Second, one can approximate the empirical distribution of socioeconomic variables and level-of-service variables in the population by a histogram, with each cell in the histogram corresponding to a fairly homogeneouls market segment. Then the aggregate forecast is approximately equal to a sum over these market segments. This segmentation can be as coarse or as fine as desired; the finer the structure, the more accurate the

Table 6. *Change in Mode Shares when North Side Feeder*
Headway is Cut from 20 Minutes to 5 Minutes

Segment	Walk	Bus	Driven	Proportion in Pupulation
North	-.15	+.24	-.09	.75
South	0	.0	0	,25
Total	1.11	+.18	-.07	

Mean Utility = 3.110(if walk)+4.950(if bus) -.110(traveling time) -.080(headway) -.200(cost) +.672(no. of drivers, if driven)

segmentation. If a very coarse segmentation is used, then the method is close to an aggregate procedure. Third, one can approximate the empirical distribution of attributes of homogeneous market segments by using series expansions in terms of statistical moments, so that aggregate shares are written as functions of choice probabilities at average arguments and moments of the distribution of explanatory variables. Fourth, one can sample randomly from the empirical distribution of characteristics of homogeneous market segments, and form the sample expectation as an approximation to the population expectation. The first and third methods require information on moments of the distribution of explanatory variables. The second requires data on the size of market segments, and the fourth requires a representative sample from the population. The first method is not feasible except in special cases. Segmentation method two is feasible, and simple to apply for quick, rough answers when the number of explanatory variables is not too large. The third method does not converge rapidly, or perhaps not even at all, unless the distribution of explanatory variables is relatively concentrated. The fourth method is the most flexible. The required data for this method can be supplied from a calibration data base provided that the base is representative of the population, or from other data sources such as U.S. Census data, provided these sources contain the variables used in the forecasting model. In contrast to calibration, forecasting requires no data on actual transportation choices. Those are predicted by the model. Hence one can utilize socioeconomic data sets which are not specifically transportation-oriented to provide explanatory variables. A method of synthesizing socioeconomic data from Census data has been developed by Cosslett, Duguay, Jung, and McFadden (1977).

In summary, the sampling method of approximating statistical expectations is the most flexible tool for aggregate forecasting from disaggregate models,. The method can be combined with survey or synthesized data to provide aggregate forecasts at reasonable cost.

The basic principles of behavioral disaggregate modelling, in summary, are that aggregate travel demand can be expressed as the sum of the demands of homogeneous market segments, and that the demand within a homogeneous market segment has a structure determined by behavioral regularities that are stable over time and space. How different are disaggregate and aggregate models in concept? They differ primarily in degree. Disaggregation carries market segmentation to the extreme. It emphasizes the regularity of individual choice behavior, in contrast to conventional modelling which emphasizes the physical regularity of aggregate flows. Aggregate and disaggregate models differ significantly in the number and form of explanatory variables, consistency across different aspects of travel behavior, calibration methods, and forecasting techniques. These differences are, however, primarily technical; the result of historical development and the practical limitations of data compilation and computation. Behind every good aggregate model stands a disaggregate model, and vice versa. The discovery of empirically valid regularities which simplify and extend forecasting methodology, and the relaxation of empirically invalid restrictions, should be a goal of every transportation analyst. From this point of view, disaggregate behavioral forecasting is a natural evolution of traditional aggregate demand analysis.

Calibration of behavioral disaggregate models requires less data than aggregate model calibrations. In forecasting, disaggregate models need to consider both the explanatory variables for each homogeneous market segment, and the computation of each segment's mode split. Fortunately, a variety of analytic or statistical methods, or a coarse market segmentation, can provide forecasts of aggregate mode shares. The range of answerable policy questions is limited by the extent of level-of-service variables affecting the choice probability. The planner's ability to translate policy changes into level-of-service changes is another potential limitation.

Aggregation predictions in disaggregate models can be adapted to comprehensive analysis of large-scale transportation system changes, or to "quick and dirty" analysis of limited aspects of travel behavior and incremental policy changes. In short behavioral disaggregate forecasting methodology can provide a multi-channel forecasting system. The theory of individual behavior provides a blueprint for the construction of disaggregate models. The methodology has the flexibility to meet the varied policy analysis needs of the planner.

It must be stressed that disaggregate behavioral analysis is neither a model nor model system; it is an approach to the development of model systems. There will never be "best" or "final" disaggregate models. Model systems will continue to evolve as experience accumulates. Not all model systems developed from behavioral principles will be "good." The method is open to abuse and misuse, as are aggregate model systems. Given that the analytic and statistical methods employed in disaggregate behavioral modelling will be new to many planners, and given that many planners are not well-grounded in the "folk theory" of behavioral modeling from economics and psychology, one can predict that the unsuccessful disaggregate models will outnumber the successful ones. On the other hand, there is now a track record of success with these models. They have proved that they can provide accurate and flexible forecasts, and that used with judgment, they can provide a useful tool for organizing and systematizing policy analysis.

CHAPTER 4

STATED PREFERENCE ANALYSIS
OF TRAVEL CHOICES:
THE STATE OF PRACTICE*

*David A. Hensher***

Abstract

Stated preference (SP) methods are widely used in travel behaviour research and practice to identify behavioural responses to choice situations which are not revealed in the market, and where the attribute levels offered by existing choices are modified to such an extent that the reliability of revealed preference models as predictors of response is brought into question. This chapter reviews recent developments in the application of SP models which add to their growing relevance in demand modelling and prediction. The main themes addressed include a comparative assessment of choice models and preference models, the importance of scaling when pooling different types of data, especially the appeal of SP data as an enriching strategy in the context of revealed preference models, hierarchical designs when the number of attributes make single experiments too complex for the respondent, and ways of accommodating dynamics (i.e. serial correlation and state dependence) in SP modelling.

---

*Reprinted from *Transportation*, vol. 21 (1994), no. 2, pp. 107-133.
**Institute of Transport Studies, Graduate School of Business, University of Sydney.

Acknowledgment: A longer version appeared in *Transportation* (Vol. 21, No. 2, 1994). Permission to reproduce the paper is gratefully acknowledged. All footnotes are removed and parts of the text are reduced in content. Readers may wish to consult the full paper published in *Transportation*.

I. Introduction

It is twenty years since the seminal papers by Davidson (1973) and Louviere et al (1973) in transportation were published which alerted us to the appeal of methods for evaluating an individual's response to combinations of levels of attributes of modes of transport which are not observed in the market, but which represent achievable levels of service. Widespread interest in this "new" approach to travel behaviour modelling, however, was slow in developing, in part due to the high agenda interest in the development of discrete-choice models and activity approaches to the study of the continuous sequences of human actions over a period of time (see Hensher and Stopher 1979). Indeed, until the early eighties, the transport contributions were dominated by publications from Louviere and his colleagues (see Louviere 1979 for a summary) with an almost universal application to the study of mode choice (Meyer et al 1978).

Although it is always difficult to pinpoint the major events which heralded in the beginning of a widespread interest in SP methods, the motivation seems to have evolved from a number of applications in which the behavioural response involved an alternative which was either not currently available (e.g. Louviere and Hensher 1983, Hensher 1982) or where there was difficulty in assessing substantially different attribute mixes associated with existing alternatives to those observed (e.g. Kocur et al 1982, Hensher and Louviere 1983, Bradley and Bovy 1985, Louviere and Kocur 1983). An important paper by Lerman and Louviere (1978) demonstrated the theoretical links between revealed preference and stated preference models.

Prior to the paper by Louviere and Hensher (1983), the emphasis had been on judgmental tasks in which a respondent was asked to rate or rank a number of attribute mixes associated with a particular choice context. The modelling of this data using standard regression-based estimation procedures required simulation of choice environments in order to predict market share. Louviere and Hensher showed how a preference experiment (i.e. a number of alternative mixes of attributes) could be extended to incorporate choice experiments in which an individual chooses from among fixed or varying choice sets, enabling estimation of a discrete-choice model and hence direct prediction of market share. Stated *choice* experiments are now the most popular form of SP method in transportation and are growing in popularity in other areas such as marketing, geography, regional science and tourism. The papers by Louviere and Hensher (1982) and Louviere and Woodworth (1983) have become the historical reference sources for stated choice modelling in transportation.

The introduction of stated choice modelling using the set of established discrete-choice modelling tools routinely applied with revealed preference data widened the interest in SP-methods. For the first time travel behaviour researchers could see the benefit of stated-preference data in enhancing their travel choice methods. This I would argue was the major watershed which after 10 years has resulted in widespread acceptance of SP methods in practice in transportation. A number of monographs and special issues of journals are now available which capture the major contributions up to the late eighties (Pearmain et al 1991, Louviere 1988, Bates 1988, and Louviere 1992). Louviere, Hensher and Shocker (1992) run an annual short course, covering all aspects of stated-preference modelling (i.e. relevance, design, estimation, and application). Batsell and Louviere (1991) and Louviere (1993) have recently reviewed the state of the art in experimental analysis of choice experiments. Green and Srinivasan (1978, 1990) are the recognised review sources in marketing. Louviere and Timmermans (1990) provide an overview in the context of tourism.

With this brief historical perspective behind us, this paper concentrates on some of the important developments in recent years which crystallise the state of practice in stated preference modelling. In particular, we evaluate the pros and cons of alternative response metrics (namely ranks, rates and choice), the major considerations in the design of an experiment (i.e. attribute selection, attribute levels, main and interaction effects, hierarchical designs and making the exercise comprehensive and comprehendible), approaches to model estimation (especially individual models, and individual choice models based on a sample of individuals where the data is maintained at a disaggregate level or aggregated within each observation to choice proportions), and the scaling of data with different metric dimensions to enable data aggregation and enrichment. We also refer to the growing software capability for experimental design, model estimation and market share prediction. Throughout the paper the emphasis is on the practice of SP analysis.

II. Defining the Response Dimension

There are two broad categories of stated response of interest in travel behaviour research: (i) An individual is asked to indicate his *preferences* among a set of combinations of attributes which define services or products. This judgmental task, usually seeks a response on one of two metric scales—a rank ordering or a rating scale. (ii) An individual is asked to *choose* one of the combinations of attributes. Information is not sought on the ordering or rating of each of the non-chosen combinations. This is often called a first-preference choice task.

In both stated preference and stated choice experiments, each combination of attributes can be defined as an *alternative* in the sense of representing a product or service specification which may or may not be observed in the market. The attributes can include not only well-defined sources of (indirect) utility such as travel times and travel costs, but also aggregators such as name of product (e.g. car, train) which represent the respondent's perception of the attributes of the alternatives which are not represented by the explicitly defined attributes. In both preference and choice experiments it is feasible to vary both the combinations of attributes and levels as well as the subsets of mixes to be evaluated. This can be achieved by either designing varying numbers of combinations or asking the respondent to a priori eliminate any combinations which are not applicable before responding (soliciting criteria for non-applicability—see Louviere and Hensher 1983).

In practice, it is common in preference experiments to hold the number of alternative attribute mixes constant and only vary the attribute levels. However, in choice experiments, it is common to vary the number of alternatives, while either holding the attribute levels associated with each alternative constant, or varying them, producing varying choice sets (e.g. Hensher et al 1989). Fixed choice set designs are also widely used (e.g. Louviere and Hensher 1983, Gunn et al 1992).

The decision on which type of response strategy to pursue must be addressed at the beginning of an SP study, because it will define the available outputs. A major consideration is the need for predictions of behavioural response, especially market shares. Rank order and ratings "predictions" must be transformed to accommodate useful predictive outputs (except where the interest centres on the image of, or attitude towards, a service or product—see Hensher 1991). Choice responses are directly translated into predictions, through the application of discrete-choice models such as multinomial logit (MNL), and are also relatively easier for the respondent. However, the advantage of the direct translation comes at the expense of information loss. In a first-preference choice experiment, no information is available on the ordering of all of the alternatives in contrast to ranking and even rating. In recognition of this information loss, a number of studies have investigated ways of maximising the information content of a response metric while both maintaining the ability of the respondent to handle a more difficult task and have the capability of estimating a model which can provide useful predictive outputs in the form of market shares (and attribute elasticities) (e.g. Elrod et al 1992, Ben-Akiva et al 1992).

1. Rank-Order Data

Rank order (non-metric) data is popular with analysts who subscribe to the view that individuals are more capable of ordering alternatives than reporting, by a rating task, their degrees of preferences. A choice experiment is a first-order ranking task. A procedure proposed by Chapman and Staelin (1982) for translating rank order data into choice responses, referred to as 'rank explosion,' enables one to translate the full depth of R ranks into R-1 choice observations. Each choice set in a sequence excludes the alternative(s) ranked above each level in the rank as we redefine each rank level as the "chosen" from the set below the rank of the "previously chosen." For example, if we have four alternatives and each is ranked 1 to 4, the reconfigured sequential choice sets are the chosen as rank = 1 and the remaining 3 alternatives, the chosen as rank = 2 and the alternatives ranked 3 and 4, and the chosen as rank = 3 and the alternative ranked 4. Automatic explosion and estimation as a multinomial logit model can be executed in the LIMDEP package

(Econometric Software, 1992).

The usefulness of preference ranking data has recently been questioned by Ben-Akiva et al (1992). They found that response data from different ranking depths are *unequally* reliable, and that different ranks produce statistically significantly different estimates of the (indirect) utilities. To conform with the underlying properties of discrete-choice models, that is consistency with random utility maximisation and the well known properties of MNL models, the estimated indirect utilities from the full choice set should be proportional to the utilities estimated from any other choice set of another ranking depth. This requirement is rejected by Ben-Akiva et al (1992) for several of the depths of comparisons. Although this evidence is based on only one empirical study, there is a growing view that rank order data provides limited information, at least below rank 4 (Hensher and Louviere 1983), a position corroborated by Bradley and Daly (1992). It suggests the potential value of confining choice analysis to the first preference choice.

Further research is required to decide on the fate of ranking data as a basis of translation of a full or part profile of ranks into choice responses, to enable direct prediction of market shares. The usefulness of rank order responses *analysed as ranks* however is not under question *per se*, except to the extent of the reliability of the lower-order ranks. Hensher and Louviere (1983) proposed a way of transforming ranking responses into expected choice frequencies for analysis in the random utility framework. The translation produces choice proportions representing the responses of a sampled individual when faced with an alternative in every possible choice set. Iterative weighted least squares regression can be used to obtain parameter estimates. To my knowledge, the method has not been used by anyone else.

2. Ratings Data

Ratings are, prima facie, the richest response metric, giving both order (including ties) and degree of preference. Analysts typically select a 5 or 10 point scale (and occasionally 100 points), to represent an underlying (i.e. latent) continuous distribution of interval scaled rates. A rating task is also the most demanding on a respondent, since the magnitude of the response associated with each attribute mix can vary across the entire rating scale. Ratings data are often assumed to have a monotonic translation into a utility scale, and after model estimation using techniques such as generalised least squares regression, the parameter estimates are applied via a logit transformation to obtain choice probabilities. The validity of this transformation is questionable, at least because of the discrete-nature of the ordered sets of ratings available to the respondent. There are also different distributional assumptions for the error components of GLS and MNL.

A preferable approach to utilising ratings data in the derivation of choice probabilities is to treat the observed ratings as a non-linear rating scale in an ordered response model which defines points on the *observed rating scale* as thresholds (Henry 1982, Winship and Mare 1984, Crask and Fox 1987). Empirical rating scales are best viewed as discrete realisations of unmeasured continuous variables. The ordered probit or ordered logit model allows one to include ordinal dependent variables into the preference model in a way that explicitly recognises their ordinality and avoids arbitrary assumptions about their scale (Johnson 1990). The essence of the approach is an assumed probability distribution of the continuous variable that underlies the observed ordinal dependent variable. Ordered probit or logit also takes into account the ceiling and floor restrictions on models which include ordinal variables, whereas a linear regression does not.

In specifying an appropriate preference model, we assume that the observed rating scale is a nonstrict monotonic transformation of an unobserved interval variable. Thus one or more values of an interval-level variable are mapped into the same value of a transformed ordinal variable. An underlying continuous variable is mapped into categories that are ordered but are separated by unknown distances. We cannot, for example, say that the difference between ratings 5 and 4 is identical to the difference between ratings 4 and 3, or 3 and 2. This method has been implemented in Hensher (1991), and Ortuzar and Garrido (1993). One possible practical limitation of the ordered probit model is that it does not have a closed-form solution. This means that each change in an attribute level must be evaluated through integration of the open-form choice probability model. LIMDEP fortunately can perform this task with ease.

3. Choice Data

The attraction of choice responses in part evolves from the discussion of rank and rating data. Ultimately, the majority of travel behaviour practictioners want predictions of the demand or market share for a service or product. Individuals in reality make decisions by comparing a set of alternatives and selecting one. With this simple requirement in mind and the commentary above, the appeal of a first preference choice modelling approach is clear.

An appealing feature of stated choice (SC) data is the ability to view the experiment as the stated response counterpart to revealed preference (RP) data, the mainstay of econometric modelling. In addition to the capability of stated choice experiments to extend evaluation beyond observed attribute levels, the essential difference is one of scale. The recognition of the relative strengths and weaknesses of both types of data suggest that the joint utilisation of both data should enrich the modelling activity and further our understanding of choice behaviour. In particular SP data can be used effectively to enrich the predictive capability of a base RP model, especially where the market share for a new alternative is being evaluated.

Whereas RP data describes actual choices in terms of a set of market-based measurements of attributes of alternatives (which by definition are restricted to the currently available feasible set), the SC data describe potential choices in terms of a set of constructed measures of combinatorial mixes of attributes of real and/or hypothetical alternatives. The opportunity to position an SC data set relative to an RP data set within the one empirical analysis on the common choice problem enables the modeller to extend and infill the relationship between variations in choice response and levels of the attributes of alternatives in a choice set, and hence increase the explanatory power of the RP choice model.

The mixing of sources of data however is not a matter of "naive" pooling. It requires careful consideration of the unit of the (indirect) utility scale. For example, the utility scale in an MNL model is inversely related to the variance of the unobserved influences, summarised as the random error term; hence the parameter estimates of two identical indirect utility specifications obtained from two data sources with different variances will necessarily differ in magnitude, even if the choice process that generated the indirect utilities is identical. The notion of scaling is not new. Horowitz (1981), for example, alluded to it. However prior to the contribution of Morikawa (1989), the scaling discussion was not specifically directed to the opportunity to enrich RP data with SC data. Some recent applications using mixed data are Morikawa (1989), Bradley and Daly (1991, 1992), Hensher and Bradley (1993) and Swait and Louviere (1993). Given the importance of this enrichment strategy, it is discussed in more detail in section four.

III. Experimental Choice Design

The *engine* of stated preference analysis is a controlled experiment, out of which comes a series of survey questions eliciting a response to alternative combinations of levels of attributes. A good experiment is one which has a sufficiently rich set of attributes and choice contexts, together with enough variation in the attribute levels necessary to produce meaningful behavioural responses in the context of the strategies under study.

There is a logical sequence of tasks required to design a choice experiment. This should be distinguished from the issue of statistical design complexity. The latter may require specialist support; whereas the overall process can be executed almost mechanically once the options within each task are known and understood. Importantly, the tasks must be undertaken with some broad awareness of the downstream implications of a decision taken at each stage. Hence a considerable amount of revision is likely to occur before finalising an experiment. The key steps are summarised below, using commuter mode choice as the example context.

Task 1 involves the *identification of the set of attributes* which need to be considered as sources of influence on mode choice. There may well be a large number of these attributes, requiring an early decision on which attributes to include in the experimental design and which to exclude, treating the latter as *contextual* or *covariate* effects. For example, we might exclude the number of transfers associated with the use of a public transport mode, because it is unlikely to vary within a mode. It may be better accommodated by describing a fixed level for a mode in the context-setting statement accompanying the experiment.

One way of preserving a large number of design attributes is to partition the attributes into generic groups, with each group defined by elemental attributes, and to design a number of linked hierarchical experiments (e.g. Hensher 1991, Louviere and Gaeth 1987, Hague Consulting Group 1988, Kroes and Sheldon 1988, Timmermans 1988). The hierarchical approach assumes that individuals classify attributes into a set of generic decision constructs (e.g. comfort, convenience, cost and time). They then choose among the alternatives based on the generic attributes. A separate experiment for each generic attribute involves the repondent rating each of the elemental attributes associated with each mode, in order to give some substantive interpretation to the sources of utility underlying the generic constructs. Choosing a mode is not so meaningful for a subset of sources of influence on choice.

The **second task** involves *selecting the measurement unit* for each attribute. In most cases the metric for an attribute is unambiguous; however there are situations where this requires consideration of alternative metrics. This is particularly true for generic attributes such as comfort. For example, one could define an ordinal scale of high, medium and low (which may be problematic if the analyst does not describe precisely what each level represents). Alternatively one could endogenise the construction of the metric scale by asking each respondent to first place values on each of the generic attributes, possibly on a satisfaction rating scale, to define one of the levels as the current level (not necessarily the medium level), and then the analyst can construct the other two levels as variations from the reported level. This is not so clear for a new alternative; however one way is to use a very clear description of the new mode as the surrogate for current awareness/experience. It may be as good as reliance made on *experience* with available alternatives which have never been used.

Well-defined attributes such as wait time can be treated in a number of ways, although in practice the selection is decided primarily by the number of levels. For example, a two-level attribute could be "zero" and "greater than zero"; a three-level attribute could be "zero," 5 and 10 minutes. There is more information in the latter, although the complexity of the experiment and/or the accuracy required on this attribute and/or the inability of a respondent to perceive any noticeable difference between levels may have a bearing on the selection.

Task 3 involves the *specification of the number and magnitudes of attribute levels*. As a rule of thumb, one should be extremely cautious about choosing attribute levels which are well outside the range of both current experience and believability. For existing alternatives one should construct a range which contains the level currently faced by an individual, no matter how the attribute is measured, and define it as one of the levels in the design. Consideration of the magnitude of an attribute to be evaluated in an application is also crucial to ensure that the design can assess behavioural response in the new attribute level regime. When new alternatives are being evaluated, making the attribute levels believable (and deliverable) becomes a primary consideration.

The number of levels for each attribute will be decided by the overall complexity of the design. This involves consideration of the combinations of attribute levels generated, the manner in which they are exposed to a respondent (i.e. partitioned or in their entirety), the need to investigate non-linearity (which is not possible with only two levels), and the extent to which interaction effects between pairs of attributes may be important. The final selection and format of implementation must be decided by the criterion of being comprehensible to the respondent.

Task 4, *statistical design,* is where the attribute levels are combined into an experiment. A combination of attribute levels describes an alternative, referred to in the literature as a *profile* or treatment. The alternative can be abstract in the sense of being an attribute mix which is not defined for a particular mode (e.g. a travel time and cost); or it can be mode-specific (e.g. travel time and cost by car). The former is often referred to as an *unranked alternative* and the latter as a *ranked alternative*.

Alternatives are generated with the aid of statistical design theory. In a statistical experiment each attribute has levels, and it is these levels that are the input data required to construct a factorial design (i.e. combinations of attribute levels for all attributes in the design). A *full factorial design* contains descriptions of all possible alternatives, enabling one to independently estimate the statistical effects of each attribute on the choice response. In practice the full number of combinations is impracticable to evaluate, and so a *fractional factorial design* is constructed. The price one pays for making the experiment manageable is that some statistical efficiency is lost. In designing a fractional factorial experiment, the analyst has to assume that certain interaction effects among the attributes are not statistically significant. This is a very reasonable non-testable assumption for a large number of possible interactions, especially interactions of more than two attributes (e.g. three-way interactions), and indeed for many two-way interactions. If interactions are statistically significant, their effects in a fractional factorial design will be loaded onto the individual *main effects*, giving erroneous results. This is referred to as *confounding* main effects with interaction effects. The analyst has to be creative in selecting a limited number of two-way interactions which enable one to include up to that number of interactions to test for statistical significance. It is important to note that the two-way interactions can be any two attributes, up to the maximum allowed for statistical independence.

The most common fractional factorial design is a main *effects* plan. The majority of previous applications in transportation are of this structure. A main effects plan does not, in a statistical design sense, provide a sufficient number of alternatives to be able to detect unobserved but possibly significant interaction effects, preventing determination of whether the estimated main effects are statistically biased. Main effects plans assume that individuals process information in a strictly additive way, such that there are no significant interactions between attributes. A main effects plan does enable the analyst to define a linear and higher-order dimensions (e.g. quadratic) for each attribute. Higher-order effects are important where the marginal rate of substitution between two attributes (e.g. the value of travel time savings) is a function of the magnitude of a design attribute (e.g. the value of travel time savings is a function of the level of travel time).

The fractional factorial designs are given in standard experimental design tables (e.g. Hahn and Shapiro 1966), which indicate to the user (i) if all the main effects are independent of two-way interactions, (ii) the number of independent interactions permissable for each fraction, (iii) the residual degrees of freedom, and (iv) the actual combinations of levels of attributes. For example, 3 attributes at 3 levels gives a full factorial of 27 combinations. This can be reduced to a one-third fraction of 9 combinations in which all the main effects are independent of two-way interactions, but there are no independent two-way interactions.

To appreciate the importance of an awareness of possible statistical correlation between main effects and interactions, assume a situation where we have 5 attributes each of 2 levels. This is a 2^5 design giving 32 possible alternatives. To reduce the number of combinations to a more manageable size without loosing essential information, an orthogonal main effects design can be developed from only a 2^3 factorial if we make certain assumptions about interaction effects. By assuming that some interaction effects are not significant, we can use these "interaction effects" to represent the two main effects which would otherwise be missing from the 2^3 design. For example, the 8 combinations in the 2^3 design are as follows (using orthogonal coding to represent the levels of each of the two-level attributes).

To include the cost attributes in the fractional factorial (i.e. the 8/32 or one-quarter fraction), we can use the 4th and 5th columns which represent interactions between two of the time attributes to construct the extra main effects IVC and PC only if the interactions IVT*WT and IVT*WK are equal to zero. It is obvious why these two interaction effects must be excluded: the interactions of the cost main effects with IVT are prefectly correlated with the main effects WT and WK, as shown by comparing columns 3 and 6 and columns 2 and 7. This is the underlying rationale for fractional factorial designs. If some interaction effects may be significant, you will have to construct a larger design such as a 2^4 factorial. A repeat of the process outlined above will enable you to identify the number of two-way interactions which are independent of the main effects. All pairs of interest can be evaluated to identify

Invehicle time (IVT)	Wait time (WT)	Walk time (WK)	IVT*WT (Invehicle-Cost-IVC	IVT*WK (Parking-Cost-PC)	IVT*IVC (=WK)	IVT*PC (=WT)
−1	−1	−1	+1	+1	−1	−1
−1	−1	+1	+1	−1	+1	−1
−1	+1	−1	−1	+1	−1	+1
−1	+1	+1	−1	−1	+1	+1
+1	−1	−1	−1	−1	−1	−1
+1	−1	+1	−1	+1	+1	−1
+1	+1	−1	+1	−1	−1	+1
+1	+1	+1	+1	+1	+1	+1
0	0	0	0	0	0	0

the number of permissable independent two-way interactions are orthogonal with the main effects.

One of the important issues in statistical design is *orthogonality*, which ensures that the attributes presented to individuals are varied independently from one another. This property of zero-correlation between attributes enables the analyst to undertake tests of the statistical contribution of main effects and interactions, and is promoted as a major appeal of SP data compared to RP data. There is a view that although this is a desirable property, it is not a necessary condition for useful SP modelling. RP modellers have had to live with some amount of correlation, and have suitable tests for multicollinearity to identify when correlation is a problem. Mason and Perreault (1991) show in a cross-sectional context that fears about the harmful effects of collinear attributes often are exaggerated. Indeed the major benefit of SP methods is the ability to capture the response to diverse attribute combinations which are not observed in the market. One suspects that this is the dominating reason for the popularity of SP methods in transportation.

Hensher and Barnard (1990) have made a distinction between design-data orthogonality (DDO) and estimation-data orthogonality (EDO) in order to highlight that DDO is not always preserved in model estimation. This is very important for the most common procedure in travel behaviour modelling of estimating an MNL model with three or more alternatives on the individual response data, namely pooling all data (i.e. number of individuals in the sample by number of stated choice replications per individual) across the sampled population, but *not* aggregating the response data within a sampled individual. Estimation orthogonality using individual data and discrete choice models requires that the *differences* in attribute levels be orthogonal, not the absolute levels. Techniques such as MNL estimated on individual data require the differencing on the attributes to be *the chosen minus each and every non-chosen*. Since the chosen alternative is not known prior to design development, it is not possible to design an experiment which has DDO, and which also satisfies EDO (Hensher and Barnard 1990).

The innovative method proposed by Louviere (1988) for overcoming EDO is not feasible where individual data are applied in estimation. The Louviere method defines a base alternative and derives all attribute combinations from a given *difference of attribute levels* satisfying an orthogonal-difference design. It is however suitable when the choice responses are aggregated within each individual's set of replications to derive choice proportions for each alternative. In this case, logit regression is a suitable estimation methods, which does not require any further differencing in estimation. Transportation modellers have tended to opt for the preservation of the individual discrete-choice responses, and hence (without realising it in most cases), accepting some amount of correlation.

There are a growing number of software packages which can be used to design fractional factorial experiments. The user defines each attribute by the number of levels, and then follows menu-driven screen instructions on how to select a particular fractional factorial which has the statistical properties the analyst requires. The most popular packages in transportation are SPEED/MINT (Hague Consulting Group, The Netherlands), CONSURV (Intelligent Marketing Systems—Canada and Econometric Software-Australia), and GAME GENERATOR (Steer, Davies Gleave-U. K.).

In **task 5**, the experiment designed in task 4 has to be translated into a set of *questions and showcards for execution in the data collection phase*. The survey instrument can be designed for either a notebook computer or non-computerised administration. Whatever the preferred collection strategy, the design must be translated from a set of orthogonal or near-orthogonal design attribute levels into real information for respondents to comprehend and respond. Where feasible, it is suggested that a respondent be asked to both choose an alternative and either rank or rate the full set of alternatives (or a subset derived from a prior question on applicability or non-applicability of particular alternatives). The subset issue is particularly important where there are too many alternatives to rank or rate, although it may be of interest in a choice response context to ascertain some additional information on relevant sets. If the request for ranking or rating responses may jeopardise the cooperation acrosss the replications of the experiment, it is more important to limit the task to the first preference choice.

Where there are a lot of replications, it is popular to *block or randomise* the experiment in such a way that subsets of respondents are asked to respond to either a fixed subset or a random subset in a way which ensures that all replications have equal representation. The only concern about this strategy is the extent of segmentation heterogeneity with respect to response profile, which could lead to a distortion of the population's response profile.

Task 6. The selection of an appropriate *estimation procedure* will be dependent on the metric of the response variable and the level of aggregation of the data for modelling. The main approaches are summarised in Table 1.

Exploded ranks involves converting data derived from a preference ranking task into choice data for modelling. This procedure has been described above in section 2.1. Approaches B, D and F can use regression based estimation methods such as generalised least squares because the response variable is continuous. However, aggregating data derived from repeated observations on each individual introduces a number of statistical problems due to the non-independence of intra-individual observations (Louviere and Woodworth 1983). Approach A should be estimated by techniques such as ordered logit or ordered probit; GLS would produce biased parameter estimates.

Unexploded ranking data *analysed* as individual observations (approach C), can be utilised in a choice context by assuming the independence of irrelevant alternatives (IIA) property, and transitivity in the unobserved choice sets implied by the rankings (Hensher and Louviere 1983). A simple translation of rankings into choice proportions for each alternative is then possible. If there is doubt about the use of rules for ranking which violate the IIA assumption, then the translation is dubious (Louviere 1988). The resulting choice proportions can be used in the estimation, by generalised least squares or ordered logit/probit, of an individual level choice model.

Table 1. Alternative Model Estimation Methods

Data Response Dimension	Rating	Rank-Order Unexploded	Rank-Order Exploded	First-Preference
Modelling Strategy: Aggregated Sample Choice Proportions [Grouped Data]	B	D	F	
Individual Choices [Individual Data]	A	C	E	G

In approach G (or equivalently E) the data relate directly to discrete choice responses, and estimation takes place using the repeated observations on each individual. The MNL model has been used in the majority of the stated choice applications (e.g. Louviere and Hensher 1983, Bates et.al 1987, Wardman 1988, Bradley and Bovy 1986). All of the statistical procedures are available in LIMDEP (Econometric Software 1992). Specialised software is readily available for logit modelling such as ALOGIT (Hague Consulting Group, the Netherlands), PCLOGIT which superseded BLOGIT (Institute of Transport Studies, University of Sydney), and NTELOGIT (Intelligent Marketing Systems—Canada and Econometric Software—Australia).

The final task, **task 7**, uses the estimated parameters in a *simulated choice* context to obtain choice probabilities for each alternative for each sampled individual, which together with population weights can be used to obtain predictions of market shares or total demand. To obtain predictions of total demand, it is important to allow for a no-choice response in the experimental design (Louviere and Hensher 1983) .

IV. Scaling and Enrichment

The behavioural framework underlying discrete-choice models such as MNL is applicable for both RP and SP data. The definition of the observed and unobserved influences on the choice outcome however varies. First, the observed levels of the attributes of alternatives typically obtained in an RP study are sought directly from the decision maker or taken from exogenous data such as posted prices. The responses are reported perceived levels, which may vary from the "actual" levels. By contrast, the attribute levels associated with an SP study are fixed by the analyst, and are by definition "actual" levels. Thus we have at least one source of variation in the metric of the observed attributes of alternatives. Second, the choice outcome in the RP study is the known outcome, whereas for the SP study it is the potential outcome or the outcome with the highest likelihood of occurrence given the combination of attribute levels offered in an experimental replication. Third, the SP study elicits choice responses from a repeated measures experiment in which the attribute levels (and even the choice set) are varied, in contrast to the single response in an RP study. Thus there is a greater amount of information on decision maker response to a range of possible attribute profiles.

After recognising the likely sources of observed variation between RP and SP data, the remaining unobserved sources of indirect utility are most unlikely to display identical distribution profiles within the common sampled population. Hence the *"naive* pooling of the two types of data cannot be treated as if they display identical unobserved effects. Given that the variance of the unobserved effects is an important piece of information used in the derivation of the functional form of a probabilistic discrete choice model (McFadden 1981), this variance deviation has to be recognised and accommodated. One solution proposed originally by Morikawa (1989) is to scale the variance of the unobserved effects associated with the SP data so that the equality of variances across the RP and SP components of a pooled model is reinstated. The indirect utility expressions are defined as (Morikawa 1989):

$$V_{rp} = \alpha + \beta X_{rp} + \psi Y + \varepsilon_{rp}$$
$$; \theta^2 = var\ (\varepsilon_{rp})/var\ (\varepsilon_{sp})$$
$$V_{sp} = \delta + \beta X_{sp} + \gamma Z + \varepsilon_{sp}$$

where

X_{rp}, X_{sp} = a vector of observed variables common to rp and sp data
Y, Z = vectors of observed variables specific to one data set or the other
$\beta, \alpha, \delta, \psi, \gamma$ = unknown parameters
$\varepsilon_{rp}, \varepsilon_{sp}$ = the unobserved effects associated with the rp and sp data configurations
θ^2 = the scaling parameter, enabling the scaling of V_{sp} equal to V_{rp}, and hence joint estimation of the two data sets.

The probability of a decision maker selecting an alternative out of the available set of alternatives is defined as the probability that the observed and unobserved indirect utility of an alternative is greater than or equal to the observed and unobserved indirect utility of each and every other alternative in the choice set:

$$Prob_j = Prob\ \{(V_j + \varepsilon_j) \geq (V_{j'} + \varepsilon_{j'});\ j \in J;\ j \neq j'\}$$

Particular assumptions on the distribution of the unobserved effects within the sampled population lead to a particular functional form of the discrete choice model (see below). A priori the relative magnitudes of the variances is unknown, due to the many sources of differences between the RP and SP contexts. The equality of variances is a permissable empirical outcome, but not one to be assumed ex ante.

1. The Econometric Specification

The distribution of the unobserved effect in an indirect utility expression has always been an important consideration in econometrics. Within the family of random utility models centred on discrete choices, the multinomial logit (MNL) form requires that the unobserved effects are independently and identically distributed (IID) across the alternatives in the choice set, according to the extreme value type I distribution (Hensher and Johnson 1991, Borsch-Supan 1986, Ben-Akiva and Lerman 1985). The violation of this constant variance condition (alternatively referred to as the independence of irrelevant alternatives property) resulted in the development of the nested (or hierarchical) logit (NL) model, which permitted differential variance between levels and/or branches within a level of the nested structure but a common variance within a branch (Hensher 1986, 1991, Borsch-Supan 1986). The explicit accommodation of differential variance within a nested-logit model provides a means of identifying the scale parameter required to rescale parameter estimates associated with data derived from more than one source which are combined in a single empirical model.

The RP parameters to be estimated are the simple values of α, β, and ψ, the SP parameters are $\theta\delta$, $\theta\beta$ and $\theta\gamma$. This scaling has no other effect on the distributional assumptions or on the conversion of the indirect utility expressions to choice probabilities. The scaling of $\theta\beta$ is the essential link betwen the two data models. The SP model, however, is nonlinear. This estimation problem can be solved by available nested-logit software, by setting up an *artificial tree structure* as follows (Bradley and Daly 1991). The artificial nest is constructed to have *at least* twice as many alternatives as are observed in reality. One subset is labelled as RP alternatives, the other subset as SP alternatives. The SP subset can include additional new alternatives not in the RP subset. The indirect utility functions in each case are defined by the Vrp and Vsp expressions, defined above without theta. The RP alternatives are placed just below the "root" of the nest, whereas the SP alternatives are each placed in a single-alternative "next." For the SP observations, the average indirect utility of each of the "dummy composite" alternatives (Figure 1 – after Bradley and Daly 1991) uses the theoretical basis of the inclusive value concept associated with linking levels in a nested logit model (McFadden 1981) to define

$$\text{Vcomp} = \theta \log \sum_{j=1}^{J_{sp}} e^{V_{sp}^j}$$

in which the summation is taken over all alternatives in the nest corresponding to the composite alternative. Because each nest contains only one SP alternative, V^{comp} reduces to θV_{sp}, the expression for a single SP alternative, with every parameter including the unobserved component associated with an SP alternative scaled by θ. It is because the approach operates as if we are estimating a traditional nested logit model and drawing on the empirical content of the inclusive value which links levels in a tree structure that we refer to the estimation of the scaling approach as an *artificial* nested (logit) model. The scaling θ does not have to lie in the unit interval, the condition for consistency with random utility maximisation (Hensher and Johnson 1981, Ben-Akiva and Lerman 1985), because individuals are not modelled as choosing from the full set of RP+SP alternatives. The scale for SP relative to RP can be greater than one.

Figure 1. The Estimation Structure

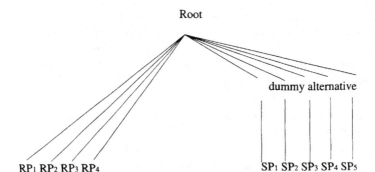

The joint estimation using two types of data involves a choice out-come associated with the RP data and a number of choice outcomes associated with the SP data. This is not a typical discrete choice applica-tion where there is only one choice outcome in either an MNL or NL configuration. To allow for this multiple response the observations are *stacked* in such a way that for each RP observation there is a null choice set for the SP observation, and for each SP observation there is a null choice set for the equivalent RP observation. The 'hierarchical' struc-ture, given in Figure 1, ensures that each of the parameter estimates associated with the SP data are scaled by the ratio of the variances. The different thetas on each dummy node are constrained to take the same value, a requirement for the scaling condition. Different theta's can be allowed for each *additional* type of SP data set.

The concentration on the unobserved effects is deliberate, given that the scaling of *all* parameters associated with one type of data is neces-sary to enable joint estimation of two or more types of data within an IID model framework. Any additional sources of variation between attributes can be accommodated by the inclusion of data-type specific dummy variables such as a fatigue effect dummy for SP data (measured for example by the sequence of replications) (see Bradley and Daly 1992). The scale parameter can be normalised to unity on either the RP or SP side.

To scale the variance of the unobserved effects in the SP component relative to the RP component, a sequential or a simultaneous scaling approach can be used. Simultaneous estimation of the "nested" structure using the method of full-information maximum likelihood (FIML) is the most efficient approach; although sequential estimation can also be used, both allowing us to normalise the variance of the one data source to unity and allowing the variance of the other data source to be empiri-cally determined around unity. In sequential estimation, the calculated standard errors are not efficient and are likely to be underestimated lead-ing to inflated t-statistics (Hensher 1986). Morikawa (1989) cites under-estimates by a factor of 10 to 500%. Sequential estimation is also ineffi-cient in the sense of loss of sample points if differential choice sets are permitted across the sample, since one encounters parts of the tree struc-ture without a chosen alternative or a single alternative (Hensher 1986). As an enrichment strategy for RP modelling, one anticipates a burgeon-ing literature of RP-SP applications.

V. Conclusions and New Challenges

There are many challenges still to be faced in making the existing set of tools both more user-friendly and capable of assisting in the resolution of further issues emanating from state of the art research. In concluding this paper, we have selected two topics of particular importance in ongoing research to highlight the richness of stated preference modelling. Other important topics not discussed herein are transferability of models over time and location, (e.g. Hensher and Battellino 1993) using SP experiments to value environmental effects (e.g. Adamowicz et al 1992), defining consideration sets and an efficient number of alternatives (e.g. Bunch and Batsell 1989) and external validity (e.g. Horowitz and Louviere 1993).

1. Incorporating Uncertainty in an Experiment

It is widely acknowledged that the levels of many attributes actually offered in the marketplace have an element of uncertainty. This is especially the case for services where the variability in total demand affects the ability to deliver a certain level of service. There are many examples in transportation, such as the reliability of travel times due to traffic congestion, the breakdown of a bus, and an accident on the train system. In these circumstances, a fixed attribute level in a design experiment may be more realistically redefined to account for the expectation of variation (i.e. uncertainty). This issue has been addressed in a general way in the theoretical literature on risk and uncertainty, and only recently has there been a serious effort in designing uncertainty into a choice experiment.

Senna (1992) is one example of recent efforts. He gave each respondent a set of five travel times for the same trip repeated five times, and allowed the levels to vary across the five trips. No variability implied certainty. The design had three levels of mean travel time, three levels of travel time variability and costs, with a modified rating scale of 5 levels. By treating uncertainty as an additional attribute with obvious links to another mean level attribute, the property of orthogonality becomes attractive in statistical estimation to enable identification of the role of uncertainty in choice response.

2. Introducing Dynamics into Stated Preference Model Estimation

Some RP-SP choice models incorporate the endogenous choice variable from the RP choice set as an exogenous variable in the SP indirect utility expressions to represent inertia; which implies the presence of state dependence. Furthermore, it is well known in the econometric's literature that true state dependence is not transparent if (serial) correlation exists between the random components of the RP and SP indirect utility expressions. Morikawa et al (1992) propose a method of handling state dependence and serial correlation in a discrete choice modelling context and apply it in an intercity mode-choice context.

Hensher (1993) proposes a panel-data approach for handling these correlated sources of potential bias in parameter estimates in repeated measures SP data when ratings data is used; drawing on the analogy to the time series of cross-sections data profile common in econometrics (i.e. a panel). The panel approach is only applicable to SP data except where the RP alternatives have been rated. This approach recognises that there are unobserved effects which are constant within an individual between replications. These can be defined either as fixed (ω_i) or random (μ_i) individual-specific effects. With a large sample, it is likely that a random-effects formulation would be used. In addition there could be a replication order effect which can be allowed for by the inclusion of an order-specific fixed (τ_r) or random (η_r) effects variable. The panel data estimator for a fixed effect specification is:

$$R_{ir} = \alpha_0 + \beta'x_{ir} + \omega_i + \tau_r + \varepsilon_{ir}$$

and for a random-effects specification is:

$$R_{ir} = \alpha + \beta'x_{ir} + \mu_i + \eta_r + \varepsilon_{ir}$$

where R_{ir} is the rating response for replication r and individual i, x_{ir} is the set of attributes from the experimental design and contextual/covariate influences, ε_{ir} is the residual error effect, and α and the β matrix define unknown parameters, to be estimated. τ_r and η_r can capture sources of replication bias including order effects. μ_i and ω_i can capture inertia effects as well as other person-specific effects such as fatigue.

3. A Final Word

Stated preference analysis has come a long way. It is now widely accepted as a logical approach to extending the behavioural response space for studies of traveller behaviour and travel demand. .

References

Adamowicz, W., Louviere, J.J. and Williams, M. (1992) combining revealed and stated preference methods for valuing envoronmental amenities, Working Paper, *Department of Rural Economy, University of Alberta*, Edmonton (unpublished).

Anderson, N.H. (1981) *Foundations of Information Integration Theory*, Academic Press, New York.

Anderson, N.H. (1982) *Methods of Information Integration Theory*, Academic Press, New York.

Bates, J. (guest editor) (1988) Stated preference methods in transport research, *Journal of Transport Economics and Policy*, XXII (1), January, 1-137.

Bates, J.J. et. al. (1987) *The Value of Travel Time Savings*, Policy Journals, United Kingdom.

Batsell, R.R. and Louviere, J.J. (1991) Experimental analysis of choice, *Marketing Letters*, 2 (3), 199-214.

Beaton, W.P., Meghdir, H. and Carragher, F.J. (1992) Assessing the effectiveness of transportation control measures: use of stated preference models to project mode split for work trips, *Transportation Research Record* 1346, 44-1346.

Ben-Akiva, M E and Lerman, S (1985) *Discrete Choice Analysis: Theory and Application to Travel Demand*, MIT Press, Cambridge.

Ben-Akiva, M. E. and Morikawa, T. (1990) Estimation of switching models from revealed preferences and stated intentions, *Transportation Research*, 24A (6), 485-495.

Ben-Akiva, M., Morikawa, T. and Shiroishi, F. (1992) Analysis of the reliability of preference ranking data, *Journal of Business Research*, 24 (2), 149-164.

Borsch-Supan A. (1986) *Econometric Analysis of Discrete Choice*, Springer-Verlaag, Berlin.

Bradley, M. A. and Bovy, P.H.L. (1985) A stated preference analysis of bicyclist route choice, *PTRC Summer Annual Meeting*, Sussex, 39-53.

Bradley, M. A. and Daly, A. J .(1991) Estimation of logit choice models using mixed stated preference and revealed preference information, paper presented to the *6th International Conference on Travel Behavior*, Quebec, May 22-24, 1991.

Bradley, M. A. and Daly A. J. (1992) Uses of the logit scaling approach in stated preference analysis, paper presented at the *7th World Conference on Transport Research*, Lyon, July.

Bradley, M. A. and Hensher D. A. (1992) Stated preference surveys, In Ampt, E.S., Richardson, A. J. , and Meyburg A. H. (eds.) *Selected Readings in Transport Survey Methodology* Eucalyptus Press, Melbourne, 31-35.

Bunch, D.S. and Batsell, R.R. (1989) How many choices are enough?: the effect of the number of observations on maximum likelihood estimator performance in the analysis of discrete choice repeated measures data sets with the multinomial logit model, Working Paper, *Graduate School of Management, University of California*, Davis (unpublished).

Chapman, R.G., and Staelin, R. (1982) Exploiting rank ordered choice set data within the stochastic utility model, *Journal of Marketing Research*, 19, 288-301.

Crask, M.R. and Fox, R.J. (1987) An exploration of the interval properties of three commonly used marketing research scales: a magnitude estimation approach, *Journal of the Market Research Society*, 29, 317-339.

Davidson, J.D. (1973) Forecasting traffic on STOL, *Operations Research Quarterly*, 24, 561-9.

Econometric Software (1992) *LIMDEP 6.0*, Econometric Software Inc., New York and Sydney.

Elrod, T., Louviere, J.J. and Davey, K.S. (1992) An empirical comparison of ratings-based and choice-based conjoint models, *Journal of Marketing Research*, XXIX (3), 368-377.

Green, P. E. and Srinivasan, V. (1978) Conjoint analysis in consumer research: issues and outlook, *Journal of Consumer Research*, 5, 103-123.

Green, P.E. and Srinivasan, V. (1990) Conjoint analysis in marketing reserach: new developments and directions, *Journal of Marketing,* 54 (4), 3-19.

Greene, W H (1990) *Econometric Analysis,* MacMillan, New York.

Gunn, H. F. , Bradley, M. A. and Hensher, D. A. (1992) High speed rail market projection: survey design and analysis, *Transportation ,* 19, 117-139.

Hague Consulting Group (1988) A stated preference analysis of public transport service, station and vehicle improvements in Stockholm, Report prepared for *Stockholm Transport,* October 1988 (mimeo)

Hahn, G.J. and Shapiro, S.S. (1966) A catalogue and computer programme for design and analysis of orthogonal symmetric and asymmetric fractional experiments, *General Electric Research and Development Centre Report No 66-C-165,* Schenectady, New York.

Henry, F. (1982) Multivariate analysis and ordinal data. *American Sociological Review,* 47, 299-304.

Hensher, D.A. (1982) Functional measurement, individual preference and discrete-choice modelling: theory and application, *Journal of Economic Psychology,* II (3), 323-335.

Hensher, D A (1986) Sequential and full information maximum likelihood estimation of a nested logit model, *Review of Economics and Statistics,* LXVIII (4), 657-667.

Hensher, D.A. (1991) Hierarchical stated response designs and estimation in the context of bus use preferences, *Logistics and Transportation Reviews* 26 (4), 299-323.

Hensher, D.A. (1993) Treating the replications of a stated preference experiment as a panel specification, *Institute of Transport Studies,* Graduate School of Business, The University of Sydney (in preparation).

Hensher, D. A. and Barnard, P. O. (1990) The orthogonality issue in stated choice designs, in Fischer, M., Nijkamp, P and Papageorgiou, Y (eds.) *Spatial Choices and Processes,* North-Holland, Amsterdam, 265-278.

Hensher, D.A. and Battellino, H.C. (1993), The use of discrete choice models in the determination of community preferences towards sub-arterial traffic management devices, *Proceedings of the 7th World Conference on Transport Research,* Lyon, France.

Hensher, D.A. and Louviere, J.J. (1983) Identifying individual preferences for international air fares, *Journal of Transport Economics and Policy*, XVII (2), 225-245.

Hensher, D.A. and Stopher, P.R. (eds.) (1979) *Behavioural Travel Modelling*, Croom Helm, London.

Hensher, D.A ., Barnard, P., Milthorpe, F. and Smith, N. (1989) Urban tollways and the valuation of travel time savings, *The Economic Record*, 66 (193), 146-156.

Horowitz, J. L. (1981) Sampling specification and data errors in probabilistic discrete-choice models, Appendix C of Hensher, D.A. and Johnson, L.W. (1981) *Applied Discrete-Choice Modelling*, Croom Helm (London) and Wiley (New York), 417-435.

Horowitz, J. L. and Louviere, J.J. (1993) Testing predicted probabilities against observed discrete choices in probabistic discrete choice models, *Marketing Science* (in press).

Johnson, L.W. (1990) Discrete choice analysis with ordered alternatives, in Fischer M.M., Nijkamp, P and Papageorgiou, Y.Y. (eds.) *Spatial Choices and Processes*, North-Holland, Amsterdam, 279-289.

Kocur, G., Adler, T., Hyman, W. and Audet, E. (1982) *Guide to Forecasting Travel Demand with Direct Utility Measurement*, UMTA, USA Department of Transportation, Washington D.C.

Kroes, E. and Sheldon, R. (1988) Are there any limits to the amount consumers are prepared to pay for product improvements?, paper presented at the *PTRC Annual Summer Meeting*, July.

Lerman, S.R. and Louviere, J.J. (1978) On the use of functional measurement to identify the functional form of the utility expression in travel demand models, *Transportation Research Record* No. 673, 78-86.

Louviere, J.J. (1979) Attitudes, attitudinal measurement and the relationship between attitudes and behaviour, in Hensher, D.A. and Stopher, P.R. (eds.) (1979) *Behavioural Travel Modelling*, Croom Helm, London, 782-794.

Louviere, J.J. (1988) *Analysing Decision Making: Metric Conjoint Analysis*, Sage University Paper No. 67, Newbury Park, Beverly Hills.

Louviere, J.J. (guest editor) (1992) Special issue on experimental choice analysis, *Journal of Business Research*, 24 (2), March, 89-189.

Louviere, J.J. (1993) Conjoint analysis, in R. Bagozzi (ed.) *Handbook of Marketing Research* , Academic Press, New York.

Louviere, J.J. and Gaeth, G.J. (1987) Decomposing the determinants of retail facility choice using the method of hierarchical information integration: a supermarket illustration, *Journal of Retailing*, 63, 25-48.

Louviere, J.J. and Hensher, D.A. (1982) On the design and anlaysis of simulated or allocation experiments in travel choice modelling, *Transportation Research Record*, No. 890, 11-17.

Louviere, J.J. and Hensher, D.A. (1983) Using discrete choice models with experimental design data to forecast consumer demand for a unique cultural event, *Journal of Consumer Research*, 10 (3), 348-361.

Louviere, J.J. and Kocur, G. (1983) The magnitude of individual level variation in demand coefficients: a Xenia , Ohio, case example, *Transportation Research*, 17A, 363-374.

Louviere, J.J. and Timmermans, H. (1990) Stated preference and choice models applied to recreation research: a review, *Leisure Sciences*, 12, 9-32.

Louviere, J.J. and Woodworth, G.G. (1983) Design and analysis of simulated choice or allocation experiments: an approach based on aggregate data, *Journal of Marketing Research*, 20, 350-367.

Louviere, J.J., Meyer, R., Stetzer, F. and Beavers, L.L. (1973) Theory, methodology and findings in mode choice behaviour, *Working Paper No. 11, The Institute of Urban and Regional Research*, The University of Iowa, Iowa City.

Louviere, J.J., Hensher, D.A. and Shocker, A. (1992) *Conjoint Measurement: A Short Course*, Course offered annually in Australia and the USA.

Madden, G.G. (1992) Social experimentation in economics: an overview of the stated-preference experimental design method, paper presented to the *Fourth Conference of the Australian Centre for Experimental Economics*, University of Adelaide, 19-21 June.

Mason, C.H. and Perreault, W.D. (1991) Collinearity, power, and interpretation of multiple regression analysis, *Journal of Marketing Research*, XXVIII, 268-80.

McFadden, D. (1981) Econometric models of probabilistic choice in Manski, C.F. and McFadden, D. (eds.) *Structural Analysis of Discrete Data*, MIT Press, Cambridge, 198-272.

Meyer, R. J., Levin, I.P. and Louviere, J.J. (1978) Functional analysis of mode choice, *Transportation Research Record* No. 673, 1-7.

Morikawa, T. (1989) *Incorporating Stated Preference Data in Travel Demand Analysis,* PhD Dissertation, Department of Civil Engineering, M.I.T.

Morikawa, T, McFadden, D and Ben-Akiva, M E (1990) Incorporating psychometric data in econometric travel demand models, *Kyoto University Working Paper,* Department of Civil Engineering, University of Kyoto, Japan.

Morikawa, T., Ben-Akiva, M.E. and Yamada, K. (1992) Estimation of mode choice models with serially correlated RP and SP data, paper presented at the *7th World Conference on Transport Research,* Lyon, July.

Ortuzar, J. de Dios and Garrido, R.A. (1993) On the probabilistic interpretation of semantic scales in stated preference rating experiments, *Department of Transport Engineering, Pontifica Universidad Catolica de Chile* (unpublished).

Pearmain, D., Swanson, J., Kroes, E. and Bradley, M. (1991), *Stated Preference Techniques: A Guide to Practice,* Second Edition, Steer Davies Gleave and Hague Consulting Group.

Senna, L. A.D.S. (1992) Traveller's willingness to pay for reductions in travel time variability, paper presented at the *7th World Conference on Transport Research,* Lyon, July.

Swait, J. and Louviere, J.J. (1993) The role of the scale parameter in the estimation and comparison of multinomial logit models, *Journal of Marketing Research* (in press).

Timmermans, H.J.P. (1988) Hierarchical information integration applied to residential choice processes, paper presented at the *Annual Meeting of the American Association of Geographers,* Phoenix, Arizona.

Wardman, M. (1988) A Comparison of revealed and stated preference models of travel behaviour, *Journal of Transport Economics and Policy,* XXII (1), 71-92.

Winship, C. and Mare, R.D. (1984) Regression models with ordinal variables, *American Sociological Review,* 49, 512-525.

CHAPTER 5

TRIP SCHEDULING IN
URBAN TRANSPORTATION ANALYSIS*

Kenneth A. Small**

Transportation economists have long known how to determine equilibrium configurations of travel demand and system behavior on static congested road networks. Yet applications consistently overpredict the effects that trends or policies will have on the maximum severity of peak-period congestion. A typical case is when a capacity expansion is predicted to lower congestion markedly during peak travel times but what actually occurs is a narrowing of the period of peak congestion: an example of the *shifting-peak phenomenon*.

The basic mechanism is aptly explained by Anthony Downs (1962) in terms of what I call *latent demand*. The equilibrium usage pattern of a highly congested facility entails many people being deterred by congestion itself. Some of these people choose alternatives that are included in standard modeling techniques, such as public transit. Many, however, choose to alter their schedules, combine several purposes into one trip, settle for less than ideal residential locations, or forgo discretionary

Discussants: Donald Dewees, University of Toronto; Randall J. Pozdena, Federal Reserve Bank of San Francisco; Steven Morrison, Northeastern University.

*Reprinted from *American Economic Review*, Vol. 92, No. 2 (May 1992), pp. 482-86.

**Department of Economics, University of California, Irvine, CA 92717. This paper was written during a visiting appointment at Harvard University. I am grateful to Richard Arnott, John Meyer, and Randall Pozdena for comments on an earlier draft.

trips. If the equilibration model fails to incorporate these adaptations, it cannot predict the substantial shifts into peak-period road travel that occur as soon as congestion is eased slightly.

One of the adaptations, trip scheduling, appears to be particularly important. It is now well enough understood so that practical equilibrium models of urban travel can begin to incorporate it. There is reason to believe that doing so would produce some interesting surprises, because certain known results for highly stylized cases differ dramatically from ordinary intuition.

For example, suppose identical commuters trade off queueing delay at a bottleneck against the inconvenience of arriving early for work, regarding both as costs of travel. It turns out that the aggregate cost of scheduling inconvenience is comparable to the aggregate cost of queueing delay, becoming equal to it when people are identical in their scheduling preferences. More surprisingly, the total cost of travel is independent of the unit value people place on queueing delay, a situation in stark contrast to standard cost-benefit analysis.

This paper presents evidence for the importance of endogenous scheduling, discusses the effects of ignoring it, and describes recent advances in modeling it. These advances include analysis of the welfare benefits associated with policies that modify scheduling choices.

I. Evidence of Endogenous Scheduling

Two kinds of evidence have accumulated. The first is indirect, from observing the outcomes of changes in the transportation environment that seem explicable only in terms of scheduling shifts. The second is direct analysis of survey data that contain information about the times people travel.

The indirect evidence includes a number of studies in which a new bridge or rapid transit line failed to produce the expected decline in the number of peak-hour travelers using an existing parallel highway. See Small (1992 pp. 113-4) for citations. One study surveyed users of the newly opened Bay Area Rapid Transit (BART) line between Oakland and San Francisco, as well as users of the parallel San Francisco—Oakland Bay Bridge. The immediate impact of the BART opening was a diversion of 8,750 peak automobile trips from the bridge to BART;

but within a few months, 7,000 new peak-hour auto trips were generated. This brought peak congestion nearly back to its original level, although its duration diminished. Similar peak narrowing is reported following bridge openings near London and at Vianen, Netherlands.

Conversely, many studies have observed a spreading of the peak as exogenous growth in travel demand exceeds growth in capacity, or when capacity is suddenly reduced due to a road closing. These include a cross-sectional study of U.S. metropolitan areas, a time-series study of London, and observations of a bridge closing in Edmonton, Alberta.

Direct survey evidence supports the conclusion that an important cause of these observations is endogenous rescheduling of trips. For example, residents of western Holland reported a desire to travel during the peak hour, if congestion were eliminated, that represented latent demand equal to 27 percent of current peak volumes. Nearly half of this was due to schedule shifting.

A few studies have estimated econometric models of scheduling choices by commuters. For example, my 1982 article estimates a logit model of choice among 12 travel intervals, each of 5 minutes duration. The model measures a utility function which depends on travel time and on the amount that the work-arrival time associated with a hypothetical scheduling choice deviates from the official work-start time (this deviation is known as *schedule delay*). In one model that fits well, the dependence on schedule delay, divided by a constant disutility of travel time, looks like Figure 1. The marginal rates of substitution are $\Delta/v_T = 5.47$ minutes, $\beta/v_T = 0.61$, and $\gamma/v_T = 2.40$; here v_T denotes the value of in-vehicle time, which can be inferred from many other studies. More generally, these rates of substitution are found to vary with socioeconomic characteristics, travel situation, and employer's flexibility toward late arrivals.

II. Effects of Ignoring Endogenous Scheduling

The conventional static model for analyzing congestion assumes a fixed speed-flow relationship, with demand constant over a predetermined time interval. The same failure described earlier applies when it is used to analyze any policy that removes cars from the peak-hour traffic stream without altering the relative desirability of peak versus off-

Figure 1. Disutility of Schedule Delay Relative to Travel Time

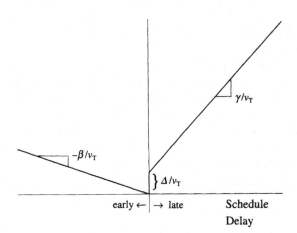

peak travel. Transit and car-pool incentives, gasoline taxes, parking fees, and growth controls do nothing to prevent any "spare" highway capacity from being appropriated by people who previously traveled outside the peak period.

The static model's mispredictions are likely to be especially severe when the assumed speed-flow relationship is very steep, as is common when analyzing expressways. The model then predicts that small demand shifts produce large changes in average speed. As a result, it is sometimes falsely claimed that inducing just a few percent of drivers to switch to car pools or mass transit would eliminate most congestion.

Such mispredictions affect normative as well as positive analysis. Consider, for example, the benefits from a capacity increase. If the predicted reduction in peak travel times is partly illusory, so are the associated benefits in the form of travel-time savings. On the other hand, important benefits may be reaped in the form of more convenient schedules, which the analysis fails to recognize. The net effect of these offsetting biases is not obvious but can be determined within the specific alternative models described next.

III. Recent Modeling Advances

Two approaches to incorporating endogenous scheduling have made their way into the economics and engineering literature, both focusing on the journey to work. (Only occasionally have departures from work been considered.) Both approaches have been used to investigate the shifting-peak phenomenon, the effects of time-of-day pricing, and the biases inherent in a cost-benefit analysis that ignores scheduling behavior. Most applications assume that utility is piecewise linear in schedule delay, as shown in Figure 1, but usually set the discrete lateness penalty Δ to zero.

Instantaneous Equilibria

The most natural extension of the standard model is to view it as describing instantaneous equilibria between supply and demand at any given time of day. Endogenous scheduling is then added as part of the demand model. The equilibration process forces consistency between the pattern of congestion over time and the scheduling choices given this pattern. This approach, developed by J. Vernon Henderson (1977 Ch. 8), can incorporate a speed-flow curve of any shape and is amenable to simulation modeling. A disadvantage is that it is not fully consistent with the dynamics of road travel, as it allows a commuter who departs home during a period of declining congestion to overtake one who departed earlier. Henderson (1992) shows that if this model is the correct one, the conventional analysis of benefits from an incremental capacity expansion will always overstate them.

Queueing at a Bottleneck

The second approach has been to model queueing behind a bottleneck. Traffic is assumed to flow at a constant speed as long as volume V is less than a fixed capacity C; but when V exceeds C, a queue builds at rate $V-C$ vehicles per unit time. A commuter who encounters a queue containing N vehicles suffers queueing delay N/C. The model was pioneered for analyzing equilibrium schedule choices by William Vickrey (1969) and has subsequently been elaborated in a dozen or so articles in the economics and engineering literatures (see Small [1992] for a review). While this approach is very stylized, it leads to surprising results with important economic intuition; it also has been extended to several routes and to heterogeneous commuters, potentially bringing it within the realm of practical planning models.

Perhaps the most interesting results for economists are those in two articles by Richard Arnott et al. (1990, 1992). In their model, as extended in Small (1992), there are Q commuters, and the times they prefer to pass through the bottleneck are uniformly distributed over a period of duration q. If Q/q exceeds capacity C, a queue develops, inducing some commuters to choose schedules that get them to work before or after their preferred times. Those choosing to go early must balance the marginal reduction in schedule-delay cost from starting a bit later against the marginal increase in travel-time cost; this can happen only if traffic enters the queue at rate $Cv_T/(v_T-\beta)$, in which case capacity is exceeded and the queue builds. Similarly, toward the end of the rush hour, traffic enters at the smaller rate $Cv_T/(v_T+\gamma)$, allowing the queue to dissipate gradually. The earliest and latest commuters incur no travel-time delay and identical schedule-delay costs $\delta[(Q/C)-q]$, where $\delta \equiv \beta\gamma/(\beta+\gamma)$ is a kind of composite unit cost of scheduling inconvenience. Only one commuter avoids schedule-delay cost altogether, and that person incurs the maximum travel-time cost, namely $\delta Q/C$. In the special case $q=0$, in which everyone wants to pass through the bottleneck at the same time, they all incur identical total travel costs; in that case the aggregate travel cost $\delta Q^2/C$ consists half of schedule-delay cost and half of travel-time cost.

The remarkable thing about these equilibrium costs is that they are independent of the value of time v_T. This is because the bottleneck is at capacity throughout the period in which anyone travels, the duration of which, Q/C, is independent of v_T. This duration determines the travel costs of the first and last commuters, to which other commuters' costs are tied through the conditions for scheduling equilibrium. If the value of time were higher, commuters would try harder to spread out their travel schedules to avoid congestion; but in so doing they would decrease the amount of queueing and leave unchanged the time at which it begins and ends. The net result would be less congestion but, because it is valued more highly, the same congestion costs.

The optimal time-varying price is one that maintains outflow from the bottleneck precisely at capacity, but with no queueing; it does so by exactly mimicking the path taken by queueing-delay cost in the absence of pricing. This causes each person to choose the same work-arrival schedule as before and to incur the same total perceived price as before. However, in that perceived price, a money price has been substituted for the queueing-delay cost; so the aggregate social costs of travel decline by precisely the amount of those queueing-delay costs. In other words, congestion is eliminated, while schedules remain unaltered. This property of the optimal-price schedule was noted by Vickrey (1969); it contrasts with the Henderson model, in which optimal pricing causes the peak period to spread. Gordon Newell (1987) shows that the existence (though not necessarily the optimality) of such a pricing scheme characterizes a much more general set of distributions of desired travel schedules.

Arnott et al. (1992) show further that if total demand Q is elastic with respect to average travel cost, the pricing problem can be broken into two parts. They consider the case $q=0$ (identical schedule preferences). In the first part, some price schedule (not necessarily the optimal one) is chosen; the scheduling equilibria are then determined for each value of total demand Q, and total travel costs $TC(Q)$ thereby determined. In the second part, an additional uniform price is chosen so as to maximize net social benefits, including the consumer surplus under the demand curve for Q. This second part turns out to be identical to the conventional model for congestion pricing, with output now measured as Q rather than as vehicle flows. For example, with optimal time-varying pricing, $TC(Q) = \frac{1}{2}\delta Q^2/C$ as noted above, and the usual analysis applies; but note that average cost $\frac{1}{2}\delta Q/C$ rises linearly with Q and so does not become as steep as is usually assumed in analyses based on speed-flow curves. Conventional cost-benefit and second-best analyses can also be applied to the second part of this problem, because the scheduling adjustments are incorporated into $TC(Q)$.

Small (1992 pp. 134-7) shows that if equilibrium is correctly described by this bottleneck model, benefits from an incremental capacity expansion may be either over- or underestimated using the conventional model. For example, if the conventional analysis assumes that speed is proportional to $(V/C)^k$, as is common, then benefits are overestimated if $k>2$ and underestimated if $k<2$. This occurs because the higher is k, the greater is the overstatement of travel-time reductions. A different result is derived for the planner who recognizes that a queueing model applies but believes erroneously that the times people enter the queue are exogenous. In that case, the planner overestimates marginal benefits if $(v_T/\delta) > 2$ and underestimates them if $(v_T/\delta) < 2$.

IV. Conclusion

There are many ways these models can be made more realistic. One is to embed them in a network with endogenous route choice. Another is to incorporate more fully the heterogeneity that is found in the empirical studies of scheduling choice, both in parameters and in unobservable preferences for particular schedules. Yet another is to allow capacity to be random, depending for example on weather conditions or traffic accidents. Considerable progress has been made on these fronts, for example by Moshe Ben-Akiva et al. (1986). Another desirable extension, awaiting better empirical measurements, is to incorporate the reliability of travel schedules.

Despite these limitations, the work described here is sufficiently advanced that it can be incorporated into practical traffic studies and into standard economic theories of traffic congestion. Doing so promises to bring new predictive accuracy and new insights into transportation analysis.

References

Arnott, Richard, de Palma, André and Lindsey, Robin, "Economics of a Bottleneck," *Journal of Urban Economics*, January 1990, 27, 111-30.

_____, "A Structural Model of Peak-Period Congestion: A Traffic Bottleneck with Elastic Demand," *American Economic Review*, 1992 (forthcoming).

Ben-Akiva, Moshe, de Palma, André and Kanaroglou, Pavlos, "Dynamic Model of Peak Period Traffic Congestion with Elastic Arrival Rates," *Transportation Science*, August 1986, 20, 164-81.

Downs, Anthony, "The Law of Peak-Hour Expressway Congestion," *Traffic Quarterly*, July 1962, 16, 393-409.

Henderson, J. Vernon, *Economic Theory and the Cities*, New York:

Academic Press, 1977.

_____, "Peak Shifting and Cost-Benefit Miscalculations," *Regional Science and Urban Economics*, 1992 (forthcoming).

Newell, Gordon F., "The Morning Commute for Nonidentical Travelers," *Transportation Science*, May 1987, 21, 74-88.

Small, Kenneth A., "The Scheduling of Consumer Activities: Work Trips," *American Economic Review*, June 1982, 72, 467-79.

_____, *Urban Transportation Economics, Fundamentals of Pure and Applied Economics*, Vol. 51, Chur, Switzerland: Harwood, 1992.

Vickrey, William S., "Congestion Theory and Transport Investment," *American Economic Review*, May 1969 (*Papers and Proceedings*), 59, 251-60.

PART II

TRANSPORT COSTS AND
COST ANALYSIS

CHAPTER 6

COMPETITION, NATURAL MONOPOLY, AND SCALE ECONOMIES*

*Keeler, Theodore E.***

When discussing the railroad industry, the terms "competition" and "monopoly" are often tossed about loosely. Kolko states that railroad regulation came about in the late nineteenth century not because the railroads were too monopolistic, but because they were too competitive.[1] He is referring to the fact that regulation aided the railroads in preserving a cartel and preventing rate wars. But in even the simplest economic theory, what do "too monopolistic" and "too competitive" mean? Are they as inconsistent as Kolko indicates? Similarly, it is often said about the railroads in the last half of the twentieth century that the industry is no longer a monopoly because of the competition of highway, water, and air transportation.[2] While this statement may be true in a broad sense, it still does not address the issue of whether railroads represent a natural monopoly in the narrower sense of economic theory, that is, it does not make it clear whether the private market can or will generate

* Reprinted from Keeler, T.E. (1983), *Railroads, Freight, and Public Policy*, Brookings Institution, Ch. 3 (Competition, Natural Monopoly, and Scale Economies), pp. 43-61.
** Department of Economics, University of California at Berkeley.

1. Gabriel Kolko, *Railroads and Regulation, 1877-1916* (Princeton University Press, 1965).
2. This is stated, for example, in the Staggers Rail Act of 1980 (49 U.S.C., sec. 10101a, note).

an economically efficient solution. It is the existence of a natural monopoly in that sense that determines whether the railroad industry requires public intervention to be efficient.[3] Of course, public intervention might occur whether it were efficient or not. But it is best to clearly understand whether the structure of the railroad industry is or is not competitive in the economic sense of the term, and if it is not, just what the structure is. This boils down to the matter of scale economies relative to the size of markets for rail transportation.[4] There is a sizable amount of empirical evidence on this issue, but first, it is necessary and appropriate to review some basic economic theory.

Market Structure

The theory presented here is so basic that something like it can be found in introductory economics textbooks. Yet because elaborate theoretical studies and econometric analyses often fail to take account of this theory, it is worth reviewing. This and the next chapter will expand on it with both empirical evidence and theoretical refinement.

I start with the simple case wherein there is only one market for rail services in which potential rail firms can operate. In this case the market includes shipments of a single commodity between two cities, with no intermediate service. Output (Q) is the flow of shipments of the commodity per unit of time, and long-run unit costs, marginal and average ($LRMC$ and $LRAC$), are as shown in figure 1. The figure represents a natural monopoly. As the density of traffic flows on the route increases, the average cost to a single firm ($LRAC$) declines over the entire area under the demand curve (D). There is room for only one low-cost firm in this market.

For such a natural monopoly to exist, it must always be cheaper for a single firm to produce the relevant output than for two or more firms to

---

3. If firms' entry into and exit from the market are sufficiently easy, even a natural monopoly can achieve efficient results. See William J. Baumol, "Contestable Markets: An Uprising in the Theory of Industry Structure," *American Economic Review*, vol. 72 (March 1982), pp. 1-15.

4. Scale economies and indivisibilities are only one category of problems causing market failure. See Francis M. Bator, "The Anatomy of Market Failure," *Quarterly Journal of Economics*, vol. 72 (August 1958), pp. 351-79.

Figure 1. A Natural Rail Monopoly

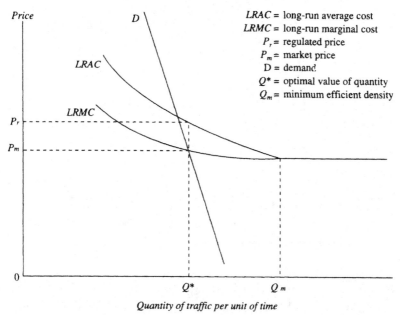

Quantity of traffic per unit of time

produce it.[5] It is not necessary that the average cost curve be falling over the entire range of output under the demand curve, as shown in figure 1—it can be flat or even rise where it hits the demand curve. But in the last case, the average cost curve must have been falling over some lower levels of output; otherwise, the above-mentioned conditions for natural monopoly will not be met.

Figure 2 shows a potentially competitive market. Economies of route density are exhausted when a relatively small amount of the market is accommodated. If there were free entry of firms into this market and if potential entrants had knowledge of the profits to be made and equal access to factor inputs, a competitive equilibrium would be achieved. In between the cases of "natural monopoly" and "naturally competitive" markets is the case of "natural oligopoly" wherein a small number of

5. This condition for natural monopoly is called "sub-additivity." See Robert D. Willig, "Multiproduct Technology and Market Structure," *American Economic Review*, vol. 69 (May 1979), p. 349.

Figure 2. A Competitive Rail Market[a]

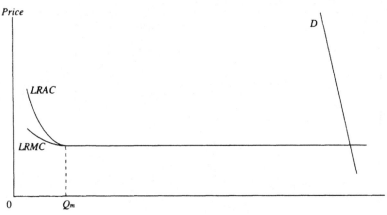

Price

D

LRAC

LRMC

0   Q_m

Quantity of traffic per unit of time

a. See figure 1 for explanation of variables.

efficient firms will "fit" into the market.

Simplistic though such graphic representation is, it reveals some important things about the market for rail transportation that are often ignored.

First, these figures make it evident that economies of route density (the potential for lower costs as more traffic flows over a given route) are intimately connected with the potential existence of natural monopoly problems in the railroad industry. Although other economies of integrated operation are also relevant to the functioning of rail markets, any analysis of the potential for natural monopoly in transportation that fails to take account of economies of traffic density will not arrive at a logically correct resolution of the issue.

Second, the figures, combined with a rudimentary knowledge of theories of oligopoly and competitive pricing,[6] offer a potential explanation for Kolko's statement that railroads were regulated because they were too competitive rather than too monopolistic. Suppose that two natural monopolists, having jointly entered a market, attempt to compete. Note that under these circumstances marginal cost (*LRMC*) for each firm will

---

6. This is, strictly speaking, Bertrand-type oligopoly behavior.

be below average cost. Note also that if one firm cuts its price but that price cut is not matched by the other firm, the price-cutting firm will make money from any additional traffic won, so long as the reduced price is still above marginal (not average) cost.[7] Unless collusion is achieved, there will be a natural tendency for price to fall to marginal cost. In a competitive industry this will produce a stable equilibrium, because marginal and average costs are the same. In a natural monopoly, however, marginal cost will be below average cost in the range of production, since, as defined, the average cost curve falls through the output range behind the demand curve. Thus when natural monopolies try to compete, there is a distinct possibility of rate wars, characterized by price cuts designed to avoid immediate matching by competitors (It is not surprising that, during nineteenth century rate wars, secret rate kickbacks were often offered to large shippers). This simple analysis can easily be generalized to show that noncollusive, Bertrand-type pricing behavior will always result in losses as long as there are "too many" firms in an industry, for example, three entrants into a natural duopoly, and so forth.[8]

The outcome of this process, wherein excess capacity is driven out of a natural monopoly market, is often called destructive or cutthroat competition, because it could so easily cause at least one of the rivals to go bankrupt. Furthermore, once the rival was driven out, the incumbent firm could be expected to reap the full monopoly rents achievable from controlling the market. Recent theoretical developments, however, show that such outcomes do not necessarily hold.[9]

Consider the case of a natural monopoly market in which entry and

---

7. For a more elaborate discussion of the relationship between cutthroat competition and excess capacity, see F. M. Scherer, *Industrial Market Structure and Economic Performance* (Rand McNally, 1980), chap. 8.

8. Ibid.

9. A good summary of the literature on contestable markets is in Baumol, "Contestable Markets." Paradoxically, entry of new firms into natural monopolies can also cause market failure. See John C. Panzar and Robert D. Willig, "Free Entry and Sustainability of Nature Monopoly," *Bell Journal of Economics*, vol. 8 (Spring 1977), pp. 1-22. See also William J. Baumol, Elizabeth E. Bailey, and Robert D. Willig, "Weak Invisible Hand Theorems on the Sustainability of Multiproduct Natural Monopoly," *American Economic Review*, vol. 67 (June 1977), pp. 350-65; and William J Baumol and John C. Pnzar, *Contestable Markets and the Theory of Industry Structure* (Harcourt Brace Jovanovich, 1982).

exit are both easy and in which a new entrant is at no cost disadvantage. In this case, the loser in a fight such as this one, entailing destructive competition, can pull out easily before any significant losses are incurred and well before bankruptcy. So the loser is not nearly so badly off as in the story told above. But the winner is not so well off either. If it charges a price yielding any profits at all (beyond a normal return on capital), it will induce the entry of at least one other firm, and price rivalry will continue until all profits are eliminated—price will be driven down to average costs in the case of a single-product firm or to a welfare-maximizing combination of zero-profit prices in the case of a multiproduct firm (these are referred to in a later chapter as "second-best," or Ramsey, prices).

In short, Baumol and the others have documented that, with very easy entry and exit, a natural monopoly has almost all the attractive characteristics of a competitive market, eliminating the need for regulation. They appropriately call such a natural monopoly a "contestable" natural monopoly.

If railroads constituted a contestable natural monopoly, it would greatly simplify the task of regulating them, because the marketplace could then be trusted to accomplish a large part, if not all, of the task of achieving efficient pricing and resource allocation in the industry. Common sense, however, indicates that the railroad industry is not contestable: entry entails a long and tedious process of buying up parcels of land, generally requiring powers of eminent domain (which, in turn, requires some government intervention). Engineering and building a railroad line also require considerable time and expense. So entry into the industry is anything but easy.

Exit is also difficult, largely because of public regulatory policies. But even without regulation, exit from the industry would be difficult by the standards of many other industries: heavy sunk costs, often financed with debt, are incurred to serve a specific market, without the opportunity to transfer them to other markets easily. While bridges, ballast, rails, and ties can be moved from one route to another, they can be moved only at great expense.

Overall, then, rail markets seem unlikely candidates for contestability. As firms are driven out of rail markets by rate wars, losing firms are likely, because of sunk costs, to go bankrupt rather than exit easily. And the entry of new firms into a given market should not be expected to be fast or easy.

Nevertheless, the theory of contestable markets is far from irrelevant to the railroad industry. A scheme wherein right-of-way was publicly owned, with privately owned locomotives and cars (and more than one firm competing on a given right-of-way), might allow contestable markets. Furthermore, to the extent that competing technologies, including trucks, barges, and coal slurry, have cost levels somewhere near rail costs, they may be able to impart to rail markets some of the characteristics of contestable markets.

The crude model of competition in the railroad industry just developed can, with one additional complication, be used to explain the Interstate Commerce Commission's concern with preserving weak carriers and preserving service on low-density lines. The analysis above assumes only service between two cities, with no intermediate service. But suppose that the abandonment of one of the railroads generated loss of service for intermediate cities not served by the other railroad. The ICC would then have a political incentive to try to maintain the first railroad, and indeed, there may be economic benefits to subsidizing it.[10]

Scale Economies

With a few exceptions, a railroad firm is likely to be larger and more complicated than the one discussed above. Specifically, it will probably haul a number of different types of commodities (with different costs) for different lengths of haul at different times between different points. And the overall size of the firm is likely to be quite independent of the amount of traffic that travels on a given route of that firm—that is, a large firm may have short or long hauls and high or low traffic densities between different points. Some commodity trips entail travel over high-density and low-density routes, with long and short trains.

Economies of route density can produce a natural monopoly on a given route, though in the absence of any other economies of scale, the national railway system could be made up of a large number of small firms, each with a local monopoly.

---

10. Markets do fail when the demand curve hits the social average cost curve (or the cost curve for a single firm in a natural monopoly) where it is declining, so that the marginal cost is below the average cost. See Bator, "Anatomy of Market Failure."

Another type of economy of firm integration that might be observed in the railroad industry is economies of length of haul. With fixed terminal expenses, longer hauls should mean lower costs per mile. If these economies exist, a railroad that has an integrated nationwide system will have an advantage over a railroad that must make and accept interline shipments to and from other railroads.

Still another type of scale economy is that of firm size. In rail transportation, economies of firm size would mean lower costs for larger firms, when length of haul and route density are held constant. If there were substantial economies of firm size without economies of traffic density, it would be economic to have a number of integrated nationwide (or international) railroads that competed on all their routes.

Finally, railroads, like most other modern corporations, are multiproduct firms. Indeed, it is possible to view each different type of commodity trip (depending not only on commodity type, but also on the specific terminal points connected by the trip, on the time at which the shipment occurs, and on the quality of service) as a different product of the rail firm.[11] In the late 1970s a new literature developed on the theory of multiproduct monopolies, which extended the relatively simple criteria for single-product natural monopoly to a somewhat more complicated set of criteria for multiproduct natural monopoly. For this analysis, it is important to take adequate account of this literature and of these criteria. However, the literature allowing rigorous testing of the hypothesis of multiproduct natural monopoly is not yet well developed, and most studies of scale economies in the industry have not been structured to adequately test the hypothesis of multiproduct monopoly.

Therefore, for the purposes of this study, I first survey most of the available literature on this topic from a single-product perspective, treating as the single product net ton-miles of freight hauled and assuming a

---

11. Transportation economists have been aware for some time that different passenger or commodity trips constitute very different types of output. See, for example, John R. Meyer, John F. Kain, and Martin Wohl, *The Urban Transportation Problem* (Harvard University Press, 1965), especially the appendix. The ICC has for some years estimated the costs of commodity trips using accounting procedures, but the only study to estimate the costs of such commodity trips directly from an econometric cost function is Sergio Jara-Diaz and Clifford Winston, "Multiproduct Transportation Cost Functions: Scale and Scope in Railroad Operations" (Massachusetts Institute of Technology, April 1981).

commodity of "typical" weight, bulk, length of haul, and other characteristics. Once this survey is complete, I will present both a summary of the multiproduct theory and evidence on how my conclusions on natural monopoly in the industry can be affected by a more accurate multiproduct perspective.

Empirical Evidence on Scale Economies

In 1850 Dionysius Lardner wrote *Railway Economy: A Treatise on the New Art of Transport, Its Management, Prospects, and Regulations,* quite possibly the first systematic application of economic analysis to railroads. He set forth three basic principles of railroad economics, one of which was the following: "Railroad expenses do not vary in proportion to the volume of business handled."[12] In other words, Lardner asserted that rail transportation is subject to scale economies.

Ever since the time of Lardner, students of the railroad industry have debated whether there are scale economies in the industry.[13] Appendix B [not reprinted here] contains a critical survey of a number of studies on railroad costs conducted over the past thirty years. It shows that most of the studies conducted during the 1950s and 1960s found few economies of scale; they found that there were no economies of firm size and that economies of traffic density, if they were measured at all, appeared to be exhausted at very low traffic densities, so that practically all the mainline rail mileage in the country was operated subject to constant returns.

However, not everyone studying these matters agreed with this, and even those who did indicated some doubt. Meyer, Peck, Stenason, and Zwick, in one of the most important rail cost studies in the late 1950s, noted that the indivisibility of the rail plant was an important factor, making marginal and average costs different.[14] In general, studies that found constant returns to scale in the railroad industry suffered from

---

12. Cited in Stuart Daggett, *Principles of Inland Transportation* (Harper, 1928), p. 53.

13. Indeed, the first statistical work on railroad costs was as early as 1916. M. O. Lorenz, "Cost and Value of Service in Railroad Ratemaking," *Quarterly Journal of Economics,* vol. 30 (February 1916), pp. 205-18.

14. John R. Meyer, Merton J. Peck, John Stenason, and Charles Zwick, *The Economics of Competition in the Transportation Industries* (Harvard University Press, 1959), pp. 159-63.

methodological problems: they sometimes confused returns to firm size with returns to traffic density, or they allocated costs between freight and passenger service in questionable ways.

Studies of railroad costs from the 1970s tell a different but consistent story about returns to traffic density. They all give strong evidence of increasing returns, up to a rather high traffic density relative to tonnages moving over most route-mileage in the United States. These studies are based on differing econometric methods and specifications, although most are based on the same data set: lager Class I railroads in the United States for the late 1960s and early 1970s.

Some summary results of the analysis in appendix B are given in table 1, which shows the estimated percentage of costs that are variable (total revenues achievable through marginal cost pricing divided by total costs) evaluated at mean traffic density for each study, as well as estimated minimum efficient traffic density.[15] The table also indicates, where relevant, whether each study found increasing, decreasing, or constant returns to firm size when traffic density was held constant. Although there is a considerable variation in some of the figures shown in the table, it tells a reasonably consistent story.

First, consider the results on the percent of costs variable. Except for the Friedlaender and Spady study (for which the percent variable applies to high-density main-line trackage), all percent variables are evaluated at mean traffic densities for all firms in the sample. And the results of these studies are reasonably consistent—they indicate that, as of the late 1960s and early 1970s, on the average a railroad could recover 55 to 65 percent of its total costs with marginal cost pricing. As one might expect, however, all the studies found that as traffic densities rise, approaching minimum efficient density, the percent of costs variable rises. Thus in Harmatuck's study a doubling of the traffic density from the mean (roughly from 3.5 million to 7 million net ton-miles per route-mile) results in the percent of costs variable rising from 52 to 97.5. Similarly, Friedlaender and Spady's estimate of the percent of costs variable, because it imposes a large, discrete drop in costs between "low-density" and "high-density" lines, is most applicable to main-line operations with higher-than-average densities (see appendix B for a fuller explanation of this).

Properly interpreted, the evidence on cost elasticities seems to tell a

---

15. For citations of all these studies, see appendix A.

Table 1. Some Evidence on Scale Economies from
Cross Sectional Studies of U.S. Railroads[a]

Study	Year of study	Years of data set	Mean long-run cost elasticity (Percent)	Minimum efficient density (millions of net tons)
Caves, Christensen,		1955	61.2[b]	n.a.
and Swanson	1981	1963	60.5[b]	n.a.
			71.6[b]	n.a.
Friedlaender and Spady	1981	1968-70	89.5	8.2
Harmatuck	1979	1968-70	51.7	7-8[c]
Harris	1977	1972-73	64	Over 30[d]
Keeler	1974	1968-70	57[e]	15
Sidhu, Charney, and Due	1977	1973	67	1.7

Sources: Douglas W. Caves, Laurits R. Christensen, and Joseph A. Swanson, "Productivity Growth, Scale Economies, and Capacity Utilization in U.S. Railroads, 1955-74," *American Economic Review*, vol. 71 (December 1981), pp. 994-1002; Ann F. Friedlaender and Richard H. Spady, *Freight Transport Regulation: Equity, Efficiency, and Competition in the Rail and Trucking Industries* (MIT Press, 1981); Donald J. Harmatuck, "A Policy-Sensitive Railway Cost Function," *Logistics and Transportation Review*, vol. 15 (May 1979), pp. 277-315; Robert G. Harris, "Rationalizing the Rail Freight Industry: A Case Study in Institutional Failure and Proposals for Reform," Sloan Working Paper 7705 (University of California at Berkeley, Department of Economics, September 1977); Theodore E. Keeler, "Railroad Costs, Returns to Scale, and Excess Capacity," *Review of Economics and Statistics*, vol. 56 (May 1974); and Nancy D. Sidhu, Alberta Charney, and John F. Due, "Cost Functions of Class II Railroads and the Viability of Light Traffic Density Railway Lines," *Quarterly Review of Economics and Business*, vol. 17 (Autumn 1977), pp. 7-24.

n.a. Not available.

a. All railroads are Class I (revenues of over should be $5 million a year in these years), except Sidhu, Charney, and Due, which are Class II short lines.

b. These are short-run cost elasticities, judged to be nearly equivalent to long-run cost elasticities in other studies. See appendix B.

c. These are the estimated densities at which 97.5 percent of costs are variable in the Harmatuck study. See appendix B.

d. In the Harris study 93 percent of costs are variable at 30 million net ton-miles per route-mile.

e. Referred to as a short-run elasticity in the Keeler study, but equivalent to a long-run function below minimum efficient density, as explained in appendix B.

consistent and reasonable story: for all but rather high-density main-line trackage, rail routes in this country operated at increasing returns to scale, with marginal costs below average costs. On the other hand, while a relatively large portion of the nation's route-mileage is the low-density sort, with marginal costs below average costs, relatively more of the traffic flows over higher-density routes, where this is not a problem.

Before considering this evidence on traffic densities, let us consider the evidence from the various studies on minimum efficient traffic density. As indicated in appendix B, estimates range from a low of 8 million to 10 million net ton-miles per route-mile (Friedlaender and Spady) to as much as over 30 million net ton-miles (Harmatuck, Harris). The cause of this seemingly distressing variation in results is not difficult to find; Friedlaender and Spady state it succinctly for all studies: "Since the standard errors of the coefficients ... are large, and since one is extrapolating far beyond the sample range, these calculations [of minimum efficient density] may well be meaningless."[16] In other words, because the average route densities for most railroads are well below whatever the minimum efficient density may be, all calculations of minimum efficient density entail extrapolating along an estimated function. Naturally, under these circumstances, the estimates are likely to be quite sensitive to the specification of the cost function used. If this is so, one might be tempted to conclude that nothing can be said about minimum efficient density. Fortunately, the evidence contradicts this.

Specifically, in practically all studies the average cost curve starts to flatten out well before it reaches minimum efficient density, so that even if it is not completely flat within the observed range of traffic densities, it becomes almost flat. This is especially true of estimates based on the most sophisticated and flexible of functional forms, the translog function. Harmatuck found that at twice the mean traffic density in his study, equivalent to 7 million to 8 million net ton-miles per route-mile, 97.5 percent of costs were variable.[17] Similarly, Friedlaender and Spady found that for main-line operations of a number of large, high-density railroads almost all costs (95 to 100 percent) were variable (Firms for which they found this to be true include the Santa Fe, the Missouri

---

16. Ann F. Friedlaender and Richard H. Spady, *Freight Transport Regulation: Equity, Efficiency, and Competition in the Rail and Trucking Industries* (MIT Press, 1981), p. 156.

17. Donald J. Harmatuck, "A Policy-Sensitive Railway Cost Function," *Logistics and Transportation Review*, vol. 15 (May 1979), pp. 303-04.

Table 2. Freight Density for U.S. Line-Haul Railroads, Selected Years,
1929-80 Millions of net ton-miles per route-mile

Year	Freight density
1929	1.82
1939	1.44
1944	3.29
1950	n.a.
1960	n.a.
1970	3.74
1974	4.26
1979	5.02
1980	n.a.

Sources: Calculated from Association of American Railroads, *Yearbook of Railroad Facts*
(Washington, D.C.: AAR, 1981), pp. 36, 46.
n.a. Not available.

Pacific, the Southern Pacific, the Southern, and the Union Pacific).[18]
While the exact density at which railroad costs flatten out completely is
not known, it is known that the cost curve for freight services becomes
almost flat at around 7 million to 10 million net ton-miles per route-
mile, depending on commodity type and other circumstances.

The determine the current importance of these economies of traffic
densities in the railroad industry, table 2 looks at trends in those densities, and table 3 at recent estimates of those densities for various firms.
As table 2 indicates, overall route densities have increased rather
sharply in recent years, the mean value having risen by over 60 percent
in the last decade (after many of these cost studies were completed)
alone. Table 3, which presents traffic densities for individual railroads
for 1969 and 1980, indicates even more clearly that some railroads,
especially on their main lines, have probably reached or surpassed minimum efficient density for all practical purposes. But a large fraction of
the nation's rail system operates at densities far below that. In 1975
fully 75 percent of the nation's rail network was operating below 8 million net ton-miles per route-mile.[19]

---

18. *Freight Transport Review*, p. 147.
19. Ibid., p. 220. Friedlaender and Spady's figures are in gross ton-miles per route-mile,

Table 3. Freight Densities of Major Railroads, 1969 and 1980
Millions of net ton-miles per route-mile

Railroad	1969	1980
Atchison, Topeka & Santa Fe	3.67	6.03
Baltimore & Ohio	5.29	4.46
Burlington Northern	2.61[a]	6.11
Chesapeake & Ohio	6.67	6.12
Chicago & Northwestern	1.63	3.10
Colorado & Southern	1.98	10.66
Denver & Rio Grande Western	4.26	5.97
Detroit, Toledo & Ironton	2.78	2.80
Fort Worth & Denver	1.10	6.55
Grand Trunk Western	3.05	3.49
Kansas City Southern	3.77	5.96
Louisville & Nashville	4.80	5.97
Maarine Central	1.14	1.11
Missouri-Kansas-Texas	1.66	3.81
Missouri Pacific	2.98	5.01
Norfolk & Western	6.97	6.58[b]
Pittsburgh & Lake Erie	7.28	5.52[b]
St. Louis-Southwestern	5.74	7.75
Seaboard Coast Line	3.36	4.26
Soo Line	5.64	6.27[b]
Southern	4.22	5.35
Southern Pacific	5.64	6.27[b]
Union Pacific	4.91	7.87[b]
Western Maryland	4.11	1.80
Western Pacific	4.15	3.20

Sources: 1969 (or 1971) data, Interstate Commerce Commission, *Transport Statistics*(Government Printing Office, 1970, 1972); 1980 (or 1979) data, *Moody s Transportation Manual* (1981).
a. First entry for Burlington Northern is 1971.
b. Second entry for these railroads is 1979.

---

but are equivalent to the figures mentioned in the text with a conversion factor of 2.6 gross ton-miles per net route-mile. See Robert G. Harris, "Rationalizing the Rail Freight Industry: A Case Study in Institutional Failure and Proposals for Reform," Sloan Working Paper 7705 (University of California at Berkeley, Department of Economics, September 1977), p. 52.

Table 4. Evidence on Short-Run Rail Costs

Study	Year of study	Years of data set	Range of cost elasticities
Braeutigam, Daughety, and Turnquist	1980	1969-77	15.8
Charney, Sidhu, and Due	1977	1963-73	0-75
Freidlaender and Spady	1981	1968-70	58-150
Jara-Diaz and Winston	1981	1975-80	35.2-78.7a

Sources: Ronald R. Braeutigam, Andrew F. Daughety, and Mark A. Turnquist, "The Esti-
mation of a Hybrid Cost Function for a Railroad Firm," *Review of Economics and
Statistics*, vol. 64 (August 1982), pp. 401-02; Alberta H. Charney, Nancy H. Sidhu,
and John F. Due, "Short Run Cost Functions for Class II Railroads," *Logistics and
Transportation Review*, vol. 13 (December 1977), p. 352; Friedlaender and Spady,
Freight Transport Regulation, p. 147; and Sergio Jara-Diaz and Clifford Winston,
"Multiproduct Transportation Cost Functions: Scale and Scope in Railroad Opera-
tions" (Massachusetts Institute of Technology, April 1981).

a. These numbers are the reciprocals of Jara-Diaz and Winston's estimates of global scale
economies, S_m. Thus for firm I, $S_m = 1.27$. So the cost elasticities are $1/2.84=0.352$ and
$1/1.27=0.787$, respectively.

The studies discussed so far can best be interpreted as providing evidence on the long-run costs of rail services, with the route structure held
constant (some of the results of Keeler and of Caves and others were
described as short-run costs, but their short-run cost functions are best
interpreted as long-run ones below minimum efficient density; see
appendix B). Recently, however, there have been some important time
series studies of short-run rail costs, including those of Braeutigam,
Daughety, and Turnquist; Jara-Diaz and Winston; and Charney, Sidhu,
and Due.[20] These studies are useful on three counts. First, they give
some indication of the relationship between average and marginal costs
for existing levels of investment in rail plant. Since many of these costs
will be sunk for some time to come, it is useful to know what these
short-run costs are. Second, because all these studies are based on highly

20. Ronald R. Braeutigam, Andrew F. Daughety, and Mark A. Turnquist, "The Estimation of a Hybrid Cost Function for a Railroad Firm," *Review of Economics and Statistics*, vol. 64 (August 1982), pp. 394-404; Jara-Diaz and Winston, "Multiproduct
Transportation Cost Functions"; and Alberta H. Charney, Nancy D. Sidhu, and John
F. Due, "Short Run Cost Functions for Class II Railroads," *Logistics and Transportation Review*, vol. 13 (December 1977), pp. 345-59.

disaggregated data for small firms, they give an idea of how aggregating data for cross sectional studies of larger firms has affected the results. Third, also because of their disaggregation to small firms with simple route networks, these studies allow the testing of other relatively specialized hypotheses about the nature of rail technology. Braeutigam and his colleagues, for example, analyze the impact of service quality (operating and yard-processing speed) on rail costs. Jara-Diaz and Winston test for the existence of multiproduct natural monopoly. (Once again, a more detailed discussion of all these studies may be found in appendix B). The results of these studies, in terms of short-run cost elasticities, are presented in table 4. Also included in the table are the results of the only cross sectional study to analyze true short-run costs (that is, with both route structure and plant capital held constant), that of Friedlaender and Spady.

The results of the short-run cost studies are consistent on only one count—they show a wide range of variation in the percent of costs variable. As pointed out by Friedlaender and Spady, this is apparently because many poorer railroads have neglected their plants, making the marginal costs of using them relatively high. On the other hand, railroads that have maintained their plants well tend to have short-run cost elasticities at or below the equivalent long-run levels. The results of the disaggregated short-run studies also indicate that the cost characteristics of a shipment depend fairly heavily on the circumstances—the relevant gradients, commodity types, urbanization, and so forth. The more aggregative studies may not always be accurate about costs of specific shipments, although the importance of these effects is not known.

In summary, then, based on a single-product approximation, a large fraction of the nation's rail system operates subject to increasing returns to traffic density, while the more important main lines are more likely to operate at near-constant returns to traffic density.

The Nature and Causes of Scale Economies

For purposes of subsequent analysis, and especially to understand how generalization of the preceding analysis to a multiproduct framework would affect the results, it is useful to analyze the reasons for the existence of scale economies in the railroad industry.

For many years those who believed that there were economies of traffic density assumed that they stemmed from a high level of "fixed" costs, mainly the capital and maintenance expenses of road property. It could be argued that if this was true the problems of destructive competition should no longer exist if these costs were written off: the only remaining costs should then be ones that vary with the amount of traffic carried. Since the industry is a declining one, so the argument goes, it will never need to recover these written-off costs.

The main problem with this argument is that its premise—that scale economies in the industry derive exclusively from fixed capital costs—is untrue. Miller first noted in 1973 that a large part of the economies of density in the railroad industry derive from costs other than capital and maintenance costs of way and structures.[21] Specifically, he found that part of them come from line-haul operations, such as engine crew costs, and another part from equipment maintenance and capital costs.

Although at first this may seem strange, in fact it makes good sense. As traffic densities rise, trains tend to get longer, thereby reducing line-haul crew costs per ton of freight carried. Train frequencies also rise, and this allows for better utilization of both labor and equipment. All these things appear to cause significant economies of traffic density, at least below densities of 8 to 10 ton-miles per route-mile.

The evidence on economies of density that Miller first noted have since been confirmed by many subsequent studies, including those of Friedlaender and Spady, Harmatuck, Harris, and Keeler.[22]

However, to some degree the economies of traffic density observed here stem from restrictive work rules. The economies of operation for long trains arise largely because a train must generally have a crew of from three to seven, who are paid a full day's wage for only 100 miles of work. If the crew numbered only two and if they were paid lower, market-clearing wages, scale economies from long trains would be far less important.

---

21. Edward Miller, "Economies of Scale in Railroading," *Proceedings Fourteenth Annual Meeting, Transportation Research Forum*, vol. 14, no. 1 (1973), pp. 683-701.
22. Friedlaender and Spady, *Freight Transport Regulation*; Harmatuck, "A Policy-Sensitive Railway Cost Function"; Harris, "Rationalizing the Rail Freight Industry"; and Theodore E. Keeler, "On the Economic Impact of Railroad Freight Regulation," Sloan Working Paper 7601 (University of California at Berkeley, Department of Economics, September 1976).

Finally, economies of route density can take the form not only of lower costs, but also of better service at the same costs. If higher density allows a railroad to operate more frequent trains, it may not achieve lower costs, but it may well make more money because shippers value better service. Harris and Keeler confirm that whether it comes from better service or lower costs, a high route density contributes to a high level of profitability, all other things being equal.[23]

Scale Economies in a Multiproduct Framework

In recent years a substantial body of literature has developed on natural monopoly in a multiproduct setting. This literature shows that the criteria for natural monopoly in a multiproduct setting are considerably more complicated than the single-product criteria discussed so far in this chapter.[24]

Because little work has been done to empirically test the criteria for multiproduct natural monopoly in the railroad (or any other) industry, I cannot provide anything close to definitive evidence on the extent to which analysis in a multiproduct framework would affect the results. Nor is this the place for a detailed, technical discussion of the theoretical criteria for natural monopoly—that should be (and is) the subject of another book.[25] Nevertheless, I can provide a brief, nontechnical review of the criteria for multiproduct natural monopoly and summarize what evidence is available so far on the extent to which multiproduct analysis would change my results on railroads.

Although the technical criteria for natural monopoly with multiprod-

23. Robert G. Harris and Theodore E. Keeler, "Determinants of Railroad Profitability: An Econometric Study," in Kenneth D. Boyer and William G. Shepherd, eds., *Economic Regulation: Essays in Honor of James R. Nelson* (Michigan State University Press, 1981), pp. 37-54.

24. The references on this topic are numerous. See, for example, William J. Baumol, "On the Proper Cost Tests for Natural Monopoly in a Multiproduct Industry," *American Economic Review*, vol. 67 (December 1977), pp. 809-22. A useful summary of this literature may be found in Robert D. Willig, "Multiproduct Technology and Market Structure," *American Economic Review*, vol. 69 (May 1979, *Papers and Proceedings, 1978*), pp. 346-51.

25. William J. Baumol, John C. Panzar, and Robert D. Willig, *Multiproduct Technology and Market Structure* (Harcourt Brace Jovanovich, 1982).

uct firms can be complicated, the ideas behind these criteria are simple. At the most basic level, the criteria are the same for singe-and multiple-product firms: for there to be a natural monopoly for a collection of goods and services, it must be cheaper for one firm to produce that collection than for more than one firm to produce it. But except for that similarity, the criteria for natural monopoly for multiproduct firms are much more complicated than for single-product firms.

For multiple-product firms, unlike single-product firms, there are several potential definitions of scale economies, no one of which is sufficient to assure the existence of natural monopoly. Two types of scale economies, however, when they occur together, are sufficient (though not necessary) to assure natural monopoly. The first of these, called product-specific economies of scale, are very like decreasing average costs for a single-product firm. To define them, the avoidable costs of one product (say, X) of a multiproduct firm are first defined as the costs that could be avoided if the firm's output of X went down to 0, when all other outputs are held constant at some given level. The average avoidable costs for some output level X are then total avoidable costs divided by that output level. A firm has product-specific economies of scale for product X if over all output levels for that product, and for all combinations of outputs for other products, there are declining average avoidable costs associated with increased outputs of X.

Unlike the case of a single-product firm, however, product-specific scale economies are not in themselves sufficient to guarantee natural monopoly in the case of multiproduct firms. This is easy to show intuitively. Consider the case of a railroad providing two products only, hauling freight and passengers between points A and B. Suppose total costs for the railroad are simply the sum of two separate cost functions, each with marginal costs below average costs throughout all relevant ranges of output:

$$TC = F(P) + G(F),$$

where TC is total costs, P is passengers, and F is tons of freight. Such a market would tend to have separate natural monopolies in passenger and freight traffic, because there are product-specific scale economies in each. That is, a market combining all passenger services in one firm will have lower costs than a market with two passenger firms. The same is true of freight.

But these product-specific scale economies offer no incentive for aggregating both passenger and freight services under one firm. For a multiproduct natural monopoly to occur, it is necessary to have another type of economy, described by Panzar and Willig as economies of scope.[26] Essentially these represent economies of aggregation of the production of many services or goods under one firm.

A natural monopoly must have a combination of product-specific scale economies and economies of scope (Just as scale economies alone are not sufficient for natural monopoly, so economies of scope alone will not allow it either—if there were only economies of scope and no scale economies, production could occur in many small, diversified firms).

Because the empirical study of multiproduct natural monopoly is in its infancy, there is relatively little evidence on which to base any empirical conclusions. Only one study, that of Jara-Diaz and Winston, has been specified to test for the existence of multiproduct natural monopoly in the railroad industry, and it is based exclusively on a sample of tiny Class III railroads.[27] Nevertheless, its evidence is revealing. It shows that if one ignores the fixed maintenance and capital costs for way and structures, there are insufficient economies of scale and scope to cause natural monopoly in the industry. On the other hand, Jara-Diaz and Winston hypothesize that if these way-and-structures costs were included, there would be enough economies of scale and scope to guarantee natural monopoly at the low densities at which the Class III railroads in their sample operate. But they state that this result is tentative and subject to further confirmation.

In any event, Jara-Diaz and Winston's results are at least roughly consistent with the following hypothesis: below the point at which a single-track main line is fully utilized, there are sufficient economies of scale and scope to guarantee natural monopoly. Beyond this point, the natural monopoly disappears. At least one study of the industry, dating from 1974 and hence preceding the literature on the multiproduct natural monopoly, was specified to yield this result.[28]

---

26. John C. Panzar and Robert D. Willig, "Economies of Scale in Multi-Output Production," *Quarterly Journal of Economics*, vol. 91 (August 1977), pp. 481-94.
27. "Multiproduct Transportation Cost Functions."
28. Theodore E. Keeler, "Railroad Costs, Returns to Scale, and Excess Capacity," *Review of Economics and Statistics*, vol. 56 (May 1974), pp. 201-08.

This makes good intuitive sense: at low densities, different types of freight share both trains (with more than one type of commodity on a train) and track. As more commodity types are carried on a given route, they are carried at lower costs, because the trains are longer and the tracks are better utilized. And as increases in any one commodity type allow for longer trains and better plant utilization, scale economies as well as economies of scope result.

Thus it is reasonable to believe that the same results hold in a multiproduct setting as in a singe-product setting: below minimum efficient density, there are sufficient economies of scale and scope to guarantee natural monopoly. Beyond that level natural monopoly may no longer exist. However, in a multiproduct setting the concept of minimum efficient density is an ambiguous one: it could be, say, 7 million net ton-miles per route-mile for new automobiles, or 10 million net ton-miles per route-mile for coal, or some number in between for some given combination of autos and coal. Because the evidence based on multiproduct criteria is incomplete, these conclusions are tentative.

All the evidence presented here and in appendix B confirms the hypothesis of increasing returns to traffic density over most route-mileage in the railroad industry and, along with the simple model presented earlier in the chapter, suggests that scale economies are likely to play an important role in the railroad industry, both in the market behavior of the firms and in the regulatory policy of the government.

CHAPTER 7

ECONOMIES OF DENSITY VERSUS ECONOMIES OF SCALE: WHY TRUNK AND LOCAL SERVICE AIRLINE COSTS DIFFER*

Douglas W. Caves**, Laurits R. Christensen**
and Michael W. Tretheway***

I. Introduction

In the literature on the U.S. airline industry there are two widely held beliefs regarding the structure of costs. First, there are rapidly declining unit costs of service within any city-pair market (Bailey and Panzar, 1981; Keeler, 1978; White, 1979). Second, there are approximately constant returns to scale for airline systems that have reached the size of the U.S. trunk carriers (Caves, 1962; Douglas and Miller, 1974; Keeler,

* Reprinted from *Rand Journal of Economics* (Winter, 1984), pp. 471-489.

   An early version of this article entitled "A Reexamination of Scale Economies for U.S. Trunk Airlines" was presented at the Econometric Society Meetings in Denver, Colorado, September, 1980. Our research has benefited greatly from financial support from the National Science Foundation, the University of Wisconsin Graduate School, and the Civil Aeronautics Board, from research assistance by Robert Windle, Kenneth McClelland, Paul Feldman, and Chris Lankey, and from helpful discussions with Gary Chamberlain, John Geweke, Trevor Heaver, and Joseph Swanson. We are also indebted to numerous past and present staff members of the Civil Aeronautics Board for assistance in data development.

** University of Wisconsin-Madison and Christensen Associates.

*** University of British Columbia.

1978; White, 1979). A third, more tentatively held belief is that there are scale economies available to be exploited by carriers smaller than the trunks (which is to say, smaller carriers have higher unit costs than the U.S. trunk carriers) (Keeler, 1978).

The first belief is largely a matter of faith or *a priori* reasoning, since data are not available on costs for particular routes. The second has been borne out by several studies that show very similar unit costs for trunk airlines which differ greatly in size. The third view derives principally from the finding by Eads, Nerlove, and Raduchel (1969) of substantial system scale economies for the U.S. local service airlines. This finding appears to be confirmed by a casual inspection of airline costs. For example, in 1978 variable costs came to 7.7¢ per passenger-mile for the trunk airlines but 11.2¢ per passenger-mile for the local service airlines.[1]

This substantial difference in cost would seem to imply that the local carriers would have difficulty competing with the trunk carriers in the newly deregulated environment. Similarly, the still smaller new carriers should have even higher unit costs than the locals. These implications, however, are belied by two developments since deregulation. First, the locals have been able to gain market share at the expense of the trunks (Graham and Kaplan, 1982). Second, new carriers have entered the market and have been able to compete successfully against both the local service and trunk carriers.

The purpose of this article is to explore the apparent paradox of small air carriers with a purported unit cost disadvantage competing successfully against the large trunk carriers. We do this by developing a model of costs for airline services. The model is based on a panel data set for the years 1970 through 1981 comprised of all trunk and local service airlines.[2] Our model of airline costs is novel in that it includes two dimensions of airline size—the size of each carrier's service network and the magnitude of passenger and freight transportation services provided. This allows us to make the crucial distinction between returns to

---

1. Variable costs include fuel, labor, and materials costs, which account for more than 80% of airline costs. The categories "trunk" and "local service" are no longer used by the CAB, but they continue to be used in the literature. Carriers included in these two categories are listed in Table 1 in Section3.

2. It would be desirable to include new carriers in the panel, but this is precluded by insufficient data. The new carriers are not required to file the same data as the trunks and locals.

density (the variation in unit costs caused by increasing transportation services within a network of given size) and returns to scale (The variation in unit costs with respect to proportional changes in both network size and the provision of transportation services).

We find substantial economies of density for air carriers of all sizes within our sample. This confirms the belief in declining unit costs for specific airline markets. We also find constant returns to scale for the trunk carriers, thus confirming the second belief. Our final finding is that constant returns to scale also hold for the local service carriers. This finding refutes the third belief, and is consistent with the observed ability of the locals to compete with the trunks in markets of equal density and length. We cannot willy-nilly extrapolate these results to smaller networks, such as those of the new carriers. But the fact that several new carriers appear to have a good chance of surviving might lead one to believe that there is no substantial cost disadvantage even for airlines with very small networks.

Although our findings seem to contradict the trunk-local cost differential cited above, the contradiction is explained by differences in the network characteristics between trunks and local service carriers. The average number of cities served by the locals is virtually the same as that of the trunks, but the density of traffic is much lower, and the average distance between takeoff and landing (stage length) is much shorter. Unit costs decline markedly as density of service and average stage length increase. Costs also vary inversely with average load factor, and until recently the locals had lower load factors than the trunks.

In Section 2 we develop a general model of airline costs that emphasizes the important role of the airline network. Section 3 describes the panel data used to estimate the parameters of the cost structure. Parameter estimates and basic conclusions are presented in Section 4, and the robustness of the conclusions with respect to model form and type of estimator is explored in Section 5. Section 6 uses our estimated cost model to explain the difference in trunk and local service airline costs. In Section 7 we draw upon the recent development of contestability theory and its application to the airline industry to analyze the welfare implications of our cost function results for the deregulated airline industry.

II. A General model of Airline Costs

All previous studies of airline costs of which we are aware have used data either for large carriers (the trunks) or for small carriers (the locals). None of the studies attempted to estimate a model that would simultaneously explain the structure of airline costs for both large and small carriers. The prevailing view seemed to be that large and small carriers faced different cost structures, which could only be modelled separately.

We have not encountered any cogent argument to support the position of size-related differences in cost structures. We believe that it should be possible to capture any differences that do exist by specification of a sufficiently general model of airline costs. Accordingly, we introduce the general total cost function:

$$CT = f(Y, P, W, Z, T, F),   \qquad (1)$$

where CT is total cost, Y is output, P represents the network, W is a vector of factor prices, Z is a vector of control variables, T is a vector of time shifts, and F is a vector of firm-specific shifts in the cost function, as described below. The model that we propose is general in several senses. First, we choose a translog form for f so that the model is a second-order approximation to any general cost function. Second, we introduce control variables (Z) to reflect airline characteristics. We include average stage length and average load factor, both of which have been emphasized by previous investigators.[3] We also include the number of points served, as an indicator of the size of the airline network.[4] Third, we take advantage of the fact that our panel data set (a time series of cross sections) allows specification of intercept shifts for each firm and for each year. The inclusion of these shift factors (binary variables) precludes biases in the coefficients of the included explanatory variables that might arise from the exclusion of variables such as unmeasurable

---

3. Average stage length is the average distance between takeoffs and landings. load factor is the ratio of seat miles sold to seat miles actually flown.

4. In the parlance of logistics, the number of points served is a measure of the number of nodes in a network. Average stage length is a measure of the length of the links between the nodes. In addition, by including both output and load factor in the model, one can make inferences concerning the impact on costs of increased service offerings on links.

aspects of network that are constant over time for a given firm.[5]

Traditionally, the level of output has been used to represent firm size in industry cost studies. Recently, however, writers have begun to distinguish between firm size and level of output. We believe that it is particularly important to make such a distinction for industries in which services are provided over a network of geographically distributed points. Cost per unit of output may vary substantially among firms, depending on the nature of the networks they serve. For example, one might expect a lower level of unit costs if a given level of output were provided over a smaller number of cities.

Several authors have used route-miles as a measure of network size in studies of the railroad industry.[6] This measure is ambiguous for airlines, however. It is not clear how many city-pair routes should be counted in determining route-miles. Furthermore, the route-miles data that are available do not conform to any particular standard.[7]

Airline networks can be described according to numerous attributes. A common distinction in recent literature is hub-and-spoke networks vs. linear networks, but much greater detail of description would be possible. To be useful for econometric analysis, however, distinctions must be simple and readily quantifiable. After considering a number of alternatives, we settled upon the number of points served (P) as the single most important attribute of an airline network.[8]

---

5. When using time series data, researchers generally include a time trend or annual time effect to prevent bias of the output coefficient arising from shifts of the cost function due to technical progress, an unmeasurable variable. A similar effect may occur in the cross section dimension. The cost function may shift from one firm to the other because of unmeasured variables–perhaps some unmodelled aspect of a carrier's network. As with the technical progress case, this poses an estimation problem if the shifts are correlated with output or other regressors. See Mundlak (1961, 1978) for discussion of proper estimation techniques.

6. See Caves, Christensen, Tretheway, and Windle (1984) for a review of studies of network effects in the railroad industry.

7. The last year for which the CAB compiled a route-miles measure for each airline was 1978. The individuals responsible for compiling the data indicated to us that route-miles were not comparable from carrier to carrier or even from year to year.

8. An airport, rather than a city, constitutes a point. Thus, an airline serving two airports in New York City would have two New York points. Points that a carrier was authorized to serve but did not actually serve during the year were not counted. We obtained the number of points data from the CAB publication, *Airport Activity Statistics* (December 31 issue for each year).

The inclusion of points served in the cost function along with output permits us to distinguish between returns to density and returns to scale in airline operations. We define returns to density as the proportional increase in output made possible by a proportional increase in all inputs, with points served, average stage length, average load factor, and input prices held fixed. This is equivalent to the inverse of the elasticity of total cost with respect to output:

$$RTD = \frac{1}{\varepsilon_y},$$

where ε_y is the elasticity of total cost with respect to output. Returns to density are said to be increasing, constant, or decreasing, when RTD is greater than unity, equal to unity, or less than unity, respectively. We use the terms increasing returns to density and economies of density interchangeably. Economies of density exist is unit costs decline as airlines add flights or seats on existing flights (through larger aircraft or a denser seating configuration), with no change in load factor, stage length, or the number of airports served.

We define returns to scale as the proportional increase in output *and points served* made possible by a proportional increase in all inputs, with average stage length, average load factor, and input prices held fixed. This is equivalent to the inverse of the sum of the elasticities of total cost with respect to output and points served:

$$RTS = \frac{1}{\varepsilon_y + \varepsilon_p},$$

where ε_p is the elasticity of total cost with respect to point served.[9] Returns to scale are said to be increasing, constant, or decreasing, when RTS is greater than unity, equal to unity, or less than unity, respectively. We use the terms increasing returns to scale and "scale economies"

---

9. Under this definition RTS is conditional on the firm-specific shifts, F, in the sample. Caves, Christensen, Tretheway, and Windle (1984) Generalized RTS to account for possible relationships among output, network, and the firm-specific shifts. They found that the generalization did not substantially alter the estimate of RTS for U.S. railroads. Estimation of the more general concept of RTS requires a large cross sectional dimension to the sample so that "between" estimates can be computed. We attempted to use the approach with our airline data set. but the degrees of freedom wee estimation of RTS.

interchangeably. Scale economies exist if unit costs decline when an airline adds flights to an airport that it had not been serving, and the additional flights cause no change in load factor, stage length, or output per point served (density).

Estimation of (1) requires that we specify a functional form. We adopt the translog functional form proposed by Christensen, Jorgenson, and Lau (1973), which has been widely used in recent cost studies. Christensen and Greene (1976) and several others have demonstrated the favorable attributes of the translog for studying scale economies. The translog is a flexible form in the sense of providing a second-order approximation to an unknown cost function. We write the translog total cost function with time and firm intercept shifts of effects included as:

$$\ln CT = \alpha_0 + \sum_T \alpha_T + \sum_F \alpha_F + \alpha_y \ln Y + \sum_i \beta_i \ln W_i + \sum_i \phi_i \ln Z_i$$

$$+ \frac{1}{2} \delta_{YY} (\ln Y)^2 + \frac{1}{2} \sum_i \sum_j \gamma_{ij} \ln W_i \ln W_j + \frac{1}{2} \sum_i \sum_j \psi_{ij} \ln Z_i \ln Z_j$$

$$+ \sum_i \rho_{Yi} \ln Y \ln W_i + \sum_i \mu_{Yi} \ln Y \ln Z_i + \sum_i \sum_j \lambda_{ij} \ln W_i \ln Z_j , \quad (2)$$

where $\gamma_{ij} = \gamma_{ji}$, $\psi_{ij} = \psi_{ji}$ the α_T are time-period effects, and the α_F are firm effects. A cost function must be homogeneous of degree one in input prices, which implies the following restrictions on the parameters of the translog cost function:

$$\sum_i \beta_i = 1, \quad \sum_i \gamma_{ij} = 0, \quad (\forall_j), \quad \sum_i \rho_{Yi} = 0, \quad \sum_i \lambda_{ij} = 0, \quad (\forall_j), \quad (3)$$

Shephard's (1953) lemma implies that the input shares (C_i) can be equated to the logarithmic partial derivatives of the cost function with respect to the input prices:

$$C_i = \beta_i + \sum_j \gamma_{ij} \ln W_j + \rho_{Yi} \ln Y + \sum_j \lambda_{ij} \ln Z_j \qquad (4)$$

It has become standard practice to specify classical disturbances for (2) and (4) and to estimate the parameters of the cost function by treating (2) and (4) as a multivariate regression. We follow this procedure, using a modification of Zellner's (1962) technique for estimation. To overcome the problem of singularity of the contemporaneous covariance matrix, we delete one of the share equations before carrying out the second stage of Zellner's technique for estimation. The resulting estimates are asymptotically equivalent to maximum likelihood estimates. Moreover, the use of all equations at the first stage ensures that the estimates are invariant to the choice of equation to be deleted at the second stage.

III. Data

Our data consist of annual observations on all the trunk and local service airlines from 1970 through 1981. There are 15 airlines in the sample for the full period and six additional airlines for shorter periods. See Table 1 for details. There are a total of 208 observations.

We employ five categories of inputs: labor. fuel, flight equipment, ground property, and equipment (*GPE*), and all other inputs. We refer to the last category as materials. Labor price is formed as a multilateral

Table 1. *U.S. Trunk and Local Service Airlines**
(Observations Available for 1970-1981, Unless Otherwise Noted)

Trunk Airlines		Local Service Airlines	
American		Air West[1]	1970-1980[4]
Braniff		Frontier	
Continental		North Central	1970-1978[5]
Delta		Ozark[1]	
Eastern[1]		Piedmont	
National[1]	1970-1979[2]	Republic	1979-1981[5]
Northeast	1970-1971[3]	Southern	1970-1978[5]
Northwest[1]		Texas International[1]	
Pan American		U.S.Air	
TWA[1]			
United[1]			
Western			

*These designations were used by the CAB until 1981.

1. Except the following years, which were deleted due to strike in excess of 25 days: Eastern, 1980: National, 1970, 1974, 1975; Northwest, 1970, 1972, 1978; TWA, 1973; United, 1979; Air West, 1972, 1979; Ozark, 1973, 1979, 1980; Texas International, 1974, 1975.
2. National merged with Pan American on January 1, 1980.
3. Northeast merged with Delta on August 1, 1972.
4. Air West merged with Republic on October 1, 1980, but reported data separately for 1980 .
5. North central and Southern merged on July 1, 1979, to form Republic.

index of 15 categories of employees.[10] Fuel price is dollars per gallon. Flight equipment price results from a multilateral index of nine aircraft categories with value shares based on the current annual cost to lease one plane of the appropriate type. *GPE* cost is measured by applying a capital service price reflecting interest, economic depreciation, capital gains, and taxes to a stock of *GPE* capital formed by using the perpetual inventory method.[11] Within each year the price of materials is assumed constant across firms. Annual change in materials prices is given by a Tornqvist index of seven categories of materials input. To reduce the number of parameters we must estimate we used the multilateral index procedure to aggregate materials and the two types of capital. We refer to the resulting input as capital-materials.[12]

We recognize four categories of output: revenue passenger-miles (*RPM*) of scheduled service, *RPM* of charter service, revenue ton-miles (*RTM*) of mail, and *RTM* of all other freight. Scheduled service accounts for the bulk of revenues for all trunk and local service carriers. Because of the small revenue shares for the other outputs, we do not believe that cost function estimation using the distinct outputs would be fruitful. Thus, we have aggregated the four output types by using the multilateral index procedure.

The model incorporates two characteristics of airline operation, load factor and average stage length. Average stage length is the average distance between takeoffs and landings. Load factor is the ratio of seat miles sold to seat miles actually flown.

In Table 2 we give means of the data for the trunks, locals, and combined airlines for the year 1976, one of the midyears of the sample.[13]

---

10. See Caves, Christensen, and Diewert (1982) for a theoretical discussion of multilateral index procedures. Caves, Christensen, and Tretheway (1981) apply this theory to the measurement of airline inputs.

11. We note that both types of capital are measured on a replacement cost method. Fight equipment uses what could be described as a "one-plane-of-size-*k* method. If technical change makes a particular type of aircraft obsolete, however, its lease cost will fall, and thus our measure of capital used in production will fall.

12. We explored models which disaggregate these inputs and found they did not alter our conclusions regarding returns to density or scale.

13. Our procedures for data development are discussed in more detail in Caves, Christensen, and Tretheway (1981), which also displays a considerable amount of data for the trunk carriers. These procedures were refined, updated, and extended to the local service carriers in Caves, Christensen, and Tretheway (1983).

Table 2. Means of Variables Used in the Study for the Year 1976

	Combined Airlines	Trunks	Locals
RPM Scheduled Service(billions)	9.33	15.01	1.52
RPM Charter Passenger(billions)	.63	1.04	.07
RTM Mail(billions)	.052	.086	.005
RTM Other Freight(billions)	.21	.35	.01
Number of Points Served	63	66	59
Average Stage Length(miles)	480	685	197
Load Factor*(%)	.54	.55	.52
Total Cost(billions of $)	.91	1.42	.20
Number of Employees	15,300	23,700	3,800
Average Wage(pilots and copilots)	48,200	54,700	39,300
Fuel Price($/gal.)	.32	.32	.31
Gallons of Fuel(million)	498	789	98

*Scheduled passenger service.

IV. Estimates of the Structure of Airline Cost.

Using the model developed in Section 2 and the data described in Section 3, we proceed to estimate the U.S. airline total cost function. The regressors are all normalized by removing their sample means. There are 53 parameters to be estimated, and we present full details of the regression results in the Appendix. In Column 1 of Table 3 we present the first-order coefficients of the translog function explaining airline costs.

Since total cost and the regressors are in natural logarithms and have been normalized, the first-order coefficients are all interpretable as cost elasticities evaluated at the sample mean. All of these coefficients have the expected signs and are highly significant. The elasticities of cost with respect to the factor prices are equivalent to shares in total cost. Thus, at the sample mean, labor accounts for approximately 36% of airline costs, while fuel accounts for nearly 17% and capital and materials account for 48%.[14] Both stage length and load factor have the expected negative relationship with total cost. A 1% increase in average stage

---

14. The fuel share grew from 11% to 27% for the trunks from 1970 to 1981. For the locals it grew from 10% to 26%.

Table 3. First-Order Coefficients of Cost Functions*
(Standard Errors in Parentheses)

Regressor	(1) Unrestricted Translog Total Cost Function	(2) Total Cost Function Restricted to First-Order Terms	(3) Unrestricted Translog Variable Cost Function	(4) Translog Total Cost Function Restricted to Zero for Firm Effects
Output	.804	.824	.719	.922
	(.034)	(0.29)	(0.43)	(.019)
Points Served	.132	.128	.139	.155
	(.031)	(.029)	(.033)	(.024)
Stage Length	-.148	-.140	-.046	-.220
	(.054)	(.039)	(.055)	(.024)
Load Factor	-.264	-.261	-.145	-.284
	(.070)	(.066)	(.071)	(.079)
Labor Price	.356	.357	.422	.357
	(.002)	(.003)	(.002)	(.018)
Fuel Price	.166	.166	.196	.166
	(.001)	(.004)	(.001)	(.001)
Capital-Materials Price**	.478	.478	.382	.477
	(.002)	(.003)	(.002)	(.002)
Capacity			.153	
			(.045)	

* See Appendix for full regression results.
** Materials price for the variable cost function

length implies a decrease in cost of .15%, and a 1% increase in load factor implies a decrease in cost of .26%.

As one would expect, there is a strong positive relationship between total cost and output when all other factors are fixed. A 1% increase in output leads to a .80% increase in cost. The inverse of this, 1.24 with a standard error of .05, is returns to density at the sample mean. For a given level of output and the other factors, we find a positive and statistically significant relationship between cost and points served; the elasticity is .13. The sum of the first-order coefficients on output and points served provides the elasticity of total cost with respect to a proportionate change in output and points served in the neighborhood of the sample mean. The sum is .94 with a standard error of .04. The inverse of the sum is 1.07 with a standard error of .05. Thus, we cannot reject the hypothesis of constant returns to scale at the sample mean.

The finding of constant returns to scale at the midpoint of our sample does not necessaryily imply that either the trunks or local airlines have constant returns to scale. The sample mean reflects an averaging of the characteristics of the trunks and locals. To assess the scale and density characteristics of the trunks and locals we must evaluate them at points that are relevant to the two sets of carriers.

In Table 4 we present the means of the output characteristics for the trunks and locals for the total observation period 1970-1981. Over the full sample period output for the average trunk carrier was nearly ten times as great as for the average local service carrier, while average

Table 4. Returns to Density and Scale at Sample Means of Trunks, Locals, and Pooled Data set (Standard Errors In Parentheses)

	Total Cost		Means of Covariates				Variable Cost	
1970-1981	Returns to Density	Returns to Scale	Output*	Points	Stage Length	Load Factor	Returns to Density	Returns to Scale
Pooled Mean	1.243(.053)	1.068(.049)	.288	64.9	407	.540	1.179(.061)	.988(.057)
Trunks Mean	1.235(.061)	1.068(.052)	.733	66.3	673	.556	1.119(.071)	.965(.060)
Locals Mean	1.254(.073)	1.069(.077)	.074	62.9	197	.517	1.265(.083)	1.019(.085)
1970								
Pooled Mean	1.271(.060)	1.058(.055)	.167	63.0	338	.447	1.241(.072)	.980(.064)
Trunks Mean	1.253(.061)	1.025(.050)	.516	61.2	639	.520	1.124(.077)	.917(.061)
Locals Mean	1.295(.090)	1.101(.093)	.041	65.2	152	.427	1.379(.114)	1.050(.098)
1976								
Pooled Mean	1.225(.052)	1.046(.051)	.273	60.0	390	.543	1.161(.062)	.966(.060)
Trunks Mean	1.218(.060)	1.054(.055)	.731	61.9	651	.553	1.016(.075)	.952(.065)
Locals Mean	1.234(.073)	1.035(.075)	.070	57.4	193	.529	1.234(.084)	.983(.084)
1981								
Pooled Mean	1.235(.055)	1.093(.048)	.505	71.9	571	.578	1.105(.056)	1.003(.054)
Trunks Mean	1.235(.065)	1.109(.056)	.968	75.3	797	.584	1.075(.067)	1.010(.062)
Locals Mean	1.236(.059)	1.068(.059)	.171	66.6	328	.568	1.154(.058)	.991(.063)

*Output scaled to 1.000 for Delta 1977.

stage length for the trunks was more than triple that of the locals. On the other hand, point served and average load factor were quite similar for the trunks and locals—the trunks being approximately 10% greater in both cases. Evaluation of returns to density and scale at the trunk and local means reveals negligible differences at these two widely separated points. Returns to scale are 1.07 for both the trunks and the locals, while returns to density are 1.25 for the locals and 1.24 for the trunks.

It is possible that focusing on the means for the full 1970-1981 period obscures some important differences during the period. Thus, we also present results in Table 4 for trunk and local means for individual years. For the sake of brevity, we present only the first and last year and one of the middle years-1970, 1976, and 1981.[15] The disparity in output and stage length between the trunks and locals was greatest in 1970 and declined substantially by 1981. The trunk-to-local-mean-output ratio was 12.6 in 1970 and 5.7 in 1981, the corresponding stage length ratios were 3.4 in 1970 and 2.4 1980. The mean load factor for the locals was considerably lower than that of the trunks in 1970 (.43 vs. .52), but by 1981 they were practically identical (.57 and .58). The trunk mean of points served grew from 61 in 1970 to 75 in 1981, while the local mean was in the mid-60s in both years (in spite of a decline into the 50s in 1976). For none of these different sample points is it possible to reject the hypothesis of constant returns to scale. On the other hand, the hypothesis of constant returns to density must be rejected at each of the points observed. In

Table 5. Own-Price Elasticities and Elasticities of Substitution Computed at Sample Mean for Unrestricted Translog Total Cost Function (Standard Errors in Parentheses)

Own-Price Elasticities		Elasticities of Substitution*	
Labor	-.17	Labor vs. Fuel	-.29
	(.07)		(.09)
Fuel	-.01	Labor vs. Capital-Materials	.46
	(.02)		(.14)
Capital-Materials	-.21	Fuel vs. Capital-Materials	.24
	(.05)		(.06)

* Positive indicates substitutes, negative indicates complements.

15. We have compiled the results for the rest of the years. There are no significant differences between these years and those appearing in Table 4.

all cases the point estimate is between 1.21 and 1.28.

In Table 5 we present the estimated own-price elasticities of each of the three inputs and the Allen-Uzawa cross elasticities of substitution for the sample mean. The own-price elasticities are all of the correct sign and relatively small in absolute value, indicating inelastic demand. Capital-materials is found to be substitutable for both labor and fuel. Labor and fuel are found to be complements, however.

V. Robustness of Estimates of the Structure of Airline Costs

In this section we explore the robustness of our central findings with respect to returns to scale and density. We estimate both less restrictive and more restrictive versions of the translog model. In all cases we continue to find constant returns to scale and increasing returns to density for both trunk and local airlines.

The translog cost function contains numerous second-order and interaction terms. The coefficients on these terms do not enter directly into out computations at the sample mean, but they have an indirect effect because they are estimated simultaneously with the coefficients on the first-order terms. An unrestricted translog form often provides results that are dominated by second-order and interaction terms at extreme sample points. This raises the legitimate concern of whether the estimated first-order effects are unduly affected by the second-order terms.

In our current investigation the estimated translog form does have some undesirable features at the extremes of our sample. In particular, although the neoclassical curvature or regularity conditions are satisfied in the neighborhood of the sample mean and for 105 out of 208 observations, the conditions are violated at extreme sample points.[16]

---

16. See Caves and Christensen (1980) for discussion of regularity conditions in the context of the translog form. The positive coefficients on the first-order price terms are sufficient for regularity at the sample mean. The further a data point is from the sample mean, the more important the second-order term becomes in the calculation of the regularity condition. The concavity problems in this study are due to the very rapid increase of fuel prices during the 1970s. Models which allowed more flexibility in the functional form for input prices were successful in increasing the number of observations satisfying the conditions. Since these models did not change the estimate of *RTS* and *RTD*, we opted to present the less complicated model.

Wales (1977) has shown that curvature problems at extreme data points do not necessarily undercut the validity of elasticity estimates at the sample mean. Nonetheless, we believe that the credibility of our elasticity estimates will be increased if we can show that they do not depend strongly on the particular set of second-order coefficients that we have estimated. To this end we have estimated several restricted versions of the translog form to assess the robustness of the elasticity estimates. We have found them to be extremely robust. To illustrate we present in Column 2 of Table 3 the parameter estimates from the most restricted version of the translog form—that with all of the second-order and interaction coefficients restricted to be zero.[17]

The coefficients for the simplified translog form (Column 2 of Table 3) are remarkably similar to the first-order coefficients from the basic translog model (Column 1 of Table 3). The output and load factor coefficients are increased slightly in absolute value, and the stage-length coefficient is decreased, but the changes are small relative to the standard errors of the coefficients. The simplified model has constant elasticities of cost with respect to output and points served. They imply returns to scale of 1.05 everywhere (with a standard error of .04); thus, on the basis of this model we cannot reject constant returns to scale anywhere within (or outside) our sample. Returns to density are 1.21 everywhere (with a standard error of .043)

We have found that our results are robust with respect to substantial simplification of our model of airline costs. We now explore whether the results are robust to some further complications of the model. Caves, Christensen, and Swanson (1981) have discussed the estimation of returns to scale under the specification used above (static equilibrium) and the alternative specification of partial static equilibrium. The latter specification allows the possibility that firms are not in static equilibrium with respect to one or more factors of production.

There are two plausible arguments supporting the position that airlines have not maintained the optimal level of capacity throughout the 1970s. First, demand for airline services is highly variable over business cycles. Even though there is an active second-hand market for aircraft, airlines are reluctant to dispose of temporary excess capacity because

---

17. The *F*-test for testing the restrictions implied by the first-order only model was 134.5. The 1% critical value of this test is 1.92.

asset prices are depressed during recessions. Second, it is widely held that CAB regulation led airlines to maintain excess capacity. In light of these arguments, we follow the approach of Caves, Christensen, and Swanson (1981) in specifying a variable cost function, conditional on the level of airline capacity.[18]

The translog variable cost function takes the same form as the total cost function, with the following exceptions: (a) variable cost replaces total cost as the regressed, (b) the price of capital and materials is replaced by the price of materials as a regressor, and (c) a capacity variable is introduced as a regressor, which interacts with all the other regressors in addition to having its own first- and second-order coefficients.[19]

In Column 3 of Table 3 we present the first-order coefficients of the translog variable cost function. Full details of the regression are presented in the Appendix. The coefficient on capacity is .15, indicating that at the sample mean, *ceteris paribus,* a 1% increase in capacity would result in a .15% increase in variable costs. This is consistent with excess capacity for the airline industry. The estimated variable cost function implies that a movement to the optimal level of capacity would lead to total costs which were only 83% as high as those observed.[20] The elasticity of variable cost with respect to capacity is larger for the trunk airlines before deregulation, .24 in 1970 and .23 in 1976, but declines to .16 by 1981, a value near the sample mean.

With the introduction of capacity into the cost function, the roles of stage length and load factor are reduced both in terms of magnitude and statistical significance. The points served coefficient is virtually unchanged, but the output coefficient is reduced by approximately 10%. The labor and fuel price coefficients have increased, thereby reflecting the larger shares of labor and fuel in variable cost than in total cost.

---

18. See Brown and Christensen(1981) for further discussion of the translog variable cost function

19. Capacity is measured as the sum of the annual service flows (measured in constant 1977 dollars) from flight equipment and ground property and equipment. This, rather than a constant dollar valuation of the capital stock, is the correct measure of capacity to produce output in any given year.

20. For given values of output, input prices, and control variables we find the level of capital that equates capital's value of marginal product with its price. Variable costs are simulated with this quantity and then added to capital costs to get total costs with an optimal level of capital.

We must compute returns to density and scale from the variable cost function by using formulas that correspond to the same concepts discussed in Section 2 for the total cost function. The formulas involve the same coefficients as for the total cost function except for the additional multiplicative factor of unity minus the elasticity of variable cost with respect to capacity.[21] Thus, returns to density are simply:

$$RTD = (1 - \varepsilon_k) / \varepsilon_y \qquad (5)$$

For the full period sample mean this is $(1-.153)/.719 = 1.18$ (with a standard error of .06). Returns to scale have the same formula, except that the elasticity of variable cost with respect to output is replaced by the sum of elasticities of variable cost with respect to output and points served:

$$RTS = (1 - \varepsilon_k) / (\varepsilon_y + \varepsilon_p). \qquad (6)$$

For the full period sample mean this is $(1 - .153) / (.719 + .139) = .99$ (with a standard error of . 06).

We see that, like the total cost function, the variable cost function yields an estimate of returns to scale at the sample mean that is very close to unity—constant returns to scale. Also like the total cost function, the variable cost function indicates increasing returns to density, although the estimate is somewhat lower for the variable cost function. In the right-hand panel of Table 4 we present returns to density and scale from the variable cost function evaluated at all the same points as for the total cost function. We find no significant departures from constant returns to scale for either the trunk or local carriers. All of the estimates of returns to density show significant economies of density for the local carriers. The point estimates for the trunks also indicate economies of density, but none of them is sufficiently significant to cause rejection of a test of constant returns to density.

All of our estimating equations include a constant effect for each firm. Mundlak (1961, 1978) advocated this approach to prevent bias in the coefficients due to the omission of variables that are constant over time for a given firm and correlated with the other explanatory variables. An unmeasurable aspect of network might be an example of such a variable. To demonstrate the bias that can arise from omitting correlat-

---

21. See Caves, Christensen, and Swanson (1981) for discussion.

ed firm effects we show in Column 4 of Table 3 the first-order coefficients that result from imposing the restriction this the firm effects, α_F, are zero.[22] It is readily apparent that this model yields very different conclusions regarding returns to scale and density. Specifically, without firm effects one is led to the erroneous conclusions that there are diseconomies of scale (RTS = .93) at the sample mean, and that returns to density are much lower, 1.08 versus 1.24.

VI. Explanation of the Difference in Total Costs for Trunk and Local Service Airlines.

In Section I we noted that variable costs for the local service carriers exceeded those of the trunk carriers by a substantial amount—11.2¢ vs. 7.7¢ per passenger-mile in 1978. This translates into a percentage difference of 38%. [100 (ln 11.2—ln 7.7)]. We return to the question of the cost difference between the trunks and locals on the basis of our figures for total cost, and the explanation in terms of an estimated total cost function.

Using the cost function estimates in Column 1 of Table A1 in the Appendix, we predict total cost at the sample mean of the covariates for both the trunks and local carriers, and find a difference of 44%. This difference in trunk and local unit costs is even larger than the previously discussed 38% variable cost difference. We emphasize that this large difference is not a result of differences in carrier size, since we have found constant returns to scale. Rather, it is due to differences in service characteristics, as we now show.

The 44% difference in fitted total cost is the sum of differences explained by the covariates and differences that are unexplained except by the firm dummy variables. The firm dummy variables indicate that at any given level of the covariates unit costs for the local service carriers would be 14% below those of the trunk carriers.[23] This represents fac-

---

22. Hausman and Taylor (1981) proposed a x^2-test statistic for the presence of correlated firm effects. Our computed value of this statistic is 80.2. whereas the 1% critical value is 48.25.

23. The 14% is obtained by averaging the individual firm effects across the locals and across the trunks, with each effect weighted by the number of times the firm enters the sample. The difference between the average trunk and average local effect is .142.

tors not included explicitly in our model, such as differences in managerial efficiency, differences in network structure not captured by the points-served variable, etc. The 14% difference is in the opposite direction of the overall difference in unit costs. Therefore, there is a 58% difference in unit costs that is explained by the covariates in the total cost function; that is, the model provides an explanation, based on firm characteristics, for unit costs of the locals to be 58% higher than those of the trunks.

The 58% difference cannot be directly assigned to individual firm characteristics because the regressors include interactions of pairs of characteristics. Caves, Christensen, and Diewert (1982) have shown, however, that the components of the Tornqvist (1936) index provide a decomposition into portions attributable to specific characteristics that is exact for an aggregator function of the translog form, even with a full set of interaction terms. Therefore, we use the Tornqvist index to decompose the 58%. The portion due to characteristic X is given by:

$$- 1/2[(\partial \ln CT / \partial \ln X)_T + (\partial \ln CT / \partial \ln X)_L](\ln X_T - \ln X_L),$$

where T denotes trunk, L denotes local, and X is any characteristic except output. For output ($X = Y$) the same formula would apply if we were decomposing total cost. Since the decomposition is for average cost (CT / Y), the term ($\ln Y_T - \ln Y_L$) must be added.

The decomposition of the 58% difference in unit costs between trunks and local service airlines is presented in Table 6. An overwhelming portion of the total difference, 45%, is explained by the difference in level of output, that is, density of service for a given size of network. The only other factor of major significance is average stage length, which accounts for 18% of the unit cost difference. The differences in average load factor and points served account for only 2% and—1%, respectively. Trunk airlines pay, on average, higher prices per unit for labor, materials, and capital services, but the same price for fuel. Taken together, this givers the locals a 6% advantage in unit costs.

From this decomposition we see that the observed difference between trunk and local average unit costs is explained by differences in characteristics of the firms, particularly by lower density of service and shorter stage lengths for the locals. Casual comparison of trunk and local unit costs might lead one to conclude that the locals operate in a region of increasing returns to scale. By distinguishing between density and scale

Table 6. Difference in Unit Cost for Trunk and Local Service Airlines Explained by Fitted Total Cost Function

Amount of Difference to Be Explained		
Difference between Local Service and Trunk Fitted Unit Cost (Total Cost Model)		43.5%
Less Amount Due to Firm Dummy Variables		-14.2%
Amount to Be Explained by Regressors		57.7%
Difference in Unit Costs As Explained by:		
Output		45.0%
Average Stage Length		17.6%
Average Load Factor		1.7%
Points Served		-.7%
Input Prices		
Labor Price	-3.8	
Capital-Materials Price	-2.1	
Fuel Price	.0	
Subtotal		-5.9%
Total Explained Difference		57.7%

economies, we see that this is not the case. The locals will not lower unit cost by increasing the scale of their operations. Only by increasing traffic density and stage length can they significantly lower their average costs.

VII. Welfare Analysis of the Structure of Airline Cost

We conclude with a brief discussion of the implication of our findings for the likely behavior of the airline industry under deregulation. The key question of interest with respect to airlines is whether one should expect unregulated markets to produce socially desirable outcomes. The relevant concept of a market is, we believe, a city-pair. Although our analysis has been conducted by using a firm's systemwide cost data, our results can be used to provide some evidence on conduct in city-pair markets.

Our finding of significant economies of density, at least for the local service airlines which typically operate in the less dense markets, confirms the belief in declining unit costs within a given network and therefore within city-pair markets. Traditional economic theory held that such a characteristic requires entry and price regulation to achieve an acceptable outcome in terms of social welfare (Scherer, 1980). But the recent analysis of Baumol and Willig (1981) challenges the traditional position. They develop a model of a market characterized by declining unit costs and show that there are conditions under which such a market will produce socially desirable results. Two conditions that are sufficient for such an outcome are first, contestability of airline markets, and second, the existence of a sufficient magnitude of fixed (but not sunk) costs.

In the recent literature on contestability and industry structure, the airline industry has frequently been used as a illustration of an industry with a high degree of contestability (Bailey, 1981; Baumol, Panzar, and Willig, 1982). The essence of the case is that under deregulation, airline entry and exit are characterized by relatively low costs, few of which are sunk (Bailey and Panzar, 1981). The transition to a deregulated equilibrium characterized by contestable markets has not been instantaneous. Bailey and Baumol (1984. pp.130-131) discuss several factors that have diminished contestability during the period immediately following deregulation. The importance of these factors, such as nonoptimal networks and widely divergent cost structures among carriers, should decline as the regulatory era recedes into history. If this happens, the contestability of airline markets will be enhanced.[24]

With regard to the second condition, our model confirms the existence of fixed costs associated with airline networks. That is, an air carrier incurs substantial costs associated with the size of the network to be served, regardless of the level of output provided within that network. The model of Baumol and Willig (1981) indicates that if these fixed costs are of sufficient magnitude and are not sunk, then prices are sustainable and there can exist a welfare optimum without government regulation. Sustainable prices are prices that will cover costs yet not invite entry or "cream-skimming." Several observers have argued that few if any airline costs are sunk, but further analysis is required to determine whether the fixed costs of particular networks are of sufficient size to

---

24. As Bailey and Baumol (1984) note. one factor which may continue to impede contestability is the nonmarket allocation of landing slots at major airports.

achieve the favorable result spelled out by Baumol and Willig(1981).[25]

Such determination requires global knowledge of the cost surface. Our analysis, by integrating the local service and trunk carriers into a single model, provides information on the nature of cost over a much wider range of output than previous studies. But a definitive welfare analysis will require information on cost for carriers such as the recent entrants, which have very small networks and low levels of output within these networks. Further research in this area is required.

Appendix

*Table A1. Estimated Coefficient of Translog Cost functions
(Standard Errors in Parentheses)*

Regressor	Unrestricted Translog Total Cost Function	Total Cost Function Restricted to First-Order Terms	Unrestricted Translog Variable Cost Function	Translog Total Cost Function Restricted to Zero for firms Effects
First-Order Terms				
Constant	13.243	13.216	13.006	13.153
	(.045)	(.035)	(.049)	(0.19)
Output	.804	.824	.719	.922
	(.034)	(.0.29)	(.043)	(.013)
Points Served	.132	.128	.139	.155
	(.031)	(.029)	(0.33)	(0.24)
Stage Length	-.148	-.140	-.046	-.220
	(.054)	(.039)	(.055)	(0.24)
Load Factor	-.264	-.261	-.145	-.284
	(0.70)	(.066)	(0.71)	(.-0.79)
Labor Price	.356	.356	.422	.357
	(.002)	(.003)	(.002)	(.002)
Fuel Price	.166	.166	.196	.166
	(.001)	(.004)	(.001)	(.001)
Materials-Capi -tal Price*	.478	.478	.382	.477
	(.002)	(.003)	(.002)	(.002)

25. With regard to the absence of sunk costs, see Bailey and Panzar (1981). Also see Eads(1972), who argues that used aircraft markets are nearly perfect.

Table A1 (Continued)

Regressor	Unrestricted Translog Total Cost Function	Total Cost Function Restricted to First-Order Terms	Unrestricted Translog Variable Cost Function	Translog Total Cost Function Restricted to Zero for firms Effects
Capacity			.153 (.045)	
Second-Order Terms				
$(Output)^2$	.034 (.054)		.092 (.343)	-.114 (.048)
$(Points)^2$	-.172 (.152)		-.219 (.150)	-.429 (.114)
Output-Points	-.123 (.064)		.182 (.121)	.205 (.058)
$(Labor Price)^2$	.166 (..026)		.170 (.0.27)	.170 (.025)
$(Fuel Price)^2$	.137 (.003)		.156 (.004)	.136 (.003)
$(Materials-capital Price)^2$	.150 (.022)		.142 (.024)	.153 (.021)
Labor-Fuel	-.076 (.005)		-.092 (.006)	-.076 (.005)
Labor-Materials	-.090 (.023)		-.078 (.025)	-.093 (.022)
Fuel-Materials	-.060 (.005)		-.064 (.006)	-.060 (.005)
$(Stage Length)^2$	.068 (.155)		-.201 (.174)	-.139 (.125)
$(Load Factor)^2$	.047 (.617)		-.602 (.935)	-.758 (.842)
Stage Length-Load Factor	-.354 (.190)		-.572 (.261)	-.1.022 (.240)
Output-Labor	-.009 (.005)		-.087 (.018)	-.008 (.005)

Table A1 (Continued)

Regressor	Unrestricted Translog Total Cost Function	Total Cost Function Restricted to First-Order Terms	Unrestricted Translog Variable Cost Function	Translog Total Cost Function Restricted to Zero for firms Effects
Output-Fuel	.018 (.003)		.057 (.011)	.017 (.003)
Output-Materials	-.010 (.004)		.031 (.018)	-.009 (.004)
Points-Labor	.036 (.007)		.030 (.008)	.035 (.007)
Points-Fuel	-.032 (.004)		-.042 (.005)	-.030 (.004)
Point-Materials	-.004 (.007)		.012 (.008)	-.005 (.007)
Stage Length-Labor	-.028 (.008)		-.014 (.009)	-.028 (.008)
Stage Length Fuel	-.003 (.005)		-.011 (.006)	-.001 (.005)
Stage Length-Materials	.031 (.007)		.025 (.009)	.029 (.007)
Load Factor-Labot	.073 (.024)		.131 (.030)	.070 (.024)
Load Factor-Fuel	-.063 (.014)		-.116 (.019)	-.059 (.014)
Load Factor-Materials	-.011 (.024)		-.016 (.030)	-.011 (.023)
Output-Stage Length	-.050 (.085)		.239 (.189)	.178 (.173)
Output-Load Factor	.036 (.119)		.057 (.448)	.449 (.129)
Points-Stage Length	.218 (.111)		.173 (.114)	-.217 (.091)
Points-Load Factor	.118 (.154)		-.215 (.176)	-.768 (.195)

Table A1 (Continued)

Regressor	Unrestricted Translog Total Cost Function	Total Cost Function Restricted to First-Order Terms	Unrestricted Translog Variable Cost Function	Translog Total Cost Function Restricted to Zero for firms Effects
(Capacity)^2			.440 (.276)	
Capacity-Labor			.083 (.017)	
Capacity-Fuel			-.031 (.010)	
Capacity-Materials			-.053 (-.016)	
Capacity-Output			-.262 (.301)	
Capacity-Points			-.334 (.097)	
Capacity-Stage Length			-.134 (.149)	
Capacity-Load Factor			.239 (.384)	
<u>Time Dummies</u>				
1970	.169 (.018)	.162 (.017)	.186 (.019)	.213 (.023)
1971	.159 (.017)	.164 (.016)	.174 (.018)	.204 (.022)
1972	.105 (.014)	.115 (.015)	.121 (.015)	.134 (.021)
1973	.111 (.014)	.118 (.014)	.126 (.014)	.138 (.021)
1974	.086 (013)	.088 (.014)	.088 (.013)	.089 (.021)
1975	.077 (.013)	.080 (.013)	.075 (.013)	.082 (.021)

Table A1 (Continued)

Regressor	Unrestricted Translog Total Cost Function	Total Cost Function Restricted to First-Order Terms	Unrestricted Translog Variable Cost Function	Translog Total Cost Function Restricted to Zero for firms Effects
1976	.043 (.012)	.044 (.013)	.040 (.012)	.046 (.020)
1978	-.043 (.015)	-.051 (.014)	-.045 (.015)	-.153 (.022)
1979	-.083 (.019)	-.100 (.016)	-.105 (.019)	-.097 (.024)
1980	-.022 (.017)	-.011 (.016)	-.060 (.017)	-.035 (.022)
1981	-.033 (.018)	-.016 (.017)	-.084 (.020)	-.037 (.022)
Firm Dummies				
American	.063 (.044)	.153 (.022)	-.032 (.054)	
Braniff	-.084 (.042)	-.165 (.033)	-.025 (.047)	
Continental	-.121 (.048)	-.125 (.038)	-.081 (.051)	
Eastern	.125 (.025)	.101 (.019)	.088 (.027)	
National	-..064 (.061)	-.088 (.043)	.021 (.063)	
Northeast	-.088 (.091)	-.110 (.069)	.157 (.017)	
Northwest	-.177 (.038)	-.159 (.027)	-.251 (.038)	
Pan Am (premerger)	.031 (.081)	.014 (.046)	-.135 (.085)	
Pan Am (postmerger)	.034 (.068)	.008 (.040)	-.148 (.072)	

Table A1 (Continued)

Regressor	Unrestricted Translog Total Cost Function	Total Cost Function Restricted to First-Order Terms	Unrestricted Translog Variable Cost Function	Translog Total Cost Function Restricted to Zero for firms Effects
TWA	.151 (.051)	.144 (.027)	-.139 (.060)	
United	.137 (.041)	.097 (.024)	-.087 (.057)	
Western	-.104 (.048)	-.122 (.039)	-.064 (.051)	
Air West	-.101 (.071)	-.047 (.061)	.082 (.082)	
Frontier	-.245 (.074)	-.186 (.058)	-.060 (.085)	
North Central	-.092 (.075)	-.060 (.061)	.097 (.084)	
Ozark	.149 (.079)	-.102 (.067)	.030 (.091)	
Piedmont	-.144 (.078)	-.091 (.064)	.057 (.089)	
Republic (premerger)	.091 (.082)	.017 (.049)	.298 (.088)	
Republic (postmerger)	.163 (.086)	.035 (.049)	.336 (.093)	
Southern	-.155 (.081)	-.119 (.070)	.043 (.093)	
Texas International	-.195 (.083)	-.164 (.071)	.013 (.097)	
U.S.Air	-.057 (.055)	-.009 (.041)	.115 (.064)	

*Materials price for the variable cost function.

References

BAILEY, E.E "Contestability and the Design of Regulatory and Antitrust Policy." *American Economic Review Papers and Proceedings*, Vol. 71 (May 1981), pp. 178-183.

_____, AND BAUMOL, W.J."Deregulation and the Theory of Contestable Markets." *Yale Journal on Regulation*, Vol. 1 (1984), pp. 111-137.

_____, AND PANZAR, J. C. "The Contestability of Airline Markets during the Transition to Deregulation." *Law and Contemporary Problems* (Winter 1981), pp. 125-145.

BAUMOL, W.J. AND WILLIG, R.D., "Fixed Costs, Sunk Costs, Entry Barriers, and Sustainability of Monopoly." *Quarterly Journal of Economics*, Vol. 95 (August 1981), pp.405-431.

_____, PANZAR, J.C., AND WILLIG, R.D. *Contestable Markets and the Theory of Industry Structure*. New York: Harcourt Brace Jovanovich, 1982.

BROWN, R.S. AND CHRISTENSEN, L.R. "Estimating Elasticities of Substitution in a Model of Partial Static Equilibrium: An Application to U.S. Agriculture, 1947-1974" in E.R. Berndt and B.C. Field, eds., *Measuring and Modelling Natural Resources Substitution*, Cambridge: MIT Press, 1982.

CAVES, D.W. AND CHRISTENSEN, L.R. "Global Properties of Flexible Functional Forms." *American Economic review*, Vol. 70 (June 1980), pp. 422-432.

_____, _____, AND DIEWERT, W.E. "The Economic Theory of Index Numbers and the Measurement of Input, Output and Productivity." *Econometrica* Vol. 50 (November 1982), pp. 1393-1414.

_____, _____, AND SWANSON, J.A. "Productivity Growth, Scale Economies and Capacity Utilization in U.S. Railroads, 1955-1974." *American Economic Review*, Vol. 71 (December 1981), pp. 994-1002.

_____, _____, AND TRETHEWAY, M.W. "U.S. Trunk Air Carriers, 1972-1977: A Multilateral Comparison of Total Factor Productivity." in T Cowing and R. Stevenson, eds., *Productivity Measurement in Regulated Industries*, New York: Academic Press, 1981.

_____, _____, AND _____, "Productivity performance of u.s. Trunk and Local Service Airlines in the Era of Deregulation." *Economic Inquiry*, Vol. 21 (July 1983), pp. 312-324.

_____, _____, _____, AND WINDLE, R.J. "Network Effects and the Measurement of Returns to Scale and Density for U.S. Railroads" in A.F. Daughety, ed., *Analytical Studies in Transport Economics,* Cambridge: Cambridge University Press, 1984.

CAVES, R.E. *Air Transport and Its Regulators.* Cambridge; Cambridge; Harvard University Press, 1962.

CHRISTENSEN, L.R. AND GREENE, W.H. "Economies of Scale in U.S. Electric Power Generation." *Journal of Political Economy,* Vol. 84 (August 1976), pp. 655-676.

_____, JORGENSON, D.W., AND LAU, L.J. "Transcendental Logarithmic Production Frontiers." *Review of Economics and Statistics,* Vol. 55 (February 1973), pp. 28-45

DOUGLAS, G.W. AND MILLER, J.C., III. *Economic Regulation of Domestic Air Transport: Theory and Policy.* Washington, D.C.: Brookings Institution, 1974.

EADS, G.C. *The Local Service Airline Experiment.* Washington, D.C.:Brookings Institution, 1972.

_____, NERLOVE, M., AND RADUCHEL, W. "A Long-Run Cost Function for the Local Service Airline Industry." *Review of Economics and Statistics,* Vol. 51 (August 1969), pp. 258-270.

GRAHAM, D.R. AND KAPLAN, D.P. *Competition and the Airlines: An Evaluation of Deregulation.* Washington, D.C.: Office of Economic Analysis, Civil Aeronautics Board, December 1982.

HAUSMAN, J.A. AND TAYLOR, W.E. "Panel Data and Unobservable Individual Effects." *Econometrica,* Vol. 49 (November 1981), pp. 1377-1398.

KEELER, T.E. "Domestic Trunk Airline Regulation: An Economic Evaluation." *Study on Federal Regulation.* Washington, D.C.: U.S. Government Printing Office, 1978.

MUNDLAK, Y. "Empirical Production Functions Free of Management Bias." *Journal of Farm Economics,* vol. 43 (February 1961), pp. 44-56.

_____, "On the pooling of Time Series and Cross Section Data." *Econometrica,* Vol. 46 (January 1978), pp. 69-85.

SCHERER, F.M. *Industrial Market Studies and Economic Performance.* Chicago: Rand McNally, 1980.

SHEPHARD, R.W. *Cost and Production Functions.* Princeton: Princeton University Press, 1953.

TORNQVIST, L. "The Bank of Finland's Consumption Price Index."

Banks of Finland Monthly Bulletin, No. 10 (1936), pp.1-8.

WALES, T.J. "On the Flexibility of Flexible Functional Forms: An Empirical Approach." *Journal of Econometrics*, Vol. 5 (1977). pp.183-193.

WHITE, L.J. "Economies of Scale and the Question of "Natural Monopoly' in the Airline Industry." *Journal of Air Law and Commerce*, Vol. 44 (1979), pp. 545-573.

ZELLNER, A. "An Efficient Method of Estimating Seemingly Unrelated Regressions and Tests for Aggregation Bias." *Journal of the American Statistical Association*, Vol. 58 (December 1962), pp. 977-992.

CHAPTER 8

STATISTICAL COSTING IN TRANSPORTATION*

*W. G. Waters, II***

Costing is the process of ascertaining the relationship between costs and output in a way which is useful for making decisions. Knowledge of the cost implications of alternative situations are needed in order to analyze a wide variety of problems within a private firm as well as in formulating or assessing public policies. This paper reviews the major approaches to costing, in particular, the application of the statistical technique of regression analysis to determining costs. Some conceptual as well as practical problems in the use of costing methods are examined and the diverse uses of statistical costing in transportation are illustrated.

I. Costs and Decision Making in Transportation

The relevant costs for decision-making are the changes in costs which

*Reprinted from *Transportation Journal* (Spring, 1976), pp. 49-62.

**Mr. Waters is with the Centre for Transportation Studies, The University of British Columbia, Vancouver. This study was supported in part by funds from the Centre for Transportation Studies. The author wishes to thank C. Loren Doll, Trevor D. Heaver, Terry J. Norman, and Spencer Star of U.B.C., and Joseph A. Swanson of the University of Iowa for their helpful comments on a previous draft.

will be associated with a change in the level of some activity or service. For expansions in output this will be the marginal or incremental costs of expanding that service. For reducing or eliminating an output or activity the relevant concept is avoidable costs.

Determining costs in transportation is often difficult because of (1) the heterogeneous nature of output and (2) indivisibilities in production. The heterogeneous nature of output refers to the diverse products which are produced in transportation, e.g., a ton-mile involving opposite directions is not the same product, the movement of perishable commodities is not necessarily in the same market as the movement of bulk materials. The implication is that one must specify accurately just what is being supplied in order to cost it properly. The degree of accuracy required will depend on the particular question being addressed. For example, costing for rate-making purposes requires estimating accurately the specific dollar magnitudes whereas testing for the presence of economies of scale need only establish the ratio of changes in costs to changes in output.

Indivisibilities in the production process have two aspects. First, a trip or single act of supplying transportation can satisfy several demands simultaneously. Second, expenditures on imputs may occur less frequently than the number of trips: the costs of some inputs are spread over several trips. As a result of these characteristics a variety of different outputs are provided and a composite of costs are incurred over some period of time; but it is difficult, and may be impossible, to identify a specific level of expenditure with a specific output. For decision-making it is necessary to have estimates of both types of costs: those which can be identified with particular outputs, and those which can only be identified with groups of outputs.

Costing methods are used to estimate the specific relationship between certain outputs and costs when that relationship is not obvious from available information. There are three basic approaches to costing: accounting, engineering and statistical. This paper concentrates on the third approach but the role of statistical costing cannot be understood without reference to the other two. So we begin by briefly reviewing some salient characteristics of the accounting and engineering approaches to costing. Following that, the problems and uses of statistical costing are addressed.

II. The Accounting and Engineering Approaches to Costing

1. Accounting Costs

The accounting approach to costing simply compiles the cost categories relevant to the output or service in question and uses that information to estimate or predict the costs associated with a change in the specific output level. This is generally the cheapest and most convenient method, providing data exist. However, there are three potential shortcomings of this approach: (1) there is the potential difficulty that the historical or recorded book costs of assets may not be an accurate guide to the actual opportunity costs of those assets; (2) the cost accounts may not distinguish between costs which vary with changes in output levels from costs which remain fixed; (3) the accounting process itself might obscure the relationship between costs and specific outputs, that is, the aggregation in the accounts prevents identifying what proportion of costs can be identified with particular outputs.

The first problem, that recorded values of assets may not be a reliable indicator of the opportunity costs of those assets is a familiar difficulty and needs little elaboration here. Opportunity costs are the relevant con-

Figure 1 Fixed and Variable Costs Separated

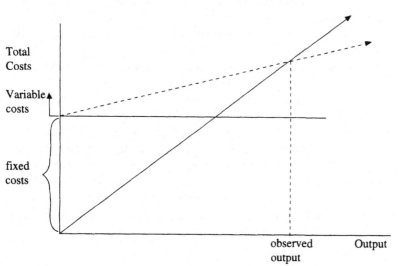

cept for decision-making so accounting figures may need modification to reflect actual opportunities forgone.

The second potential shortcoming of accounting costs (the accounts might not distinguish between fixed and variable costs) is illustrated in Figure 1. A concept such as total costs divided by total output as a predictor of costs corresponds to the cost function drawn from the origin through point A. Classification of costs as fixed or variable might yield a considerably different prediction such as the dashed line in Figure 1. The behavior of costs as output changes in either direction from point A is quite different from that predicted by average total costs.

The third potential problem with accounting costs is that the accounting process could obscure the causality between particular outputs and cost categories. This is not necessarily the fault of the accounting system. If costs are incurred in common with supplying several outputs it may be impossible to identify costs with specific outputs regardless of the costing method employed. But the aggregation in accounting systems may give rise to additional misleading instances of common costs. A fundamental purpose of accounting is a systematic ordering and recording of the financial transactions of an enterprise. Accounting categories tend to be determined by the nature of the expense or revenue class. For example, costs may be categorized as fuel, labor expenses of various types, etc., while revenues are likely classified by different types of service provided. But there may be little correspondence between cost categories and revenue accounts for specific outputs provided. Some (or all) costs might be traceable to specific outputs but the association becomes obscured in the accounting process. In these circumstances accounting costs are unable to reveal accurately either the level of costs which can be directly identified with a particular output or the level of costs which can be directly identified with a particular output or the level of costs which are unavoidably incurred in common with other outputs. It is important to keep these categories separate. Frequently, some accounting rules will be adopted deliberately to apportion the common costs among the various outputs, e.g., allocate such expenses in proportion to the relative size of each of the common outputs. Such practices can actually thwart efficient decision-making because such apportionments are economically arbitrary and will be misleading predictors of cost-output relations.

2. Engineering Costing

This second basic approach to costing begins by ascertaining the technical coefficient between inputs and outputs. Combining such coefficients with the cost of those inputs yields the cost function for the particular output.[1] Ready examples are estimating fuel requirements for different speeds, gradients, loads, etc. Charts or tables are often prepared by vehicle manufacturers; firms make use of these in selecting and operating their equipment (commercial aircraft operators may make in-flight adjustments in speed and altitude to minimize in-flight fuel costs).

There are two approaches to engineering costing. The first is to derive the technical coefficients from physical laws or precise engineering relationships.[2] The second is to establish empirically the technical relationship by controlled experiment. An example of the latter would be the tests of highway wear associated with different-weight vehicles. Test sections of roads are built and subjected to controlled use by various sizes and numbers of vehicles. This will establish wear coefficients which can then be tied to the costs of providing and maintaining roads. The two approaches in engineering costing can be used in conjunction with one another.

The major shortcoming of the engineering approach is that it is fairly data- and time-intensive; therefore, it is a rather costly procedure. It should be highly accurate, and it is used in instances where the desired accuracy is deemed to warrant the cost of achieving it. A further possible shortcoming is the non-stochastic nature of this approach (particularly the mathematical preciseness of the first approach although the same objection can be directed at any single, detailed experiment to establish cost-output relationships). The engineering approach does not have to be deterministic. One could incorporate predicted variance in performance or repeat controlled experiments to establish reliability. But these make the engineering approach all the more expensive. Finally, engineering costing necessarily deals only with outputs and inputs which are readily related in a physical way so that costs are necessarily traceable to out-

---

1. If there is substitutability among inputs there is the necessary additional step of seeing that inputs are combined in optimal proportions.
2. Cf. Joseph De Salvo, "A Process Function for Rail Linehaul Operations," *Journal of Transport Economics and Policy,* (JAN. 1969), PP. 3-28.

puts. Engineering costing will not do away with situations where multiple outputs exist such that specific cost-output relations are impossible to identify. A careful study of production relationships and related cost functions might dispel false instances of what appear to be untraceable costs (e.g., instances where accounting methods obscure causality between costs and services provided) but it cannot eliminate genuine instances of untraceable costs. The engineering approach might identify more precisely the level of common (or joint) costs with levels of multiple outputs.

III. Statistical Costing

1. Introduction

The third costing method which has found extensive use in transportation (and other industries) is statistical costing.[3] Basically, it is the

---

3. Statistical costing has been used in one way or another for all modes except pipelines (where engineering costing is more appropriate). The most extensive use has been for railways. Some recent examples are: Association of American Railroads, Bureau of Railway Economics. *A Guide to Railroad Cost Analysis.* Washington, D.C., December, 1964; G. H. Borts, "The Estimation of Rail Cost Functions." *Econometrica*(January 1960) pp. 108–31; Z. Griliches, "Cost Allocation in Railroad Regulation." *Bell Journal of Economics and Management Science,* (Spring, 1972), pp.26–41; T. E. Keeler, "The Economics of Passenger Trains." *Journal of Business* (April, 1971) pp. 148–174; T.E. Keeler, "Railroad Costs, Returns to Scale, and Excess Capacity," *Review of Economics and Statistics* (May, 1974), pp. 201–208; J. R. Meyer, et al., *The Economics of Competition in the Transportation Industries* (Harvard, 1964); J.R. Meyer, "Some Methodological Aspects of Statistical Costing as Illustrated by the Determination of Rail Passenger Costs." *American Economic Review,* (May 1958) pp. 209–222; E. Miller, "Economies of Scale in Railroading" *Transportation Research Forum Proceedings,* 1973, pp. 683–701; and J. Stenason & R.A. Bandeen, "Transportation Costs and Their Implications: An Empirical Study of Railway Costs in Canada," In *Transportation Economics* (National Bureau of Economic Research) 1965.

    Some applications to air transportation include: G. Eads, M. Nerlove and W. Raduchel, "A Long Run Cost Function for Local–Service Airline Industry: An Experiment in Non-Linear Estimation," *The Review of Economics and Statistics,*, (Aug. 1969), pp. 258–70; R.J. Gordon, "Airline Costs and Managerial Efficiency" in *Transportation Economics* (National Bureau of Economic Research) 1965; T.E. Keeler, "Airline Regulation and Market Performance," *Bell Journal of Economics and Management Science,* (Autumn, 1972), pp. 399–424; C.E. Sarndal and T.H. Oum, "A Stause of statistical techniques (usually multiple regression analysis)[4] to infer cost-output relations from a sample of actual operating experiences. A compilation of instances of different cost-output (and/or different combinations of multiple outputs) is subjected to statistical techniques to identify the variability of costs with output measures. Statistical costing generally makes use of accounting information (with possible adjustments such as disaggregating cost categories, revaluation of assets to equal their opportunity costs, etc.). The sample of observations must, of course, consist of cost-output experiences relevant to the relationship being estimated. Observations may consist of a comparison of different branches of a firm's operations (e.g., different regions), experience over a period of time, or a cross-section of the cost-output experience of different firms. Each of these sets of observations has particular

tistical Analysis of Airline Operating Costs," Working paper no. 16, Centre for Transportation Studies, (University of British Columbia, Vancouver); C.E. Sarndal and W.B. Statton, "Factors Influencing Operating Cost in the Airline Industry," Working Paper No. 11, Centre for Transportation Studies (University of British Columbia, Vancouver) and *Journal of Transport Economics and Policy* (forthcoming); and M.R. Straxheim, *The International Airline Industry,* (Brookings) 1969. Appendix B.

Two Examples for water transportation are: L.S. Case & L.B. Lave, "Cost Functions for Inland Waterway Transport in the U.S.," *Journal of Transport Economics and Policy,* (May 1970) pp. 181–91; and B. Foss, "A Cost Model for Coastal Shipping: A Norwegian Example," *Journal of Transport Economics and Policy,* (May 1969), pp. 195–222.

Some examples for motor transportation are: J. Johnston, "Scale, Costs and Profitability of Road Passenger Transport," Journal of Industrial Economics(June, 1956) pp. 207-23; R. K. Koshal, "I. The Cost of Trucking: Econometric Analysis, II. Bus Transport: Some United States Experience," Journal of Transport Economics and Policy, (May 1972) pp. 147-153; R. K. Koshal, "Economics of Scale in Bus Transport: Some Indian Experience." *Journal of Transport Economics and Policy,* (January 1970), pp. 29-36; N. Lee and I. Steedman, "Economies of Scale in Bus Transport: Some British Municipal Results," *Journal of Transport Economics and Policy* (January 1970) pp. 15-28; and S. L. Warner, "Cost Models, Measurement Errors and Economies of Scale in Trucking," Chapter 1 in M. L. Burstein, et al., *The Cost of Trucking: Econometric Analysis* (Transportation Center: Northwestern University Evanston) 1965, on motor carriers.

4. An exception are the recent papers by Sarndal and Stattop, "Factors Influencing Operating Cost in the Airline Industry," and Sarndal and Oum, "A Statistical Analysis of Airline Operating Costs" They make use of *path analysis* to explore the directional causality among various factors (e.g. network characteristics, technology, etc.) which affect airline costs.

advantages depending upon the purpose of costing but each also entails disadvantages in that it may introduce a systematic bias to the estimate of cost-output relations.

Statistical costing is not an ideal method but is a substitute for detailed engineering studies and/or controlled experiments. It is a less costly technique and the degree of precision depends on: (1) the sample size; (2) the fundamental predictability of the relationship being investigated; (3) correct specification of the variables measured; (4) the accuracy of measurement; and (5) the validity of the assumptions which underlie the statistical method employed (usually regression analysis). This last influence is very important. If one or more of the underlying assumptions are not satisfied this will undermine the accuracy and/or reliability of the estimate of the cost-output relationship.[5] In some cases, there are techniques which can be used to correct for violations of assumptions. An analyst must be alert for these complications and be aware of their implications. Computers will perform the calculations regardless of all but catastrophic errors, but the validity of the results depends upon whether or not subtle, but important, underlying statistical conditions are satisfied.

We turn now to a discussion of the problems and uses of statistical costing. The first section reviews problems in the formulation and estimation of cost functions; the second section discusses the diverse uses of statistical cost functions.

2. Problems in the Formulation and Estimation of Statistical Cost Functions

This section points out a number of problems in the formulation and estimation of cost functions. The first part deals with general problems in formulating the cost function as well as problems with the data used to estimate it. The second group of problems is related to the selection

---

5. The conceptual validity of the ordinary least squares regression model requires a number of assumptions about the interrelationships among variables (e.g., explanatory variables must be independent of one another) and the behavior of stochastic components which inevitably appear is our non-deterministic world (e.g., errors of disturbances to the hypothesized relationships must be randomly distributed with a mean value of zero and a constant variance); A useful reference to principles of econometrics applied to cost analysis is J. Johnston, *Statistical Costing* (McGraw-Hill, 1960).

and measurement of variables in the cost function. The third part looks at problems associated with the aggregation of data.

(a) Formulation of a Cost Function and Data Problems

Cost functions can be "short run" or "long run." Actual experience does not correspond exactly to this precise dichotomy of theory but it is a useful working distinction. They are *short run* if some inputs to the production process cannot be varied over the time period considered; they are *long run* if all (or at least nearly all) inputs can be adjusted for a change in the level of output.

Short run cost functions are generally estimated using time series data. During a limited time period, a firm would not be able to adjust fixed assets in response to changed levels of demand thus the observed cost-output variability is short run in nature. But unless the time period is very short some assets will have been changed within some firms in the sample. A time series may also be associated with changes in technical knowledge, input combinations and/or the prices of inputs. Thus a time series estimate may not yield an accurate prediction of a cost function based on present knowledge, equipment and input costs.

Another potential statistical problem with the time series data is that of auto-correlation. If temporary disturbances tend to carry over from one period to the next (i.e., disturbance terms in successive years are not independent), this will reduce the calculated standard error of estimate of the regression coefficient; therefore the coefficient appears more significant than is warranted. Special statistical techniques or procedures must be employed to surmount this difficulty (the simplest approach is to use the "first-differences" or *changes* in costs and outputs between periods rather than the cost-output figures themselves).

Most statistical studies of costs focus on long run estimates. Long run cost functions generally are estimated using a cross-section of firms or across separable branches or divisions of a firm (e.g., different geographic areas of operation). One must assume that firms (or divisions) operating at different output levels will have adjusted their fixed assets (capital equipment) to optimal levels with only random deviations;[6] thus

---

6. This is a questionable assumption for rail costing studies given the excess capacity present in many railways. Cf., Keeler, "Railroad Costs, Returns to Scale, and Excess Capacity."

an estimated cost function across these firms should be a long run variety. This approach avoids some of the difficulties of time series, but it may bring other difficulties.[7] Data may be more difficult to obtain, particularly for non-regulated firms. For regulated firms, there is always the suspicion that data supplied to regulators might not be as accurate or reliable as it could be. Accounting procedures differ among firms, thus the accounts may not be exactly comparable.[8] One cannot expect all firms to be operating precisely at design capacity. Some expenses occur less frequently than once a year or else are postponable for a time. As a result, a particular year's expenditures might not be an accurate indication of the true costs (one might be able to correct for this source of error by averaging two or three years' data for each firm in a cross-section). Such short run variations can give rise to biased estimates of the relationship between costs and outputs.[9] If there are systematic differences among firms which go unnoticed, this can result in biased estimates of the "true" relationship between costs and output.

Some studies estimate both long run and short run cost functions. A data sample could include both cross-sectional and time series data and the long run and short run estimates are estimated using the appropriate subsample of the data.[10] A promising alternative approach is to derive the long run cost function from estimated short run cost functions.[11]

Aside from the short run versus long run question, there are a number of other problems in formulating statistical cost functions. There is the

---

7. For a general critique of the use of cross-sectional data for estimating cost functions (particularly for estimating economies of scale) see M. Friedman, "Theory and Measurement of Long-Run Costs' in G. C. Archibald, ed., *The Theory of the Firm* (Penguin Books) 1971, pp. 44-52.

8. Differences can arise even with a "uniform system of accounts." Some expenses inevitably overlap accounts thus can be recorded differently among firms.

9. If the variation in observed costs from designed capacity costs varies with the size of the firm, this can result in a biased estimate of the coefficient of costs and output (this is the so-called "regression fallacy"). Cf., Borts, "The Estimation of Rail Cost Functions," Johnston, *Statistical Costing*, pp. 188-93, J. R. Meyer and G. Kraft, "The Evaluation of Statistical Costing Techniques as Applied in the Transportation Industry," *American Economic Review* (May 1961), p. 322-4.

10. For example, A. F. Friedlaender, "The Social Costs of Regulating the Railroads," *American Economic Review* (May, 1971) pp. 226-34.

11. Cf. Eads, Nerlove and Raduchel, "A Long-Run cost Function for Local-Service Airline Industry: An Experiment in Non-Linear Estimation," and Keeler, "Railroad Costs, Returns to Scale, and Excess Capacity."

choice of the functional form of the relationship, i.e., whether costs are a linear or some more complex mathematical function of output. Not much experimentation has taken place on this matter but it would usually be resolved on empirical grounds (best fit) although one might argue on *a priori* ground instead (e.g., the limited knowledge of the production function might be sufficient to imply a particular relationship between costs and output).[12] Short run cost functions are expected to be non-linear; but the shape of long run functions is less certain. If there are positive fixed costs in a postulated linear total cost function, the average cost curve must be non-linear.

The last point is related to the question of whether one should estimate *total* cost functions or deflate by size or output levels and thus estimate an *average* cost function. In situations where the relationship between costs and outputs implies that one form of the cost function is linear and the other is not, one would adopt the linear form since linear relationships are often easier to estimate than non-linear. Where other functional forms are postulated it is usually possible to transform the data in such a way as to use linear regression methods. Most costing studies estimate total cost functions. It is preferable to express the dependent variable (costs) directly rather than in ratio form (cost per unit).

An argument for the use of average cost function is if the expected variability of total costs about a regression line is greater for higher levels of output. This violates one of the underlying assumptions for the use of linear regression analysis. Dividing total costs by output can correct for this[13] but it can also give rise to other statistical difficulties (see the discussion in part *b* below concerning the ICC's practice of expressing their cost data on a per mile of track basis). This problem of increasing size of the deviations from a regression line can be dealt with by other methods such as converting the data to logarithms before using linear regression analysis.

---

12. The necessary assumptions which underlie the use of least squares regression techniques cannot be satisfied simultaneously for different functional forms; hence there is an econometric objection to trying to settle the question of function form by experimentation.

13. Miller "Economies of Scale in Railroading." uses this argument as justification for dividing by miles of track.

(b) Selection & Measurement of Variables for the Cost Function

The choice of alternative output measures is a persistent problem. There is no unique best measure of the output of a transportation enterprise even for disaggregated components of costs. The most commonly used measure is the gross ton mile for freight and the seat-mile for passenger traffic. But some categories of costs can be better related to some other output measure, e.g. vehicle miles, number of journeys, etc. The ICC has been criticized for their reliance on gross ton miles as a measure when other variables are more appropriate for certain types of expenses.[14]

Size of firm (or size of divisional operations within a firm) is often listed as a separate variable in a cost function. But "size" can be measured in various ways e.g. fleet size, miles of track of railways, total assets. The selection among competing measures is usually resolved on an empirical basis, i.e., choose the measures which yield the best statistical fit (as indicated by the R^2 or coefficient of determination). The U.S. Interstate Commerce Commission has been criticized for its treatment of the size variable in its railway costing studies.[15] The Commission deflates the data by a size variable (miles of track) before regressing costs on output. It is preferable to capture the influence of size by listing it as a separate variable in the regression rather than arithmetically transforming the date into averages. Deflating by size can lead to biased results. For example, suppose costs (E) are related to output (Q) and size (S) as in equation (I):

$$(I) \quad E = a + bQ + cS$$

---

14. Griliches, "Cost Allocation in Railroad Regulation." is the most recent critic.

15. Cf., Meyer, et. al., *The Economics of Competition in the Transportation Industries*, Chapter 3 and Appendix A; Meyer and Kraft, "The Evaluation of Statistical Costing Techniques as Applied in the Transportation Industry"; Ann Friedlaender, *The Dilemma of Freight Transport Regulation* (Brookings, 1969) Chapter 2 and Appendix A; Griliches, "Cost Allocation in Railroad Regulation." The principal reference to ICC procedures is Interstate Commerce Commission, Bureau of Accounts, *Explanation of Rail cost Finding Procedures and Principles Relating to the Use of Costs.* St. 7-63. Washington, D.C. November, 1963; Presumably in response to the many criticisms over the years, in 1970 the Commission authorized a task force to investigate the possibility of new research into costing methods. Interstate Commerce Commission, docket No. 34013. *Rules to Govern the Assembling and Presenting of Cost Evidence.* Decided July 13, 1970. Served July 30, 1970.

Divide both sides of (I) by S

$$\frac{E}{S} = \left(\frac{a}{S} + c\right) + b\frac{Q}{S}$$

This is estimated as

$$\text{(II)} \quad \frac{E}{S} = k + b\,\frac{Q}{S}$$

"... to identify k with c... essentially means overestimating the effects of the size variable since a can be normally assumed to be greater than zero (because it usually represents the average effect of minor omitted influences on cost and costs are always positive)"[16] Griliches compared a regression of form (I) with that of the ICC (II) and found c was significant but b was not. He concludes that "... (size) appears in a 'significant' form... only because the other variables were divided by it."[17]

Introducing additional independent variables to increase the explanatory power of a regression often raises the problem of *multicollinearity*. This is where variations of some or all of the alleged independent variables are correlated with one another. In the extreme this can completely undermine regression analysis. When variables are strongly correlated with one another their simultaneous presence in a regression obscures the relationship between the dependent variable (costs) and the correlated "independent" variables. If one must choose between alternative variables this might be done either by *ex ante* specification of which variables is expected to be more important or by *ex post* selection of the variable which gives best statistical fit. Neither approach is completely satisfying because there may be good reason to expect a certain variable to contribute some independent explanation of costs but that variable must be excluded from regression analysis because it is strongly correlated with some other variable.

---

16. Meyer, et. al., *The Economics of Competition in the Transportation Industries*, p. 37.
17. Griliches, "Cost Allocation in Railroad Regulation." p. 32. Borts, "Discussion: (of J. R. Meyer, 'Some Methodological Aspects ...')." *American Economic Review* (May, 1958) pp. 235-8 questions the theoretical justification for including "size" in long run cost functions.

(c) Problems Associated with the Aggregation of Data

If detailed information on cost accounts is available there is the problem of determining the appropriate level of disaggregation. What accounts can be added together and treated as an aggregate with respect to output measures? Extensive disaggregation is costly but aggregating accounts might conceal variability. Railways use quite extensive disaggregation in their cost investigations.[18] Cost accounts can be aggregated if found to vary together with a common output measure. This process of examining and aggregating accounts generally proceeds by gradual experimentation.[19] Often, cost accounts are aggregated already but not in a manner ideal for costing studies. This is unfortunate but unavoidable and will generally reduce the explanatory power which can be achieved. Of course, recognizing such problems is the first step in redesigning accounting systems to provide more useable information for decision-making.

Many studies employ total costs with total output for each firm as a single observation in a cross-section (e.g., studies investigating the possible presence of economies of scale). Studies which employ such highly aggregated data do so generally because that is all that is available.

A different problem arising from aggregating data is if the sample of observations does not really represent a single population. Statistical costing studies often suffer from a small sample size, either too few years' data (indeed, a longer time period increases the chances of difficulties with such data) or too few firms or branch operations for a cross-section. Very small sample sizes (e.g., less than 15 observations) have

---

18. For example, see the discussions on railway costing in Canada reported in Vol. III of the Royal Commission on Transportation, *Royal Commission on Transportation*, vol. III, Ottawa, 1962. A summary of extensive cost investigations for the Canadian railways was reported by J. Stenason and R. A. Bandeen, "Transportation Costs and Their Implications: An Empirical Study of Railway Costs in Canada." For detailed studies across U.S. railroads see Meyer, et. al., *The Economics of Competition in the Transportation Industries*, appendices B & C, Association of American Rail-roads, *A Guide to Railroad Cost Analysis*, and Miller, "Economis of Scale in Railroading.

19. An exception is Meyer and Kraft, "The Evaluation of Statistical Costing Techniques as Applied in the Transportation Industry,' who explored the use of "principle components" analysis to assist in determining what railway accounts could be aggregated. This is a technique which constructs a minimum number of composite or index variables based on a combination of two or more of what would have been separate independent variables.

few degrees of freedom and therefore reduce the reliability of regressions as well as the ability to explore additional explanatory variables. As a result, studies will pool observations whenever possible. Situations where this practice may prove troublesome include: (1) including both large and small firms in the sample; (2) including firms or branch operations from different regions of the country; (3) pooling cross-section and time series data. Some studies have shown that small and large firms exhibit different cost-output behavior; hence it is inappropriate to include them in a single sample.[20] Data on U.S. Railways are sufficiently numerous to investigate whether or not there are significant differences among regions. Both Borts and Friedlaender found these differences exist.[21] The problem of pooling cross-section and time series data has not been given much attention but it is a potentially serious problems.[22] One is combining data with different sorts of bias and statistical problems (e.g., autocorrelation in time series and possible systematic differences across some firms). These problems are hidden within the sample, and there is the possibility of bias in the estimates of regression coefficients and their significance tests.[23]

3. Making Use of Statistical Cost Studies

There are two basic methods of using statistical results: (1) projection or prediction of a change in costs with a change in output based on regression results; and (2) analysis of deviations of particular observations from the norm or regression equation. These are discussed in turn.

---

20. For example, Griliches, "Cost Allocation in Railroad Regulation,' finds this among the U.S. railroads. There appears to be significant differences between small (local service) airlines and major trunklines (see Straszheim, *The International Airline Industry*, pp. 95-6 for a concise summary of findings; also Sarndal and Oum, "A Statistical Analysis for Airline Operating Costs.')

21. Borts, "The Estimation of Rail Cost Function," and Friedlaender, "The Social Costs of Regulating the Railroads,' p. 229.

22. An exception is Keeler, "Airline Regulation and Market Performance," p. 407 ff., who carefully investigates the problems of pooling time series with cross-sectional data in his analysis of airline costs.

23. Warner, "Cost Models, Measurement Errors and Economies of Scale in Trucking,' has explored some of the difficulties of combining cross-section with time series data.

(a) Predictions Based on Regression Results

The statistical result of primary interest is the estimated regression coefficient which expresses the change in costs with a change in output. This is the slope of the simple regression (one independent variable) line in Figure 2. Predictions can be made with or without the constant term, that is, one can make predictions based on the regression line itself (e.g., point A in Figure 2) or one could just employ the co-efficient between costs and output to predict from any initial cost-output position (e.g., prediction from point B in Figure 2). Figure 2 includes the confidence interval for predictions such as point A. Note that the reliability of predictions declines as one forecasts beyond the range of observed experience. Extrapolations must be made with caution.

Generally there is less interest in the constant term itself if one is estimating a *total* cost function. One might focus on the constant term specifically as an attempt to identify the "threshold" costs necessary before any output could be forthcoming.[24] Less faith is attached to the particular value for the intercept because it generally is some distance

Figure 2 Predictions Based on Regression Results

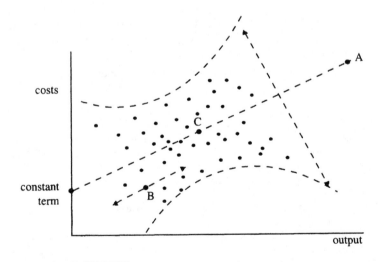

24. Cf.: Meyer, et. al., *The Economics of Competition in the Transportation Industries*, Chapter 3 and Meyer and Straszheim, *Pricing and Project Evaluation*, p. 37.

from any of the observations in the regression sample and the assumed mathematical relationship or functional form is much less certain outside the range of actual observations. Nevertheless, the presence of a significantly positive constant term in a "long run" total cost function implies that average costs will be declining with volume, i.e., marginal costs will be below average costs.

A different use of regression results for predictive purposes is the ICC's practice of estimating the "percent variable" of railway costs. In economics terms, this is the cost elasticity with respect to output expressed on a percentage basis.[25] A percent variable less than 100 indicates increasing returns or decreasing unit costs. The ICC multiplies its estimate (80%) times average total costs (or fully allocated costs) of railways involved in rate hearings. The result is the Commission's estimate of "out of pocket" or "variable" costs for the carrier.[26] There are serious problems which undermine the validity of the Commission's approach[27] but this does illustrate a use of statistical results for predictive purposes.

A difficulty with statistical costing is that the coefficients are only estimates rather than precise values. However, statistical theory predicts the magnitude of probable error in estimating the coefficient. For hypothesis testing (e.g., hypothesized presence of economies of scale) it is generally sufficient to confirm that an estimated coefficient is significantly different from some particular value. For example, an estimated cost elasticity significantly less than unity indicates a declining average cost.[28] In situa-

---

25. This can be calculated as incremental costs divided by total costs (or, on a per unit of output basis, as incremental costs divided by average costs). If costs (E) are related to output (Q) in the form: $E=a+bQ$, the percent variable (calculated at the average size of output Q of firms in the sample data) would be $\frac{b}{a+bQ} \times 100$

26. Since 1970 the term "out of pocket" has been replaced by "variable," Interstate Commerce Commission, *Rules to Govern the Assembling and Presenting of Cost Evidence.*

27. The criticisms include: the ICC's practice of deflating data by the size of firm (discussed earlier), excessive aggregation of data and use of a single output measure, small and large railways included in the sample, the percent variable is calculated for the average output of railways in the sample but applied in specific cases where output levels do not equal this average; see Griliches, "Cost Allocation in Railroad Regulation," also footnote 15.

28. The term "economies of scale" is often used to refer to any situation of decreasing average costs. Technically, this is incorrect. "Economies of scale" is a more restrictive term referring to actual increasing returns when all inputs are increased equiproportionately. The positive constant term in a linear long run cost function indicates the presence indivisible inputs not being increased as volume expands.

tions where one does make use of the specific estimate of the coefficient, the standard error of estimate of the coefficient enables confidence limits to be drawn. An illustration using the estimated regression coefficient for points B and C is in Figure 2. For larger sample sizes (30 or more) one is 95 percent confident that the actual change in costs with a change in output will lie within twice the standard error of the estimated coefficient. In practice, there is a tendency to use the estimated coefficient (perhaps to several decimal places) but to ignore or overlook a sizeable standard error. This is a dangerous situation because of the false sense of accuracy conveyed by the precise value of the regression coefficient. It could lead to decisions made without regard for the consequences of possible error in cost estimates.

An occasional practice which results in less confident predictions is that of "pyramiding." Costs of one category are estimated as a function of some other costs, e.g., maintenance expenses of buildings might be statistically estimated as a function of expenditures on building themselves. This may be a useful predictor in itself but if the "other costs" (e.g., the building costs) are then estimated as a function of output measures, then one is "pyramiding" estimates on top of estimates to predict the initial category and margins of error are being compounded in the process.

Accounting and engineering estimates of costs generally do not have a confidence interval attached to them but that is not to imply that such results are known with certainty; it is a weakness that one does not have a feel for how unreliable they can be. But it is generally true that statistical costing contains more sources of error and bias; therefore one would not employ statistical methods when a more direct or accurate method of costing were available.

(b) Examining Deviations from Regression Results

The analysis of deviations from the regression results (the "residuals") is a second basic method of utilizing statistical results. It is illustrated for a simple regression in Figure 3. This method of analysis is used primarily with cross-section data. One attempts to assess relative performance by the position of particular observations relative to the regression results. This is an improvement over merely comparing deviations from an average and should be more reliable. One examines and

Figure 3 Analysis of Deviations From Regression Results

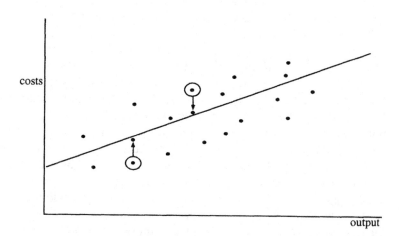

searches for explanations for the deviation of a particular observation from the regression results. Is it purely a random deviation which must be expected, or are there non-random explanations which should be incorporated? For example, repairs and maintenance expenses might be consistently higher for firms or plants which experience more severe winters. A frequent cause of differences in (average) cost levels among firms is unfavorable route characteristics, e.g., shorter stage lengths will make an equally efficient airline show higher unit costs. If other possible explanations are exhausted one might credit superior or poor performance to differing managerial skills.[29] Of course, if one only has one observation for a firm then there are weak grounds for drawing such conclusions. The particular result could be explained as a random occurrence such as a "bad year." If one finds consistent poor (or superior) performance in several different cost categories and/or consistent relative performance over several time periods, then one becomes more confident that some explanation is in order (which still may prove to be other than managerial efficiency). If analysis does reveal non-random

---

29. Gordon, "Airline Costs and Managerial Efficiency," examines the relative performance of U.S. trunk airlines by this approach. However, this sample size is very small so his results must be regarded as tenuous.

explanations which were not explicitly included in the regression estimates, then the regression co-efficients cannot be accepted at face value
because they will be biased estimates due to the omitted variables.

The possibility of differing managerial efficiency across an industry
has prompted some to argue for special statistical techniques to be
employed when estimating cost functions for regulatory purposes. Regulators should employ guidelines based on the most efficient observations; therefore they should establish cost-output estimates based on the
lowest observed cost-output experience rather than the "average" relationship that ordinary regression techniques yield.[30] This is an appealing
argument provided the expected variability in cost for any given level of
output is entirely explained by inefficiencies of different firms. The
validity of this assumption is questionable at least. But the issue points
out the problem that a cross-section of inefficient firms would yield an
excessively high prediction of cost levels. To adopt such cost estimates
for regulatory purposes (e.g., for determining minimum rate levels)
would sanction existing inefficiency.

IV. Statistical Costing and Decision-Making in Transportation

Statistical costing studies can be used for a variety of purposes by
both private firms and public agencies. One can employ statistical costing: (1) to predict expenditure levels for cost accounts in an enterprise;
(2) predict cost behavior with specific output decisions (this includes
both general tests for economies of scale as well as studies to measure
accurately the costs of specific outputs); and (3) as a basis for comparative evaluation of different firms or operations.

The degree of accuracy required varies with particular circumstances.
Predicting the level of expenditures for various cost accounts of an
enterprise generally is not so demanding of precision. For example, the
problem of heterogeneous outputs is not so important. A measure relating costs to aggregate activity levels may suffice to forecast expenditures for general financial purposes.

On the other hand, if the costing study is to assist firms or regulatory

---

30. Meyer and Kraft, "The Evaluation of Statistical Costing Techniques as Applied in the
Transportation Industry," pp. 321-2 examine this argument.

agencies in examining the prices for transporting specific commodities the accuracy required is greater. This is the purpose of many costing studies, particularly for railway costs.[31] If accurately and successfully pursued, costing studies yield a measure of those costs which are identifiable with, and vary with, a particular output. In situations of homogeneous outputs this procedure also identifies the level of fixed costs associated with that output (i.e., the constant term). For heterogeneous or multiple outputs the coefficients indicate the variable costs traceable to specific outputs. This then enables one to establish more accurately the untraceable costs common to the specific output in question. Note that statistical costing is *not* a method for eliminating or allocating untraceable costs. There must be measurable association between costs and outputs before a regression coefficient can emerge. For optimal pricing and output decisions, managers need knowledge about both traceable and untraceable variable costs.

On the subject of costing and pricing it should be pointed out that establishing the traceability and variability of costs on the supply side does not necessarily establish traceability to the demand side. Operating costs might be established precisely for, say, a vehicle mile but supply consists of round trip journeys. These costs are not traceable to the fronthaul and backhaul demands served. Therefore, measuring the variable costs with output measures does not, in itself, constitute a minimum below which rates are not permitted. The advances in costing techniques do not change this fundamental problem in transportation rate-making.

Many costing studies have been aimed primarily at establishing the presence or absence of economies of scale and not the cost-output coefficient per se. This may not require the degree of precision required for setting specific freight rates. In other circumstances estimates of economies of scale may need to be precise. Perhaps there are economies of scale only at low levels of output and/or diseconomies encountered beyond some size level. Identifying these critical output levels requires closer attention in formulating and estimating the cost function. Significant evidence of the presence of economies of scale might be taken as sufficient

---

31. The results need not be for revising or setting prices. In Canada, railways can be required to provide a service at a price which does not cover costs. If so, they are entitled to a subsidy to help offset this loss. Statistical costing is used extensively to establish costs which are then used in determining the amount of subsidy. The procedures are outlined in H. L. Purdy, *Transport Competition and Public Policy in Canada* (University of British Columbia Press: Vancouver) 1972, Chapter XIV.

grounds for relaxing regulations restricting mergers among firms in an industry. However, policy implications can be very sensitive to the results of studies of economies of scale. Suppose economies of scale are found to exist up to a point. It is important to know how large is the minimum efficient size plant relative to the market. Is a single monopoly firm all that the market justifies? Do economies of scale relative to the market result in only a few large firms (oligopoly)? Or, are economies of scale sufficiently small that the market can be served by a large number of competitors? These alternative possibilities imply very different implications for public policy regarding mergers and competition.

The third major use of statistical costing is as a basis for comparative evaluation of different firms or operations. Analysis of results reveals firms (or branches of a firm) which deviate from "normal" experience. These deviations are examined in an attempt to explain their relative performance, e.g., is it because of inherent advantages or disadvantages of particular operations or can the differences in observed performance be traced to superior or inferior management? Once, again, the degree of precision required will vary with particular circumstances.

Statistical costing is an important tool of analysis. The shortcoming of statistical costing for decision-making is that it requires some technical expertise both in preparation as well as in use. Even then, the results or answers are not exact. This imprecision leads some to doubt the usefulness of this method of costing. But if statistical costing is only used where other methods are not possible or are prohibitively expensive, the procedure sheds light on situations which are otherwise obscured. "In cost estimation, as in most decision problems, the objective is not to attain perfection but rather to attain the best possible estimates within the stipulated time and cost constraints."[32] The use of statistical estimates is not a substitute for judgment by managers of firms or government regulators, but information to assist them in decision-making. Surely an estimate with confidence intervals is more useful than a state of ignorance or false accuracy.

32, Meyer and Kraft, "The Evaluation of Statistical Costing Techniques as Applied in the Transportation Industry," p.313.

CHAPTER 9

DEVISING BUSINESS STRATEGY FOR RAILWAYS*

*Beesley, Michael E. and Peter B. Kettle**

I. Introduction

The study, of VicRail's system in Australia, was undertaken in 1980 for Victoria's Minister of Transport by Transmark's Economics Group.[†] Its findings were directed to a major Government review of railway policy. In consequence it dealt with questions of the chief information requirements, and their intended use by top management, for devising a strategy for future business development. In considering current financial performance, and the scope for improvement during the 1980s, the study had to address issues of traffic costing methods and pricing policy, the railway's future financial viability and its required level of public expenditure support. To draw conclusions for the business as a whole, this meant giving attention to all of the railway's activities, including ancillary functions such as property management and station trading.

* Reprinted from *Transportation,* Vol. 13, No. 1 (1986), pp. 53-83.

† Transmark is a subsidiary of the British Railways Board, acting as its international consultancy. The authors, who were respectively study director and manager, wish to thank Bernard Warner (an independent consultant), Richard Eccles (of Transmark) and Adrian Balkyn-Rackowe (of British Rail) for their valuable contributions, The study report, titled Rail Cost—Pricing Options, was released by the Minister in April 1981.

**London Business School, U.K.

The study was prompted by a search for means to reduce VicRail's large and growing financial losses. Estimates in its annual report put the proportion of working expenditures covered by customer receipts at 46% for the passenger, parcels and mails business and 71% for freight. VicRail is not atypical. Eight out of ten European systems recently reviewed generated customer revenues sufficient to cover between only 32 to 61% of total system costs (including capital outlays): few have subsidy payments confined to specific non-commercial purposes or specific aspects of operation (Gwilliam *et al.*, 1979). And in Australia the financial position of all seven systems has deteriorated since the mid-or late-1960s. All but Westrail have made significant losses on working expenditures alone from the early 1970s or before.[1] Even after proper recognition and compensation for "public service obligations," now under discussion, most of these systems would still be in substantial deficit.

The problem is certainly not confined to railways which are closely controlled by government or which effectively function as government departments. There is widespread pressure among government treasuries to reduce rail deficits, so the arguments pursued here are pertinent for many systems. But a move towards a break-even position should also be viewed as beneficial to railways in their current environment. In particular, greater freedom from government controls, and corresponding gains in managerial integrity and motivation requires on the one hand a shift in most cases to a far more specific from of subsidy management. On the other hand, this rests on being able to demonstrate that the railway system has a potentially profitable core of services, which can survive independently of a subsidized set. Without this, a stand-off relationship is unlikely to be feasible. So, in effect, assessing potential for financial improvement tests whether it is possible to remove external constraints of various forms on a railway's management.

In moving from typical loss situations now experienced, a railway business must spend a considerable time with negative total cash flow before it gets to break-even, and possibly makes a profit. Thus, we see reasons for a railway to develop plans, usually for the coming 5 to 10 years, covering all constituent parts of its business and setting out a fea-

---

1. Comparative data for the period 1965-75 are discussed in J.S. Dodgson. *The Economics of Australian Railway Deficits*. Economic Research Bulletin No. 7, University of Wollongong, Australia, 1978.

sible programme of action. Such plans must rest on decisions taken about which services the railway should withdraw from, which it should develop, and ways of dealing with the several markets collectively in such a manner as to minimize losses.

VicRail was an appropriate system to tackle because of its modest scale (6200 route km and 23000 staff in 1980) and a relatively uncomplicated rail network and service routings. A comprehensive treatment was feasible with the scale of resources available in a normal consultancy assignment. Ours spanned 6 months, consuming 15 months of professionals' time plus routine computational assistance

II. Principal tasks and information needs

1. Specification of sectors

The framework of analysis we advocate (see Fig. 1) depends foremost on distinguishing types of business, or markets, for a railway which can usefully be defined in revenue and cost terms. We call these "sectors." It follows that if subsidies are granted for social purposes, they will be related specifically to individual sectors, and will refer to the whole of that defined activity and its potential loss—not merely to, say, capital inputs or to elements of running expenses. This implies a significant change of subsidy-providers' behaviour away from general deficit financing. to adopt a business-specific subsidy system would be most unusual, if not unique, among Governments facing substantial railway deficits.

The distinction between sectors of the business to be reviewed is helped by a typically high concentration of revenue and activity. Thus, VicRail's annual reports itemize revenue for 30 classes of goods. For 1979/80, the top ranking 5 classes accounted for 56% of freight revenue, and the top 10 classes for 78%. Freight comprised 60% of total system revenue, while passenger services, mostly comprising urban operations, accounted for 28% of revenue.

Partitioning activity has also to recognize the different means of rail production which govern costs, as well as the nature of the outputs themselves, For example, large scale Australian movement of coal, grain, or logs usually entails a distinctive type of operation, with loading

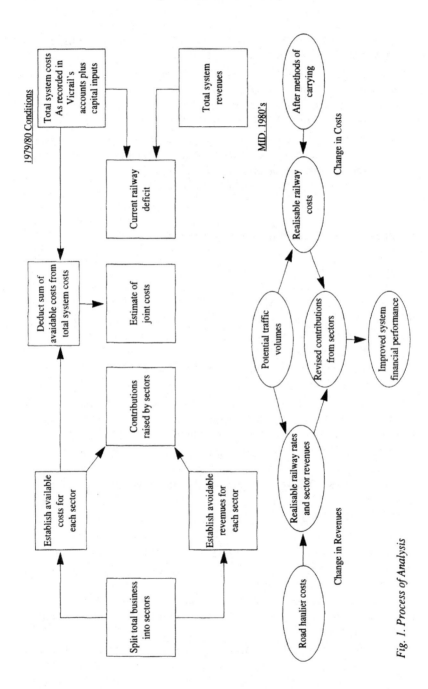

Fig. 1. Process of Analysis

and terminal facilities and frequently much of their own track. Among passengers, urban services call for highly specialized activity and there is usually a strong degree of geographical separation between different types of operation. All activity needs to be covered, so there will be some untidiness. But, in nearly all cases, it will turn out that distinctive production methods account for a large proportion of operating costs, whilst also being associated with distinctive markets. Whilst the customers will naturally be far more numerous than sectors, it is consideration of the sector which produces the basic information on business costs which, with market data, govern the terms on which the railway has to approach the task of contracting.

Decisions to improve financial performance involve, first, calculating the costs incurred in undertaking the business represented by each sector, and the corresponding revenues each generates. Deduction of costs from revenues defines the scale of positive contribution that each sector makes to any remaining costs of the rail system which are "joint" to all sectors, or combinations of them. Secondly, from a knowledge of present sector performance, one must consider possible improvements in cost-recovery, including potential modifications to amounts of traffic carried. On the costs side, the search for superior production processes needs to focus on improving operating practices as well as available equipment, and maybe extend to research and development activity. In parallel, pricing and hence revenue possibilities should be explored chiefly through analysis of customers' transport alternatives. The whole analysis needs to be geared to what it is feasible to change within the time scale deemed relevant.

We stress the importance of including the totality of railway activity for investigation. Unless this is done, there will be neglected costs. Uncovered activities represent voids into which unknown quantities of cost tend to be relegated. Moreover, a constant overview of total activity is required since what needs to be done in respect of any particular sector depends on what can be achieved for others. For example, a decision to reduce carryings of a particular product, or to withdraw from the business, needs to be reviewed in the light of what changes may be required elsewhere in the system, so that total costs can still be covered. There is, therefore, a dual requirement: to compare present and potential revenues and costs for the different sectors and to aggregate results over the whole organization. The need to aggregate results means that the number of separate sectors it is feasible to distinguish for analysis is necessarily quite limited. As seen later, we distinguished 20 main sectors in our study of VicRail's system.

2. Traffic costing

Identifying relevant costs, and their measurement, depends on the purposes to which the information is to be put. Improving finances means defining costs to match possible actions—planned changes to output levels, up or down, as well as changed ways of producing particular outputs. Costs imply the existence of options to refuse potential business or to disengage from existing services for customers. They are therefore to be viewed as potentially avoidable outlays associated with feasible decisions. To be useful for decisions affecting customers, the outlays must refer to specific periods for which contracts are negotiated, which may be long or short term.

It follows that there is no one "correct" set of costs which are attributable to the respective sectors. What are to count as relevant outlays will depend fundamentally on the nature and quantity of the contemplated change in traffic levels, and the associated length of commitment to carry the traffic. Failure to recognize this can cause much confusion!

Thus, recent estimates of costs associated with VicRail's task of carrying grain have produced the following statements; In VicRail's grain business (a) "Customer revenues cover 73 to 80% of costs," (b) "Customer revenues cover 54% of costs," (c) "Customer revenues cover well over 100% of costs." Statements (a) and (b) come from earlier Transmark work[2] and (c) is the output of cost modeling work done by VicRail's own planning and marketing staff. To most readers, this would indicate inconsistency, but actually each statement is quite defensible. They refer respectively to three types of cost and revenue changes: those associated with VicRail withdrawing altogether from the grain business; those associated with discontinuing the movement of peak loads offered, during the silo overflow period, equivalent to some 20% of VicRail's usual output; and those associated with providing single

---

2. Reported in Transmark, *The Movement of Grain by VicRail: An Assessment of Costs in Relation to Charges*, April 1980. Study for Victoria's Minister of Transport, to assist with a review of rail's grain rates.

extra trains to move grain.

All three calculations are potentially relevant in a negotiation with a customer, being the Australian Wheat Board in the grain case cited. Thus, the organization must aim to be better off with a client's business than without it (calculation a); there may be at any one time particular modifications of the contract which are desirable (calculation b, which indicated the need for early attention to the peak); and one might want to be in a position to accept or refuse specific movements (calculation c).

These examples underline three simple, fundamental points. Costs are measurable, and only measurable, with respect to a specified output change; the decision to change output must always simultaneously involve a potential change to revenues; and the final choice among options will, in principle, involve consideration of more than one estimate of cost.

Whilst the notion of avoidability may seem straightforward enough, one implication is that a traffic's costs depend critically on the actual scope for adjustment within the system following its hypothesized loss or diminution. Identifying what in practical circumstances can be done to reduce the resources used in catering for all other traffics which are assumed to remain requires rigorous investigation. It includes, for instance, possible changes in total administrative staff and track requirements. Traffic in a given sector may occupy so much of a network that, in the event of total withdrawal, it would pay to close a number of lines. If so, the costs associated with keeping these lines are avoidable for that sector. Alternative yields from the assets released are relevant too. However, in shrinking the railway, some of the remaining traffic will be likely to find itself bereft of track. For it the least cost means of maintaining deliveries has to be computed, which is an offset to the putative saving from withdrawal of the sector in question.

Calculation of avoidable costs for an existing business involves an iterative, subtractive process. One asks how far costs can be reduced by eliminating (or scaling down) a particular class of traffic. This exercise is repeated for each class of traffic in turn, over the entire business. A traffic's cost is the difference between total outlays now required to operate the whole system and those required for its contemplated scale of carryings. All other rail services are to be assumed constant in amount and quality in the comparison. Because of the need to sum across the whole business a time horizon for establishing cost avoidability must, when defined, be consistent between all sectors.

The same approach applies to choices about increasing, as well as reducing, existing outputs, including entry into new markets. In present railway circumstances, though, consideration of adding new markets will be far less important than testing the existing ones.

Contrary to traditional railway costing practices, this approach is strongly against seeking to allocate an observed set of costs, themselves exhaustive of all outlays, to classes of traffic. Moreover, the costs to be entered are strictly *ex ante*, though past expenditures are generally a very useful source of evidence about what costs to expect. Because future costs are in question, issues of future input prices and productivity arise. Principal opportunities to substitute new technology, technical practices, etc. must be incorporated with the assessment of potential.

In measuring costs, there are three basic requirements; that they be relevant; be correctly valued; and that their structure be known. Discussion so far has been mainly about *relevance*: costs can only be measured with respect to a specific output change which must reflect potential decisions about changing one's business. Our approach does not start with categories of "long-term" and "short-term" costs, or "fixed" and "variable" costs. We ask, instead, what consequences flow from a specific type of decision involving choice among options. We suggest that, for most rail systems, the aim should be to describe the cost implications of three output changes: a movement to zero from the present total level of a traffic; a major change in its output, say around 20 to 30% of its total level; and a small change, represented by the addition or subtraction of a smaller customer.

When relevance has been settled, costs must be *valued*. The appropriate concept is the opportunities foregone in using resources to match the specified output change. This is often simply thought of as the price which is paid to hire factors of production—i.e. directly observable financial outgoings. Yet the concept is far wider than this. It can, for instance, refer to what could be realized in selling assets which would be made redundant if a sector's business were discontinued, or refer to revenues foregone when a decision is made to switch resources from one use to another. There will often be a variety of opportunities foregone by a production decision. The appropriate cost is represented by the most valuable course of action precluded (i.e., the greatest sacrifice).

Thus, for locomotives associated with a particular traffic, cost is

given by the most valuable of three options: sale to other railways second-hand; use on one's own system for other traffics (e.g. working the
whole fleet less intensively, or catering for extra demand); and scrap-
ping. If capacity constraints apply, say on track, a major consideration
will be the potential earnings of other traffics forced out, which might
give a better return on the resources employed. This is, for example, an
issue in serving Australian grain during the harvesting season. In dealing with a total set of railway activities, it will be found that values
chiefly depend on opportunities outside the rail business and hence on
what is viewed to be rail's legitimate scope of action.

Finally, there is the question of the *structure* of costs—i.e. how production costs behave with changes in output levels of different sectors.
This has to be related to output variation within the limits of interest,
and so requires that issues of relevance and valuation are already settled.
Variation in cost per unit of output will mostly depend on whether technically indivisible items are present. Thus, if one chooses to use high
rather than low strength rail track there will be levels of production at
which total operating costs, per unit output, will be smaller because
other—more divisible—items can be combined with it in service production. Thus, there may be savings to be gained from being able to run
longer and heavier trains over routes, manifest in crew costs for
instance. But these savings can be realized only if one does produce the
required level of output.

The anticipated structure of costs therefore presents a problem of
dealing with risk, implying a trade-off between risk acceptance and
prospective financial return in contracting with customers. The principal
risks are that output will vary more than anticipated around a mean,
either up or down, and second that output will not be big enough and
thus fail to realize the promised reduction in unit costs. With big customers, one cannot rely on the law of large numbers to minimize the former risk. However, if production were guaranteed at the looked-for
level, higher margins could be achieved. A knowledge of cost structure
is thus required for making the necessary judgements in negotiating contracts, involving such devices as guaranteed take-offs, and contingent
ways of coping with unexpectedly high demands.

Unfortunately, the literature—economic or other—on costs is not particularly illuminating for problems of strategy. Issues of cost structure
often preoccupy to the false exclusion of relevance and value. Certainly

for our problem of deficit reduction, relevance will have to take precedence. Also "fixed" and "variable" costs, which describe elements in structure (the "fixed" lumpy input and the factors which have to be combined with it), are unfortunately very often associated with the avoidable/unavoidable distinction. "Fixed" tends to become synonymous with "unavoidable" costs, due to a failure to consider potential adjustments to throughput capacity in line with changes to traffic volumes. Similarly, in drawing on the accounting tradition, it is easy to confuse budgetary procedures, concerned with accountability and commitment, with the problem of illuminating contingent decisions.

3. The aggregation problem and pricing

The sum of the costs calculated for separate sectors is unlikely to equal the total outlays associated with all of a railway's activity, though we set out to be comprehensive. When summing over the sectors, two possibilities of systematic deviation from total recorded outlays arise, namely an *under*-exhaustion and an *over*-exhaustion. The most usual is the first, denoting the presence of joint costs between sectors. These arise from different traffics sharing the same resources or equipment such as locos, rolling stock or trackwork, whereby advantage is taken of the possibility of lowering unit output costs by combining production of two or more types of service.

In contrast, over-exhaustion of total outlays denotes the likelihood that parts of the rail system are under capacity strains. that is, when a given sector is withdrawn, costs for other sectors are less, for instance because traffic congestion is relieved. Also, the prices to be paid for resource inputs may be a function of aggregate railway output. Thus, unit labour costs might rise because of overtime payments for drivers produced by the additional demands of seasonal traffics. Normally, however, in Western Railways one expects joint costs to predominate over such effects.

For the system being studied, the various sources of resulting under- or over-exhaustion should be identified in respect of different cost categories. This is necessary because no independent check is available on the magnitude of divergences thrown up by the calculations. They have to be justified by reference to reasoned argument about why joint, or congestion costs are to be expected. Thus, if joint costs arise for trackwork they may reflect engineering practices which do not properly recognize such determinants of track wear as the frequency and weight of trains.

There are similar possibilities on the revenue side. Typically, sector calculations will tend to show an over-exhaustion of total revenues. This is due to effects of withdrawal of a particular sector for any connecting services—e.g. suburban passenger services which feed inter-city services. But sectors can also have important competitive features, where by the loss of one service has a revenue generation impact on another, e.g fast "skip-stop" commuting services and those stopping at all stations, and highly discretionary services such as tourism.

The presence of joint costs, and their expected predominance over congestion effects for most systems, has important implications for pricing. Since these costs have to be covered for the system to be viable, the traffics *together* must raise at least sufficient extra revenue (over the sum of their individual costs) to do this between them. We stress that how this sum is to be raised has nothing logically to do with the relative scale of the various sectors and supposed "shares" in the joint costs, which cannot be allocation between them. Elimination of a major traffic because it only exceeds its avoidable costs by a very small margin would nonetheless result in a *worse* financial outcome.

Avoidable cost exercises indicate the minimum revenues which particular traffics must generate to survive. This sets lower limits to their respective prices. Having discarded sectors failing to meet their avoidable costs, one can then seek ways of raising the necessary total contribution to meet the system's joint costs. Whether this is possible depends on what the respective markets will yield, which in turn will largely depend on customers' alternatives, most notably road haulage. Since rail markets differ widely, it is to be expected that, as a result of this search to cover costs and make profits, there will be substantial differences in the relation of charges set to avoidable costs in each sector.

For a given system, the more detail in which the outputs are specified for investigation the greater the occurrence of joint costs will tend to be. The approach we have outlined should be used to examine the viability of different *combinations* of sectors, as well as of individual sectors, since joint costs have to be covered at different levels of aggregation within the business. In principle, one wishes to test for as many combinations as there are sets of joint costs.

III. An application to VicRail, Australia

VicRail has experienced rapidly rising deficits since the late-1960s, with receipts from users covering only 59% of total working expenses in 1979-80. Capital expenditure that year amounted to A$ 54 million, financed directly by government, giving a total subvention of A$ 215 million or A$ 9400 per staff member. Victoria's Ministry of Transport decides on revisions to published tariffs and fare scales (though these serve serve as maxima, and most freight business is done on lower negotiated rates); it also sanctions proposals to close lines or withdraw services. Legislation introduced in 1981, however, meant the lifting of VicRail's common carrier obligation. It permits road hauliers to compete freely with VicRail, throughout the State, for all but five bulk commodities; these also may be freed in due course at the discretion of the Minister. Financially, the railway has, nevertheless, continued to function as a government department, with customer revenues being channeled directly to the Treasury.

Since the early-1970s, VicRail's Board has sought a clearer definition of its supposed public service obligations and specific compensation for carrying them out. Its annual reports took up the philosophy of specific subsidies following the 1972 Bland Report into State transport policy (Bland, 1972). More recently, in evidence to the Lonie Inquiry (1980), VicRail has argued for subsidy via a major infrastructure grant, principally to meet trackwork costs, in order to help it compete "more fairly" with growing road haulage competition. However, progress in this whole area has been very show. Subsidy continues to be paid on a global basis, though VicRail monitors the relation between user payments and government's "revenue supplement" in meeting the costs allocated to each of six categories of service (four for passenger/parcels activity and two for freight).

1. Process of analysis

The process followed, and the main links between tasks, is represented by the flow chart in Figure 1. The top half deals with base year (1979/80) conditions, starting with sector specification. Sectors were assessed initially in relation to existing traffic tasks and charges, and the existing technology and operating practices. Each sector's respective avoidable costs were first calculated and their sum then compared against an independently arrived at estimate of total outlays entailed in maintaining current output levels of the whole system. This revealed that joint costs do exist for VicRail on a significant scale. By making estimates for different categories of cost-such as crews and locomotives—the compositions of jointness by type of expenditure was also assessed. Next, the revenues earned by each sector were measured. Comparison with respective avoidable costs indicated how far each contributed—or fell short of contributing—to the identified joint costs of system operation. The net impact of their contributions, when viewed in relation to joint costs, is revealed in the current system deficit. (There were found to be no major interactions between sectors on the revenue side.)

Attention was then turned to prospects for improvement by the mid-1980s. Since policy options for passengers were being debated by government, it was thought most useful to focus on the potential for freight activity. This work is represented in the lower half of the chart. Possible changes to rail pricing and productivity were considered in relation to a changed set of traffic tasks, taken to be representative of likely future conditions.

On the costs side, the potential for improving operating practices was examined, in particular methods of train operation and traffic handling. This is an area in which a high pay-off could be expected and was not dependent on much additional investment. The changes postulated to operations themselves had an effect on the nature of the traffic tasks to be costed. Consequent change to sectors' avoidable costs, and also impacts on system joint costs, were calculated—assuming, for purposes of analysis, unchanged operation of the passenger and ancillary businesses. On the revenue side, analysis of freight pricing possibilities was made chiefly by reference to customers' options to use road haulage services. Estimates were made of the likely future level of haulier charges for the relevant commodities, and judgements then made about the rail rates which could be sustained in competition for the various freight sectors, by typical lengths of haul. By setting each sector's potential revenue against its avoidable cost, revised contributions were calculated. These demonstrated the extent of financial improvement, for the total business, which the reforms could bring about. Finally, the analysis enabled exploration of the effects of possible decisions to withdraw from unremunerative sectors and of agreements that might be reached on specific subsidy support.

We now discuss what was carried out to generate the required information, and its use in devising a strategy to contain, and reduce, losses for VicRail.

2. Investigation of present performance

(1) Partitioning the business

A total of 20 sectors were distinguished as being most relevant to the railway's market decisions, this was done chiefly by similarity of production methods. Thus, the carriage of grain on VicRail entails a distinct operation, with specialized loading and discharge facilities, much of its own track and a specially prepared train plan for the three month peak. General merchandise (less than car load lots) is dealt with through a set of over 30 freight centers, whilst container traffic has its own specialized equipment and organization (see Figs. 2 and 3).

Eleven categories of freight were distinguished in this way, accounting for 79% of total tonne-kilometers, and 77% of freight revenue in 1979/80, as listed in Table 1. The remaining traffic was put in a residual category, chiefly comprising motor vehicles, chemicals, rice, stone, gyp-

Fig. 2. Road Haulage Costs in Mid-1980s and Rail Rates at 1979-80 Group A commodities

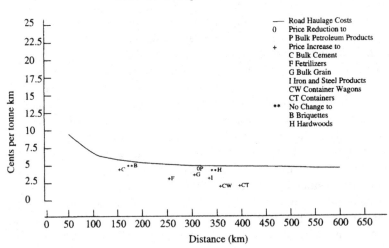

Fig. 3. Road Haulage Costs in Mid-1980s and Rail Rates at 1979-80 Group B commodities

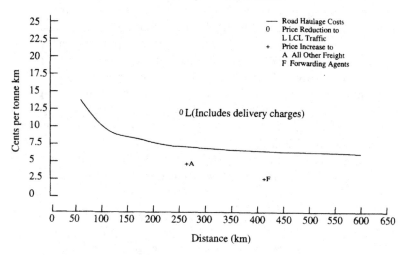

Table 1 . Freight Sectors

1979/80 data	Million tonne-kilometres	% of total	Revenue A$ million	% of total
Bulk grain	1500	38.6	50.5	37.1
Containers	369	9.5	6.5	4.8
Iron and steel products	223	5.7	5.5	4.0
Container wagons	208	5.3	3.6	2.6
Fertilizers	159	4.1	4.4	3.2
Forwarding agents	135	3.5	2.6	1.9
Coal Briquettes	132	3.4	6.2	4.6
L.C.L. traffic*	121	3.1	15.0	11.0
Bulk cement	91	2.3	3.9	2.9
Bulk petroleum products	89	2.3	3.7	2.7
Hardwood	50	1.3	1.9	1.4
All other freight	811	20.9	32.4	23.8
Totals	3888	100	136.2	100

* Less than car load.

sum, and sand. Grain (of which most is wheat) has traditionally been by far the major product, although the year taken had a record harvest.

Within passengers, suburban movement has a particular mode of traction and geographic area (Metropolitan Melbourne) and a high service frequency. For country services, we distinguished predominantly daily commuter travel between Melbourne and outside towns (termed "country commuter") from other services. Country commuters are provided with only a skeleton off-peak service. Finally,there are daily long-distance services from Melbourne to Sydney and Adelaide, operating with high grade coaching stock. Suburban carryings are by far the largest of these, as shown in Table 2.

There remained various ancillary activities, together comprising 13% of VicRail's total earnings, which were categorized as shown in Table 3.

Table 2. Passenger Sectors

1979/80 data	Million passenger kms	% of total	Average Journey length (km)	Revenue A$ million	% of total
Suburban	1480	70.4	16	44.9	70.2
Country	400	19.0	128	10.9	17.1
Country comuter	35	1.7	59	2.1	3.3
Inter-State	187	8.9	374	6.0	9.4
Totals	2102	100	22	63.9	100

Table 3 . Ancillary Sectors

1979/80 data	Revenue(A$ million)	% of total
Parcels and mails	9.4	32.1
Station trading and catering	7.0	23.9
Property rentals and advertsing	5.4	18.4
Miscellaneous activities*	7.5	25.6
Totals	29.3	100

*consist principally of the Mt. Buiffalo Chalet, a holiday concern, and contract work for related organisations

(2) Sector Costs and Testing for Jointness

We focussed on the most fundamental calculations, those relating to potential withdrawal from a sector. Except for *ad hoc* studies of hardwood and livestock traffics, and our own earlier investigation of grain, the financial consequences on VicRail as a whole of possible policies to disengage entirely from such sectors had not previously been tested. It was recognized that various modifications are likely to be desirable to contracts or conditions of carriage for a business sector, as with the peak period for grain carriage. However, we were unable, within available time, to make the calculations associated with less-than-total output changes.

Since our assessments involved a prospectively permanent change in output, the costs relate to outlays that could be avoided when all possible adjustments to the loss of a given traffic have been worked through. This includes desired changes to manning levels, locomotive fleets, number of stations, scale of technical support services, and so forth. This aim, of establishing the likely change in finances when the new equilibrium is reached, raises the question of changes in revenues and outlays over time—i.e. the railway's prospective cash flow. We adopted an equivalent of discounted cash flow calculations for this, as enlarged on below. Capital as well as operating expenditures were included. Whilst the former are funded by the State Treasury, they inevitably enter decisions on business development and bear directly on the pricing policy for VicRail.

To establish the relevant outlays, a review was made of all items of expenditure associated with the railway's operation, as reported in its annual accounts and in supporting statements of capital expenditures. We sought to identify all items which, in principle, could be affected to a significant degree by the withdrawal of any business sector.

In all cases, withdrawal would enable a reduction in levels of train movement, mainly affecting outlays for provision and operation of motive power, rolling stock and train crews. Use is also made of road transport for collection and delivery of general merchandise, and to supplement rail for certain commodities in peak periods. Feeder bus services are also run. Second, some reduction in administrative and technical back-up services could also be expected upon a sector's withdrawal. Third, reduced traffic flows would mean less use of freight yards, trackwork, ancillary infrastructure and stations, affecting expenditure on maintenance and renewal work. Finally, specific to "dedicated" lines, being those we deemed would close without a particular traffic, is the possibility of selling off or leasing redundant assets—including elements of track, land and buildings. This represents revenue gained from withdrawal, to be added to the estimated cost savings from line closure.

Measurement of operating costs was based on analysis of working expenditures incurred during the 1979/80 year. These were taken as representative of what would *continue* to be spent in future years, if current methods of running the railway, its technology and the traffic tasks themselves were to remain unchanged. In a particular year external factors might have made prevailing conditions unusual, for instance highly adverse weather holding back scheduled track maintenance work. It was found that standardizing for such factors was not required for 1979/80.

Capital (once-and-for-all) costs had to be regarded as a stream of future outlays required to sustain particular sectors. To present these in a form directly comparable with estimates of operating costs, the time stream calculated was discounted using a suitably derived cost of finance. The capital costs so arrived at are therefore the equivalent annuity of the sum of discounted future outlays. Thus, taking wagons, we assessed what future outlays would be required to maintain each sector's output at its recorded 1979/80 level. This time stream of outlays, made for a 30-year period, reflected the existing age of the relevant wagon fleets and recognized that replacement will often not be on a like-for-like basis. We then found the amount which, if incurred each year in perpetuity, would be equivalent to the present value sum obtained.

To aid subsequent investigation, we adopted a basic distinction for costing and reporting between single commodity and mixed-load freight trains. This reflected our expectation about the main influences on train running costs, and the need to make the costing work responsive to ideas for change in operating practice. To help test hypotheses on jointness for particular types of cost also, the findings were provided in respect of six major expenditure categories—train running, bus operations, trackwork, station operations, support services and assets on dedicated lines. A comparison of total system outlays, of A\$ 492 a year, with the sum of sector costs indicated the presence of substantial joint costs. These totalled A\$ 92 million a year of 19% of system outlays. By far the most important—as may be expected—concern jointness in permanent way (A$ 29 million), signalling and communications (A$ 13 million) and administrative and technical support services (A$ 10 million). Together these account for over half the total jointness found. The evidence given of under exhaustion of system outlays for various elements of cost confirmed the view of VicRail operating staff that congestion is not serious, though it does arise on some parts of the network, most notably during the peak months of grain carriage.

Nonetheless, as Fig. 4 shows, most of the principal cost elements have a high degree of avoidability. And whilst major jointness was found in trackwork and support services, it is smaller than usually thought. Indeed, they are usually treated as virtually unaffected by traffic changes, mostly because it is assumed that capacity cannot be adjusted in response[3]. Potential capacity reduction was certainly important in our study, reflecting the possibility of shutting down some lines entirely

Fig. 4. Degree of Jointness for Main Cost Elements (1979-1980 Conditions)

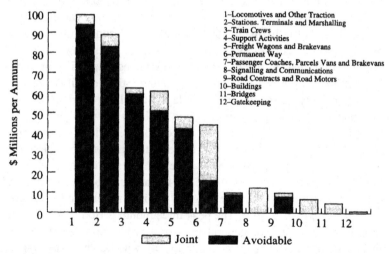

3. See, for instance, *Measuring Cost and Profitability in British Rail* (British Railways Board, London, February 1978). This notes that track and signalling costs are seen not to vary much in response to traffic volume changes within existing line capacity. but it does not deal with the contrary point. namely that the volume changes in traffic being costed are often large enough to permit substantial reductions in capacity - without, that is to say, entailing major works to simplify track layout, signalling arrangements, etc.

upon sector withdrawal, and also potential for reducing the number of tracks required elsewhere on routes in the network. Most notably, the withdrawal of grain would imply the closure of as much as 1800km of track (20% of the system total) on which it predominates or is the sole user. Alternative means for carrying the small volumes of remaining traffic were found to be considerably less expensive than keeping these lines open. Other lines were found to be "dedicated" in a similar manner to hardwood, suburban and country passenger services—as shown on Fig. 5.

By making a separate assessment of total outlays required to operate the existing system, and analyzing the composition of system costs, we sought to satisfy ourselves that the apparent residual of unaccounted-for costs were truly joint between the sectors, and were not simply the result of errors in estimating avoidability which rested extensively on sampling. We considered the findings against our expectations of how the presence of jointness is likely to vary as between different elements of cost, and produced reasons to explain the degree of jointness revealed. VicRail accounts gave a control on working expenditure for the system as a whole and also, by manipulation of the data, a control on individual cost elements. No control totals existed for capital costs, however.

Some of the reasons established for the jointness identified are therefore worth noting. for instance, in train running, that identified for traction was chiefly associated with haulage of railway engineering and other materials, and light running (with no load) between servicing or repair depots and stations, as established from records of train performance. That for train crews reflects these factors plus some slack in rosters. For wagons, jointness mostly arises as a result of fluctuations in carrying requirements during the year—in particular between grain and other users of general purpose wagons (mainly super-phosphate, coal briquettes, and LCL traffic). The peak three month period in grain carrying overlaps a trough in general industrial production; grain can use much slack then. So when grain is notionally withdrawn, many wagons which grain uses remain. For recent conditions, we found that some 40% of the system's general purpose wagons would be redundant if grain traffic were abandoned, yet in terms of commodity volumes hauled grain represents as much as 75% or more of their usage.

Estimates of sectors' permanent way maintenance and renewal costs were derived from an available regression model of total tonne-kilome-

Fig. 5. Victorian Railways network

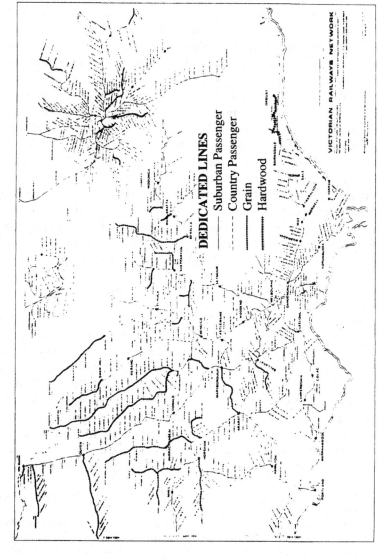

trage. The estimates had a significant constant term, indicating unexplained costs; these showed up in the aggregation exercise as sizeable unaccounted for outlays connected with track, confirming that joint costs are present. In reviewing these and other sources of jointness, we find most of that identified arises from choice of production method (i.e. economic convenience) rather than, as is often supposed, from strict technical necessity; around 70% of jointness in permanent way costs, for instance, is of this type.

Finally, we must stress the importance for cost measurement of gaining a thorough understanding of how the system actually functions,and the technical practices adopted. This point is illustrated in our subsequent review of rather different findings obtained from ourselves by the Australian Railway Research and Development Organization (ARRDO) for cost-recovery, and contributions generated, by major sectors of VicRail's business.[4] Within freight activity, it was established that different accounts of system operation, particularly the supposed incidence of single as against mixed-load movement, provided a major explanation of the differences between us. This accounted for one quarter of the A\$ 36 million discrepancy in findings on sector contributions.[5]

(3) Sector Revenues and Contributions to Joint Costs

Analogously to costs, estimates were made of customer receipts which would be lost upon a sector's withdrawal. This was straightforward for freight and ancillary activities. In freight, receipts were recorded for a detailed commodity breakdown (120 different classes), distinguishing less-than-wagon-load consignments in each class. However, for passengers there was both interaction between the sectors, as well as basic data problems, to consider. Within the metropolitan area jointness area arises between country and suburban sector services. In various cases journeys could be made by either, since some country trains make stops at a number of suburban stations, However, owing to comparative-

---

4. Transmark, *Assessments of Revenue—Cost Relationships in VicRail.* A review prepared for VicRail management. May 1981 (confidential).

5. The discrepancy quoted was after the two sets of results had been standardized for differences in the precise way the freight business was divided up for analysis (affecting sector content), for the use of data for 1978/79 conditions (by ARRDO) rather than for 1979/80 conditions(by Transmark), and after adjustments were made to allow for different treatments of capital outlays.

ly low frequency of stopping country services, the degree of jointness was judged very small.

Cases of service complementarity, giving rise to possible revenue losses beyond a particular sector, were present for inter-state and country services which are fed by suburban trains, The degree of interaction was, however, found to be generally small. Thus, the loss of suburban sector revenue upon withdrawal of inter-state services would add, at most, 4% to the receipts lost from interstate trains themselves. Unfortunately, the absence of origin—destination data precluded such measurement for country services. So, in the event, no complementarity effects were included in the sector revenue estimates.

The results were expressed as cost-recovery rates (CRR) for the twenty sectors, indicating the proportion of costs entailed in service provision which are met from user payments. All four passenger sectors were shown to have CRRs below 50%. Inter-state and suburban services, at 43 and 42% respectively, were doing considerably better than country services (24%) and country commuter services (14%). The absolute shortfalls on avoidable costs were greatest by far for the suburban sector (A$ 63 million), and smallest for the low volume country commuter and inter-state sectors (A$ 13 million and 8 million respectively).

Details of findings for the freight and ancillary sectors are confidential. But freight performance in covering avoidable cost was generally much better than for passengers, with most sectors having a CRR in the 60-100% range. Only one made a positive contribution to the system's joint costs. Shortfalls for the other freight sectors totalled A$ 57 million, compared with that of A$ 119 million for passenger sectors. Ancillary sectors generally achieved CRRs well over 100%, with one producing a shortfall on avoidable cost. Thus, only four of all twenty sectors were found to be making positive contributions to joint costs—all being modest.

Finally, from comparison of total revenues and costs, the system deficit was revealed to be running at A$ 262 million a year. The overall position may be summarized thus for 1979/80 conditions (Table 4).

Table 4.

	A$ million per annum
Sum of sectors' avoidable costs	399.7
System joint costs	92.3
Total system costs	492.0
Total system revenues	229.5
Overall deficit	262.5

3. Market prospects and potential performance

(1) Traffic Prospects

It was necessary to consider traffic tasks which were representative of likely market conditions 5-8 years ahead. The forecasts had to stand for a set of average expectations then, recognizing that there may be substantial year-to-year fluctuations in some sectors, most notably for grain. What levels of traffic could rail attain in view of industrial production prospects, and likely mode shares?

We had to do this in the absence of any available medium or long-term statements. Three main sources were used:

 – Information on how rail's share of traffic carryings has been changing over the last 15 years, generally showing modest to substantial reductions in market share, concurrent with developing road competition.
 – Against this background, we considered output prospects in particular industries and likely future movements in GDP.
 – A set of new business opportunities identified by VicRail's commercial managers.

As a result, we foresaw the following *potential* tasks, with a substantially smaller grain task than in the record year of 1979/80, but considerable growth in a number of other sectors.

Its was recognized that to retain or attract certain traffics, it might be necessary for rail to reduce some rates charged, because of de-regulation measures then afoot and the likelihood of productivity improvements for road hauliers. In other sectors, rail might be able to raise its rates in real terms, or wish to reject attainable traffic for reasons of high cost operation—as now examined.

Table 5. Potential Freight Tasks in the Made Mid-1980s.

Sector	Net tonne Kmmillions	% Change on 1979/80 levels
Bulk grain	1071	-29
Containers	428	+16
Iron and steel products	335	+50
Container wagons	274	+32
Forwarding agents	193	+43
Fertilizers	185	+16
Bulk cement	151	+66
Coal Briquettes	144	+ 9
Bulk petroleum products	101	+13
LCL traffic	60	-50
hardwood	44	-12
All other freight	985	+21
Totals	3971	+ 2

(2) Scope for Operating Improvements

We concentrated on the scope for introducing more "block" train working, with trains comprised of blocks of five or more wagons, each block conveying traffic between a particular origin and destination. This idea was strongly supported by our earlier findings, a close association being found between train running cost per tonne-kilometer shifted and the proportion of a sector's traffic dealt with in point-to-point train loads.

To give customers a minimum of once a week delivery or collection service, origin/destination flows needed to amount to 5000 tonnes or more a year. Any traffic smaller than this would be discarded. The hoped-for benefits stem from expected use of fewer terminals, less frequent working between sidings and yards and effects for rolling stock utilization. Rejecting the small flows implies a reduction in some inherently high cost traffic, such as fertilizers—with a wide dispersal of rail destination points. Second, lower operating costs would tend to be realized for most of the surviving traffic.

We assessed that this meant an overall cut of 13% in potential tonne kms, implying an 11% smaller total freight task than in 1979/80. For most sectors, the cut in potential volumes was modest. But there were major effects on hardwood, bulk petroleum products, the residual freight category and fertilizers. Surviving volumes represented the future freight tasks for costing and price assessments.

The realizable cost savings for these traffics depend largely on the size distribution of the various flows. The heavier flows, of 40000 tonnes per annum and over, were considered large enough to realize the benefits—in actual movement costs—of existing single commodity train working (although greater terminal costs would usually be entailed for mixed loads). The remainder was costed, on average, at the same rate per tonne-kilometer as that of existing mixed commodity trains. These estimates rested on a number of broad judgements, reflecting operators' experience. The judgements used need testing with reference to a fully specified train plan, though sensitivity tests showed that they do indicate the order-of-magnitude improvement to be expected. Calculations were also made for changes to other costs, including trackwork, support services, road contracts and the extent of line dedication.

Working in 1979/80 price levels, we found that in real terms the reduction in the sum of freight sectors' avoidable costs would amount to 26% per tonne-kilometers, or some A$ 67 million a year in respect of the 11% smaller total task. In addition, some change will occur to the joint costs of system operation, since traffics that share the same infrastructure and equipment are being varied in combination. Jointness is also affected by changes in the way the task is assumed to be performed. A reduction in these costs of 8% (i.e., A$ 7 million per annum) was estimated. As a result, the proportion of jointness within system costs rose a little, to just over 20%. Overall, then, total costs were expected to fall by around A$ 74 million per annum by the mid-1980s, or by 15%, assuming unchanged passenger and ancillary businesses.

(3) Pricing Possibilities

We investigated what combination of rates for sector traffics could be sustained in competition, without substantial risk of their loss to other modes. By establishing revenue potential, this assisted review of the long-term viability of sectors, and decisions on whether to develop particular markets or withdraw from them should there be little prospect of covering future costs. The findings would also help management set price and revenue targets for those responsible for individual sector performance, and help identify the ceiling rates that major customers would be prepared to pay, this being essential information for negotiating their contracts.

As for most railways, the limits on attainable freight revenue for VicRail are most strongly influenced by road haulage competition. This provides the chief option to rail for customers to move their goods, though shipping is also important for certain products. Our approach called for much more emphasis on price discrimination between products and customers than previously in VicRail. Thus, rates for its major sector—grain—had been the outcome of a series of *ad hoc* adjustments over time with no machinery for formal negotiations between the railway and consumer interests. Charges for other traffics arose from similar historical developments. Some form of price discrimination by VicRail was necessary if many rail users were to receive a service at all. Moreover, the extent of possible "discrimination" between customers was limited by the degree to which those in the competitive road haulage industry had, by the nature of their operations, different costs than rail for the various movements.

Revenue potential was based primarily on forecasts of road haulage operating costs for the mid-190s, enabling us to judge what competitive haulage rates will be for different commodity classes. Our approach was not based on direct rate data, partly because of the scarcity of suitable haulage quotations at each end of the relevant distance scale. But it also reflected difficulties of interpreting short-term and cyclic demand influences on rates at the time the observations are recorded. Freight de-regulation measures mentioned will reinforce the already strong degree of competition in Victoria's road haulage industry. So we assumed that road prices will closely reflect the costs of giving the particular service in the mid-1980s. In so doing, it was necessary to dispel some myths about rate setting in the haulage industry, most notably to demonstrate that rail is a "price-taker" rather than as many believe a price-leader for freight carriage.

Having established likely road rate structures we assessed attainable revenues for freight traffics, consistent with safeguarding the business. This was made in respect of an "average" rail rate for each sector—i.e. that chargeable (per tonne-kilometer) for the distance corresponding to its mean length of haul. We judged that safe pricing implies setting rail rates at around 15 to 20% below those of road (depending on the traffic and distance) to allow for service quality differentials. In practice, railways can rarely match road rates for major commodities because of lower service quality. Comparison of State road and rail rates for contrasting sets of commodities showed that road hauliers do generally command a significant premium over rail rates, for long as well as short distance hauls.

The relation between our estimates of road haulage costs (and thus prices) for the mid-1980s and the average rates which VicRail was charging in 1979/80 for its freight traffics is shown on the two graphs overleaf.

Results showed that real reductions to present rail rates are required in particular to retain LCL traffic, but also for bulk petroleum products due to productivity gains foreseen for road. Little change is implied to coal briquettes and hardwood traffic. But there was found to be substantial scope for rises elsewhere—up to 60% on average rates. This was particularly so for the long—distance interstate movements of forwarding agents and container traffics, reflecting effects of the existing tariff taper.

In specifying rate potential where terminal road distribution is involved, allowance was made for these additional customer costs—mainly affecting LCL, container, forwarding agent and fertilizer traffics. We looked to shipping as the prime competitor for iron and steel products, being guided by quotations on commercial shipping rates for inter-capital movements, since these rather than costs of company-owned ship operation are likely to confront VicRail in future.

The new combination of rates would raise, net, an extra 13% of revenue per annum for *future tasks*, compared with the case if 1979/80 rates were applied. Rate rises would generate an extra A$ 20 million, with reductions producing A$ 5 million less per annum. Owing to the smaller overall task, total freight revenues would be 3% down on their 1979/80 level.

(4) Effects on Financial Performance

The pricing and operating changes outlined would enable six freight sectors to meet their avoidable costs, rather than only one under 1979/80 conditions, representing 61% of forecast freight tonne kms. Four other sectors would meet over 90% of their respective avoidable costs; only two would perform badly, recovering less than 70% of their costs. This is illustrated in Fig. 6, in relation to the 1979/80 performance of VicRail's passenger and ancillary business sectors. The latter are labelled A-D since specific findings remain confidential.

In consequence, positive freight contributions totalling A$ 7 million per annum would be raised to meet the new, lower joint costs of system operation. For those sectors failing to meet avoidable costs, shortfalls would amount to a greatly reduced A$ 6 million.

On the basis of the initiatives outlined so far, a substantial improvement in *overall* financial performance is seen to be possible by the mid-1980s. This is illustrated in Fig. 7. Working in real terms and allowing for productivity changes on both road and rail, we found that the system deficit could be cut by A$ 66m, or one-quarter in relation to its assessed level for 1979/80 condition. This primarily reflects reductions in freight sector shortfalls on their avoidable costs. The potential reduction in system joint costs (A$ 7m) and additional contributions generated to meet them (£ 5m) are very modest by comparison.

Fig. 6. Sector Financial Performance

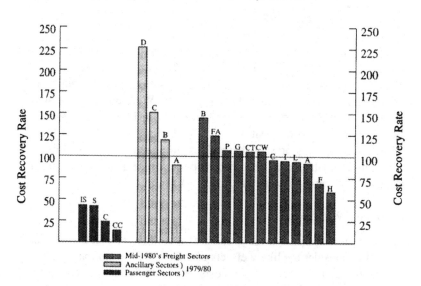

Fig. 7. Impact of Changes on Business Performance A$ millions Per Annum

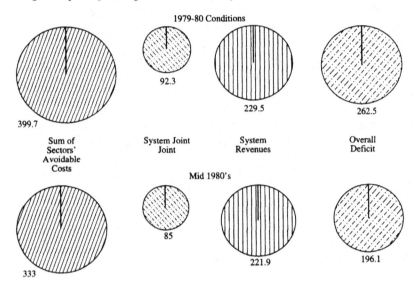

1979-80 Conditions

399.7 — Sum of Sectors' Avoidable Costs

92.3 — System Joint Joint

229.5 — System Revenues

262.5 — Overall Deficit

Mid 1980's

333

85

221.9

196.1

4. Developing the strategy

These measures would, nevertheless, still leave a large overall deficit, of close to A$ 200 million per annum in the mid-1980s. The approach advocated earlier (section2) can be pursued to consider what additional actions should be taken to reduce it further. We start with the main option for VicRail's future business and then consider tactical issues of how to reach the desired position.

Two basic options present themselves: to abandon traffics failing to meet their avoidable costs, or to continue to provide them subject to specific payment from government.

(1) Possible Withdrawals

On the first option—to abandon traffics—further calculations are required to consider the likely effects of different *combinations* of sector withdrawals on the system's joint costs. We identified six freight sectors which would be unable to cover their avoidable costs by the mid-1980s. Since their shortfalls sum to only A$ 6 million a year, potential financial improvement would mostly depend on effects for joint costs were these sectors to be withdrawn together. Because they would then account for nearly 40% of freight tonne-killometres, we would expect a fairly substantial reduction in joint costs—perhaps by a further 25%, or some A$ 20 million a year.

Such withdrawals will have to be treated very carefully, however, and reviewed in the light of other options. For example, fertilizers, with a deficit, have much geographically in common with grain which by the mid-1980s could be a positive contributor. The cost calculations for grain already contain a high degree of line dedication, so withdrawing them both together would be unlikely much to affect joint costs. If so, financial logic would indicate withdrawal only from fertilizers. Other sector combinations probably possess more substantial potential for financial gain, depending largely on the extent of route overlap and the possibility of closing lines.

There are, we note, highly promising *longer-term* possibilities of rationalizing the handing and distribution of some major bulk commodities, involving substantial pruning of branch lines. This chiefly concerns grain, fertilizers, and petroleum products. Major investment would be required, but viability during the late-1980s, and beyond, will be heavily influenced by such ideas.

A further requirement in developing strategy is that less-than-total output changes are examined, representing reductions of say 20-30% to total tasks. This is chiefly to recognize the existence of sub-sectors which have rather different cost and market characteristics—e.g. different cereal grains and components of our residual freight sector. Thus, some sectors might be improved further by restructuring to discard the least remunerative traffics. Other, related, tasks would be to test for changes affecting particular routes, or different ways of dealing with peaks in volume such as for grain—e.g. by encouraging storage at rail receival points, at ports or intermediate locations. The ability to make such calculations, and integrate them with the other investigations, has to grow with time and increasing familiarity, the discovery of computational short-cuts, and so on.

(2) Passenger services and subsidy

It is plain, by contrast, that by far the most important financial problems for VicRail will concern passenger services, especially if the foregoing reforms of freight are carried out. Here, specific subsidy is most relevant.

The outstanding candidates for this are the suburban and country passenger services, which together accounted for nearly A$ 100 million of negative contribution in 1979/80. If these are made the subject of specific government payments, a major step towards achieving a financial break-even for the system will have been taken. Much else, of course, would need to be done, in particular the mentioned rationalization of the way much bulk freight is dealt with. But there would emerge a realistic target for financial self-sufficiency. This raises the question of what would be involved in specifying the subsidy. It needs much more investigation, but the bearing of our model on it it as follows.

A sensible starting point would be to consider the combination of suburban and country passenger services. We expect their impact on system joint costs to be considerable so that, when taken together, avoided costs would probably be in the order of A$ 120 million a year. This represents the minimum subsidy required for their financial viability. As seen, there must be a positive contribution to other system costs also. If the other, non-subsidized, services have already been adjusted to get the most from market opportunities, the remaining requirements for system viability will become clear.

If government is satisfied that no further sectors deserve explicit public subsidy, and that the most is being done to get positive margins form them, then logically it could increase the passenger subsidy for the sectors mentioned beyond their avoidable costs (as recalculated). The limit on this would be set, in a stand-off relationship, by government's valuation of the social benefit of these particular services. In negotiation between government and VicRail, it would be necessary for the implications of the quite complex calculations to be transparent. This, amongst many other things, is required for managing such a relationship, in order that both subsidy giver and receiver are satisfied.

(3) Path to the desired position

The strategy will indicate which sectors are worth cultivating in the long-term; commercial prudence calls for a policy of gradual adjustment to the attainable pricing position in these cases. However, some traffics which either alone or in combination cannot justify replacement of assets, or long-term retention of capacity, may be well worth retaining until for instance major renewals are due or much labour can be shed, or in view of favorable immediate market prospects. Thus, the charging floor for these traffics in the next, say, 3 to 5 years might be much below their avoidable costs as we calculated for, on a long-term basis.

For sectors with doubtful longer-term prospects, a choices has to be made between a planned run down of traffic (in such a way as to minimize the lag between the act of shedding traffic and reducing costs), and the alternative tactic of speeding up the transition by aggressive price increases. With the latter, it is hoped that inflexibility in demand in the immediate future will more than offset any difficulties of quickly reducing costs. Short-term avoidable cost calculations are therefore required to determine which solution will suit particular cases. In general, we consider that the more appealing of these solutions, and probably much more profitable one, would be to adopt an aggressive pricing policy. this could apply, for instance, to much of VicRail's LCL sector.

Finally, we should stress the need for overall balance in developing information for forming the strategy and its implementation. Progress on one front must be matched by progress on others. So far at VicRail, attention to principles of subsidy management and to issues of traffic forecasting and modal competition has lagged well behind efforts in other area. Systematic knowledge of road haulage operations, in particular is conspicuously lacking. There is a pressing need, as in most rail organizations, to be better informed about major customers' transport (as well as business) options, and about the nature of haulage operations in corridors relevant to its main commodity flows. It is hoped that work on hauliers' costs of carriage and service quality aspects will be actively pursued, alongside the other work indicated, and its data requirements made an integral part of future management information systems within VicRail.

IV. Lessons for railway managements

In considering the problem of improving finances, we have argued that a railway system may be viewed as analogous to any business at present making large losses. Whilst performance is defined in terms of those; items directly entering financial accounts for railway activity, these may, of course, reflect the creation of external benefits via specific subsidy payments negotiated with government—as with ordinary commercial corporations.

We do not think that the means to improve financial performance. as reported here for VicRail, have been adopted in any railway system so far. Although the concepts of avoidable and joint costs are of long standing,[6] traffic costs have rarely been worked out for a whole rail system.[7] And nowhere have we found the approach used to consider future possibilities in the manner of our case study. Why is this so?

First, we observe that railways do not—as many suppose—face costing problems which are uniquely difficult. They are not exceptionally different from ordinary industry in either market or cost characteristics. Complex peak loading issues are confronted for instance in the electricity, telecommunications, and a variety of leisure industries, and joint cost problems for oil refineries make those encountered in railways seem minor! This, and the strides made in electronic data handing, means that little excuse can be made of system complexity or size. The answer partly lies in a lack of commercial attitude and motivation, often stemming from inherited social obligations and political controls. For many railways, the whole manner in which it does business is conditioned by

---

6. Discussion of jointness and its significance for railways goes back to papers by Harbeson 30 years ago and by Tausig much earlier. See R.W. Harbeson, Cost-finding in rail transportation: some lessons from American experience, *The Transport and Communication Review*, Vol. 6. No. 4(Oct-Dec 1953): and F.W. Tausig. Railway rates and joint costs once more, *Quarterly Journal of Economics*, Vol. 27, No. 2 (Feb. 1913).

7. Three comprehensive studies are known to us:
   ARRDO's recent investigations of contribution margins, though its work has focussed on working expenditures. This comprised a programme of studies to identify the main contributors to Australian state rail deficits. A general description of the work and findings is given in ARRDO's 1981 Report on Rail. The approach used is explained in *A Contribution Analysis of VicRail*(Part 1, Methodology Report), ARRDO, Melbourne, July 1981.
   R. Travers Morgan and Partners' studies of the New South Wales system made during 1977-79. The freight modeling work is summarised by R.G. Bullock, A.W. Wardrop and R.A Galbraith in *The Analysis and Costing of Rail Freight Operations* paper given at the 6th Australian Transport Research Forum, Brisbane, October 1980.
   British Rail's assessment of costs attributable to different parts of its business, using a six-fold division (4 passenger sectors, freight and parcels activity). Report by the Board's management accounting staff, *Rail Sector Avoidable Costs Study*, London, July 1980.

"public service" commitments, sometimes voluntarily assumed rather than imposed by legislation. However, the major stumbling block has been a concern with a single set of financial accounts, i.e. those underlying typical annual report statements. Since cost calculations need to relate to decisions which often have different purposes, a variety of cost informations systems is usually desirable. The problem has been managements' reluctance to accept that the required information systems are indeed complementary. Different possibilities have usually been viewed as competitive. Naturally, they have been unwilling to jettison the traditional accounting systems which serve them well in various ways; but this has had the effect of blocking the introduction of others. Our study had to construct what amounted to a new information system, starting virtually from scratch, and geared specifically to illuminating the net impact of feasible changes to VicRail's system. Conventionally, as in VicRail, management information is dominated by requirements of budgeting, the control of cash flow and resource use, encouraging a very short-term view.

The line of attack adopted depends on distinguishing sectors of activity, comprehending the whole business, which represent both distinct production processes and separate markets based on customer requirements. Its acceptance requires a major shift from managements' traditional concern with technical functions, in which departmental planning predominates—as reflected in the still widespread autonomy of the engineering branches and the power which their heads wield. For example, it involves rejecting the evaluation of investment in terms of groups of assets such as rolling stock and locomotive fleets, in favour of evaluation within a context of revenue and cost forecasts by sector. A prerequisite for successful transition to "sector management" will be basic organizational changes to alter the balance of prevailing influences, especially those bearing on cost control and technical practices, in order that planning and investment decisions reflect a paramount concern for specific sectors and overall business performance. It also implies that subsidies paid by government should generally become far more specific than now, to be capable of application to a given sector and hence integrated with management's plan to move towards profitability.

The most important calculations to be made concern withdrawal from a business sector, because the basic strategic question is whether or not a particular class of business should be undertaken at all—i.e. whether it is be retained (or taken on) and developed, or be abandoned. Successful negotiation of prices means that there must be a credible possibility of refusing the business, and hence that the consequences of this for the railway's finances are known.

Given a commitment to a particular sector, costs such at those associated with peaks or different sub-markets should then be investigated with a view to improving performance by a possible re-structuring of activity. Whilst revenue and cost calculations have to be developed iteratively, as information allows, at all stages in forming the strategy an overview of the whole business must be maintained. This implies a capability, which is absent in present systems, to sum information across the several sectors.

In considering improvement via pricing policy, our study emphasizes the need for price discrimination between, and also within, different sectors. To achieve this requires a different approach to dealing with large as opposed to small customers. Customer size is an important determinant both of the nature of information required to assess revenue potential, and for deciding how pricing decisions are to be handled in the rail organization.

For large customers, especially, knowledge is needed of their own marketing opportunities as well as of the potential contribution of road or sea transport in satisfying them. For them, the aim should be to establish the limits of bargaining for contracts, set respectively by rail's avoidable costs of carrying the traffic and by the net potential advantage to the customer of using rail, which in some cases may include a premium for superiority over road. This enables ways of sharing the potential benefits to be devised, including reduction of risks by sharing capital outlays, and agreed ways to deal with future fluctuation of traffic. The future cost estimates for VicRail's sectors were intended to be used by management, alongside our assessments of competition, for this purpose. In dealing with large *public* customers, additional information will be required about external effects of proposed price changes. Small customers have to be dealt with by establishing rules to be followed by lower level managers. There should, we suggest, be target prices for contracts, themselves derived from the strategic calculations for the sectors. The lower levels should not be given cost calculations reflecting potential results of their sales, but rather be given information about road costs and prices, and other customer oriented information, relevant for seeking improvements on the target price. There could be an instruction to refer upwards any proposals to deviate below this target. With this procedure, salesmen could be motivated by incentives based on the total custom they generate. Our estimates of future road rates confronting VicRail provide a basis, together with judgements about service quality differences, for setting these target prices.

Traditionally, railways have favored centrally established but delegated pricing rules, in preference either to fully centralized price determination, which we argue for, or to decentralized solutions. Because of the inability to aggregate over the whole business in reviewing pricing decisions, this has led to an endemic failure to exploit competitive advantages, characterized by weak selling. In our approach, aimed at redressing this, a key role must be played by the chief executive. He has, in essence, to deal directly with the large customer and set the sectoral targets which will determine the basis from which lower managers deal with the smaller customer.

References

Bland, H. A. (1972). *Report of the Board of Inquiry into the Victorian Land transport system*. Melbourne: Government Printer.

Gwilliam, K. M., Prideaux, J. D. C. A., et al.(1979). *A Comparative Study of European Rail Performance*. London: British Railways Board.

Lonie, W. M. et al., (1980). *Victorian Transport Study: Final Report*. Melbourne: Ministry of transport.

PART III

PRICING OF TRANSPORT SERVICE

CHAPTER 10

THE ROLE OF COST IN THE MINIMUM
PRICING OF RAILROAD SERVICES*

*William J. Baumol and Nine Other Economists***

Original Editor's note.—Over the past fifteen years, settled patterns of regulation of transport rates and services have been subjected to increasing scrutiny and criticism not only from academic economists but also from producers and users of transportation, public officials, and the public in general. The largest single reason for this heightening of interest has been the increasingly severe competitive and financial position of the railroad industry. While the operation and regulation of any one mode of transportation cannot be considered in isolation, much of the present discussion of transport regulation properly centers on the railroads. An important

---

*Reprinted from *Journal of Business*, 1962, pp. 357-66.

**William J. Baumol, professor of economics, Princeton University, and member of Mathematica; James C. Bonbright, professor of finance, emeritus, Columbia University; Yale Bronzen, professor of business economics, Graduate School of Business, University of Chicago; Jole Dean, professor of business economics, Columbia University, and economic consultant, Joel Dean Associates; Ford K. Edwards, transportation consultant, Edwards and Peabody; Calvin B. Hoover, professor of economics, Durham, North Carolina; Dudley F. Pegrum, professor of economics, University of California at Los Angeles; Merrill J. Roberts, professor of transportation, Graduate School of Business, University of Pittsburgh; Ernest W. Williams, Jr., professor of transportation, Graduate School of Business, Columbia University.

topic has been the search for regulatory principles and procedures which would yield the maximum public benefit from railroad plant and technology under present competitive conditions.

The following statement was prepared under the auspices of the Association of American Railroads, an obviously interested party and one that has done much to stimulate broad interest in the regulatory problems of its members. The statement represents a consensus of ten economists, most of whom will need no introduction to readers of this *Journal*. It is published here as a contribution to the discussion of the business and regulatory economics of transportation and of other industries, both within and outside the public utility field. Specifically, the panel of economists undertakes to clarify the economic principles of costs that are relevant as a guide to the pricing of particular railroad services. The statement, concerned with concepts of cost, should help to provide an essential groundwork for the development of improved techniques for the measurement of relevant costs in specific situations.

Foreword

Recognizing the growing attention to cost considerations in railroad rate-making, the Board of Directors of the Association of American Railroad requested Burton N. Behling, Economist, Bureau of Railway Economics of the Association, to arrange for a study of the relevant concepts in determining cost floors for rates and to seek the advice and counsel of a group of outstanding and disinterested economists in this matter.

To collaborate with him in this undertaking, he engaged the following distinguished consultants:

William J. Baumol, professor of economics, Princeton University, and member of Mathematica

James C. Bonbright, professor of finance, emeritus, Columbia University

Yale Brozen, professor of business economics, Graduate School of Business, University of Chicago

Joel Dean, professor of business economics, Columbia University, and economic consultant, Joel Dean Associates

Ford K. Edwards, transportation consultant, Edwards and Peabody

Calvin B. Hoover, professor of economics, Durham, North Carolina

Dudley F. Pegrum, professor of economics, University of California at Los Angeles

Merrill J. Roberts, professor of transportation, Graduate School of Business, University of Pittsburgh

Ernest W. Williams, Jr., professor of transportation, Graduate School of Business, Columbia University

They began their task early this year, and the results of their work are now presented in the attached statement entitled "The Role of Cost in the Minimum Pricing of Railroad Services." All the participants "subscribe to it in substance and they specifically agree with the conclusions as set forth in the summary at the end of the statement."

I. Introduction

Increasing competitiveness in transportation has stimulated debate regarding the principles which should guide the determination of any floor below which particular railroad rates will not be permitted to fall. A central issue in this debate is whether particular rates should be cost or market oriented. This statement examines the issue—bringing to bear accepted principles of economics that apply throughout the economy. It sets forth the role of cost in pricing and in so doing shows that prices must be *both* cost and market oriented.

Examining first the basic cost concepts and then the nature of railroad costs, the analysis concludes that incremental costs provide the valid cost guide for minimum pricing and that "fully distributed" costs must be rejected as an economic test of any particular price or rate. These conclusions are reached by reference to the interest both of the pricing carrier and of society as a whole, and they have the same force and relevance for pricing within modes of transport as among modes.

II. Underlying Cost Principles

The increase in total costs resulting from an expansion in a firm's volume of business is commonly referred to as *incremental cost*. This cost is of vital economic significance. For to businessman it provides an essential guide to his production and pricing policy. If he is considering a reduction in price, he needs to know whether the increase in total revenues from greater volume will more than cover the additional costs that will be incurred, For the whole economy it is incremental (not fully distributed) cost that is the relevant cost guide to how much of what shall be produced and how much should be invested in various lines of production. This cost, which is measured by the value of the additional resources that will be used up when more of anything is produced, represents the real cost to society.[1] Incremental costs indicate (by comparison with the incremental revenues they will bring) whether additional outputs of any commodity are worth producing and (by incremental cost comparisons) which of the alternative ways of satisfying wants or requirements is the most efficient.[2]

But not all costs can be identified causally with specific quantities of production. Much of the controversy over cost concepts stems from the false notion that all costs can be traced and attributed to specific blocks of output. Although many costs are *traceable*, there are also *non-traceable* costs which simply do not lend themselves to this method of identification:

a) *Fixed costs*—Some costs, called *fixed costs*, do not change in magnitude when the quantity of output for a given plant varies. Hence, it is impossible to assign any specific portion of these costs to a particular unit of output (e.g., to a particular ton-mile of traffic). Rather, a fixed cost must be imputed to the entire supply of the type or types of service with which it is associated.

b) *Joint costs*—Different services may sometimes share their costs, as, for example, when the same roadbed is employed to transport both food products and lumber.

---

1. Social cost which are escaped by the enterprise must also be included in the calculation.
2. In addition to those costs which vary with rate of output for a given investment level, incremental costs include cost increments associated with new investment. For example, if special equipment is acquired in order to handle certain additional traffic, the costs are incremental to that traffic.

Such common and joint cost conditions are frequently encountered in the railroad industry as well as elsewhere. Wherever incremental costs are also either joint or common costs, the resulting difficulties of allocation cannot be side-stepped. Here the standard distinction between common costs and joint cost can have practical importance. *Common costs* are outlays devoted to either of two or more classes of services which may be variably proportioned at the discretion of management, with the result that it is, in principle at least, possible to trace them to individual services. *Joint costs*, in contrast, are costs for which the proportions of output are not variable, so that supplying one class of service in a given amount results automatically in making available another class of service in some unalterable amount. The practical consequence is that incremental joint costs are not traceable to individual railroad services and can be allocated only arbitrarily. In contrast, those common costs which are incremental are traceable in principle, although it may be impossible over a considerable range to do so in practice.

For any business or industry there is no rigid division between variable costs and fixed costs. Some cost elements which are fixed in the very short term or with small changes in output may over a somewhat longer period or a broad range of output become incremental if additional investments or other inputs are required. However, an indefinitely longterm view of incremental costs is not appropriate, for some fixed costs may be expected to remain fixed over any time period and range of output that is reasonable to consider in setting a price floor. Depending on the particular circumstances, incremental costs might contemplate a range of short terms. The only general rule for deciding which measure of incremental cost to use as a *cost* guide for minimum pricing is that the choice of incremental cost functions must be geared to the duration of the expected revenue change.[3]

Each particular situation requires its particular cost analysis by management. For example, a cost structure will be affected significantly by the extent of unused capacity in the production factors involved. Where unused capacity is substantial and persistent, the fixed cost elements per

---

3. More specifically, the decision is governed by such revenue dimensions as the nature and amount of the contemplated change in volume, the length of the commitment to carry the traffic, the duration and geographic scope of the changed rate, the alterations of the service that might require added investments, and the time period in which changes may legally or practically take place.

unit of output are correspondingly greater and more enduring, and the incremental costs proportionately smaller.

Arbitrary apportionments of nontraceable costs among fully particular kinds of outputs must be employed in the calculation of "fully distributed cost." This measure will be further considered later in particular reference to railroad ratemaking. However, it is apparent from what has been said that fully distributed costs have no true economic content because their derivation falsely assumes that all costs can be traced to particular kinds or quantities of output and can rationally enter directly into pricing decisions. The greater the degree of nontraceable costs, the more inappropriate is the use of fully distributed costs as a guide to minimum prices.

III. Nature of Railroad Costs

Fixed costs, which are independent of volume and are not attributable to specific amounts of traffic, are an important characteristic of railroad cost structures. Large portions of railroad investment costs represent expenditures for longlived facilities that have been "sunk" in the enterprise at various times in the past. The facilities involved are of such specialized nature that they are not generally transferable to other pursuits without great loss. Fixed costs associated with sunk physical investments, as well as organizational or other cost factors which are underutilized, are irretrievably committed to an essential public service unless disinvestment, organizational shrinkage, or, as a last resort, abandonment occurs.

Because of the long but varied lives of their facilities and the inherent uncertainties of forecasting, adjustment of railroad capacity to changing requirements is difficult. Unutilized railroad capacity is a chronic problem which demands effective steps to retain existing traffic and to attract additional traffic. Moreover, railroad investments in recent years which were intended for modernization and greater efficiency have in many instances also increased capacity, although this has not usually been the purpose. Significant technological improvemets include heavier rail and track structures, electronic yards, centralized traffic control, and better communications, as well as improved locomotive power and higher-capacity freight cars. Realizaion of the potential economies of these and other interrelated improvements depends on large and increasing traffic volumes.

The railroads own, and hence must fully pay for, the costly plant facilities they use. In contrast, highway, water, and air carriers use publicly owned rights of way and facilities. To the extent that they repay the economic cost of these facilities furnished to them, their payments are mainly through use charges which make their costs of this sort predominantly variable. For these and other reasons, these rival carriers can adjust their capacities to fluctuating demand more promptly and precisely than can the railroads.

The rapid growth of electrical utility volume has been due to a steady reduction of real prices on average and to promotional pricing designed to utilize capacity effectively and to expand sectors of demand that are price-elastic. These achievements have been made possible, on the cost side, by sustained technological progress and economies of scale in the generation and transmission of electricity and, on the demand sisde, by strong markets and commendable regulatory in sight. This kind of economic performance, generally regarded as serving the public interest, is no less socially desirable for the failroads. And even though it is more difficult to attain because of their highly competitive environment, such performance is at least equally urgent because of the railroads's financial plight.

The public interest requires maximum economic utilization of the vast capacity of the railroads's plant and operating organization. To this end it is essential that the burden of fixed costs be spread over as large a volume of traffic as can be developed with attractive rates in excess of the relevant incremental costs. This mode of operation is desirable not only for the railroads in providing them with the opportunity for reasonable investment returns. It may also be advantageous to the shippers in lower shipping costs. Above all, it is in the public interest because it provides the maximum amount of transportation service for the resources which are employed for this purpose.

IV. Relevant Incremental Costs

In determining incremental costs, it is necessary to distinguish between sunk and prospective investments. Sometimes the pertinent incremental cost involve making added inbestment (e.g., cars or locomotive). In that event all the added costs to be incurred (including use-depreciation and cost of capital) should be recognized as incrementa. Sometimes capacity is so excessive that the traffic at issue can be handled without added investment. The investment costs then are sunk and may become fixed for long periods. Once the commitment has been made, and if a plethora of capacity subsequently develops, the recovery of anything more than incremental cost is better than nothing.

Prudent railroad management should certainly be aware of the threat to longterm profitability, and even survival, from fixing rates on a substantial proportion of traffic near strictly short-term incremental costs. Nevertheless, in the complex and varied circumstances of the railroads, there will be some situations where pricing of particular services on the basis of short-term considerations will improve utilization and will yield accretions to net income not otherwise obtainable. In view of their primary responsibility to make effective use of their vast facilities through volume retention and development, railroad maangements require considerable latitude in estimating relevant costs as well as in pricing decisions. There is no single cost formula which will always and automatically be appropriate.

In rapidly expanding industries operating with short-lived facilities and highly flexible organization, recognition of the transitory nature of fixed costs and their tendency to be transformed rather quickly into incremental costs is an essential costing precept for pricing purposes. But railroad costs cannot be cast in such a simple mold. The reality of their fixed costs cannot be made to disappear with a general assumption of variability with traffic volumes if the time period is stretched out long enough. With the persistent and serious underutilization of capacity which is characteristic of the railroads' basic plant and organization, large amounts of fixed costs remain fixed indefinitely. The least effective way to cope with unutilized railroad capacity would be to include its fixed costs in floors for pricing. For the high prices which would result could only discourage utilization of these facilities and aggravate the condition.

Neither extremely short-run nor extremely long-run incremental cost is an economic concept of general applicability to all minimum pricing problems encountered in the railroad industry. The determination of the relevant incremental costs appropriate for a particular pricing decision is not simple[4] but must reflect complex railroad cost conditions that arise from persistent excess capacity, irrelevant fixed-cost elements, and such interrelated dynamic factors as changing volume, changing labor and material costs, technological innovations, and improved operating techniques. Where such dynamic forces are at work the incremental costs of additional traffic, which may be induces by a reduced rate, may be quite different from those indicated by past experience.

More penetrating analysis of specific cost elements in needed for a better understanding of their relationship to traffic volumes. Such analysis, which is beyond the scope of this statement on cost concepts, should be intensified by the railroads. Particularly urgent is the need for cost determinations which are "tailored" to specific situations instead of the commonly used general measures which are vitiated by excessive averaging.

V. Costs and Pricing

Forward-looking costs are essential because the pricing decisions they must guide necessarily look to the future. The estimation of such costs must reckon with changes in operating techniques which may result from expanded volume and associated or unassociated technological innovations. Because of these factors, historical experience provides no sure basis for determining those future incremental costs which alone

---

4. The relevant incremental costs are a function principally of the prospective volume in relation to present volume and unutilized capacity in existing plant and organization. The rate over time at which the prospective volume is likely to be achieved, the prospects for its continuance over the longer term, and its distribution over stated time periods (for example, seasonality and peaking characteristics) are all relevant to the determination of appropriate incremental costs. From consideration of the prospective volume and its characteristics it may be feasible to estimate those elements of plant and organization which will require ultimate replacement, allowances for the use of which should figure currently in costs. If volume promises to build up substantially over time, the likelihood and cost of the required expansion in capacity must be recognized in the computation of the price floor.

are relevant in setting price floors.

As a general rule, any rate below incremental cost is both unprofitable and socially wasteful off resources because the additional (incremental) revenue obtained is less than the additional cost incurred.[5] However, this does not mean that the railroads should set rates *at* that cost level or that they should be required to do so. On the contrary, this cost reference is uniquely important as a guide in determining the specific rates which will provide the maximum contribution to the overhead burden and thus to net income. The margin above incremental costs which maximizes this contribution depends upon the price sensitivity of demand, determined primarily by the alternatives available to shippers. The judgment of management should be relied upon to make this determination, subject to limitations imposed by regulation of maximum rates and discrimination Thus, while incremental costs should not *determine* prices or rates, they set the lower boundary (and demand conditions and regulation the upper boundary) within which pricing decisions should be made.

Railroads produce a multiplicity of different services in many markets with dissimilar demand characteristics. For example, the demand for the transportation of coal for three hundred miles eastbound may be entirely different from the demand for the transportation of the same commodity three hundred miles westbound because of competitive or market influences. Basing rates on demand (as well as on incremental costs) to attain the maximum contribution means, therefore, that rates for all services will not be the same either abolutely, or in relation to cost, or in contributions to the net income of the carriers.

Since demands for rail services have become increasingly elastic as alternative means of transportation (both for-hire and private) have become ever more available, the greatest total contribution to net income will for many items and hauls result from a low unit margin above incremental cost and a large volume. Estimating the volume of traffic which might move at different levels of rates and the effect on net

---

5. The application of this principle in particular situations may require special care in estimating the pertinent incremental costs and incremental revenue. Especially in the short run they may be different from what they superficially appear. Example the hidden incremental costs of dismissing and the reassembling a key work-force; and the hidden, from gone incremental revenue that may result in losing a profitable customer by refusing to take an occasional order below incremental cost.

income is a key aspect of pricing. This vital function is a primary management responsibility which should be performed on the basis of managerial and not regulatory judgment. Rates so determined, however, can legitimately continue to be subject to regulation of maximum rates and to legal rules against unjust discrimination.[6]

Differential pricing is consistent with the public interest in the economical utilization of resources. It can yield significant benefits to the users of rail services by encouraging the retention of traffic and the development of greater traffic volumes and improved profits, thus fostering the adoption of improved technology and service, as well as lower rates.

Pricing designed to achieve such results should not be condemned as "destructive" or "unfair" competition Rather it is necessary for constructive competition and maximal economy and efficiency in the utilization of resources. By the very nature of competition some are hurt by it. It may well be that realistic assessments of incremental costs as a pricing guide would encourage rate reductions where carrier or regulatory policies have stressed preservation of historic rate structures or keeping rates high enough to maintain "fair" market sharing. Indeed, reductions designed directly to improve profits may do so mainly by shifting traffic away from firms operating by other modes, which are thereby hurt or even destroyed. But this does not constitute predatory competition. Predatory practices must be taken to refer to temporary price reductions designed to eliminate competition in order to clear the way for high and monopolistic rates in the future. Ease and low costs of re-entry of trucks and other modes make predatory competition by the railroads unprofitable and hence unlikely. Moreover, such undesirable practices constitute a legitimate concern of the regulatory authorities. Regulatory powers should not, however, be used to prevent price reductions which are designed to improve or maintain profits by increasing or retaining traffic volume. Such prevention is particulary undesirable socially, because of the low rates of utilization of the large property investments of the railroads.

---

6. The railroads also are subject to the limitation a reasonable over-all "return," but this regulatory limitation has not for many years of low earnings been a matter of real concern. If excessive profits were ever achieved, it would be the lawful responsibility of the regulatory authorities to apply the appropriate restraints.

VI. "Fully Distributed" Cost an Invalid Basis for Minimum pricing.

The relevant incremental cost constitute all the cost information pertinent to the determination of floors in the pricing of particular railroad
services. "Fully distributed" cost, measured by some kind of arbitrary
statistical apportionment of the unallocable costs among the various
units or classes of traffic, is an economically invalied criterion for setting minimum rates, from both a managerial and a regulatory standpoint.
No particular category of traffic can be held economically responsible
for any given share of the unallocable costs. Whether any particular rate
is above or below some fully distributed cost is without real economic
significance for minimum pricing.

Stated differently, the appropriate aim of the railroads is to determine
that margin above incremental costs, traffic volume considered, at
which a rate produces the maximum total contribution toward fixed
costs and net income. Fully distributed costs cannot serve this vital economic purpose. They present an entirely false picture of traffic profitability. Their use would drive away great quantities of profitable, vol-
ume-moving traffic now handled at rates below fully distributed costs.

Another misconception is the view that if some railroad rates are
below fully distributed costs a burden in imposed on other traffic which
must pay more to make up the "deficiency." But, when the true significance of unallocable costs is understood, it becomes apparent that a particular rate which maximizes the contribution to such costs over and
above the relevant incremental costs cannot possibly burden other traffic
even though rates on the latter may be higher. If such contributions from
lower-paying traffic were lost because of unattractive rates, railroad
earnings and expenditures for improvements would suffer, and the ability to provide good service would be impaired. Traffic which is not
moved cannot possibly help to bear the unallocable costs. It is the fully
distributed cost doctrine which, by pegging minimum rates on a false
economic premise, would burden not only railroad shippers but the
economy as a whole and would tend to bankrupt the railroad system by
artificially restricting the economic use of railroad facilities and services.

Especially in competitive industries, no cost system can really assure
that all costs will be covered and a "normal" profit earned, for sales vol-

ume will play a significant role. If guaranteed coverage of all costs and a normal profit are the objectives of fully distributed cost pricing, it cannot succeed. For that matter, neither can pricing based on relevant incremental costs plus a maximum contribution to fixed costs and net income, as determined by conditions of market demand, provide such a guarantee. But if these contributions are maximized throughout the pricing structure, the best result has been achieved and no further improvement is possible under prevailing market conditions.

Thus, the fully distributed cost doctrine does not reflect valid principles of pricing, where fixed costs are significant. Application of this false criterion in the railroads' present competitive environment would bring about prices which (for much traffic) would shrink volume. If the same total constant costs were then distributed on the shrunken traffic volume, even greater fully distributed unit costs would result, and if this should cause the railroads to raise rates still higher relative to the prices of other modes of transport, then rail traffic volume would probably be still further reduced. A costing procedure which can inaugurate such a destructive cost-price spiral is not qualified to serve as a basis for pricing in the railroad business or in any other with unallocable costs and unused capacity.

The social costs of such a pricing method could be enormous. The railroads could not function economically and quite possibly could not survive the use of this misguided basis of pricing. Under it, much traffic either would not move at all or would be moved only by modes of transportation with higher actual economic costs. The end result would be a greater total transportation cost borne by the whole economy in return for a reduced total volume of transportation service.

VII. Full Cost of Low-Cost Carrier Also a False Standard

An offshoot of the fully distributed cost fallacy is the contention that rail rates should not be permitted to go below the "full cost of the low-cost carrier"(such carrier being determined on the basis of comparative fully distributed cost), whether it be that of a railroad or a different mode of transport. This contention, also, has no validity as a measure of "inherent advantage" or relative economy in the utilization of economic resources of the nation. For the reasons pointed out above, the low-cost carrier is properly identified by incrementa! cost not by so-called "full" cost.

Only a railroad's own incremental cost s are of any significance as a guide in establishing its minimum rates; and this same principle applies as well to other modes of transport and other industries. Imposing a different and higher *cost* standard deprives railroads of traffic which they can transport more economically, artificially stimulates the growth of uneconomic transportation by other means including private transportation, deprives the shipping public of the benefits of low-cost service, and imposes higher commodity prices on the consuming public. However computed, the use of fully distributed costs would be wasteful of economic resources by misdirecting their use and by keeping them idle or underutilized.

In addition to its inherent defect, this specious "cost" proposal has another deficiency. To whatever extent carriers which operate on public facilities may not have to meet full economic costs in conducting their business, their "fully distributed costs" are not consistent with those computed for the railroads. For the railroads a fully distributed cost computation embraces the entire costs. The effect of the use of the "full cost of the low-cost carrier" doctrine is to obstruct the railroads in pricing their services in competition with other modes to the extent that they may be subsidized. Thus, this proposal constitutes umbrella rate-making to protect any subsidized modes of transportation from legitimete compertition by the railroads.

VIII. Summary

1. In the determination of cost floors as a guide to the pricing of particular railroad services, or the services of any other transport mode, incremental costs of each particular service are the only relevant costs.

2. Rates for particular railroad services should be set at such amounts (subject to regulation of maximum rates and to legal rules against unjust discrimination) as will make to greatest total contribution to net income. Clearly, such maximizing rates would never fall below incremental costs.

3. Pricing which is not restricted by any minimum other than incremen-

tal cost can foster more efficient use of railroad resources and capacity and can therefore encourage lower costs and rates. This same principle applies to other modes of transportation.

4. The presence of large amounts of fixed costs and unused capacity in railroad facilities makes it especially important that railroad rates encourage a large volume of traffic.

5. Reduced rates which more than cover incremental costs and are designed by management to maximize contribution to net income do not constitute proof of predatory competition.

6. "Fully distributed" costs derived by apportioning unallocable costs have no economic significance in determining rate floors for particular railroad services. The application of such a criterion would arbitrarily force the railroads to maintain rates above the level which would yield maximum contribution to net income and would deprive them of much traffic for which they can compete economically. For similar reasons, restriction of railroad minimum rates according to the "rull cost of the low-cost carrier" is economically unsound.

The undersigned economists and transportation specialists have issued the foregoing statement on the role of costs in railroad rate-making. All the signatories subscribe to it in substance, and they specifically agree with the conclusion as set forth in the summary at the end of the statement.

CHAPTER 11

OPTIMAL DEPARTURES FROM MARGINAL COST PRICING*

*William J. Baumol and David F. Bradford***

The need for this paper is a paradox in itself and indeed it might be subtitled: *The Purloined Proposition or The Mystery of the Mislaid Maxim*. For the results which it describes have appeared many times in the literature and have been reported by most eminent economists in very prominent journals. Yet these results may well come as a surprise to many readers who will consider them to be at variance with ideas which they have long accepted.

The proposition in question asserts that, *generally, prices which deviate in a systematic manner from marginal costs will be required for an optimal allocation of resources, even in the absence of externalities.* The reason for the difficulty into which marginal cost pricing is likely to fall is rather well known. What is not widely recognized is that there exists a highly sophisticated and well-developed body of literature indicating what should be done in such circumstances.

---

* Reprinted from *American Economic Review* (1970), pp. 265-283.

** The authors are members of the department of economics, Princeton University. We are grateful to the National Science Foundation whose grant greatly facilitated completion of this paper. We must also express deep appreciation to our colleagues, Charles Berry, Stanley Black, William Branson, and W. Arthur Lewis, and to Ralph Turvey, whose comments and suggestions helped enormously in the development of its ideas.

To see how the problem arises, consider an economy in which all industry has been nationalized and in which the central planning agency is dedicated to the maximization of social welfare. Suppose, accordingly, that it is decided to set all prices *equal* to marginal costs and to make up any deficits by subsidy out of the governmental treasury. If these funds are derived by excise taxes this is obviously a decision to make some prices depart from marginal costs after all. Or if it is obtained by an income tax, it is the price of labor which is forced away from its marginal cost. Any tax, except a Pigouvian poll tax—which might perhaps more felicitously be called an "inescapable tax"—will unaviodably affect some price. There is no way out of it. Any level of tax revenue which the government is determined to collect, whether as a means to make up a deficit resulting from a marginal cost pricing arrangement or for any other purpose, must in practice produce some price distortion.

Once this difficulty is recognized it becomes clear that one is dealing with a problem in the area of the second best. We are now faced with a problem involving maximization *in the presence of an added constraint.* Resource allocation is to be optimal under the constraint that governmental revenues suffice to make up for the deficits (surpluses)[1] of the individual firms that constitute the economy.

The theorems which have been developed to deal with this issue derive added interest from the fact that they are (virtually) the only concrete prescriptions for any second-best problem which have so far

---

1. Presumably, as a practical matter, there is an asymmetry between the problems posed by surpluses and those resulting from deficits. The real difficulty arises when we try to collect resources to cover the deficits without distorting consumers' and producers' choices. Since it is not possible in practice to levy lump sum taxes whose magnitude is independent of the decisions of those who pay them, we are forced to consider second-best solutions to the tax problem. A surplus can presumably be distributed more easily in a "lump sum" manner. One can, for example, distribute shares in future surpluses to all members of the economy on the basis of their incomes at some point in the past, or one can simply divide them equally among all individuals.

It should be emphasized also that the deficit problem need not arise only in the case of decreasing costs where the revenue yielded by marginal cost pricing will fall short of the total costs of the firm. For example, in practice revenue requirements of the firm are often based on historical accounting cost figures which management feels it must recover. Similarly, governmental tax requirements may exceed any profits obtained from nationalized firms subject to diminishing returns when they price at marginal costs.

appeared in the literature. The discussion of this paper differs from the earlier writings in several ways. First, it deals with an important case not explicitly covered in most of the other papers in the area: quasi-optimal pricing when commodity prices throughout the economy are all adjusted as far as is possible. Second, it attempts a simplified exposition which is, of course, possible only at a cost in terms of loss of generality. Third, it brings together, explicitly, all three strands of the discussion: the welfare theoretic, the regulatory, and the public finance contributions. Finally, as far as we know, it offers the first overview of the extensive literature that has grown up in the area.

I. Sources of the Analysis

The preceding formulation of the problem suggests why the results described in this paper are not widely recognized. For they arise not out of the literature of welfare economics but from two more specialized fields—the theory of taxation and the analysis of public utility regulation.

The connection of the analysis with the theory of taxation is easy to understand. For the investigation, as it has just been described, is tantamount to a study of a system of optimal excise and income taxes. Only a small modification in our statement is needed for this purpose: instead of requiring the governmental revenue to equal the (algebraic) sum of the deficits of the firms constituting the economy, the revenue constraint can be generalized to require the tax system to bring in whatever revenues the government has decided it needs. The taxes which are optimal subject to this more general revenue requirement constraint then can be shown to follow the same necessary condition as that which replaces the marginal cost pricing rule in our previous discussion.

Similarly, there is a direct line between the more general welfare analysis and the theory of public utility regulation. For one reason or another, various public or regulated private monopolistic or partially monopolistic enterprises are operated under what amounts to a fixed profit constraint. Examples are turnpike authorities (required to cover costs and pay back invested capital), and regulated electricity, water, and telephone systems. The enterprises cited as examples are all firms that market a number of commodities. The turnpike sells easy driving between many different pairs of points, and, perhaps more important, at various times of day. Similarly, the telephone system sells ordinary telephone services for various uses over various distances and at various times, and, in addition, sells private wire, teletype, television signal transmission, and other services related to, but not identical with, telephone services as usually conceived. In each example the demands for the different services are very obviously strongly interrelated, and they are obviously produced under conditions involving common costs.

If we assume that the net revenue allowed these enterprises is less than the amount profit maximization would yield, some degree of freedom is introduced into the pricing of the commodities produced.[2] A wide variety of output combinations and sets of prices can then be chosen, each of which would just meet the net revenue constraint. The problem, then, is to determine which of these is optimal (second best) from the point of view of the use of resources to serve consumer desires. A similar problem obviously arises in a nationalized industry which is required to earn enough to cover its costs.

II. The Nature of the Theorem

In this section we shall describe the rules indicating whether a particular price-output combination that satisfies the profit constraint is socially optimal, i.e., whether from the point of view of the economy it yields the most effective allocation of resources permitted by the constraint.[3] A solution to this constrained maximum problem will be called

---

2. Of course, some amount of freedom is also introduced into the choice of method of production. We assume throughout that good will, pride of service, patriotism or the shrewdness of regulators assure that whatever output combination is chosen is produced at minimum cost.

3. It is not suggested that profit-constrained firms will by themselves tend to institute such optimal policies. When profits are eliminated or reduced in importance, other objectives presumably guide decision makers. For one thing, they may be able to afford stupidity in production decisions as pointed out by Harvey Leibenstein. A well-known alternative goal is sales maximization, the implications of which have been discussed *ad nauseam* by one of the present authors. Other possibilities have been examined by Herbert Simon, Robin Marris, Oliver Williamson, Armen Alchian, and Reuben Kessel and by others. For a bibliography and an excellent discussion see Williamson.

"quasi-optimal," because it is a second-best solution forced upon us by the revenue requirement.

A problem such as ours is usually framed in terms of the determination of appropriate output levels, but it can also be treated in terms of the choice of a price set for the outputs. Given the relevant demand functions, the choice of prices is tantamount to the choice of (salable) output levels. The two problems are, of course, formally identical, but, as we shall show, the pricing decision approach avoids a number of difficulties and yields a surprisingly simple optimality rule. In most conventional and familiar terms this rule asserts that Pareto optimal utilization of resources in the presence of an absolute profit constraint requires (considering substitution effects alone) that all outputs be reduced by the same proportion from the quantities that would be demanded at prices equal to the corresponding marginal costs. The rule takes an even simpler form in the event cross elasticities of demand are zero. It then requires that each price be set so that its percentage deviation from marginal cost is inversely proportionate to the item's price elasticity of demand. According to this result, the social welfare will be served most effectively not by setting prices equal or even proportionate to marginal costs, but by causing unequal deviations in which items with ealstic demands are priced at levels close to their marginal costs. The prices of items whose demands are inelastic diverge from their marginal costs by relatively wider margins.

This result is surely not immediately acceptable through intuition. It strikes us as curious, if for no other reason, because it seems to say that ordinary price discrimination might well set relative prices at least roughly in the manner required for maximal social welfare in the presence of a profit constraint. Since the objective of the analysis can be described as the determination of the optimally discriminatory set of prices needed to obtain the required profit, some degree of resemblance is perhaps to be expected. The case studied here is, thus, in a sense the obverse of the problem of profit maximizing price discrimination, and while the two solutions bear some qualitative resemblance, it can be shown that they may in fact differ substantially in quantity.

The theorem can be reformulated and generalized in a number of ways. Instead of utilizing the producers' and consumers' surplus concepts with all their theoretical limitations, the analysis can be framed in terms of the Hicksian compensating variation. Or a Pareto optimality approach can be utilized, both of these procedures obviating any need for interpersonal utility comparisons. Similarly, the theorem has been extended to cover cases involving nonzero cross-elasticities of demand, to deal with input prices and the prices of intermediate goods, etc. Of course, once this is done the result loses some of its simplicity and the preceding statement requires considerable modification. But even then, surprisingly simple versions remain possible, as we shall see.

III. The Formal Theorem

In previous discussions, the basic theorem has been stated in a number of different ways. The objective itself has been described alternatively as: a) maximization of the sum of consumers' and producers' surpluses; b) determination of a set of prices from which it is *not* possible to change in a way that permits the gainers to compensate the losers; and c) maximization of the level of satisfaction of any one individual, given the utility level of each other individual (Pareto quasi-optimality). Each of these maximizations is, of course, constrained by the revenue requirement.

We will discuss the following four variants of the theorem, each of which gives a set of necessary conditions for quasioptimal pricing:

1) If prices are quasi-optimal the ratio between the marginal profit yields of unit changes in the *prices* of any two goods will be equal to the ratio between their output levels.

2) For each product, the deviation of the quasi-optimal price from marginal cost must be proportionate to the difference between the product's marginal cost and marginal revenue (i.e., its marginal social welfare cost must be proportionate to its marginal contribution to the profit requirement). This result holds only in the case where cross-elasticities are all zero.

3) For each product, the percentage deviation of quasi-optimal price from marginal cost must be inversely proportionate to its price elasticity of demand. This result also holds only where cross-elasticities of demand are zero.

4) Quasi-optimal prices must yield outputs that deviate by (approximately) the same proportion from those which would result from pricing at the marginal costs corresponding to the quasi-optimal output levels. This last form of the proposition, which is the variant most frequently

encountered in the literature, is more general than the second and third versions of the theorem.

In demonstrating these propositions we shall utilize a comparatively straight-forward manner of proof which has not previously appeared in the literature.[4] To facilitate the exposition we start with a partial equilibrium approach. That is, we demonstrate that socially optimal pricing by a multi-product monopolist operating under a profit constraint is described by the preceding propositions. The monopolist is assumed able to set the prices of his final good outputs, but to purchase inputs at prices which remain fixed throughout the analysis. It will be celar that his optimal policy is the same as that which would be induced by the imposition of excise taxes equal to the derived divergence between output price and the marginal costs which would obtain if the outputs were to be produced by perfect competitors. This establishes the correspondence between the monopoly regulation and the excise taxation interpretations of the theorems.

If the monopolist is taken to be very large (e.g., if substantially all of the economy is operated by the government), or correspondingly, if the commodities taxed account for a large share of total output, the assumption of fixed input prices must clearly be relaxed. This has been recognized and dealt with in the literature (for a simple statement see A. C. Pigou (1947, pp. 105-09); a sophisticated treatment is found in M. Boiteux 1956). We do not go into detail on this problem, but we do show in a subsequent section that the same line of reasoning used in our proof can readily be extended to a general equlibrium model.

The demonstration proceeds as follows:

Let $p_1, \ldots, p_n$ and $x_1, \ldots, x_n$ be the prices and outputs of the n commodities produced by the monopolist and, as indicated above, take as fixed the prices of his inputs. Let $Z(p_1, \ldots, p_n)$ be our (unspecified) measure of consumer benefit which is to be maximized subject to the profit constraint[5] $\Pi(p_1, \ldots, p_n) = M$ where the profit function has now been

---

4. To simplify the exposition we have dispensed with some theoretical niceties in the proof presented here, especially in the definition of the objective function. These are discussed and the objective function is examined in greater detail in our forthcoming paper.

5. If the revenues permitted by regulation are based on total investment rather than being fixed in absolute amount, this constraint may require some modification. If (as is at least ostensibly the goal of regulation) gross profits are required to be no greater

expressed in terms of prices rather than outputs. As usual in such constrained maximization problems, Z will be maximal subject to this constraint only if

(1) $$\frac{\partial Z}{\partial p_i} = \lambda \frac{\partial \Pi}{\partial p_i}, \ (i = 1, 2, \ldots, n)$$

That is the intuitively obvious first-order requirement that the marginal welfare gain from a given price change (price reduction) must be proportionate to its marginal profit cost.

We can make the preceding equation much more explicit by examining more specifically the nature of the consumer benefit function $Z(p_1, \ldots, p_n)$. While we will not be able to say much about that function itself, we can be rather specific about its partial derivatives, which is all we need for our present purposes.

We need a basis on which to estimate the gain to consumers from price-quantity data. A one dollar reduction in the price of a commodity will enable a consumer who is presently consuming x units of that commodity to continue buying exactly his original bundle of goods with a budget that is smaller by x dollars than his original budget. Thus x dollars is a lower limit to the relevant compensating variation since this is the least he would be willing to pay for that price change, and he would probably pay more since the x dollar reduction in his budget accompanied by the one dollar reduction in the specified price would certainly permit him to buy his original bundle and might perhaps enable him to buy one which he prefers but which he could not previously afford. Similarly, if an individual is currently purchasing the respective amounts $x_1, \ldots, x_n$ of our n commodities at prices $p_1, \ldots, p_n$, the amount he would pay to confront instead prices $p_1 + \Delta p_1 \ p_2, \ldots, p_n$ will be at least $-x_1 \Delta p_1$. John Hicks (p. 330 ff.) shows rigorously in this same general

---

than the cost of capital, then net profits (over the cost of capital) will be zero and the constraint will hold as stated with $M=0$. If, however, the profit rate is permitted to exceed the cost of capital and the firm's total capital varies with output levels we may end up with M, the total profit permitted by regulation, itself varying with output levels. Our formal results remain unchanged if in the profit constraint $\Pi = R - C = M$ (where R=total revenue and C=total cost) we use C^* to represent $M+C$ and rewrite the constraint as $\Pi = R - C^* = 0$. We can then express all of our results in terms of C^* instead of C. Economic interpretations are, however, clouded by this modification.

manner that the *rate* of consumer gain per dollar *increase* in the price of any commodity is precisely the negative of the amount of the commodity initially consumed, times one dollar. We may then take as our expression for the derivative of the benefit function the compensating variation corresponding to the price change

$$\partial Z/\partial p_i = -x_i$$

Hence, substitution into the previous equation (1) yields

(2) $$-x_i = \lambda \partial \Pi/\partial p_i$$

or, dividing by the corresponding condition for any other item j, we obtain

(2a) $$\frac{1}{x_i} \frac{\partial \Pi}{\partial p_i} = \frac{1}{x_j} \frac{\partial \Pi}{\partial p_j}$$

as the required condition for quasi-optimality.

Equation (2a), then is the first of the four variants of the theorem described at the beginning of this section. This necessary condition for quasi-optimality requires marginal profit yields of price changes to be proportionate to output levels. It may perhaps claim the virtue that it is relatively operational. If the firm has some notion of the likely marginal profit yield of a change in any one of its product prices, management can readily check whether (2a) is approximately satisfied.

We can now proceed directly from (2) to a derivation of the other variants of the basic theorem. We use MRi, MCi, and Ei to represent, respectively, the marginal revenue, marginal cost, and price elasticity of demand of output i, and for simplicity assume that all cross-elasticities of demand are zero, though this is not necessary for the more general analysis, and is certainly not required for the preceding variant of the theorem.

Since[6]

---

6. It is here that the zero cross-elasticities enter our exposition. In the more general case, of course, $MRi=pi+\sum_j x_j \partial p_j/\partial x_i$. In our forthcoming paper we have dealt in some detail with this more general case which clearly complicates the analysis but does not change its nature in any fundamental way.

(3) $MR_i = p_i + x_i \partial p_i / \partial x_i$

then

$$\partial \Pi / \partial p_i = (MR_i - MC_i) dx_i / dp_i$$
$$= (p_i + x_i \partial p_i / \partial x_i - MC_i) dx_i / dp_i$$

Substituting this into our basic condition (2) we have

$$- x_i dp_i / dx_i = \lambda (p_i + x_i dp_i / dx_i - MC_i)$$

or adding $(p_i + x_i dp_i / dx_i - MC_i)$ to both sides we obtain

$$p_i - MC_i = (1 + \lambda)(p_i + x_i dp_i / dx_i - MC_i)$$
$$= (1 + \lambda)(MR_i - MC_i)$$

This is the second form of the quasi-optimality theorem: the difference between price and marginal cost[7] should be proportionate to the difference between marginal revenue and marginal cost.

Next we may rewrite the preceding equations as

(4) $- \lambda (p_i - MC_i) = (1 + \lambda) x_i dp_i / dx_i$

or

$$\frac{p_i - MC_i}{p_i} = \frac{1 + \lambda}{\lambda} \frac{1}{E_i}$$

---

7. Some care must be exercised in interpreting the various forms of the theorem described here because marginal costs are not generally constant. Let $MCi(q)$ represent marginal costs corresponding to the quasi-optimal output levels while $MCi(M)$ represent the marginal costs corresponding to the equilibrium outputs when all prices are set equal to marginal costs. Then in our proposition we have $\Delta pi = pi - MCi(q)$ and they are thus *not* necessarily equal to the $pi - MCi(M)$. That is, the propositions do not contrast quasi-optimal prices with the prices corresponding to a marginal cost pricing equilibrium as ordinarily conceived. They refer instead to the differences between the quasi-optimal prices and the marginal costs corresponding to the quasi-optimal output levels.

since by the usual formula, $E_i = -(p_i/x_i)(dx_i/dp_i)$ which is the third form of the result.[8] Note that it implies that if all elasticities in question are equal, prices should be set proportional to marginal costs.

For the final form of the proposition, write the deviation of price from marginal cost as Δp_i, i.e., set $p_i - MC_i = \Delta p_i$. Then equation (4) can be written after a minor rearrangement of terms as

$$\frac{dx_i}{dp_i} \Delta p_i = -\frac{1 + \lambda}{\lambda} x_i$$

But the left-hand side of the preceding equation may be interpreted as an approximation to the change, Δx_i, in the ith commodity demanded which would result from a shift from the actual prices to current marginal cost levels. We thus obtain the last version of our theorem:

$$\Delta x_i = k x_i, \quad \text{where } k = (1 + \lambda)/\lambda.$$

The more sophisticated discussions have generally emphasized this last form of the theorem, the assertion that quasi-optimal pricing requires (after compensation for income effects) a proportionate change in all purchases from the levels that would be observed if prices were set at marginal costs.[9] This interpretation has usually been preferred to the two

---

8. It should be reemphasized that this form of the derivation deliberately ignores the supply side for the sake of expository simplicity. However, the analysis is easily extended to take supply into account, and this was done from the very beginning of the discussion, by Frank Ramsey and by A.C. Pigou in 1947. For example, Pigou states "Writing η (definded as negative) for the elasticity of demand in respect of pre-tax output, er for the corresponding elasticity of supply of the rth commodity and tr for the ad valorem rate of tax on it, it can be proved that, in the conditions supposed (the optimum system of such taxes yielding a given revenue require) rates of tax ... such that $tr/(1/ei-1/\eta)$ has the same value for all values of r" (pp. 107-08).

9. In accord with the comments of fn. 6, this third form of the theorem should be read as follows: a change in prices from their quasi-optimal levels to *the corresponding marginal cost levels* should reduce all outputs in (approximately) the same proportions.
   If we estimate demand changes on the assumption that the slope of each demand curve is constant over the relevant range, our proposition is valid for large as well as for small price changes. It nows asserts that the divergence between price and marginal cost must be such that the estimated percentage changes in demand resulting from a drop in all prices to the given marginal cost levels are the same for all commodities.

variants that precede it because, as has been shown by M. Boiteux (1956), Paul Samuelson (1951), and others, this form of the theorem holds quite generally and does not depend on the simplifying assumptions needed to arrive at the two special forms of the theorem described before this last variant. Only our first relationship (2a), which requires the marginal profit yields of commodity price changes to be proportionate to their output levels, is of the same order of generality.[10]

IV. Intuitive Rationale

Though at first blush the rationale underlying the preceding propositions may not be entirely transparent, it is not too difficult to account for them intuitively. The last form of the theorem is perhaps the most helpful in offering us a grasp of the entire matter. We need merely think of the consequence of a deviation of price from marginal cost as a distortion of relative demand patterns. This immediately suggests the last form of the theorem for it implies that the damage to welfare resulting from departures from marginal cost pricing will be minimized if the *relative* quantities of the various goods sold are kept unchanged from their marginal cost pricing proportions. If we accept this plausibility argument, then the elasticity form of the theorem clearly follows. If we propose to (say) contract the demands for A and B each by precisely k percent, then if A's demand is much more elastic than B's, clearly A's price must be raised by a substantially smaller percentage than that of B.

A bit moe light is shed on the matter by a simple graphic discussion that follows rather loosely and analysis first presented by Ursula Hicks (p. 167 ff) and developed fully by William Vickrey in 1968. In Figure 1

---

10. Note that application of the theorem in any of its forms does not rule out a two-part or a multi-part tariff. On the contrary, it tells us how to determine the quasi-optimal value for each of the multiplicity of prices that composes such a tariff. For example, when the consumer pays one charge for the rental of a telephone and another for each of his calls, this can be interpreted either as a two-part tariff or as a pair of prices for two distinct but related services each of which has a quasi-optimal price. This discussion is, of course, based on the observation that one cannot in reality impose a Pigouvian poll tax as one part of the multi-part tariff. Indeed, if such a lump sum tax were possible there clearly would be no need for the theorems under discussion. Marginal cost prices plus lump sum taxes could then satisfy the revenue requirement and yield an optimal allocation.

consider the segments of two demand curves D_aK and D_bK through point K. Let us use the Marshallian measure of consumers' surplus to compare the psychic loss to consumers from a given price (tax) rise with the resulting increase in (tax) revenues. Then, if demand is in fact given by the less elastic curve D_bK and price rises from P_o to P_1, the loss of consumers' surplus will be $P_oKE_bP_1$. On the other hand, assuming for simplicity that marginal costs are constant at level OC, net revenue will be increased as a result of the price change by the quantity $P_oK_bE_bP_1$ minus R_bRKK_b. Thus the positive portion of the net revenue change, $P_oK_bE_bP_1$, may be considered to be offset by an approximately equivalent loss to consumers. This means that with the less elastic demand curve the rise in price will have caused a net reduction in net revenue plus consummers' surplus that is measured by the shaded area, R_bRKE_b.

Similarly, with the more elastic demand curve, D_aK, the rise in price from P_o to P_1 will decrease the sum of the revenue net of consumers' surplus by the greater area R_aRKE_a. In general, then (with marginal costs constant), a given price rise will exact a larger social cost in consumers' surplus not offset by increased revenues the more elastic the

Figure 1

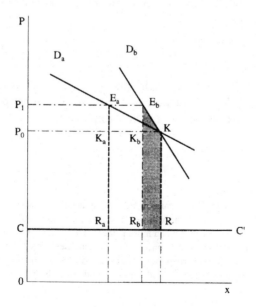

demand curve. That is essentially the reason for the theorem that calls for a relatively small deviation between the price and marginal cost of any commodity whose demand is comparatively elastic.

V. A Simple General Equilibrium Model

Our interest in conveying the central results of the literature discussed in our paper to a wide readership in an intuitively convincing fashion leads us to couch our argument of Section IV in terms of partial equilibrium analysis. It is desirable, however, to sketch out the way it all works in general equilibrium terms. A simple reinterpretation of the terms used in the derivation of the theorems will show that our proof is sufficient to establish the propositions in the special general equilibrium case in which there is only one input factor, labor, and all the productive activities are in the hands of the government. Accordingly, let $p_1, ..., p_n$, be the prices in terms of labor hours at which the n final outputs other than leisure, $x_1, ..., x_n$, all produced by the government, are sold to the consumer-laborers. The government is assumed to operate with a profit constraint in the form of a fixed number, M (which may be zero), of units of labor. In addition, of course, there is a production constraint, which we may write as.[11]

$$(5) \qquad C = F(x_1, ..., x_n),$$

where C is the minimum labor input sufficient to produce the output vector, $x_1, ..., x_n$. The problem is to maximize "consumer benefit" subject to this production relation and the profit constraint,

$$(6) \qquad \pi = p_1 x_1 + ... + p_n x_n - C = M$$

---

11. Notice that in putting this constraint in the form of an equality, we have ruled out production inefficiency. Although this is a plausible requirement and makes things easier, it is not always innocuous when more is meant by "consumer benefit" than attainment of Pareto optimality—the concept utilized here. See Peter Diamond and James Mirrlees for a proof that production efficiency will be called for under almost all "reasonable" assumptions about production, individual utility, and social welfare relations.

Now let us treat the government as an ordinary firm that imagines it can buy all the labor it wants at a price of one per unit. The additional labor it would have to buy to produce an additional unit of good is then the marginal cost of that good, both in the accounting sense and in the sense of its leisure opportunity cost, all other outputs held constant.

There will be, in general, a large set of price vectors compatible with both (a) clearing of the markets for goods and factors and (b) satisfaction of the government's profit constraint. It is useful to spell this statement out in somewhat more detail. If the aggregate labor sold is L, we can write the set of demand equations as

$$L = L(p_1, \ldots, p_n)$$
$$x_1 = x_1(p_1, \ldots, p_n)$$
$$\ldots\ldots\ldots\ldots\ldots$$
$$x_n = x_n(p_1, \ldots, p_n),$$

where, necessarily (Walras' Law),

$$p_1 x_1 + \ldots + p_n x_n = L$$

For a set of prices to be market-clearing, the government must buy exactly the specified amount of labor and produce exactly the specified quantities of goods. By (5) and (6) "feasible price vectors" are those which satisfy the profit constraint conditions

$$L - F(x_1, \ldots, x_n) = M,$$

or, equivalently,

$$p_1 x_1 + \ldots + p_n x_n - F(x_1, \ldots, x_n) = M$$

The task is to find among these an optimal price vector, where we have taken this to mean a vector which consumers in the aggregate would be unwilling (after costless negotiation among themselves) to bribe the government to change. The solution to this problem is found in the propositions set forth in Section III above. The entire analysis in that section continues to hold when the profit constraint as just described is used in place of the usual partial equilibrium construct.

VI. The Taxed and the Untaxed Sectors

Now we are equipped with a genuine, if very simple, general equilibrium apparatus, but one which in most respects can be manipulated in partial equilibrium terms. The key to this is the form in which we have expressed the production relation (as a cost function), the fixing of the government's profit constraint in terms of labor, and the corresponding choice of labor as price numeraire (so that the price of the single input factor, the "all other prices" of partial equilibrium analysis, is fixed at unity). In this model the government can be taken to tax the output of producers of the n non-leisure goods (where the tax is the difference between price and marginal cost), and hence these goods make up the "taxed sector." The untaxed sector here may reasonably be described as the production of negative labor input to the taxed goods-production sector, i.e., the production of leisure. In a rather trivial sense, in the latter sector marginal cost and price are always equal at unity.

It is illuminating at this point to reconsider "our" results in light of the following comment by Abba Lerner, who derives two special rules for quasi-optimality, each applicable to a special case:

[One] rule [equalize tax elasticities] is appropriate where the shifting is only from a taxed to an untaxed sector, while the [other] rule [maintain proportionality of price to marginal cost] is appropriate where the shifting is only to another part of the taxed sector (as would be the case if all uses of resources could be, and were, taxed).

What we need is a rule that is applicable whether the resources shifted by a tax remain in the taxed sector or go to the untaxed sector or are divided between the two sectors. [p. 285]

Documentation of the fact that a general rule for optimal excise taxation has long been available in the literature, and presentation of a simplified derivation of several forms of such a rule are precisely our objectives. It is easy to show that in those situations where Lerner recommends prices in proportion to marginal cost, our theorems do likewise; where Lerner recommends equalization of tax elasticities, so do our theorems; and where Lerner calls for something in between the two, our theorems provide an exact prescription.

In the case of the model which has just been described,[12] the state-

---

12. Two things should be noted. First, when Lerner speaks of "tax elasticity" he is refer

ment that a tax change has as its only effect a shifting of resources from taxed to untaxed sectors is clearly equivalent to the assertion that the only output affected in the taxed sector is the one whose tax rate has changed. If the effect of varying any one tax is only to shift resources into the non-taxed sector then only own elasticities of the taxed goods, and not their cross-elasticities with one another, can be non-zero. In this case, Lerner and we (most directly in variant 3 of the theorem) conclude that the percentage deviation of price of any taxed commodity from marginal cost should be inversely proportional to its own price elasticity of demand.

We turn now to the next case where the alternative use of resources induced by tax changes can be said to be entirely in the taxed sector. This is obviously equivalent to the assertion that labor is perfectly inelastically supplied over a wide range of price vectors.[13] In this situation, Lerner and our theorems agree that prices proportional to marginal costs, i.e., relative prices equal to marginal rates of transformation between (non-leisure) commodities, is clearly optimal. This result follows easily for the case when cross-elasticities between (non-leisure) goods are all zero. Then, since a change in the price of a given good results in no change in either the purchases of other goods or of labor sold, it must lead to no change at all in labor expenditure on the good in

ring to what might better be called "own tax elasticity," that is, the relative change in the tax revenue (here, profit) collected on commodity x_i, when the tax on xi (divergence between price and marginal cost of xi) is raised by one unit. The change in tax revenue collected on other commodities, which arises via cross-elasticity of demand, is not included.

Second, it should be observed that although the term "resources" is often not definable in general equilibrium models of the type described above (since choice is made from among alternative vectors of social aggregates of final goods, without reference to the underlying mechanics of production), in this simple case we may presumably equate them with "labor."

13. Note that unless this inelasticity of supply results from some kind of artificial constraint, such as a legal maximum working day, of from a kink in the individuals' utility functions, commodity taxes will in this case *not* yield the same result as lump sum taxes. For if the inelasticity results from the offsetting of income and substitution effects, a doubling of prices will generally have a different effect from the subtraction of half (or any other portion) of the individuals' original labor income, leaving prices unchanged. This is obviously so because the (alternative) new price lines will not have the same slope and so they cannot be tangent to the same indifference curve at the same point.

question. That is, all goods must be demanded with equal, in fact, with unit elasticity. Our third form of the theorem states that in this case the relative deviation of price from marginal cost should be the same for all commodities.

More generally, admitting non-zero cross elasticities, the zero elasticity of labor supply means that any change in profit resulting from a price change comes purely from the change in labor cost of goods sold, since there can be no change in the total revenue received by the firm or government: the fixed quantity of labor offered in exchange for their products. We have, for all price vectors in question, by the inelasticity of labor supply at quantity L_0:

(7)
$$\sum_j p_j x_j(p) = L_0;$$

$$\text{i.e.,} \quad \sum_j p_j \frac{\partial x_j}{\partial p_i} + x_i = 0$$

for all i. Furthermore, as just noted, price changes can affect profits only through their effect on costs:

(8)
$$\frac{\partial \pi}{\partial p_i} = \frac{\partial}{\partial p_i}(\sum_j p_j x_j - C)$$

$$= 0 - \sum_j \frac{\partial C}{\partial x_j} \frac{\partial x_j}{\partial p_i}$$

Recall now the first form of "our" theorem which asserts that optimality requires, for all i,

$$-x_i = \lambda \frac{\partial \pi}{\partial p_i}$$

In the case now under consideration, this becomes by (8)

$$-x_i = -\lambda \sum_j \frac{\partial C}{\partial x_j} \frac{\partial x_j}{\partial p_i}$$

But by (7)

$$-x_i = \sum_j p_j \frac{\partial x_i}{\partial p_j}$$

Together these results imply that the first-order conditions can be written for all i,

$$\sum_j \left(p_j + \lambda \frac{\partial C}{\partial x_j} \right) \frac{\partial x_j}{\partial p_i} = 0$$

Since $\partial C/\partial x_j$ is the marginal cost of x_j, this asserts that prices bearing the proportion $-\lambda$ to marginal cost satisfy the first-order conditions.

In the more general case where shifting takes place both between sectors ($\partial C/\partial p_j \neq 0$) and within the taxed sector ($\partial x_i/\partial p_j \neq 0$, at least sometimes), an analogous algebraic chain of steps leads to the following first-order conditions, for all i:

$$\sum_j \left(p_j + \lambda \frac{\partial C}{\partial x_j} \right) \frac{\partial x_j}{\partial p_i} = (1 + \lambda) \frac{\partial L}{\partial p_i}$$

Only by chance will these conditions be satisfied by prices proportional to marginal cost, or by prices deviating from proportionality by a simple function of own elasticity. In this we agree with Lerner. However, the theorems prescribe definite prices which do optimize, given the constraints, and there is no necessity to resort to a rough compromise between two polar rules. One rule prescribes for the polar situations as well as for intermediate ones. This does not mean that a more precise spelling out of Lerner's compromise would not yield the same (correct) conclusions: it means only that the task which remains is not to find the general rule. That is already accomplished by (9). Rather, it is only necessary to translate this rule into a form compatible with Professor Lerner's very illuminating intuitions.

VII. The Case Where All Items are Taxable

Finally, we must yet deal with the case excluded from our discussion thus far, in which "*all* uses of resources" can be taxed. In view of our preceding agreement with Lerner that when tax changes result in resource shifts only within the taxed sector, prices proportional to marginal costs are optimal, our assertion that this is generally not the case when all goods are taxable may come as a surprise. The explanation is, however, relatively simple overall marginal cost pricing will not, as rule yield the necessary revenue.[14] This follows from a basic assumption of the entire analysis: that lump sum taxes are impossible. In terms of our general equilibrium this requires (by Walras law) that the net value of consumers' sales and purchases of all commodities, *including labor*, add up to zero. In that case, a proportionate tax, leading to a proportionate change in prices, will still leave the net consumer expenditures at zero and hence will yield no revenue to the government.

In formal terms, let P_i be the price of commodity i ($i=1, ..., n$) facing the consumer, no longer expressed in labor terms, and let P_L be the price of labor. Following the sign convention that positive numbers represent net purchases of desired goods, negative numbers, net sales, let $a_1, ..., an, a_L$, be the vector of net transactions carried out by a consumer. Our no-lump sum tax assumption can be expressed as the requirement that $P_1a_1+P_2a_2+...+P_na_n+P_La_L=0$ (This implies, of course, that the aggregate net transactions vector, summed over all consumers, satisfies the same condition, expressed above as the condition on the demand functions $p_1x_1+...+p_nx_n=L$, where prices were expressed in labor terms). Obviously, here it makes absolutely no difference to the consumer whether he faces prices $P_1, ..., P_n, P_L$ or prices ten times as high; only relative prices count. If the government were to collect the difference between these two price vectors (P and $10P$) as a tax, it would collect precisely $9(\sum_i p_i a_i+P_L a_L)$, which is zero. A tax vector which is a scalar multiple of the price vector facing consumers will, under our zero-transfer assumption, *always* yield zero revenue.

With consumer budgets equated to zero, the vector of taxes thus cannot be proportional to consumer prices if there is to be any tax yield, and hence consumer prices cannot be proportional to marginal costs. Now we are back where we started. If the government wishes to obtain, say, a quantity M of labor for its own uses, and can only work with commodity taxes, it must get consumers to settle at an equilibrium with an aggre-

---

14. We shall say that "overall marginal cost princing prevails when the price vector confronting consumers a scalar multiple of the vector of first partial derivative of the transformation function evaluated at the associated social total net output vector.

gate net transaction vector $x_1, \ldots, x_n, -L$, satisfying $L-F(x_1, \ldots, x_n)=M$, i.e., such that the leisure given up for production exceeds that necessary to produce the other desired goods by M.

VIII. An Analysis in Terms of Quantity Changes

Some readers may find it instructive to see a derivation of the propositions carried out explicitly in a general equilibium context and in terms of quantity changes rather than price changes. This is easily done within our present model if it is assumed that lump sum redistributions maintain a socially optimal distribution of alternative social totals of goods and leisure. Then we can employ a Samuelsonian social utility function relating social welfare to these totals, with the property that the tangent plane to any social indifference surface is also a "budget plane" associated with prices at which that point will be sustained as a competitive equilibrium. Thus prices can be written as a function of quantities. The analysis is made more transparent if we assume that there is a certain fixed total, $\overline{L}$, of labor time which must be allocated among production, leisure, R (for recreation), and government surplus, yielding the constraint:

$$F(x_1, \ldots, x_n) + R + M = \overline{L}$$

where $F(x_1, \ldots, x_n)$ is obviously the (labor) cost function for the output bundle $(x_1, \ldots, x_n)$.

The problem is to maximize over output-leisure bundles the social utility function, $U(x_1, \ldots, x_n, R)$, subject to this constraint, and subject to the constraint that exactly the required government surplus is obtained as profit:

$$\sum_{i=1}^{n} p_i x_i - F(x_1, \ldots, x_n) = M,$$

where the p's are equilibrium labor-prices associated with the chosen output-leisure bundle. Associating the Lagrange multiplier λ with the first constraint, and the multiplier, μ, with the second, we can write out the Lagrangian expression:

$$V(x_1, \ldots, x_n, R, \lambda, \mu)$$
$$= U(x_1, \ldots, x_n, R)$$
$$+ \lambda[\overline{L} - F(x_1, \ldots, x_n) - R - M]$$
$$+ \mu \left[M - \sum_{i=1}^{n} p_i x_i + F(x_1, \ldots, x_n) \right]$$

Taking partial derivatives we obtain the first-order conditions:

$$\frac{\partial U}{\partial x_i} - \lambda \frac{\partial F}{\partial x_i}$$

$$- \mu \left[\frac{\partial}{\partial x_i} \left(\sum_{j=1}^{n} p_j x_j \right) - \frac{\partial F}{\partial x_i} \right] = 0,$$

$$i = 1, \ldots, n$$

$$\frac{\partial U}{\partial R} - \lambda = 0$$

Dividing each of the first n conditions by the $(n+1)$st and noting that equilibrium of the consumer requires $\partial U/\partial x_i / \partial U/\partial R = p_i/p_r = p_i$ (since labor is the numeraire, its price unity) we have

$$p_i - \frac{\partial F}{\partial x_i} = \frac{\mu}{\lambda} \left[\frac{\partial}{\partial x_i} \left(\sum_{i=1}^{n} - p_j x_j \right) - \frac{\partial F}{\partial x_i} \right]$$

Employing with their usual meanings, the symbols MC and MR (the latter including the effect on revenue of variations in *all* prices), the preceding condition implies

$$p_i - MC_i = \frac{\mu}{\lambda}(MR_i - MC_i),$$

$$i = 1, \ldots, n$$

which is the second form of our theorem from which the other forms can be obtained exactly as before. Thus we have derived the results explicitly from a general equilibrium model. Note that the term "marginal revenue" is definable here because we have normalized prices to labor dimensions and have assumed behind-the-scenes income distribution, making determinate the effect on equilibrium prices of changes in any of the desired outputs. Note also that under these conditions, the second version of the theorem, proved in Section III for the case of independent demands, is shown to hold generally.

IX. Notes on the History of the Discussion

There is some point in going briefly into the antecedents of the discussion because this history makes it all the more difficult to understand why the proposition in question have achieved so little recognition by the profession. The general line of argument has appeared widely for the better part of a century. The formal theorems themselves date dack more than forty years. As we will see, this work has appeared in some of our leading journal under the authorship of some of the luminaries of our profession and was clearly no limited to a backwater of the literature.

There is an informal proposition very closely related to the results under examination that has a long history going back at least to the 1870's. With the establishment of the Railway and Canal Commision in England in 1873, and of the discussion preceding the establishment of the Interstate Commerce Commission in the subsequent decade there arose a rich literature examining utility pricing in relation to the public interest. A number of author advocated prices that vary directly with demand *in* elasticity ("value of service").

The mainstay of the early discussion was an argument only loosely related to the formal propositions in which we are interested. In brief, it was maintained that a relatively low price in elastic markets, provided it covers more than incremental cost, may well permit lower prices in other markets and hence be beneficial to everyone. For (particularly if the firm is subject to a constraint on its overall profit) the opening of a market which makes any net contribution may permit or may even

---

15. For some examples see A. T. Hadley (ch. 6); Porter Alexander (esp. pp. 2-5, 10-11) and W. Acworth (ch.3, esp. pp. 57-60). Hadley, the American economist who went on to become a president of Yale, is the author of what is apparently the classic discussion of the period, in which he coined the phrase "not charging what the traffic can *not* near." There is in fact a hint of the argument much earlier than this in the work of Dupuit who advocates the separation of consumers into different classes each paying a different price, remarking "suppose that (railroads) offered nothing but first class tickets, what a loss for the public and for the companies" (pp. 124-27).

require a reduction in prices elsewhere.[16]

Discussion along these lines has since appeared throughout the literature of public utility economics (See, e.g., James Bonbright, esp. chs. 5, 17-20). The various forms of the proposition have also appeared at least implicitly in a number of the standard writings of economic theory, notably in Joan Robinson's work and that of W. Arthur Lewis.[17]

However, the formal mathematical propositions which are derived from optimality considerations and which are the subject of this paper, themselves have a substantial history. As propositions on optimal taxation they first appear in 1927 in Frank Ramsey's pathbreaking article on taxation.[18]

---

16. "If the (New York to San Francisco) price is more than the *additional outlay* involved in doing it, as against leaving it alone, it is profitable to the railroad, and the business is moreover advantageous to the whole inland community served by the railroad. For it adds to the number of men employed along the line and ... the more prosperous the road, the lower the local rates may be made" E. P. Alexander (p. 4) [author's italics]. The author adds (p. 5) that between the limits of "unreasonable" profits and net loss, actual profit rates "should be adjusted in proportion to value of service rendered" (inelasticity of demand).

17. See Joan Robinson (p. 207). Since she is dealing with a single product and does not utilize any explicit revenue constraint, the result she gives is not quite what is needed for our purposes but it is closely related to the theorem under discussion.
Lewis' statement (pp. 20-21), on the other hand, is precisely on target: The principle ...is that those who cannot escape must make the largest contribution to indivisible cost, and those to whom the commodity does not matter much...get off lightly.... When there are escapable indivisible expenses to be covered the case for discrimination is clear. It secures an output nearer the optimum and levies the indivisible cost on those who get the greatest benefit (measured by their consumers' surplus).... Moreover, it is possible in some cases that the net result may be that everyone pays a lower price.... *If the undertaking is out merely to cover its costs*...reducing the price to some persons with elastic demands may increase the surplus over marginal cost which they contribute...(emphasis added).

18. The theorem seems to have made its greatest impact on the literature of public finance. A.C. Pigou (1928, pp. 126-28); (1947, pp. 105-09) reports Ramsey's results, offers an intuitive explanation and translates the theorem into elasticity terms. He also argues that except in the case of linear supply and demand functions the argument holds only if the taxes are small.
Ursula Hicks (pp. 167 ff) provides a very similar result on the basis of an elementary graphic argument. Yet even Richard Musgrave in his classic volume (p. 148) devotes only a footnote to the theorem and dismisses it as being "arrived at within the framework of the old welfare economics of interpersonal utility comparison." His characterization of the argument as part of the ability-to-pay approach is surely rather misleading. Cf. R. Bishop's comment on Musgrave, p. 212n.

Thus, more than a decade before the publication of Hotelling's historic discussion of marginal cost pricing, Ramsey had in another context provided at least implicitly a solution to the optimal pricing problem for an industry in which marginal cost prices do not cover total costs.

A. C. Pigou took up the Ramsey discussion in the following year in his book on public finance, providing a very lucid and rather extensive summary of the argument. It was independently approached by Ursula Hicks in her 1947 book on the same subject. Her analysis is largely diagrammatic and is based entirely on the Marshallian consumers' surplus, just as Ramsey's and Pigou's had been. However, as far as we have been able to tell, the formal analysis did not reappear until 1951 in an article by M. Boiteux which was the first to dispense with the notion of consumers' surplus. Apparently in the same year, Paul Samuelson submitted to the U.S. Treasury a closely related paper containing a generalization of Ramsey's results.[19] Samuelson's approach differs from that which we are discussing in that he employs no explicit revenue requirement. Instead he requires some preselected quantity of each output to be left unused by the private sector and made available to the government. His result, however, is essentially the same as those of the other contrib-

---

19. Samuelson's own brief description of the history of the analysis (1964) is worth reporducing:

   ... Consider an optimal *laissez faire* situation that maximizes a social welfare function with zero government expenditure and taxes. Now introduce government services as a (vector) function of a small or large parameter y, $G(y)$. Suppose excise taxes (on goods or services) to be alone feasible, and introduce a (vector) pattern of excises $T(y)$ sufficient to provide resources for the G. What is the optimal $T(y)$ pattern to maximize the welfare function $W(y)=W(T, G)$? This is the problem set by Pigou to Frank Ramsey in the 1920's. Approximate answers were given by Ramsey, Boiteux (and in unpublished form by Hotelling and Hicks). In a pearl cast before the U.S. Treasury in 1950, I gave an exact solution for large and small programs; namely, that the optimal pattern is the one at which the response of all goods and factors to a further compensated-Slutsky price distortion would result in equal percentage (virtual) reductions.

   My literary wording is loose, but there is no need for approximative consumer's surplus at all...

   Though the reported date of the Samuelson memorandum may seem to imply some ambiguity about the order of appearance of this and the first Boiteux article, this issue is cleared up by Samelson's explicit reference to the Boiteux article on page 5 of his memorandum in which he expresses his debt to the "brlliant analysis by M. Boiteux."

utors under discussion.

In 1952 there appeared a particularly simple derivation of the theorem in its most elementary form in a note by Alan Manne. His discussion assumes that cross-elasticities of demand are all zero and it measures and aggregates consumers' and producers' surplus in an unabashed Marshallian manner, but his derivation compensates for these simplifications by its great lucidity. Boiteux and Manne were also the first to present the analysis in the form of a discussion of public utility pricing. One year later Marcus Fleming provided an independent and illuminating derivation.

Meanwhile, Gerard Debreu had contributed analytic materials which led Boiteux to employ a Pareto optimality approach to the matter. On this basis Boiteux was then able to complete his definitive analysis of the subject. In Boiteux' classic 1956 article the analysis is, as a result, independent of any interpersonal comparison. The notions of consumers' and producers' surplus are dispensed with altogether. He is able to deal with goods whose demands are interdependent, with the pricing of inputs and intermediate goods as well as with outputs. It has also been emphasized by a subsequent writer (Jacques Drèze) that by his general equilibrium approach to the matter, Boiteux was contributing an explicit second-best solution, one of the few to be found to date in any area of welfare economics. Of course, no piece of analysis can answer every relevant question, and Boiteux left unsettled some matters of detail. There is a moderately mysterious role played in his analysis by the numéraire commodity; he has not dealt with problems of nonnegativity of outputs, etc. All this has left room for subsequent work by R. Rees, William Vickrey (*Testimony* and other unpublished work), the present authors, and by a number of others.[20]

---

20. Among those who have also written on the subject are Diamond and Mirrlees and Bishop. Recall in this connection Samuelson's reference to unpublished work by Hicks and Hotelling, on which more light is shed by the following excerpt from a letter which the authors received from Professor Hicks:

It was just as well that you sent me the cutting from Samuelson [the preceding footnote], or I should have found it hard to recollect the matter. But with this refreshment it comes back. I think the story is as follows.

In December 1946 (in the last week of my first visit to the United States) I stayed for a couple of days with Hotelling at Chapel Hill. I then told him that I had worked out (using a quite crude consumers' surplus method) that if a given sum had to be raised in excise taxes, the least-sacrifice way of doing it was the proportional all-round

However, there is no need to go beyond Boiteux' work for a basis for the welfare discussion contained in this paper. The generalization to optimal pricing for an entire economy requires only one small modification in Boiteux' two-sector analysis. In his model there are two sets of firms, the first composed exclusively of perfect competitors, while the second are subject to the author's rules for quasi-optimal pricing. For our purpose we need merely take all firms to fall into the second category and our interpretation follws at once. In sum, it follows for the economy as a whole that unless marginal cost pricing happens to provide returns sufficient to meet the social (governmentally determined?) revenue requirement, a quasi-optimal allocation calls for systematic deviations of prices from marginal costs *throughout the economy* in the manner specified by the theorems that this paper has described.

X. Concluding Comment

We conclude our survey of the relevant literature as we began—at a loss to explain how a set of results flowing from the pens of so distinguished a set of authors and appearing and reappearing in the profession's leading journals, should so long have escaped general notice. This is all the more curious in light of the importance of the subject and the elegance of the theory.

As a theoretical matter, the theorem we have discussed seems fundamental not only for the analysis of public finance and the regulation of utilities, but also for some of the basic precepts of welfare economics.

---

reduction in consumption, as compared with an optimum position. For if the burden of the tax is

$$\frac{1}{2}\Sigma q_{ij}dp_idp_j$$

this is minimised subject to $G=\Sigma q_idp_i$ if

$$dq_i=\Sigma q_{ij}dp_j=\lambda q_i$$

where λ is the Lagrange multiplier. Not much more than this, except that I had allowed (in the spirit of the old Hotelling article) that the qij could incorporate supply as well as demand reactions.

I remember he told me I ought to publish this, but I didn't—mainly, I suppose, because I was conscious of the qualifications to which Samuelson alludes in his paper, and which, if I had set them out in my style, would have whittled away the result so near to nothing.

Earlier we spoke of the result as a proposition in the theory of the second best. But it is more than this. In a world in which marginal cost pricing without excise or income taxes is normally not feasible, the solution we have usually considered to characterize the "best" is none too good, because it is simply unattainable. In that case, the systematic deviations between prices and marginal costs that the theorem calls for may truly be optimal because they constitute the best we can do within the limitations imposed by normal economic circumstances.

Appendix
Comments on Lerner's Appendix

In the Appendix to his paper, Lerner asserts that our analysis overemphasized demand elasticities. In addition, the Appendix contains a wider range of lesser criticisms. To deal in depth with all of these would require us to impose on the reader's time and patience. We propose to touch briefly on what appear to us to be the more important issues raised by Lerner, and trust that our failure to respond to other points will not be taken as a sign of general agreement.

Two criticisms appear recurringly in Lerner's Appendix and they are best disposed of at the outset. The first is that we have somehow used as a standard of welfare a measure of *consumers loss*, and have left out any measure of *social damage*. Since our economy was taken to consist entirely of consumers, i.e., we use the terms "consumer" and "person with utility function" here interchangeably, we would use the two terms "consumers' loss" and "social damage" interchangeably as well. We would use neither without a grain of salt. The touchstone of quasi-optimality is plain and simple Pareto optimality, given the profit or tax revenue constraint. As is by now generally recognized, Pareto optimality cannot be comfortably equated with a "higher ethical good," and we apologize if we give the impression that a quasi-optimal price structure (for the monopolist) or tax structure was "good" in any sense other than Pareto optimality.

The second assertion that occurs in several places is that our analysis assumes constant marginal costs. This is simply incorrect. The only point at which marginal costs are taken to be constant is in our Section IV, the graphical presentation, which is intended solely as an aid to intuition. Elsewhere there is no assumption of any sort about marginal costs and none of the results depend on such an assumption. Lerner seems to suggest that our assumption that the prices of inputs are fixed can be equated to the premise that marginal cost is constant. We fail to see any connection between the two. Our assumption that input prices are constant is another, perhaps mistaken, compromise in the direction of intuitive appeal.[21]

Incidentally, the point of our footnote 7 is not, as Lerner suggests, to acknowledge in passing that marginal costs might in fact be variable. Rather, it is intended to point out that the marginal costs in question in the various forms of the theorem are *not* those which prevail in some initial situation before any taxes are imposed, but those which in fact rule at the solution values. Rather than apologizing for assuming marginal costs constant, we are, on the contrary, saying that marginal costs will very likely change as taxes are varied, so one must watch out and be sure to use the correct values in testing for optimality.

The basic task undertaken by Lerner in his Appendix relevant to the discussion here is derivation of our four forms of the "mislaid maxim" from his second rule. Since all four are derivable from either the first $(\partial \pi / \partial p_i = \lambda x_i,$ all $i)$ or the fourth $(\sum_j (\partial x_j / \partial p_j) (p_j - MC_j) = \gamma x_i,$ all $i)$ it is reasonable that he sould be able to do this. It is nevertheless somewhat surprising that he did not in the process notice that his second rule takes into account only "own tax elasticity" and hence implicitly assumes the zero cross elasticities which he finds so objectionable in our second and third forms. It is probably because of this that he comes to the conclusion that our first form holds only when cross-elasticities are zero, which is simply incorrect.

Lerner's handling of our first form of the theorem (which, incidentally, is the one form we did *not* distill from the literature although since deriving it, we have seen essentially the same variant in Diamond and Mirrlees) is altogether curious. Almost paradigmatic of the economist's

---

21. Analytically, it does serve to a set a price level so that the government profit constraint in pecuniary form is pinned down. In the case of more than one input factor it does, however, hide rather strong assumptions about the transformation function in a full general equilibrium treatment. In any event, the pecuniary variant of the government's budget constraint is perhaps not the most felicitous for use in such a treatment. The theorems in question are, however, in no way sensitive to these assumptions. Again we recommend perusal of the literature on this point.

approach to a welfare problem, say, how large a park to build, is the following: "Clearly our rule should be, enlarge the park until the incremental social gain from enlargment by an additional unit is just balanced by the social loss from the space and other resources thereby foregone. But that is, of course, purely tautological. What we now need to do is clothe the concepts of social gain and social loss with operational measures...." In this case Lerner goes backwards: "The equalization of the ratio between marginal yield and output level turns out to be an obscure way of expressing the equalization of marginal tax yield and marginal social damage—an equalization that minimizes the total social damage for a given total tax yield" (p. 289). We were, as it happens, especially pleased with the first form of the theorem which we think is new, precisely because it seemed to promise more than the others a degree of operational applicability. Our feeling was that experienced tax officials (or monopoly managers) would have a much better chance of estimating at least roughly the magnitudes that enter that expression—the effect on the total tax take (profit) (including cross effects) of a change in a given tax (price) than econometricians would have of estimating the full matrix of cross elasticities, just as it seems plausible that a businessman may come close to maximizing profits even though he is pretty vague about quantities such as marginal cost and marginal revenue. If this is misplaced faith it doesn't matter, because the first form of the theorem, being equivalent to the others (and for more forms see our forthcoming paper), is at least no harder than they to put into practice. One thing is clear, the operational meaning of the first form is easier than the others (except, perhaps, for the fourth) to explain to a non-economist.

The derivations of the second and third forms of our theorem, like those of the first and fourth, make no use of and in no way depend upon constancy of marginal cost. The second and third variants do, however, involve an assumption of zero cross elasticities of demand among the goods whose prices are in question. Lerner is quite properly disturbed by the implication of extending this assumption to *all* goods. The demand relationship being traced out by variations in the price vector is simply the aggregate offer curve of the economy with the initial commodity vector of each citizen specified (generally at zero) and no net transfers. Independent demands for the individual goods are impossible here except in the trivial case in which the demanded vector is completely independent of the price vector, a vector which would in turn have to be the zero net transactions vector. The implication is not that the results are incorrect but that the second and third forms are not relevant when all goods are taxable and there are no net transfers.

Again, contrary to Lerner, the fourth form of the theorem is as general as the first, and more general than the second and third (*not* because it doesn't depend upon constant costs—they don't either—but because it does not assume zero cross-elasticities). Given the parenthetical word "approximately" its generality would seem assured. But we were willing to go farther than that, and took great pains to make precise in Section III, in the algebraic development of the fourth variant, what operationally was meant by "approximately" here. In footnote 9 we spell this out still further.

References

W. M. Acworth, *The Railways and the Traders*. London 1981.

E. P. Alexander, *Railway Practice*. New York 1887.

R. Bishop, "The Effects of Specific and ad valorem Taxes," *Quart J. Econ.*, May 1968, 82, 198-218.

D. F. Bradford and W. J. Baumol, "Quasi-optimal Pricing with Regulated Profit and Interdependent Demands," forthcoming.

M. Boiteux, "Le 'revenue distribuable' et les pertes économiques," *Econometrica*, Apr. 1951, 19, 112-33.

———, "Sur la gestion des Monopoles Publics astreints à l'équilibre budgétaire," *Econometrica*, Jan. 1956, 24, 22-40.

J. Bonbright, *Principles of Public Utility Rates*. New York 1961.

G. Debreu, "The Classical Tax-Subsidy Problem," *Econometrica*, Jan. 1952, 20, 00.

P. A. Diamond and J. A. Mirrlees, "Optimal Taxation and Public Production," mimeo. working paper 22, M.I.T. 1968.

J. H. Drèze, "Some Postwar Contributions of French Economists to Theory and Public Policy, with Special Emphasis on Problems of Resource Allocation," *Amer. Econ. Rev.*, June 1964, 54, 1-64.

J. Dupuit, *Trait th orique et pratique de la conduite et de la distribution des eaux*. Paris 1854.

J. M. Fleming, "Optimal Production with Fixed Profits," *Economica*, Aug. 1953, N.S. 20, 215-36.

A. T. Hadley, *Railroad Transportation*. New York and London 1886.

J. R. Hicks, *Value and Capital*, 2d ed, New York 1956.

Ursala Hicks, *Public Finance*. New York 1947.

H. Hotelling, "The General Welfare in Relation to Problems of Taxation and of Railway and Utility Rates," *Econometrica*, July 1938, 6, 242-69.

H. Leibenstein, "Allocative Efficiency vs. 'X-Efficiency,'" *Amer. Econ. Rev.*, June 1966, 56, 392-415.

A. P. Lerner, "On Optimal Taxes With an Untaxable Sector," *Amer. Econ. Rev.*, June 1970, 60, 284-94.

W. A. Lewis, *Overhead Costs*. London 1949.

A. Manne, "Multiple-Purpose Public Enterprises—Criteria for Pricing," *Economica*, Aug. 1952, N.S. 19, 322-26.

R. Musgrave, *The Theory of Public Finance*. New York 1957.

A. C. Pigou, *A Study of Public Finance*, (a) 1st ed., London 1928; (b) ed ed., London 1947.

F. Ramsey, "A Contribution to the Theory of Taxation," *Econ. J.*, Mar. 1927, 37, 47-61.

R. Rees, "Second-Best Rules for Public Enterprise Pricing," *Economica*, Aug. 1968, N.S. 35, 260-73.

Joan Robinson, *The Economics of Imperfect Competition*. London 1933.

P.A. Samuelson, "Theory of Optimal Taxation," unpublished, approx. 1951.

_____, "Principles of Efficiency—Discussion," *Amer. Econ. Rev. Proc.*, May 1964, 54, 94-95.

W. Vickrey, *Testimony*, F. C. C. Docket No. 16258, Networks Exhibit No. 5, Appendix I. Washington 1968.

O. Williamson, *The Economics of Discretionary Behavior*. Englewood Cliffs 1964.

CHAPTER 12

AN INTEGRATED FARES POLICY
FOR TRANSPORT IN LONDON*

Stephen Glaister** and David Lewis***

Abstract

A common but disputed justification for public transport subsidy
is that lower fares will encourage transfer from private vehicles,
alleviating the congestion externality. A quantitative method is
developed to judge the validity of this 'second best pricing' argument and it is applied to the best available evidence on peak and
off-peak bus, rail and private car models in Greater London. A total
operating subsidy not exceeding £150m per annum may be justified
despite low private traveller response to public transport fares. Substantial reallocation of public traffic between times and modes
would also be desirable, but current car traffic and subsidy levels
seem broadly correct.

*Reprinted from *Journal of Public Economics*, Vol. 9 (1978), pp. 341-355.

**The London School of Economics, London, England. We have benefitted enormously
in writing this paper from advice and discussions with many individuals including
David Quarmby, Paul Flower and Malcolm Fairhurst of London Transport, Paul
Godier and Alexander Grey of the Greater London Council, Christopher Simpson and
John Collings of the Department of Transport and Peter Mackie, Institute for Transport Studies, Leeds. Whilst we have attempted to make full use of the information
they have kindly given us the views expressed here are entirely our own. We are
aware of weaknesses in our approach and would only regard our results, at the very
best, as indications of rough orders of magnitude.

***The Electricity Council, London, England.

I. Introduction

The fixing of fare structure and subsidy levels for urban public transport services promises to remain a contentious issue for a long time. Arguments of many kinds have been advanced on the subject. The 'second best' argument in favour of setting fares differently from marginal social costs on the grounds of economic efficiency is a common one. This argument suggests that since private car users are charged less than their marginal social costs in congested conditions, there is an advantage in holding public transport fares down so as to encourage marginal car users to switch modes. This has often been challenged on the grounds that whilst it is theoretically valid it is quantitatively unimportant. For example, the recent UK *Transport Policy* white Paper (1977, paragraph 58) says that 'it is sometimes argued that subsidies should be paid to public transport to attract travellers out of cars and so reduce congestion on the roads... The evidence is that there are few places where [the necessary] conditions are met and that subsidies paid for this reason are, on the whole, misplaced.'

The validity of this conclusion turns on the actual magnitudes of the marginal social costs of car use, of the cross-elasticities between the modes and upon the way in which these quantities should be used in calculating the optimum fare structure. The purpose of this paper is to extend the results derived by Glaister (1974) and to combine traffic elasticities obtained by Lewis (1977, 1978) with the best available estimates of the other relevant quantities to explore the likely quantitative importance of the second best argument in the Greater London area.

The provision of transport services in London is complicated. The Greater London council provides an annual lump sum subsidy to the London Transport Executive (LT) which is the sole provider of stage carriage bus services. LT also operates an extensive underground railway system. British Rail (BR) is responsible for the substantial network of surface commuter railways in addition to main line inter-city services. BR receives subsidies directly from Central Government. In this paper we identify three modes, private car, bus and rail taken as a whole. We thus leave the important taxi mode, which is privately owned, out of our consideration. This is for simplicity. The propensity to switch to the 'walk' mode is implicit in the price elasticities used below.

The available evidence indicates that own and cross-price elasticities, as well as marginal costs, differ very significantly between the peak and the off-peak. Thus the possibilities of transferring trips between periods as well as between modes means that an adequate treatment of even a highly aggregate and simplistic system will require consideration of the three modes and peak and off-peak times of day. As we shall show this requires knowledge of twenty demand elasticities, which is at the limit of our current empirical knowledge. Further, the way in which the various elasticities should be combined in analysing such a complicated interrelated system is not at all intuitively obvious.

II. Theoretical Development

A detailed discussion of the justification of a special case of the following approach is to be found in glaister (1974). In keeping with the notation used there we use the following indices:

Index	Transport mode
1	on-peak private
2	off-peak private
3	on-peak bus
4	off-peak bus
5	on-peak rail
6	off-peak rail

Then if p_i are the corresponding prices in £ per passenger mile, $X^i(p_1, ..., p_6)$ would be the demand per hour for the six types of transport. We shall also use the notations.

$$\eta^i_j = \frac{P_j}{X^i} \frac{\partial X^i}{\partial P_j} = \frac{P_j}{X_i} X^i_j, \qquad i, j = 1, 2, ..., 6, \tag{1}$$

for the elasticity of demand for service of type i with respect to price of service of type j. For example η^1_4 would be the elasticity of demand of peak car use with respect to off-peak bus fare.

Consider the following problem:

$$\max_{p_3, p_4, p_5, p_6} \{G\left(\alpha_3, \alpha_4, \alpha_5, \alpha_6, X^l(\alpha_3, ..., \alpha_6), X^3(\alpha_3, ..., \alpha_6), \hat{p}, u\right)$$

$$-G(p_3, p_4, p_5, p_6, X^l(p_3, ..., p_6), X^3(p_3, ..., p_6), \hat{p}, u)$$
$$-[C^3(X^l, X^3)-p_3X^3]-[C^4(X^4)-p_4X^4]$$
$$-[C^5(X^5)-p_5X^5]-[C^6(X^6)-p_6X^6]\} \qquad (2)$$

The function $G(p, X^l, X^3, \hat{p}, u)$ is the expenditure function aggregated across individuals [c.f. Diamond and McFadden (1974)]. The variable prices are $(p_3, ... , p_6)$ and $\hat{p}$ is a vector of all other, fixed prices including p_1 and p_2. Thus we are assuming that the money costs of car use cannot be varied. u is a vector of constant utility levels. The expenditure function is taken to depend upon peak car and bus traffic levels because of the congestion externality–for a given set of prices and increase in peak traffic levels would require a compensating increase in expenditure (income) to maintain given utility levels because of time and other losses sustained by peak travellers. We assume that off-peak congestion effects are negligible. Peak car traffic levels as well as peak bus traffic levels appear in the peak bus cost function because of the effect of congestion on bus operating costs. Rail travel causes no externality. The α_3, ..., α_6 are a set of 'base' prices–say prices considerably higher than those under consideration. Thus the difference between the expenditure function evaluated at the two different points is the compensating variation. That is, the amount of money that would be required to compensate for an increase from $p_3, ..., p_6$ to $\alpha_3, ..., \alpha_6$.

The remaining four terms in square parentheses are the operating subsidies required on the peak and off-peak bus and rail services. To put the objective another way, the sum of the compensating variation and the gross revenues is the total 'willingness to pay' from which must be subtracted the various operating costs.

The treatment of time losses and congestion effects in this way has the following justification.[1] Individual h's utility will depend upon passenger miles travelled by the various modes, x_h^i and the time and inconvenience of travelling by each mode, t^i, $i = 1, 2, ..., 6$. But because of the congestion effects the t^i will depend upon the total demand for each mode on the system-that is, there will be 'speed-flow' relationships of

---

1. We are indebted to a referee for this exposition of the point.

the form

$$t^i = f^i (X^1, ..., X^6) \tag{3}$$

where

$$X^i = \sum_h x_h^i \tag{4}$$

Then utility functions can be written in the form $u_h(x_h^i, ..., x_h^6, X^1, ..., X^6)$, where the X^i can be treated parametrically to the individual. Hence, Aggregate compensated demand functions will be given by

$$X^i = \sum_h x_h^i (p_1, ..., p_6, X^1, ..., X^6, u_h), \quad i = 1, ..., 6. \tag{5}$$

Eqs. (5) can be solved for the X^i to yield compensated 'reduced-form' market demand function, $X^i(p_1, ..., p_6, u_1, ..., u_h)$. Similarly the individual expenditure functions can be written $g_h(p_1, ..., p_6, X^1, ..., X^6, u_h)$, and aggregating,

$$G = (p_1, ..., p_6, X^1, ..., X^6, u_1, ..., u_n) = \sum_h g_h \tag{6}$$

These are the expressions appearing in (2). They represent the long run demand and expenditure responses to prices, after any system readjustment due to congestion effects have taken place.

Differentiating (2) with respect to peak bus fare, p_3, yields one necessary condition for a maximum:

$$-\frac{\partial G}{\partial p_3} - \frac{\partial G}{\partial X^1} X_3^1 - \frac{\partial G}{\partial X^3} X_3^3 - C_1^3 X_3^1 - C_3^3 X_3^3 + X^3$$
$$+ P_3 X_3^3 - C_4^4 X_3^4 + P_4 X_3^4 - C_5^5 X_3^5 + P_5 X_3^5 - C_6^6 X_3^6 + p_6 X_3^6 = 0. \tag{7}$$

But it is an elementary property of the expenditure functions in (6) that

$$-\frac{\partial G}{\partial p_i} = \sum_h \frac{\partial g_h}{\partial p_i} = \sum_h x_h^i = X^i \tag{8}$$

We are indebted to a referee for this exposition of the point.
Using (8) and collecting terms in (7) we have

$$(p_3 - S_3)X_3^3 + (p_4 - C_4^4)X_3^4 + (p_5 - C_5^5)X_3^5 + (p_6 - C_6^6)X_3^6 = S_1 X_3^1, \tag{9}$$

where

$$S_1 = \frac{\partial G}{\partial X^1} + \frac{\partial C^3}{\partial X^1} \quad \text{and} \quad S_3 = \frac{\partial G}{\partial X^3} + \frac{\partial C^3}{\partial X^3} \tag{10}$$

are the marginal social costs of a peak car passenger mile and a peak bus passenger mile respectively.

Similar expressions are obtained by differentiating with respect to the other choice variables, p_4, p_5 and p_6. On converting to elasticity form, the set of four first order conditions can be written as:

$$\begin{bmatrix} \eta_3^3 & \eta_3^4 & \eta_3^5 & \eta_3^6 \\ \eta_4^3 & \eta_4^4 & \eta_4^5 & \eta_4^6 \\ \eta_5^3 & \eta_5^4 & \eta_5^5 & \eta_5^6 \\ \eta_6^3 & \eta_6^4 & \eta_6^5 & \eta_6^6 \end{bmatrix} \begin{bmatrix} (p_3-S_3)X^3 \\ (p_4-C_4^4)X^4 \\ (p_5-C_5^5)X^5 \\ (p_6-C_6^6)X^6 \end{bmatrix} \frac{1}{S_1 X^1} = \begin{bmatrix} \eta_3^1 \\ \eta_4^1 \\ \eta_5^1 \\ \eta_6^1 \end{bmatrix} \tag{11}$$

This is a linear system of equations determining the four price-marginal social cost margins in terms of the traffic levels and all the own-price and cross price elasticities. This resolves the formal problem of how the various elasticities can be combined into a calculation of the overall 'second best' optimum price structure.

Detailed interpretation of the general expression in (11) is complex. However, assuming that

$$\eta_3^5 = \eta_3^3 = \eta_3^6 = \eta_6^3 = \eta_4^3 = \eta_5^5 = \eta_4^6 = \eta_6^4 = \eta_5^1 = \eta_6^1 = 0,$$

the solution for (p_3-S_3) and $(p_4-C_4^4)$ reduces to that obtained in Glaister(1974) because the rail mode is, in effect, removed. Eq. (11) can then be written as

$$p_3 = S_3 + \frac{S_1}{(1-\rho)} \frac{X^1}{X^3} \left(\frac{\eta_3^1}{\eta_3^3} - \frac{\eta_3^4 \eta_4^1}{\eta_3^3 \eta_4^4} \right) \tag{12}$$

$$p_4 = C_4^4 + \frac{S_1}{(1-\rho)} \frac{X^1}{X^4} \left(\frac{\eta_4^1}{\eta_4^4} - \frac{\eta_4^3 \eta_3^1}{\eta_3^3 \eta_4^4} \right) \tag{13}$$

where

$$\rho = \frac{X_3^4 X_4^3}{X_3^3 X_4^4} = \frac{\eta_3^4 \eta_4^3}{\eta_3^3 \eta_4^4} > 0 \qquad (14)$$

Assuming that $\rho < 1$ and that the modes are substitutes, (12) and (13) indicate that both peak and off-peak prices will be below respective marginal social costs of car use, both because of the possibilities of attracting peak car users directly (through η_3^1 and η_4^1) and reallocating demand between periods (through η_3^4 and η_4^3) so as to allow further adjustment to car traffic. Analogous interpretations apply to the solutions to the full system in (11).

III. The Demand data used

The simultaneous eqs.(11) do not give explicit solutions for the optimum prices. However, we found it a relatively simple matter to compute numerical solutions for a variety of assumed functional forms for the demand and cost relationships. For reasons of inadequate data rather than computational convenience we assumed that all marginal costs are constant, except that marginal social costs of car use were allowed to rise with increasing road traffic now. Strictly, as shown in (10) it would be desirable to acknowledge that marginal peak bus cost are influenced by car traffic levels but we were unable to obtain reliable information on this effect so we neglected it. The effect of this will be, other things being equal, to lead to an underestimate of the desirable level of subsidy.

In much of what follows we also assume all of the demand elasticities to be constants, because the constant elasticity demand curve is the most commonly estimated functional form in the studies from which we draw our values. We do, however, mention the results of some experiments with linear demand curves which we carried out for comparison. There would be no difficulty in principle in using alternative forms for marginal cost and demand relationships, except that there might be some problems with the convergence of the numerical techniques and some increase in computing costs.

Various authors have investigated demand relationships for bus, rail and private car travel in Greater London for the period 1970–1975. The models are all single equation estimates which relate bus and rail receipts and car traffic levels to real travel cost on various modes, vehicle miles run on bus and rail(as a proxy for service frequency), real incomes, demographic factors and, in some cases, weather and seasonal variations. If it is fair to assume that vehicle miles run are exogenously determined then these estimates would be correctly specified estimates of the reduced form equations in (5) and (8) except that in some cases relevant variables are unfortunately omitted. A difficulty with simultaneous determination of vehicle miles run would occur if the allocation of fixed resources between modes of travel and other sectors of the economy changed because of a change in demand–itself caused by a revision in prices or service quality. In the long-term this interaction between supply and demand does take place. In London, however, London Transport and British Rail adjust fare and service levels to new demand conditions at least one year after such changes are perceived. Likewise, the Greater London Council as the local highway authority is by necessity sluggish in adjusting road capacities. Further, severe staff shortages experienced by the operators over the period of estimation were the dominant factor in determining supply levels. Thus it is probably reasonable to assume that prices and service levels (and all other explanatory variables) are principally exogenously determined and hence that the estimates we use approximate to the correct reduced form estimates. Selection of values from unrelated studies is the best that we are able to do at the moment. Table 1 summarises the results obtained in some of the studies from which we have taken our elasticities.

Fairhurst and Morris (1975) and Glaister (1976) have used London Transport weekly bus and rail receipts data. Collings, Rigby and Wels by (1977) use four-weekly data from various bus operators around the UK. Although all the studies are founded on the assumption of constant point fare elasticities there are differences between the results which are partly due to differences in estimation technique. Fairhurst and Morris (1975) and Collings et al. (1977) used year-on-year proportionate changes throughout, whilst Glaister (1976) used a standard loglinear form with dummy variables to correct for seasonality and estimated by generalised least squares because of evidence of significant first order serial correlation. Other sources of difference between the estimates obtained are differences in the treatment of lags and cross-elasticities.

*Tabel 1. Estimated Monday-Friday 24 Hour Fare Elasticities and
95 Percent Confidence Limits.*

| | | With respect to: | | | |
| | | Bus | Rail | Durbin-Watson statistic | R^2 |
Elasticity of:					
Fairhurst and Morris (1975)	Bus	-0.60 (±0.30)	0.25 (±0.52)	1.16	0.94
	Rail	0.25 (±0.83)	-0.40 (±0.21)	1.33	0.95
Glaister(1976)	Bus	-0.56 (±0.35)	0.30 (±0.24)	1.98	0.96
	Rail	1.11 (±0.52)	-1.0 (±0.37)	2.05	0.93
Collings Rigby and Welsby(1977)	Bus	-0.405 (±0.5) (average of 48 operators	Not in Model	0.55-2.68 (range of 48 operators)	various
Lewis(1978)	Peak road traffic	0.025 (±0.079)	0.056 (±0.060)	1.60	0.73

Lewis (1977, 1978) used similar techniques with road traffic data
obtained from automatic road counters by the Greater London Council.
He was able to distinguish between peak and off-peak flow rates and
elasticities. Although all the evidence on rail elasticities shown in table
1 relates to London Transport data we have seen unpublished work on
British Rail data which is consistent with these results.

It is clear that the available sources do not yield a single 'correct' set
of estimates, so we chose values for computational purposes which are
consistent with table 1 but which cannot be regarded as definitive.
Because of this uncertainty we thought it important to carry out an
exhaustive analysis of the sensitivity of our results to the elasticity values used, and we report the results of this in section 6.

We required peak, off-peak and between period elasticity values.
Research by London Transport and the Greater London council suggests
that off peak elasticities are some 2–3 times peak elasticities. We took

an estimate of roundly 2.5 in drawing peak and off-peak values from 5-day 24 hour relationships. Estimates of peak to off-peak elasticities do not exist. On the assumption that these values are very small in relation to the 'within period' estimates, each was taken to be roughly 5 percent of the corresponding within-period elasticity.

The elasticities obtained in this way were uncompensated, whilst the analysis is in terms of elasticities compensated for income effects. The appropriate adjustment was carried out using income elasticities (from the studies already referenced) and shares in Greater London house-holds' expenditure (from 1975 Family Expenditure Survey data) shown in table 2. This adjustment made very little difference, only affecting the first significant figure in two cases. Table 2 also shows hourly flow rates which were obtained from Greater London Transportation study data. These all relate to travel throughout the Greater London area, the rail figure including British Rail passenger-miles in the area.

To ensure a measure of overall consistency of the demand relations the elasticity matrix was converted to a substitution matrix to test for its symmetry. Given the diverse nature of the sources it was not to be expected that the matrix would be exactly symmetrical, but we were gratified that it was so nearly so. In any case the Slutsky symmetry conditions would not necessarily be expected to hold when aggregating across individuals. Symmetry was enforced by replacing off-diagonal pairs by their average values. On converting back to compensated elasticity form we obtained the values which are shown in table 3, together with 95% confidence intervals derived by scaling the confidence intervals estimated in the original demand studies pro rata. This scaling involved a minor adjustment in all cases. It must be emphasised that elasticities obtained in this way are far from definitive and in any case

Table 2. *Income elasticities, expenditure shares and traffic flow fates.*

Mode	Income elasticity	Share in expenditure	Passenger-miles/ hour(millions)
Car	0.13	Not required	1.46
Peak bus	0.4	0.0053	0.70
Off-peak bus	0.4	0.0027	0.18
Peak rail	0.8	0.0076	1.76
Off-peak rail	0.8	0.0033	0.22

Table 3. Adopted compensated elasticities and 95 percent confidence limits.

		Bus		Rail		Car
		Peak	Off-peak	Peak	Off-peak	Peak
Bus	Peak	-0.35 (±0.11)	0.04	0.14 (±0.13)	0.01	0.025 (±0.079)
	Off-peak	0.029	-0.87 (±0.50)	0.009	0.28 (±0.74)	0.0016 (±0.0013)
Rail	Peak	0.143 (±0.378)	0.013	-0.30 (±0.17)	0.05	0.056 (±0.06)
	Off-peak	0.008	0.28 (±0.74)	0.018	-0.75 (±0.42)	0.0034 (±0.0028)

can only represent medium-term demand responses. Long run adjustments to residential and work place location and hence to travel patterns are to be expected.

IV. Costs and Traffic Levels

Several studies have recently run into difficulties because of renewed uncertainties about marginal social cost of private vehicle use in large conurbations such as London. In view of the importance of the topic for policy considerations there is surprisingly little evidence available. On the basis of the advice received, and our best information on speed/flow relationships and time values, we considered two alternatives: case (a) where the marginal social cost of a peak passenger mile would decline linearly from £0.21 at current traffic levels to £0.07 at half that level, and case (b) declining from £0.15 to £0.11. Case (b) might be the more appropriate for the 'average' Greater London trip. The corresponding figure for a peak bus passenger mile was taken to be a constant £0.05.

Marginal operating cost data have been provided by London Transport, but no information has been available from British Rail. Therefore, to the extent that the marginal costs of a British Rail and a London Transport passenger mile differ, we inevitably introduce distortions. Calculations were carried out with two sets of operation cost data. Case

1 is intended to represent estimates of short-run marginal costs (including social costs) while in case 2 we attempt to make some allowance for the marginal capacity costs of an extra passenger-mile, The costs used are shown in table 4.

The bus operation cost data were obtained from a sophisticated bus scheduling model by London Transport, and are a weighted average of figures for one man and crew operated buses. Both the peak figures include the allowance of £0.05 per passenger mile for congestion cost caused by buses. Rail data were less precise than the bus data. In London, the conventional wisdom that off-peak capacity exists so that the marginal cost of an extra off-peak passenger mile is much lower than that for a peak passenger-mile may no longer hold, because a large proportion of (London Transport) maintenance work is carried out during the off-peak, significantly reducing the number of trains available. In addition there are considerable problems in drawing the line between short-run marginal cost involving no capacity costs and increases in capacity brought about in the short or medium term by investment in, say, computer control systems, improved signalling and better trains, which increase capacity without additional track or duplicate tunnels. (Part of the justification of the first section of the Jobilee line, which is now under construction, is to relieve congestion on the nearby Bakerloo line.) Case 1 estimates assume simply that marginal costs are some fraction of average costs. Case 2 estimates attempt to take some account of capacity costs although the estimates will need to be revised as further evidence becomes available.

V. Results

The results are displayed in table 4. This gives the marginal costs used, the computed optimum fares, the 'subsidies' in £ per hour to each of the modes, the resulting rates of traffic flow, the ratios of flow rates to subsidy rates in passenger miles per £ and the total annual subsidy assuming a 5-day week and a 52 week year. The 'subsidies' referred to are subsidies on operating costs, so fixed costs would require additional subsidy. Since marginal operating costs are assumed constant they are also average operating costs so that a price equal to marginal operating cost will imply a zero operating subsidy. It should be noted that in case

Table 4. Results

Case	Marginal costs (Pence per passenger mile)				Fares (Pence per passenger mile)				Subsidies (£ per hour $\times 10^4$)				Traffic flows (Passengers per hour $\times 10^6$)					Passenger miles (per £ subsidy)				Total annual subsidy (£m)
	Bus		Rail		Bus		Rail		Bus		Rail		Car	Bus		Rail		Bus		Rail		
	Peak	Off-peak	Peak	Off-peak	Peak	Off-peak	Peak	Off-peak	Peak	Off-peak	Peak	Off-peak		Peak	Off-peak	Peak	Off-peak	Peak	Off-peak	Peak	Off-peak	
Present					4.3	4.3	4.3	4.3					1.46	0.7	0.18	1.76	0.22					
1a	11	6	2	4	3.4	3.1	0.3	0.5	1.35	0.36	5.89	0.42	1.25	0.51	0.13	3.53	0.86	38	35	60	207	137
1b	11	6	2	1	4.31	3.44	0.47	0.58	0.84	0.31	5.02	0.35	1.28	0.50	0.12	3.29	0.83	59	39	65	230	112
2a	14	6	30	1	5.22	2.21	20.4	0.39	2.97	0.64	1.04	0.73	1.59	0.79	0.17	1.08	1.20	26	26	10	164	251
2b	14	6	30	1	7.38	2.95	23.5	0.52	1.16	0.44	7.14	0.50	1.61	0.72	0.14	1.09	10.5	62	33	15	292	159
3b	14	6	10	1	7.02	3.12	6.11	0.54	1.20	0.39	6.35	0.45	1.50	0.60	0.14	1.63	0.97	50	35	26	218	144

1 marginal capacity costs are not allocated to peak users so that they are being implicitly treated as fixed costs and therefore do not appear in the calculation of the 'subsidies' for case 1. The 'passenger miles per £' figure is quoted because this statistic is currently used as a measure of performance for management purposes by the London Transport Executive [see Quarmby (1977)].

The results for case 1a illustrate the substantial gap between computed optimum fares and assumed marginal costs. It will be noted that in this case marginal costs for rail are considerably below those for bus, which explains the rather low peak and off-peak rail fares of 0.3 and 0.5 pence. The highest rate of subsidy is to peak rail and this achieves a doubling of peak rail traffic and a quadrupling of off-peak rail traffic, whilst reducing both car and bus traffic. Such an increase in peak rail traffic would be infeasible in practice, but the result is a consequence of failing to allocated true marginal capacity cost to peak rail users. The overall subsidy level, neglecting capacity costs, for a five day week would be £137m per annum. It is interesting to note that the assumed cost structure here is such that it is optimum to have a peak rail fare below the off-peak fare in spite of it having double the marginal cost. Case 1b produces results which are not significantly different.

The allocation of marginal capacity cost to peak users in case 2a results in an increase of peak marginal social bus costs from 11 pence to 14 pence and a substantial increase of peak rail costs from 6 pence to 30 pence. Compared with cases 1a and 1b this leads to a modest increase in peak bus fares (although they remain less than one half of marginal costs) and a substantial increase in explicit subsidy to this mode. Peak rail fares rise substantially, but only to two thirds of their allocated costs. Both off-peak fares fall because of the increased advantage in attracting public transport traffic out of the peak. This fares structure would cause a 9 per cent increase in car traffic, a 13 percent increase in peak bus traffic, a small decrease in off-peak bus traffic, a substantial decline in peak rail traffic and a large increase in off-peak rail traffic. Peak rail traffic attracts a very large subsidy which pushes the total subsidy up to £251m per annum. Case 2b is similar, except that peak rail attracts a rather smaller subsidy.

It was felt that in respect of peak rail marginal cost cases 1 and 2 represented extreme positions. As a compromise results of a 'case 3b' are presented, which is as for case 2b, except that peak rail costs are reduced to 10 pence per passenger mile. We feel this to be the most reasonable case and it is used in the sensitivity analysis in the next section. Relative to current fare levels it would suggest an increase of peak bus fares from 4.3 pence to 7.0 pence but a reduction of off-peak bus fares to 3.1 pence. Similarly peak rail fares would be increased to 6.1 pence but off-peak rail fares reduced substantially to about 0.5 pence. This would lead to a very marginal increase in car use, a 17 percent fall in peak bus traffic, slight falls in off-peak bus and peak rail traffic and a four-and-a-half fold increase in off-peak rail traffic. The overall subsidy level would be about £144m per annum, 69 percent of which would be attributable to peak rail services.

The whole exercise was repeated using linear rather than log-linear demand relations. The results were, in general, similar, except that isolated small but negative fares were generated—something which is precluded by assuming constant elasticities.

VI. Sensitivity

Since considerable uncertainty attaches to the values used in this analysis it is impossible to assess the practical value of such results as have been obtained without a knowledge of their sensitivity to changes in those values. Some limited indication has already been given of the sensitivity to the marginal costs. This leaves the elasticities. Generally these were taken or interpolated from econometric studies where their estimates were known to have t distributions with estimated standard errors. Hence it seemed reasonable to allow the elasticities used to 'vibrate' according to their estimated probability distributions and investigate the properties of the frequency distributions of the solution prices that were generated. Thus for each of the 20 elasticities 100 drawings were taken from a normal distribution (rather than the t for simplicity–in most cases there would be sufficient degrees of freedom for this to make little difference) with the appropriate mean and standard error. Frequency distributions of each of the four price solutions were then generated using case 3b cost assumptions. The mean, standard deviation, third and fourth moments were calculated together with the ratio of mean to standard deviation as a means of comparing the relative variabilities induced by the varying elasticities. Some of these results are summarised in table 5.

Table 5. Summary of sensitivity analysis.

Elasticity	Mean	S.D.	p_3/S.D.	P_4/S.D.	P_5/S.D.	P_6/S.D.
η_3^3	-0.35	0.056	5.8	12.7	17.3	16.3
η_5^3	-0.143	0.193	3.1	4.8	2.9	4.7
η_4^4	-0.87	0.255	12.9	2.9	25.0	4.6
η_6^4	-0.28	0.37	37.2	2.0	75.6	2.8
η_3^5	0.14	0.07	4.6	10.6	18.6	14.0
η_5^5	-0.3	0.085	4.8	7.1	4.1	6.8
η_4^6	0.28	0.38	60.5	3.4	116.3	4.2
η_6^6	-0.75	0.21	85.6	6.6	95.7	3.0
η_3^1	0.025	0.04	1.7	3.6	5.7	4.9
η_4^1	-0.0016	0.0007	888.4	33.5	2375.3	73.5
η_5^1	0.056	0.031	5.0	6.6	4.4	6.6
η_6^1	-0.0034	0.001	896.7	38.6	1258.1	17.8

The distributions generated in this way showed considerable skew in many cases, but the mean values were very close to the values obtained in the 'deterministic' case. Table 5 shows that the optimum fares calculated are reasonably robust in most cases, the few cases of low ratios of means to standard errors indicating those elasticities for which better estimates are most needed. In particular the large standard error of the elasticity of private car use with respect to peak bus fare (η_3^1) causes considerable uncertainty about the optimum peak bus fare.

VII. Summary

We have collected the best evidence we can find on demand responses and social costs for three competing modes, private car, bus and rail in the Greater London area. Taking into account the differences between peak and off-peak conditions we have attempted to integrate this evidence into a simplistic general equilibrium system. The aim was to explore the implied prices and subsidy levels to see if there is any substance in the 'congestion reducing' argument against charging public transport users their full marginal costs. Within the limited validity of our method and the data, we have found that whatever view one takes about the allocation of marginal capacity costs there is a defensible case for a subsidy to the operation of public transport, but that this would be unlikely to exceed, say, £150m per annum (for a 5 day week) for the whole system. The solutions are dominated by the marginal cost of the modes and, in as far as rail has a lower marginal cost than bus our results would suggest some advantage in a general lowering of rail fares relative to bus fares in order to encourage some redistribution of traffic to the cheaper mode. This is in spite of our use of *lower* elasticities for the rail mode. A differential of 4 to 5 pence per passenger mile between peak and off-peak on both modes is indicated. Current private car traffic levels and overall subsidy levels are quite close to the optimum calculated from our case 3b.

We would emphasise that these conclusions are predicated on the assumption that alternative policies towards traffic, such as road pricing, traffic management and parking restraint, are either infeasible or interior. It would be interesting to compare the resource and welfare implications of these various alternatives. We would anticipate that the 'second best' policies suggested in this paper would be shown to be inferior to some form of road pricing or supplementary licencing in the case of London. There are other interesting questions which we have not considered, such as the extent to which the policies we have proposed would simultaneously affect such other objectives as income redistribution, land use, urban densities and employment patterns.

References

Collings, J.J., D. Rigby and J.K. Welsby, 1976, Passenger response to bus fares, Department of Environment, Directorate General Economics and Resources, No. 24.

Diamond, P.A. and D.L. Mcfadden, 1974, Some uses of the expenditure function in public finance, Journal of Public Economics 3, no. 1, 3-22.

Fairhurst, M.H. and P.J. Morris, 1975, Variations in the demand for bus and rail travel up to 1974, R 210, London Transport Executive.

Fairhurst, M.H. and J.R.F. Stee, 1976, London Transport's passenger markets: An analysis of GLTS data, T.N. 107, London Transport Executive.

Glaister, S., 1974, Generalised consumer surplus and public transport pricing, The Economic Journal, December.

Glaister, S., 1976, Variations in the demand for bus and rail travel in London, 1970 to 1975, Manuscript, The London School of Economics.

Greater London Council, 1976, Financing London Transport, Department of Planning and Transportation, May.

Department of Environment, 1970, Transport policy; a Consultation Document, (H.M.S.O.).

Lewis, D.L., 1977, Estimating the influence of public policy on road traffic levels in Greater London, Journal of Transport Economics and Policy, May.

Lewis, D.L., 1978, Public policy and road traffic levels: A rejoinder, Journal of Transport Economics and Policy, January.

Quarmby, D.A., 1977, The contribution of economic research to transport policy decisions, European Conference of Ministers of Transport, September.

London Transport Fares, 1970, National Board for Prices and Incomes, Report No. 159.

Transport Policy, 1977, Cmnd 6836, June, (H.M.S.O.)

CHAPTER 13

OPTIMAL BUS FARES*

Ralph Turvey** and Herbert Mohring[†]

This paper[1] is about optimal fares on buses under first-best conditions. Traffic congestion and the non-optimal pricing of petrol, of parking, of railway journeys and so on are thus simply ignored. They are, of course, enormously important, but they are better understood than the problem on which this paper concentrates.

This problem is to find out what marginal cost pricing of bus service consists of. One apparently obvious answer, which is wrong, is that if a bus run costs X and carries γ passengers. and if all these passengers travel the same distance, the marginal cost per passenger and hence the optimal fare is X/γ. This ignores the point that X is a joint cost. Demand, unlike costs, is a matter of individual passenger journeys; but it is a function not only of fares but also of travel times. These, once the passengers have got to the bus stops, depend on frequency and speed.

---

* Reprinted from *Journal of Transport Economics and Policy* (1975), pp. 280-286.

** Economic Adviser. Scicon. when this paper was written. Now Economic Adviser, Bureau of Economic and Social Policies, International Labour Office, Geneva.

† Professor, University of Minnesota.

1. We are indebted to E.V. Morgan, J. K. Welsby, Geoffry Mole, Tony Churchill, and T.M. Coburn for comment on earlier drafts.

Passenger's Time Costs

The right approach is to escape the implicit notion that the only costs which are relevant to optimisation are those of the bus operator. The time-costs of the passengers must be included too, and fares must be equated with marginal *social* costs. This appoach has already been put foward in a paper by one of us [1, p.591]. The present paper differs by not including in the analysis the time cost of getting to and from bus stops, since we here assume their number and location to be given.

As a preliminary, let it be noted that the overall average bus speed depends on the following factors:

(a) Average traffic speed, which influences the speed of the bus between stops.

(b) The rates of deceleration to a stop ar.d acceleration from it.

(c) The time spent at each stop. This depends linearly upon the number of passengers boarding and alighting (in the case of single doorway buses) or upon either the one or the other (in the case of two-doorway buses). The values of the constant and of boarding and alighting times per passenger depend upon the type of bus and the fare-collecting system. On all these matters see the authoritative Report LR 521 [2].

Take (a) and (b) as given and assume that single-doorway buses are used. Then the extra time added to a bus trip by a stop can be written as:

$$T + b.B + a.A$$

That is, the sum of the extra time caused by deceleration and acceleration and of the deadtime, plus (boarding-time times number boarding) plus (alighting-time time number alighting). The time spent by any particular passenger from arriving at the bus stop until he alights at his destination will be the sum of the following items:

(1) Waiting time, which varies inversely with frequency;

(2) Length of journey divided by mean speed between stops;

(3) A time depending on the number of stops made during his journey and the numbers of other passengers boarding and alighting at each.

This total time is a cost which is borne by the passenger himself. It is the excess of marginal social costs over this which ought to be reflected in the fare he pays, if the fare is to help to make his individual journey decision the socially optimal one. This excess is the increase in journey times which he imposes on other passengers plus any increase in the bus operator's costs necessary to preserve other services. If, for example, the slowing down of a bus would shorten the turn-round time available before the scheduled departure time of the subsequent run, adding to crew costs, or would raise fuel costs, then these additional costs of traversing the bus route without adversely affecting other services constitute part of marginal cost. Thus the excess marginal social cost consists of the following items:

(1) b times the number of passengers already on the bus when he boards and boarding behind him at his stop (or $T + b$ times the former when the bus stops specially for him) plus a times the number of passengers on the bus when he alights (or $T + a$ times this number when the bus stops specially for him).

(II) The interval between buses if the bus leaves some one behind when he is on it (since he then makes that passenger wait for the next bus).[2]

(III) The additional cost, if any, to the operator of preserving the quality of his services for all other passengers.

By boarding or alighting, the passenger will cause some people further along the route to wait longer. But he will also cause othe people to wait for a shorter time, since they would have had to wait for the next bus if this one had not been delayed. So, if passengers' arrivals at bus stops are random in relation to bus timings, these two effects cancel out on average. (On infrequent services where timetables mean something to passengers as well as to the operators, arrivals are not random and the analysis would be different. This paper, however, concentrates entirely on the case where passengers do not know when the next bus will come.)

Frequency

We are now in a position to look at optimal fares. First let us look at optimal fare level in relation to the bus operator's costs, and repeat an important point made in the earlier paper [1]. This requires us to turn

---

2. This is a simplification. If A on the first bus caused B to wait for the second bus, B in turn may make C wait for the third bus.

from the marginal condition for the optimal number of passengers, given the number of bus runs, to the marginal condition for the optimal number of bus runs, given the number of passengers. One bus run less will involve a certain gross marginal cost saving which must be equated with the following marginal effects:

(i) Increased travel times due to greater stop-times and a larger number of stops caused by more passengers boarding and alighting from each remaining bus on average.

(ii) Increased probability of each remaining bus being full, so that some waiting passengers have to wait for the next bus.

(iii) Increased costs of maintaining the services provided by the remaining buses as a result of their increased stop times and increased number of stops.

(iv) Increased waiting time. (Waiting time on average equals half the interval between buses, and this interval is increased by the subtraction of one run.)

Now suppose both that the fares are optimal, so that the number of passengers is optimal, and that the number of bus runs is optimal. Then we can say that the value of $[(I) + (II) + (III)] \times$ (number of passengers per run) is equal to the fare revenue per bus run. We can also say that the value of (i) to (iv) is equal to the marginal cost of a bus run. So if the value of $[(I) + (II) + (III)]$ times the number of passengers per run were the same as the value of (i) to (iv), the fare revenue from a bus trip would just equal the marginal cost of a bus trip. But they are not the same. There is an asymetry between the disbenefits of more passengers with the same number of bus runs and the disbenefits of fewer bus runs with the same total number of passengers. Fewer buses mean increased waiting time because of a longer average interval between buses. Items (i), (ii) and (iii) correspond with (I), (II) and (III), but item (iv) corresponds to nothing. Hence $[(I) + (II) + (III)]$ times the number of passengers falls short of (i) to (iv), and this means that the optimal fare revenue from a bus run falls short of marginal cost.

The point then is that, even if there are constant private costs to scale of bus operation, there are decreasing social costs. If the number of bus runs and the number of passengers both went up by x per cent, total waiting time would not go up by x percent. So marginal social costs are below average social costs. We have a classical case for subsidy in order to achieve optimal resource allocation. This case has nothing to do with congestion. It is just coincidence that considerations arising from congestion also point in the same direction, to subsidising buses or to taxing or restraining private car use. Conversely, a failure to subsidise buses or tax car-use sufficiently accelerates a shift from buses to cars for two quite separate reasons. One is a matter of congestion costs. The other which is the subject of this paper, is that a decline in the total number of bus journeys which results in fewer runs causes a further decline, frequency being an important factor in determining demand. Less means worse and worse means less.

In explaining marginal social less private cost of a bus passenger in time terms as the sum of (*I*, (*II*) and (*III*), we are looking at marginal costs when the size of the system is given. If we wish instead to look at costs when the system size is adjustable, i,e, to examine long-run rather than short-run marginal costs, we immediately meet the difficulty that the system cannot be adjusted to provide for just one passenger more or less. The correct way round this is to say that optimal fares should always be determined by "short-run" marginal costs and that this pricing rule has to be supplemented by an investment rule.[3] Our investment rule was formulated above in terms of equating the value of (i) to (iv) with the marginal costs of an extra bus run along this route. Point (iv) is the effect of the increase in frequency in decreasing waiting times, so we can say that the value of this decrease must be subtracted from the cost of the extra buses, crews, fuel, tyres, etc., in order to get the marginal social cost. It is the failure to make this subtraction which vitiates the proposition referred to at the beginning of this paper.

The distinction between the (short-run) pricing rule and the (long-run) investment rule may help to explain a difficulty about operating costs which bothered a reader of an earlier version of this paper. By "investment" we here mean decisions about system size, including how many runs are made along each route during each period, so the term "long run" is rather inappropriate. But, terminology aside, a rise in, say, fuel costs does not *of itself* dictate a rise in fares according to the pricing rule. This may seem baffling. Yet the fact is that one passenger more or less will cause no noticeable change in fuel consumption, so that the price of fuel is not directly relevant to the optimal fares for influencing

---

3. A similar point applies fairly generally to all optimal pricing by public enterprises, as explained in [3] chapter 7.

passengers' individual decisions. However, the rise in fuel costs may, by the operation of the "investment" rule, make some runs on some routes extra-marginal, so that they are suspended. If the consequence is that bus loadings increase, the operation of the pricing rule will then dictate some fare increases. So a rise in fuel costs will result in a rise in optimal fares after all. Fuel cost, crew wages and the cost of new buses all affect system size; this helps to determine bus loadings, and it is bus loadings which are relevant in setting fares. We now consider how fares should be set in more detail.

Time Costs in Optimal Fares

It must be recognised that a difficulty of the pricing rule is that it requires valuations of passengers' time, both waiting at bus stops and when the buses they are in are delayed. For cost-benefit analysis in transport it is customary to use standard uniform values, waiting time being treated as, say, three times more valuable than time spent in a bus. While this is a sensible pragmatic procedure, we have to recognise that it is a lack of uniformity, that is to say a dispersion round the average which partly generates the problem in the first place! An important reason why reduction in fares or increases in service frequency will attract new passengers is that new passengers implicitly attach higher values to time than the existing passengers.

Having noted this complication, we have to ignore it in discussing the structure of optimal bus fares in terms of the time costs. These(to remind the reader) are:

(I) Delay Caused to passengers on the bus by boarding and alighting,
(II) Delay caused to people waiting at bus stops because the bus is full.

An idea of the possible magnitude of these items can be obtained by using data from the admirable investigation by Cundill and Watt of boarding and alighting times [2]. Consider first the ordinary two-man red London buses with a single open entrance at the rear. In the peak hours these buses carry 38 passengers on average and have a typical service frequency of 4 minutes. Their stop-time in seconds is 0.95 plus 1.15 time number boarding plus 1.0 times number alighting. If to this dead-time of 0.95 seconds we add a numerically convenient guess of 20.05 seconds for the extra time involved in decelerating to a halt and accelerating from rest instead of carrying on, then, in terms of the symbols used earlier, we have $T = 21$ seconds, $b = 1.15$ seconds and $a = 1.0$ second. Thus the marginal time-costs imposed on others by a passenger are:

(I) $38 \times (1.15 + 1.0) = 81.7$ seconds for other people in the bus plus
$38 \times (0.95 + 20.05) = 798$ seconds if the bus stopped specially for him.

(II) 4 minutes' extra wait for any person he prevents from getting on the bus by being on it when it is full.

Different results are naturally obtained with other types of buses and other fare systems. The one-man-operated flat-fare Red Arrow in London, for example, has a stop-time in peak hours equal to whichever is the greater of the following:

5.65 + 3.3 times number boarding;
8.2 + 1.4 times number alighting.

Higher Fares on Full Buses

Since optimal fares depend on time-costs, which depend partly on fare-collection systems, which both determine what fare structures are possible and help to determine costs which affect the optimal system size, it is clear that complicated inter-dependencies are involved. But, whatever bus type is used, one primary feature of optimal fare systems is obvious enough. That is that the fare should be higher:

(α) The greater the expected number of people on the bus when passengers board and alight;

(β) The greater the probability that the bus is full when there are people at bus stops who want to get on it.

Although this is a simple principle, it is a fruitful one to apply. *Firstly*, it means that fares should be higher in the crowded direction, i.e. inward to work and outward in the evenings, than in the reverse direction.[4] (It is, incidentally, interesting to consider how cities would have developed if the rule had always been applied.) *Secondly*, it means that peak fares should exceed off-peak fares. It is, however, less clear whether weekend and evening fares should be low, since higher wage

---

4. There are possible exceptions to this. The probability of an extra passenger causing a bus to stop specially for him may be greater when flows are low than when they are high, as pointed out on page 599 of Mohrings paper [1].

costs may cause these services to have such high operating costs that the operation of the investment rule cause them to be few and hence crowded. *Thirdly*, and this is the most novel conclusion, fares should be positively related to distance only when the probability of buses being full is non-negligible along the whole route. This is because item (α) above has nothing to do with the distance travelled; only (β) has. A passenger travelling two crowded miles is twice as likely to prevent a waiting pas-

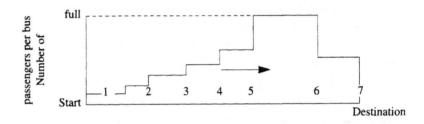

senger from boarding as a passenger travelling only one crowded mile.

To illustrate all this, consider the example of the main direction of travel during the peak. We can draw a curve showing the average number of passengers on the inward buses during the morning rush-hour on the route segments bounded by seven stops. The fares from 1, 2, 3, 4, and 5 to 7 should be successively *higher* beacuse at each of them the boarding time of an additional passenger will delay successively more existing passengers. The boarding delay imposed at 6, however, is below that at 5, so the fare from 6 to 7 should be below that from 5 to 7.

All Journeys, including segment 5 to 6, involve a probability of imposing cost type (β), i.e. more waiting delay.

Taking both (α) and (β) costs together, therefore, optimal fares are *not* positively related to distance in this example. Not only should the fare from 3 to 6 fall below that for the shorter distance 5 to 6; both should exceed the fare for the longer distance from 1 to 5. What matters is not distance, but how full the buses are. The highest fares should be for journeys going past those stops where queues sometimes last longer than the interval between the buses.

For the outward journey in the morning (α) is lower than on the inward journey and (β) is negligible. Hence a very low fare is justified. In the evening peak everything is the other way round.

The example relates only to a radial feeder route. However, at least along the routes studied by Cundill and Watts [2], no such systematic variations were observed in the numbers of passengers on buses. As explained above, a positively distance-related element does then come into optimal fares. But the fares should vary less than proportionately with distance, since the (α) element is not distance-related.

Revenue Constraints

In practice, no bus undertakings receive general subsidies calculated along the lines which our analysis would suggest. Many, Indeed, are supposed at least to break even. Hence in practical terms their aim to maximise welfare, i.e. (under our first-best assumptions) willingness to pay less costs, is constrained by a net revenue requirement. In such cases, the pricing rule involves departing from the optimal tariffs in the way that brings in the extra net revenue with the least effect on resource allocation. So fares could be designed by first constructing an optimal fare structure and then modifying it so as to meet the financial constraint. Alternatively, and more realistically, one might begin with an existing non-optimal fare structure which does meet the financial constraint. Alternatively, and more realistically, one might begin with an existing non-optimal fare structure which does meet the financial constraint, and then improve it by putting some fares up and others down in a way which does not spoil financial performance but as far as possible reflects the principle suggested here.

In either case, some of the common differences between actual fare structures and unconstrained optimal ones appear to be capable of rationalisation in simple "what the traffic will bear" terms. In particular, it seems plausible that passengers going in the opposite direction to the main stream are able to pay as much as the majority of passengers. Off-peak passengers, on the other hand, may be more sensitive to fare levels than commuters are; so off-peak fare concessions are much more common. The conflict between distance-related fares and flat fares, finally, involves additional complications in the choice of fare system. which can have a very large influence on costs. It is interesting to recall that many years ago London tramways, which had distance-related fares, also had a flat twopenny fare between the hours of 10 in the morning and 4 in the afternoon. This fitted in very neatly with the second and third implications of the principle put forward above.

Finally, let us revert to the investment rule. The number of bus runs on a route constitutes only one of many types of decisions about the service to be provided. The other types include answers to such questions as:

What time in the morning should the service start?

What time in the evening should it cease?

Should the route start nearer to the centre of town?

The effect on total passenger time-costs of different answers to one of these questions will vary from case to case. To determine the optimal extent of the service is thus as difficult as determining the optimal frequency and fares for a given extent of the service. Furthermore, the other aspect of the investment rule has been passed over rather lightly in this paper: that is, the analysis of the bus operator's costs. In discussing the optimal number of bus runs along a route during a certain period, we assumed that the marginal cost of one extra bus run was known. In fact, indivisibilities in hiring of crews and, still more, in the purchase of buses mean that crew costs and annual bus costs are joint over a large number of runs. Investment decisions are thus far more complicated than they have been represented as being. The marginal cost of a single run (per-run costs such as extra fuel apart) largely consists of the shadow-values of crew-time and bus-time, which can only emerge from system-wide optimisation.[5] But failure to explore these matters does not impugn the suggested pricing rule. The fuller the bus, the more should a passenger pay for getting on it, being on it and alighting from it.

References

[1] Mohring, H.: "Optimisation and scale economies in urban bus transportation." *American Economic Review*, September 1972.
[2] Cundill, M. A., and P. F.Watts: *Bus boarding and alighting times*. Transport and Road Research Laboratory, Report LR 521, 1973.
[3] Turvey, R.: *Economic analysis and public enterprises*. Allen and Unwin, 1971

---

5. It is what Littlechild calls a *mutatis mutandis* marginal cost, as explained in [3], chapter 7.

CHAPTER 14

INTER-FIRM RIVALRY AND FIRM-SPECIFIC PRICE ELASTICITIES IN DEREGULATED AIRLINE MARKETS*

*Tae Hoon Oum, Anming Zhang and Yimin Zhang**

I. Introduction

Since deregulation in 1978 the U.S. airline industry has undergone major structural changes. A series of mergers and hub-and-spoke network development have increased market concentration at major airports as well as at industry level. The industry is still being consolidated. Analysts express concern regarding the increasing market power of a few airlines, especially in route markets connected to major hub airports. There is clear evidence that major U.S. airlines attempt to solidify

* Reprinted from *Journal of Transport Economics and Policy*(May, 1993), pp.171-192.

** Tae Hoon Oum is a member of the Faculty of Commerce and Business Administration at the University of British Columbia; Anming Zhang is in the Department of Economics at the University of Victoria, Canada; and Yimin Zhang is in the School of Business at the University of New Brunswick. The authors thank anonymous referees; Jim Brander, Keith Head, Murray Frank, Mike Tretheway, and W.G. Waters; and the participants in the seminars at the University of British Columbia, University of Victoria, University of California at Berkeley, and Osaka University, for useful comments and suggestions. The research grant support from the Social Science and Humanities Research Council of Canada (SSHRCC) is gratefully acknowledged.

their market power by intensifying hub-and-spoke networks, offering commission overrides to travel agents (a system that rewards agents for directing a high proportion of their business to an airline), using skillful dynamic pricing and seat allocation techniques (scientific yield management) and frequent-flyer bonus programmes for rewarding brand-loyal customers.

A large number of routes are served by three or fewer airlines, indicating that a small-numbers oligopoly is the dominant market structure in the industry, particularly on the routes directly connected to major hubs. Furthermore, recent evidence shows that dominant airlines at hub airports have sustained higher average fares for the local traffic than their competitors (see Borenstein, 1989, 1990; and Berry, 1992). This suggests the importance of understanding competitive interaction among airlines in order to explain their pricing behaviour and price differentials between airlines serving the same route markets.

This paper examines the pattern of firm conduct in different market (route) circumstances and estimates price elasticities of the firm-specific demand (the demand an individual firm faces) and aggregate market demand, taking into account explicitly the form of inter-firm rivalry being practised. This is accomplished by estimating the market demand jointly with the firm-specific first-order conditions for profit maximisation. The estimation is carried out using firm-specific panel data for a set of monopoly and duopoly airline routes connected to American Airlines' and United Airlines' Chicago hub. Our first objective is to calculate the price elasticity of the firm-specific demand by estimating airline "conduct parameters" (often called "conjectural variations"). The estimated conduct parameters will also allow us to test how close each airline's pricing behaviour has been to the Bertrand, Cournot and cartel (collusion) strategies in each route market, in addition to computing price elasticity of the demand faced by each airline in each market.

Our second objective is to examine the pattern of an individual airline's conduct in various market situations. Is there a major difference in pricing behaviour between American Airlines and United Airlines in a similar market situation? Are there systematic differences in pricing behaviour between short and long-distance routes? Is the duopolist pricing behaviour related to its current market share? Is the duopolist pricing behaviour on leisure-oriented routes different from that of other routes? What role does the intensity of activity of fringe airlines and charter services play in shaping the pricing behaviour of the duopolists? These are the questions to be examined using the estimated conduct parameters for the two airlines. The results of these examinations may allow us to make some generalisations about the pricing behaviour in other airline duopoly cases, including the situation in Canada between Air Canada and Canadian Airlines International.

Airline demand and pricing have been the subject of considerable empirical study. Significant effort has been expended in the estimation of airline demand (see Verledger, 1972; De Vany, 1974; Ippolito, 1981; Mutti and Murai, 1977; Strazheim, 1978; Anderson and Kraus, 1981; Abraham, 1983; Hensher and Louvière, 1983; Oum and Gillen, 1983; Morrison and Winston, 1985; Agarwal and Talley, 1985; Oum, Gillen and Noble, 1986; Haitovsky, Salomon and Silman, 1987; Talley and Schwartz-Miller, 1988; and Fridstoöm and Thune-Larsen, 1989).[1] All these studies, however, focused on aggregate market demand, fare class demands, or consumer choice of modes, not firm-specific demand. What distinguishes this paper is the explicit estimation of price elasticities of the demand an individual airline faces on each route, taking into account the nature of the inter-firm rivalry being practised.

Pricing behaviour in the airline industry has been studied by, among others, Panzar, 1979; Abraham and Keeler, 1981;[2] Call and Keeler, 1985; Bailey, Graham and Kaplan, 1985; Borenstein, 1989, 1990; Borenstein and Rose, 1989; Dresner and Tretheway, 1992; and the U.S. Department of Transportation, 1990. In particular, Borenstein (1989, 1990) and Berry (1990) investigated the relationship between hub-and-spoke route structure and market power. Berry (1990) concludes that both cost advantage and market power lead to airport dominance; McShane and Windle (1989) quantify the effect of hubbing on cost efficiency. Levine (1987) gives comprehensive discussion on various issues of imperfect competition in deregulated airline markets. Several authors, including Bailey and Baumol (1984), Call and Keeler (1985), Morrison and Winston (1989), Whinston and Collins (1992), and Berry (1992) investigate whether airline markets are "contestable." These price and

---

1. Survey of airline demand and mode choice studies is included in Oum, Waters and Yong (1992).
2. Abraham and Keeler (1981) are probably the first writers who predicted correctly that there would be consolidation of the U.S. airline industry into five or six airlines as a consequence of deregulation.

contestability studies are concerned with market conduct, at least implicitly. Our paper, distinctly, deals with the explicit estimation of conduct parameters and associated firm-specific price elasticities and attempts to isolate a single strategic setting by focusing only on monopoly and duopoly routes.

Recently Brander and Zhang (1990, 1993) investigated airline conduct in a doupoly airline market, taking into account the inter-firm rivalry explicitly. The latter paper focused on the dynamic aspects of airline pricing behaviour. However, in both papers the authors calculate conduct parameters using the price elasticity of market demand estimated by previous researchers rather than estimating conduct parameters econometrically. What distinguishes the current paper is that we estimate the firm-specific first-order conditions for profit maximisation jointly with the route demand function. This allows us to identify a firm's conduct parameters separately for each route, and compute price elasticities of the firm-specific demand directly from the estimated equations. In our model, the conduct parameters and demand elasticities vary across routes. In addition, the current paper focuses on examining the pattern of pricing behaviour with respect to route characteristics and the competitive situation under which firms operate.

Section 2 describes the theoretical structure of our investigation. The econometric model is derived in Section 3, while Section 4 describes the data. Empirical results are described in Section 5. A summary, and concluding remarks, are given in Section 6.

II. The Theoretical Structure

Consider an industry which consists of two firms producing a homogeneous product. Let x^i be the ith firm's output, $i = 1,2$. Total output, denoted as X, is the sum of x^1 and x^2, and the inverse demand is written as:

$$p = p(X) \tag{1}$$

Using $C^i(x^i)$ to denote total cost, firm i's profit function can be written as:

$$\pi = x^i p(X) - C^i(x^i) \tag{2}$$

If we regard output as the choice variable, then the Nash equilibrium is represented by the following first-order conditions:

$$p + x^i p' = c^i \qquad (3)$$

where c^i denotes marginal cost and p' the derivative of market price with respect to output. This Nash quantity (or "Cournot") solution yields, by equation (3), a positive price-cost margin. Furthermore, when there is only one firm in the industry, the term on the left hand side of equation (3) reduces to monopoly marginal revenue.

In this Cournot model, equilibrium arises when each firm optimally selects its output, given the output of the other firm. The alternative conjectural variation framework arises by assuming that each firm views the firm's output as a function of its own output, yielding first-order conditions:

$$p + x^i p' (1 + v^i) = c^i \qquad (4)$$

where $v^i \equiv dx^j / dx^i$ ($j \neq i$) is often called the "conjectural variation." From equation (4), parameter v^i may be used to index the degree of competitiveness (or collusiveness) of firm conduct. The higher the level of v^i, the greater the price-cost margin and hence the more collusive the firm conduct. The Cournot solution corresponds to zero conjectural variations, so that if a firm behaves more competitively (collusively) than Cournot, $v^i < (>) 0$. In particular, if price rather than quantity is the choice variable, the Nash price (or "Bertrand") solution will yield marginal cost pricing. If the two firms have the same marginal costs, this implies that $v^i = -1$ in equation (4). In other words, the Bertrand model yields the same outcome as under the perfectly competitive strategy, which leads a firm to believe that it can sell as much output as it likes at the current market price. At the other extreme, if firms manage to collude tacitly and maximise their joint profits, the resulting "cartel" solution will imply, under identical costs, that $v^i = 1$. In general, we would have $-1 < v^i < 1$. Following Brander and Zhang (1990) we refer to v^i as a "conduct parameter."

The knowledge of firm conduct is, thus, essential in discussing and predicting prices in oligopolistic markets. Notice that equation (4) can be rewritten as:

$$(p - c^i)/p = s^i (1 + v^i)/\eta \qquad (5)$$

where $\eta \equiv -(dX/dp)(p/X)$ is the (positive) price elasticity of market demand and s^i is firm i's market share. Further, we can define the (positive) reciprocal of firm i's perceived elasticity of demand as $1/\eta^i \equiv -(dp/dx^i)(x^i/p)$. Simple manipulation of this expression yields:

$$\eta^i = \eta s^i (1 + v^i) \qquad (6)$$

Combining equations (5) and (6) shows that each firm's price-cost margin ratio is given by the reciprocal of its perceived elasticity of demand. Under the monopoly market structure, firm-specific elasticity η^i reduces to the market elasticity and equation (5) becomes:

$$(p^M - c^M)/p^M = 1/\eta \qquad (7)$$

where M denotes monopoly. In oligopoly, however, η^i may or may not equal market elasticity η, depending on conduct parameters. $\eta^i = \eta$ if firms manage to achieve the cartel solution. Otherwise, $\eta^i > \eta$ Thus, even if we observe price-inelastic demand in a market, each oligopolist may face an elastic demand; this makes it difficult to raise prices. Here the extreme case is the Bertrand solution in which η^i approaches infinity. In general, the price elasticity perceived by each firm is positively related to the aggregate price elasticity and inversely related to its market share and conduct parameter. In the Cournot solution, each firm's elasticity is the market elasticity divided by its output share.

III. The Econometric Model

Our principal objectives in this paper are to calculate firm-specific price elasticities by estimating market-specific and firm-specific conduct parameters for a set of Chicago-based airline routes involving American airlines and United Airlines, and to relate the estimated conduct parameters to market characteristics (such as route distance). The data points, described more fully later, are characterised by duopoly and monopoly only, with a large majority of them being duopoly.

In Section 2 we considered the case of single, homogeneous products. In fact, airlines produce "product lines" consisting of numerous fare classes (first-class, standard economy, various levels of shallow discounts and deep discounts). This makes it difficult, if not impossible, to carry out complete investigations on airline pricing behaviour, particularly in the context of an oligopoly model. It is impossible to fathom an airline's pricing strategy by examining all fare levels and their volumes because they are so numerous. All airlines use sophisticated "yield management" programmes, which allow them to allocate seats of a flight dynamically over time as they watch the progress of the actual booking for a given flight (see Brumelle *et al.*, 1990). Since the seat allocation for a flight among numerous fare levels changes daily, if not hourly, the prices an airline charges are not transparent even to expert travel agents (let alone consumers). This makes it easier for an airline to charge a high average fare for essentially the same packages of fare classes in a given route market, which is embedded in its scientifically designed yield management programme. Therefore, it is our opinion that the only feasible way to investigate a firm's pricing conduct is to look at the overall result of the firm's yield management practices on a route. The weighted average price charged per passenger on a given route is the single most important indicator for the firm's pricing strategy in that market. This is the reason we chose to use average yields per passenger on each route.

Since traffic volume of the first-class category is very small, we exclude it from our analysis. Standard economy and discount categories are aggregated together and treated as a single output. It is possible to treat them separately, but the distinction between them is unreliable and not consistent across airlines, as they now practise a sophisticated form of seat allocation across numerous fare classes (yield management). This suggests that aggregating the two categories is a better practice, especially when the purpose of the research is to study the strategic pricing behaviour of the firm and the price elasticities perceived by the firms. An airline's (weighted) average fare is used as the product price for the airline.

We use "local traffic" as our measure of output. Our local traffic, or trips with single plane service, for a city-pair consists of passengers who originate in one city and terminate in the other without changing planes (but allowing stops). Total origination-destination (O-D) traffic would, however, also include "connecting" passengers who change planes, especially on long-distance routes. We assume that connecting traffic, if any, is exogenous to the major firms in the local market.

We treat the outputs of American Airlines and United Airlines as homogeneous, noting that the two carriers are reasonably symmetric in factors which might affect non-price product attributes including network.[3] Chicago is a major hub for both airlines while the connecting cities in our data set are not significant for either airline.

Our approach to econometric specification is within the general framework discussed in a survey paper by Bresnahan (1989). Consider market k at the tth observation. We convert first-order conditions in equation (5) to the stochastic specification,

$$p_{kt}^i = \frac{c_{kt}^i \eta_k}{\eta_k - (1 + v_k^i) s_{kt}^i} + \varepsilon_{kt}^i \qquad (8)$$

where $i = 1$ for American Airlines (AA) and 2 for United Airlines (UA), and ε_{kt}^j is a random error term. It is worth noting that the error terms in equation (8) allow observed prices to be different between competing airlines even though the first-order condition (equation (5)) implies the same price. Suppose quantity and price data are available. Then conduct parameters v_k^i can be estimated, using equation (8), if we know marginal cost c_{kt}^i and the price elasticity of route demand η_k. Consider first the determination of route demand elasticities. One approach is simply to use the results from existing airline demand studies, as in Brander and Zhang (1990, 1993). However, this approach has two potential drawbacks. First, all the existing airline demand studies we could find (for example, Oum, Gillen and Noble, 1986; Anderson and Kraus, 1981; Straszheim, 1978; and Mutti and Murai, 1977) used pre-deregulation data. As our analysis focuses on firm rivalry in the post-deregulation

---

3. In fact, airlines compete both in terms of price and quality of service (mainly frequency). Although it is possible to extend our model to include competitive choice of frequency, it is difficult to implement such a model empirically as it requires not only extensive data on frequency but also the information about how costs vary with frequencies. For a given route competing airlines tend to use aircraft of similar size. As a result, the frequency variables would be highly correlated with market shares. This would pose a problem in estimating the system.

era, demand elasticities might have changed over the time period. Second, the airline routes considered by these studies do not nest ours, so the best we can do is use an average estimate of elasticity for all our routes. To the extent that elasticities differ systematically across the routes under investigation, this approximation would introduce a source of error in estimating conduct parameters for each route.

Our approach here is to estimate demand elasticities by using the current data set. We approximate market demand (the inverse of equation (1)) with a log-linear functional form as follows:

$$\log X_{kt} = A - \eta_k \log p_{kt} + g(Y_{kt}) + \varepsilon_{kt} \qquad (9)$$

where A is an (unknown) parameter associated with the demand intercept, Y_{kt} is a vector of variables shifting demand, $g(\cdot)$ is some function to be determined, and ε_{kt} is a random error term. Note that the market demand elasticity, η_k, enters demand equation (9) as route-specific. Thus, we impose no restrictions on the way η_k may vary across routes as well as on their levels: η_k are estimated from the data.

As indicated above, estimation of conduct parameters requires marginal cost information for each carrier on each route. Brander and Zhang (1990) have proposed a method in which the route-specific marginal cost is calculated as follows:

$$c_{kt}^i = cpm_t^i \, (D_k/AFL_t^i)^{-\theta} D_k \qquad (10)$$

where cpm_t^i is each carrier's cost per passenger-mile for an "average" route in the U.S. domestic market, AFL_t^i is each carrier's average flight length for the U.S. market as a whole, and D_k is the distance of route k. From equation (10), calculation of route-specific marginal costs requires knowledge of θ. If $\theta = 0$, then the cost per passenger is simply equal to the cost per passenger-mile multiplied by flight length, indicating a linear relationship between cost and distance. However, it is well known in airline economics that costs are strictly concave in distance rather than linear, implying $0 < \theta < 1$.[4] This phenomenon is called the "cost taper,"

---

4. One obvious reason for this lies in the fact that airline costs can be separated into line-haul costs and terminal costs, where terminal costs are those related to the amount of traffic carried but independent of the mileage travelled. A less apparent reason may have something to do with passenger load factor (an indicator of aircraft seat utilisation). The optimal load factor is shown to be higher on long-distance routes than on short-distance routes (see Douglas and Miller, 1974), but a high load

and θmay be used to capture the "tapering effect." The higher the value of θ, the stronger the tapering effect. Several studies in the airline literature suggest a value of about 0.5 for θ, and Brander and Zhang (1990) use θ = 0.5 in their "base case" analysis.

We use equation (10) as our marginal cost formula, but treat θ as an unknown parameter of the cost function. Substituting (10) into (8) yields:

$$p_{kt}^i = \frac{[cpm_t^i(D_k/AFL_t^i)^{-\theta}D_k]\eta_k}{\eta_k-(1+V_k^i)s_{kt}^i} + \varepsilon_{kt}^i \qquad (11)$$

When firm i is a monopoly on route k at observation t, use of equation (10) gives:

$$p_{kt}^M = \frac{[cpm_t^M(D_k/AFL_t^M)^{-\theta}D_k]\eta_k}{\eta_k-s_{kt}^M} + \varepsilon_{kt}^M \qquad (12)$$

where s_{kt}^M is the firm's market share in the route market. Note that the monopoly pricing behaviour implied by equation (12) generalises that given in (7): if the firm is a "pure" monopolist, then $s_{kt}^M = 1$ and the former reduces to the latter. We use equation (12) because although a single firm may have a substantial market presence, it is empirically rare for the firm to have 100 percent market share. Given that all the other output is exogenous to the major firm, monopoly pricing (7) can be shown to extend to (12).[5] Although our main concern is firm conduct in

---

factor tends to reduce the cost per passenger, suggesting that long-distance routes tend to have lower costs per passenger-mile than short-distance routes.

5. The profit function for the major firm ("monopolist") is:

$$\pi^M = p(x^M + x_o)x^M - C^M(x^M) \qquad (13)$$

where x_o denotes the output other than the major firm. The first-order condition for the monopolist, assuming x_o is exogenous, requires that

$$p^M + x^M p' - c^M = 0 \qquad (14)$$

where $p^M = p(x^M + x_o)$. This can be rewritten as:

$$(p^M - c^M)/p^M = s^M/\eta. \qquad (15)$$

Substitution of (10) into (15) gives (12).

oligopolistic markets, data on monopoly routes contain valuable information in determining econometrically the cost and demand functions noting that, given the market share, monopoly conduct, unlike oligopoly conduct, is well specified.

The first-order conditions of equation (11) ((12) in the case of monopoly) and demand equation (9) are jointly estimated by a maximum likelihood method using a pooled cross-sectional and time-series data set of the Chicago-based airline routes.[6]

IV. The Data

We obtained price and quantity data from I.P. Sharp Associates. The I.P. Sharp data are derived from Databank 1A of the U.S. Department of Transportation (DOT) *Origin and Destination Survey*. This data set, OD1A, is a 10 percent sample of all tickets that originate in the U.S. on significant domestic carriers. The basic unit of our price data is the directional fare, which is taken to be half of the excursion (or round-trip) fare. Our volume information contains the number of directional local passengers in the 10 percent sample for each airline on each route.

We used the following procedure to obtain airline routes in our data set. Twenty routes were selected by taking all Chicago-based city-pair routes for 1985 on which American and United together had a market share exceeding 90 percent, and on which each carrier had at least 100 passengers per quarter in the 10 percent sample.[7] The quantity data for the 20 routes were then collected for each quarter from 1981 to 1988.[8]

---

6. Note that, theoretically, there are three equations (two price equations and one demand equation) for a duopoly route but only two equations (one price equation and one demand equation) for a monopoly route. Our econometric model is a three-equation system. In particular, a third equation will be created when the estimation switches to a monopoly route, and this equation is essentially an identity.

7. Many studies (including Call and Keeler, 1985; Levine, 1987; Morrison and Winston, 1990; Borenstein, 1989, 1990; Berry, 1990; and U.S. DOT, 1990) conclude that the degree of airport dominance affects airline pricing behaviour as a result of such factors as market power, consumer's valuation of higher departure frequency, and cost advantage, all of which come with high presence in a major airport. For this reason, we also excluded major hub airports (such as Denver and Dallas/Fort Worth) from the data.

8. OD1A data are quarterly, beginning on 1 January 1981, and are updated and revised regularly but with a substantial lag.

The data for the first and third quarters of 1988 contained errors and were not usable. This left us with thirty quarters and a total of 20 x 30 = 600 potential data points.

Useful data points for our purpose are those that are characterised as duopoly (between AA and UA) or monopoly (AA or UA). We classified an observation (a quarterly data point) as duopoly if the combined market share of AA and UA exceeded 75 percent, each "duopolist" had at least 30 percent of the combined share, and the quarterly traffic volume for each airline in the 10 percent sample was a least 100 passengers. An observation is classified as monopoly if AA (or UA) alone had at least 90 percent market share and its quarterly traffic volume in the 10 percent sample was at least 100 passengers. All other observations were excluded from our econometric estimation.[9]

After applying the above filtering rule, the total number of observations used for econometric implementation is 359 quarterly data points spanning 20 routes for the 1981-88 period. Of the 359 data points, 308 (about 86 percent) are in the duopoly category, while the remaining 51 are in the monopoly category. Therefore, duopoly is the primary feature of this data set. The eight-year quantity data set also reveals structural changes on several routes over time, especially between the earlier and later years. All 51 monopoly observations were in the first half of the sample period (that is, before the fourth quarter of 1984) while the duopoly data points spanned the entire period, with about two-thirds of them in the second half of the sample period. Table 1 lists the names of each connecting city and the distance of each route, in ascending order of distance. It also shows, using data on duopoly routes only, the mean prices for American Airlines and United Airlines on each route. The mean passenger volumes in each market are given in column 5 while the last column contains the combined mean market share of the two carriers.

As discussed in Section 3, estimation of marginal costs needs data on a carrier's overall cost per passenger-mile, cpm_r^i, and on a carrier's aver-

---

9. Defining duopoly as having jointly at least 75 percent market share and monopoly as having at least 90 percent market share is somewhat arbitrary. U.S. DOT (1990) used 90 percent market share to define a monopoly route, whereas Brander and Zhang (1990) used 75 percent market share to define a duopoly route. We have conducted sensitivity analysis using slightly different market share criteria (80 or 70 percent for oligopoly, 95 or 85 percent for monopoly) and found that, at least for this data set, the results reported below are not sensitive to these small changes.

age flight length for the U.S. market, AFL_t^i. Following Brander and Zhang (1990) we used operating expenses as a proxy for variable cost. U.S. DOT reports operating expenses for each carrier based on its Form 41 (see *Air Carrier Financial Statistics*).[10] The DOT also reports revenue passenger-miles, which is equal to available seat miles multiplied by load factor (see *Air Carrier Traffic Statistics*). We obtained cpm_t^i by dividing operating costs by passenger miles for each year. AFL_t^i was obtained by dividing aircraft revenue miles by aircraft revenue departures performed in each year (*Air Carrier Traffic Statistics*). Our calculation shows that the average cost per passenger-mile and the average stage length are very similar between the two airlines, with an overall average cost of 12.56 cents for American and 11.93 cents for United, and an overall average distance of 778 miles for American and 773 miles for United.

In equation (9) we specified the route aggregate demand as a function of the average market price and the demand-shifting factors, $g(Y_{kt})$. In order to incorporate the market demand function into the system of estimating equations, we need to choose the variables Y_{kt} and the functional form g(•). Typically, aggregate airline demand models using route data include the three usual components of gravity-type of transport interaction model between cities: population, income of the origin and destination cities, and one or more measure of impedance between the two cities. Since an average air fare variable is already included in (9) and Chicago is one end of all the routes included in our sample, we only considered population and income of the cities on the other end of the route. Since both population and per-capita income were not statistically significant at any reasonable level on the basis of a likelihood ratio test, it was decided to include the airport catchment area's total income (that is, the product of population and per-capita income). In addition, we incorporated two dummy variables: a dummy variable indicating high demand seasons (second and third quarters) and a dummy variable indicating vacation-oriented routes (Las Vegas and Reno routes).

A statistical test using Box-Cox transformation of the total income variable in $g(Y_{kt})$ indicated superiority of the logarithmic transformation

---

10. Operating expenses are costs incurred in the performance of air transport and air transport related services. This includes direct aircraft operating expenses, ground expenses and indirect operating expenses.

Pricing of Transport Services

Table 1. Route, Distance, Mean Price and Volume on Duopoly Routes

Route	Distance (miles)	AA Fare	UA Fare	Local Passenger	AA and UA Share
Grand Rapids	134	112	117	1452	0.970
Des Moines	306	131	138	2539	0.995
Omaha	423	127	128	2539	0.946
Buffalo	467	150	144	2071	0.980
Rochester	522	159	157	1639	0.994
Tulsa	587	134	133	1500	0.972
Wichita	591	173	171	964	0.985
Syracuse	601	164	163	1371	0.996
Oklahoma	692	159	160	1627	0.963
Albany	717	176	177	1352	0.996
Hartford	778	180	185	3745	0.980
Providence	842	165	171	1549	0.988
Austin	972	150	156	1141	0.850
Phoenix	1440	176	156	7061	0.871
Tucson	1441	160	154	1400	0.966
Las Vegas	1521	148	116	4982	0.874
Reno	1680	166	151	769	0.945
Ontario, CA	1707	199	194	1432	0.955
Sacramento	1790	195	195	846	0.980
San Jose	1837	222	218	1418	0.991

of that variable over the linear form. Therefore, the log of total income variable and the two dummy variables indicated above enter in the route aggregate demand function (9).

Measurement of population and per-capita income raises a difficulty of defining the "proper" catchment area of each airport. For most airports, we collected the data from *Local Area Personal Income* published by the U.S. Department of Commerce, Bureau of Economic Analysis. This source reports population figures for the metropolitan statistical area (MSA). However, for some airports MSA may not be a good indicator for the airport catchment area.[11] For these airports (San Jose and Ontario, California) it was necessary to adjust the population figures.

V. Empirical Results

Two hypotheses were tested concerning conduct parameters of the two airlines. The first hypothesis was to test whether or not American and United adopted identical pricing strategy on all routes in the sample. This can be tested by constraining the equality of conduct parameters on each route, that is, $v^1_k = v^2_k$ for all routes $k = 1,...,20$ (20 degrees of freedom). The second hypothesis concerns whether or not a given airline adopted identical pricing strategy on all routes. This is tested by constraining equality of each airline's conduct parameters across all 20 routes (38 degrees of freedom), that is, $v^i_1 = v^i_k$ for $k = 2,...,20$ and $i = 1,2$. The asymptotic likelihood ratio test was employed to test these hypotheses. Both hypotheses are rejected overwhelmingly.[12] These test results indicate that American and United do not apply the same pricing strategy on all the routes, and neither airline applies an identical pricing strategy in all markets. Therefore, in the remainder of this paper, our discussion will be based on the unconstrained econometric model.

Table 2 reports the maximum likelihood parameter estimates for the (unconstrained) econometric model with the standard errors of the estimates in parentheses. The nonlinear estimation converged to these estimates from several different sets of starting values, indicating that the global maximum was (probably) located. Below we discuss the key empirical findings.

---

11. For example, multiple airports exist near San Jose and Ontario, CA. Many passengers who travel to and from San Jose use other airports in the San Francisco area (see Harvey, 1987), and many who travel to and from Ontario use Los Angeles area airports.

12. The likelihood ratio test statistics are as follows. The test statistic for the hypothesis of equality of conduct parameters between the two airlines is $-2(L_0 - L_1) = 2(3472 - 3425) = 94$, where L_0 is the value of the log-likelihood function under the null hypothesis and L_1 the value of the log-likelihood function for the unconstrained model. Since the critical value of x^2_{20} at $\alpha = 0.01$ is 38, we reject the null hypothesis of equal conduct parameters overwhelmingly. The test statistic for the hypothesis of equal conduct parameters across 20 routes for both airlines is $-2(L_0 - L_1) = 2(3504 - 3425) = 158$. Since the critical value of x^2_{38} at $\alpha = 0.01$ is 63, we reject the null hypothesis overwhelmingly.

Table 2. Parameter Estimates of the Econometric Model
(Standard Errors in Parentheses)

Route	Elasticity	AA Conduct Parameter	UA Conduct Parameter
Grand Rapids	1.671(0.070)	0.636(0.140)	0.829(0.156)
Des Moines	1.475(0.070)	0.730(0.239)	0.094(0.156)
Omaha	1.492(0.068)	0.668(0.374)	0.038(0.209)
Buffalo	1.515(0.067)	0.061(0.122)	0.148(0.159)
Rochester	1.542(0.065)	0.023(0.103)	0.329(0.131)
Tulsa	1.564(0.067)	-0.203(0.172)	0.494(0.296)
Wichita	1.623(0.068)	0.029(0.164)	-0.072(0.154)
Syracuse	1.553(0.065)	-0.042(0.103)	0.437(0.139)
Oklahoma	1.523(0.064)	-0.182(0.118)	0.423(0.170)
Albany	1.543(0.064)	-0.049(0.102)	0.460(0.135)
Hartford	1.356(0.067)	0.131(0.149)	-0.135(0.102)
Providence	1.581(0.065)	-0.437(0.207)	-0.307(0.179)
Austin	1.589(0.068)	-0.440(0.253)	-0.019(0.298)
Phoenix	1.241(0.067)	-0.853(0.163)	-1.014(0.263)
Tucson	1.523(0.064)	-0.813(0.134)	-0.661(0.206)
Las Vegas	2.032(0.251)	-0.693(0.604)	-1.493(0.572)
Reno	2.336(0.240)	-0.509(0.325)	-0.893(0.272)
Ontario, CA	1.500(0.062)	-0.412(0.126)	-0.476(0.117)
Sacramento	1.589(0.062)	-0.538(0.168)	-0.548(0.109)
San Jose	1.461(0.061)	-0.283(0.106)	-0.363(0.087)
Intercept(A)	13.375(1.189)		
Total income(g_1)	0.163(0.125)		
Seasonal dummy(g_2)	0.080(0.026)		
Vacational dummy(g_3)	3.634(1.194)		
Tapering factor(θ)	0.432(0.029)		
Log-likelihood	-3425.062		

Route Demand Functions

The price elasticity estimate for the route aggregated demand ranges between 1.24 and 2.34 with the vacation routes (Las Vegas and Reno) assuming the highest values. (For routes other than Las Vegas and Reno, the price elasticity ranges between 1.24 and 1.67.) The average price elasticity for the 20 sample routes is 1.58. These elasticity estimates are very close to the estimates reported in previous studies (see, for example, Oum, Gillen and Noble, 1986[13]), which used pre-deregulation data. The higher price elasticities for vacation routes are expected because a higher proportion of the users of those routes are leisure travellers, who tend to be more price-sensitive than non-leisure (business) travellers. We also note that for the majority of the routes the elasticity estimates are fairly uniform. All the demand-shifting variables (total income, seasonal and vacational dummies) have expected signs and are statistically significant for the two dummy variables.

Cost Function

The estimate for θ (distance tapering factor for the cost) is 0.43, with a standard error of 0.03. As expected, a hypothesis test would strongly reject both $\theta = 0$ (linear relationship between cost and distance) and $\theta = 1$ (cost per passenger being unrelated to distance). Furthermore, $\theta = 0.5$, which was used by previous researchers, would also be rejected at the 5 percent level of significance.[14] Our estimate, 0.43, lies between 0.15 estimated by Caves *et al.* (1984) and the value 0.67 estimated by Borenstein (1988). Our costing model in equation (10) gave very similar predicted costs for American and United on most of our sample routes. This justifies using the firm conduct value of -1 and 1 to indicate the

---

13. They estimated a two-stage consumer demand system for U.S. domestic air travel routes, using a cross-sectional sample of 200 routes in 1978. Fare classes were subdivided into first-class, standard economy and discount. Their estimated elasticities for the discount fare class range from 1.5 to 2.0, and the range for regular economy is 1.2 to 1.4.

14. The likelihood ratio test rejects the null hypothesis of $\theta = 0.50$ at $\alpha = 0.05$ level: $-2(L_0 - L_1) = 2(3428.27 - 3425.06) = 6.42 >$ critical value of $\chi^2_1 (0.05) = 3.84$, where L_0 is the value of the log-likelihood function under the null hypothesis. But the hypothesis of $\theta = 0.50$ is not rejected at $\alpha = 0.01$ level ($\chi^2_1(0.01) = 6.63$).

Bertrand and cartel behaviour, respectively.[15] The cournot conduct parameter (which equals 0) is not affected by marginal cost differences.

Conduct Parameter Estimates

All 40 route-specific conduct parameters are in the "reasonable range" of -1 (Bertrand) and 1 (cartel) as predicted by our theoretical structure. There are two possible exceptions involving United's conduct parameters for Phoenix (-1.01) and Las Vegas (-1.49). Statistically, both are not different from -1. As discussed earlier, a conduct parameter close to -1 would indicate marginal cost pricing, while a conduct parameter less than -1 would suggest pricing below marginal cost. The actual record shows that United's average yield on the Las Vegas route was $116, as compared to $148 charged by American (see Table 1). The estimated marginal cost figures, on the other hand, were $134 for United and $137 for American. One possible explanation is that United was reacting to the active competition from charter carriers and fringe scheduled carriers as well as trying to maintain its dominant position over American.[16]

Table 3 reports 95 percent confidence intervals for the conduct parameters. It may be worth noting that almost one half (19 out of 40) of the conduct parameters include the Cournot value of 0 in their 95 percent confidence intervals. Eight conduct parameters (involving four routes—Phoenix, Tucson, Las Vegas and Reno—which may be referred to as "sunspot" destinations) include the Bertrand value of -1. Thus oligopolistic conduct may be described as being Bertrand behaviour in leisure-oriented (sunspot) markets. Only three out of 40 conduct parameters (involving Grand Rapids, Des Moines, and Omaha, the three shortest routes in the sample) include the cartel value of 1 in the 95 percent confidence intervals. However, the 95 percent confidence interval for American in the Omaha route also includes the Cournot value of 0. In sum, the competitive behaviour for American and United may be described as being between Bertrand and Cournot behaviour, but closer

---

15. Different marginal costs for duopolists could affect the values of firm-specific conduct parameters under the Bertrand solution and the cartel solution.
16. There was active competition from charter carriers in the Chicago-Las Vegas market. Furthermore, as the data in Table 1 show, this route has an unusually high presence of fringe scheduled carriers as compared to other duopoly routes.

Table 3. 95 Percent Confidence Intervals for Conduct Parameters

Route	AA Conduct Parameters	UA Conduct Parameters
Grand Rapids	0.362, 0.910	0.524, 1.078
Des Moines	0.262, 1.198	-0.211, 0.343
Omaha	-0.064, 1.400	-0.371, 0.372
Buffalo	-0.178, 0.300	-0.163, 0.402
Rochester	-0.179, 0.225	0.073, 0.538
Tulsa	-0.540, 0.134	-0.086, 0.967
Wichita	-0.292, 0.350	-0.374, 0.174
Syracuse	-0.244, 0.160	0.165, 0.659
Oklahoma	-0.413, 0.049	0.090, 0.695
Albany	-0.249, 0.151	0.196, 0.676
Hartford	-0.161, 0.423	-0.335, 0.028
Providence	-0.842, -0.032	-0.657, -0.021
Austin	-0.935, 0.055	-0.602, 0.457
Phoenix	-1.182, -0.544	-1.529, -0.594
Tucson	-1.075, -0.551	-1.064, -0.332
Las Vegas	-1.876, 0.490	-2.613, -0.579
Reno	-1.145, 0.127	-1.426, -0.458
Ontario, CA	-0.659, -0.165	-0.705, -0.289
Sacramento	-0.867, -0.209	-0.761, -0.374
San Jose	-0.491, -0.075	-0.533, -0.224

to Cournot, on most of the sample routes we investigated. This result is not inconsistent with the result of Brander and Zhang (1990), who obtained Cournot behaviour by using a different methodology and a single period data set.

The average values of the conduct parameters of all routes are -0.16 for American and -0.14 for United. These are more competitive than the Cournot conduct while being very close to it. If we assume that costs are roughly the same between monopoly and duopoly routes for the same airlines, then our results can show that moving from duopoly to monopoly routes would raise prices by about 17 percent. This result is consistent with the estimates obtained in the literature.[17] Also, since the

Figure 1. Differential Conduct Parameters vs. Differential Market Shares

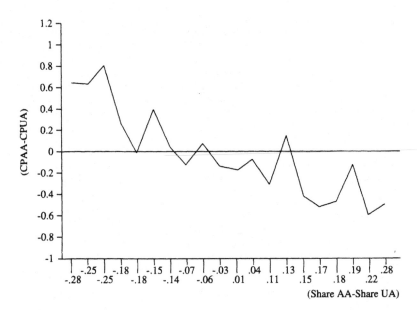

(Share AA-Share UA)

number of actual competitors does affect prices, it is another endorsement of the almost unanimous findings of the recent studies which conclude that deregulated airline markets are not perfectly contestable (see, for example, Call and Keeler, 1985; Morrison and Winston, 1989; Levine, 1987; and Hurdle *et al.*, 1989).

It can be seen from Table 2 that, although being close to each other overall, conduct parameters of the two airlines (at least their point estimates) are quite different in some route markets. This may imply that, in these markets, the two airlines perceive competition differently and thus employ different pricing strategies. A careful examination of the corre-

---

17. For example, Hurdle *et al.* (1989) find, using 850 non-stop city-pair routes in the U.S., that a reduction from two to one firms raised prices on average by 20 percent. Borenstein (1992) reports that in 1990, prices on routes with two active competitors averaged about 8 percent lower than on monopoly routes. Our estimate of 17 percent is between the estimates of the above two studies.

lation between conduct parameters and market share distribution led us to make the following inferences.

- The conduct parameters tend to be different between American and United in markets with unequal division of market shares, while they are similar in markets with similar market share divisions (see Figure 1). In fact, the correlation between the difference in the conduct parameters and the differential market shares of the two carriers is 0.90 (*t*-ratio of -8.6).

- The observed relationship between conduct parameters and the firm's market shares (see Figure 2) suggests that, in these essentially duopoly markets, the carrier with the higher market share tends to have lower conduct parameters. This negative correlation (the correlation coefficient is -0.27 for American and 0.44 for United) may be interpreted in two alternative ways: (a) the airline with the higher market share behaves more competitively than its opponent; (b) the firm that prices more aggressively succeeds in securing a higher market share.

Figure 2. Estimated Conduct Parameters vs. AA s Market Share

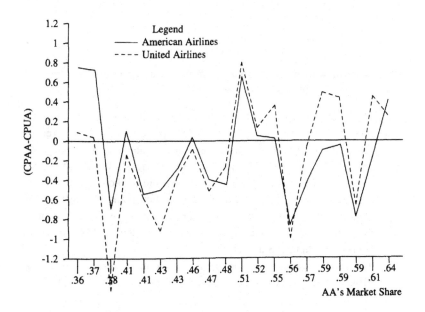

Figure 3. Estimated Conduct Parameters vs. AA and UA s Market Share

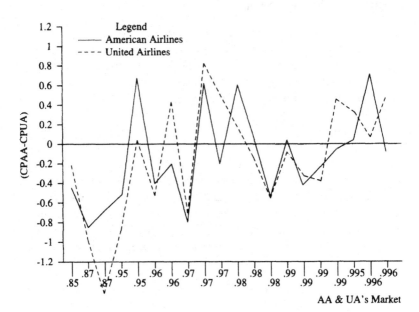

An examination of the conduct parameters and route characteristics led us to make the following observations.

- There is fairly strong evidence that conduct parameters are inversely related to distance, implying that firms price more competitively in longer distance routes. (Similar findings are obtained by, among others, U.S. DOT, 1990). This may result from the additional competition posed by other carriers serving the same route markets, using connecting flights through their respective hubs. For example, Western Airlines (now a part of Delta) served Chicago and Las Vegas out of its Salt Lake City hub. Chicago-Las Vegas passengers could have taken a connecting flight at Salt Lake City.
- The conduct parameters tend to be negative in the markets with a significant presence of fringe airlines (for example, Phoenix and Las

Vegas).[18] Figure 3 demonstrates graphically that the conduct parameters of both American and United increase (become less competitive) as their combined market share increases.

A regression of the conduct parameters on the combined market share of American and United and distance variables confirms the above results, that is, a positive and significant coefficient for the combined market share (*t*-ratio of 2.70), and a negative and highly significant coefficient for distance (*t*-ratio of -7.28).

Firm-specific Price Elasticities

The price elasticities of demand each firm faces are computed using the estimated conduct parameters, the market shares of the two firms, and the price elasticities of market demand (see equation (6)). Table 4 reports these firm-specific elasticity results in the last two columns, and the market demand elasticity (from Table 2) in the first column. It is possible to make the following observations from the firm-specific price elasticity results.

- The firm-specific elasticities are similar between American and United. This is a striking result in view of the quite different conduct parameters observed in some of our sample routes. A closer examination reveals that the similarity in elasticities between the two carriers is caused by similar performance in price-cost margin ratios by the two airlines in most routes. Equations (5) and (6) show that the firm-specific elasticity is equal to the inverse of the margin ratio of the airline. This indicates that the duopolists appear to use pricing strategy which equalises the ratio of margin to price. This is indeed a surprising discovery.
- The price elasticity faced by each carrier is very high in sunspot markets (Phoenix, Tucson, Las Vegas and Reno). For the cases of Phoenix and Las Vegas, United's elasticities reach infinity because the point estimates of the conduct parameters were smaller than -1 (see equation (6)).

18. This is expected because fringe airlines disciplined the duopolists by offering cheaper fares or by acting as a spoiler in the market. This happened in Canada where Wardair, a minor player in the trans-Canada market, disciplined the duopolists (Air Canada and Canadian Airlines) before being acquired by Canadian. This result is also consistent with the findings of Graham, Kaplan and Sibley (1983) and Borenstein (1990) who conclude that airlines find it more difficult to collude tacitly in markets with three carriers than in markets with two carriers.

• The firm-specific elasticities increase with distance. This is primarily because the conduct parameters decrease with distance. The effect remains even after we control for both the sunspot market effect and the fringe-firm effect.

A regression of the firm-specific price elasticities (excluding the two infinity cases) on distance, the combined share of American and United, and sunspot market dummy shows that the distance coefficient has the expected positive sign and is statistically significant (t-ratio of 1.99).

VI. Summary and Concluding Remarks

We have examined the pattern of firm conduct and associated price elasticities perceived by each firm in a sample of 20 routes to and from Chicago which were dominated by American Airlines and United Air-

Table 4. Estimated Firm-Specific Elasticities

Route	Market	AA	UA
Grand Rapids	1.671	2.015	1.853
Des Moines	1.475	2.355	2.113
Omaha	1.492	2.398	2.292
Buffalo	1.515	2.735	2.761
Rochester	1.542	2.721	2.602
Tulsa	1.564	2.076	2.892
Wichita	1.623	3.372	3.286
Syracuse	1.553	2.743	2.642
Oklahoma	1.523	3.054	2.741
Albany	1.543	2.764	2.559
Hartford	1.356	2.935	2.650
Providence	1.581	5.806	4.419
Austin	1.589	4.943	3.802
Phoenix	1.241	16.090	∞
Tucson	1.523	13.723	11.052
Las Vegas	2.032	17.603	∞
Reno	2.336	11.134	38.121
Ontario, CA	1.500	5.510	5.331
Sacramento	1.589	8.389	5.958
San Jose	1.461	4.722	4.034

lines. The conduct parameters and the aggregate market demand parameters were estimated through an econometric model which takes into account explicitly the form of inter-firm rivalry being practised. The estimation was carried out using firm-specific quarterly data for a set of monopoly and duopoly airline routes for the 1981-88 data.

Statistical tests rejected two hypotheses: (a) identical conduct between American and United, and (b) identical conduct for a given airline in all routes. This led us to believe that the airlines adjust their pricing strategies to the competitive conditions on each route. The overall results indicate that the duopolists' conduct may be described as somewhere between Bertrand and Cournot behaviour, but much closer to Cournot, in the majority of our sample observations. This has an important policy implication in that rigorous competition is not being practised on some of the duopoly routes. The main results for the pattern of conduct parameters are summarised below.

- Conduct parameters tend to be different between American and United in the markets with unequal division of market shares.
- The carrier with a higher market share tends to have a lower conduct parameter, or alternatively, the carrier exercising aggressive pricing tends to secure a higher market share.
- Conduct parameters are inversely related to route distance, implying that firms price more competitively on longer distance routes.
- Conduct parameters tend to be negative in markets with a significant presence of fringe airlines and/or charter services.

The price elasticity for the route aggregate demand ranges between 1.24 and 2.34 with an average value of 1.58. (The price elasticity ranges between 1.24 and 1.67 for routes other than Las Vegas and Reno, the two vacation routes.) The firm-specific elasticities are very similar between American and United, increase with route distance and are very high for leisure-oriented routes.

Our econometric model represents a small improvement over the airline demand models estimated in the past in two respects. First, this paper estimates the market demand model jointly with the individual firm's first-order conditions for profit maximisation. Second, inter-firm rivalry is explicitly incorporated in the model.

It could be argued that in order to understand inter-firm pricing rivalry in the airline industry it is necessary to look at the time-series behaviour of the conduct parameters. This paper focused on the effects of route characteristics on the pattern of inter-firm pricing rivalry and the associated firm-specific price elasticities. To accomplish this main objective, it was necessary to formulate the econometric model in such a way as to allow for variation of the price elasticity of the route aggregate demand and the conduct parameters across routes. This made it impossible econometrically to investigate the dynamic pricing behaviour over time. In contrast, Brander and Zhang (1993) were able to investigate the pattern of dynamic pricing behaviour over time because they computed the conduct parameters by using price elasticities estimated by others (Oum, Gillen and Noble, 1986), rather than estimating them econometrically. Since we found that airline pricing behaviour is different from route to route, future work will be necessary to develop and econometric method that will allow the estimation of conduct parameters which vary over time and across routes.

References

Abraham, M. (1983): "A Service Quality Model of Air Travel Demand: An Empirical Study." *Transportation Research*, 17A(5), pp. 385-93.

Abraham, M. and T.E. Keeler (1981): "Market Structure, Pricing and Service Quality in the Airline Industry Under Deregulation." In W. Sichel and T. Gies (eds.): *Application of Economic Principles in Public Utility Industries*. Michigan Business Studies, vol. II, no. 3, pp. 103-20. Ann Arbor, University of Michigan Press.

Agarwal, V. and W. Talley (1985): "The Demand for International Air Passenger Service Provided by U.S. Air Carriers." *International Journal of Transport Economics*, vol. 12, no. 1, pp. 63-70.

Anderson, J.E. and M. Kraus (1981): "Quality of Service and the Demand for Air Travel." *Review of Economics and Statistics*, vol. 63, pp. 533-40.

Bailey, E.E. and W.J. Baumol (1984): "Deregulation and Theory of Contestable Markets." *Yale Journal of Regulation*, vol. 1, no. 2, pp. 111-37.

Bailey, E.E., D.R. Graham and D.P. Kaplan (1985): *Deregulating the Airlines*. Cambridge, Mass., MIT Press.

Berry, S. (1990): "Airport Presence as Product Differentiation." *Ameri-

can Economic Review (Papers and Proceedings), vol. 80 (May), pp. 394-99.

Berry S. (1992): "Estimation of a Model of Entry in the Airline Industry." *Econometrica*, vol. 60, no. 4, pp. 889-917.

Borenstein, S. (1989): "Hubs and High Fares: Dominance and Market Power in the U.S. Airline Industry." *Rand Journal of Economics*, vol. 20 (Autumn), pp. 344-65.

Borenstein, S. (1990): "Airline Mergers, Airport Dominance, and Market Power." *American Economic Review* (Papers and Proceedings), vol. 80 (May), pp. 400-404.

Borenstein, S. (1992): "The Evolution of U.S. Airline Competition." *Journal of Economic Perspectives*, vol. 6 (Spring), pp. 45-73.

Borenstein, S. and N.L. Rose (1989): "Price Discrimination in the U.S. Airline Industry." Discussion Paper 306, Institute of Public Policy Studies, University of Michigan.

Brander, J.A. and A. Zhang (1990): "Market Conduct in the Airline Industry: An Empirical Investigation." *Rand Journal of Economics*, vol. 21, no. 4 (winter), pp. 567-83.

Brander, J.A. and A. Zhang (1993): "Dynamic Oligopoly Behaviour in the Airline Industry." *International Journal of Industrial Organization*, forthcoming.

Bresnahan, T.F. (1989): "Empirical Studies of Industries with Market Power." In R. Schmalensee and R.D. Willig (eds.): *Handbook of Industrial Organization*, chapter 7, pp. 1011-57. New York, North-Holland.

Brumelle, S., J. McGill, T.H. Oum, K.Sawaki and M.W. Tretheway (1990): "Airline Seat Allocation with Dependent Discount/Full Fare Demands and Overbooking." *Transportation Science*, vol. 24, no. 3 (August), pp. 825-36.

Call, G.D. and T.E. Keeler (1985): "Airline Deregulation, Fares, and Market Behaviour: Some Empirical Evidence." In A.F. Daughety (ed.): *Analytical studies in Transport Economics*. Cambridge: CUP.

Caves, D.W., L.R. Christensen and M.W. Tretheway (1984): "Economies of Density versus Economies of Scale: Why Trunk and Local Service Airline Costs Differ." *Rand Journal of Economics*, vol. 15, pp. 471-89.

De Vany, A. (1974): "The Revealed Value of Time in Air Travel." *Review of Economics and Statistics*, vol. 56, pp. 77-82.

Douglas, G.W. and J.C. Miller (1974): *Economic Regulation of Domestic Air Transport: Theory and Policy*. Brookings Institute, Washington D.C.

Dresner, M. and M.W. Tretheway (1992): "Modelling and Testing the Effect of Market Structure on Price: The Case of International Air Transport." *Journal of Transport Economics and Policy*, vol. 26, no. 2, pp. 171-84.

Fridstroöm, L. and H. Thune-Larsen (1989): "An Econometric Air Travel Demand Model for the Entire Conventional Domestic Network: The Case of Norway." *Transportation Research*, vol. 23B, no. 3, pp. 231-24.

Graham, D.R., D.P. Kaplan and D.R. Sibley (1983): "Efficiency and Competition in the Airline Industry." *Bell Journal of Economics*, vol. 14 (Spring), pp. 118-38.

Haitovsky, Y., I. Salomon and A. Silman (1987): "The Economic Impact of Charter Flights on Tourism to Israel: An Econometric Approach." *Journal of Transport Economics and Policy*, vol. 2, no. 2, pp. 111-34.

Harvey, G. (1987): "Airport Choice in a Multiple Airport Region." *Transportation Research*, vol. 21A, no. 6, pp. 439-49.

Hensher, D.A. and J.J. Louvière (1983): "Identifying Individual Preferences for International Air Fares." *Journal of Transport Economics and Policy*, vol. 17, no. 3, pp. 225-45.

Hurdle, G.J., R.L. Johnson, A.S. Joskow, G.J. Werden and M.A. Williams (1989): "Concentration, Potential Entry, and Performance in the Airline Industry." *Journal of Industrial Economics*, vol. 38, pp. 119-39.

I.P. Sharp Associates Ltd. (1988-89): *Department of Transportation Origin and Destination Survey*, Data Bank 1A.

Ippolito, R.A. (1981): "Estimating Airline Demand with Quality of Service Variables." *Journal of Transport Economics and Policy*, vol. 15, no. 1, pp. 7-16.

Levine, M.E. (1987): "Airline Competition in Deregulated Markets: Theory, Firm Strategy, and Public Policy." *Yale Journal of Regulation*, vol. 4, pp. 393-494.

McShane, S. and R. Windle (1989): "The Implications of Hub and Spoke Routing for Airline Costs and Competitiveness." *Logistics and Transportation Review*, vol. 25, no. 3, pp. 209-30.

Morrison, S.A. and C. Winston (1985): "An Econometric Analysis of the Demand for Intercity Passenger Transportation Research." *Transportation Economics*, vol. 2, pp. 213-37.

Morrison, S.A. and C. Winston (1989): "Empirical Implications and Tests of the Contestability Hypothesis." *Journal of Law and Economics*, vol. 30 (April), pp. 53-56.

Morrison, S.A. and C. Winston (1990): "The Dynamics of Airline Pricing and Competition." *American Economic Review* (Papers and Proceedings), vol. 80 (May), pp. 389-93.

Mutti, J. and Y. Murai (1977): "Airline Travel on the North Atlantic: Is Profitability Possible?" *Journal of Transport Economics and Policy*, vol. 11, no. 1, pp. 45-53.

Oum, T.H. and D.W. Gillen (1983): "Structure of Intercity Travel Demands in Canada: Theory, Tests and Empirical Results." *Transportation Research*, vol. 17B, no. 3, pp. 175-91.

Oum, T.H., Gillen and D. Noble (1986): "Demand for Fareclasses and Pricing in Airline Markets." *Logistics and Transportation Review*, vol. 23 (September), pp. 195-222.

Oum, T.H., W.G. Waters II and J. Yong (1992): "Concepts of Price Elasticities of Transport Demand and Recent Empirical Estimates: An Interpretative Survey." *Journal of Transport Economics and Policy*, vol. 26, no. 2, pp. 139-54.

Panzar, J. (1979): "Equilibrium and and Welfare in Unregulated Airline Markets." *American Economic Review* (Papers and Proceedings), vol. 69, pp. 92-95.

Straszheim, M.R. (1978): "Airline Demand functions in the North Atlantic and Their Pricing Implications." *Journal of Transport Economics and Policy*, vol. 12, no. 2, pp. 179-95.

Talley, W.K. and A. Schwartz-Miller (1988): "The Demand for Air Services Provided by Air Passenger-Cargo Carriers in a Deregulated Environment." *International Journal of Transport Economics*, vol. 15, no. 2, pp. 159-68.

U.S. Department of Commerce (1981-88): *Local Area Personal Income.* Various issues, Washington D.C.

U.S. Department of Transportation (1984-88): *Air Carrier Financial Statistics* and *Air Carrier Traffic Statistics.* Various issues, Washington D.C.

U.S. Department of Transportation (1990): "Industry and Route Structure" and "Pricing." *Secretary s Task Force on Competition in the U.S. Domestic Airline Industry*, vol. 1 (February).

Verledger, P.K. (1972): "Models of the Demand for Air Transportation." *The Bell Journal of Economics and Management Science*, vol. 3, no. 2 (Autumn), pp. 437-57.

Whinston, M.D. and S.C. Collins (1992): "Entry, Contestability, and Deregulated Markets: An Event Study Analysis." *Rand Journal of Economics*, vol. 23 (winter), pp. 445-62.

Date of receipt of final type script: February 1993.

PART IV

INFRASTRUCTURE PRICING
AND INVESTMENT

CHAPTER 15

PRICING AND CONGESTION: ECONOMIC PRINCIPLES RELEVANT TO PRICING ROADS*

*David M. Newbery***

I. Introduction

The road network is a costly and increasingly scarce resource. For the UK the Department of Transport (1989a) calculates that total road expenditures (capital and current) or 'road costs' averaged £4.34 billion per year at 1989/90 prices for the period 1987/8-1989/90. Public expenditure on roads has been fairly stable recently, increasing by about 6 per cent in real terms between 1982/3 and 1988/9, but with no strong trend (Department of Transport, 1989b, Tables 1.18, 1.22, 1.23). From the 24.6 million vehicles registered, road taxes of £12.7 billion were collected (including the £1.4 billion car tax), or 2.9 times the Department's figures for 'road costs.' In 1987 15.1 per cent of consumers' expenditure was on transport and vehicles, and 11.3 percent was on motor vehicles alone. Clearly, road transport is of major economic significance. Car ownership per 1,000 population in the UK appears to be catching up on the rates in the larger European countries and is now about 83 percent of

* Reprinted from *Oxford Review of Economic Policy*, Vol. 6, No. 2, 1990, pp. 22-38.
** Department of Applied Economics, University of Cambridge.

French and Italian levels and 73 percent of West German levels. Over the decade 1979-89, the number of private cars increased from 14.3 to 18.5 million, or by 29 percent. From 1978-1988, the number of total vehicle-km driven rose from 256 to 363 billion or by 42 percent. As the length of the road network increased rather less, the average daily traffic on each km of road rose by 34 percent over the same decade on all roads and by 52 percent on motorways. Traffic on major roads in built-up areas (i.e. those with a speed limit of 40 mph or less) increased by 13 percent (Department of Transport, 1989b, Tables 2.1, 2.3).

As road space is a valuable and scarce resource, it is natural that economists should argue that it should be rationed by price—road-users should pay the marginal social cost of using the road network if they are to be induced to make the right decisions about whether (and by which means) to take a particular journey, and, more generally, to ensure that they make the correct allocative decisions between transport and other activities. If road-users paid the true social cost of transport, perhaps urban geography, commuting patterns, and even the sizes of towns would be radically different from the present. The modest aim here is to identify these social costs, provide rough estimates of their magnitude for Britain, and hence identify the major policy issues.

One way to focus the discussion is to ask how to design a system of charges for road use. The problem of designing road charges can be broken down into various sub-problems. First, what is the marginal social cost (that is, the extra cost to society) of allowing a particular vehicle to make a particular trip? Part will be the direct cost of using the vehicle (fuel, wear and tear, driver's time, and so forth) and will be paid for by the owner. This is the private cost of road use. Other costs are social: some will be borne by other road-users (delays, for example); some by the highway authority (extra road maintenance); and some by the society at large (pollution and risk of accidents). These are called the *road-use costs*—the social costs (excluding the private costs) arising from vehicles using roads. It seems logical to attempt to charge vehicles for these road-use costs, in order to discourage them from making journeys where the benefits are less than the total social costs (private costs plus road-use costs). The first task, therefore, is to measure these road-use costs.

The second question is whether road-users should pay additional taxes above these road-use costs. One argument is that road-users should pay the whole cost of the highway system, not just the extra cost of road use, either to be 'fair' in an absolute sense or to achieve parity or equity with, say, rail-users (in those rare countries whether the railway is required to cover its total costs without subsidy). Another argument is that the government needs to raise revenues and some part of this revenue should be collected from road-users, since to exempt them would be to give them an unreasonable advantage over the rest of the population. Both arguments appeal either to the desire for equity or fairness, or to the need for efficiency in the allocation of resources (road versus rail), or both.

Relevant Principles of Taxation

The modern theory of public finance provides a powerful organizing principle for taxing and pricing. Under certain assumptions policies should be designed to achieve production efficiency, with all distortionary taxes falling on final consumers. Broadly, the conditions for this result, set out formally in Diamond and Mirrlees (1971), are (a) that production efficiency is feasible, and (b) that any resulting private profits are either negligible or can be taxed away. The feasibility condition would be satisfied if the economy were competitive and externalities could be corrected or internalized.

The theory has immediate implications for road charges and taxes. Road-users can be divided into two groups: those who transport freight, which is an intermediate service used in production, and those who drive their own cars or transport passengers who enjoy final consumption. Freight transport, which is roughly and conveniently synonymous with diesel-using vehicles, should pay the road-use costs to correct externalities and to pay for the marginal costs of maintenance. Additional taxes (comprising the *pure tax element*) on (largely gasoline-using) passenger transport can be set, using the same principles that guide the design of other indirect taxes. We shall show below that one would expect a close relationship between road-use costs and total road expenditures. There is no logical reason to attribute the taxation of passenger transport to the highway budget, since it is a component of general tax revenue. But if all road taxes and charges are taken together, there are good reasons to expect that they will exceed total highway expenditure. In short, in a well-run country no conflict need arise between the goals of designing an equitable and efficient system of road-use charges and taxes and the desire to cover the highway system's costs.

The theory provides a useful framework for the study of road-user charges. The first step is to identify the road-use costs. The second is to see what methods are available for levying charges and how finely they can be adjusted to match these costs. The third step is to examine how far these methods have repercussions outside the transport sector and, where these occur, how to take them into account. These three steps will suffice for freight transport. For passenger transport, one other step is needed: to determine the appropriate level of (and method of levying) the pure tax element.

II. Quantifying the Social Costs of Road Use

Vehicles impose four main costs on the rest of society—accident externalities, environmental pollution, road damage, and congestion. Accident externalities arise whenever extra vehicles on the road increase the probability that other road-users will be involved in an accident. To the extent that accidents depend on distance driven and other traffic these accident costs can be treated rather like congestion costs. Newbery (1988a) argued that accident externalities could be as large as all other externality costs taken together, and are thus possibly of first order importance. There are two reasons for this high estimate, both disputed. The first is that the figure critically depends on the value of a life saved or the cost of a life lost. If one bases this on apparent willingness to pay to reduce risks, then the cost per life saved might be between £650,000 and £2 million at 1989 prices, based on the survey results of Jones-Lee, reported in this issue. The lower figure is over double that originally used by the Department of Transport, who based their earlier estimates on the expected loss of future earnings of a representative victim. Apparently the Department of Transport has been persuaded of the logic behind the willingness-to-pay approach, and now uses a figure of £500,000 (Jones-Lee, 1990).

The second reason is that in the absence of convincing evidence, the estimate assumed that the number of accidents increased with the traffic flow as the 1.25 power of that flow. (That is, if the traffic is twice as heavy, the risk of an accident happening to each car is increased by 19 percent. Compare this with the number of pairwise encounters between vehicles, which rises as the square of the flow.) This in turn means that a quarter of the cost of mutually caused accidents is an uncharged externality, even if each driver pays the full cost of the accident to him. (To the extent that society pays through the NHS, these individual costs are borne by society and attributable as part of 'road costs.' The Department of Transport includes direct costs. It might be argued that their earlier valuation of life was based on the loss of earnings which might have to be made good through the social security system to survivors.) Note that it is important to relate the accident rate to traffic levels in order to identify the size of the externality. Indeed, one might argue from the fact that the accident rate has fallen as traffic has increased that this 1.25 power law is invalid, and that at best there is no relationship between traffic and the accident rate. If so, then there would be no externality between motor vehicles (other than that already counted in the cost falling on the NHS). This would be the case if one took seriously the explanation of 'risk compensation,' according to which road-users choose a desired level of perceived risk with which they are comfortable—too little risk is boring, too much is frightening. Improvements in road safety then induce compensating increases in risk taking, while deteriorating road conditions (ice, snow, heavier traffic) induce more caution. Of course, one should be wary of using time series information about accident rates as road improvements are continuously undertaken to improve road safety. The relationship between accident rate and traffic should be derived from a properly estimated cross-section analysis.

Jones-Lee, in his article in this issue, does indeed assume that the accident *rate* (i.e. the risk of an accident per km driven) is independent of the traffic flow, from which it follows that there is no externality between motor vehicles (except those caused by the system of social and health insurance). He also assumes that the probability of any vehicle having an accident involving a pedestrian or cyclist is constant per km driven, in which case it follows that the accident rate experienced by cyclists and pedestrians is proportional to the number of vehicle km driven. If this is the case, then motor vehicles do impose an externality on non-motorized road-users (though not on other motorists), which Jones-Lee calculates to be quite large—perhaps 10-20 percent of total road costs. Of course, we remain relatively uncertain about the relationship between accidents to other road-users and traffic. It has been remarked that not so long ago children were allowed to play in the street, and cycle or walk unaccompanied to school. The number of accidents to such children was quite high. Now it is so obviously insane to allow such activities that the number of accidents may have fallen with the increase in traffic. Of course, that accident externality is still there, though hidden in the form of the extra costs of ferrying children to school, and not allowing them to play or cycle unsupervised.

The main problem therefore lies in identifying the relationship between traffic and accidents—in the words of the US Federal Highway Cost Allocation Study 'Quantitative estimation of accident cost and vehicle volume relationships, however, has not yet proved satisfactory...' (US Federal Highway Administration, 1982). Given the huge costs involved and the potential gains from lowering accident rates, identifying such relationships should have overwhelming research priority.

Similarly, pollution costs share many of the same features as congestion costs (and tend to occur in the same places). Where they have been quantified (for the US) they appear to contribute less than 10 percent of total road costs. They are normally dealt with by mandating emission standards, and by differential taxes on the more polluting fuels (for example, by having higher taxes on leaded petrol). A new European Directive on vehicle emissions, known as the Luxembourg Agreement, will be implemented in the UK. This mandates NO_x levels of half the current limit, and reductions in hydrocarbon releases of three-quarters, at an estimated cost to the motorist of £800 million or about 4 percent of motoring costs (Department of the Environment, 1989). Provided the pollution costs are reflected in fuel taxes, and given the requirement to meet emissions standards, these costs will have been satisfactorily internalized. One should, however, be rather cautious about mandating stringent emissions standards without a careful cost-benefit analysis. Crandall *et al.* (1986, pp. 114-15) estimate that the programme costs for the US of the more stringent 1984 emissions standards might be about $20 billion per year with a replacement rate of 10.5 million cars, which is several times greater than rather optimistic estimates of the potential benefits of reducing pollution. (Safety regulations in contrast, though expensive, seem to have been justified on cost-benefit criteria.) Some of these issues are discussed further in Newbery (1990).

Road Damage Costs

These are the costs borne by the highway authority of repairing roads damaged by the passage of vehicles, and the extra vehicle operating costs caused by this road damage. The damage a vehicle does to the road pavement increases as the fourth power of the axle load, which means that almost all damage is done by heavy vehicles such as trucks. Increasing the number of axles is a potent method of reducing the damaging effect of a vehicle—doubling the number of equally loaded axles reduces the damage to an eighth of its previous level. Consequently most highway authorities closely regulate the axle configuration and maximum legal axle loads. Increasing the road thickness dramatically increases the number of vehicles that can be carried before major repairs are required—doubling the thickness increases this number by 2 to the power 6.5 or so (Paterson, 1987). Consequently the most damaging and therefore costly combination is a heavy vehicle on a thin road.

The theory which allows these costs to be quantified is set out in Newbery (1988a, b). The road-damage costs of a vehicle will be proportional to its damaging power (and will be measured in terms of Equivalent Standard Axles, or ESAs). Britain, in common with most advanced countries, follows a condition-responsive maintenance strategy in which the road is repaired when its condition reaches a predetermined state. In such cases, the road-damage costs will be equal to the average annual costs of maintaining the road network in a stable state, multiplied by the fraction of the road deterioration caused by vehicles, as opposed to weather, allocated in proportion to ESA-miles driven. The fraction of total costs allocated to vehicles will depend on the climate, the strength of the road, and the interval between major repairs, and the formula is given in Newbery (1988a, b). In hot, dry climates it will be between 60 and 80 percent, while in freezing temperate climates the proportion will be between 20 and 60 percent, the lower figures corresponding to more stringent maintenance criteria or lower traffic volumes. For Britain, Newbery (1988a) argued that the appropriate fraction was 40 percent. If maintenance is condition-responsive then it is not necessary to charge vehicles for the damage they do indirectly to subsequent vehicles which experience increased operating costs on the damaged pavement—on average the condition of the pavement will remain unchanged.

It is simple to update the road-damage costs given in Newbery

Table 1. Road Costs at 1989/90 Prices (£ million)

Cost category	Annual average	
	5% TDR	8% TDR
Interest on capital	4,000	6,400
(Capital expenditure)	(1921)	
Maintenance		
less costs attributable to pedestrians	2,093	2,093
Policing and traffic wardens	327	327
Total road costs	6,420	8,820
of which attributable to		
road damage costs	314	314
gross vehicle mass	495	495
VKT	225	225
Balance attributable to PCU	4,884	7,284
PCU km	375 billion km	
Cost per PCU km	(1.30 p/km)	(1.94p/km)

Sources: Department of Transport (1989a).
Notes: Figures are annual averages for the years 1987/88 to 1989/90.
     TDR: Test Discount Rate.
     VKT: Vehicle km travelled.
     Costs attributable to gross vehicle mass and VKT taken from Department of Trans-
     port (1989a), adjusted in the same way as those given in Newbery (1988a, Table 5).

(1988a) using the latest estimates of road-track costs provided in Department of Transport (1989a, Table 5). The total cost identified is £785 million, or 8.7 pence/ESAkm. The allocable fraction is 0.4, giving £314 million or 3.5 pence/ESAkm. As such, road-damage costs are a small fraction of total road costs. To provide a quick estimate of how large a fraction, Table 1 above updates the results from 1986 to 1990 from Newbery (1988a, Table 2). There the value of the road network was estimated at £50 billion excluding land. Updated to 1990 prices this is £62 billion, and annual capital expenditure of £2 billion brings it to £70 billion. The cost of land is estimated at 14 percent of this, to give a total of £80 billion. In Newbery (1988a) the rate of interest on this capital value was taken to be the then Test Discount Rate of 5 percent real, and if this figure is again used, then interest on the value of the road network would be £4,000 million, compared to the actual capital expenditures of only £1,921 million. Recently, the Test Discount Rate has been revised upward to 8 percent real (presumably reflecting the perceived higher real rate of return in the rest of the economy), and at this rate the interest costs would rise to £6,400 million.

There is little logic in combining current and capital expenditures as the Department of Transport does in estimating 'road costs,' and Table 1 only includes imputed interest at the two different rates of 5 percent and 8 percent. It will be seen that allocable road-damage costs amount is 3.5-5 percent of total road costs, and are thus essentially negligible (which is not to deny that it is important to charge them appropriately to heavy goods vehicles).

This estimate is quite close to that for 1986 of 3.5 percent given in Newbery (1988a). Even if repair costs currently allocated by the UK Department of Transport in proportion to gross vehicle weight are included (and the theoretical justification for so doing is rather unclear) the figure only rises to 9-13 percent (depending on the choice of the TDR). Small *et al.* (1988) estimate that pavement costs, including construction and periodic resurfacing, are less than 16 percent of road costs in their simulations of an optimized US road system, and road-damage charges would only account for 2 percent of total charges. Far and away the largest element (again ignoring accident costs, which might also be very large) are the congestion costs.

Congestion Costs

These arise because additional vehicles reduce the speed of other vehicles, and hence increase their journey time. The standard way of calculating the short-run marginal congestion cost (MCC) of an extra vehicle in the traffic stream starts by postulating a relationship between speed (v kph) and flow (q vehicles or PCU/h) where PCU are passenger car units, a measure of the congestive effect of different vehicles in different circumstances (e.g. higher for heavy lorries on steep hills than on the level). If the travel cost per km of a representative vehicle is

$$c = a + b/v, \tag{1}$$

where b is the cost per vehicle hour, including the opportunity cost of the driver and occupants, then the total cost of a flow of q vehicles per hour is $C = cq$. If an additional vehicle is added to the flow, the total social cost is increased by

$$dC/dq = c + q*dc/dq. \qquad (2)$$

The first term is the private cost borne by the vehicle and the second is the marginal externality cost borne by other road-users.

The next step is to establish the speed-flow relationship, $v = v(q)$, and here one must be careful to pose the right question. Engineers designing particular sections of the road network are concerned with flow at each point, and most of the relationships estimated are of this form. They show that traffic flow is heavily influenced by junctions, where additional traffic enters or disrupts the smooth flow, and it is possible for the speed-flow relationship to be backward bending, as in Figure 1.

Figure 1. Speed Flow Relationship for a Link

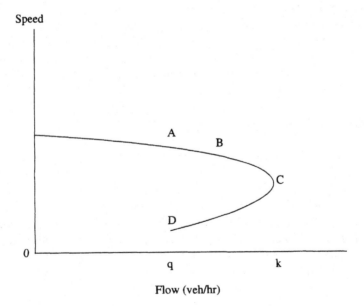

The curve is to be interpreted as follows. As traffic increases above q the speed is given by points such as A, B. As traffic nears the capacity of the link, k, at the point C, the flow changes to a condition of stop-start, and traffic flow through the bottleneck drops, to a point such as D, associated with a lower speed. This is an unstable situation, and as flow falls, so the traffic leaving the bottleneck will accelerate, and eventually clear the blockage. At that time, the speed will jump back up to point A (Further details are given in Newbery, 1987, and Hall *et al.*, 1986.)

Useful though this relation is for road design, it is not what is wanted for estimating the cost of congestion, where we need a measure of the total extra time taken by the remaining traffic to complete their planned journeys, not their speed at a particular point on the road network. The Department of Transport, when planning roads to alleviate congestion, uses formulas estimated by the Transport and Road Research Laboratory, and reported in Department of Transport (1987). These are based on 'floating car' methods, in which the observing vehicle remains in the traffic stream for a period of time, and hence give a better estimate of the average relationship between speed and flow. They find a reasonably stable linear relationship of the form

$$v = \alpha - \beta q, \tag{3}$$

where q is measured in PCU/lane/hr. The estimated value of β for urban traffic is 0.035. This agrees closely with a careful study of traffic flows within zones of Hong Kong, reported in Harrison *et al.* (1986), itself commissioned as part of Hong Kong's road-pricing experiment.

This linear relationship can be used to quantify the average and marginal costs of traffic and hence to determine the MCC. Figure 2 below gives this relationship for suburban roads at 1990 prices, based on the estimated COBA 9 formula. The left-hand scale gives the speed associated with the traffic flow, and on such roads average speeds rarely fall below 25 kph, so the relevant part of the diagram is to the left of that speed level. Another, quite useful way of representing this limitation is to suppose that the demand for using suburban roads becomes highly elastic at this level, an idea pursued further below.

In some ways a better measure of the congestion relationship is given by the marginal time cost (MTC) in vehicle-hours per vehicle-km, which can then be multiplied by the current value of the time use of the vehicle, b in (1). From (3), the MTC is just $\beta q / v^2$. Given data for q and *v*, the MTC can be estimated.

Newbery (1988a, Table 1) estimated these costs for Britain for the year 1985. Rather than repeat the rather time-consuming calculations reported there, the following short-cut has been adopted. If *m* is the MCC as a function of *q*, and if Δq is the increase in traffic over some period, then the revised estimate of the MCC is $m + dm/dq \cdot \Delta q$. The factor by which to scale up the original estimates of MCC can be found from the above equations and is

$$\{1 + (2\beta q/v)\} \,(\Delta q/q). \tag{4}$$

The results of this updating procedure are given in Table 2. If anything, the estimate will be on the low side, as the relationship is very non-linear. If some roads have an above-average increase in traffic while others have a below-average increase, then taking the average increase $\Delta q/q$ will underestimate the average of the costs on each road.

Table 2 shows in a vivid way the great variation in marginal congestion costs by time of day and location. Urban central areas at the peak have an *average* congestion cost of 10 times the average over all roads, and more than 100 times that the average motorway or rural road.

Figure 2. Average and Marginal Cost of Trips
(Urban non-central roads, 1990 prices)

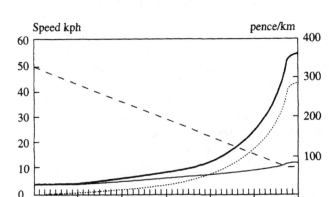

Table 2. Marginal Time Costs of Congestion in Great Britain, 1990

	MTC (veh h/ 100 PCUkm)	VKT fraction	MCC p/PCUkm	Index of MCC
Motorway	0.05	0.17	0.26	8
Urban central peak	5.41	0.01	36.37	1,070
Urban central off-peak	4.35	0.03	29.23	860
Non-central peak	2.36	0.03	15.86	466
Non-central off-peak	1.30	0.10	8.74	257
Small town peak	1.03	0.03	6.89	203
Small town off-peak	0.63	0.07	4.20	124
Other urban	0.01	0.14	0.08	2
Rural dual carriageway	0.01	0.12	0.07	2
Other trunk and principal	0.04	0.18	0.19	6
Other rural	0.01	0.11	0.05	1
Weighted average			3.40	100

Source: Updated from Newbery (1988a, Table 1)

The table shows that the average congestion cost is 3.4 pence/ PCUkm, and, given the 375 billion PCUkm driven from Table 1, if road-users were to be charged for congestion, the revenue collected would have been £12,750 million. If we add to this sum the road-damage costs (£314 m), the amounts allocated according to gross vehicle mass (£495 m), and VKT (£225 m), all taken from Table 1, then the appropriate level of road charges should yield £13,784 million. Total road taxes were £12,700 million, or 92 percent of the required level. Congestion charges would amount to 92 percent of the total appropriate road charge.

It is interesting to compare these estimates with those given in Newbery (1988a). The estimated congestion charges for Britain for 1986 were £6,203 million out of the total appropriate charge (excluding accident costs) of £7,033 million, or 88 percent. The figures are high as the amount of time wasted is so high, though the costs are frequently ignored by highway authorities, as they are entirely borne by highway-users. The Confederation of British Industries has calculated that traffic congestion costs the nation £15 billion a year, or £10 a week on each household's shopping bill (*The Times*, 19 May 1989). This figure is comparable to the £13 billion for the appropriate congestion charge calculated above, though the question of how best to measure the true social cost of congestion is discussed more fully below.

Small *et al.* (1989) cite evidence that suggests congestion costs are also high in the US. Thus average peak-hour delays in crossing the Hudson River to Manhattan have roughly doubled in the past ten years, while congestion delays in the San Francisco Bay Area grew by more than 50 percent in just two years. In 1987, 63 per cest of vehicle-miles were driven on Interstate Highways at volume to capacity ratios exceeding 0.8, and 42 percent on other arterials. Although their study does not quantify the congestions costs they suggest figures of some tens of billions of dollars annually—a figure which squares with the evidence in the next paragraph.

The correct charge to levy on vehicles is equal to the congestion costs they cause (in addition to other social costs like damage costs). If roads experience constant returns to scale, in that doubling the capital expenditure on the road creates a road able to carry twice the number of vehicles at the same speed, and if roads are optimally designed and adjusted to the traffic, then it can be shown that the optimal congestion charge would recover all of the non-damage road costs (Newbery, 1989). These include interest on the original capital stock, as well as the weather-induced road-damage costs not directly attributable to vehicles, and other maintenance expenditures, collectively identified as 'road costs attributable to PCU' in Table 1. The available evidence supports constant returns to scale or possibly rather mildly increasing returns, of the order of 1.03–1.19. (This always surprises highway engineers, who *know* that it does not cost twice as much to double the capacity of a highway, as many costs—embankments, etc.—are fixed, and the capacity of a two-lane divided highway is considerably greater than of a one-lane divided highway. But most capacity increases are needed in congested urban areas where the costs of land acquisition can be extremely high. The econometric estimates pick this factor up. See Keeler and Small, 1977, and Kraus, 1981.) If we take the estimates as supporting constant returns, then the result is directly applicable, and provide a useful benchmark against which to judge the estimated congestion charges. If we assume increasing returns to scale, then road charges would not cover road costs of an optimal road network.

In 1986 the estimated average congestion charge was 1.42 times as high as the road costs attributable to PCU, suggesting either that the road network was inadequate for the level of traffic, or that the correct rate of interest to charge was higher than 5 percent real. (At 8 percent the ratio was only 1.0.) The corresponding ratio for 1990 is 2.82 (or 1.75 at 8 percent interest). In short, if roads were undersupplied in 1986, they are becoming critically scarce as traffic volumes increase faster than road space is supplied. Notice that assuming that there are increasing returns to capacity, expansion strengthens the conclusion that roads are undersupplied.

III. Charging for Road Use

Ideally, vehicles should be charged for the road-use cost of each trip, so that only cost-justified trips are undertaken. In practice it is not too difficult to charge for road damage, which is largely a function of the type of vehicle and the extent to which it is loaded. Ton-mile taxes as charged by some of the states of the US can approximated the damage charge quite closely, provided they are made specific to the type of vehicle. Vehicle-specific distance taxes would be almost as good, provided axle loading restrictions were enforced. Fuel taxes are moderately good in that they charge trucks in proportion to ton-miles. As they charge different types of vehicles at (almost) the same ton-mile rate, they must be supplemented by vehicle-specific purchase taxes or license fees and combined with careful regulation of allowable axle configurations and loading (Newbery *et al.*, 1988, Newbery 1988c).

The more difficult task is to charge for congestion, which varies enormously depending on the level of traffic, which in turn varies across roads and with the time of day, as Table 2 shows dramatically. The most direct way is to charge an amount specific to the road and time of day, using an 'electronic number plate' which signals to the recording computer the presence of the vehicle. The computer then acts like a telephone exchange billing system, recording the user, the time and place, and hence the appropriate charge, and issuing monthly bills. The cost per number plate is of the order of $100, or perhaps a quarter of the cost of catalytic converters which are now mandatory for pollution control in many countries. Such systems have been successfully tested in Hong

Kong (Dawson and Catling, 1986) but there was initially some pessimism at the political likelihood that they would ever be introduced (Borins, 1988). The stated objection was that the electronic detectors could monitor the location of vehicles and hence would violate the right to privacy. This objection may be valid in a society suspicious of (and not represented by) its government, though evidence suggests that this is not likely to be much of a problem in Europe (ECMT, 1989). The objection could be levied against telephone subscribers once itemized bills are introduced, and the objection can be overcome in much the same way by the use of 'smart cards,' rather like magnetic telephone cards. The electronic license plate would be loaded with the smart card and would debit payments until exhausted. Only thereafter would the central computer monitor and bill for road use.

A more plausible explanation for the lack of success in Hong Kong may have been that it was not clear to car owners that the new charges (which were quite high, of the order of $2-3 per day) would replace the existing and very high annual license fee. Faced with a doubling of the cost of road use, commuters understandably objected. But the whole point of charging for road use by electronic license plates is to replace less well-designed road charging schemes, such as fuel taxes and license fees. The proposition that needs to be put to the public is that in exchange for the entire system of current road taxes (fuel taxes in excess of the rate of VAT, the special car purchase tax, and the license fee), road-users will be charged according to their use of congested road space, at a rate which for the average road-user will be roughly the same. (For the UK this is still just about feasible on the figures given above, at least if the pure tax element on private motorists is allowed to fall to zero.) As more than half the road-using population drives less than the average number of miles in congested areas, this should command majority support.

An alternative method of selling the use of electronic license plates might be to offer rebates for tax on fuel used (at the estimated rate per km, or on production of receipts) and to waive the license fee for those installing the license plates. This might be necessary as an interim measure when their use is confined to major urban centres, notably London. It is noticeable that despite the claim by Channon as Minister of Transport that the Government had no plans to introduce road pricing because of the perceived public hostility, that hostility seems to be diminishing, at least in London. A recent opinion survey conducted by the Metropolitan Transport Research Unit showed 87 percent in favour of some form of traffic restraint, and 53 percent in favour of a fixed charge to drive into Central London. Charging per mile was widely supported, and 48 percent said they would use public transport if such charges were introduced (*Independent*, 26 January 1990).

Until road pricing is introduced, alternative and less satisfactory methods of charging are necessary. One such is selling area licenses which grant access to congested zones such as city centres during rush hours. This solution has been used in Singapore for over a decade, with considerable success. Heavy parking charges and restricted access may also be effective to varying degrees (World Bank, 1986). At the moment, however, the only way to charge vehicles for the congestion they cause is in proportion to the distance they drive, by fuel taxes and/or vehicles purchase taxes (which approximate reasonably well to distance charges for heavily used vehicles, but less well for automobiles). Such taxes, combined with access charges (area licenses, or even annual licenses) achieve the desired effect of charging road-users on average for congestion, but do little to encourage them to drive on less congested roads or at less busy times of the day (or, indeed, to take public transport instead).

Figure 3. Cost of Congestion
(Urban Non-Central Roads, 1990 Prices)

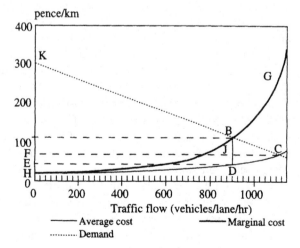

In Britain, the estimates above suggest that road taxes might usefully be increased somewhat. It is worth remarking that there are clear advantages in raising such corrective taxes to their efficient level, as they allow other distortionary taxes, which incur deadweight losses, to be reduced.

IV. Measuring the Costs of Congestion

So far we have avoided discussing the actual cost of congestion in Britain, and instead calculated the revenue that would be generated if vehicles were to be charged for the congestion they caused. Figure 3 shows how the equilibrium demand for trips is established in the absence of such charges. If road-users pay only the private costs of the trip, their costs are given by the average cost schedule, which meets the demand schedule at point C. At that point the willingness to pay by the marginal road-user is equal to the cost of the trip. The efficient congestion charge would be an amount *BD*, which, if levied, would cause demand to fall to the level associated with point *B*. The revenue then raised would be *ABDE*, and this is the amount referred to above as the revenue attributable to the congestion charge. In the figure it would amount to £600 per lane-hour. But is this the correct measure of the congestion cost? Consider various alternative measures. Once measure frequently cited in newspaper accounts of the cost of congestion is the extra costs involved in travelling on congested rather than uncongested roads. This might be measured by *FC* times *FH*, the excess of the average actual cost over the cost on a road with zero traffic. On the figure this would amount to £530 (per lane-hour). But this is an unrealistic comparison, as it would be uneconomic to build roads to be totally uncongested. Instead one might compare the extra costs of the excessive congestion at point *C* above that which would be efficient, at point *D*. These extra costs might be measured as *CF* times *EF*, or £270. This is not satisfactory either, as fewer trips would be taken at the efficient level of charges. A better alternative is the loss in social surplus associated with excessive road use. The efficient total social surplus associated with point *B* is the consumer surplus triangle *KBA*, plus the tax revenue *ABDE*. The social surplus associated with point *C* is just the triangle *KCF*, and the difference is the rectangle *FJDE* *less* the triangle *BCJ*, or £198. This is also equal to the area of the standard deadweight loss triangle *BCG*. In this case the deadweight loss is equal to one third of the revenue measure.

There is one important case in which the revenue measure accurately measures the deadweight loss, and that is where the demand for trips becomes perfectly elastic beyond its intersection with the marginal social cost schedule at point *B*. In this case there is no gain in consumer surplus in moving from the efficient level of traffic to the equilibrium level, and hence the loss is just equal to the forgone tax revenue. Put another way, by not charging the efficient toll in this perfectly elastic case, the government forgoes revenue but the consumer makes no gain. In crowded urban areas this is a plausible situation. The equilibrium level of traffic is found where the marginal road-user is indifferent between using a car or some alternative—public transport or walking. Thus traffic speeds in London are about the same as they were in the nineteenth century, and the time taken to get to work (or, more properly, the total perceived cost) for many commuters is no better by road than alternatives. Figure 4, which is taken from a graph in *The Times*, 5 December 1988, itself based on work by Martin Mogridge, illustrates this graphically for central London. The average door-to door time taken between points in central london is remarkably similar for all three modes of transport, so car speeds in equilibrium are determined by the speeds of alternative public transport.

In such circumstances, the social costs of congestion may even be understated by the revenue measure. Consider the situation portrayed in Figure 5. Initially demand is *GC* and equilibrium is established at *C* with commuting cost of 0*F*. But if road-users were charged an amount *BD* then some road-users would switch to public transport, reducing demand for private road use. This increased demand for public transport would, after appropriate investment and expansion, lead to an improved frequency of service, while the reduced traffic would lead to a faster public transport service, lowering the cost of travel. Given this lower public transport cost, the demand for private transport would fall from *GC* to *GD*, and the willingness to pay for private commuting would fall, from the level 0*F* to 0*A* for the marginal commuter. In this case charging the congestion tax would yield tax revenue (a social gain) while reducing the cost of commuting (an additional consumer gain). The tax forgone thus understates the cost of congestion.

Figure 4. Equilibrium Trip Speed

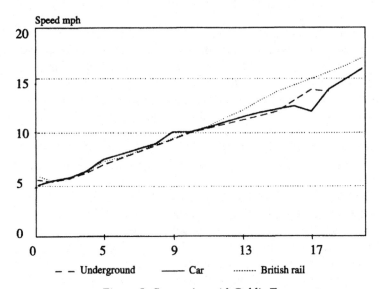

Figure 5. Congestion with Public Transport
(Urban central areas, 1990 prices)

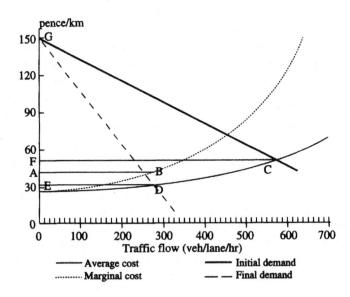

V. Cost-Benefit Analysis of Road Improvements

The average road tax paid by vehicles per km is now somewhat below the average efficient level. On roads of below average congestion, vehicles may be overcharged, but in urban areas they are certainly undercharged, in many cases by a large margin. Faced with growing congestion, one natural response is to increase road capacity. Figure 6 illustrates the pitfalls in simple-minded cost-benefit analysis. If the road capacity is doubled, then the average and marginal cost schedules will move from 'before' to 'after'. The initial equilibrium will be at *B*, where demand is equal to the initial average cost (*AC*), and traffic will be *BG*. If the *AC* is lowered to *E*, then the apparent cost-saving is *GBEF*, to be compared with the cost of the improvement. But the lower *AC* will induce increased traffic and the new equilibrium will be at point *D*, not *E*. The benefit will be *GBDH*, which may be significantly lower.

Figure 7 shows that where traffic increases come from previous users of public transport, as in Figure 4, the effect of the road 'improvement' may be to increase traffic volumes but to raise average costs, making everyone worse off, and adding negative value. It is hard to escape the

Figure 6. Cost-Benefit of Road Improvemtnts

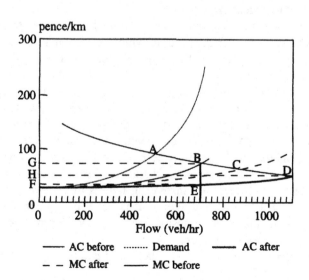

Figure 7. Perverse Road Improvement

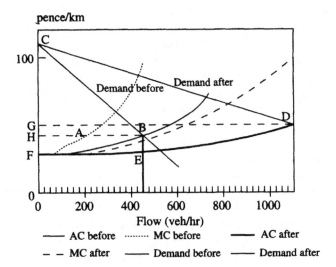

pence/km

AC before ······· MC before ——— AC after
— — MC after ——— Demand before ——— Demand after

conclusion that as journey speeds in London are now below their level at the turn of the century, before the introduction of the car, much of the road investment has been self-defeating.

The situation is radically changed when road-users pay the efficient congestion charge. Consider Figure 8, in which the demand for trips is perfectly elastic along *AC*, and congestion charges at the rate *AB* (marginal cost *less* average cost) are levied by means of an electronic number plate. If road capacity is expanded, but the charge maintained, then the social gain is the increase in the revenue collected, *ACDB*, which can be compared with the cost. If there are constant returns to capacity expansion and the road improvement is self-financing, it is justified. This is another application of the proposition that with constant returns to road expansion, congestion charges will recover the costs of the road investment. If there are increasing returns to expansion, then expansion may still be justified even if it is not self-financing—one should compare the marginal expansion costs with the marginal benefit measured by the increased revenue.

The implications of this are clear—without road pricing, road improve-

Figure 8. Road Improvements with Charges

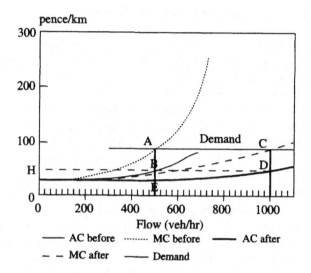

ments may yield low or even negative returns, but with efficient pricing, not only are improvements easy to evaluate, they should also be self-financing, at least if there are constant or diminishing returns to expansion, as is likely in congested areas.

VI. Pricing Public Transport

If private road-users are significantly undercharged for using the road in urban areas, then commuters face the wrong relative prices when choosing between public and private transport. If it is hard to raise the price of private driving, why not lower the price of public transport to improve the relative price ratios? There are a number of problems with this proposal. First, it is hard to compute the second-best public transport subsidies given the great variation of congestion costs by time of day and location. Second, the subsidies have to be financed by taxes which have distortionary costs elsewhere (Note that congestion charges would reduce the distortionary costs of the tax system). Third, subsidies to public transport appear to be rather cost-ineffective. Few motorists are attracted off the road into private transport, with much of the increase in public transport use coming from those previously not using either mode.

There are also political economic problems with operating public bus companies at a loss—there is a temptation to ration them and lower the quality, thus defeating the purpose of making them more attractive to commuters. It becomes more difficult to gain the benefits of deregulation and privatization. It may just lead to rent-dissipation by the supplier of public transport—as seems to have happened to some extent when the London Underground was heavily subsidized. The same applies to subsidizing rail travel—it becomes unattractive to expand capacity if this just increases the size of the loss.

A more promising approach is to make private transport relatively less attractive and public transport more attractive, by improving the quality of the latter, possibly at the expense of the former. Bus lanes which reduce road space to other road-users have this effect, as would electronic signalling to give priority to public transport at traffic lights. Banning private cars from congested streets during the working day has a similar effect. Arguably the greatest obstacle to overcome is that of making private road-users aware of the true social costs of their road use. Table 2 reveals that *average* congestion charges of 36 pence/km would be appropriate in urban centres at the peak, and 30 pence/km during the off-peak, with higher charges appropriate on roads with higher volume and/or lower speeds. Figure 2, which is plotted for 1990 costs for suburban areas, shows that when traffic speeds have fallen to 20 kph, then congestion charges of 50 pence/km are in order. It is hard to make public transport 50 pence/km cheaper than its unsubsidized level, and thus it is more productive to think of ways of raising the cost of private transport at congested periods, or directly reducing its level.

It was argued above that road pricing gives rise to sensible cost-benefit rules for road improvements. The same is also true for other transport investments, especially in public transport and that most capital intensive form, rail transport. If road-users paid the full social cost of road use, then there would be every reason to charge users of public transport the full social marginal cost, including congestion. It is unlikely that there are economies of scale in peak-period road or rail use in London, or in peak-period bus use in other cities, and this would lead to fares that would cover the full operating costs, including interest on capital. It would therefore again be easier to apply commercial criteria to investment in public transport, and, indeed, there would no longer be a strong case for keeping these services in the public sector.

VII. Conclusion

Road pricing is the best method of dealing with congestion, and would have far-reaching implications for the viability and quality of public transport, for the finance of urban infrastructure, and ultimately for the quality of life. The average road charges might not need to increase above current levels, for if roads were correctly priced, demand for the use of the most congested streets would fall, and with it the efficient charge to levy. Current road taxes are heavy and yield revenue greater than the average cost of the current road system. In equilibrium, with efficient road pricing and an adequate road network, one would expect road charges to be roughly equal to road costs, so either road charges would fall below current tax levels, or substantial road investment would be justified, and possibly both.

A shift to road pricing would cause a fall in the cost of driving in non-urban areas, and an increase in the cost of urban driving. In the medium run the quality of urban public transport would improve, and the average cost of urban travel by both public and private transport might fall below current levels. Energy consumption would increase, as there would no longer be any reason to have heavy fuel taxes (other than those needed to reflect the costs of pollution, and this problem is arguably better addressed by mandatory emissions standards). A shift to road pricing matched by offsetting adjustments to other taxes to raise the same total tax revenue is unlikely to be inflationary, both because the average road tax/charge would be almost unchanged, and because any increase in charge leading to higher travel costs could be matched by lower taxes on other goods, leading to a fall in those elements of consumer expenditure.

Similarly, the impact on the distribution of income is likely to be slight and probably favourable. Urban private travel costs would rise, at least in the short run, and urban public transport quality-adjusted costs might fall (depending on how rapidly any subsidies were phased out, and how quickly the increased demand for public transport were translated into more supply at higher average quality). Rural transport costs would fall. As urban car-owners are richer than average, and users of public transport are poorer, the redistribution should be favourable. The government would have to decide on the fate of the car tax, which raised £1.4 billion in 1989/90, and which is a fairly progressive form of indirect tax, being levied at an *ad valorem* rate on the purchase price. Its logic as a method of rationing access to road space would disappear, but it could be retained as a pure consumer tax if it were thought to be justifiable on redistributive grounds.

References

Borins, Sandford F. (1988), 'Electronic Road Pricing: An Idea whose Time may Never Come,' *Transportation Research*, 22A(1) : 37-44.

Crandall, R. W., Gruenspecht, H. K., Keeler, T. E., and Lave, L. B. (1986), *Regulating the Automobile*, Brookings, Washington DC.

Dawson, J. A. L., and Catling, I. (1986), 'Electronic Road Pricing in Hong Kong,' *Transportation Research*, 20A (March) : 129-34.

Department of the Environment (1989), *Environment in Trust : Air Quality.*

Department of Transport (1987), *COBA 9*, Department of Transport, London.

_____ (1989*a*), *The Allocation of Road Track Costs 1989/90*, Department of Transport, London.

_____ (1989*b*), *Transport Statistic Great Britain 1978-88*, Department of Transport, London.

Diamond, P. A., and Mirrlees, J. A. (1971), 'Optimal Taxation and Public Production, I : Productive Efficiency,' *American Economic Review*, 61 : 8-27.

ECMT (1989), European Conference of Ministers of Transport Round Table 80, *Systems of Infrastructure Cost Coverage*, Economic Research Centre, OECD, Paris.

Hall, F. L., Allen, B. L., and Gunter, M. A. (1986), 'Empirical Analysis of Freeway Flow-Density Relationships,' *Transportation Research*, 20A : 197-210.

Harrison, W. J., Pell, C., Jones, P. M., and Ashton, H. (1986), 'Some

Advances in Model Design Developed for the Practical Assessment of Road Pricing in Hong Kong,' *Transportation Research,* 20A : 135-44.

Jones-Lee, M. W. (1990), 'The Value of Transport Safety,' *Oxford Review of Economic Policy,* 6(2) : 22-38.

Keeler, T. E. and Small, K. (1977), 'Optimal Peak-Load Pricing, Investment and Service Levels on Urban Expressways,' *Journal of Political Economy,* 85(1) : 1-25.

Kraus, Marvin (1981), 'Scale Economies Analysis for Urban Highway Networks,' *Journal of Urban Economics,* 9(1) : 1-22.

Newbery, D. M. G. (1987), 'Road User Charges and the Taxation of Road Transport,' *IMF Working Paper WP/87/5,* International Monetary Fund, Washington DC.

_____ (1988a), 'Road user Charges in Britain,' *The Economic Journal,* 98 (Conference 1988) : 161-76.

_____ (1988b), 'Road Damage Externalities and Road User Charges,' *Econometrica,* 56(2) : 295-316.

_____ (1988c), 'Charging for Roads,' *Research Observer,* 3(2) : 119-38.

_____ (1989), 'Cost Recovery from Optimally Designed Roads,' *Economica,* 56 : 165-85.

_____ (1990), 'Acid Rain,' *Economic Policy,* 11, October.

_____ Hughes, G. A., Paterson, W. D. O., and Bennathan, E. (1988), *Road TRansport Taxation in Developing Countries : The Design of User Charges and Taxes for Tunisia,* World Bank Discussion Papers, 26, Washington, D. C.

Paterson, W. D. O. (1987), *Road Deterioration and Mainterance Effects : Models for Planning and Management,* Johns Hopkins University Press for World Bank, Baltimore.

Small, K. A., Winston C., and Evans, C. A. (1989), *Road Work : A New Highway Pricing and Investment Policy,* Brookings, Washington DC.

US Federal Highway Administration (1982), *Final Report to the Federal Highway Cost Allocation Study,* US Government Printing Office, Washington, DC.

World Bank (1986), *Urban Transport,* Washington DC.

CHAPTER 16

ROAD PRICING FOR CONGESTION MANAGEMENT : THE TRANSITION FROM THEORY TO POLICY*

*Small, Kenneth A., and Jose A. Gomez-Ibanez***

Abstract

This paper reviews a variety of examples of road pricing covering a wide range of sites, objectives, and implementation strategies. Objectives range from raising revenues to reducing traffic externalities. Locations include single facilities, city centers, and entire metropolitan regions. Five of the projects are in place, two are in the process of implementation, and four were seriously considered proposals. We focus on the political, institutional, and operational features that shed light on how urban governments are able to approach congestion pricing.

* This paper draws extensively from research supported by the Transportation Research Board and the American Association of State Highway and Transit Officials, through the National Cooperative Highway Research Program. We are grateful to Richard Arnott, Roy Bahl, Amihai Glazer, and Clifford Winston for comments on an earlier version, which was presented at the Taxation, Resources and Economic Development (TRED) conference, Lincoln Institute of Land Policy, Cambridge, Massachusetts, Sept. 30—Oct. 1, 1994. We alone are responsible for the results and opinions expressed.

** The authors are at University of California at Irvine and Harvard University respectively.

We find evidence that significant pricing incentives can produce major changes in behavior, and that even small incentives can produce targeted changes, such as small shifts in the time of day of travel. Furthermore, experience shows that road pricing can operate smoothly given thorough planning, attention to detail, and a willingness to learn from prior experience.

Projects that are politically acceptable show several characteristic traits. They tend to be fairly simple in design, to build incrementally on previously existing arrangements or experience, to address clearly understood and widely supported objectives, and to involve transparent financial flows that facilitate public trust in the use of the monies. Too simple a design may reduce the possible congestion savings and other benefits, but great complexity does not add much to the benefits and can increase political opposition. The incremental accumulation of experience and public trust in Scandinavia has facilitated the progressively more sophisticated applications of toll rings around city centers in Norway and Sweden. This same experience may have facilitated the serious consideration given to more ambitious proposals in the London and Randstad regions. In France and southern California, time-varying tolls were seen as a way to solve particular problems of a toll road operator; in each case the rationale was transparent and acceptable to the public given the particular context.

I. Introduction

Traffic congestion is a classic externality, especially pervasive in urban areas. The theoretical and empirical relationships governing it have been thoroughly studied. As a result, there is a consensus among urban economists, and a growing number of other analysts, that the best policy to deal with it would be some form of congestion pricing. Such a policy involves charging a substantial fee for operating a motor vehicle at times and places subject to peak demands. The intention is to alter people's travel behavior enough to reduce congestion.

Discussion of congestion pricing of roads benefits from a long history of practical policy development that supplements the theoretical and empirical base. The work of William Vickrey (1955, 1963, 1965, 1973) stands out, but is by no means alone: other notable contributions addressing policy design and evaluation include Walters (1961), U.K.

Ministry of Transport (1964), Mohring (1965), May (1975), Gcmez-Ibañez and Fauth (1980), Kraus (1989), and Small (1992). A comprehensive two-year study by the National Research Council (1994) is almost entirely concerned with implementation. Together, these works address technology and institutions for implementation, relationship to road investment, welfare evaluation of ideal and not-so-ideal policies, financial policies for using revenues, and practical steps that could take us from current policies toward congestion pricing.

Recent years have witnessed sharply increased practical interest in congestion pricing and related policies involving pricing incentives, including innovative road tolls and parking fees. This broader group of policies is called road pricing. Interest has arisen especially from the urgent need to find new revenue sources for transportation investments, and from the failure of alternative policies to significantly stem the growth of traffic congestion.

It therefore seems an opportune time to assess the practical experience with road pricing worldwide. For many years, the only example of congestion pricing was Singapore, a case that has received mixed reviews. Today there is considerably more experience to draw from, as well as several quite detailed plans that made considerable progress in the political sector. These cases cover a wide range of sites, objectives, and details of implementation. Many are reviewed by Hau (1992),

Table 1. Cases of Road Pricing Studied

Type of road pricing	Degree of implementation		
	In place (date)	Scheduled (date)	Under Study
City center: congestion pricing	Singapore (1975)		Hong Kong Cambridge, UK
City center: toll ring	Bergen (1986) Oslo (1990) Trondheim (1991)	Stockholm (1997)	
Single facility: congestion pricing	Autoroute A1, France (1992)	State Route 91, California (1995)	
Area-wide: congestion pricing			Randstad London

Lewis (1993), and Gomez-Ibañez and Small (1994).

This paper summarizes eleven such cases, including Singapore, and from them draws lessons about implementation. In particular, we examine how well the theory of congestion pricing holds up in the transition to practical and politically achievable policies. The cases are divided into four broad categories: congestion pricing of a center city, center-city toll rings for raising revenue, congestion pricing of a single facility, and comprehensive area-wide congestion pricing. Table 1 lists our cases according to these categories, and shows whether each case is already implemented, scheduled for implementation at a definite date, or only under study.

II. Pioneers: Congestion Pricing of City Centers

Three cities have seriously considered congestion pricing of a congested central area. Each was the pioneer of an important new concept, the evaluation of which sheds light on what is required to make the theory of congestion pricing work. For Singapore, the concept was congestion pricing itself, and the implementation was very simple: the priced area is defined by a single cordon line surrounding the city center, the technology consists of paper windshield stickers, and enforcement is performed visually by traffic officers. For Hong Kong, the new concept was an operational one: electronic road pricing (ERP), a flexible and comprehensive system involving multiple cordons and fully automated charging through the electronic identification of devices attached to vehicles. For Cambridge, England, the new concept was congestion-specific charging, an attempt to more closely approximate the theoretical ideal of congestion pricing by making the charge vary in real time in a manner reflecting the severity of congestion actually encountered while inside the priced area.

Only one of these systems is operational. Singapore's Area License Scheme (ALS) was inaugurated in 1975 and still operates today; the city has recently taken bids on an electronic system to replace its manual charging and enforcement. Hong Kong's ERP scheme was subjected to extensive technological field trials as well as exhaustive desk studies for prediction and evaluation, but was withdrawn due to public opposition. Cambridge has also been the site of a technological field trial and at one point the scheme had the support of the County Council; but many details remained to be filled in when a new and unsupportive Council came to power in 1993.

1. Singapore's Area License Scheme

The Singapore scheme, begun in June 1975, is part of an extremely stringent set of policies designed to restrict automobile use in this crowded island city-state with a population of 3 million. The scheme was chosen by the national government, dominated by a strong executive, following a review of options including conventional road tolls and higher parking charges. These alternatives were rejected because space for toll stations was lacking and parking charges were believed ineffective in the face of heavy through traffic and numerous chauffeur-driven cars.

The size and structure of the fee has varied over the years. It is imposed on vehicles entering the restricted area during certain hours, originally just the morning peak period. For cars, the fee has ranged from approximately $1.50 to $2.50 per day in U.S. currency equivalent.[1] Carpools and taxis carrying four or more people were originally exempted, as were motorcycles and commercial trucks. In 1989, charges were extended to include these vehicles and the restraint hours were extended to the afternoon peak (but still in the inbound direction, since that produced the desired effect on through traffic). In 1994, the hours were extended to include the time between the morning and afternoon peaks. Collection costs are modest, amounting in the early years to about 11 percent of the US$2.7 million annual revenue.

Effects on modal choice and on traffic within the zone have been dramatic. Among commuters to jobs in the restricted zone, the share commuting in cars with less than four passengers dropped from 48 percent to 27 percent during the first few months of operation, while the combined modal shares of carpool and bus rose from 41 percent to 62 percent (Watson and Holland, 1978, p. 85). As shown in Table 2, traffic

---

1. The exchange rate between the Singapore dollar and the U.S. dollar was S$1=US$0.48 in 1975, and S$1=US$0.55 in 1992. For a complete account of changes in fee structure and level over the years, see Gomez-Ibañez and Small (1994), especially Table A-4. For other reviews see Toh (1992) and Menon et al. (1993).

entering the zone during restricted hours declined by 44 percent. During the half-hour preceding the restraint period, in contrast, traffic rose 13 percent, and it probably rose also during the hours after the peak. (In fact, the original restraint hours of 7:30-9:30 a.m. had to be extended by 45 minutes after the first month of operation because so many people were postponing trips until just after the restraint period.) Some of the road space released during the restraint hours was taken by trucks, whose peak-period entries increased by 124 percent during the first few months of operation (Watson and Holland, 1978, p. 48). Furthermore, afternoon traffic failed to decline significantly until afternoon restraint hours were established in 1989; before that, many people with destina-

Table 2. Effects of the Singapore Area License Scheme

	1975 initiation: morning only		1989 changes: morning and afternoon	
	Before (Mar. 1975)	After (Sept.-Oct. 1975)	Before (May 1989)	After (May 1990)
Daily traffic entering restricted zone (1000's):				
7:00-7:30 a.m.	9.8	11.1	9.7	9.7
7:30-10:15 a.m.[a,b]	74.0	41.2	51.8	44.8
10:15-11:00 a.m.	NA	NA	22.1	21.8
4:00-4:30 p.m.	NA	NA	12.9	12.4
4:30-6:30 p.m.[b]	NA	NA	51.5	23.8
6:30-7:30 p.m.	NA	NA	22.3	24.1
Average commute time to jobs in restricted zone for those not changing mode (minutes):				
Solo driver	26.8	27.9	NA	NA
Carpool[c]	28.2	31.5	NA	NA
Bus Rider	40.4	41.0	NA	NA

a: Restraint hours in effect Aug. 1975–May 1989.
b: Restraint hours in effect Feb. 1990–Dec. 1993.
c: Average for carpool drivers, carpool passengers, and other car passengers, weighted by number in sample.
NA: data not available.
Sources: Watson and Holland (1978), pp. 41, 133; Menon and Lam (1993), p. 29.

tions on the far side of the zone apparently avoided the zone during the morning but traveled through it during the afternoon.

While traffic speeds rose dramatically in the zone itself, a large portion of the resulting time savings appears to have been dissipated by increased congestion outside the zone. As shown in Table 2, average commuting time to jobs in the zone increased for each mode of travel from May to October, 1975. We suspect that subsequent road improvements outside the zone have modified this pessimistic finding, but data are lacking.

The Singapore experience demonstrates that travelers respond dramatically to sufficiently high pricing incentives. However, it does not necessarily prove that a scheme as simple as a single cordon and a single time period is a good idea. Problems of spillover across spatial and time boundaries may make this scheme too crude an approximation of marginal-cost pricing to provide the net economic benefits achievable in theory. On the other hand, the problem could be simply that the fee was set too high, as argued by Watson and Holland (1978), Wilson (1988), Toh (1992), and McCarthy and Tay (1993).

2. Hong Kong's Electronic Road Pricing Trial

Nearly a decade after the inauguration of the Singapore area license scheme, Hong Kong, a slightly larger city with population 4 million, proceeded with plans for a more complex system using electronic charging and video enforcement. Hong Kong's field trial succeeded in thoroughly verifying the ability of electronic charging mechanisms to operate with very high degrees of accuracy. The system, now somewhat obsolete, used radio-frequency communications through loop antennas buried in the pavement, and required vehicles to be channeled into lanes when they passed the charging points. Systems for automatic charging, billing, and enforcement through closed-circuit television all performed extremely well (Catling and Harbord, 1985).

A variety of pricing structures and charging locations were considered. Results were predicted for three such schemes based on a simulation model designed by the MVA Consultancy in London (Harrison, 1986). These schemes varied in complexity (see Table 3), but all included at least five zones. (Hong Kong has two dense commercial districts, one on the tip of the Kowloon Peninsula and the other on the north shore of Hong Kong Island, making a single cordon like Singapore's less practical.) Scheme A had five zones and several cordon "tails" extending the zonal boundaries to discourage travel along the outer ed ge of the zones; 130 distinct charging points would have had to be equipped, each imposing an identical charge which varied by time of day. Schemes B and C imposed higher charges for crossing in the direction of peak flow than for crossing in the opposite direction. Scheme C also had more zones and charging points than either A or B. In all three schemes, two levels of charges were to be assessed: a higher one during the morning and afternoon peaks and a lower one before, between, and after the peaks. No charge would be assessed at other times.

Peak travel was predicted to decline by 20 to 24 percent (Table 3). Total daily car trips would be reduced by 9-13 percent. Using Scheme B as a middle prediction that is not too different from the others, about 41 percent of all daily trip makers would be unaffected by the charging scheme; another 42 percent would pay the charge, and the remaining 17 percent would alter their trips, two-thirds by changing mode and one-

Table 3. Predicted Effects of Hong Kong Electronic Road Pricing Schemes

	ERP scheme		
	A	B	C
Design of restraint scheme:			
Number of zones	5	5	13
Number of charging points	130	115	185
Peak direction more expensive?	*no	yes	yes
Average monthly payment (US$ equivalents, 1985)[a]	15.60	18.20	20.80
Predicted effect on travel:			
Change in peak-period car trips	–20%	–21%	–24%
Economic evaluation:			
Gross revenue (US$ millions/year)[a]	51	60	70
Net benefits before collection costs (US$ millions/year)[a]	95	113	119

a: The 1985 exchange rate was HK$1 = US$0.13 (International Monetary Fund, 1992).
Source: Transpotech, Ltd. (1985), pp. 2.69, 2.70, 2.74, 2.79.

third by changing time of day of travel (Transpotech, 1985, pp. 2.69-2.79).

Projected net benefits, ignoring collection costs, are shown in the last row of the table. Taking the most complex (Scheme C) as a benchmark for the possible benefits, we see that the simplest (Scheme A) achieves 80 percent of these benefits, while Scheme B achieves 95 percent. This suggests that five zones and two charging levels are sufficient to reasonably well approximate marginal-cost pricing; charging more in the peak direction (Scheme B) does substantially better, but further refining the geography (Scheme C) makes little difference. Of course, all these schemes are far more complex than Singapore's.

Ultimately none of the schemes were adopted. A number of factors worked to defeat them. The policy deliberations took place during the early stages of a transfer of power from the British colonial government to popularly elected officials; the government was slow to consult newly elected members of local district boards, giving them an issue on which to assert their independence. Poor economic conditions in the early 1980s had lowered automobile ownership and so relieved some of the urgency for strict policies to reduce congestion. Many people objected to the potential invasion of privacy made possible by the electronic monitoring equipment. Finally, many did not perceive that the revenues from the project would benefit them; only belatedly did the government propose to use these revenues to reduce the annual license fee.

Analysts have debated the extent to which Hong Kong's failure to implement any of the proposed schemes represented tactical errcrs, bad luck, or inherent political weaknesses of congestion pricing.[2] What seems clear is that any successful implementation in a democracy will require anticipating and resolving likely objections early in the planning process, including making clear just how the revenues will be used to benefit the population.

3. Congestion-Specific Charging for Cambridge, England

Cambridge, a historic city of 100,000 people located 60 miles north of London, was the site for a unique proposal that would carry congestion pricing close to its theoretical extreme. Within a ring encompassing the congested city center, charges would vary in real time to match the

---

2. See Ho (1986), Fong (1986), Borins (1988), and Hau (1989).

amount of congestion actually experienced by the individual vehicle (Sharpe, 1993). The rationale for this was that the amount of congestion experienced by a vehicle may be closely related to the externality imposed by that vehicle on others. (This proposition is debatable given the dynamics of congestion formation.) The proposal, put forth in 1990 by Brian Oldridge, then Director of Transportation for Cambridgeshire, won preliminary approval of the Cambridgeshire County Council, but subsequently has been shelved for further study.

Real-time congestion pricing was to be implemented by means of an in-vehicle meter, which contains a clock and is connected to the car's odometer. For example, under one suggested charging regime, the meter would assess a charge of £0.20 ($0.36 at the 1990 exchange rate) whenever a distance of 0.3 mile is traversed either (a) at a speed less than 16 miles per hour or (b) with more than four stops.[3] Charges would be deducted from the balance contained in a prepaid "smart card" or "electronic purse," thereby preserving the user's anonymity and overcoming one source of resistance encountered in Hong Kong.

Oldridge retired in 1993 and his replacement, J. Michael Sharpe, widened the range of schemes under consideration to include more conventional forms of road pricing, such as cordon charges or zone fees, as alternatives to congestion metering. Sharpe apparently recognized the potential for public outrage when charges are unpredictable. From the user's point of view, real-time charging means that on those very days when travel conditions are unexpectedly poor, a financial penalty is added to the aggravation already experienced. It seems likely that many citizens would blame politicians or traffic planners for incidents of severe congestion rather than accepting the idea that they should pay more because they are imposing higher marginal costs on others.

The metering technology was tested in 1993 as part of the ADEPT project within the European Union's DRIVE-II program (Blythe and Hills, 1994). However, moves toward implementation ended in 1993 with a change in the shire government. Modeling studies of various road pricing possibilities for Cambridge have continued; preliminary results suggest that the use of congestion-specific charges does significantly increase the benefits beyond those achievable from a cordon-type pricing system (Milne et al., 1994), presumably by increasing the precision

---

3. See "SERC Funds Research" (1990) or Oldridge (1994).

with which prices approximate marginal costs.

Cambridge has served as a useful setting for demonstrating the technical feasibility of more sophisticated forms of road pricing. However, there is a need to develop grass roots support simultaneously with concrete proposals, especially ones as radical as the original Cambridge plan. It seems to us unlikely that any locality would accept a real-time pricing proposal with unpredictable charges, at least in the absence of lengthy prior experience with more prosaic pricing policies.

III. The Scandinavian Toll Rings

The previous discussion illustrates the evolution of increasingly sophisticated proposals for congestion pricing. Meanwhile, a more modest type of road pricing has emerged as a serious tool for highway finance in Scandinavia. Toll rings now surround three Norwegian cities, and one is planned for Stockholm, Sweden.

The Scandinavian toll rings do not represent congestion pricing according to our definition because they are designed mainly to generate revenue. Congestion management is not among the objectives in Norway, and is only secondary in Sweden. Rather, in each case the primary motivation is to generate revenue to finance desired transportation infrastructure improvements. As a result, Norway's tolls are low, ranging from approximately $0.70 to $1.75 per entry,[4] and do not vary much by time of day. Furthermore, the locations of toll stations were chosen not to optimize traffic management, but to achieve a rough distributional balance among residents of city and suburban jurisdictions while altering people's trip-making as little as possible.

Revenue generation is also the dominant factor in the proposed Stockholm toll ring, although in this case traffic reduction for environmental reasons is another objective. Congestion management is a lower priority, and so tolls are not planned to vary by time of day, although this remains an option for later consideration.

Despite these modest beginnings, the Scandinavian toll rings may evolve into a system of congestion pricing. Except for the low levels

4. We use the average exchange rates for 1992: NOK 1 = US$0.16 for Norway, and SEK 1 = US$0.17 for Sweden.

and limited variation of the toll rates, they are virtually identical to a cordon scheme for congestion pricing. Furthermore, each Scandinavian toll ring has been more technologically sophisticated than its predecessor. Two of the three Norwegian toll rings offer electronic toll collection as an option. The Swedes plan to go further by collecting the tolls from free-flowing traffic on multilane roads without physical lane barriers. This gradual progression of technologically more sophisticated implementation offers the opportunity for local planners to examine a number of practical issues that anyone planning a large scale urban congestion pricing scheme would face.

1. Norway's Three Urban Toll Rings

Norway has long used toll financing for special projects such as tunnels and bridges. The toll rings extend the concept of toll finance to cities as a whole. Each is part of a financial package of major regional road improvements. For each, the ability to toll inbound movements is facilitated by the existence of natural barriers created by mountains and fjords. An operational and financial summary is contained in Table 4.

Bergen, with an urban area population of 300,000, instituted in 1986 a manual system operating 16 hours per day on weekdays. It initially used just six toll stations, with a seventh added following completion of a new highway link. Oslo, the nation's capital with area population 700,000, followed four years later with a system of 19 toll stations charging at all times. Among the road projects funded by the Oslo ring is the Oslo Tunnel, an express bypass for congested downtown arterials that opened the previous month with bond financing, to be paid off by toll revenues; this and other tunnels are regarded in part as environmental improvements. An electronic charging option, available by subscription at reduced daily or monthly rates, adapts a microwave technology pioneered in 1987 at the Ålesund tunnel on the western coast; subscribers are billed monthly and enforcement is by video camera.

Trondheim instituted a more complex system in 1991. It operates 11 hours per day on weekdays, with a discount for trips entering after 10:00 a.m. and ceilings on the number of charges that can be incurred in any hour and in any month. The discounts and ceilings apply only to electronic subscribers, who now account for 85 percent of all tolled crossings. No seasonal pass is available in Trondheim. These features could enable Trondheim's system to approximate congestion pricing. However, the charges per crossing are only $1.12 for prepaid subscribers and the off-peak discount is only $0.32, so the scheme does not accomplish much congestion management.

Table 4. Overview of Norway s Toll Rings

	Bergen	Oslo	Trondheim[a]
Urban area population, '000s	300	700	136
–% inside toll ring		28	40
Starting date of toll ring	Jan. 2, 1986	Feb. 1, 1990	Oct. 14, 1991
Number of stations	7	19	11
Entry fee for cars (NOK)[b]			
Single trip (manual or coin)[c]	5	11	10
Per trip (subscription):[d]			
With prepayment[e]	4.50	7.43	7
Off-peak discount (after 10 a.m.)	NA	NA	2
Monthly pass[f]	100	250	NA
Times charges are in effect:			
Days	Mon-Fri	all days	Mon-Fri
Hours	6 a.m.-10 p.m.	all hours	6 a.m.-5 p.m.
Average daily crossings during			
toll hours ('000s)	68	204.4	40.5
% by subscription	59	63	85
1992 gross revenue, NOK millions	63	628	70.7

a: Figures exclude the pre-existing Ranheim toll station, which has higher rates (not shown) applicable in both directions and at all times.

b: For 1992. Exchange rate: NOK 1 = $0.16.

c: Bergen: all stations manned. Oslo: all stations manned, 8 also have coin lanes. Trondheim: 1 station manned, others coin or magnetic card only.

d: In Trondheim, subscribers are charged for no more than one trip per hour and no more than 75 per month. Trondheim subscription rates rose in 1994 for people making 10 or fewer crossings per month.

e: Charges shown are for the following prepayment quantities. Bergen: booklets of 20. Oslo: 350 trips. Trondheim: NOK 2500 prepayment. A postpayment option is also available in Trondheim.

f: Six- and twelve-month passes are also available, at lower rates.

NA: not applicable.

Sources: Larsen (1988), Waersted (1992), Tretvik (1992), and personal communications with E. Backer-Røed (Bro- og Tunnelselskalpet A/S, Bergen), K. Waersted (Directorate of Public Roads), G. Fredriksen (Trøndelag Toll Road Company, Trondheim), T. Tretvik (SINTEF, Trondheim).

Evasion of the video license plate enforcement is possible but rare except in Bergen, which lacks electronic collection but still allows non-stop passage by seasonal pass holders. Privacy for electronic subscribers is protected by the Data Inspectorate, which has strict regulations on all government data registers containing personal information. Use of electronic billing information for criminal enforcement, for example, would require a court order.

As expected, the impact of these pricing systems on traffic has been modest, reducing vehicle crossings by no more than 5-10 percent (Ramjerdi, 1994). The Trondheim system does seem to have induced some afternoon peak spreading, as people delay inbound trips until the end of the charging period at 5:00 p.m. (the normal work day ends at 4:00 p.m.); downtown shop owners have even extended their hours of operation to accommodate this response. The small price reduction at 10 a.m. in Trondheim has little or no effect on travel.

Public response has been surprisingly muted, despite survey evidence showing that support is lukewarm at best. A few incidents of vandalism accompanied the opening of the Oslo system, but other startup problems have been minor. As shown in Table 5, attitudes toward the toll rings in both Oslo and Trondheim were strongly negative, although less so after the systems opened than before. Attitudes toward the entire package of tolls and road improvements in Trondheim, however, are more evenly balanced, according to a survey taken in Trondheim which showed a

Table 5. Public Attitudes toward Toll Rings

	Positive	Negative	Unsure
Oslo toll ring:			
Before (1989)	29	65	6
After (1992)	39	56	5
Trondheim toll ring:			
Before (April/May 1991)	7	72	21
After (Dec. 1991)	20	48	32
Trondheim package:			
Before (April/May 1991)	28	28	44
After (Dec. 1991)	32	23	45

Source: A/S Fjellingjen (Oslo); Surveys by NOREAKTA (Trondheim), as reported by Tretvik (1992), p. 7 and figure 4.

slight plurality in favor after the system had been in operation for about two months.

2. The Dennis Package for Stockholm

Swedish interest in road pricing has arisen in a quite different political context than Norway's. Sweden has little history of toll finance of roads, bridges, tunnels, or even ferries; but it does have a strong and politically potent environmental movement. As a result, the Swedish program has stressed reducing environmental problems associated with traffic, especially in inner cities.

Notwithstanding these differences, Sweden has decided to create a toll ring for the capital city, Stockholm, which in many respects resembles the Oslo toll ring. Discussions are also underway for two other cities, Gothenberg and Malmö. The fact that different goals have produced similar policies illustrates the appeal of pricing schemes that are relatively simple and that build incrementally on experience elsewhere.

Stockholm is more than twice the size of Oslo, with a regional population of 1.64 million. Since the late 1980s, city politicians have been floating various proposals to restrain automobile traffic in order to reduce congestion, pollution, accidents, and noise, and to increase the speed of transit buses. In 1990, the national government convened negotiations among the chief political parties in each of the three largest metropolitan areas, leading to three separate agreements in 1991. All three include toll financing, and Gothenberg's includes a "green zone" in the inner city with limited road investments and various traffic restraints.

The Stockholm agreement has evolved into a toll ring instead of just tolls on new facilities. Stockholm's appointed negotiator was Bengt Dennis, Governor of the Bank of Sweden, and the resulting three-party agreement is known as the Dennis package. This package and the process producing it provide evidence that allocation of toll revenues can play a critical role in designing politically acceptable pricing schemes.

The central components of the agreement are improvements to public transit, new bypass roads, and road pricing as the chief financing mechanism. The total 15-year investment package (including some subsequent cost reestimates) is $6.9 billion (1992 prices and exchange rate). Somewhat over half is for roads, the rest for public transit, primarily rail.

The road investments include two controversial elements, both designed to divert through traffic from the inner city: completion of an inner ring road within the city limits, and construction of a tolled north-south bypass route west of the city. A third controversial element, designed in part to reduce all forms of inner-city traffic, is the toll ring. It will lie just outside the ring road, charging inbound vehicles, and will require about 28 toll stations. The ring toll, scheduled to go into effect in 1997, is expected to be set initially at $2.55 (1992 prices) and will be adjusted automatically for inflation. Discounts of an undetermined structure may be offered (Cewers, 1994).

The final package required compromise by each of the three main political parties. The Moderate Party (a conservative party) objected to the toll ring and proposed instead to finance the inner ring road with conventional tolls. But by placing the cordon line just outside the ring road, a conceptual compromise was attained: the toll will help limit traffic coming into the inner city, while still being viewed partly as a toll on the ring road itself, since most people using that road will come from outside the cordon.

The Dennis agreement states that toll collection initially will allow for either cash or electronic payment. However, the agreement also directs the Swedish National Road Administration to undertake technical development of a fully automated electronic fee-collection system for eventual use. The system is to allow fees to be varied by time of day and by type of emission control on the vehicle (Social Democratic Party et al., 1991, p. 30). It is eventually to operate in a free-flow multilane environment with video enforcement, and to permit a single smart card to pay for the toll ring, public transport, and parking.

Modeling studies suggest that the toll ring will complement the bypass routes' goal of reducing motor-vehicle travel in inner Stockholm, and will mitigate the effects of additional traffic caused by construction of the new roads (Johansson and Mattsson, 1994). The package therefore offers both improved travel conditions and a limitation on congestion and adverse environmental effects of road traffic.

3. Lessons from the Scandinavian Toll Rings

Norway and Sweden have adopted a pragmatic approach to road pricing. Initiated primarily to finance transportation investments, the policy has increasingly been enriched to ameliorate congestion and environmental effects of traffic. While Bergen's and Oslo's schemes are strictly meant to raise revenue, Trondheim's applies a mild incentive to spread the afternoon rush hour, and Stockholm's is designed to significantly reduce inner-city traffic.

This pragmatism has produced pricing schemes of impressive scope. Each surrounds an entire large city center, affecting many of the region's motorists. Oslo handles 200,000 crossings per day, while Stockholm anticipates more than 350,000 (Cewers, 1994). This large scale spreads the burden of financing road improvements widely. The use of seasonal passes or caps on the number of charges incurred further limits the burden on any one household.

The evolving features of the toll rings highlight the benefits of building on others' experience. Each project has been carefully planned and has used methods and equipment that are sufficiently simple and well tested to promote a smooth, relatively problem-free introduction. At the same time, each has taken advantage of the experience of its predecessors by adding new features that increase the convenience to users and the effectiveness of congestion management. Public confidence in the reliability of increasingly sophisticated pricing systems has been built, while the schemes remain closely tied to well articulated and widely shared objectives.

IV. Congestion Pricing of a Single Facility

We now turn to two innovative experiments that resulted from specific problems with financing or operating a congested expressway. In each case a form of congestion pricing arose out of the needs of a private operator.

1. Autoroute A1 in Northern France: Weekend Peak Spreading

Autoroute A1 is an expressway connecting Paris to Lille, about 120 miles to the north. It is part of a network of toll expressways operated by the Société des Autoroutes du Nord et de l'Est de la France (SANEF), one of seven government-owned but quasi-commercial toll road operators. As with many state turnpikes in the United States, vehicles receive a ticket upon entering the expressway and pay at a toll booth upon exiting, the amount depending on the length of the trip.

The A1 is subject to heavy inbound peaking near Paris on Sunday afternoons and evenings. In April 1992, after a period of extensive public consultation and publicity, SANEF confronted this congestion problem by implementing a time-varying toll scheme for Sundays only. A special "red tariff" is charged during the Sunday peak period (4:30-8:30 p.m.), with toll rates 25 to 56 percent higher than the normal toll. Before and after the peak there is a "green tariff" with rates 25 to 56 percent lower than the normal toll. For example, the tariff from Lille to Paris is normally $9.88;[5] but on Sunday it falls to $7.41 at 2:30 p.m., rises to $12.35 from 4:30 to 8:30 p.m., then falls again to $7.41 before returning to its normal value at 11:30 p.m.

These hours and rates were designed so that total revenues are nearly identical to those collected with the normal tariff. This property was believed essential for public acceptance, which in fact has been largely favorable.

The impact of the scheme is mainly on the timing of trips. Comparisons of traffic counts show that southbound traffic at the last mainline toll barrier near Paris declined approximately 4 percent during the red period and rose approximately 7 percent during the green period, relative to a six-year trend for comparable Sundays. The most pronounced shift was from the last hour of the red period to the later green period (Groupe SEEE, 1993, pp. 11, 18). A survey in November 1992 confirmed that many people . about one-fifth of those traveling during the green period . sought to lower their toll by shifting the timing of their trips, sometimes by stopping for meals at service areas along the highway (Centre d'Etudes Techniques de l'Equipement Nord-Picardie, 1993).

Although many people traveling during the early green period (2:30-4:30 p.m.) said that they had advanced their trips, traffic levels during these two hours grew little if at all. A likely explanation is that as congestion during the red period lessened, some people who previously had traveled early in order to avoid congestion now found it more convenient to travel during the peak and were willing to pay the higher toll to do so. This is an example of the kind of efficient reallocation of peak traffic, to those for whom timing is most important, that is predicted by the theory of congestion pricing (Arnott et al., 1988).

---

5. Using the 1992 exchange rate of 1 france = $0.19.

2. California's Private Toll Lanes: Riverside Freeway Median

California is about to become the first site of congestion pricing in the United States. This also will apply to just a single facility, but it will be more temporally refined than the French experiment and is being accomplished through a very different process.

In 1989, California's conservative Governor pushed through a program permitting the construction of four private transportation projects, subsequently selected in a bidding process in which private consortia submitted detailed proposals including locations and pricing structures. All four selected projects were for toll expressways, including two on which tolls would vary by time of day.[6]

One of those two is under construction at the time of this writing, and is scheduled to open in December 1995. It is in the median strip of the existing Riverside Freeway (State Route 91), an extremely congested commuter route connecting rapidly growing remote suburbs in Riverside County to employment centers in Orange and Los Angeles Counties. The existing four lanes in each direction carry about 250,000 vehicles per day with one-way delays of as much as 50 minutes (Perlman, 1993). The project will add two lanes in each direction along a ten-mile stretch in Orange County, and will link publicly built high-occupancy vehicle (HOV) lanes in Riverside County to planned HOV lanes further west in Orange County.

The project was controversial in Riverside County, whose residents will pay most of the tolls, even though it adds new capacity and the existing lanes will remain free of charge. The reason is that it substitutes for an originally planned single HOV lane in each direction, which was supposed to be funded by Orange County. (Riverside County has already funded and partly built the HOV lane on its side of the border.) This objection is partially ameliorated by an arrangement in which vehicles with three or more people will pass at reduced rates, or even for free if financial results from the road are sufficiently favorable.[7]

The design and collection of tolls are the responsibility of a private French toll road company, Cofiroute, which is part of the consortium

---

6. Gomez-Ibañez and Meyer (1993), pp. 172-193.
7. See California Department of Transportation and California Private Transportation Corporation (1992), p. 2; or Fielding (1994), p. 392.

that is building the project. Prcfits are constrained by a flexible ceiling on rate of return, negotiated with the State in a franchise agreement, but otherwise the toll rates and structure are freely determined by the company. This freedom was crucial to the project's viability and, in particular, to the builders' ability to apply time-varying tolls.

Of course, the existence of free parallel lanes just a few feet away greatly constrains the tolls that can be profitably charged. As a result, the company is planning to set toll rates that vary in fine increments in response to real-time measurements of congestion levels. This will be accomplished by restricting entry to cars equipped for electronic charging. Unlike the Cambridge scheme, the price of a given trip will be announced on electronic message signs prior to the entrance to the priced lanes, so that motorists can decide whether to opt for the priced or unpriced lanes. The signs will also provide information about delays on the free lanes. The maximum toll is expected to be $2 (Perlman, 1993).

3. Lessons and Future Prospects for Congestion Pricing
on Single Facilities

France and California have produced the only two instances of true congestion pricing other than Singapore's. Neither came about from any comprehensive theory of social welfare. Rather, both are narrowly targeted responses to specific problems: a peaking problem in France and a funding problem in California. Each turned to pricing as a common-sense adaptation of ordinary toll financing to the specific needs of the situation. In France, political considerations called for revenue neutrality and so an intuitive (though non-optimal) three-tiered toll structure was developed. In California, financial viability in the face of parallel free lanes required fine-tuned time-varying tolls.

A number of other congestion pricing projects are under consideration in the United States. Another of the approved private projects in California, thus far held up by environmental and financial considerations, would extend State Route 57 as an all-new elevated expressway along the Santa Ana River channel in Orange County; eleven miles in length, it would charge tolls tentatively proposed to vary between $1 at night and $5 during the peak (Gomez-Ibañez and Meyer, 1993, p. 173). The San Diego Association of Governments has proposed to allow low-occupancy vehicles to travel on HOV lanes on Interstate Route 15 for a fee (Duve, 1994). With funding for demonstration projects authorized by federal highway legislation, planning is underway for congestion pricing on the San Francisco Bay Bridge (Dittmar et al., 1994), although as of this writing no sponsor was found for state enabling legislation. A program of private highways in the State of Washington resulted in several congestion pricing proposals being approved for consideration by the state's Transportation Commission (Washington State Department of Transportation, 1994).

V. Big Plans for The Randstad and London

Two very large metropolitan areas, in The Netherlands and England, have been the sites of proposals, plans, and studies of comprehensive congestion pricing. The scale and scope of these potential pricing schemes make them qualitatively different from the schemes discussed earlier. Neither appears to have prospects for implementation in the near future.

1. The Netherlands' Randstad Region [8]

The Randstad region of The Netherlands, shown in Figure 1, is a sprawling urban region that covers more than 2,000 square miles and is home to some 6 million people. It includes the nation's four largest urban areas: Rotterdam and Amsterdam, with one million people each, and The Hague and Utrecht, each with over half a million. In both its urban form and its degree of road congestion, the Randstad resembles the larger Los Angeles region in the United States:[9] both areas are polycentric with multidirectional peak flows, both areas contain vital international ports and airports, and planners in both areas have turned to congestion management strategies to cope.

---

8. The information in this section relies primarily on Stoelhorst and Zandbergen (1990), Pol (1991), Int't Veld (1991), Hau (1992), and personal communications with H.D.P. Pol, Director of Project Spitzbijdrage, Ministry of Transport and Public Works, The Netherlands.

9. See Clark and Kuijpers-Linde (1994) for an explicit comparison.

Figure 1. Randstad Holland

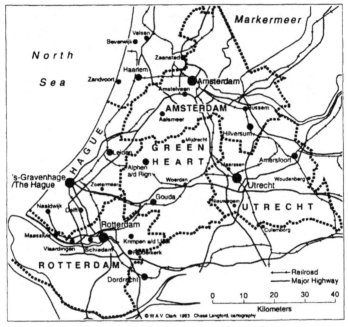

Source: Clark and Kuijpers-Linde (1994). Reprinted by permission.

During the late 1980s, The Netherlands Government developed a proposal called "road pricing" for the region. It involved a multiple cordon
system with 140 charging points and time-varying tolls, and was expected to reduce vehicle travel by 17 percent during peak hours. Considerable development work was undertaken on the technology and on models to predict impacts. However, critics questioned its technical feasibility, its immunity to invasions of privacy, and its ability to prevent
spillover traffic onto local streets. Unable to obtain support in Parlia-
ment, the Government in 1990 substituted a more modest plan for conventional road tolls.

Further study, however, convinced the Ministry of Transport and Public
Works that conventional tolls would require too much land for toll plazas
and would cause even more traffic diversion. In 1992, the Ministry developed a new proposal called "peak charging." It would again incorporate

congestion pricing, this time in the form of a daily supplementary license for travel on the main arterial system during the morning peak. The fee would be about $2.85 per day[10] and apply during the hours 6-10 a.m. The purchase of a daily, seasonal, or annual pass would be recorded by license plate and enforcement would be by random video pictures.

A new government, elected in 1994, has tabled further consideration of this proposal. Hence it appears that in the end these proposals were all too radical to attain the needed political support.

2. Greater London

Greater London, with seven million people and nearly four million jobs, has been the site of a remarkable series of comprehensive studies of congestion pricing, covering a variety of time periods, policies, and models. The resulting proposals have garnered considerable political support, but none has been adopted.

During the 1970s, the Greater London Council became interested in restraining traffic through supplementary licensing, a form of congestion pricing in which a daily license is required to drive within a defined area during peak hours. The favored options all involved a daily charge of around $2.00 (1973 prices)[11] to drive in Central London between 8 a.m. and 6 p.m. on weekdays; in some variations, an additional charge would apply in Inner London (a larger area surrounding Central London) during the morning peak only. Because Central London is only 3.4 miles in diameter, and because it has extensive transit service, these charges were expected to dramatically reduce traffic there, raising peak-hour speeds by as much as 40 percent (May, 1975).

In 1985, the Greater London Council was abolished and its planning functions devolved to the newly created London Planning Advisory Committee, composed of representatives of local boroughs and other authorities. This group in 1988 proposed a transportation strategy with considerably less road building than was planned by the national government under Prime Minister Margaret Thatcher. The strategy relied heavily on traffic restraint, including pricing measures. This time the congestion pricing proposal involved three concentric cordon rings, the

---

10. 1992 prices, using the 1992 exchange rate of 1 guilder = $0.57.
11. Exchange rates per British pound were $2.45 in 1973, and $1.78 in both 1988 and 1990.

innermost surrounding Central London and the outermost surrounding Inner London. In addition, screenlines would divide Central London into six cells. A charge of $0.89 (1988 prices) would be assessed for crossing a cordon or screenline; for Central London this would apply all day in both directions, whereas for the outer two cordons it would apply only during the peak period and in the peak direction (London Planning Advisory Committee, 1988).

Analysis isolating just the pricing measures showed dramatic predicted reductions in inbound traffic, by 15 percent into Inner London and 25 percent into Central London (May et al., 1990). More recent analysis shows that the distributional impacts of such a scheme would be concentrated among suburban car-owning households. Restricting the charges just to Central London would lower total benefits and shift the adverse impacts more toward poorer households (Fowkes et al., 1993); it would also make benefits more sensitive to the charging level, creating a greater likelihood of overdoing the policy as apparently happened in Singapore.

The most recent study of congestion pricing was a massive three-year research program begun in 1991 under the sponsorship of the U.K. Department of Transport. It investigated technology, public attitudes, changes in travel behavior, effects on reliability of travel times, effects on goods vehicles, and many other aspects (U.K. Department of Transport, 1993). These studies generally verified the behavioral responses expected from theory. However, at the conclusion of the study the Minister of Transport declared that no congestion pricing would be undertaken in London at least for the remainder of the decade.

3. Assessment

Despite the commitment of some important political figures, neither The Netherlands nor the United Kingdom has yet put in place any of the ambitious schemes for congestion pricing that have been proposed. The magnitude of the operation is so large, the technical and operational details so numerous, the effects so far-reaching, and the interest groups so many, that it appears to be exceedingly difficult to find a viable plan to introduce comprehensive pricing all at once. Meanwhile, much is being learned about how road pricing might be administered and what effects it would have.

VI. Conclusion

Both studies and actual experience have shown beyond a doubt that congestion pricing can substantially affect behavior and reduce traffic congestion. At the risk of over-generalizing, it appears that in the nations reviewed here, charges of $2 to $3 per day for entry to a restricted area during peak periods would reduce traffic by 20 percent or more. Charges can be targeted to divert traffic around certain areas or to shift it from one time period to another. In most cases it is feasible to offer customers a choice of collection options. Operating costs can be kept reasonable, around 10-12 percent of revenues.

For any road pricing project, no matter how limited, careful attention to the details of design and implementation is important. The level of fee, the potential for evasion or diversion, the security of information about people's travel, and the degree of public understanding all greatly influence the project's viability.

Regardless of how well planned, winning political approval for any congestion pricing project is difficult in a democracy. Many reasons have been suggested, but perhaps the most fundamental is that many motorists stand to lose, especially if they do not perceive that they are benefitting from the uses of toll revenues. One obvious solution is to use toll receipts to finance widely desired transportation improvements, to lower other taxes paid by motorists, or to reduce other toll charges. When the tolled facility is new and is financed directly by the revenues, people are likely to clearly understand the relationship between their payments and tangible benefits.

People are suspicious of plans to change arrangements they are comfortable with. The progression of innovations that we have reviewed here offers the possibility of overcoming this barrier through incremental change. The Norwegian toll rings began as means of financing transportation infrastructure, but the progressive increase in sophistication has made it possible to include traffic management as a subsidiary goal. The accumulated experience has enabled Stockholm to pursue a conscious traffic management strategy in a city considerably larger than any in Norway, while still giving prominence to the objective of financing infrastructure. It seems likely that similar spillovers from the projects in France and California could easily occur, giving pricing mechanisms the degree of credibility needed for other toll road operators to adapt them to their needs. These considerations make the approach of demonstration projects, embodied for example in U.S. federal legislation, an attractive one.

However, there is always the danger that an ill advised project will focus attention on the potential drawbacks of congestion pricing without revealing its potential benefits, and thereby provide ammunition to opponents. One advantage of the comprehensive studies in The Netherlands and Britain is that they enable the essential elements of a successful program to be identified in advance, thereby reducing the likelihood of unexpected problems arising during the course of implementation.

In sum, the international experience with congestion pricing is both cautionary and encouraging. While suggesting important pitfalls and political limitations, it also demonstrates that pricing can be practical and effective at managing congestion, and that the political problems, while difficult, may not be insoluble.

References

Arnott, Richard, André de Palma, and Robin Lindsey, "Schedule Delay and Departure Time Decisions with Heterogeneous Commuters," *Transportation Research Record* 1197 (1988) 56-67.

Blythe, Philip T., and Peter J. Hills, "Electronic Road-Use Pricing and Toll Collection: The Results of the ADEPT Project," in *Proceedings of the International Conference on Advanced Technologies in Transportation and Traffic Management*, Centre for Transportation Studies, Nanyang Technological University, Singapore (May 1994), 309-318.

Borins, Sanford F., "Electronic Road Pricing: An Idea Whose Time May Never Come," *Transportation Research*, 22A (1988), 37-44.

California Department of Transportation and California Private Transportation Corporation, *Amendment 1, Development Franchise Agreement: State Route 91 Median Improvements* (January 8, 1992).

Catling, Ian, and Brian J. Harbord, "Electronic Road Pricing in Hong Kong: The Technology," *Traffic Engineering and Control*, 26 (1985), 608-615.

Centre d'Etudes Techniques de l'Equipement Nord-Picardie, "Modulation des Péages sur A.1," study prepared for Service d'Etude Technique des Routes et Autoroutes (SETRA), Government of France (1993).

Cewers, M., "Stockholm Toll Collection System," in *Proceedings of the International Conference on Advanced Technologies in Transportation and Traffic Management*, Centre for Transportation Studies, Nanyang Technological University, Singapore (May 1994), 143-150.

Clark, William A.V., and Marianne Kuijpers-Linde, "Commuting in Restructuring Urban Regions," *Urban Studies*, 31 (1994), 465-483.

Dittmar, Hank, Karen Frick, and David Tannehill, "Institutional and Political Challenges in Implementing Congestion Pricing: Case Study of the San Francisco Bay Area," in National Research Council, Committee for Study on Urban Transportation Congestion Pricing, *Curbing Gridlock: Peak-Period Fees to Relieve Traffic Congestion*, vol. 2, Transportation Research Board Special Report 242, Washington, D.C.: National Academy Press (1994), 300-317.

Duve, John L., "How Congestion Pricing Came To Be Proposed in the San Diego Region: A Case History," in National Research Council, Committee for Study on Urban Transportation Congestion Pricing, *Curbing Gridlock: Peak-Period Fees to Relieve Traffic Congestion*, vol. 2, Transportation Research Board Special Report 242, Washington, D.C.: National Academy Press (1994), 318-333.

Fielding, Gordon J., "Private Toll Roads: Acceptability of Congestion Pricing in Southern California," in National Research Council, Committee for Study on Urban Transportation Congestion Pricing, *Curbing Gridlock: Peak-Period Fees to Relieve Traffic Congestion*, vol. 2, Transportation Research Board Special Report 242, Washington, D.C.: National Academy Press (1994), 380-404.

Fong, Peter K.W., "An Evaluative Analysis of the Electronic Road Pricing System in Hong Kong," *Hong Kong Economic Papers*, 17 (1986), 75-90.

Fowkes, A.S., D.S. Milne, C.A. Nash, and A.D. May, "The Distributional Impact of Various Road Charging Schemes for London," Institute for Transport Studies Working Paper 400, University of Leeds (June 1993).

Gomez-Ibañez, José A, and Gary R. Fauth, "Downtown Auto Restraint Policies: The Costs and Benefits for Boston," *Journal of Transport Economics and Policy*, 14 (1980), 133-153.

Gomez-Ibañez, José A., and John R. Meyer, *Going Private: The International Experience with Transport Privatization*, Washington, D.C.: Brookings Institution (1993).

Gomez-Ibañez, José A., and Kenneth A. Small, *Road Pricing for Congestion Management: A Survey of International Practice*. National Cooperative Highway Research Program Synthesis of Highway Practice 210. Washington, D.C.: Transportation Research Board (1994).

Groupe SEEE, "Evaluation Quantitative d'une Expérience de Modulation de Péage sur l'Autoroute A1: Note de Synthèse," Note 90601800-4f, prepared for Service d'Etude Technique des Routes et Autoroutes (SETRA), Government of France (April 1993).

Harrison, Bil, "Electronic Road Pricing in Hong Kong: Estimating and Evaluating the Effects," *Traffic Engineering and Control*, 27 (1986), 13-18.

Hau, Timothy D., "Road Pricing in Hong Kong: A Viable Proposal," *Built Environment*, 15 (1989), 195-214.

Hau, Timothy D., *Congestion Charging Mechanisms for Roads*. World Bank Working Paper No. WPS-1071, Washington, D.C. (1992).

Ho, L.-S., "On Electronic Road Pricing and Traffic Management in Hong Kong," *Hong Kong Economic Papers*, 17 (1986), 64-74.

Holland, Edward P., and Peter L. Watson, "Traffic Restraint in Singapore," *Traffic Engineering and Control*, 19 (1978), 14-22.

In't Veld, R.J., "Road Pricing: A Logical Failure," in *Environmental Protection: Public or Private Choice*, D.J. Kraan and R.J. in 't Veld, eds., Kluwer Academic Publishers, Dordrecht (1991), 111-121.

International Monetary Fund, *International Financial Statistics Yearbook*, vol. 45 (1992).

Johansson, Börje, and Lars-Göran Mattsson, "From Theory and Policy Analysis to the Implementation of Road Pricing: The Stockholm Region in the 1990s," in Börje Johansson and Lars-Göran Mattsson, eds., *Road Pricing: Theory, Empirical Assessment and Policy*, Boston: Kluwer Academic Publishers (1994), 181-204.

Kraus, Marvin, "The Welfare Gains from Pricing Road Congestion Using Automatic Vehicle Identification and On-Vehicle Meters," *Journal of Urban Economics*, 25 (1989), 261-281.

Larsen, Odd I., "The Toll Ring in Bergen, Norway—The First Year of Operation," *Traffic Engineering and Control*, 29, (1988), 216-222.

Lewis, Nigel C., *Road Pricing Theory and Practice*, London: Thomas Telford (1993).

London Planning Advisory Committee, *Strategic Planning Advice for London*, London, (1988).

May, A.D., "Supplementary Licensing: An Evaluation," *Traffic Engineering and Control*, 16 (1975), 162-167.

May, A.D., P.W. Guest, and K. Gardner, "Can Rail-Based Policies Relieve Urban Traffic Congestion?" *Traffic Engineering and Control*, 31 (1990), 406-407.

McCarthy, Patrick, and Richard Tay, "Economic Efficiency vs Traffic Restraint: A Note on Singapore's Area License Scheme," *Journal of Urban Economics*, 34 (1993), 96-100.

Menon, A.P.G., and S.H. Lam, "Singapore's Road Pricing Systems, 1989-1993," Transportation Research Report NTU/CTS/93-2, Centre for Transportation Studies, Nanyang Technological University, Singapore (Nov. 1993).

Menon, A.P. Gopinath, Soi-Hoi Lam, and Henry S.L. Fan, "Singapore's Road Pricing System: Its Past, Present and Future," *Institute of Traffic Engineers Journal*, 63, No. 12 (Dec. 1993), 44-48.

Milne, D.S., A.D. May, and D. Van Vliet, "Modelling the Network Effects of Road User Charging," in *Proceedings of the International Conference on Advanced Technologies in Transportation and Traffic Management*, Centre for Transportation Studies, Nanyang Technological University, Singapore (May 1994), 113-120.

Mohring, Herbert, "Urban Highway Investments," in *Measuring Benefits of Government Investment*, ed. by Robert Dorfman. Washington, D.C.: The Brookings Institution (1965), 231-275.

National Research Council, Committee for Study on Urban Transportation Congestion Pricing, *Curbing Gridlock: Peak-Period Fees to Relieve Traffic Congestion.* Vol. 1: Committee Report and Recommendations; Vol. 2: Commissioned Papers. Transportation Research Board Special Report 242. National Academy Press (1994).

Oldridge, Brian, "Congestion Metering in Cambridge City, United Kingdom" in Börje Johansson and Lars-Göran Mattsson, eds., *Road Pricing: Theory, Empirical Assessment and Policy*, Boston: Kluwer Academic Publishers (1994), 131-140.

Orange County Transportation Commission (OCTC), "91 Median, 57

Extension are Private Toll Road Sites," *Newsline* (October 1990), p. 3.

Perlman, Jeffrey A., "Persistence Paves the Way for Toll Lane," *Los Angeles Times*, Orange County Edition (August 1, 1993), B3, B11.

Pol, H.D.P., "Road Pricing: The Investigation of the Dutch Rekening Rijden System," Netherlands Ministry of Transport and Public Works (Feb. 1991).

Ramjerdi, Farideh, "The Norwegian Experience with Electronic Toll Rings," in *Proceedings of the International Conference on Advanced Technologies in Transportation and Traffic Management*, Centre for Transportation Studies, Nanyang Technological University, Singapore (May 1994), 135-142.

Sharpe, J. Michael, "Demand Management: The Cambridge Approach," Transportation Studies, Cambridgeshire County Council, Cambridge, U.K. (May 1993).

Small, Kenneth A., "Using the Revenues from Congestion Pricing," *Transportation* 19 (1992), 359-381.

Social Democratic Party, Moderate Party, and Liberal Party, "The Greater-Stockholm Negotiation on Traffic and Environment: The Dennis Agreement," signed by O. Lindkvist et al., transmitted by Bengt Dennis to The Minister of Transportation and Communication, Stockholm, Sweden (Jan. 23, 1991).

Stoelhorst, H.J., and A.J. Zandbergen, "The Development of a Road Pricing System in The Netherlands," *Traffic Engineering and Control*, 31 (1990), 66-71.

Toh, Rex S., "Experimental Measures to Curb Road Congestion in Singapore: Pricing and Quotas," *Logistics and Transportation Review*, 28 (1992), 289-317.

Transpotech, Ltd., *Electronic Road Pricing Pilot Scheme: Main Report*, Report prepared for the Hong Kong Government (May 1985).

Tretvik, Terje, "The Trondheim Toll Ring: Applied Technology and Public Opinion," SINTEF Transport Engineering, Trondheim, Norway. Presented at the joint OECD/ECMT/GVF/NFP Conference on The Use of Economic Instruments in Urban Travel Management, Basel, Switzerland (June 1992).

U.K. Department of Transport, "London Congestion Charging Research Programme Progress Note No. 4," London: U.K. Department of Transport (July 1993).

U.K. Ministry of Transport, *Road Pricing: The Economic and Technical*

Possibilities, Her Majesty's Stationery Office, London (1964).

Vickrey, William S., "Some Implications of Marginal Cost Pricing for Public Utilities," *American Economic Review, Papers and Proceedings,* 45, (1955), 605-620.

Vickrey, William S., "Pricing in Urban and Suburban Transport," *American Economic Review, Papers and Proceedings,* 53 (1963), 452-465.

Vickrey, William S., "Pricing as a Tool in Coordination of Local Transportation," in *Transportation Economics: A Conference of the Universities-National Bureau Committee for Economic Research,* ed. by John R. Meyer. New York: Columbia University Press (1965), 275-296.

Vickrey, William S., "Pricing, Metering, and Efficiently Using Urban Transportation Facilities," *Highway Research Record,* 476 (1973), 36-48.

Waersted, K., "Automatic Toll Ring No Stop Electronic Payment Systems in Norway—Systems Layout and Full Scale Experiences," Directorate of Public Roads, Norway, paper presented to the Sixth Institution of Electrical Engineers International Conference on Road Traffic Monitoring and Control, London, (April 1992).

Walters, A.A., "The Theory and Measurement of Private and Social Cost of Highway Congestion," *Econometrica,* 29 (1961), 676-699.

Watson, Peter L., and Edward P. Holland, *Relieving Traffic Congestion: The Singapore Area License Scheme,* World Bank Staff Working Paper No. 281, Washington, D.C. (1978).

Washington State Department of Transportation (WSDOT), "Public Private Initiatives in Transportation: Status Report," Public Private Initiatives in Transportation Program, WSDOT (August 19, 1994).

Wilson, Paul W., "Welfare Effects of Congestion Pricing in Singapore," *Transportation,* 15 (1988), 191-210.

"SERC Funds Research on Congestion Pricing, with Cambridge a Possible Candidate Site for Demonstration," *Traffic Engineering and Control,* 31, No. 10 (1990), 532-533.

CHAPTER 17

EFFICIENT TRANSPORTATION INFRASTRUCTURE POLICY*

*Clifford Winston***

Spending public funds to revitalize America's worn and congested roads and runways ranks high on nearly everyone's list of ways for government to raise the nation's productivity. The Governors' Task Force calls for outlays of $1 trillion to $3 trillion over the next 20 years—well above current capital spending—to build more roads and airports. The Joint Economic Committee received a letter signed by more than 300 economists and heard testimony from Alan Blinder and James Tobin, among others, urging an immediate increase in public investment in physical infrastructure.

However, the consensus that public investment must be increased breaks down when it comes to how to raise the money. Some argue the federal government should raise taxes or user fees; Transportation Secretary Samuel Skinner has called on the nation's governors to raise state gasoline taxes. But gasoline tax increases are hard to get through state legislatures, and the federal government is reluctant to spend money on

* Reprinted from *Journal of Economic Perspectives*, Vol. 5, No. 1, Winter 1991, pp. 113-127.

** *Senior Fellow, The Brookings Institution, Washington, D.C. I am grateful to C. Evans. S. Morrison, and K. Small for helpful comments and collaboration on much of the research reported here. I also received useful suggestions from H. Aaron, J. Meyer, C Shapiro, J. Stiglitz, and P. Viton. B. Szittya and T. Taylor provided valuable editorial assistance.*

infrastructure because of the deficit.

This paper offers a different perspective on paying for and investing in the transportation infrastructure. The following example illustrates the need to move away from the current national mind set. Pick any pothole-laden, congested two-land road in an urban area. Suppose public funds are used to widen the road to four lanes and to repave it. Benefits will immediately flow from this investment in the form of lower travel time and less vehicle damage. But many travelers who previously avoided the road during peak travel periods will now find the road attractive and want to use it. The improvements will also induce long-lived land-use and vehicle purchase decisions. Before long the road may again fill to capacity and steadily deteriorate. Generalizing from this example, the trillion dollars spent over the next 20 years might result in expanded transportation capacity that eventually faces the same problems as before. This is an illustration of Downs's (1962) law: On urban commuter expressways, peak-hour traffic congestion rises to meet maximum capacity, because commuters shift from less preferred modes and times of day.

This cycle can be broken only if infrastructure is priced and invested in more efficiently. If the pothole-laden road is kept to two lanes when it is repaved but vehicles are required to pay efficient tolls based on congestion and pavement wear, then the road's capacity is far less likely to be exceeded during peak periods and its pavement will remain in good condition. Making efficient use of current transportation capacity will reduce the need for massive public investment in airports and roads and will prevent the recurrence of infrastructure problems.

Surprisingly, the belief of most economists that public infrastructure spending should be substantially increased is not based on efficient pricing and investment principles. Instead, it appears to be based on either personal observations or on a suspicion that because uncongested infrastructure is a public good, society has tended to invest too little in it. Both perspectives have diverted many economists and policymakers from realizing there are surprisingly large but plausible benefits from *efficient* infrastructure pricing and investment.

These benefits arise because airports and roads are characterized by pricing systems that do not reflect economic costs and by poor design decisions that have resulted in higher costs of use. If road and airport systems are priced and invested in efficiently, then the long-run requisite increases in investment are quite modest, the systems would be roughly self-financing in places where some congestion is optimal, and the federal budget deficit is reduced. Efficient infrastructure policy can also complement the beneficial effects that deregulation of the transportation industries has had on competition and firms' operations, and help to address the primary sources of current discontent with deregulation.

I. The Theory of Efficient Infrastructure Policy

Transportation infrastructure provides *capacity*, in the form of traffic lanes and runways, for highway and air trips, as well as *durability*, in the form of thick pavement, to facilitate trips in heavy motor vehicles and large aircraft. Users of the infrastructure impose costs on themselves and others by contributing to congestion, which increases travel time, and by wearing out the infrastructure, which necessitates maintenance expenditures to repair pavement and vehicles. Efficient infrastructure policy maximizes the difference between social benefits and the costs of use, including the costs that users impose on others, by specifying pricing guidelines to regulate demand and investment guidelines to specify design. (Winston (1985) presents a mathematical derivation of these guidelines.)

Although the literature on optimal pricing and investment has a long and distinguished history that dates back to the writings of Pigou and Knight among others (see Winston (1985) for a survey), Mohring and Harwitz (1962) were the first to determine optimal pricing and investment policies in a rigorous long-run framework. Although recent work has extended their model to account for demand uncertainty, lumpy investment and so on, their basic insights remain intact. The efficient marginal cost pricing rule recognizes that when infrastructure users make travel decisions, they will ignore their contributions to congestion and infrastructure wear. As a result, the social costs of a trip will exceed private costs, and the infrastructure authority must therefore set congestion tolls and infrastructure wear charges to close this gap. The efficient investment rule calls for capacity and durability to be produced to the point where the marginal benefit from increasing investment in each dimension equals its marginal cost. The pricing and investment rules jointly constitute an efficient long-run policy, in which a user's full marginal cost is determined at the optimal level of capacity and durability.

Mohring and Harwitz also showed that the financial viability of a public infrastructure facility under optimal pricing and investment depends upon its cost function. If capacity and durability costs are jointly characterized by constant returns to scale, then the facility's revenue from marginal cost pricing will fully cover its capital and operating costs. If costs are characterized by increasing returns to scale, then marginal cost pricing will not cover costs; conversely, if costs are characterized by decreasing returns to scale, marginal cost pricing will provide excess revenue. The analysis that follows discusses the effects of implementing optimal pricing and investment guidelines.

II. Efficient Highway Pricing and Investment

The United States has nearly four million miles of roads, but roughly half of the nonlocal roads are currently in fair or poor condition, and traffic during commuter rush-hours approaches capacity on one-half of the urban interstates and one-third of the other main arterial highways(Small, Winston, and Evans, 1989). Efficient highway pricing and investment could dramatically improve the condition and performance of our roads, while requiring only a small increase in capital spending.

Historically, gasoline taxes have been used to charge vehicles for their use of the roads and to finance expenditures. The gasoline tax was a reasonable way to raise revenue as long as roads were uncongested and in good condition. But fuel tax receipts fluctuate with economic conditions and fuel prices, and recent shortfalls in gas tax revenues have made it increasingly necessary to supplement the gas tax with state and local revenues.[1] These periodic shortfalls and continual uncertainty are one reason to move away from the fuel tax as a source of highway revenue. A more important reason is that the fuel tax does not reflect the pavement damage and congestion caused by vehicles.

---

1. Tolls are levied on some roads and eight states have adopted taxes that assess trucks according to their total weight and distance traveled, but such charges account for only a small share of highway revenues.

Pavement Wear Charges

Pavements become worn as vehicles pass over them and eventually require resurfacing. Pavement damage itself depends on *vehicle weight per axle*, not total vehicle weight. The damage caused by an axle is defined in terms of the number of "equivalent standard axle loads" (esals) causing the same damage; the standard is a single axle of 18,000 pounds. Small and Winston (1988) report that this damaging power rises exponentially to the third power with its load. (This differs from the conventional belief that the damaging power rises exponentially to the fourth power.) Thus, for example, the rear axle of a typical 13-ton van causes over 1000 times as much damage as that of a car. Since trucks and buses cause almost all of the pavement damage, discussion of pavement wear charges is usually limited to them.

A marginal cost pavement wear charge can be assessed by multiplying a vehicle's esal-miles by the marginal cost of an esal-mile. For example, Small, Winston, and Evans (1989, p. 42) estimated the (average) marginal cost of an esal-mile on rural interstate highways to be 1.5 cents.[2] Thus, a truck equivalent to 2 standard axles traveling 100 miles on a rural interstate would accrue 200 esal-miles and a charge of $3.[3] Such a pavement wear charge would reflect much more accurately the damage caused by vehicles using the road. It would also give truckers an incentive to reduce axle weights by shifting to trucks with more axles, thus extending pavement life and reducing highway maintenance expenditures.

The fuel tax currently in use provides truckers with the opposite incentive: the tax rises with a vehicle's axles, since trucks with more axles require larger engines and get a lower fuel economy. Another counterproductive incentive is that many state turnpikes charge more for a given weight if it is carried on a vehicle with many axles.

---

2. The National Cooperative Highway Research Program calculated the average maintenance cost per esal-mile to be 1.6 cents (Transportation Research Board, 1986).
3. New devices for weighing trucks in motion and improvements in microelectronic identification make it possible for firms and auditors to tabulate esal-miles accurately.

Optimal Pavement Durability

The damage that a truck does to pavement depends not only on its axle weight but also on the durability (thickness) of the pavement.[4] Pavement thickness has been strongly influenced by guidelines from the American Association of State Highway and Transportation Officials (AASHTO). Small and Winston (1988) examined these recommendations, and found that AASHTO had failed to incorporate economic optimization into the design procedure (failing to minimize the sum of capital and maintenance costs) and had developed a relationship between pavement life and pavement thickness that was statistically flawed. As a result, they found that optimal thicknesses were significantly higher than current thicknesses, especially for heavily traveled interstates. For example, the optimal thickness for heavily traveled rigid concrete pavements is 13.8 inches compared with AASHO's estimate of 11.2 inches. Increasing thickness by 2.6 inches more than doubles the life of the pavement. Greater road thicknesses would substantially reduce annual maintenance expenditures and, because they would lower the marginal cost of an esal-mile, would also soften the impact of efficient pavement wear taxes on truckers.

The economic effects of building roads to optimal durability and of charging marginal cost pavement wear taxes to truckers are shown in Table 1. The effects of the first-best policy are shown in the first column of the table, while columns two and three show the results of partial implementation. Gains in net welfare from the first-best policy total $7.75 billion annually (in 1982 dollars), nearly 18 percent of total 1982 highway expenditures. The source of these benefits is a huge, roughly 75 percent, annual reduction in maintenance costs of nearly $10 billion, which is achieved with only a $1.2 billion annualized increase in capital costs. This policy is also politically attractive because it entails little redistribution; in fact, all major highway interests gain. Truckers and their customers gain because increased durability *lowers* the efficient road-wear charges from the charges that apply on today's roads. The public sector gains because trucking firms distribute their loads over

---

4. Besides making pavement thicker, durability can also be improved by improving drainage, using better construction materials and other methods. Aging and weathering leave a pavement more vulnerable to heavy loads.

Table 1. *Annual Economic Effects of Efficient Infrastructure Policy for Roads*
(change, relative to current pracice, in billions of 1982 dollars except as
noted; positive dollar values indicate improvement)

Item	Efficient Pricing and Investment	Efficient Pricing with Current Investment	Efficient Investment With Current Pricing
Investment Costs			
Maintenance Savings	9.428	6.441	8.536
Annualized Capital Savings	-1.276	–	-2.236
Total Savings	8.152	6.441	6.300
Trucking Firms' and			
Shippers' Welfare[a]	0.134	-5.586	–
Government Revenues	-0.574	3.884	–
Modal shifting[b]			
Modal surplus	0.029	0.204	–
Rail Profits	0.011	0.411	–
Total Welfare	7.752	5.354	6.300
Change in Standard			
Loadings[c] (percent)	-38.12	-48.38	0.0

Source: Small, Winston, Evans (1989)

a: These estimates do not include changes in user costs (vehicle damage and slower speeds due to damaged pavement). Small, Winston, and Evans (1989) point out there are difficulties in obtaining reliable estimates of this effect. Their rough estimates indicate that under optimal pricing and investment user costs are reduced by $3.03 billion when they are optimized along with maintenance and capital costs. User costs still fall by $1.8 billion under optimal pricing and investment when they are not explicity optimized.

b: Modal surplus measures the benefits to shippers who shift freight to or from railroads in response to the change in truck taxes.

c: The reduction in standard loadings is accomplished with only a small change in ton-miles that results from modal shifting; most of the reduction is from truck-type shifts.

more axles (change vehicle types) reducing standard loadings (esals) by 38 percent, reducing highway maintenance expenditures. Railroads gain slightly from an increase in traffic,[5] and the federal government's budget

---

5. Railroads gain because truck charges tend to rise on intercity traffic shipped long distances in large quantities; hence their business grows despite a small overall decrease in truck charges.

balance is improved because the reductions in maintenance expenses greatly offset the loss in highway revenues and increase in capital expenses.

The table also shows the importance of combining optimal pricing and investment. Setting efficient pavement wear taxes at current highway durability (middle column) would produce a smaller welfare gain and generate substantial redistribution from the trucking industry to the public treasury. This finding confirms that truckers are currently being undercharged for their use of the roads, but it also reveals how inadequate infrastructure investment can penalize an industry.

Building roads to optimal durability while maintaining current pricing (last column) also produces a smaller welfare gain and requires greater capital outlays. Because optimal investment is a long-run policy and the benefits from reduced maintenance expenses will be seen only several years after initial capital outlays, the present value of which must all be incurred when a road is upgraded, extra capital expenses could arouse short-term budgetary concerns. Nonetheless, society would save $4 for every $1 spent, including interest, which is a healthy return.

Congestion Charges

Regardless of what policies are implemented to fight traffic congestions—from high-occupancy vehicle lanes to subsidies for public transit—delays get longer and drivers and passengers get angrier. At first sight, increasing highway capacity may appear as sensible as increasing highway durability, but capacity and durability inadequacies have different effects on road users. Few vehicles are discouraged from using a road because of its durability problems, so optimal durability produces benefits without significantly increasing use. On the other hand, because many motorists are discouraged from using a congested road, traffic will be attracted when capacity is expanded to relieve congestion. Benefits may be accrued by expanding capacity but congestion will persist in the long run (Downs's law). The only way to reduce congestion permanently is to set an explicit price for capacity.[6]

---

6. Some have argued that the fuel tax is a surrogate for congestion pricing because cars tend to get lower fuel economy in heavy traffic. But fuel economy could actually improve if, for example, congestion forces cars to travel at moderate speeds (30 miles-per-hour) instead of higher speeds.

Congestion pricing has been advocated by economists for many years, but policymakers have either ignored it or dismissed it on political and practical grounds. For example, congestion pricing is not mentioned in *Time*'s (1988) eight-page cover story on gridlock. Ross Sand-ler, New York City Commissioner of Transportation (Pitt, 1989), dismissed the idea by saying, "What would you do—put tolls on all the highways?"

However, Small (1983) shows that objections by those who protest that lower income drivers would be unfairly penalized are unfounded. If toll revenues are used to lower property taxes, invest in public transit, or replace registration fees or fuel taxes, congestion pricing can benefit all income classes. Objections that tolls are impractical are also overstated. Congestion tolls varying by time of day, and imposed when congestion would otherwise persist, can be implemented without disrupting a traveler's journey. An automated vehicle identification (AVI) system, in which an electronic number plate is mounted underneath each vehicle, can be used to transmit a vehicle's numbered identification to a control center each time it passes over a power loop embedded beneath a toll site. The vehicle owner is then sent a monthly bill similar to a phone bill. Such a system has been tested in Hong Kong and found to perform exceptionally well. A sample of conclusions from the test includes the following: more than 99.7 percent of vehicles crossing a given toll site were correctly identified; security features could detect attempted fraud; and manual supplementary police enforcement at toll sites was proven feasible (Catling and Harbord, 1985). In the United States an AVI system is currently operating on the North Dallas Tollway and in New Orleans.

Because the effects of congestion pricing vary widely by locale, owing to different traffic densities and road systems, most studies of its effects have been site-specific. But a study by Lee (1982) made a rough estimate of the effect of adopting congestion pricing nationwide and found that it would generate $5.65 billion (1981 dollars) in annual net benefits, mostly in the form of annual travel delay savings of approximately one billion vehicle-hours. If congestion pricing were accompanied by optimal investments in road capacity, then annual net benefits would be even higher and the initial redistribution from road users to the road authorities would probably be less.

Highway Finance and Additional Benefits

Although efficient road pricing and investment would generate sub-stantial benefits, one must estimate the degree of scale economies in highway production to determine whether this policy would enable highways to be financially self-sufficient. Highways produce two "prod-ucts:" traffic volume requiring capacity (number of lanes) and standard loadings requiring durability (thickness). Determining the economies of scale in this multiproduct case requires finding the economies for each specific product, and then the economies of joint production, commonly referred to as economies of scope. Small, Winston, and Evans (1989) find strong economies associated with producing standard loadings, because a pavement's ability to withstand traffic increases far more than proportionally with its thickness. They find evidence from the literature that there are mild economies from producing traffic volume. (A com-mon explanation is that capacity goes up faster than the number of lanes; for example, two lanes in a given direction have more than twice the capacity of one lane.) However, they also find diseconomies of scope from jointly producing volume and standard loadings, because as the road is made wider to accommodate more traffic, the cost of any additional thickness required to handle heavy vehicles rises, since all lanes must normally be built to the same thickness. The result of com-bining these components is that the product specific economies are vir-tually offset by the diseconomies of scope, which leads to approximate-ly constant returns to scale in highway production.[7]

These constant returns to scale imply that urban roads that are some-times congested could be self-financing, in the long run. For uncongest-ed rural roads, additional charges such as license and registration fees would be required to attain a balanced highway budget.

This finding reveals an important additional benefit from congestion pricing. If efficient marginal cost pricing for road wear is undertaken alone, the road authority would face a deficit for urban roads, as well as rural roads, because of the economies of pavement durability.[8] But when

---

7. Small, Winston, and Evans (1989) discuss the possible efficiency gain from a road system that separates truck and auto traffic, which is motivated by their finding of diseconomies of scope. Such a system could be like the split of autos and trucks on the New Jersey Turnpike outside of New York City.

8. Small, Winston, and Evans (1989) find that the "pavement deficit" is reduced by opti-

efficient road wear pricing is combined with efficient congestion pricing, the (marginal) cost of building the pavement itself is effectively charged twice: once from trucks because they require a thicker pavement and once from cars because they require a wider pavement. The result is that losses from pavement durability economies are eliminated.

As a further benefit, congestion pricing could substantially reduce the public transit operating deficit, which approached $9 billion in 1985 according to the Urban Mass Transportation Administration. Higher congestion tolls will cause some motorists to shift to public transit. For example, Viton (1983) finds that congestion pricing in the San Francisco Bay Area would raise mass transit's share of downtown commuters by 10-20 percentage points. This increased ridership will probably lead to buses or trains running more frequently, which will increase convenience and allow transit agencies to raise fares above inefficiently low levels but still attain more ridership.

Efficient highway infrastructure policy could also complement the effects of trucking deregulation. Instituted in 1980, motor carrier deregulation has benefited shippers by some $14 billion annually (1988 dollars) in lower shipping costs and better service (Winston, Corsi, Grimm, and Evans, 1990). Because of shippers' increased use of just-in-time inventory methods, which attempt to keep inventories to a minimum by bringing in raw materials just in time for production, frequent and reliable service has become especially important. Deregulation has also stimulated the trucking industry to make innovations in equipment, routing, scheduling, and communications.

Congested and damaged roads thwart the effectiveness of carrier innovations, cause travel delays that disrupt the just-in-time inventory process, and raise carrier operating costs through wasted fuel and vehicle damage. All these costs are eventually borne by consumers. Some recent proposals to combat congestion and pollution would ban trucks from downtown areas during certain parts of the day and raise shipping costs even higher. Efficient highway infrastructure policy could supplant potentially counterproductive proposals, and facilitate carriers' continu-

mal pavement wear pricing and investment from its current level of $16.6 billion (1982 dollars) to $9.84 billion (1982 dollars). The pavement deficit is defined for the optimal and current policy as the difference between tax revenues and the annualized value of resurfacing expenditures and the cost of the paving material itself.

ing efforts to minimize shipping costs.[9]

Efficient highway infrastructure policy is designed to make the best use of scare durability and capacity. Scarce durability arises because roads can only withstand a finite number of standard loadings before they need resurfacing. Efficient road wear pricing attempts to reduce loadings by forcing shifts to trucks with fewer loadings; efficient investment recommends road design that allows roads efficiently to withstand a greater number of loadings. Each policy extends road life and saves society maintenance expenses; together they reduce maintenance expenses even more and, most importantly, they minimize redistribution and thus political problems. Scarce capacity is effectively rationed by congestion pricing; such capacity only can be used by those motorists willing to pay an efficient premium for it. With efficient highway infrastructure policy in place, authorities are able to make efficient decisions about whether building new roads can be economically justified.

III. Efficient Airport Pricing and Investment

Airport congestion and flight delays are receiving increasing public attention. The Department of Transportation has tried to coax airlines into improving their reliability by publicizing each carrier's on-time performance. Many observers argue the problem stems from a lack of airport capacity, citing the fact that no new major airports have been built since 1974. There are many supporters of federal subsidies for a new Denver airport, estimated to cost $2.5 billion.

Although additional airport capacity is not likely to attract as much traffic as additional highway capacity, the tremendous increase in aircraft departures of more than 25 percent during the past decade, partly

---

9. Although they are not analogous to the problems with publicly owned roads, infrastructure problems could also arise in railroad freight service because rail infrastructure is privately owned and maintained. Winston, Corsi, Grimm, and Evans (1990) point out that rail's financial performance has improved because of deregulation and that no major changes in rail policy are currently warranted. But they also suggest that a radical policy initiative, separating ownership of the rail infrastructure from ownership of the operating companies, could be necessary in the event of an economic downturn to preserve rail's financial viability and to facilitate sufficient railroad competition.

spurred by deregulation, and the high cost and long lead times associated with new airports suggest that society will be faced with a difficult and expensive catch-up task if it commits itself to reducing air congestion by building more airports. A less costly and more effective solution is to price and invest in existing airports more efficiently.

Efficient Runway Pricing and Capacity

The most common way of assessing landing fees at airports is by aircraft weight. Thus, a commercial jumbo jet pays considerably more to land during a given hour than a small private plane (general aviation). Weight-based landing fees were probably a reasonable way to allocate airport costs and raise revenue when airports were uncongested, but today, the principal cost that an aircraft imposes when it takes off or lands is that it delays other aircraft. (Runway damage caused by aircraft is small.) Morrison and Winston (1989b) found that this delay can be substantial. For example, the elasticity of average departure delay, defined as the percentage change in average departure delay caused by a 1 percent change in aircraft departures, is 2.9 for commercial carriers. This is similar to general aviation's elasticity of 2.5. Current weight-based landing fees undercharge aircraft in inverse proportion to their weight because they do not account for the congestion externality.

An airport's capacity is primarily determined by its number of runways, although terminal facilities and gate space can also have some effect. If an airport already owns the land, an additional 10,000 foot x 150 foot runway can be constructed for roughly $40 million in 1987 dollars (Morrison and Winston, 1989b). Optimal runway capacity is reached when the marginal cost of an additional runway is equated with the marginal benefit of reduced delay. The benefits of reduced delay are mainly the time saved by air travellers. Morrison and Winston (1989b) estimate average delay to be just a few minutes at some airports but as high as 27 minutes at New York (La Guardia) airport. They also estimate commercial air travelers' hourly value of time to be $42 (1988 dollars) and account for the number of passengers carried by different types of aircraft. Thus, for example, the passenger delay cost imposed on a commercial jet landing at La Guardia approaches $2,000. The effects of replacing weight-based landing fees with marginal cost congestion fees and of building the optimal number of runways at airports is shown in

Table 2.[10] The effects of efficient runway pricing and investment are shown in the first column of the table, and the effects of adopting efficient runway pricing at current runway investment are shown in the second column.

Optimal airport pricing and investment policy could generate roughly $11 billion (1988 dollars) in annual benefits. Travelers reap $8 billion in reduced delay and also would pay lower fares because the expansion in runway capacity called for under optimal investment combined with congestion pricing would reduce congestion to such an extent that, on average, landing fees would fall.[11] The annualized cost of the additional runway investment is only about $1.5 billion. Carriers benefit from the lower operating costs from reduced delay. Airports' net revenues would fall slightly, but, as we argue below, they would become financially self-sufficient.

The combination of efficient pricing and efficient investment policies is again economically and politically important. If airports adopted efficient congestion fees alone, there would be considerable redistribution from travelers—who would primarily absorb the higher takeoff and landing fees through higher fares—to airports. The losses to commercial travelers could be softened by reductions in the 8 percent ticket tax used to support air traffic control and airport construction. But general aviation, which would face the largest user fee increase, would remain uncompensated and mount heavy opposition to this change.[12]

Combining efficient pricing and investment would postpone the need

10. Optimal runway capacity is determined under the assumption that no additional land is needed for runway expansion. Although this assumption is unreasonable for some airports, other capacity-enhancing mechanisms are or will be available that could by themselves produce a similar effect or enable runways to be built closer together at airports with limited room for growth. These mechanisms include high-speed runway exits, microwave landing systems, phased array radar, and digital pilot-air traffic control communications. In any case, this assumption produces an upward bias in the estimate of net benefits.

11. General aviation travelers will face higher landing fees. But the Morrison-Winston model does not account for the greater flexibility that general aviation travelers have in their choice of airport and arrival and departure time, thus their loss is overstated.

12. General aviation was successful in its opposition to the landing fee increase at Logan(Boston) Airport. But the revised prices at Logan were only applied to small aircraft (fees were actually lowered for larger planes to keep the plan revenue neutral) and were not differentiated by time of day.

Table 2. *Annual Economic Effects of Efficient Infrastructure Policy for Airports*
(change, relative to current pracice, in billions of 1988 dollars; positive
values indicate an improvement)

Item	Efficient Pricing and Runway Investment	Efficient Pricing Current Runway Investment
Consumer surplus change from landing and takeoff fees[a]	1.10	-12.53
Reduced delay to travelers	7.91	3.62
Carriers' operating cost savings	2.77	1.23
Airport revenues less costs	-0.77	11.50
Total welfare change	11.01	3.82

Source: Morrison and Winston (1989b), pp. 61-112.
a: The consumer surplus change measures the effect of changes in landing and takeoff fees on travelers who continue to fly and those who are driven from or attracted to airline travel.

to build expensive new airports. The FAA estimates that the new Denver airport will reduce current delays at the Denver Stapleton airport by 35 percent to 50 percent. Optimal pricing and investment at Stapleton would lower delays by at least that much at lower costs (Morrison and Winston, 1989b). Continued growth in air travel will eventually necessitate constructing new airports, but these decisions will be made more efficiently if we make better use of our current airport capacity.

Because airports are characterized by overall constant returns to scale(Morrison, 1983), they would be financially self-sufficient under optimal pricing and investment. Their self-sufficiency would help lower the federal government deficit because airports would not need funds from the government to finance improvements.

Efficient Air Transportation Policy and Deregulation

Deregulation of the airline industry has been a success. Morrison and Winston (1986, 1989a) find that deregulation has provided travelers and carriers with $14.9 billion of annual benefits (1988 dollars).[13] But by lowering fares and accelerating the development of hub and spoke route structures, deregulation has increased the flow of traffic at major airports, which has strained airport capacity and caused delays. Despite popular belief, the source of the delays in not deregulation per se but the failure of airports to undertake optimal pricing and investment. The increased flying activity in the deregulated environment makes this failure all the more costly; Morrison and Winston (1989b) estimate that the potential benefits of deregulation have been lowered by at least $2 billion because of greater travel time.

Today, all airports in the U.S. are publicly owned, usually by local government agencies. Airports' contributions to investments in capacity are financed by bonds that are effectively guaranteed by the airlines. Efficient pricing and investment could reduce the airlines' control over airport investments, especially ones that would enable competitors to have easier access to the airport, because airports would be financially self-sufficient. It has been argued that under use agreements between airlines and airports, airlines can block airport investments in capacity that require them to pay additional fees. By expanding capacity, efficient pricing and investment could also reduce entry barriers that exist at certain airports because carriers are unable to get takeoff and landing slots.(Of course, these additional competitors would need to obtain gate space, also.) New entry could be facilitated, putting downward pressure on fares and adding to the benefits from deregulation.

IV. Toward Efficient Infrastructure Policy

The potential exists to realize substantial benefits from an efficient infrastructure policy. The annual welfare gain from efficient pricing and investment of highways and airports advocated here approaches $25 billion, and it can be obtained for only about $2.7 billion in annualized capital expenditures to increase road thickness and to build more runways. Benefits would actually be higher than these estimates suggest

---

13. This positive conclusion has been corroborated by a recent study (Morrison and Winston, 1990) that compares deregulated and hypothetically regulated air fares since deregulation in 1978 through 1989.

because performance in the deregulated airline and trucking industries would improve. And efficient infrastructure policy can at the same time effectively address the major concerns with deregulation, air travel delays and entry barriers at airports. The conclusion is clear and inescapable: public spending on infrastructure should certainly be increased, but it should be done efficiently and be accompanied by efficient pricing. Indeed, efficient pricing is a prerequisite to making efficient infrastructure investments.[14]

Leadership at the federal level would help shape an efficient infrastructure policy. One useful step would be for the federal government to require that requests for federal grants for highway and airport capacity improvements include a plan to reduce capital needs by efficient pricing and efficient investment. Unfortunately, current federal policy as stated in the National Transportation Plan (U.S. DOT, 1990) only mentions efficient pricing and investment in a vague way, if at all, and usually refers to it in connection with inefficient policies.

The best hope for sensible policy reform may reside with the states. Oregon has recently introduced an axle-weight tax for selected trucks and several locales in California are seriously exploring congestion pricing. There has also been support in California newspapers for congestion pricing (see the editorials cited in Small, Winston, and Evans (1989), p.92). These states have recognized (and perhaps others will too) that the current federal emphasis on supporting increases in infrastructure spend-

---

14. Some readers may be familiar with the work of Aschauer (1989), who estimates time series regressions that attempt to explain the impact of the nonmilitary public capital stock on the nation's productivity, and finds very powerful effects. In fact, the effects he finds are too powerful.

Consider a one-time lump-sum $60 billion increase in infrastructure spending. An increase of this magnitude in 1985 would enable public works capital spending to regain its 1960 share of GNP. This lump-sum investment represents a 6 percent increase in the value of the infrastructure stock. Using Aschauer's elasticity estimate of .24 for the change in productivity with respect to the change in the infrastructure capital stock leads to a 1.4 percent increase in current output from the investment or a $70 billion gain in the first year. With conservative parameters, the present value of the gain in future years would exceed $600 billion, for a benefit-cost ratio of 10:1.

This return is implausible. Charles Schultze (1990) argues Aschauer's findings simply demonstrate that the time pattern of productivity and public investment growth are similar (both rising in the 1950s and 1960s, and both falling in the 1970s and 1980s) and that this correlation generates grossly inflated estimates of the return to public infrastructure investment.

ing with such means as higher state gasoline taxes will fail to provide a permanent solution to recurring infrastructure problems. Steps must be taken to stop passing these problems on to future generations.

References

American Association of State Highway and Transportation Officials, *AASHTO Guide for Design of Pavement Structures*, Washington: AASHTO, 1986.

Aschauer, David Alan, "Is Public Expenditure Productive?" *Journal of Monetary Economics*, March 1989, 23, 177-200.

Catling, Ian, and Brian J. Harbord, "Electronic Road Pricing in Hong Kong, 2: The Technology," *Traffic Engineering and Control*, December 1985, 26, 608-615.

Downs, Anthony, "The Law of Peak-Hour Expressway Congestion," *Traffic Quarterly*, July 1962, 16, 393-409.

Governors' Task Force Report, Presented to National Governors Association, Chicago, IL, August 1989.

Joint Economic Committee, United States Congress, "Public Investment in Infrastructure," July 1989.

Lee, Douglass B., "New Benefits From Efficient Highway User Charges," *Transportation Research Record*, 1982, no. 858, 14-20.

Mohring, Herbert, and Mitchell Harwitz, *Highway Benefits: An analytical Framework*. Evanston, IL: Northwestern University Press, 1962.

Morrison, Steven A., "Estimation of Long-Run Prices and Investment Levels for Airport Runways," *Research in Transportation Economics*, 1983, 1, 103-130.

Morrison, Steven, and Clifford Winston, *The Economic Effects of Airline Deregulation*. Washington, DC: The Brookings Institution, 1986.

Morrison, Steven A., and Clifford Winston, "Airline Deregulation and Public Policy." *Science*, August 1989a, 245, 707-711.

Morrison, Steven A., and Clifford Winston, "Enhancing the Performance of the Deregulated Air Transportation System," *Brookings Papers on Economic Activity: Microeconomics*, 1989b, 61-112.

Morrison, Steven A., and Clifford Winston, "The Dynamics of Airline

Pricing and Competition.:" *American Economic Review, Papers and Proceedings,* May 1990, 80, 389-393.

Pitt, David E., "Tolls or No, Traffic Gets Worse," *New York Times,* September 1989.

Schultze, Charles L., "The Federal Budget and the Nation's Economic Health." In Aaron, Henry, ed., *Setting National Priorities: Policy for the Nineties.* Washington, DC: The Brookings Institution, 1990.

Small, Kenneth A., "The Incidence of Congestion Tolls on Urban Highways," *Journal of Urban Economics,* January 1983, 13, 90-111.

Small, Kenneth A., and Clifford Winston, "Optimal Highway Durability," *American Economic Review,* June 1988, 78, 560-569.

Small, Kenneth A., Clifford Winston, and Carol A. Evans, *Road Work: A New Highway Pricing and Investment Policy.* Washington, DC: The Brookings Institution, 1989.

Time, "Gridlock! Congestion on America's Highways and Runways Takes a Grinding Toll," September 12, 1988, 52-60.

Transportation Research Board, National Cooperative Highway Research Program, "Relationships Between Vehicle Configuration and Highway Design," National Research Council, Washington, DC, November 1986.

United States Department of Transportation, *Moving America: New Directions, New Opportunities.* Washington, DC, February 1990.

Viton, Philip A., "Pareto-Optimal Urban Transportation Equilibria," *Research in Transportation Economics,* 1983, 1, 75-101.

Winston, Clifford, "Conceptual Developments in the Economics of Transportation: An Interpretive Survey." *Journal of Economic Literature,* March 1985, 23, 57-94.

Winston, Clifford, Thomas M. Corsi, Curtis M. Grimm, and Carol A. Evans, *The Economic Effects of Surface Freight Deregulation.* Washington, DC: The Brookings Institution, 1990.

CHAPTER 18

OPTIMAL PEAK-LOAD PRICING, INVESTMENT AND SERVICE LEVELS ON URBAN EXPRESSWAYS*

*Theodore E. Keeler and Kenneth A. Small***

Abstract

Optimal tolls, capacities, and service levels for highways can be determined jointly by way of an integrated peak-load pricing model. In this paper, such a model is developed and estimated with data for roads in the San Francisco Bay Area. The results suggest optimal peak user tolls of 2-7 cents per automobile mile on rural highways, 2-9 cents on suburban highways, and 6-35 cents on central city highways. Although our results are to some degree dependent on the interest rate, time value, and peak demand configuration assumed, one basic conclusion holds up under all alternative assumptions: current user charges are well below optimal peak tolls. However, our results also suggest considerably higher rush-

* Reprinted from *Journal of Political Economy*, 1977, Vol. 85, No. 1, pp. 1-25.
** University of California at Berkeley and Princeton University, respectively. Work for this paper was done with the support of National Science Foundation grant GI-37181. The authors are very much indebted to G. Cluff, J. Finke, and P. Viton for research assistance, and to S. Peltzman, W. Vickrey, M. Webber, and the referee for helpful comments. Also, we wish to thank various members of the staff of the Institute of Urban and Regional Development at the University of California for clerical assistance.

hour speeds than currently prevail on Bay Area roads, and the lower travel time costs suggested by our analysis (relative to the current situation) should to some degree offset the corresponding higher user charges.

Given the crowded condition of most metropolitan freeways during rush hours in this country, the question of optimal pricing and investment policies for urban roads is a topic of some interest and controversy. It is the aim of this paper to derive a long-run model of highway pricing and investment to shed light on these issues. The model is developed and estimated, using data from a sample of freeways in the San Francisco Bay Area.

In brief, the model is concerned with trading off the cost of providing urban expressway capacity against the value of travel time to minimize total system costs. Out of the model comes a set of long-run peak-load tolls (equal to optimal short-run tolls when investment is made correctly), as well as an optimal service level (as a function of time values and capacity costs). These results give some indication as to whether auto transportation in a given corridor is priced efficiently and whether capacity provided is appropriate.

In Section I the model is set forth, consistent with the previously established theory of peak-load pricing, but particularly suited to highways. Sections II-V are concerned with empirical estimation of the parameters of this model. More specifically, Section II is concerned with the estimation of capital and maintenance costs and with determining returns to scale in the provision of freeway services. Section III is concerned with estimating the technological trade-off between travel time and capacity utilization. Section IV discusses briefly the issues involved in valuing travel time and presents the assumptions made in this study, as well as some evidence to support them. In Section V attention is directed to the peaking characteristics of demand for Bay Area freeway services.

Section VI pulls together the theoretical and empirical work of the previous sections, discusses the optimization procedure used, and presents the results. Section VII presents a comparison of optimal and existing prices and service qualities on the relevant freeways, and Section VIII discusses the policy implications of our results.

I. The Theory of Optimal Highway Pricing and Investment

As was first shown by Mohring and Harwitz (1962), the optimal pricing and investment decision for highways can be dealt with analytically in a single model. This model was extended to include peak-load pricing by Vickrey (in Fitch 1964), Strotz (1964), and Mohring (1970). The present model draws from all these previous ones, although it is not identical with any of them in every detail.[1]

To start, we make two simplifying assumptions. First, we assume that highway construction can be done without problems of plant indivisibility. Although this is not strictly realistic, it is not an unreasonable assumption for large urban highways, for the wider the roads in the system, the less relevant indivisibilities become to the analysis. Second, we assume that demand in each period is independent of prices in other periods. The implications of dropping these assumptions will be considered in detail later.

We assume, then, that over an annual period there are T subperiods over which demand varies: let $P_t = P_t(Q_t)$ be the demand function for period t, where Q_t is the flow of vehicle tips over a given urban route per unit of time and P_t is the total user cost of a trip on the route, including cost of travel time.

The rental cost of the road used for these trips includes interest and amortization on the investment, plus those maintenance costs which are variable with road size (as opposed to traffic volume using the road). It is thus

$$\rho(w) = \frac{r}{1 - e^{-rL}} K(w) + M(w) + rA(w), \tag{1}$$

where r is the interest rate, L is the effective lifetime of the road, $K(w)$ is the construction cost (as a function of width, w), $M(w)$ is the maintenance cost varying with width, and $A(w)$ is the land acquisition cost.

We now define an average variable cost function, which includes all expenses of user-supplied inputs—variable ownership, maintenance, and operating costs of the autos, plus the value of in-vehicle travel time for

---

1. Strotz's analysis, couched completely in terms of utility functions, is quite rigorous, but empirically unworkable. Mohring (1970) works out the solution starting with utility functions, then translates the results into intertemporally dependent demand functions. The reader seeking a more complete derivation of the basic results shown here is directed to his work.

the average number of passengers in each vehicle. In addition, it includes the cost of publicly supplied inputs whose costs vary with vehicle-miles and not lane capacity (police costs, for example). Let this variable cost function be

$$C_t = C_t(Q_t, w), \tag{2}$$

where $\partial C_t / \partial Q_t > 0$, and $\partial C_t / \partial w < 0$. That is, additional traffic, holding land capacity constant, will slow everyone down, thereby raising costs; additional lane capacity, on the other hand, will allow everyone to speed up, holding traffic constant (when the road is uncrowded, however, these effects may be very small).

We also assume that $C_t(Q_t, w)$ is homogeneous of degree zero in Q_t and w; this is equivalent to assuming that the speed of traffic on the road is dependent only on the volume-capacity ratio of the road and not the absolute size. There is considerable evidence to support this assumption, at least for roads with widths of two or more lanes in each direction (since our analysis is strictly for expressways, this is reasonable; see Highway Research Board [1965, p. 76]).

We wish to maximize net benefits of all trips on the route over the life of the road:

$$NB = \sum_{t=1}^{T} \left[\int_0^{Q_t} P_t(Q_t) \, dQ_t - Q_t C_t(Q_t, w) \right] - \rho(w) \tag{3}$$

Necessary conditions for the maximum may be found by differentiating (3) with respect to each Q_t, and with respect to w, and setting each derivative equal to zero.

Differentiating with respect to each Q_t, setting the result equal to zero, and rearranging, we have

$$P_t = C_t + Q_t \frac{\partial C_t}{\partial Q_t}, \qquad (t = 1, \dots T). \tag{4}$$

This condition is simply that total price paid in each period should be equal to short-run marginal cost. The second term after the equal sign is the optimal congestion toll, the difference between optimal price and average variable cost.

Optimizing (3) with respect to w yields the following condition:

$$-\sum_{t=1}^{T} Q_t \frac{\partial C_t}{\partial w} - \rho'(w) = 0. \tag{5}$$

This states that the lane capacity should be expanded to the point where the marginal cost of an extra unit of capacity is equal to the marginal value of user cost savings brought about by that investment.

It is now worth considering the relationship between the revenues from optimal tolls charged on the road and the costs of owning and maintaining it. To do so, we multiply equation (4) by Q_t and sum over all time periods. By use of condition (5), and of Euler's theorem on homogeneous functions C_t, we obtain the following equation for toll revenues:

$$\sum_{t=1}^{T} [P_t(Q_t) - C_t] Q_t = w\rho'(w). \tag{6}$$

If there are constant returns to scale in highway construction, then $\rho(w)=aw$, where a is a constant, so $w\rho'(w)=\rho(w)$, and total tolls from the road will just cover its rental costs. With increasing returns, the road will have to be subsidized for efficient operation, and similarly, with decreasing returns the road will earn a surplus.

We are now in a position to consider qualitatively the implications of relaxing our assumptions regarding demand interdependencies and plant indivisibilities.

As Mohring (1970) has shown, the existence of intertemporal demand dependencies does not alter the short-run pricing rule (4), but it will affect the magnitude of the toll in long-run equilibrium. By taking the current demand distribution over time as given and fixed, we should obtain reasonable first-round approximations to optimal tolls for each period. To get an idea of what the effect would be of "demand spreading" on equilibrium tolls, we also recalculate our results with a much flatter peak than the existing one. While this procedure is not a precise one, it should tell something about the likely effects of potential demand interdependencies.

The main impact of indivisibilities is to force construction of roads either too large or too small for the amount of traffic using them. This means, as Neutze (1966) has shown, that if there are constant returns to scale in constructing and maintaining the road some roads will make money and others will lose, but with a large group of roads they should tend to break even overall. Similarly, with increasing returns to scale the system will lose money, and with decreasing returns it will make money. In ignoring indivisibilities, our work may thus give misleading results for any one road, but for a system as a whole, the results are likely to be suggestive of what would happen under a regime of optimal pricing and investment.

II. Estimation of the Highway Capacity Cost Function.

This section is concerned with estimation of the function $\rho(w)$, mentioned above. This is done by way of three statistical cost models, one for construction, one for land acquisition, and another for maintenance.

A. *Construction Costs*

In estimating construction costs for urban highways, it is necessary to disentangle several effects which cause the cost per lane-mile to differ for different stretches of road.

First, scale economies or diseconomies may exist, making wider roads cheaper or more expensive per lane-mile than narrower roads. Evidence from previous studies of this question leaves the answer in dispute.

On the basis of prior engineering considerations, Meyer, Kain, and Wohl (1965, pp. 200-204) find considerable economies of width. But this result would seem to stem more from their initial engineering assumptions than from empirical evidence. They also do not take account of the fact that when wide roads meet they require a more elaborate and expensive interchange system than smaller roads. Thus, they state that, especially for autos (as opposed to buses), their method could considerably overstate costs for a four- or six-lane freeway relative to an eight-lane freeway.

And it is difficult to separate the effects of urbanization and scale in determining highway costs. Walters (1968, p. 184), looking at a data sample of construction costs compiled by Meyer, Main and Wohl, finds considerable evidence of decreasing returns to scale in the figures, which seem to imply higher cost per lane for a wider road. Meyer, Kain, and Wohl, on the other hand, attribute all these cost differences to the effects of urbanization (1965, p. 204).

In another study, Fitch and Associates (1964, p. 131) find evidence of decreasing returns to scale for urban freeways. They examine the costs of two highway plans for Washington, one with far more freeway capacity than the other. They find that the freeway-intensive plan is considerably costlier on a lane-mile basis than the non-freeway-intensive plan. The evidence on scale economies in freeway construction, then, is inconclusive.

Urbanization, the second important variable determining freeway capital costs, is difficult to measure. Joseph (1960) uses net residential density, which is likely to be the most reliable available measure of urbanization, but data on that are difficult to get for the Bay Area roads in our sample. In our model, the impact of urbanization is estimated by allowing construction costs per lane-mile to vary discretely between central city areas (i.e., Oakland-San Francisco,) urban but outside the central cities areas, and rural-suburban (unincorporated) areas.

The data sample over which the model was estimated includes all state-maintained roads in the nine Bay Area counties, including arterials, expressways, and rural roads.[2] Each observation consists of a single stretch of road in a given county. Thus, costs per lane-mile for State Highway 24 in Contra Costa County represent one observation (average lane widths of each road were calculated from state records). Data on 57 such observations were collected.[3]

The construction cost data used were historical in nature. The following procedure was used to convert them into 1972 dollars. Annual investments made in each of these roads over the period 1947-72 were converted to 1972 prices using the California Highway Construction Cost Index. The costs were then added up, under the assumption of a "one-horse-shay" depreciation policy, with an estimated lifetime of 25 years.

In order to separate the effects of urbanization and scale on freeway costs, two alternative specifications were used: a nonlinear one and a log-linear one. The nonlinear specification took the following form:

$$KLM = (a_1 CRS + a_2 CUC + a_3 FR + a_4 FSU + a_5 FC)w^{a6}, \quad (7)$$

---

2. The nine Bay Area counties are Alameda, Contra Costa, Marin, Napa, San Francisco, San Mateo, Santa Clara, Solano, and Sonoma.

3. Data come from California Department of Public Works (1947-72), sec. D.

where *KLM* is 1972 construction cost per lane-mile, *CRS* is the fraction of the length of the road in the sample accounted for by conventional (non-freeway) roads outside of city limits, *CUC* is the fraction of the observed road made up of conventional arterial streets or roads within city limits; *FR* is the fraction of the observed road made up by rural freeways; *FSU* is the fraction of the road made up of urban or suburban freeways, as defined by the California division of highways; *FC* is the fraction of the observed road made up of freeways within the city limits of Oakland or San Francisco (freeways in Oakland and San Francisco are counted in both *FSU* and *FC*. Thus, to get the total cost of a freeway in these cities, *FSU* should be added to *FC*); finally, *w* is the average width of the observed stretch of road in lanes.

This nonlinear regression can be used to determine the cost of a lane-mile of freeway for different degrees of urbanization and with different widths. For example, the cost per lane-mile of a six-lane freeway in Berkeley is $a_4 6^{a_6}$.

Estimation of this model requires use of a nonlinear estimator. Nonlinear least squares was used (see Malinvaud 1970, chap. 9).

An alternative specification used is a log-linear form, described by the following equation:

$$\ln(KIM) = a_1 CRS + a_2 CUC + a_3 FR + a_4 FSU + a_5 FC + a_6 \ln(w), \quad (8)$$

where all notation is the same as before, save that ln stands for natural logarithms. Exponentiation of this equation yields the following:

$$KLM = \exp\left(a_1 CR + a_2 CUC + a_3 FR + a_4 FSU + a_5 FC\right) w^{a_6}. \quad (9)$$

Again using the example of six-lane Berkeley freeway, construction cost per lane-mile would be $\exp\left(a_4 FSU\right) \cdot 6^{a_6}$.

This form has the advantage that it can be estimated linearly, while still allowing costs per lane-mile to vary depending on the degree of urbanization. But like (7) above, it still allows estimation of a degree of homogeneity a_6.

In the case of both equations, if $a_6 = 0$, that is evidence of constant returns to width; if $a_6 < 0$, that is evidence of increasing returns; and if $a_6 > 0$, that implies decreasing returns.

The results of estimation are shown in table 1. Both sets of results are consistent with the hypothesis of constant returns; in neither case is it possible to reject that hypothesis at any reasonable level of significance. Although the nonlinear equation provides some very weak evidence of increasing returns, the log-linear equation is in some ways preferable on prior grounds, given that linear regression estimators are generally more efficient than nonlinear ones and, consistent with this, that the actual lane-mile cost estimates coming from the log-linear equation are more plausible than those from the nonlinear one. For these reasons, we base our analysis and conclusions on the results of the log-linear equations.[4]

In calculating costs per lane-mile, constant returns to scale were assumed throughout on the basis of the log-linear results shown in table 1. However, in order to get an unbiased estimate of lane-mile costs using the estimation equation (9), we assumed w to have a mean of 6. As a result, all costs on the basis of coefficients a_1-a_5 were multiplied by $6^{-.0305} = .9468$. Because a_6 is so small, the estimated cost per lane-mile is highly insensitive to the value of w assumed.

One further refinement is needed to make the log-linear results useful for our purposes. All our calculations involve automobiles only. Hence, it would be inappropriate to include in them any construction costs necessary only for heavy commercial vehicles. Therefore, the costs per lane-mile derived from equation (9) should be scaled down to reflect the costs of an autos-only road. For a typical urban expressway, the United Stated Bureau of Public Roads estimates that costs for an autos-only road should be about 77 percent of costs for a general-purpose highway.[5] Therefore, all construction costs estimated above are multiplied by a factor of .77 to get the cost attributable to autos. The results are shown in table 2.

B. Lane Acquisition Costs

Conversion of land acquisition costs to 1972 value poses problems. It is clearly inappropriate to count only historical costs, given that land

---

4. It is worth noting that when the w^{a6} term was excluded from the nonlinear equation (so it could be estimated additively and linearly) the resulting estimates of the cost of lane capacity were virtually identical with those of the log-linear equation, for each degree of urbanization.

5. These calculations are especially for an urban freeway, and they are taken from data presented by Meyer, Kain, and Wohl (1965), pp. 204-6.

Table 1. Construction Cost Regression Results

Parameter Estimated	Nonlinear Equation	Log-linear Equation
a_1	116,983	11.609
	(97,193)	(0.359)
a_2	945,214	12.767
	(585,588)	(0.597)
a_3	563,649	12.993
	(388,066)	(0.729)
a_4	911,784	13.255
	(426,089)	(0.771)
a_5	2,017,817	1.1151
	(1,583,633)	(0.5389)
a_6	–0.3178	–0.0305
	(0.3399)	(0.3931)
R^2	.5262	.5183

Note: SEs shown in parentheses.
Sources: See text

Table 2. Freeway Capital Cost ($)

Capital Cost Category (per Lane-Mile)	Urban-Central City Freeway	Urban-Suburban (Outside Central City) Freeway	Rural Freeway
Construction cost............................	1,648,427	540,545	415,955
Portion of construction costs allocable to an autos-only highway	1,269,289	416,219	320,285
Annualized capital costs of an autos-only highway:			
at 6%	86,767	28,456	21,898
at 12% (35-year life)	154,599	50,695	39,010
Total land acquisition cost..............	465,829	134,439	124,787
Annualized land acquisition cost:			
at 6%	27,950	8,066	7,487
at 12%	55,899	16,133	14,914
Annual capacity-related maintenance costs...	2,917	2,917	2,917
Total annual rental per unit of capacity:			
at 6%	117,634	34,439	32,302
at 12%	213,415	69,745	56,901

Sources: See text.

costs have risen over the years. Furthermore, no satisfactory land acquisition cost index is available. However, some new roads have been built in very recent years in each county, and the land acquisition costs of these roads the probably the most reliable available guidelines for what it would cost to acquire the land anew for other roads in those locations.

Therefore, we have assumed that each observation in our cross section would have the same ratio of land acquisition costs to construction costs as the roads built in its county during the 1968-72 period. "Typical" costs for each road type (rural, urban-suburban, and central city) were calculated on this basis using the following procedure. First, for each of the nine Bay Area counties, the countywide ratio of land acquisition to construction costs was calculated for all construction undertaken during the 1968-72 period.[6] Then, a cross-section regression was estimated, using as the independent variable the fraction of the stretch of road accounted for by each road type (the same independent variables as in equation [7], save for width). The dependent variable was the countywide ratio of land acquisition to construction costs for the stretch of road involved. The results are as follows;

$$ROW/K = .267 \; CRS + .342 \; CUC + .300 \; FR$$
$$(.007) \qquad (.011) \qquad (.021)$$
$$+ .323 \; FSU + .367 \; FC \qquad\qquad (10)$$
$$(.101) \qquad (.024)$$

where *ROW/K* is right-of-way costs as a fraction of construction costs, and the fractional variables, *CRS, CUC, FR, FSU*, and *FC* are as defined below equation (7), Standard errors are in parentheses below the estimates, but they are downward biased because, given our method of calculating *ROW/K* for each observation, we really have nine rather than 57 observations on the dependent variable.

Given estimates of lifetimes and interest rate, the construction and land acquisition costs we have estimated can be converted to annual rental rates, based on equation (1). The lifetimes assumed are 25 years for construction investments and infinity for land. The choice of interest rate is difficult, for there is little agreement among economists as to the

---

6. Land acquisition cost data come from California Department of Public Works (1968-72).

discount rate appropriate to public investments. We therefore base all our calculations on two alternative interest rates, 6 percent and 12 percent. The resulting rental costs, so calculated, are shown in table 2.

C. Maintenance Costs

To estimate these costs, basically the same sample was used as for construction costs (it was possible to include a few more stretches of road, however, making the total number of stretches in the sample 66). Maintenance costs were estimated for the year 1972, and the data were tabulated from state work-order records.[7] The following equation yielded the best results;

$$MC/LM = \$2,917 + \$0.00045 \ (V/L), \quad R^2 = .20, \quad (11)$$
$$(456) \quad (.00011)$$

where MC/LM is annual maintenance cost per lane-mile, and V/L is average annual vehicles per lane on the relevant stretch of road (it was impossible to discern different marginal maintenance costs for heavy commercial vehicles relative to autos).

Total capacity costs per lane-mile are tabulated in table 2. These provide the estimates of $\rho(w)$ needed to implement empirically the model developed in Section I.

III. Road Capacity Utilization and Travel Time: The Technological Relationship

The relationship between traffic speed and capacity utilization has been estimated under varying circumstances by traffic engineers; it is commonly called a speed-flow curve, graphing the average speed of traffic on the road against the flow of traffic on the road per unit of time (usually measured as a fraction of the ideal capacity of the road and called its volume-capacity ratio). These curves are a function of such things as maximum design speed of the road, weather, terrain, vehicle types, driving habits, and the number of interchanges which the road

---

7. These data are unpublished and come from state computer-tape records.

encounters over the observed stretch.

Since our concern is with passenger commutation, we are interested mainly in speed-flow curves for radial expressways representing typical deriving conditions in this area. To estimate such a curve, it is necessary to take observations of actual speeds and volume-capacity ratios at different times for such roads. The Institute of Transportation and Traffic Engineering (ITTE) has recently completed a large-scale study doing just that for a sample of Bay Area freeways.[8] The curves estimated by the ITTE are not, however, perfectly suited to our needs as they stand. They measure instantaneous speeds on each freeway, intentionally using "straight-pipe" segments and avoiding bottlenecks. This may be useful from an engineering viewpoint, where separate calculations can account for queuing behind bottlenecks, but we are concerned here with the effects of differing levels of capacity utilization over an entire trip.

Therefore, for each of three freeways in the Bay Area we reworked the ITTE data, calculating average speeds over trips of 5-15 miles and regressing them against average volume-capacity ratios over the same stretches. ("Capacity" here refers to an engineering standard carefully defined by the Highway Research Board [1965] and calculated for each freeway segment by the ITTE staff.) The observations on speeds and volume-capacity ratios were calculated for each of the following stretches of road: the Eastshore Freeway, San Pablo to Emeryville; the Bayshore Freeway, San Mateo to Daly City; and the Nimitz Freeway, Hayward to South Oakland (calculations were also done for the Bay Bridge, but it has certain unusual characteristics which gave us reason to exclude it here). For each of the three freeways, a quadratic equation of volume-capacity-ratio (V/C) as a function of speed (S) fit the data well (see fig. 1). Note specifically that both stems of the parabola fit the data well. The backward-bending portion is a result of stop-and-start driving at bottlenecks during congested periods, and its existence has been well documented theoretically and empirically in the literature (see, for example, Walters 1961).

The two roads which could most reasonably be called typical radial

---

8. Speed-flow data come from the following reports: Ybarra and May (1968, pp. 5-6, 22-23): Nimitz Freeway northbound, Hayward to S. Oakland, October 1 and November 1, 1967; Jacobs (January 1969, pp. 23-24, 34-35): Bayshore Freeway northbound, San Mateo to Daly City, November 14-16, 1967; and Jacobs (April 1969, pp. 25, 26-27): Eastshore Freeway southbound, San Pablo to Emeryville, April 25-28, 1968.

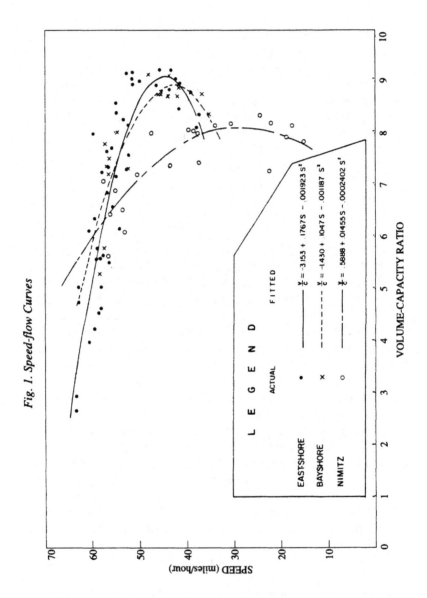

Fig. 1. Speed-flow Curves

SPEED (miles/hour)

VOLUME-CAPACITY RATIO

LEGEND

ACTUAL   FITTED

EAST-SHORE   • $\frac{v}{c} = -3.153 + .1767 S - .001923 S^2$

BAYSHORE   × $\frac{v}{c} = -1.430 + .1047 S - .001187 S^2$

NIMITZ   ○ $\frac{v}{c} = .5888 + .01455 S - .0002402 S^2$

commutation expressways are the Bayshore and the Eastshore. It is worth noting that the estimated speed-flow curves for each road are virtually identical, and it is most appropriate to use them in our calculations (the Nimitz would appear atypical in having more interchanges than the typical radial and also in having a disproportionate amount of trucks; these factors tend to congest it at traffic levels lower than the other two). For the two radials one might regard as typical, the ITTE studies on the East-shore contain more observations. We therefore use it in subsequent calculations. The details of the regression results for it are as follows:

$$V/C = -3.153 + 0.1757\,S - 0.001923\,S^2, \quad R^2 = .76. \qquad (12)$$
$$(0.791)\ (0.0311) \quad (0.000303)$$

Although the results based on this curve are not universally applicable, they should be suggestive for most radial expressways dealing mainly in automobile traffic and built with design speeds somewhere between 60 and 70 miles per hour.[9] In order to apply the curve to our model, we must choose a per lane capacity consistent with the definition used in deriving that curve and then adjust for autos-only traffic. The capacities calculated by the ITTE for the segments comprising the East-shore Freeway vary according to curves, grades, lane widths, and other factors; they averaged approximately 1,915 vehicles per hour per lane, including 4 percent trucks. Since one truck is equivalent to about two autos on level freeways (Highway Research Board 1965, p. 257), this converts to approximately 2,000 autos per lane per hour.

To convert this speed-flow curve to a relationship between volume and travel time per mile, we thus set $C = 2,000\,w$, where w is width in

---

9. It would be desirable to do alternative calculations for highways with design speeds other than 65 miles per hour, both because some downtown roads have lower design speeds and because of the 55-mile per hour speed limit which has been imposed more recently to save fuel. However, we do not have data for slower-moving roads save for the Bay Bridge, which is atypical for reasons given in the text, and the imposition of the 55-mile per hour speed limit is still so recent as to make extensive speed-flow data based on it unavailable. It would appear that the denominator of eq. (13) could be used for lower design speeds simply by reducing the intercept (46) by the reduction in the design speed minus 65 miles per hour. But the evidence on this is tentative, and other engineering evidence on the effects of differing design speeds is ambiguous, so we are not attempting to analyze the impact of differing design speeds on our analysis.

lanes in each direction, invert the upper portion of (12),[10] and take the reciprocal. The resulting travel time per mile is

$$T = \frac{1}{S} = \frac{1}{46 + \sqrt{2,111 - 520.1 \, [(V/C) + 3.153]}} \tag{13}$$

IV. The User Benefits and Costs of Speed

Faster travel confers benefits mainly because it saves time. But there are as well other highway travel costs which may vary with speed. More specifically, fuel consumption per mile (and certain related operation costs) decreases with speed starting with low speeds and then increases with high speeds.

Regarding fuel economy, the only recent field study of the relationship between fuel economy and freeway speed is that of Ybarra and May (1968). The estimated a quadratic relationship between speed and fuel economy, using a full-sized auto on California freeways. However, the curve they estimated was almost perfectly flat over any plausible range of optimal rush-hour speeds.[11] This means that in the present study optimization of speed with respect to fuel consumption is quite unlikely to be necessary. Furthermore, as Ybarra and May suggest, total operating costs are likely to be proportional to fuel consumption as a first approximation.

Thus, the only important way in which travel costs and highway speed are likely to be related for freeway travel is through the value of travel time. There is a vast literature on the theory and estimation of the value of travel time, and it is difficult to arrive at a single number for use in a given study.[12] However, based on traveler characteristics in the Bay Area and on the results of a number of studies (especially McFadden

---

10. That is, we take the positive root. The lower part (negative square root) describes the flow in queuing situations, with which we need not be concerned in a long-run optimization model, since this leg of the parabola represents the region of the production function where additional vehicles have a negative marginal product.

11. As is shown later, all the optimal rush-hour speeds found in this study range between levels of 42 and 58 miles per hour. Ybarra and May's equation yields a fuel economy of 22.34 miles per gallon of gasoline at 42 miles per hour and 22.39 miles per gallon at 58 miles per hour.

12. For surveys of much of the evidence to data on the value of travel time, see Harrison (1974, chap. 6).

1974), it is reasonable to assume that the value of in-vehicle auto travel time lies between $1.50 and $3.00 per hour per person. With an assumed average of 1.5 persons per vehicle,[13] this makes for a range of average time values between $2.25 and $4.50 per vehicle-hour. We shall do our calculations on the basis of these two alternative assumptions.

V. Demand and Peaking Characteristics

The most reliable data on hourly vehicle flows on California express-ways comes from the California Department of Public Works (1970), which takes counts at 17 points in the state. One such point is on U.S. 101, a major commutation route in San Rafael, a northern suburb, and we have used data from this route to calculate peaking characteristics on a representative commutation corridor. The results, shown in table 3, are shown in terms of a peaking ratio. This is simply the traffic per hour for each period and direction as a fraction of total average hourly traffic during the day (this average volume is defined as average daily volume in both directions divided by 48).

Peaking ratios are shown for major and minor directions over four periods: peak (7:00-8:00 A.M., 5:00-6:00 P.M.); near peak (6:00-7:00 and 8:00-9:00 A.M., 4:00-5:00 and 6:00-7:00 P.M.); daytime (9:00 A.M.-4:00 P.M.); and night (7:00 P.M.-6:00 A.M.). The data collected are representative of a typical weekday; none were collected for week-ends. This is not a serious problem, except that the assumption that there is zero traffic volume during the weekend will result in upward-biased estimates of optimal tolls during weekday periods. To compensate for this, it is not an unreasonable guess to assume hat overall, daily traffic on weekends is more or less the same as on weekdays.[14] The traffic on weekends, however, is likely to be spread out more evenly than on weekdays, except for a few shorter peaks. To account for such peaks,

---

13. Using data for the San Francisco Bay Area, McFadden (1974) finds a value of invehi-cle time of about $1.60 per person-hour. Also, using Bay Area data, Chan (1974) finds a value of in-vehicle time of $3.14 per hour, using a somewhat different specifi-cation of the model.

14. For California roads as a whole, weekend traffic is higher than weekday traffic (see California Department of Public Works [1970], blue section of appendix). However, this probably reflects patterns on intercity roads more than urban ones.

Table 3. Weekday Peaking Characteristics on Typical
Bay Area Expressway, 1967

Time Period	Length (Hours)	Definition (Actural Time)	Peaking Ratio	
			Major Direction	Minor Direction
Peak..............	2	7:00–8:00 A.M. 5:00–6:00 P.M.	3.0	1.15
Near peak	4	6:00–7:00, 8:00–9:00 A.M. 4:00–5:00, 6:00–7:00 P.M.	2.1	1.15
Day................	7	9:00 A.M.–4:00 P.M.	1.5	1.15
Night	11	7:00 P.M.–6:00 A.M.	0.4	0.4

Sources: Calculated from California Department of Public Works 1970.

Table 4. Assumed Distribution of Peaking Ratios

Period	Peaking Ratio $(X_t/\overline{X})$	Peaking Ratio as Fraction of Highest Peaking Ratio (X_t/X_1)	Hours per week Assumed in Each Direction $(n_t/52)$	Hours per week as Multiple of Peak Hours (n_t/n_1)
1..............	3.0	1.00	6.0	1.00
2..............	2.1	0.70	10.0	1.67
3..............	1.50	0.50	42.5	7.08
4..............	1.15	0.383	32.5	5.41
5..............	0.40	0.133	77.0	12.83

Sources : Calculated from table 3, plus assumptions discussed in the text.

we assume that each weekend has a single 1-hour peak each way with a peaking ratio of 3.0, the same as for a weekday rush hour. Furthermore, we assume that weekend-nights have traffic levels equivalent to those of weekday nights, for a peaking ratio of about 0.4. The peaking ration for the rest of the day during weekend periods is found by allocating remaining traffic evenly over the remaining time. This gives a peaking ratio of 1.5 in both directions for weekend daytime periods.

On the basis of the evidence and assumptions presented, it is possible to estimate the total distribution of traffic over a typical 1-week period.

In table 4, the total assumed hours per week for each peaking ratio are set forth. Also, peaking ratios for each period are calculated as a fraction of the ratio for the peak period, and the hours per week for each ratio are calculated as a multiple of the hours per week for the peak period. This estimated distribution is used in the following section to calculate optimal tolls and utilization rates.

VI. The Complete Model

We are now ready to pull together the strands of the previous sections, adapting the theoretical model developed in Section I to make it tractable with the empirical evidence assembled. The peak-load pricing and investment model will be optimized with empirical data in two steps. First, an optimal investment policy is developed, so that, for any given traffic level, total costs (agency plus user costs, peak and off-peak) are minimized according to equation (5). This yields estimates of optimal volume-capacity ratios as a function of lane capacity costs and time values. Second, once these optimal volume-capacity ratios have been calculated, the optimal long-run price for each period is determined.

A. Optimization of Capacity

As previously stated, we are including for optimization only those costs which vary with capacity utilization. These costs fall into two categories: time costs and fixed lane capacity costs. Costs of each are normalized to represent 1 mile's worth of travel over a given road type. Therefore, total time costs in a given period will be total traffic volume per unit of time, $\times$ the value of time, $\div$ by the speed (which is in turn a function of traffic flow, as estimated earlier). Capacity costs are the costs per mile shown in table 1. Therefore, the equation to be minimized, the sum of costs over all periods in the year, will be

$$TC = \sum_{t=1}^{5} \frac{Vn_t X_t}{46 + \sqrt{471 - 0.260\,(X_t/w)}} + Aw, \qquad (14)$$

where TC is total annual costs to be minimized, X_t is the one-directional hourly volume of traffic during each of the five periods indexed by t (described in the previous section), n_t is the total number of hours of the year during which flow X_t prevails, w is the width of the road in lanes in each direction, V is the value of time per vehicle-hour, and A is the estimated annual rental of a unit of lane capacity, as calculated in table 1.

In table 4, each X_t was shown as a fraction of X_1 and each n_t as a fraction of n_1. Since each of the fractions is assumed to be constant, we can then write the entire expression as a function of X_1. From table 4, we find that $n_1 = 6$ hours per week, or 312 hours per year; also, to simplify, let $x = X_1/w$. Then, using the fractions in table 4, (14) can be rewritten:

$$\frac{TC}{312X_1} = V \sum_{t=1}^{5} \frac{(n_t/n_1)\,(X_t/X_1)}{46 + \sqrt{471 - 0.260\,(X_t/X_1)x}} + \frac{A}{312x}. \quad (15)$$

It will be noted now that total cost (for all periods) per rush-hour vehicle-mile is a function of one variable and two parameters. The variable (x) is peak-hour traffic per lane-hour, and the parameters are the value of time (V), and the cost of a unit of lane capacity (A), Given available estimates of the parameters, it is possible to minimize system costs by minimizing (15). The minimization process was done numerically,[15] with the alternative parameter values previously discussed.

The results, shown in table 5, are generally consistent with what the economic theory of production says they should be: for example, an increase in the value of time reduces the optimal capacity utilization. The optimal speeds for each period implicit in the results are also shown in table 5. Not surprisingly, optimal speed rises with the value of time and falls with higher interest costs. It is also lower during rush hour than at other times.

B. Calculation of Optimal Long-Run Tolls

As was shown in Section I, the optimal congestion toll in each period is the difference between short-run marginal cost and short-run average cost. In the case of the present model, it will be recalled that the short-run average variable cost (exclusive of variable costs unrelated to capacity utilization) is

---

15. The optimization work was done with the FCDPAK program, on the University of California, Berkeley, CDC 6400 computer.

$$C_t = \frac{V}{46 + \sqrt{471 - 0.26 \, (X_t/w)}} \tag{16}$$

Therefore, the optimal capacity-related toll is

$$T_t = \frac{\partial C_t}{\partial X_t} \, X_t = 0.13V \left(\frac{X_t}{w}\right) \left[471 - 0.26 \left(\frac{X_t}{w}\right) \right]^{-1/2}$$
$$\times \left\{ 46 + \left[471 - 0.26 \left(\frac{X_t}{w}\right) \right]^{1/2} \right\}^{-2} \tag{17}$$

Estimates of the optimal tolls, based on this equation, are shown in table 5. The most striking thing about these results is the high level of the optimal peak tolls. With a 6 percent interest rate, they range from about 3 cents per vehicle-mile in the least-populated areas, to about 15 cents per vehicle-mile in Oakland and San Francisco. At a 12 percent interest rate, they range from 5 to 6 cents in rural areas up to 27-34 cents per mile in the more densely populated central city areas.

The other striking thing about the peak tools is their relationship to the assumed value of time. One would expect that a lower value of time would lead to lower toll. That is true for all the off-peak periods. But for the peak periods we get the paradoxical result (except for one case) that a lower time value *increases* the optimal peak toll. This is not so surprising as it might first seem. A lower time value means it is preferable to build fewer lanes and allow them to be more congested during each period. Given the shape of the speed-flow curve, if we allow the road to get more congested during all periods it is possible that the lower time value could cause congestion during the peak period to rise so much as to increase the optimal long-run peak toll, despite the lower time value.

C. The Effects of "Demand Spreading" Induced by Peak-Load Pricing

The result presented so far are based on the (unrealistic) assumption that the cross-elasticity between peak and off-peak demand travel is zero. Because no estimates of intertemporal cross-elasticities of demand exist, it is not possible to determine with any degree of rigor the equilibrium solution, given intertemporal demand spreading. Nevertheless, it is possible to make some intelligent guesses as to the likely effects of demand spreading on prices. For purposes of sensitivity testing, the cal-

Table 5. Results of Model: Optimal Speeds, Utilization Rates, and Capacity-Related Tolls

Road Type and Cost Assumption	Period 1			Period 2		Period 3		Period 4		Period5	
	Flow*	Speed	Toll†	Speed	Toll†	Speed	Toll†	Speed	Toll†	Speed	Toll†
Rural-suburban:											
6% interest:											
V = 4.50‡	1,427	56.0	2.7	60.5	1.1	62.9	0.6	64.1	0.4	66.5	0.1
V = 2.25‡	1,681	51.8	3.1	58.9	0.8	61.9	0.4	63.4	0.3	66.3	0.1
12% interest:											
V = 4.50	1,645	52.6	5.3	59.1	1.5	62.0	0.8	63.5	0.5	66.4	0.1
V = 2.25	1,775	49.1	6.9	58.2	0.9	61.5	0.4	63.2	0.3	66.2	0.1
Urban-suburban:											
6% interest:											
V = 4.50‡	1,512	54.8	3.3	60.0	1.2	62.6	0.7	63.9	0.5	66.5	0.1
V = 2.25‡	1,726	50.7	4.2	58.5	0.8	61.7	0.4	63.3	0.3	66.3	0.1
12%interest:											
V = 4.50	1,700	51.4	7.0	58.7	1.6	61.8	0.8	63.4	0.5	66.3	0.1
V = 2.25	1,789	48.5	9.1	58.1	0.9	61.4	0.5	63.1	0.3	66.2	0.1
Central city:											
6% interest:											
V = 4.50‡	1,777	49.0	14.5	58.2	1.8	61.5	0.9	63.1	0.6	66.2	0.2
V = 2.25‡	1,805	47.4	17.4	57.9	0.9	61.4	0.5	63.1	0.3	66.2	0.1
12%interest:											
V = 4.50	1,803	47.5	31.0	58.0	1.8	61.4	0.9	63.1	0.6	66.2	0.2
V = 2.25	1,810	46.7	34.3	57.9	0.9	61.4	0.5	63.1	0.3	66.2	0.1

Source: See text.
* Vehicle-miles per peak-period lane-hour.
† Capacity-related toll is in cents per vehicle-mile
‡ Value of time in dollars per vehicle-hour.

culations of the preceding two sections were redone based on the alternative assumption that peak-load pricing will, in equilibrium, cause rush-hour demand to spread itself evenly over the entire "peak" and "near-peak" periods, as described in table 4. Thus, in periods 1 and 2 in table 4 traffic is assumed to be of equal amount during each hour, with the same total amount of traffic over the entire period as assumed before. For all other periods, peaking patterns are assumed to be the same as before.

The results, shown in table 6, are consistent with what one would expect: tolls during the near-peak period rise, and tolls during what was previously the peak hour decline. But they still remain high, relative to any user charges paid by most U.S. commuters; they range from 2 to 3 cents per vehicle-mile on rural-suburban roads up to 6-13 cents on central city roads. Furthermore, it is worth noting that the paradoxical relationship noted before between the value of time and the optimal rush-hour toll persists: for all but two combinations of interest rate, road type, and time value, a lower value of time leads to a higher peak (and near-peak) toll. This suggests that this result is not a fluke.

D. Other Public Costs of Auto Transportation

Optimal user tolls for auto transport should include not only the capacity-related congestion costs mentioned in the previous sections but also the marginal costs of other government-provided services to highway users which vary not with capacity, but directly with use. Also, some measure of net externality cost should be included. Estimation of appropriate marginal cost figures for these variables is imprecise, and the figures which we suggest here have a higher variance than the ones just presented for capacity-related tolls.

As regards local government services whose costs should be expected to vary with auto use, there are many categories in addition to the two obvious ones, police and highway administration. In addition, these costs could include portions of the budgets for city planning, electricity, public health, coroner, city attorney, district attorney, municipal court, superior court, juvenile court, and fire department. It is not possible to determine what portions of these costs are variable with auto use, but in a previous paper (Keeler, Cluff, and Small 1974) we have estimated the average cost for these services relating to autos at $0.0045 per vehicle-

Table 6. Results with Spread-Out Peak

Road Type, Cost Assumption	Periods 1–2			Period 3		Period 4		Period5	
	Flow*	Speed	Toll†	Speed	Toll†	Speed	Toll†	Speed	Toll†
Rural-suburban:									
6% interest:									
V = 4.50‡	1,214	58.5	1.7	62.8	0.6	64.1	0.4	66.5	0.1
V = 2.25‡	1,489	55.2	1.6	61.5	0.5	63.1	0.3	66.2	0.1
12% interest:									
V = 4.50	1,442	55.8	2.8	61.7	0.8	63.3	0.6	66.3	0.2
V = 2.25	1.662	52.2	2.9	60.6	0.5	62.5	0.4	66.0	0.1
Urban-suburban:									
6% interest:									
V = 4.50	1,296	57.6	2.0	62.4	0.7	63.8	0.5	66.4	0.1
V = 2.25	1,558	45.1	1.9	61.1	0.5	62.3	0.3	66.1	0.1
12% interest:									
V = 4.50	1,516	54.8	3.4	61.3	0.9	63.0	0.6	66.2	0.2
V = 2.25	1,705	51.3	3.6	60.4	0.6	62.4	0.4	66.0	0.1
Central city:									
6% interest:									
V = 4.50	1,670	52.1	5.9	60.5	1.1	62.5	0.7	66.0	0.2
V = 2.25	1,771	49.3	6.6	60.0	0.6	62.1	0.4	65.9	0.1
12% interest:									
V = 4.50	1,763	49.6	11.7	60.0	1.2	62.2	0.8	65.9	0.2
V = 2.25	1,799	47.8	12.8	59.8	0.6	62.0	0.4	65.9	0.1

Source: See text.
* Vehicle-miles per peak-period lane-hour.
†Capacity-related toll is in cents per vehicle-mile
‡Value of time in dollars per vehicle-hour.

mile in the Bay Area.[16] To the extent that there are no economies or dis-economies of scale in the production of these services, this figure would be a reasonable estimate of the marginal cost of an auto-mile for such services. But is must be emphasized that the estimates are rough.

Externality costs are even more difficult to measure than public service costs; nevertheless, it is worth making a guess as to their size. Valu-

---

16. The 1974 paper in turn draws on Lee (1972) for some of its figures, although our esti-mates are generally more conservative than his.

ing illness and death from pollution at foregone wages and hospital bills, Small (1975) has calculated the cost of auto emissions in California urban areas at about 0.8 cents per vehicle-mile for an average-aged auto in 1974. Because of lower auto use and different meteorological conditions in other U.S. cities, the cost outside California should be lower— about 0.15 cents per auto-mile in a typical urban area. Furthermore, as older, uncontrolled autos are retired, total pollution costs should decline. Thus, a 1974 model auto in California had emissions costs of only 0.6 cents per vehicle-mile in that year, and a post-1977 auto should have costs well below 0.2 cents per vehicle-mile in California and no more than 0.03 cents outside California. The optimal toll for pollution costs is therefore likely to vary considerably depending on the situation. Suffice it to say that for now in California, autos 2 or more years old should be paying considerable tolls (0.5-1.0 cent per mile) to cover the costs of their effluents. But this problem should diminish in importance over time, assuming that emissions control devices perform as expected, and assuming future standards are not further delayed.

Overall, then, the total public costs which should be included in auto tolls would seem to range somewhere between 0.5 and 1.5 cents per vehicle-mile, depending on the considerations mentioned above.

However, the externality costs connected with highways could conceivably be offset, at least to some extent, by externality benefits. Strotz (1964) has shown that under not-too-implausible assumptions the spatial externality benefits of a transportation network can justify subsidization of it, even with constant returns to scale. The fact that such externality benefits could offset the externality costs mentioned makes the estimates given in this subsection all the more tentative. Nevertheless, the cost figures presented here are worth knowing, rough as they may be, and it must be remembered that the pollution costs are on the conservative side, valuing human life and health at no more than hospital bills plus foregone wages. It would thus require considerable externality benefits to offset these costs.

VII. Actual versus Optimal User Charges

The results of the previous three section would imply that optimal tolls charged to expressway user in the Bay Area, assuming optimal expansion of the system, should range somewhere from below 1 cent per vehicle-mile for off-peak periods up to rush-hour tolls of 2-7 cents on rural roads, 2-9 cents on suburban roads, and 6-35 cents on downtown roads. Do these results imply that roads are subsidized and/or overused?

Let us consider first the issue of subsidies. The typical auto in the Bay Area in 1972 paid user charges of 1.15 cents per vehicle-mile (Keeler et al. 1974, p. 31). This would imply that while night users are paying at least as much as they should, rush hour (and even near-peak) users are not paying tolls nearly so high as they ought to pay. Furthermore, it is worth noting from table 6 that even with considerable spreading of the peak, rush-hour tolls would still be considerably higher than they now are on most roads. In this sense, it can be said that commuter auto traffic is being subsidized.

But it does not follow from this that peak-hour auto service is being overused and should be contracted. It is true that the higher user tolls suggested here could raise toll costs considerably for commuters. However, the higher tolls would be accompanied by a much higher service quality than now exists on many routes, and it is quite conceivable that raising tolls to the levels suggested here *and* adjusting capacity to achieve the prescribed service levels could actually reduce trip costs and increase demand.[17]

Whether this actually will occur depends on how congested Bay Area freeways are during rush-hour periods. If they are so congested as to be at or near the backward-bending segment in figure 1, it is possible that higher user tolls will result in lower trip costs. Resources are not available to investigate this issue for all roads, studied, but some relevant figures are available for the year 1972 for the Eastshore Freeway, whose speed-flow curve was used for our earlier calculations on the grounds that it is likely to be fairly typical. (Details of these calculations are not

---

17. Unlike the case of a short-run congestion toll model, the present model does not achieve higher service qualities by "tolling off" some travelers from the road. Ir can do so by expanding road capacity, as well.

shown here for lack of space, but may be found in Keeler et al. 1975, p. 53). The results for this road indicate an ambiguous answer which depends on the interest rate and time value assumed: for a 12 percent interest rate, at either time value, full trip costs would rise on the East-shore Freeway under a regime of optimal pricing and investment relative to what they are now. In the case of a 6 percent interest rate, however, the result is dependent on the time value assumed. With $4.50 per hour time value, full costs would decline. With $2.25 value, they would rise. For three of the four combinations, full costs would rise, then, and for one, they would fall. But in every case, the costs of higher tolls would be to some degree offset by the benefits of a much better service quality.

VIII. Policy Implications and the Feasibility of Change

The results of this work have important implications for public policy. The most important result is that, unless Bay Area roads are grossly overbuilt, peak tolls of considerable amounts (ranging from 2 to 35 cents per vehicle-mile) should be imposed on Bay Area freeway commuters.

Previous studies of optimal short-run congestion tolls (as opposed to the long-run ones estimated here) for urban highways have generally arrived at similar conclusions—that urban freeways are underpriced during peak periods.[18]

Such conclusions have, however, incurred some significant objections, and it is worth considering these objections here to examine the extent to which our results are subject to the same criticisms.

The first objection is that, while optimal short-run tolls may be very high, that is strictly a sign of underbuilding of the freeway network; if long-run expansion policies were pursued, there would be no need for such high peak tolls. Our results show that these objections are not valid, at least for the San Francisco Bay Area.

Another objection to high peak tolls is that they discriminate against those with low time values.[19] Our results, however, show that with optimal long-run investment, the appropriate peak toll is not very sensitive

---

18. See, for example, Vickrey (1963) and Walters (1961).
19. See, for example, Nichols, Smolensky, and Tideman (1971).

to the assumed value of time; in fact, a reduction in time value actually *increases* the optimal peak toll. (Those who argue that higher time values necessitate higher peak tolls are thinking of a short-run model, where capacity is fixed; it remains true, however, that total toll revenues, over both peak and off-peak periods, will rise with an increase in the value of time.) In any event, inefficient road user charges represent a peculiar method of redistributing income.

Third, objections have been raised to short-run peak tolls because they will result in excessive profits for road authorities; even some proponents of such optimal tolls have suggested that they be returned to motorists through a lump-sum redistribution of some sort. But, on the basis of the evidence presented here, it would seem that the sum of tolls collected over all periods will just cover the cost of the road system and supporting services. To return such revenues to motorists would conflict with the reasonable principle of equity that people should pay for what they use.

A final objection to high peak user tolls on expressways regards technical feasibility. One feasible way of charging such tolls is by way of booths at interchanges, though it may be that more sophisticated metering devices are cheaper. It has been objected, however, that higher expressway tolls will induce more motorists to take parallel arterial streets, congesting them badly, and it is much harder to collect optimal tolls on these roads. Our result indicate that this problem is not likely to be an important one in the long run. The reason, simply, is that the service qualities accompanying the tolls proposed here are so much higher than those offered by rush-hour arterials that even motorists with low time values are likely to choose the tollway.

To see this, consider a numerical example: for the sake of argument, we analyze this issue with the lower-bound time value of $2.25 per hour. Let us suppose that, at existing levels of congestion, it is possible to travel during rush hour at an average speed of 15 miles per hour using arterials for the entire distance. Time cost will then be $0.15 per vehicle-mile. Adding on existing user charges would make total user-perceived costs (exclusive of auto ownership and operation) greater than $0.16 per mile.[20] However, for an urban-suburban freeway, the optimal long-run user cost (including time and tolls) is $0.086-$0.138 per mile, plus exter-

---

20. To get this, we simply add the 1.15 cents per mile user charge (mentioned above) to the time cost figure of 15 cents per mile.

nal and maintenance costs, depending on the interest rates. [21] With a higher time value, the tollway has an even greater advantage.[22] Admittedly, freeway travel usually necessitates some circuity not accounted for here; furthermore, on the most expensive of downtown expressways, optimal tolls could certainly be considerably higher than the ones shown here (although in these rare instances, average rush-hour street speeds are likely to be considerably slower than 15 miles per hour even now). The point is that the optimal tolls suggested here, combined with optimal service levels, are unlikely to result in a significant increase in congestion on parallel arterials, even assuming that pricing these arterials optimally is impossible.

In short, most objections raised to high peak tolls on urban expressways would seem to have questionable content when made to a long-run optimal toll scheme as proposed here.

The upshot of all the discussion and evidence presented in the paper is that higher peak charges (combined with higher service levels) are both feasible and desirable for Bay Area roads. Admittedly, there may be political obstacles to such tolls, but the more general understanding there is of the benefits of such tolls, the more feasible they will be. It is hoped that this paper has contributed to such an understanding.

References

California Department of Public Works, Division of Highways. *1967 Classified Vehicle Study.* Sacramento: California Dept. Public Works, December 1970.

――――. *Statistical Supplement of the Annual Report of the Department of Public Works Pertaining to the Division of Highways.* Sacramento: California Dept. Public Works, 1947-72.

Chan, L.K.P. "Derivation of a Distribution for the Marginal Value of

---

21. These time costs, plus user charges, are calculated from the optimal speeds and tolls in table 1, for an urban-suburban freeway, with a time value of $2.25.

22. This raises the interesting question as to why more urban expressways are not tollways, especially given that such tollways have been successful in large cities when no freeways were competing with them (consider, for example, the Massachusetts Turnpike in Boston). The answer to this question is outside the scope of this paper, but it is an interesting one and one worthy of further research.

Commutation Time." Mimeographed. Univ. California, Berkeley, September 1974.

Fitch, L., and Associates. *Urban Transportation and Public Policy.* San Francisco: Chandler, 1964.

Harrison, A.J. *The Economics of Transport Appraisal.* New York: Wiley, 1974.

Highway Research Board. *Special Report 87: Highway Capacity Manual.* Washington: Highway Res. Board, 1965.

Jacobs, R. "Interim Reports." In *Bay Area Freeway Operations Study.* Berkeley: Inst. Transportation & Traffic Engineering, January and March 1969.

Joseph. H. "construction Costs of Urban Freeways." *CATS Research News 4* (December 16, 1960).

Keeler, T.; Cluff, G.; and Small, K. "On the Average Costs of Automobile Transportation in the San Francisco Bay Area." Mimeographed. Univ. California, Berkeley, April 1974.

Keeler, T.; Small, K.; Cluff, G.; and Finke, J. "Optimal Peakload Pricing, Investment, and Service Levels on Urban Expressways." Working Paper no. 253, Inst. Urban and Regional Development, Univ. California, Berkeley, 1975.

Lee, D. "The Costs of Private Automobile Usage to the City of San Fransisco." Working Paper 171/BART 6. Inst. Urban and Regional Development, Univ. California, Berkeley, 1972.

McFadden, D. "The measurement of Urban Travel Demand." Working Paper no. 227, Inst. Urban and Regional Development, Univ. California, Berkeley, 1974.

Malinvaud, E. *The Statistical Theory of Econometrics.* Amsterdam: North-Holland, 1970.

Meyer, J.; Kain, J.; Wohl, M. *The Urban Transportation Problem.* Cambridge, Mass.: Harvard Univ. Press, 1965.

Mohring , H. "The Peak Load Problem with Increasing Returns and Pricing Constraints." *A.E.R.* 60, no. 4 (September 1970); 693-705.

Mohring. H., and Harwitz, M. *Highway Benefits; An Analytical Framework.* Evanston, Ill.: Northwestern Univ. Press, 1962.

Neutze, G. "Investment Criteria and Road Pricing." *Manchester School of Economic and Social Studies* 34 (January 1966): 63-73.

Nichols, D.; Smolensky, E.; and Tideman, N. "Discrimination by Waiting Time in Merit Goods." *A.E.R* 61(June 1971): 312-23.

Small, K. "Estimating the Air Pollution Costs of Transportation Modes" working Paper no. 261, Inst. Urban and Regional Development, Univ. California, Berkeley, 1975.

Strotz, R. "Urban Transportation Parables." In *The Public Economy of Urban Communities*, edited by J. Margolis. Baltimore; Johns Hopkins Press, 1964.

Vickrey, W. "Pricing in Urban and Suburban Transport." *A.E.R.* 53 (May 1963): 452-65.

Walters, A. "The Theory and Measurement of Private and Social Cost of Highway Congestion." *Econometrica* 29 (October 1961): 676-99.

_____. *The Economics of Road User Charges*. Baltimore: Johns Hopkins Press (for the World Bank), 1968.

Ybarra, W., and May, A. "Interim Report." In *Bay Area Freeway Operations Study*. Berkeley: Inst. Transportation & Traffic Engineering, June 1968.

PART V

MARKET STRUCTURE, REGULA
AND DEREGULATION

CHAPTER 19

QUALITY COMPETITION, INDUSTRY EQUILIBRIUM AND EFFICIENCY IN THE PRICE-CONSTRAINED AIRLINE MARKET*

*George W. Douglas and James C. Miller III***

Recent literature on regulated markets has focused on the ramifications of controlling price as a means of regulating a monopolist's rate of return.[1] There exist, however, a great variety of regulated *competitive* markets where the implications of price control are qualitatively different. That is, while the control of price to restrain a monopolist's profit rate may affect the technical efficiency of its production of a specifically defined output, the implications of price restraints in nonmonopoly markets are more typically manifested in the overall *quality* level of the output, an issue of allocative efficiency. There are many examples of such regulated markets (and imperfect private cartels) which, although price constrained, reach an equilibrium through vigorous nonprice competition which bids away most or all implicit rents. In these markets the

* Reprinted from *The American Economic Review*, Vol. 64, No.4, Sep. 1974, pp.657-669.
** Associate professors of economics, University of North Carolina at Chapel Hill and Texas A&M University, respectively. We gratefully acknowledge helpful comments from John Evans, an anonymous referee, and others. A portion of this research was supported by the Brookings Institution.
1. See the concise literature summary contained in William Baumol and Alvin Klevorick 2.

existence of rents (or the regulator's control of rents) is more directly related to the nature of restraints on entry rather than to the control of price. Examples include commercial banking, stock brokerage, real estate brokerage, motor trucking, taxicab service, and, of particular interest here, air transportation.

By describing industry equilibrium in these nonmonopoly markets one can identify an endogenous relationship between the regulated price and the overall general quality level of the output. For many of these markets a viable, zero-rent equilibrium can obtain over a wide range of prices, each defining implicitly an endogenous quality level. Hence, regulators indirectly control quality by the selection of the price parameter. Neither efficient costs nor optimal prices can be defined without reference to this price-quality relationship. While regulators may attempt to control tangible aspects of output quality by direct fiat, the endogenous quality determined in equilibrium is not usually amenable to direct control, if it is perceived at all. Complicating this process is the difficulty of finding an appropriate, measurable proxy for the quality dimension involved.

Equilibrium in the domestic airline markets under Civil Aeronautics Board (*CAB* or Board) regulation typifies this phenomenon and illustrates the rather wide divergence between actual and efficient prices and quality levels that may obtain under regulation. Although entry restraints have insulated the trunk carriers from new firm competition and at present the typical city-pair market is served by only a relatively small number of firms, vigorous nonprice competition has prevented the carriers from obtaining the rents which are potentially available in the regulated price structure. On the one hand, the carriers compete in the traditional, highly visible forms of nonprice rivalry such as advertising and the provision of passenger amenities. But of far greater significance in terms of per passenger cost is their use of scheduling competition in establishing market shares. While analytically similar to advertising competition, scheduling competition has a fundamental role in determining a basic characteristic of service quality in the scheduled system.[2]

---

2. The role of scheduling competition in determining equilibrium in this market has been noted by various writers, including Arthur De Vany (1968), George Eads, Miller (1969), Lawrence White, and Joseph Yance (1972). In this paper we formalize the relationship and develop the quantitative implications for service quality arising from the regulated fare.

By its very nature, scheduled transportation is nearly always characterized by some excess supply, or slack capacity. Slack capacity arises from several sources. Supply (capacity) is produced in discrete units and cannot be stored, while demand is a flow which fluctuates seasonally and stochastically. Moreover, as supply is augmented on any given route, service convenience is enhanced by the more frequent departures and the greater likelihood of the potential passenger's obtaining a seat on the preferred flight. The significance of scheduling competition among the carriers then is its effect on the system's overall level of service convenience. Since the relative slack capacity associated with equilibrium is related to the regulated price, the description of airline costs, and the selection of an efficient price level and structure require an assessment of the relationships among slack capacity, passenger costs, and overall service quality.[3] In this paper we describe and attempt to quantify these relationships, suggest the optimal level and structure of air fares, and contrast this estimated efficient solution with the market equilibrium now obtaining under regulation.

I. Quality Competition and Airline Market Equilibrium

A. The Demand for Airline Services

The demand for air travel in any market (i.e., point A to point B) can be regarded as a flow over time which fluctuates seasonally (given the time structure of prices) and stochastically. Thus, the time of consumption is a significant dimension in the definition of scheduled travel output. The expected volume of demand over any reference time period depends, as usual, on the price (fare) and the tangible aspects of quality, such as (expected) en route time, comfort, etc. But while demand arises continuously over time, any scheduled system provides capacity at discrete intervals in lumpy units; hence, most travellers must depart at a

---

3. The recent airline cost study by Theodore Keeler is a case in point. Since the cost per passenger carried varies markedly with the average load factor realized, the estimates of "efficient," cost-based fares depend crucially on the hypothesized load factor of an efficient system. We indicate in this paper why it is inappropriate to extrapolate the quasi-competitive load factors of the California intrastate markets as an efficient norm for all markets.

time other than that which is the most preferred.[4] The degree to which these discrete units of supply are matched with the continuous demand may be regarded as the "convenience" of the scheduled system. Such convenience, of course, is a highly significant determinant of total airline demand, particularly in markets where reasonably close substitutes exist. Convenience, moreover can be measured. We shall define *schedule delay* as the absolute difference between the passenger's most preferred departure time and that of his actual departure. (Thus our inconvenience measure accounts for passengers who find they must revise their preferred plans and choose either to advance their departure or delay it.)[5] Then for any equilibrium of a scheduled system, there will exist a distribution of schedule delays. An expected value of this distribution—expected schedule delay per passenger—serves as a proxy for the overall level of service convenience.[6]

Let us denote the demand for scheduled air services in a specific market as:

$$N = N(P, T, X) \qquad (1)$$

where

N = number of air passenger trips demanded per time period
P = average fare
T = expected schedule delay per passenger (i.e., (in)convenience)
X = vector of tangible aspects of service quality

Note, however, that expected schedule delay is not an exogenous variable controlled directly by any firm (in nonmonopoly markets), but is an

---

4. Herein lies the *raison d tre* for the institution of scheduled transportation: while demand for travel originates continuously over time and space, aggregation of demand over these dimensions is necessary to exploit the considerable economies of transport with respect to vehicle size and utilization.

5. Since a priori we do not know whether travellers are symmetric in their time preferences (i.e., whether on balance they view equally an adjustment to an earlier or later departure time), we shall weigh them equally per time period expended.

6. We note that schedule delay is not the only type of delay impacting on overall service quality. Certainly delays in departure, in receiving on-board services, in arrival, and in baggage claim are important. In this analysis we treat these delays as exogenous. Since reductions in such delays (or their expected value) are a means of nonprice competition, their overall levels could be treated in a way similar to the scheduling competition discussed here.

outcome of the market equilibrium. That is, schedule delay is related to the total frequency of departures in the market and to their timing. Moreover, it is also related to the probability of being unable to obtain a seat on a scheduled flight. Since demand is stochastic, we observe a typical queuing phenomenon, in which the probability of obtaining accommodation on the convenient departure flight depends on the market equilibrium's level of slack capacity, the dispersion of the demand, and the schedule frequency.[7]

Although we will describe the process more completely below, we can express the implied delay relationship generally as

$$T = T(N, \sigma_N, F, S) \qquad (2)$$

where

$T =$ expected schedule delay per passenger
   (for example, in minutes)
$N =$ number of passenger-trips demanded per time period
$\sigma_N =$ dispersion of demand
$F =$ total flight frequency
$S =$ average aircraft capacity

A priori, expected schedule delay per passenger would have the following qualitative relationships with the independent variables:

$$\partial T/\partial N > 0, \quad \partial T/\partial \sigma_N > 0,$$
$$\partial T/\partial F < 0, \quad \partial T/\partial s < 0,$$

We might suppose that the stochastic nature of demand generation for a given market would allow us to express as a function:

$$\sigma_N = \sigma_N (N) \qquad (3)$$

By substituting equations (2) and (3) into the demand equation (1), we obtain the following demand expression:

---

7. We do not infer that travellers actually form a queue in the terminal. The phenomenon is similar, however, even with the existing reservation process. Stochastic fluctuations result in excess demand for some flights, and some travellers must displace their departure time from the most preferred. Alternatively, we could measure the phenomenon as the advance time required to obtain a reservation with some arbitrarily specified level of certainty.

$$N = G(P, F, S, X) \tag{4}$$

B. The Cost of Producing Airline Services

For practical purposes, airline total costs can be dichotomized into the cost of providing capacity on a route, and the cost of providing passenger services. (See Miller (1972), pp. 224-28, and our 1974 paper, ch. 2.) Firm i costs may be written.[8]

$$
\begin{aligned}
C_i &= C_i(N_i, F_i, S_i, X) \\
&= f_i(F_i, S_i) + g_i(N_i, X)
\end{aligned}
\tag{5}
$$

To analyze equilibrium under nonprice (scheduling) competition, it is convenient to assume that for a specific market the selection of aircraft size is exogenous.[9] Moreover, a number of cross-section studies of airline costs suggest that there are no scale economies associated with firm size.[10] This allows us to rewrite cost function (5) as

$$C_i = cN_i + kF_i \tag{6}$$

where c and k are both constants.

C. The Nature of Regulatory Restraints

Although the Board has never allowed the entry of a new trunk carri-

---

8. Note that we have not made X a firm variable. There are several reasons why we might make this simplifying assumption. First, some dimensions of service-amenity competition come under direct CAB regulation (for example, "free" drinks). Second, there exists little real difference among carriers regarding the passenger amenities offered. Finally (and in partial explanation of the second reason), one observes typically that the extent of passenger service amenities varies closely with the extent of scheduling competition (i.e., both are means of attracting passengers). In short, it would appear that in price-restrained "competitive" markets, firms are "quality takers."

9. While aircraft size is endogenous to the overall equilibrium, the interdependence of production across markets served would tend to diminish the influence of specific markets. Rather, carrier fleets typically contain a small number of aircraft types, each of which dominates in certain classes of markets.

10. Studies by Richard Caves; Eads, Marc Nerlove, and William Raduchel; Mahlon Straszheim; and Miller (1970) indicate that average costs of the airline firms are not significantly related to the firm's level of aggregate output. One cannot infer from these studies, however, that scale economies do not exist in specific city-pair markets.

er, it has allowed the entry of several classes of carriers which now (to varying extent) compete with the trunks (for example, the local service carriers). More importantly for our purposes here, the Board has certificated entry of existing trunks into individual city-pair competition to the extent that presently less than 25 percent of trunk carriers' traffic is generated in quasi-monopoly markets. (See exhibits by *CAB* Bureau of Operating Rights.)

CAB control over price, however, is so pervasive that carriers tend to view price as a parameter and compete (or rival) almost entirely in nonprice dimensions, primary of which is the frequency of scheduling. (See our 1974 paper, ch. 6.) It is notable that while on various occasions the Board has limited the extent of carrier competition over passenger amenities, the Board is prohibited by law from regulating (directly) the frequency of carrier scheduling.[11]

D. A Model of Firm Behavior and Industry Equilibrium

With price P^* as a parameter, the first order condition for firm i profit maximization can be written

$$\partial \Pi_i / \partial F_i = (P^* - c)\partial N_i / \partial F_i - k = 0 \qquad (7)$$

Simply stated, the marginal revenue from an additional flight $(P^* - c)\partial N_i/\partial F_i$ must equal the marginal cost k. Alternatively profit maximization may be interpreted as equating the exogenous price P^* with the marginal cost of *attracting and carrying* an additional passenger $c + k/(\partial N_i/\partial F_i)$. Profits exist if the marginal cost as perceived by the firm exceeds the average cost per passenger $c + k(F_i/N_i)$.[12] This occurs if the perceived effect on the firm's demand of the marginal flight $\partial N_i/\partial F_i$ is less than the average number of passengers per flight N_i/F_i. For the monopoly market, we would expect this condition to hold in equilibrium, since at some point (if not from the beginning) there would be

---

11. Section 401(e) (4) of the Federal Aviation Act of 1958 (as amended) prohibits the Board from regulating carrier schedules. However, under Section 412 of the Act the Board may approve industry agreements to "self-regulate" (for example, the airport congestion agreements and the recent agreements whereby three trunk carriers have reduced capacity in four transcontinental markets).

12. This follows the analysis of nonprice competition by George Stigler.

diminishing returns to scheduling: $\partial^2 N/\partial F^2 < 0$.[13]

The extent to which scheduling competition bids away implicit rents, therefore, is determined crucially by the carriers' perception of the impact on firm demand of a unilateral increase in flight frequency. If the individual firm in a multifirm market believes that its schedule change will not be met by its rivals, then its perceived marginal cost will be less than that of a monopolist, since the effect on the firm's demand includes "diversion" from its competitors, as well as generation of new travellers.

To see this, let firm i s demand be

$$N_i = \lambda_i N(P, T, X) \tag{8}$$

where T is defined by (2) and where λ_i, the market share of firm i, is given by some function

$$\lambda i = \lambda(F_i/F, F_j/F, ..., F_n/F) \tag{9}$$

Then

$$\partial N_i/\partial F_i = \lambda_i(\partial N/\partial F) + (\partial \lambda_i/\partial F_i)N \tag{10}$$

If, for example, the firm's market share were equal to its share of the total flights scheduled in the market, equation (10) becomes

$$\partial N_i/\partial F_i = (F_i/F)(\partial N/\partial F) + (1/F - F_i/F^2)N \tag{11}$$

which may be rewritten

$$\partial N_i/\partial F_i = \{F_i/F + [1 - F_i/F] \cdot [(N/F)/(\partial N/\partial F)]\}\partial N/\partial F \tag{12}$$

Since at equilibrium $N/F > \partial N/\partial F$, the expression within the braces of (12) exceeds unity. Hence, the perceived impact of a unilateral increase in frequency by a competitor (not met by its rivals) exceeds that of the monopolist. Moreover, this perceived impact increases as the number of competitors grows (i, e., as F_i/F diminishes). Hence, the level of total market frequency at which for all firms the perceived (marginal) revenue of an additional flight equals the flight's marginal cost grows with the number of competitors.[14]

---

13. Competitive market equilibrium likewise requires that $\partial N/\partial F < N/F$, else scheduling would increase without limit.

14. Note, however, that if each firm believes that any change in flight schedules will be met by its rivals, the monopoly solution obtains.

This bias in perceived effects of scheduling is greatly amplified, more-over, by a carrier management-perceived non-linear market share func-tion. Cross-section observations of market shares in competitive airline markets would seem to imply that a carrier with the largest share of flights attracts more than a proportional share of the traffic.[15] To test this notion, cross-section observations of 137 city-pair markets in 1969 were fitted to the following market share function:[16]

$$\lambda_i = N_i / \sum_{j=1}^{n} N_j = F_i^{\alpha} / \sum_{j=1}^{n} F_j^{\alpha} \qquad (13)$$

thus yielding an estimate $\alpha = 1.233$, with a coefficient standard error of .018 and an equation $R^2 = .959$ (with 401 degrees of freedom). The esti-mate of α significantly exceeds unity, the value it would take if the mar-ket share relationship were proportional.

This market share-frequency share result has an important implication for airline scheduling strategy, for it increases a carrier's incentive to add schedules and as a result compete away industry rents. Whatever the relative market shares, as long as industry rents are being earned one or more carriers in a multifirm market can raise its own load factor (and increase its profits) by expanding service. The carrier which fails to be aggressive when others are finds its market share significantly dimin-ished. This incentive for unilateral capacity augmentation makes collu-sion difficult to orchestrate and enforce.[17] Since $\partial N/\partial F < N/F$, capacity expansion lowers market average load factor and eliminates rents. Thus, to the extent this non-linear market share-frequency share relationship is perceived by the carriers, the achievement of zero-rent equilibrium would require the existence of only a small number of competitors.[18]

---

15. This phenomenon has been described previously in cross-section studies by Gilles Renard, among others.

16. This specification is that of Renard. The data were taken from carrier reports of 1969 load factors by city pair-market as summarized in an exhibit by the CAB Bureau of Economics (1970b).

17. For example, as mentioned by Eads, when in 1971 the Board granted antitrust immu-nity to three trunk carriers for the purpose of drawing up capacity limitation agree-ments in fifteen markets, agreements could be reached on only four.

18. A vice-president of TWA, Melvin Brenner, acknowledged management's belief in this S-curve market share phenomenon in testimony before the *CAB*. He suggested, moreover, that this phenomenon generates loss equilibria in many markets in a "prisoner's dilemma" context. (See also William Fruhan, ch. 5.) This has been shown by Yance (1970) to be possible, but only in small markets with an improbably large number of competitors.

E. Evidence on the Model

Observations of market data are consistent with the above hypothesis of market equilibrium. First, over time the trunk carriers have bid away potential rents, as indicated by their reported profit rates. For example, over the period 1955 through 1970, the trunk air carriers averaged only 6.42 percent return on investment (i.e., net revenue after taxes but before interest payment on debt, as a proportion of equity-plus-debt). (See *CAB* (1972, p.76).)

Table 1. Cross-Section Analysis of Market Average Load Factors
(t-statistics in parentheses)

---

1) $ALF = 588 - 2.11 \times 10^{-5}D + 7.62 \times 10^{-7}N$
            (1.4)   (9.1)
$-7.06 \times 11^{-2}C$
   (6.5)

$R^2 = .213$
$Df = 347$

2) $ALF = .257 - .019 \ln D + .073 \ln N - 1.46 \ln C$
            (1.8)   (7.1)   (5.5)

$R^2 = .144$
$Df = 347$

Source: CAB, Bureau of Economics (1970a).

ALF = market average load factor (i.e., total passengers/total seats)
D = market distance (in miles)
N = average number of daily passengers in market
C = number of carriers in market

Second, cross-section observations of city-pair markets reveals a pattern consistent with the zero-rent hypothesis. If each specific market were independent (i. e., could be treated as a unit separate from the airlines' system of routes), we would observe in each an average load factor that approaches the break-even load factor for that market (predicted by the average fare and estimated production costs, including a normal profit). Although most airline markets are not completely independent (especially in the production of capacity), we do observe patterns in the cross-section equilibria that are consistent with those hypothesized. For example, while fares per passenger mile are lower on long hauls than on short hauls, they have not fully reflected the economies of production with respect to distance. Hence, the break-even load factors are lower for long hauls than for short hauls. As a result of intensive scheduling competition, however, actual load factors are bid down on the longer and denser routes which otherwise present the potential for the greatest rents.[19]

Third, average load factors (and rents) tend to be inversely related to the number of firms in the market. The cross-section regressions in Table 1 illustrate the effects of distance, density, and number of carriers on the markets' average load factors. (Note also in Figure 3 the hypothesized effects of distance and number of carriers.)

Finally, we do observe from time-series that actual load factors tend to equal and follow changes in the estimated break even levels. (See Air Transport Association, Slide 16.) Where substantial divergences do exist they tend to be explainable in terms of lags in equipment acquisition (or disposition) or differences between *ex ante* and *ex post* demand.

To recapitulate, in a market in which scheduling competition bids away all rents, the regulator in choosing price implicitly determines the equilibrium number of travellers and the expected per passenger schedule delay. The regulator's role, therefore, is one of serving as a proxy for the population of consumers in choosing the appropriate combination of service quality and price from the opportunity locus of these variables.[20] We consider below and attempt to quantify the opportunity locus between expected per passenger schedule delay and price.

II. Determining an Efficient Price-Quality Configuration

A. Schedule Delays and Their Cost

In order to obtain the tradeoff between equilibrium price and expected

---

19. The industry's fare structure originated from the pattern of first class rail fares prevailing thirty years ago. (See Caves.) Changes in fares have increased the "taper" of fares with distance, yet the Board's staff tends to perpetuate the phenomenon by computing average costs on the basis of previously realized load factors.

20. Insofar as quality differentiation is constrained, especially with regard to schedule delay, the regulator is obliged to choose a single common quality level for a population whose preferences for quality may be diverse. This issue is discussed by Douglas (1972) with respect to a taxicab market and is raised again in the conclusion of this paper.

schedule delay, one must first approximate delay function (2). We analyze schedule delay as arising from two sources: the difference between a traveller's desired departure time and the closest scheduled departure, and the delays caused by excess demand for the flight(s).

The former delay, denoted as *frequency delay*, we have estimated by simulation. To do this, we superimposed an assumed scheduling of F departures on a representative time pattern of demand.[21] The number of flights scheduled in the simulation was varied from unity to 50 daily. For each value of F the average *absolute* differential between the traveller's preferred departure time and the closest scheduled departure was computed as an estimate of expected per passenger frequency delay, $T(F)$. The estimated values of expected frequency delay were then fitted to the daily frequency, F, from which they were generated:[22]

$$T_f = 92(F^{-.456}); \qquad R^2 = .497 \qquad (14)$$

(standard error of exponent = .119)

The variable T_f is the expected absolute value of the time differential in minutes between a scheduled flight and the traveller's preferred time of departure.[23]

Because demand fluctuates stochastically, in some instances a specific

---

21. The time pattern employed may be found in Miller (1972, p. 233). Ideally, we wish to identify the pattern of expected flows by time of day that would be observed if there were a continuous stream of departures with excess capacity in each. Traffic data, of course, are influenced by the pattern of departures as well as demand. The time pattern used for this exercise is heuristic, reflecting, however, typical market data (See traffic data by the Department of Transportation).

22. The F flights were scheduled such that each flight faced an equal number of potential travellers. Alternatively, the flight assignment could have been made to minimize expected delays. In a real market, however, the assignment of flights would reflect the time pattern of fares and the cycling time of the system (or round trip time in a two-node system). It might be noted further that while the expected delay with a uniform time distribution of demand would be linearly related to the inverse of the flight frequency, in a market where the time profile of demand is "peaked," the relationship is not necessarily linear. Moreover, peaking of demands reduces the expected frequency delay.

23. Alternative scheduling practices may make the expected delay larger or smaller. However, the importance of the delay function is in estimating *changes* in delay as daily frequency is changed (i.e., $\partial T_f / \partial F$). While the absolute value of the estimate may be biased, its marginal change may not be.

flight faces excess demand. In such a case some travellers must look for the next best departure, and, if it is filled, the next best, etc. A simple queuing model was developed in which the process was characterized as a Markov chain. (See Douglas (1971, Appendix A) and the authors, Appendix 6–A.) From the Domestic Passenger Fare Investigation (*CAB* Docket 21866), data are available on daily passenger traffic in selected markets during February and November 1969. These data were found to be consistent with a Poisson process with the sample variance linearly related to the sample mean by:

$$\text{Var}(n) = 16.978\bar{n} \qquad (15)$$

We could thus assume that the distribution of demand arising within any time interval τ would be Poisson, with

$$\sigma_n \simeq 4.12\, \bar{n}^{1/2} \qquad (16)$$

This allows us to define a Markov process, in which the state of the system is described by Q, the number of (potential) passengers drawn from the demand distribution for that flight *plus* those passengers who were unable to obtain seats on previous flights. The steady state of the system estimates the probability distribution of the queue length facing a flight.

The probability of being delayed one flight interval, two flight intervals, etc. can thus be calculated.[24] Given the average time interval between flights, we can then estimate the expected displacement of a traveller's actual departure time from the closest scheduled departure. The absolute value of this displacement, which we denote as *stochastic delay*, was estimated over many system configurations of demand, demand dispersion, schedule frequency, and aircraft size. These estimates of stochastic delay were fitted to the function:

$$T_s = .455(Y^{.645})(X^{-1.79})(I); \qquad (17)$$
$$R^2 = .910, \quad Df = 44$$

where
T_s = expected stochastic delay per passenger (in minutes)

---

24. Using the Markov chain we are implicitly assuming that travellers always delay their departure if a flight is filled. The estimate thus overstates the expected stochastic delay if one considers that some passengers may shift to earlier flights. This becomes, in effect, a conservative bias in the later estimate of "optimal" slack capacity.

$Y = N_f/\sigma_f$

$X = (S—N_f)/\sigma_f$

I = average interval between flights (in minutes)

N_f = mean demand per flight

σ_f = standard deviation of demand per flight

(Standard errors for the exponents of Y and X were 114 and .100, respectively.)

The sum of frequency delay T_f and stochastic delay T_s we denote as (total) expected schedule delay per passenger T:

$$T = T_f + T_s = 92(F^{.456}) + .455(Y^{.645})(X^{-1.79})(I) \qquad (18)$$

In Figure 1 we indicate the estimated values of components of schedule delay as the excess capacity of the system changes in a hypothetical market.[25] We note particularly the asymptotic increase in stochastic

Figure 1

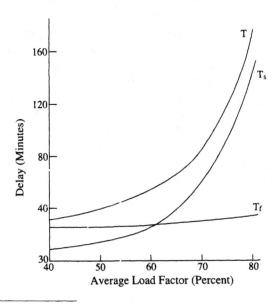

Average Load Factor (Percent)

---

25. In Figure 1, T is (total) schedule delay, T_s is stochastic delay, and T_f is frequency delay. This hypothetical market has a distance of 600 miles and serves 800 passengers per day with three-engine turbofan aircraft.

delay T_s as the relative slack capacity becomes small 'i.e., as average load factor approaches unity).[26]

B. The Price-Quality Tradeoff

In scheduled transportation, the average cost per passenger carried is quite sensitive to the utilization of capacity, or the relative level of slack capacity in the system. The relationship between average (per passenger) cost and average load factor is, of course, inverse: the higher the average load factor, the lower the per passenger cost.[27] By combining empirical estimates of the relationship between per passenger cost at various levels of slack capacity (i.e., average load factor) with the expected delay function we are able to estimate the opportunity locus between average (and marginal) cost (price) and expected schedule

Figure 2

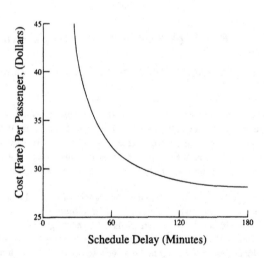

Schedule Delay (Minutes)

---

26. Note also that T_f rises slightly with increasing load factor. The reason for this is that in the figure the number of daily passengers is held constant and thus to increase load factor schedule frequency must fall and average frequency delay rises.
27. That is, $AC = c + k/L$ where L is average load factor (i. e., $L = N/Fs$ where s is the average number of seats per flight).

delay (quality).[28] The tradeoff for a hypothetical market is illustrated in Figure 2.[29]

An efficient price-quality equilibrium would be characterized by the equality of the technical tradeoff between price and quality (schedule delay) in a market with the subjective tradeoff of the passengers.[30] The latter could be derived from an appropriately estimated demand function for air travel (1):

$$\rho = (\partial N/\partial T)/(\partial N/\partial P) \qquad (19)$$

While the data required to fit the demand function specified are unavailable, we may learn much about the optimal price-quality configuration (and thus the relative efficiency of the existing market equilibrium) by assigning a reasonable value to schedule delays. In this way one can, at the very least, describe qualitatively the optimal levels of slack capacity in markets of differing distances and density. Moreover, within certain boundaries, one can appraise the overall appropriateness of prices and quality that have obtained under regulation.

III. Efficient vs. Existing Price-Quality Level and Structure

Critics have often asserted that the airline industry is characterized by

---

28. There are several sources of airline cost functions suitable for estimating the average cost–average load factor tradeoff.(See CAB, Bureau of Economics (1970b.)) For the analysis summarized in this paper we utilized the cost model developed in the authors, ch. 2. Consistent with a regulatory cost-recovery restraint, price must equal average cost. We note also that for a *given* load factor service $AC = MC = c+k/L$ where $L = N/Fs$.

29. For any given market with an underlying time pattern of demand there exists a cost function, $C=C(N, T_e, X)$, which describes the minimum cost of transporting the demand flow N, with a level of expected delay. T_e, and tangible quality X. Technical efficiency requires that the market equilibrium reach a point on this frontier. The opportunity locus descrioed in Figure 2 may be interpreted as a two-dimensional representation of the average cost function implied. Figure 2 represents a hypothetical market with distance of 600 miles, serving 800 passengers per day with three- engine turbofan aircraft.

30. If all passengers do not have the same subjective price-quality tradeoff, then a weighting problem exists. See discussion in Section V, regarding the desirability of increasing the number of price-quality options.

"excess" capacity. Clearly, such an assessment requires further analysis of the price-quality tradeoff described above. Casual observation of the interaction between the industry and the regulators, moreover, suggests why such a bias might exist. The market share competition previously described will often generate short-run losses, especially when equipment acquisition is over-optimistic or when expected demand fails to materialize. If the Board attempts to prop up carrier profits with a general rate increase, it implicitly rationalizes the lower load factors and sets the stage for another iteration of higher fares and increasing capacity. A review of the Board's rulings on fare increases confirms that carrier profits are a principal target of policy. (See Caves and William Jordan.)

Figure 3

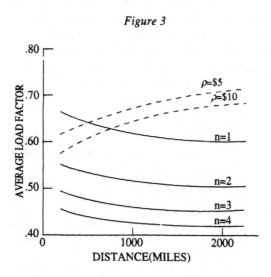

In Figure 3 we indicate the estimated optimal load factors for hypothetical markets of equal density but of variable distance. These are defined as the load factors which minimize the sum of average cost per passenger (fare) and the value of the expected schedule delay for each of two assumed values of schedule delays. In a market with average daily demand of 800, efficient load factors increase with distance, ranging in level from approximately 57-62 percent at short distances to approximately 69-72 percent in transcontinental markets. These estimates are predicated on an imputed passenger valuation of schedule delays of $5 and $10 per hour.[31]

The rise in efficient load factors with distance may be explained by the following. Expected schedule delays are a function of the relative number of empty seats carried, on the average. Since the cost of carrying an additional empty seat on a 2000 mile flight exceeds that of a 500 mile flight, one chooses to buy more quality (i.e., carry more empty seats) on the latter than on the former. This pattern is to be contrasted with that obtaining under regulation indicated by the plotted regressions in Figure 3, derived from regression 2) in Table 1.[32]

Optimal slack capacity also varies with demand density, or market size. That is, for a given level of relative slack capacity the probabilities of being delayed by *j* flight intervals is independent of market size, yet the interval between flights diminishes with market density. Hence, in larger markets one can obtain more quality with relatively fewer empty seats, and the optimal load factor increases with market size. This relationship for hypothetical markets is illustrated in Figure 4.[33] Note the contrast between optimal load factors and those existing under regulation (as derived from regression 2) in Table 1).

---

31. While we refer to ρ as the value attributed to schedule delay, we do not imply that it is equivalent to the traveller's value of en route time. The time displacement here is qualitatively different; we should expect however that having alternative uses, these delays would be valued at less than that of en route time. De Vany's 1968 measure of en route time value, $7.28 (inflated to $10 in round numbers for 1971), serves generally as an upper bound for schedule delay time value. See De Vany (1974).

32. In Figure 3 the estimated optimal values (dashed line) were computed with alternative valuations of schedule delay ρ, $5 and $10. Markets were presumed to have a demand density of 800 daily passengers; two engine turbofan aircraft were assigned for distances under 1,000 miles, three-engine turbofans for distances 1,000-1,800 miles, and four-engine turbofans for distances in excess of 1,800 miles. In the figure, *n* denotes the number of carriers in the market. We might note that while the explanatory value of the regressions in Table 1 are low, when separate regressions are run on the data segmented by number of carriers in the market the correlation coefficients generally increase. In all cases except four-carrier markets there is an inverse relationship between average load factor and distance. (See the authors, ch. 4.) Even in these markets, however, the overall levels of average load factor are much lower than reasonable estimates of the optimal levels.

33. In Figure 4, optimal average load factors (dashed lines) were estimated on the basis of two valuations of schedule delay, ρ=$5 and ρ=$10. Market distance is 600 miles and service is provided by two-engine turbofan jet aircraft. In the curves tracing out actual average load factors, *n* denotes the number of firms in the market.

The contrast between the regulated equilibrium and the efficient equilibrium is dramatically demonstrated by the intra-state California markets. A price competitive equilibrium has emerged in some of these dense markets with the activity of a maverick firm, Pacific Southwest Airlines. The prices in these markets have ranged from 40 to 50 percent less than in similar markets under *CAB* regulation. This difference can be attributed principally to the higher load factors in the California markets (in the 65-75 percent range), which is consistent with our estimate of an efficient price-quality combination for markets of this character.[34]

Implicit in this description of scheduled transport markets is an aggregate cost of service function. Technical inefficiency in the provision of service can arise from numerous sources, including inefficient timing of schedules (for example, Hotelling-type clustering), inappropriate selection of fleet composition, or inefficient routings. While the potential exists for technical inefficiency in all these forms under regulation, it is notable that an unregulated airline market might not achieve technical

Figure 4

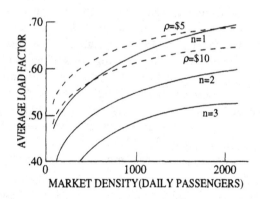

34. The California experience is described at length by Jordan. He fails, however, to relate the fare dichotomy to excess capacity and service quality. Aside from the question of X efficiency of the firms sheltered by regulation, similar results could obtain under *CAB* regulation. The low fare and high utilization which characterizes the markets to Puerto Rico is such an example.

efficiency either.[35]

Another implication of the model is that "social" scale economies exist in the production of scheduled air service even if there are no private scale economies accruing to the airline firm. That is, the average cost per passenger carried with a given level of schedule delay T and tangible quality X decreases as market size increases. Using the methodology outlined earlier we can derive a relationship between average and marginal costs of carrying an additional passenger, *while holding expected schedule delays constant*.[36] The results imply that the marginal (social) cost of a given service quality is, on average, some 10 percent less than average cost. In principle, this might suggest a rationale for the (third-degree price discriminating) discount fares now prevalent in the industry, under the assumption that the industry be operated with a cost-recovering revenue restraint. However, the implied discounts are certainly less than have existed, and in any event external costs of production might easily vitiate this result.

IV. Conclusion

A description of efficiency in price-constrained "competitive" markets requires an understanding and assessment of the endogenous relationship between quality and price. In the scheduled air transport industry, an important component of quality is endogenous to the equilibrium, and a proxy measure of this quality characteristic can be estimated. We note, however, that our estimates of the optimal price-quality configuration and thus comparisons with the existing regulated-market equilibria are based on information a good deal less complete than ideal. Specifically, we would prefer to have additional information on the value passengers place on delay time and more complete data on demand distri-

---

35. While the observed competitive markets do appear to yield a more appropriate balance of price and quality, it is not clear but that the nonproportional market share function would bias the fleet selection and scheduling practices of carriers in many nonregulated, competitive markets. See Douglas (1972) for a discussion of the competitive equilibrium likely to be found in a competitive transport market.

36. Herbert Mohring's description of the costs of a scheduled bus system arrives at a similar conclusion. His analysis, however, does not consider the stochastic component of delays.

butions by market characteristic. What we have attempted to show is that ignoring the price-quality tradeoff can lead (and probably has led) to significant divergencies between the optimal and existing price-quality options. With more complete information one could be more precise in such an efficiency assessment.

One implication of this analysis is that, *ceteris paribus*, the greater the number of price-quality options the better. We note that presently the market does provide air transportation in various configurations, characterized by wide differences in cost and schedule delay. At one end of the scale, charter flights provide the lowest price, but the greatest schedule delay. At the other extreme, corporate executives are whisked about the country in private jet aircraft at enormous cost, but with a very minimum of schedule delay. Scheduled air transportation lies between these poles, and, as we have suggested here, at the margin of excessive quality and price.

Some quality differentiation, moreover, does exist within the scheduled transport industry in this dimension. Stand-by fares and "leisure class" travel represent ways in which differentiation with regard to stochastic delays is currently practiced, although in a very limited way. Of course, additional techniques could be developed for price-quality differentiation within the regulatory environment, and in general such initiatives are to be encouraged.

Finally, it is clear that the costs of the regulated carriers are high *because* the price level is high, and not the reverse (i.e., cost is price-determined, not price-determining). Further, the proclivity of the carriers to compete intensively with scheduling rivalry implies that the regulator need not be given explicit, direct controls over capacity and quality. By controlling only the price level and structure, the regulator implicitly "controls" these quality variables. Just as there is no need for capacity controls by the regulator, collusive agreements for industry "self-regulation" should be discouraged. In short, through the control of fares, the regulator has in hand an efficient means of controlling total capacity and bringing about a more efficient level and structure of price-quality options.

References

W. J. Baumol and A. K. Klevorick, "Input Choices and Rate-of-Return Regulation: An Overview of the Discussion," *Bell J. Econ.*, Autumn 1970, 1, 162-90.

M. Brenner, *Testimony*, *CAB* Docket 21866-6, Exhibit TW 6011, Washington, Aug. 1970.

R. E. Caves, *Air Transport and Its Regulators: An Industry Study*, Cambridge 1962.

A. S. De Vany, "Mathematical Theory of the Airline Firm," in D. A. Clegg et al., eds., *A Computerized Systems Planning Process for Airports and Harbors of the State of Hawaii, 1*, Santa Barbara, July 1968, Appendix B-5.

_____, "The Revealed Value of Time in Air Travel," *Rev. Econ. Statist.*, Feb. 1974, 56, 77-82.

G. W. Douglas, *Testimony*, *CAB* Docket 21866-9, Exhibit DOT-T-3, Washington, May 17, 1971.

_____, "Price Regulation and Optimal Service Standards," *J. Transp. Econ. Policy*, May 1972, 20, 116-27.

_____, "Equilibrium in a Deregulated Air Transport Market," paper presented at Seminar on Problems of Regulation and Public Utilities, Dartmouth College, Aug. 21, 1972.

_____ and J. C. Miller III, *Economic Regulation of Domestic Air Transport: Theory and Policy*, Washington, forthcoming 1974.

G. C. Eads, "Competition in the Domestic Trunk Airline Industry: Too Much or Too Little?" in A. Phillips, ed., *Competition and Regulation*, Brookings Institution, forthcoming.

_____, M. Nerlove, and W. Raduchel, "A Long-Rum Cost Function for the Local Service Airline Industry," *Rev. Econ. Statist.*, Aug. 1969, 51, 258-70.

W. E. Fruhan, Jr., *The Fight for Competitive Advantage: A Study of the United States Domestic Trunk Air Carriers*, Boston 1972.

W. A. Jordan, *Airline Regulation in America: Effects and Imperfections*, Baltimore 1970.

T. E. Keeler, "Airline Regulation and Market Performance," *Bell J. Econ.*, Autumn 1972, 3, 399-424.

J. C. Miller III, "Scheduling and Airline Efficiency," unpublished doctoral dissertation, Univ. Virginia 1969.

_____, *Testimony*, *CAB* Docket 21866-7, Exhibit DOT-T-1, Washington, August 25, 1970.

_____, "A Time-of-Day Model for Aircraft Scheduling," *Transp. Sci.*, Aug. 1972, 6, 221-46.

H. Mohring, "Optimization in Urban Bus Transportation," *Amer. Econ. Rev.*, Sept. 1972, 62, 591-604.

G. Renard, "Competition in Air Transportation: An Econometric Approach," unpublished M.S. thesis, M.I.T., Sept. 1970.

G. Stigler, "Price and Non-Price Competition," *J. Polit. Econ.*, Jan./Feb. 1968, 76, 149-54.

M. R. Straszheim, *The International Airline Industry*, Washington 1969.

L. J. White, "Quality Variation when Prices are Regulated," *Bell J. Econ.*, Autumn 1972, 3, 425-36.

J. V. Yance, "The Possibility of Loss-Producing Equilibria in Air Carrier Markets," unpublished DOT rep., Washington 1970.

_____, "Nonprice Competition in Jet Aircraft Capacity," *J. Ind. Econ.*, Nov. 1972, 21, 55-71.

Air Transport Association of America, *Major U.S. Airlines Economic Review and Financial Outlook, 1969-1973*, Washington, June 1969.

U.S. Civil Aeronautics Board, *Handbook of Airline Statistics, 1971 Edition*, Washington 1972.

_____, Bureau of Economics, (1970a) *CAB* Docket 21866-6, Exhibit BE-6501, Washington, July 6, 1970.

_____, (1970b) "Costing Methodology, Version 6," Washington, Aug. 1970.

_____, Bureau of Operating Rights, *CAB* Docket 23852, Exhibits BOR-16, 17, Washington, March 29, 1971.

U.S. Department of Transportation, *CAB* Docket 21866-9, Exhibits DOT-D-1 through 88, Washington, Nov. 20, 1970.

CHAPTER 20

EMPIRICAL IMPLICATIONS AND TESTS OF THE CONTESTABILITY HYPOTHESIS*

Steven A. Morrison and Clifford Winston**

I. Introduction

Economics is largely concerned with the analysis of markets. Recently, Baumol, Panzar, and Willig have put forth a new view of markets that posits that, if entry and exit by potential competitors will be costless, the behavior of the incumbent firm(s) is constrained so as to establish a price configuration that maximizes market welfare.[1] Their theory has significant implications for a number of policy-related issues such as the possible anticompetitive effects of a proposed merger and the actual presence of monopoly power in particular markets.

---

* Reprinted from *Journal of Law & Economics*, Vol. XXX (April 1987), pp. 53-66.

** The authors are at Northeastern University and Brookings Institution Respectively.

1. For a complete development of this theory of contestable markets, see William J. Baumol, John C. Panzar, & Robert D. Willig, Contestable Markets and the Theory of Industry Structure (1982). Perfect contestability provides an alternative means to perfect competition for achieving a first-best welfare benchmark. For markets to be perfectly contestable, firms must be able to engage in "hit-and-run" entry without sustaining losses due to sunk costs. This requires that entrants can, without restriction, serve the same market demands and have the same technology as the incumbent firms and that entrants can enter and exit before the incumbents can respond by changing their prices. In this situation, if the market has only one incumbent firm, Ramsey-optimal prices will be charged; with two or more firms, price will equal marginal cost.

In this paper we investigate the empirical implications of the contestability hypothesis. Our paper provides a test of this hypothesis in the context of the U.S. domestic airline industry, which has been cited by proponents of the theory, and challenged by others, as an example of a contestable market. Our analysis attempts to distinguish between and characterize empirically the idea of perfect contestability, as developed by Baumol, Panzar, and Willig, and what we term imperfect contestability, as put forth by Bain.[2] The empirical issues and policy implications raised by each notion of contestability will be shown to be quite different.

II. Empirical Aspects of Perfect Contestability and Imperfect Contestability

The importance of potential competitors in influencing the conduct of incumbent firms and thus market performance has been recognized in the literature on industrial organization for many years. In his discussion of strategic aspects of market structure, Bain states that "the condition of entry, characterizing the extent to which established sellers have advantages over potential entrants, determines the relative force of potential competition as an influence or regulator on the conduct and performance of sellers in a market."[3] Baumol, Panzar, and Willig go beyond an acknowledgment that potential competition has an undetermined influence on the conduct of firms and develop the idea of a perfectly contestable market where, under certain entry and exit conditions, the presence of potential competition can generate performance that maximizes market welfare.

The empirical framework and problem that follow from Baumol, Panzar, and Willig's view of the influence of potential competition consist of determining whether the presence of potential competitors generates welfare-maximizing performance. This question could be investigated empirically by a study that compares the welfare levels of markets that (1) meet the technology and demand conditions for contestable markets

---

2. Joe S. Bain, Industrial Organization (2d ed. 1968).
3. *Id.* at 8. More explicit language was used by Joe S. Bain, A Note on Pricing in Monopoly and Oligopoly, 39 Am. Econ. Rev. 448, 452 & n.7 (1949): "[T]o argue that sellers in concentrated industries deliberately disregard the consequences of threatened entry would picture them as unbelievably stupid."

set out in note 1 above and that (2) are comparable in all respects except for the existence of at least one potential competitor. A sufficient condition for accepting the perfect-contestability hypothesis is whether only those markets that have potential competitors have also achieved welfare maximizing performance. If all markets are characterized by the presence of potential competitors, and if they also have achieved welfare maximizing performance, then the perfect-contestability hypothesis cannot be either rejected or accepted.

The empirical question that follows from Bain's model of potential competition requires determining the amount by which additional potential competitors influence market welfare. This problem can be analyzed statistically by a study in which the dependent variable, market welfare, is regressed on a number of potentially important influences that includes the number of potential competitors. A significant statistical effect of potential competitors would imply that the market is imperfectly contestable. It should be emphasized that perfect contestability does not imply that the market is also imperfectly contestable and vice versa.

Not only is the distinction between perfect and imperfect contestability an academic issue, but it has important policy implications as well. For example, consider the issue of whether an incumbent railroad should be forced to grant its competitors access to its track. If, for example, the rail market is perfectly contestable because of the presence of potential competition supplied by truck, then there is no benefit to be accrued from allowing competing railroads to have access to the track as this would establish them as potential competitors. However, if the rail market is imperfectly contestable, then the other railroads' presence as potential competitors does improve market welfare, and thus the opportunity for access should be required. We illustrate these ideas in the next section by testing the contention that airline markets are perfectly contestable. We then investigate the degree to which these markets are imperfectly contestable.

III. Contestability of Airline Markets

The question of whether the airline industry is perfectly contestable has emerged as the empirical focal point of the contestability debate. For example, Baumol, Panzar, and Willig state that "it is highly plausible that air travel provides real examples of contestable markets."[4] Bailey and Baumol assert that "in some ways the airline industry presents a particularly close approximation to contestability."[5] In response, Shepherd argues that "airline competition can be explained well by established concepts of market structure and entry."[6] Turning to empirical studies of the airline industry, Moore, Call and Keeler, and Graham, Kaplan, and Sibley have shown that various measures of efficiency (for example, price-cost ratios) depend on the number of actual competitors.[7] Because this exercise of market power is inconsistent with the (perfect) contestability hypothesis, each of these authors concluded that airline markets are not contestable. On the other hand, using similar procedures, Bailey and Panzar found that in some cases the number of actual competitors does not influence efficiency.[8] They attribute this lack of an influence of actual competitors to the presence of potential competitors. They conclude that airline markets are "basically contestable." Finally, Bailey, Graham, and Kaplan also find that market concentration influences their measure of efficiency.[9] Although they are somewhat skeptical about the power of contestability during the transition to deregulation, they are more optimistic regarding the long-run applicability of the theory.

Regardless of their conclusions, all these empirical studies share a common failure in that they do not have a direct measure of potential competition, and thus they attempt to infer the influence of potential competitors on the basis of the effect that actual competitors have on their efficiency measures. Although it is inconsistent with the hypothesis that a given market is perfectly contestable, a finding that market con-

---

4. Baumol, Panzar, & Villig, supra note 1, at 7.
5. Elizabeth E. Bailey & William J. Baumol, Deregulation and the Theory of Contestable Markets, 1 Yale J. Reg. 111, 128 (1984).
6. William G. Shepherd, "Contestability" vs. Competition, 74 Am. Econ. Rev. 585 (1984).
7. Thomas Gale Moore, U.S. Airline Deregulation: Its Effects on Passengers, Capital, and Labor, 29 J. Law & Econ. 1 (1986); Gregory D. Call & Theodore E. Keeler, Airline Deregulation, Fares and Market Behavior: Some Empirical Evidence, in Analytical Studies in Transport Economics (Andrew Daughety ed. 1985); David R. Graham, Daniel P. Kaplan, & David S. Sibley, Efficiency and Competition in the Airline Industry, 14 Bell J. Econ. 118 (1983).
8. Elizabeth E. Bailey & John C. Panzar, The Contestability of Airline Markets during the Transition to Deregulation, 44 L. & Contemp. Probs. 125 (1981).
9. Elizabeth E. Bailey, David R. Graham, & Daniel P. Kaplan, Deregulating the Airlines (1985).

centration influences efficiency does not preclude the presence of potential competition from also having an effect. Moreover, failure to include potential competitors in the model may result in a specification error, with the (biased) coefficient of the market-concentration variable capturing the influence of potential competitors. Because the "policing" function of potential competitors is at the heart of the contestability hypothesis, the contestability of airline markets remains undetermined.

A. Methodology and Data

In addition to measuring directly the influence on welfare of potential carriers, our study differs from the studies cited in at least one of the following ways. First, several of those studies were based on data collected during the transition to deregulation before firms were able to adjust fully to the changed environment. Because our study uses data from 1983, a greater degree of adjustment has occurred. Second, whereas all the other studies employed measures of efficiency, such as price-cost ratios, we use a direct measure of (the change in) consumer welfare, namely, compensating variation. This enables us to control simultaneously for the price effects and service-quality effects that are relevant for airline markets.

Our study agrees with previous findings that the airline industry meets the technology and demand conditions for contestable markets. Caves, Christensen, and Tretheway's study of the airline industry finds constant returns to scale for trunk and local carriers.[10] They conclude that there are no substantial cost disadvantages even for carriers with very small networks. Although price and nonprice (that is, service quality) effects have an important influence on demand in airline markets, Dorman has shown that a first-best social welfare maximum can be achieved in deregulated airline markets in the presence of price and nonprice competition.[11] Thus a perfect-contestability benchmark based on first-best conditions is appropriate.

The basis of the analysis is our multinomial logit model of intercity

---

10. Douglas W. Caves, Laurits R. Christensen, & Michael W. Tretheway, Economies of Density versus Economies of Scale: Why Trunk and Local Service Airline Costs Differ, 15 Rand J. Econ. 471 (1984).

11. Gary Jay Dorman, A Model of Unregulated Airline Markets, 1 Research Transp. Econ. 131 (1983).

passenger demand for business and pleasure travelers.[12] In this model the probability of choosing a particular mode of transportation (that is, auto, bus, rail, or air) is a function of, among other influences, the fare, trip time, and time between departures of all modes. The inclusion of other modes in the demand model effectively controls for the effect of intermodal competition in our analysis of contestability of airline markets. On the basis of this model we calculated compensating variation—which measured the difference between the welfare of passengers in the deregulated environment prevailing during 1983 and the optimal level of welfare—using the procedure developed by Small and Rosen.[13] Optimal welfare is attained at the combination of fares (equal to marginal cost) and flight frequency that maximizes the weighted sum of business and pleasure travelers' compensating variations for each of the city-pair routes in our sample. This welfare change between deregulation and optimality, expressed in (1977) cents per mile per traveler, is the dependent variable (DELTAW) used in the empirical analysis.[14] The technical construction of our dependent variable is presented in the Appendix.

B. Perfect Contestability

The theory of perfectly contestable markets does not motivate an econometric specification from which one can test the validity of the theory for a particular industry, but it does have implications that are empirically testable. Perfect contestability requires that our measure of welfare change be equal to zero for those markets that have at least one potential competitor. Consistent with Bailey and Baumol's discussion of

---

12. Steven A. Morrison & Clifford Winston, An Econometric Analysis of the Demand for Intercity Passenger Transportation, 2 Research Transp. Econ. 213 (1985).
13. Kenneth A. Small & Harvey S. Rosen, Applied Welfare Economics with Discrete Choice Models, 49 Econometrica 105 (1981).
14. In Steven A. Morrison & Clifford Winston, The Economic Effects of Airline Deregulation (1986), we found that carriers' welfare remained unchanged when we optimized fares and frequency. Because airlines were already earning a normal return under deregulation, and given the constant-returns-to-scale technology that characterizes the industry, carriers would continue to earn normal rates of return with optimal pricing and service levels. Thus our dependent variable actually reflects the changes in the welfare of both travelers and carriers.

the Civil Aeronautics Board's determination of potential carriers in the context of merger policy, we defined a potential carrier on a route as a carrier that served at least one of the two airports involved but that did not serve the route.[15] This definition recognizes that immediate (or, in the contestable-markets jargon, "hit and run") entry into an airline market requires that a carrier already have some presence in the market by serving at least one of the relevant airports.[16]

We calculated the welfare measure for each of the 769 randomly selected routes in our sample. Each of these routes has at least one potential competitor and has a one-way distance of at least 100 miles.[17] The calculation revealed that airline markets are not perfectly contestable because the welfare-change measure was not equal to zero for any market that had at least one potential competitor. The mean value of the welfare change was $0.014 (1977 dollars) per traveler mile.[18] For the average passenger-trip distance in the sample, this amounts to $4.61 per traveler. which, when multiplied by the estimated number of interity passenger trips during 1977 (539,289,000),[19] yields an aggregate differ-

---

15. Bailey & Baumol, supra note 5, at 132.

16. Data for the number of potential carriers were derived from the Civil Aeronautics Board's 1983 Airport Activity Statistics of Certificated Route Air Carriers. Defining a potential carrier on a route as an airline that served both airports involved (but did not serve the route) did not lead to any changes in the basic conclusions reached here. At the other extreme, one could assume that all domestic carriers are potential entrants into city-pair markets. The more restricted definition used here thus potentially biases the results in favor of perfect contestability because it eliminates some of the sunk costs that may be present in airline markets.

17. These routes covered all hub-pair classifications in airline travel. A hub classification denotes a community's share of total enplaned revenue passengers at U.S. airports. The classifications, which are determined by given shares, are large hub, medium hub, small hub, and nonhub. Although we collected a random sample of routes, each route had at least one potential competitor. For a route to have no potential competitors requires the unlikely outcome that each of the two airports involved is served by only one carrier – the carrier that serves the route connecting the airports.

18. Because of the probabilistic nature of the underlying logit model of intercity passenger mode choice, the units of welfare change are per traveler (regardless of mode chosen) as opposed to per airline traveler. Unfortunately, a standard error could not be obtained easily for this estimate. The estimate of ΔW is based on several cost-and-demand parameters, the demand parameters entering through a complicated functional form. Since almost all the individual cost-and-demand parameters were significant, this estimate of ΔW should be statisticallly reliable.

19. This figure is from the 1977 U.S. Census of Transportation National Travel Survey.

ence between deregulated welfare and socially optimal welfare of roughly $2.5 billion.[20] In all likelihood, perfect contestability is not present in the airline industry because carriers require time and must absorb sunk costs to obtain gate space and establish patronage. Establishing patronage can be particularly difficult when competing against carriers with computer-reservation systems that bias information in favor of their flights and against carriers that offer frequent-flier programs. Frequent-flier programs effectively increase the cost of switching carriers. In addition, because a potential carrier may have several profitable routes to choose from, its threat of entry into any one market is less. This probabilistic threat of entry undoubtedly reduces a potential carrier's influence on incumbent carriers' actions.

C. Imperfect Contestability

The finding that airline markets are not perfectly contestable does not preclude the possibility that they are imperfectly contestable (that is, potential competition may have an important effect on welfare). We address this question econometrically by developing a specification motivated by (imperfectly) contestable markets theory and institutional considerations. Imperfectly contestable markets theory suggests that, for a given route, our welfare-change measure is influenced by the number of both actual and potential carriers on the route. Institutional considerations suggest that the welfare-change measure will also be influenced by characteristics of a route such as the percentage of business travelers, the presence of a slot-controlled airport,[21] and unmeasured route-specific effects that we control for with hub classification dummies.[22] We defined

---

20. This figure is reasonable because, as Morrison & Winston, *supra* note 14, show, although deregulation has led to a substantial increase in welfare over regulation, it has not yet, as indicated here, achieved the socially optimal level of welfare. Indeed this outcome was predicted by some economists, for example, John C. Panzar, Equilibrium and Welfare in Unregulated Airline Markets, 69 Am. Econ. Rev.: Papers & Proc. 92 (1979).

21. These airports are New York's Kennedy and LaGuardia, Chicago's O'Hare, and Washington's National

22. For example, an unmeasured route-specific effect could be traffic density. Although density economies may be present on some routes, there are constant returns to scale at the systemwide level; see Caves, Christensen, & Robert D. Willig, Economies of Scale in Multi-output Production, 91 Q. J. Econ. 481 (1977), and is the appropriate

an actual competitor (ACTUAL) on a route as an airline that offered nonstop, or direct (that is, same aircraft), service or on-line (that is, same airline) connecting service.[23]

In an imperfectly contestable market, an increase in the number of actual and potential carriers reduces the difference between optimal and actual welfare. We also expect the presence of a slot-controlled airport on a route to reduce welfare and thus increase the welfare difference. Finally, we expect a larger share of business travelers on a route to increase the welfare difference because of these travelers' relatively inelastic demand.[24]

It is important to point out potential econometric problems that the analysis resolves. First, because the dependent variable (DELTAW) is a predicted variable, it may contain measurement error, which, if correlated with the explanatory variables, would produce biased parameter estimates. The major systematic source of measurement error that entered into the prediction of DELTAW was the omission of stochastic delay from the specification of travelers' mode choice because of a lack of data.[25] This will affect the estimates of travelers' welfare under deregulation and social optimality. A sensitivity analysis indicated, however, that this omission led to only a 2 percent error in measuring the welfare change from deregulation to social optimality.[26] The bulk of the measurement error in the dependent variable is thus likely to be random and uncorrelated with any of the explanatory variables.[27] A second econometric issue concerns simultaneity bias. Previous empirical studies of

---

welfare benchmark for fares. Note that route distance is not included in the specification because the dependent variable is normalized for distance.

23. Data for the actual number of carriers were obtained from the 1983 Official Airline Guide, North American Edition.

24. See Morrison & Winston, *supra* note 12.

25. Stochastic delay is the delay encountered by a traveler if no seats are available on the best-scheduled flight.

26. See Morrison & Winston, *supra* note 14.

27. Additional measurement error in the dependent variable could exist because marginal costs are predicted at the route level on the basis of a systemwide marginal cost function. However, this function controls largely for density effects, which are the most important source of variation in route costs. Thus these effects will be captured in the dependent variable, while any remaining measurement error is likely to be random and uncorrelated with the explanatory variables. The density effects are controlled for in the systematic (not stochastic) part of the regression by route classification dummies.

contestability postulated that the price-cost margin (the dependent variable in their analyses) was influenced by market concentration (as measured by the number of carriers serving a route). It might be argued that because the price-cost margin reflects profit opportunities for air carriers it has an effect on market concentration. However, previous work has responded to this argument. For example, Graham, Kaplan, and Sibley carried out an exogeneity-specification test and could not reject the hypothesis that concentration was uncorrelated with the error term.[28] In addition, Call and Keeler argue that concentration should be treated as exogenous because, "during the first several years of deregulation, established carriers are likely to keep much of their market shares, even with some fare cutting by new entrants."[29] These arguments should be even stronger in our case because our dependent variable, the difference between travelers' deregulated and optimal welfare, is a less accurate reflection of carriers' profit opportunities than is price-cost margin.[30]

Table 1 presents the results of an ordinary least squares regression of our model of welfare change.[31] The coefficient of ACTUAL is –0.44 and is statistically reliable, indicating that, all else constant, each additional actual competitor reduces the difference between optimal welfare and actual welfare per traveler by $0.0044 per mile. This finding of the importance of market concentration is consistent with some previous empirical studies and, of course, is inconsistent with perfectly contestable markets. However, potential entrants do serve a disciplining function as indicated by the statistically significant coefficient of PTT. Each additional potential competitor reduces the welfare change per traveler by $0.0015 per mile. Three potential competitors thus have approximately the same effect on welfare as does one actual competitor. These results provide support for the view that airline markets are imperfectly contestable.

---

28. Graham, Kaplan, & Sibley, *supra* note 7.
29. Call & Keeler, *supra* note 7.
30. For example, the welfare difference may be large in certain markets even in the presence of marginal cost pricing because of insufficient service frequency. However, low traffic density in these markets and an inability to price discriminate to the degree necessary to extract travelers' willingness to pay for increased service may discourage entry, indicating that our dependent variable is not necessarily an accurate reflection of profit opportunities.
31. A Chow test did not enable us to reject the null hypothesis of common parameters across hub-pair classifications at reasonable confidence levels.

Table 1. *Estimation Results*

Variable Definition	Mnemonic	Estimate
Hub dummy(1 if route was nonhub/nonhub, 0 otherwise)	NN	2.31 (.37)
Hub dummy(1 if route was nonhub/small hub, 0 otherwise)	NS	1.41 (.32)
Hub dummy(1 if route was nonhub/medium hub, 0 otherwise)	NM	2.16 (.40)
Hub dummy(1 if route was nonhub/large hub, 0 otherwise)	NL	2.52 (.50)
Hub dummy(1 if route was small hub/small hub, 0 otherwise)	SS	1.30 (.32)
Hub dummy(1 if route was small hub/medium hub, 0 otherwise)	SM	2.56 (.38)
Hub dummy(1 if route was small hub/large hub, 0 otherwise)	SL	3.51 (.48)
Hub dummy(1 if route was medium hub/medium hub, 0 otherwise)	MM	2.62 (.43)
Hub dummy(1 if route was medium hub/large hub, 0 otherwise)	ML	3.12 (.46)
Hub dummy(1 if route was large hub/large hub, 0 otherwise)	LL	3.42 (.50)
Slot dummy(1 if either origin or destination airport had slot restrictions, 0 otherwise)	SLOTDUM	.60 (.19)
Percentage of business travelers on route	PCTBUS	.06 (.005)
Number of airlines offering direct or on-line connecting service	ACTUAL	-.44 (.04)
Number of airlines serving at least one airport on the route (excluding ACTUAL carriers)	PTT	-.15 (.02)

Note.—No. of observations = 769; R^2 = .42. Standard errors are in parentheses.

A one-point increase in the percentage of business travelers increases the welfare change per traveler by $0.0006 per mile. As indicated above, this finding is consistent with the exercise of market power.

Since 1968, takeoff- and landing-slot allocations have been in effect at four U.S. airports. Since then, antitrust immunity has been granted to airlines to form scheduling committees and to allocate among themselves the available slots.[32] Although entry into markets serving these airports is possible, it is clearly more difficult than at non-slot-controlled airports. This is reflected by the coefficient of SLOTDUM, indicating that current welfare deviates from optimal welfare per traveler by $0.0060 per mile more on routes serving slot-controlled airports than on equivalent routes.

D. Extensions

There are two types of changes in our specifications in which the robustness of our results can be explored: greater disaggregation of the explanatory variables and interaction of the effects of potential and actual carriers. We estimated specifications that accounted for different size classifications of potential and actual carriers (for example, majors vs. nationals), different cost classifications of potential and actual carriers (for example, newly certificated, low-cost carriers vs. established carriers), and different types of service (nonstop vs. connections). These specifications led to no changes in our findings regarding imperfect contestability.[33]

It might also be argued that the effects on welfare of potential carriers increase as the number of actual carriers in a market falls or that the effects increase as the number of potential carriers rises, holding the number of actual carriers constant. Specifications that controlled for these types of possible effects again resulted in no changes in our basic

---

32. The U.S. Department of Transportation recently adopted a rule (effective April 1986) that permits airlines to buy and sell their takeoff and landing slots.

33. Disaggregation by size and cost classification for actual carriers revealed that the two largest carriers (United Airlines and American Airlines) have the greatest effect on welfare, largely because of their frequent departures, and that the newly certificated (low-cost) carriers have the second-greatest effect. An appropriate characterization of competition in deregulated airline markets is given by a combination of some version of the dominant-firm model and imperfect contestability.

findings regarding imperfect contestability. We report the results for one specification, however, that suggest that a small "critical mass" is required before the presence of potential carriers affects the behavior of actual carriers. The results in Table 2 reveal that there is a statistically insignificant effect of potential carriers until there are at least four potential carriers. If each carrier independently had a 25 percent probability of entering a given market, our results would imply that there is one expected potential entrant in a given market. Thus the required critical mass of expected potential entrants may be small for a given market, which is consistent with Harrison's experimental results.[34]

IV. Conclusion

This paper has identified and distinguished between the empirically testable implications of perfect and imperfect contestability. The empirical implications of these theories were investigated in the context of the U.S. airline industry. Our primary substantive finding is that the airline industry is not perfectly contestable but is imperfectly contestable. In this respect our conclusion supports the belief of Bailey, Graham, and Kaplan that, although "the contestability benchmark does not fully hold sway in the first years after deregulation, ... some version of the theory of contestable markets may eventually be demonstrable."[35] Our analysis shows that a version of the contestability hypothesis, as proffered by Bain, is demonstrable. [36]

From a policy perspective this finding supports the continued encouragement of actual and potential competition in the airline industry. Encouragement would not be needed if airline markets were already perfectly contestable. To take one illustrative issue, concern has arisen over biases in providing fare and flight information that have existed in the major computer-reservations systems developed by American Airlines and United Airlines. It has been alleged that one undesirable implication of allowing the provision of biased information is that travelers are not flying at the lowest possible fare. If airline markets were perfectly

---

34. Glenn W. Harrison, Experimental Evaluation of the Contestable Markets Hypothesis (unpublished manuscript, Univ. Western Ontario, Dep't Econ. 1984).

35. Bailey, Graham, & Kaplan, *supra* note 9, 171, 200–201.

36. Bain, *supra* note 2.

Table 2. Estimation Results

Variable Definition	Mnemonic	Estimate
Hub dummy(1 if route was nonhub/nonhub, 0 otherwise)	NN	2.11 (.54)
Hub dummy(1 if route was nonhub/small hub, 0 otherwise)	NS	1.38 (.33)
Hub dummy(1 if route was nonhub/medium hub, 0 otherwise)	NM	2.14 (.40)
Hub dummy(1 if route was nonhub/large hub, 0 otherwise)	NL	2.49 (.51)
Hub dummy(1 if route was small hub/small hub, 0 otherwise)	SS	1.27 (.33)
Hub dummy(1 if route was small hub/medium hub, 0 otherwise)	SM	2.53 (.38)
Hub dummy(1 if route was small hub/large hub, 0 otherwise)	SL	3.48 (.48)
Hub dummy(1 if route was medium hub/medium hub, 0 otherwise)	MM	2.60 (.43)
Hub dummy(1 if route was medium hub/large hub, 0 otherwise)	ML	3.10 (.46)
Hub dummy(1 if route was large hub/large hub, 0 otherwise)	LL	3.39 (.50)
Slot dummy(1 if either origin or destination airport had slot restrictions, 0 otherwise)	SLOTDUM	.60 (.19)
Percentage of business travelers on route	PCTBUS	.06 (.005)
Number of airlines offering direct or on-line connecting service	ACTUAL	-.44 (.04)
Number of carriers serving at least one airport on the route if less than 4, 0 otherwise	PTTLT4	-.05 (.19)
Number of carriers serving at least one airport on the route if greater than or equal to 4, 0 otherwise	PTTGE4	-.15 (.02)

Note.—No. of observations = 769; R^2 = .42. Standard errors are in parentheses.

contestable, then there would be no benefit from curtailing these practices. However, because we have found that airline markets are imperfectly contestable, it is in the public interest to foster potential and actual airline competition by eliminating biased fare and flight information.

We hope that this study has illustrated that contestability is not an all-or-nothing proposition. The development of ideas concerning the effect of potential competitors on welfare has been important; the linkage of these ideas to actual markets requires further empirical investigation.

Appendix

Construction of Welfare-Change Measure

Compensating variations that measured (in 1977 dollars) the difference between the welfare of passengers in the deregulated environment prevailing during 1983 and the optimal level of welfare were calculated using the formula developed by Small and Rosen:[37]

$$CV = -\left(\frac{1}{\lambda}\right) \left[\ln \sum_{i=1}^{n} \exp(V_i) \right] \begin{array}{c} V_f \\ V_0 \end{array},$$

where λ is the marginal utility of income,[38] V_i is the mean indirect utility associated with mode i obtained from a logit demand model, n is the number of mode alternatives, and the square brackets indicate the difference in the expression inside when evaluated at the initial (deregulated) and final (socially optimal) points.

The estimated mean indirect utility function was obtained from our model of intercity passenger demand.[39] The mode-choice specification for business and pleasure travelers included travel cost, travel time, average time between scheduled departures, and number of travelers and also included for pleasure travelers household income and age of travelers. The variables that were optimized to obtain the socially optimal level of utility were fares and frequency, which is the basis for deter-

---

37. Small & Rosen, *supra* note 13.
38. The marginal utility of income is actually equal to minus the travel-cost coefficient in our demand model.
39. Morrison & Winston, *supra* note 12.

mining the average time between departures. To maximize travelers' welfare, estimates of marginal cost were needed as a basis for the optimal fares. Further, because we are maximizing travelers' welfare with respect to both fares and frequency of service, fares must be set at optimal frequency levels. Thus we estimated an airline cost function[40] that was a function of input prices (wages, fuel price, and cost of capital), measures of output (passenger miles and seat miles), and aircraft departures that enabled us to control for economies of density. Using this function to calculate marginal costs, optimal fares for a given load factor (effectively controlling for flight frequency) were obtained for each route in our sample. The fare-frequency combination that maximized travelers' compensating variations was then determined and used as the optimized variables in the determination of V_f.

Bibliography

Bailey, Elizabeth E.; and Baumol, William J. "Deregulation and the Theory of Contestable Markets." *Yale Journal on Regulation* 1 (1984): 111–37.

Bailey, Elizabeth E.; Graham, David R.; and Kaplan, Daniel P. *Deregulating the Airlines.* Cambridge, Mass.: MIT Press, 1985.

Bailey, Elizabeth E., and Panzar, John C. "The Contestability of Airline Markets during the Transition to Deregulation." *Law and Contemporary Problems* 44 (Winter 1981): 125–45.

Bain, Joe S. "A Note on Pricing in Monopoly and Oligopoly." *American Economic Review* 39 (March 1949): 448-64.

Bain, Joe S. *Industrial Organization.* New York: John Wiley & Sons, 1959.

Baumol, William J.; Panzar, John C.; and Willig, Robert D. *Contestable Markets and the Theory of Industry Structure.* New York: Harcourt Brace Jovanovich, Inc., 1982.

Call, Gregory D., and Keeler, Theodore E. "Airline Deregulation, Fares and Market Behavior: Some Empirical Evidence." In *Analytical Studies in Transport Economics*, edited by Andrew Daughety. New York: Cambridge University Press, 1985.

---

40. See Morrison & Winston, *supra* note 14.

Caves, Douglas W.; Christensen, Laurits R.; and Tretheway, Michael W. "Economies of Density versus Economies of Scale: Why Trunk and Local Service Airline Costs Differ." *Rand Journal of Economics* 15 (Winter 1984): 471-89.

Dorman, Gary Jay. "A Model of Unregulated Airline Markets." *Research in Transportation Economics* 1 (1983): 131-48.

Graham, David R.; Kaplan, Daniel P.; and Sibley, David S. "Efficiency and Competition in the Airline Industry." *Bell Journal of Economics* 14 (Spring 1983): 118-38.

Harrison, Glenn W. "Experimental Evaluation of the Contestable Markets Hypothesis." Unpublished manuscript. London: University of Western Ontario, Department of Economics, 1984.

Moore, Thomas Gale. "U.S. Airline Deregulation: Its Effects on Passengers, Capital, and Labor." *Journal of Law and Economics* 29 (April 1986): 1-28.

Morrison, Steven A., and Winston, Clifford. "An Econometric Analysis of the Demand for Intercity Passenger Transportation." *Research in Transportation Economics* 2 (1985): 213-37.

Morrison, Steven A., and Winston, Clifford. *The Economic Effects of Airline Deregulation.* Washington D.C.: Brookings Institution, 1986.

Panzar, John C. "Equilibrium and Welfare in Unregulated Airline Markets." *American Economic Review: Papers and Proceedings* 69 (May 1979): 92-95.

Panzar, John C., and Willig, Robert D. "Economies of Scale in Multioutput Production." *Quarterly Journal of Economics* 91 (August 1977): 481-93.

Shepherd, William G. "'Contestability' vs. Competition." *American Economic Review* 74 (September 1984): 572-87.

Small, Kenneth A., and Rosen, Harvey S. "Applied Welfare Economics with Discrete Choice Models." *Econometrica* 49 (January 1981): 105-30.

CHAPTER 21
THE EVOLUTION OF U.S. AIRLINE COMPETITION*

*Severin Borenstein**

Studies by academic economists were a significant force in the movement towards deregulation of the domestic airline industry in the early 1970s (Levine, 1965; Jordan, 1970; Keeler, 1972; Douglas and Miller, 1974). During the critical 1977–78 period in which deregulation was imposed first *de facto* by the Civil Aeronautics Board (CAB) and then *de jure* by Congress, the chairman and vice-chairman of the CAB were economists. For the 14 years since deregulation, economists have continued intensive study of the industry, in part because of the unusual availability of reliable firm- and transaction-level data and in part because of the rare opportunity to observe an industry as it evolves from strict economic regulation to fairly unimpeded competition and strategic behavior.

The simplest prediction of economists about airline deregulation, and one of the few on which nearly all economists agreed, was that deregulation would improve consumer welfare in comparison to continued price and entry regulation. Fourteen years later, nearly all economists still agree on this, though the degree of enthusiasm for the deregulation outcome varies considerably. There was substantial disagreement among economists about the market structure that would result. Because

* Reprinted from *Journal of Economic Perspectives*, Vol. 6, No. 2, Spring 1992, pp. 45-73.
** Severin Borenstein is Associate Professor of Economics, University of California, Davis, Califorina.

studies of scale economies in the airline industry had concluded that none existed beyond the scale of the smaller major airlines of the 1970s (Caves, 1962; Eads et al., 1969), many economists argued that deregulation would result in more than the 11 major airlines that existed at the time of deregulation. Others predicted that only a few, or possibly only one, airline would survive at a large scale. Two noted University of Chicago economists, Sam Peltzman and Lester Telser, made a bet in 1979 on whether the 4-firm concentration ratio would be above or below 90 percent by 1985. Peltzman bet that it would be below 90 percent and, as he put it, "won the bet, but lost the war." Nationwide, concentration decreased during the first few years following deregulation, but has turned upward since then.

Though comparisons of the airline industry under regulation and deregulation continue, this is not my primary focus here.[1] As the time since deregulation grows, such comparisons to the "straw man" of regulation are increasingly speculative and decreasingly relevant to the issues at hand. Regulation under the CAB was far from ideal; if it were reimposed today, it would probably be more efficient than the pre-1978 regulation. Deregulation has also entailed missteps that would not be repeated were the process to be replayed. Therefore, an estimate of the net welfare gain (or loss) resulting from deregulation gives little guidance about the relevant choices that will face policy-makers in the future.

For the most part, the lessons that have been learned from the deregulated domestic airline industry are not about government regulation or the process of deregulation, but about the tactics, strategies, and results of competition in a dynamic, complex, and innovative service industry. These lessons are more likely to inform economists about the market process in, for instance, the hotel or fast-food industries than in electric

---

1. See Bailey, Graham, and Kaplan (1985), and Morrison and Winston (1986) for the most complete analyses of the effects of deregulation during the first half decade. Dempsey (1990) compares the trend in average prices since 1978 to the pre-deregulation trend, adjusting only for fuel price changes, and finds that prices are higher than they would have been under deregulation. The significant weakness in this comparison is that real fuel prices fell during the period Dempsey analyzes, while most other airline input prices, for which Dempsey does not control, were constant or increased in real terms. The Morrison and Winston study does a much more complete comparison and finds substantial price decrease relative to regulation.

power distribution or other traditional areas of regulation.

The next section reviews the evolution of the domestic airline industry since the late 1970s, when it was abruptly freed from most regulatory constraints on pricing, entry and exit. (International air travel is considered here only as it relates to competition in the domestic industry. This is due both to space limitations and because international air travel remains heavily and idiosyncratically regulated.[2]) The following sections will examine the competitive issues that have arisen since deregulation; the conclusions, and in some cases consensus, that economists have reached on these issues; and the public policy options in dealing with the airline industry in light of these issues.

A Brief History of the Deregulated Airline Industry

In the early 1970s, just a few years prior to deregulation, government intervention in the airline industry reached its apex. The CAB had prevented entry of new start-up airlines for many years, but in the early '70s it also imposed a "route moratorium," ceasing to assign new authority for existing airlines to serve new city-pairs and preventing many airlines from abandoning routes that they no longer wished to

Table 1. Measures of Domestic Airline Industry Concentration Since Deregulation

	1977	1982	1987	1990
4-firm Concentration Ratio	56.2%	54.2%	64.8%	61.5%
8-firm Concentration Ratio	81.1%	80.4%	86.5%	90.5%
Herfindahl Index	0.106	0.093	0.123	0.121

Source: U.S.D.O.T. Air Carrier Traffic Statistics, Revenue Passenger-Miles.
Note: The 4- and 8-firm concentration ratios are the sums of the market shares of the 4 and 8 largest firms, respectively. The Herfindahl index, the sum of the squared market shares of all firms, ranges between 0 and 1.

---

2. Those interested in whether the single European market scheduled to go into effect at the end of 1992 might offer some hope for increased international airline competition should consult the cautious view of McGowan and Seabright (1989) and Borenstein (1992).

serve. At the same time, the CAB decided that the discounts with which it had experimented in the '60s — such as student fares and discounts for a spouse accompanying a full-fare passenger—conflicted with its mandate for fair and equitable prices, so it greatly reduced the scope for such fares.

By 1976, however, the CAB began to move towards deregulation by again permitting discriminatory fare discounts. In the following two years, the Board permitted free entry of any certified carrier on a few selected routes, breaking with its history of choosing which airlines would compete in each market. It also relaxed the restrictions on chartered service to the extent that charters became close substitutes for regular scheduled flights. Just as some of the major airlines had begun to sue the CAB for violating its congressional mandate by allowing too much competition, Congress passed the Airline Deregulation Act of 1978. The Act set out a time schedule for relaxation of price and entry regulation and permitted the CAB to accelerate that schedule as it deemed appropriate.

New entry boomed and prices fell substantially on most routes, especially long distance routes. On the shorter routes, which had been cross-subsidized under regulation, real prices did not fall as much and even increased in some cases. Airline profits were at record levels in 1978, but the 1979 oil price shock dampened these gains. As the deep recession of the early 1980s set in, the profits turned to large losses. Entry of new airlines slowed markedly and came to a nearly complete halt by 1983. In the next few years, many of the new entrants and the pre-deregulation smaller carriers either merged with a major carrier or declared bankruptcy and ceased operations. Table 1 presents the evolution of three different measures of nationwide concentration in the industry. By all three measures, concentration increased between 1982 and 1990, and is now higher than it was in 1977. Figure 1 tracks the lineage of the major carriers that operated in 1991.

Measures of national concentration are convenient reference points, but the increase in concentration is less apparent at the city-pair route level, where competitors' products are effective substitutes for one another. Table 2 shows that looking at all traffic, route level concentration decreased substantially between 1984 and 1987, and showed a slight drop between 1987 and 1990. If we examine direct trips, however —those in which the passenger does not change planes—concentration

Figure 1. Chronology of Large U.S. Airlines Since Deregulation

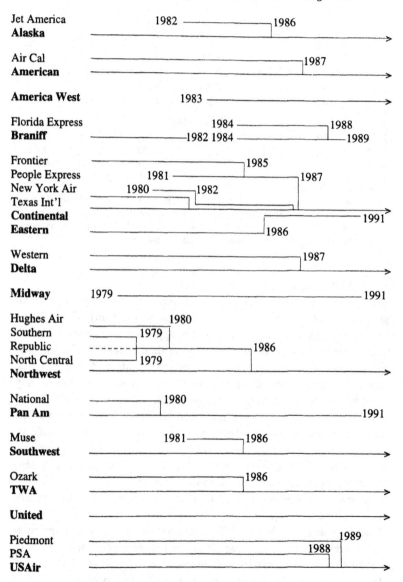

Source: Kaplan (1986) and *Wall Street Journal*, various issues

Table 2. *Average City-Pair Herfindahl Indexes*

| | Market Distance in Miles | | | | | |
	0-200	201-500	501-1000	1001-1500	1500+	ALL
Year	**All Trips**					
1984	0.600	0.588	0.537	0.479	0.415	0.531
1987	0.689	0.616	0.498	0.444	0.363	0.512
1990	0.618	0.614	0.518	0.424	0.357	0.506
	Direct Trips Only					
1984	0.601	0.598	0.601	0.581	0.536	0.590
1987	0.691	0.648	0.612	0.587	0.532	0.620
1990	0.612	0.641	0.672	0.625	0.536	0.632

Source: U.S.D.O.T. Databank IA.
Note: Excludes interline tickets and markets with less than 10 passengers per day.The numbers shown are unweighted averages across routes. The sign and approximate magnitudes of these changes are the same if routes are weighted by either passengers or passenger-miles. All data are for the second quarter of the given year.

has steadily increased from 1984 to 1990.

This outcome reflects the growth of hub-and-spoke operations. All major airlines now have one or more hubs at which many of their long-distance passengers change planes. This approach has allowed carriers to fill a higher proportion of the seats on their planes and to increase flight frequency of nonstop routes between their hubs and other airports. Since most hub airports can accommodate large-scale operations of only one airline, both logistically and economically, competition has tended to decrease on direct routes to and from the hubs. Yet, because a hub allows an airline to serve a large number of routes with a change of plane at the hub, longer routes and ones on which most passengers change planes are now served by many airlines, each channeling passengers through its particular hub airport. This explains the decline in concentration on longer routes and increase on shorter routes—usually served without a change of plane—when all trips are examined.

One drawback to hub-and-spoke operations is that a larger proportion of passengers change planes, especially on longer trips, instead of flying nonstop from their origin to their destination. The share of trips over 1500 miles that involve a flight change rose from 42 percent in 1978 to 52 percent in 1990. On trips between 500 and 1500 miles, it increased from 33 percent in 1978 to 38 percent in 1990. Gordon (1992) finds that nonstop service has increased on most of the top 500 routes since deregulation, but even on these higher density routes, the increase in nonstop flights has not kept pace with the increase in traffic. Furthermore, the loss of nonstop service is more likely to be evident on smaller routes.

Still, by allowing each airline to serve more city-pairs with change-of-plane service, hub systems have decreased the proportion of passengers who need to change airlines as well as planes during their trip. Carlton, Landes, and Posner (1980) and many passenger surveys have concluded that changing airlines imposes substantial additional costs on passengers, due to increased probability of missed connections and lost baggage. The proportion of trips that included a change of airline fell from 11.2 percent in 1978 to 6.9 percent in 1981, 4.0 percent in 1984, and 1.2 percent in 1987 and 1990. While the more recent changes are due in substantial part to mergers among major carriers, the earlier and more significant declines are explained largely by formation of hub-and-spoke systems.

Furthermore, for most travel between non-hub airports, the choice of departure times has been enhanced substantially by hub-and-spoke operations. A thinly traveled route that had one or two nonstops a day under regulation is likely now to have 10 or more possible change-of-plane routings through different hubs spread throughout the day. Finally, hub-and-spoke operations have contributed to the increased use of satellite airports such as Oakland, Burbank, or Orange County in California. Many people would rather fly to these airports with a change of plane than to San Francisco or Los Angeles airports nonstop.

Concerns about the possible anticompetitive effects of hub-and-spoke systems have been fueled by mergers and bankruptcies among some of the larger airlines in the last few years. Eight mergers among major airlines were approved in 1986 and 1987. Two of these mergers, Northwest-Republic and TWA-Ozark, involved airlines that shared the same primary hub. The Department of Transportation (DOT) approved these two combinations over the objections of participants from the Department of Justice.

The industry shakeout intensified following the August 1990 Iraqi invasion of Kuwait that increased jet fuel prices, for a brief period by more than 100 percent. Since then, America West, TWA and Continental have filed for Chapter 11 bankruptcy protection, but continued to operate. Midway, Pan Am, and Eastern have been liquidated, but only after hundreds of millions of shareholders' and creditors' dollars had been spent trying to revive these companies.

Despite the spate of airline mergers and failures, or some have argued because of them, domestic airline prices have not increased relative to costs since most new entry ended in the early 1980s. From the second quarter of 1984 to the second quarter of 1990, before the events in the Persian Gulf, prices increased 4 percent less than DOT's index of airline costs. Many managers in the industry have claimed that cash flow requirements of airlines near bankruptcy or operating under bankruptcy court protection have led to cut-throat pricing. The industry average comparison, however, hides an important dichotomy: prices on short-haul routes, under 500 miles, increased 5 percent more than the cost index between 1984 and 1990, while prices on longer routes increased 10 percent less than cost. Nearly all of these changes occurred between 1984 and 1987; from 1987 to 1990 prices moved closely in line with the DOT cost index.

Many analysts have pointed to airport capacity shortages as the most critical factor affecting competition and efficiency in the domestic airline industry. Though a few airports suffered significant congestion before deregulation, the problem has worsened dramatically since 1978. In part, the increase in airport congestion is a cost of the success of airline deregulation. From 1977 to 1990, domestic air travel increased by 120 percent.[3] During this time, no new airports were built, while expansion of existing airports was greatly hampered by environmental concerns and local zoning and noise restrictions. The formation of hubs also increased the strain on many airports. A hub operates by scheduling many incoming flights at virtually the same time and then many departures 30 to 60 minutes later, thereby increasing airport capacity demands for a given number of flights.

One approach to allocating scarce airport capacity would be to impose congestion-based landing fees, which would increase at times of peak demand. Historically, landing fees have been kept quite low; for example, from $25 for a small private plane (known as general aviation) to $800 for

---

3. Growth in travel was even greater in the 13 years prior to 1977, but this was probably due to improvements in speed and comfort of travel with the introduction of jet aircraft. Since deregulation, there have been very few technological improvements in air transport quality.

a jumbo jet at Boston's Logan airport. To date, political resistance to peak-load pricing of runway use, particularly from general aviation operators, has successfully prevented its implementation, but recent moves by the FAA indicate that this may soon change. Congestion-based landing fees would also imply that fees would cease to be a linear function of weight, as is common now, raising the cost to smaller commercial planes and general aviation and lowering the cost to large planes. This would reduce use of congested airports by aircraft carrying few passengers. An attempt to implement such a plan in Massachusetts in 1987, however, was successfully challenged in the courts for being "discriminatory."

At a few U.S. airports, permission to have a plane takeoff or land at a given time of the day has been converted into a transferable property right. Such landing slots at Washington National airport and O'Hare in Chicago have recently sold for $.5 to $1.2 million, with the higher prices going for peak time slots. Unfortunately, congestion delays appear to be just as high at "slot-controlled" airports as at similar-size airports without slots, though changing the number of slots permitted would surely affect this result. The issue of airport congestion is likely to become more important in the future.

Innovation has also occurred in the technology and strategy of selling air travel. Computer reservation systems (CRSs) used by travel agents have become a central and critical part of airline ticketing. Travel agents now write more than 80 percent of all tickets, up from about 50 percent before deregulation. There are four CRS systems currently in use, but Sabre (owned by American) and Apollo (owned principally by United, but also by USAir and some foreign airlines) have more than 75 percent of the business. Worldspan (Delta, TWA, and Northwest) is still a distant third in volume. SystemOne (Continental) is considered the poorest sister of the industry and may cease operations soon. Most tickets written by travel agents are booked through one of these systems.

The airlines, led principally by American, have also successfully explored marketing strategies to increase customer loyalty. Frequent flyer programs (FFPs) and travel agent commission override programs (TACOs) were introduced shortly after deregulation. Most travelers are aware of frequent flyer programs, which give free travel or other bonuses to passengers who have flown some preset amount with a firm. TACOs have been called "frequent booker" programs for travel agents. In a typical TACO agreement, airline X promises a travel agency a 15 percent commission rate, instead of the usual 10 percent, if that agency books more than 80 percent of its tickets on airline *X*. In a 1990 study by the General Accounting Office, more than half of all agents reported receiving commission overrides.

The biggest surprise from the first 13 years of deregulation has been the pervasive importance of hub-and-spoke operations in the logistic and competitive development of the domestic airline industry. Hubbing has enhanced the efficiency of airline operations, increased the effectiveness of marketing devices such as frequent flyer programs, changed the scale at which an airline must operate to be competitive, and exacerbated problems of congestion at major airports. For this reason, much of the economic research on the industry since deregulation has investigated issues related to the hubs and airline networks in a deregulated industry. The result has been a few well-established facts, and a growing number of questions that remain to be answered.

Nearly all of the research on airline competition addresses one or both of the two critical questions that underlie most work in applied industrial organization: "What equilibrium will evolve in the industry and what will be the speed and path of transition to that equilibirum?" and "What type or degree of government intervention will maximize social welfare?" The next two sections focus on the first question, though the observations have immediate consequences for the second. The topics divide roughly into what might be called "structure" and "strategic" issues; the former covers questions of the effect of market structure on market power—the influence of potential competition, airline networks, and mergers—while the latter includes the complexities in airline competition that result from the sophisticated marketing strategies that have developed—frequent flyer plans, TACOs, price discrimination, and computer reservation systems.

Structure Issues in Airline Competition

Many of the pre-deregulation predictions about competition in the airline industry relied on simple textbook models. The application of contestability theory to the airline industry generally assumed an industry of independent city-pair markets, failing to take account of the importance of airline networks and hub operations. Likewise, the strategic advantages to an airline of dominating service at an airport were not foreseen by many. The textbook theories generally concluded that actual or potential competition would drive all prices to the marginal costs of the most efficient firms, with less efficient airlines reorganizing or exiting the industry. The actual outcome has been quite a bit different.

The Disappointing Evidence on Contestability and Potential Competition

For many economists and policy-makers, advocacy of airline deregulation was simply a rejection of the incredibly inefficient regulation of the previous 50 years. For others, however, a cornerstone of support for airline deregulation was contestability theory, reliance on the disciplining effect of potential competition. It was argued that an airline can enter a new market quickly and with low sunk costs, particularly if the entrant already serves one or both of the endpoints of the route (Bailey and Panzar, 1981). The importance of a potential entrant serving both ends of a route before entering has been demonstrated by Berry (1990a) and Morrison and Winston (1990). Berry, for example, finds that in a sample of 281 new market entries that occurred between the first and third quarters of 1980, the new competitor already served both endpoints in 245 cases and at least one endpoint in 277 cases.

Unfortunately, potential competition appears to be no substitute for actual competition. While contestability theory in its pure form suggests that the number of actual competitors should have no effect on prices, many studies have found that the number of airlines actually competing on a route has a significant effect on the price level (Bailey, Graham, and Kaplan, 1985; Call and Keeler, 1985; Morrison and Winston, 1987; Borenstein, 1989; Hurdle et al., 1989). In 1990, prices on routes with two active competitors averaged about 8 percent lower than on monopoly routes. A third active competitor was associated with another 8 percent price drop. Nor can these effects be attributed to cost savings from higher traffic volume on more competitive routes; volume per airline is smaller on average on routes with more competitors.

Studies that attempt to explain cross-sectional variation in average prices find that a potential competitor in a market has from one-tenth to one-third the competitive impact of an actual competitor (Morrison and Winston, 1987; Borenstein, 1989; Brueckner, Dyer, and Spiller, 1990).

In retrospect, the result is not very surprising. If sunk costs are non-trivial, albeit small, and an incumbent can respond in price and quantity as quickly as a new competitor can enter, then the incumbent has little incentive to respond in advance of actual entry (Stiglitz, 1987). Advertising and the short-run losses associated with inauguration of service on a new route seem to be sufficient sunk costs to inhibit contestability in the airline industry.

Even the small estimates of potential competition effects that have been made may be too high. The measure of potential competition—the number of airlines serving one or both endpoints, but not the route itself—is almost certainly endogenous. A low price in a market will encourage well-positioned potential competitors to stay out of the market, thus increasing the number of potential competitors observed. This effect is likely to bias the analysis towards a larger estimated impact of potential competition. Reiss and Spiller (1989) make an ambitious attempt to model this problem explicitly.

A related approach to comparing the effects of actual and potential competition is to observe when entry and exit occur; that is, the result of a potential competitor becoming an actual competitor and *vice versa*. Joskow, Werden, and Johnson (1990) find that after controlling for cost factors, routes with unusually low prices are subject to more exit than others, and that exit of a competitor leads to a 10 percent average price increase for the incumbents that remain. Routes with abnormally high prices, however, are no more likely to experience new entry than are other routes. Still, they estimate that new entry on average drives down prices by about 9 percent. Morrison and Winston (1990) find that routes with lower-than-average prices, controlling for distance, are actually more likely to be entered than other routes and that routes with higher-than-average prices are more likely to experience exit of a competitor. These studies lend little support to a belief that potential competition disciplines airline markets. They do, however, strongly indicate that prices and entry are jointly determined by some process that is not well understood.

Whinston and Collins (1990) use a stock market event study to analyze the effect of entry. They look at a series of announcements by People Express during 1984-85 about specific routes that it planned to enter in the ensuing weeks. They find that the average combined equity value loss to the incumbents in these markets reflect a pretax loss in future profits of 25 percent to 43 percent of the annual revenues earned on

Table 3. Hubbing and Airport Concentration at the 30 Largest U.S. Airports

Airport	Percent Changing Planes	Airport Herfindahl	Airport Fare Premium	Rank by Size
Charlotte	75.7%	0.579	18.8%	20
Atlanta	69.0%	0.347	17.2%	3
Memphis	67.7%	0.355	27.4%	29
Dallas/Ft. Worth	65.8%	0.386	20.5%	2
Pittsburgh	62.1%	0.529	15.9%	16
Salt Lake City	61.3%	0.430	19.1%	28
St. Louis	56.2%	0.354	-4.0%	13
Chicago–O'Hare	55.7%	0.270	14.8%	1
Denver	54.1%	0.272	15.3%	7
Minneapolis	51.0%	0.418	31.5%	15
Houston–Intercontinental	49.5%	0.423	15.6%	19
New York–Kennedy	47.3%	0.202	2.9%	6
Detroit	43.6%	0.296	-0.7%	11
Baltimore	40.5%	0.299	9.1%	26
Phoenix	33.1%	0.205	-28.4%	9
Miami	31.0%	0.171	-14.3%	14
Seattle	27.3%	0.145	8.7%	24
San Francisco	25.3%	0.145	-1.5%	5
Los Angeles	25.2%	0.110	-5.3%	4
Philadelphia	24.9%	0.217	11.2%	22
Honolulu	22.4%	0.199	-20.8%	17
Newark	19.6%	0.292	11.5%	12
Las Vegas	18.9%	0.177	-27.8%	23
Houston–Hobby	17.5%	0.481	-23.4%	30
Orlando	16.8%	0.180	-15.6%	21
Boston	13.8%	0.120	9.0%	10
Washington D.C.–National	11.1%	0.125	10.7%	18
Tampa	11.0%	0.181	-12.4%	27
San Diego	6.6%	0.138	-18.1%	25
New York–La Guardia	6.2%	0.118	9.5%	8

Source: U. S. D. O.T. Databank IA, second quarter, 1990

these routes. Such a finding indicates that substantial rents were being earned prior to new entry, again reinforcing the conclusion that potential competition cannot substitute for actual competition in airline markets.

Airport Concentration and Market Power

The value of hub-and-spoke networks for the cost savings they offered was recognized before deregulation, but few saw that hubs would also be valued for the market power that they permit. For people whose origin or destination is the hub city, there is often very little competition. The hub-and-spoke networks have evolved to the point that one airline will generally fly to another airline's hub only from its own hub. United, for instance, offers nonstop service to Atlanta—Delta's major hub — only from Denver, Chicago-O'Hare, and Washington-Dulles, three of United's four largest hubs.

Table 3 lists the 30 largest U.S. airports in declining order of what might be called "hubness" — the percentage of passengers using the airport who are traveling through, rather than to or from, the city. Not surprisingly, the hubs tend to be located towards the center of the country. Table 3 also demonstrates that the markets for travel to and from hub airports tend to be more concentrated than at nonhub airports. The third column shows the Herfindahl index of to/from traffic, known as local traffic, at the airport. The correlation between the percentage of passengers changing planes at the airport and the local traffic Herfindahl is 0.74 in this list.

It has been clearly and frequently demonstrated that average prices for local traffic at concentrated airports are significantly higher than prices on other routes (Borenstein, 1989; GAO, 1990a; DOT, 1990; Berry, 1990b; Abramowitz and Brown, 1990; Evans and Kessides, forthcoming). This is illustrated by the fourth column of Table 3, which presents the average ratio of fares on local routes at these airports compared to national average fares on routes of the same distance. The correlation between this "airport fare premium" and airport concentration is 0.44 in this table. Econometric studies have found this effect while controlling for traffic volume, business/tourist mix, the number of plane changes a passenger must make, heterogeneous costs of airlines, concentration and market share on specific routes, airport-specific congestion, and many other factors. The effect, however, does not carry over to itineraries in which the passenger just changes planes at concentrated airports; "through" passengers using these airports pay prices about equal to the national average.

One of the leading explanations for this result is the market power and customer loyalty advantage that a locally dominant airline can achieve through use of frequent flyer plans and travel agent commission override programs (TACOs). One piece of evidence for this theory is that the dominant carrier at a concentrated airport charges higher average prices on routes to and from the airport than other airlines serving the same routes (Borenstein, 1989; Evans and Kessides, forthcoming). Borenstein (1991) also demonstrates that, controlling for price and service quality, the dominant airline at an airport attracts a disproportionate share of passengers who originate their trips at the airport, with the advantage being especially great on business-oriented routes. As explained below, one would expect that frequent flyer programs give a dominant airline a greater advantage in attracting business travelers than others. Other studies have included airport-level entry barriers as an explanation for the higher prices at dominated hubs. Abramowitz and Brown (1990) control explicitly for the effect of majority-in-interest (MII) clauses in gate lease contracts, which allow a dominant airline to block construction of new airport facilities. The effect of MII's is statistically significant, but small, increasing prices by less than 2 percent.

Thus, hub-and-spoke networks are not just a source of increased production efficiency; they are also associated with airport concentration and dominance of a hub airport by one or, occasionally, two airlines. This airport dominance ensures a degree of protection from competition and control over price that was not foreseen prior to deregulation and has significantly altered airlines' strategies in the deregulated industry.

Horizontal Mergers

For better or worse, the Reagan administration's *laissez-faire* views of mergers provided an experiment in industry restructuring, especially in the airline industry. In particular, two mergers between hub-sharing carriers in October 1986 were an excellent opportunity to observe the effect of increased airport dominance.

The merger between Northwest and Republic caused prices at Minneapolis, the primary hub they shared, to increase substantially faster than the national average immediately before and after the merger. The largest price increase occurred on routes where the two merging airlines had been the only competitors, increasing 23 percent faster than the national average. Overall, the average Minneapolis/St. Paul passenger's ticket price went up 11 percent faster than the national average between the year before the merger and the year after (Borenstein, 1990; see also Werden, Joskow, and Johnson, 1991).

The effect of the TWA-Ozark merger on prices at St. Louis is more mixed. When all tickets to and from St. Louis are considered, price went up 8 percent faster than the national average (GAO, 1988; Borenstein, 1990). The increase, however, is driven by a few high-volume routes on which prices increased dramatically following the merger. These were routes on which TWA and Ozark competed prior to the merger along with at least one other airline. Increases on routes with just TWA and Ozark were not faster than the national average. Finally, as Table 3 indicates, St. Louis remains a remarkably low cost city to fly to or from given that it is a concentrated hub airport dominated by TWA.

Such hub mergers appear to decrease service on routes where the merging airlines had competed. This may reflect the elimination of "redundant" service or it could be indicative of reduced competition. The interpretations are not mutually exclusive. Overall, the number of flights offered by the dominant airlines fell 7 percent at Minneapolis following the merger and 11 percent at St. Louis (Borenstein, 1990). Both mergers led to an increase in the total number of cities served from the hubs and to a large increase in the number of connections passengers could make without changing airlines (Huston and Butler, 1988).

The overall welfare effects of these and other mergers require a balancing of the increased market power that may result with the possibility of improved service and efficiency. Brueckner, Dyer, and Spiller (1990) estimate that increased traffic for a dominant airline at a hub will significantly lower the prices it charges to consumers changing planes at the hub on their way to another location. Thus, the merger of two airlines' operating hubs at the same airport would be expected to increase the volume of the traffic carried by the surviving carrier on the spokes of the network and thus decrease costs and prices to through passengers. In fact, prices for passengers traveling through Minneapolis on Northwest-Republic fell by 1.5 percent relative to industry average prices between the second quarters of 1986 and 1987, while passengers traveling through St. Louis on TWA-Ozark saw their prices increase by 0.5 percent relative to industry average during this period.

Morrison and Winston (1989) attempt to compare the costs of market power and the benefits of improved efficiency for six mergers among jet carriers that took place between 1985 and 1988. Besides the two mentioned above, these included Delta-Western, American-Air California, USAir-Piedmont, and USAir-Pacific Southwest Airlines. They find that the six mergers in total had a small positive effect on consumers. This result, however, depends on a large positive estimate of the change in the value of frequent flyer bonuses, an estimate that is probably too optimistic.

Morrison and Winston estimated that frequent flyer miles were valued by consumers at an average of 2.7¢ per mile earned in 1983, about 20 percent of the average fair paid per mile at that time, implying that the minimum 20,000 miles necessary for a free domestic ticket would produce a bonus worth $540. The estimate seems high, considering that supersaver fares for the longest transcontinental trips were under $400 at the time. More importantly, most frequent flyer mileage is never cashed in for free travel, because the consumer either never earns enough mileage for a bonus, never uses the bonus once it is earned, or uses it only for a first-class upgrade, which is likely to be a less valued use. In fact, only 5 to 8 percent of passenger miles are "non-revenue," which includes both frequent-flyer bonus tickets and employee travel. If frequent flyer program bonus trips are valued as much as paid-for trips, then the value enhancement of FFPs would be in the 3 to 7 percent range, after deducting the 1 to 2 percent of passenger miles comprised by employee travel. The actual value enhancement is probably much lower than 3 to 7 percent, since many FFP trips would not have been taken had the traveler had to pay actual fares. On the other hand, to the extent that FFP mileage is used for upgrades and other perks, the actual figure could be somewhat higher. If one assumes that FFPs enhance average ticket value by 6 percent instead of 20 percent, or about 0.8 cents per mile, the overall impact of the mergers they analyze falls from a $67 million annual increase in consumer welfare to about a $200 million loss (Morrison and Winston, 1989, Table 7).[4]

In reality, the short-run welfare effect of the mergers between direct

---

4. Furthermore, Morrison and Winston assume that the value of a FFP bonus ticket increase linearly with an increase in the number of cities that the airline serves, implying that a merger in which the surviving carrier serves 50 percent more cities than either merging carrier did would increase the value of all FFP on the carrier tickets by 50 percent. Given that one always has the option of paying for a ticket to fly where one wants, the size and unbounded nature of the value increase doesn't seem credible.

competitors was probably significantly negative. Whatever production efficiency that the mergers may have permitted does not seem to have been reflected in prices, but the increased market power was often evident. The long-run effect is much more difficult to estimate, because many of the firms—Ozark being the most notable—would probably have failed within a few years absent these mergers. Morrison and Winston (1989) point out that since mergers are extremely unlikely to be "unscrambled" once they have occurred, the appropriate long-run comparison is not to that market structure before the merger, but to the alternative possible market structures and mergers—with the potential for greater efficiency and competition increases—that are foreclosed by the merger.

Vertical Mergers with Commuter Airlines

As the much-publicized horizontal airline mergers were taking place in the mid-1980s, less-publicized vertical network mergers and joint marketing agreements were forming between major airlines and commuter carriers who serve short routes that transport passengers to larger airports. In the early part of deregulation, many commuters agreed to operate in coordination with, and under the name of, a major jet airline. These "codesharing" agreements meant that the commuter airline's flights would be timed to connect with the major airline and would be listed on computer reservation systems under the airline code of the major. In the later 1980s, these agreements were often replaced by vertical integration.

Such agreements and mergers permit greater coordination of flight schedules, baggage handling, marketing, and frequent flyer programs, which may increase the consumer's value of the joint product and may lower actual production costs. In addition, however, they can raise the costs of entry for a new airline at airports where the major and the commuter airline connect. These agreements and mergers do not lead to strict exclusivity—it is possible to connect from a United-affiliated or-owned commuter airline to an American flight—but realistically, a commuter airline cannot coordinate its schedule, airport location, and marketing with many different major airlines. If a new major carrier can compete with the commuter-affiliated major at an airport only by having its own coordinated commuter carrier, there is an associated increase in the sunk cost of starting service at the airport. The theoretical debate over whether efficiency-enhancing vertical coordination might also be used anticompetitively is far from settled.

Consumers occasionally complain that codesharing agreements are an attempt to mislead consumers about who is operating their flights. Most of these complaints are about flying on a propeller plane, however, not about the ownership or operation of the flight. Since both ownership and equipment information are available when the ticket is purchased, and since an airline will have incentive to make sure that an affiliated commuter doesn't harm the airline's good name, government intervention here does not seem wise.

Cost Heterogeneity Among Airlines

The absence of substantial economies of scale was one of the leading arguments for deregulation of the airline industry. The inference drawn by many economists was that all airlines would attain approximately the same costs of production. Yet the studies on which this conclusion was based were not very sophisticated. Essentially, they regressed the total costs of an airline on a measure of output and the costs of inputs, with little focus on the actual production process. Caves, Christensen, and Tretheway (1984) improved upon the earlier studies by distinguishing economies of de. sity—additional passengers on a given set of routes — from economies of scope—a proportional expansion of the size of the network as output expands. Using data from 1970 to 1981, they found substantial density economies, but did not find that increases in the scope of operations lowers an airline's unit costs.

One of the most remarkable results of the various cost studies has received little attention: the significant variation in unit production costs across firms. After controlling for input prices and output characteristics, the carrier-fixed effects in the study by Caves, Christensen, and Tretheway (1984) exhibit a substantial spread, with the least efficient major airline estimated to have 40 percent higher unit costs than the most efficient ones. Since none of these studies corrects for the endogeneity of wages— wages tend to decline when an exogenous cost increase causes the firm's profits to decline—these spreads might well be understated.[5]

---

5. Greenwald, Salinger, and Stiglitz (1991) argue that the cost disparities may be self-enforcing. In a theoretical model and empirical application to the airline industry, they find that firms in financial distress may be less able to invest in productivity-enhancing improvements, thus increasing their cost disadvantage.

Table 4 presents the cost per passenger-mile and per seat-mile for the 12 largest U.S. carriers during 1990. The cost heterogeneity appears to be as significant as ever, with the highest cost airline, USAir, exhibiting unit costs about 64 percent above Southwest's. Caves, Christensen, and Tretheway identify average flight length as the most significant cause of costs heterogeneity, but Southwest actually has a shorter average flight length than USAir, implying that Southwest should exhibit higher costs. America West, which operates a more traditional hub-and-spoke system than Southwest and makes greater use of travel agents and commuter reservation system ticketing also has much lower costs than the other major airlines while flying shorter average trips than most of the others.

Table 4. Cost of Major U.S. Airlines, 1990

Airline	Average Cost per Passenger-Mile	Average Cost per Seat-Mile	Average Flight Distance
Southwest	0.111	0.067	376
America West	0.122	0.075	544
Eastern	0.128	0.078	606
Midway	0.144	0.084	636
American	0.144	0.088	776
United	0.145	0.093	809
Continental	0.150	0.087	743
Northwest	0.150	0.094	665
TWA	0.151	0.089	719
Delta	0.155	0.090	626
Pan Am	0.168	0.101	693
USAir	0.189	0.112	463

Source: U.S.D.O.T. Air Carrier Traffic and Financial Statistics.

What is the source of these cost differences? One answer seems to be managerial ability. The managers of Southwest and American, which has the lowest costs among the large major airlines, are recognized in the industry for being smart and sophisticated. USAir has a reputation for poor management that dates back to the days of regulation.

Still, that just leads to the question of how the inefficient managers hold on to their jobs. Levine (1987) and others have argued that the separation between ownership and control explains the persistence of bad management at some U.S. airlines. The canonical case in the industry is Pan Am, which lost money in all but one year between 1980 and its 1991 demise—a net loss of more than $2 billion—but survived by selling off assets on which huge capital gains were realized, such as land that the company owned in Tokyo. To survive, inefficient firms must retain substantial market power. USAir is a good example. It has two significant dominated hubs, Pittsburgh and Charlotte, where it has over 80 percent of the enplanements. Eastern, which had high costs prior to its bankruptcy declaration and associated wage concessions, exemplifies the alternate outcome. Before its demise, Eastern's most significant airport position was at Atlanta, where it had to coexist with Delta, a much more efficient and sophisticated airline.

These answers, however, are *ad hoc* and the evidence is largely anecdotal. The heterogeneity of management ability and entrenchment in the airline industry, along with the detailed public data on company operations and finances, may offer an unusual opportunity to look more systematically at the internal dynamics of large corporations. These heterogeneities appear to play as large a role in the competitive evolution of the industry as the differences in market shares and concentration across firms and markets.

Strategic Developments in Airline Competition

Under government regulation, airline managers had few marketing decisions to make beyond reviewing the latest brand-image advertisements. Not only did the CAB tell each airline which products it could sell, it also dictated the ways in which they could be sold and the prices that could be charged. When these constraints were lifted, the marketing of air travel quickly became a dynamic and central part of the airline business. The airlines that innovated most quickly gained in market share and profitability.

Loyalty-Inducing Marketing Devices

The first frequent flyer program was introduced in 1981 by American Airlines, but it took until 1986 for all of the major airlines to start one. In some ways, frequent flyer programs (FFPs) are just quantity discounts: "Buy four trips, get the fifth one free." Supporters of this view have pointed out that quantity discounts are present in many industries and that they are particularly appropriate if marginal cost is below average cost, because they allow total costs to be covered while decreasing the inefficiency that results when the marginal price is above marginal cost.[6] However, FFPs also create strategic advantages for an airline with a large market share and reduce the threat of potential competition.

Strategic advantages may result both from the way frequent flyer mileage is accumulated and the way that bonuses are paid out. Because the marginal value of the reward increases as the customer builds up miles or points on a single airline, FFPs encourage travelers to choose the airline that they are most likely to fly on in the future. Thus, the airline with the most service from the traveler's home airport is particularly attractive, because it serves many markets that the consumer may need to travel in the future. Furthermore, the most common bonus—a free flight anywhere in the U.S.—will be more valuable on an airline that offers substantial service from the consumer's home airport than on an airline with little service there.

Frequent flyer programs are targeted primarily at business travelers, taking advantage of the principal-agent problem resulting when the traveler, monitored imperfectly by his employer, does not make the efficient tradeoff between lower prices, or reduced travel time, and extra FFP bonuses (Levine, 1987). In essence, the frequent flyer bonus is a kickback to the purchasing agent, in this case the employee. In a survey of travel agents conducted by the General Accounting Office (1990b), more than half said that their business customers select flights to match their frequent flyer program "always or almost always."

Bonuses earned on business travel are also untaxed fringe benefits which may jointly benefit the employer and employee while harming the government and other taxpayers. Defenders of frequent flyer programs argue that even if the employer finds it costly to monitor frequent flyer miles and bonuses directly, it can still calculate an expected value of the bonuses earned by certain types of employees, and count that toward the employees' compensation. Though this will transfer some of the agent's gains to the principal, it does nothing on the margin to lessen

---

6. This argument is frequently made in support of declining block pricing schedules for public utilities.

inefficient (and cost-increasing) schedule choices of the employee. Nor does it address the advantage that the dominant airline in an area gains through such bonuses.

What frequent flyer programs are to business travelers, travel agent commission overrides (TACOs) are to travel agents. Most travel agents earn increased commission rates from at least one airline in return for steering passengers to those airlines. No work has explicitly modeled the effect of TACOs on competition among airlines, but there is widespread belief within the industry that TACOs are most effectively used by the dominant airline in an area (Levine, 1987; Borenstein, 1991). Just as with FFPs, the rewards for increased bookings on an airline are designed to encourage the agent to concentrate bookings on a single carrier. The anecdotal evidence that exist supports the notion that travel agents will be most affected by the TACO program of the dominant airline in the area (DOT, 1988). This is due in part to the correlation between use of a carrier's computer reservation system and receipt of commission overrides from that airline, as discussed below.

Of course, salespeople of many goods and services receive different commissions on various brands and are thus biased toward the high-commission sale. Are commission overrides for travel agents any different? Probably. Most travelers are not aware of TACOs and do not realize that the agent has a reason to prefer one airline over another, so are less likely to be wary of the agent's advice. Agents hold themselves out as unbiased conveyors of travel information. Moreover, even if customers were aware, it is extremely difficult for any customer to monitor travel agent performance, due to the complexity and constant flux of prices and seat availability in a market.

Increases in brand loyalty or switching costs, such as from FFPs or TACOs, may also facilitate market division and tacit collusion (Banerjee and Summers, 1987). These programs lower the cross-elasticity of demand between products, reducing the incentive for competitive price cutting. This effect may be less important than the dominant firm advantage that the devices permit, because airlines use these strategies most aggressively in areas where they have large market shares, but the two uses are not mutually exclusive. In either case, it is clear that the airlines view these aspects of retailing their product as much more than simple price cuts or commission payments.

Information and Distribution Channels

At the time of deregulation, many industry analysts forecast a stream-lined distribution system, possibly with most ticketing done through machines similar to automatic teller machines, so that the travel agent industry would shrink or even disappear. Instead, travel agents are now more central to the distribution of air travel services than ever before, thanks to the complexity of airline fare structures and the frequency of price changes. With the current computer reservation systems, the agent can look up the schedules, fares, and seat availability on all airlines simultaneously, then reserve a ticket and seat assignment, enter the traveler's frequent flyer number, and even print out boarding passes.

The earliest entrants in the computer reservation service industry, American's Sabre and United's Apollo systems, signed up many travel agents before competing CRSs became widely available. Later entrants have never attained significant penetration in more than a few locations, areas in which the airline owning the CRS has a large share of the flights and traffic. In recent years, Sabre and Apollo have been accused of attempting to lock travel agents into exclusive use of their systems through various contract requirements: damages charged to agents who choose to switch systems may have been out of proportion to actual costs; access to an airline's TACO program may have been illegally tied to use of its CRS; and minimum use clauses may be the reason that near-ly all travel agents use only one airline's CRS for all bookings. These complaints continue, but so far have not been confirmed in court.

The earliest complaints registered against the CRSs were by airlines that didn't own a system of their own, in reaction to the biased presenta-tion of flight information. Prior to a 1984 CAB rule outlawing the prac-tice, airlines would systematically list their own flights more prominent-ly than those of their competitors, a practice known as "screen bias." A recurrent and naive view of computer reservation systems is that they are equivalent to advertising for an airline, and that every airline could start a reservation system and engage in such promotion. In reality, the sunk costs for starting a computer reservation system are substantial, because complex industry-specific software must be developed, tested, and marketed. The learning effects also appear to be significant; Sabre and Apollo systems continue to exhibit more sophistication and capa-bilities, as well as much larger market shares, than the other CRSs.

Economies of scale are quite substantial, because the software production and updating expenses are unrelated to the number of users on the system. The 1984 CAB rule forbidding "screen bias" was implicitly based on the decision that CRSs are essential facilities for selling air transport, and so should be available on a comparable basis to all airlines. Because the software that runs a computer reservation system is so complex, some screen bias almost surely remains, though it is certainly less obvious or important than before 1984.

Computer reservation systems have also become a critical tool in the administration of travel agent commission overrides. Although the 1984 rule explicitly forbids tying of TACOs to use of a carrier's CRS, such practices almost certainly continue (DOT, 1988). Ownership of the CRS used by an agent makes it easier for an airline to implement a TACO program, because most programs are based on the *share* of the agent's bookings that go to an airline, requiring reliable information on all of the agents' sales.

The bias in travel agent booking associated with the CRS it uses, called the "halo effect," was studied in 1988 by the DOT. They found that the airline owning a travel agent's CRS receives a disproportionate share of the bookings from the agent, even after a rough control for commission overrides. The strong results they get, however, could reflect factors other than CRS influence and are certainly subject to endogeneity bias. In a city with a dominant airline that owns a reservation system most of the agents in that city are likely to adopt that CRS for its superior information on the airline's flights and a greater share of agents are likely to be on the dominant airline's TACO program. Furthermore, the dominance will likely inspire greater customer loyalty through frequent flyer programs, which is not controlled for at all.

The ownership of a computer reservation system may also be a deterrent to new entry and price competition, both because of the halo effect, and also because airline B must pay a booking fee to airline A for every airline B ticket booked through airline A's CRS. Under the 1984 CAB rules, a CRS must charge the same booking fees to all airlines, but such a non-discrimination rule cannot affect the internal price or cost paid by the airline-owner for booking its own tickets. In Dallas, for instance, where more than 90 percent of the travel agent bookings go through American's Sabre system, high booking fees on Sabre could discourage entry into all Dallas routes. The DOT study found that booking fees are well above marginal or average cost.

The high-speed transmission of complex information through computer reservation systems has also raised concerns about collusion among the airlines. It appears to be common practice for an airline to announce, through the CRSs, that its price on a certain route will increase by some amount beginning on a certain date in the future. The carrier then waits to see if others will match. If they do, the price increase is implemented. If they don't, the airline suggesting the increase will either withdraw it or push back the implementation date. Other airlines might counteroffer with a smaller increase, effective a day after the first increase. Then the first airline many proceed with a smaller increase, or counteroffer again. All of this occurs without the airlines changing any prices on actual sales, because the negotiation goes on with effective dates two or three weeks hence.

Each airline's fare on the computer reservation system for each route has a descriptive code, usually a string of 5 or more letters and numbers, that may contain further information about what the airline is suggesting or at which competitor a price change might be targeted (Nomani, 1990). In one incident reported in the *Wall Street Journal*, Continental introduced a new fare on a certain route with a fare code that included "HP," the two-letter designation for America West, which Continental appeared to be attacking with the discount. The code may have included "HP" to inform other airlines that Continental was targeting the fare cut at America West and was not interested in starting a widespread fare war.

If such signalling and possible attempts at collusive price fixing exist, they give a basis for concern over the increased national concentration figures, even if route concentration has been fairly stable. The language of signalling is easier to develop and communicate if there are many opportunities for a small number of firms to interact, than if there are many firms. The impact of multimarket contact on tacit or explicit collusion and thus prices has been examined in many industries, but only Evans and Kessides (1991) has focused on domestic airlines. They find that multimarket contact has a significant effect on prices, increasing average round-trip ticket prices by more than $20. The Department of Justice has announced an investigation of airline price signalling. There is sure to be more work done in this area.

Price Discrimination and Dispersion

In the early days of deregulation, some economists called the prevalence of discount fares a sign that the new competitive equilibrium had not yet been reached. As time went by, however, and more airlines adopted complex fare structures, explanations shifted. Unlike the pre-deregulation discounts, availability of today's low fares is limited to a given number on a flight, with that number differing across flights in response to differences in demand. In this way, discounts may reflect peak-load pricing (Salop, 1978; Gale and Holmes, 1990). The restrictions on discounts have also been refined, however, so as to approach the discriminating firm's ideal: imposing prohibitive discount-qualification costs on members of the less-elastic demand group (for example, business travelers are almost never willing to stay over a Saturday night), while retaining relatively easy availability to the group with more elastic demand.

Frank (1983) suggested that the fare differentials were cost-based, because the travelers paying higher prices were those who demanded more frequent service and were thus responsible for higher fixed costs. In models of price discrimination under imperfect competition, Borenstein (1985) and Holmes (1989) have made this argument more rigorous, while clarifying that such pricing is still discriminatory in the traditional sense of differential mark-ups above marginal cost. Even though airline prices are discriminatory, there is no clear reason to believe they are less efficient than a single price set by firms with the same market power. While price discrimination necessarily results in exchange inefficiency—any given quantity produced is not allocated to the users who value it most highly—it also may increase total output compared with firms that face the same demand functions and each charge a single price.

The pattern of price discrimination in the airline industry is in itself interesting and surprising. After controlling for peak-load pricing effects, Borenstein and Rose (1991) find that discrimination is greater on more competitive routes. The theoretical works by Borenstein and Holmes predict this pattern if discrimination is based more on variations in customer willingness to switch flights—scheduling flexibility and brand loyalty—than on variations in customer reservation prices for the trip. Borenstein and Rose also find that airlines owning CRSs have significantly more price dispersion on a route, supporting the industry wisdom that effective market segmentation requires the sort of management and computer sophistication that varies widely among the airlines.

Bankruptcies, Bailouts, and Public Policy

The crisis in the airline industry that began in the last half of 1990 raised numerous public policy issues. Unsecured debt markets were closed to the weaker airlines, many of which requested financial assistance from the federal government. Did this represent a failure of capital markets, or simply a market signal that these companies should not be extended loans because they are unlikely to be able to repay them? In late 1990, the government considered several short-run fixes, including short-term loans, tapping the Strategic Petroleum Reserve specifically to lower jet fuel prices, and permitting airlines to delay remitting some of the 10 percent ticket tax to the government, thereby making interest-free loans to the airlines.

None of these steps was taken. The main reasons seemed to be that the industry was not yet so close to anticompetitive levels of concentration that the impending bankruptcies would be pivotal and, in addition, that a bailout appeared likely to spend taxpayer's money without a real hope of benefits. Bankruptcy courts handling the Eastern and Pan Am cases took a very different view, willingly spending the remaining funds of these firms to give the companies every possible chance to survive. Effectively, these courts were taxing the holders of the firms' debt. Their motivation seemed to be the preservation of competitors in the marketplace, not protection of creditors' wealth.

The bankruptcy proceedings have highlighted the fact that large corporate failures in the U.S. always involve some government intervention. The default regulator of the industry is the bankruptcy court judge. The fact that government will be involved does not mean, of course, that earlier intervention by some other government body will necessarily lead to better outcomes, but it does imply that a simple hands-off approach to the disruption and increasing concentration in the airline industry is not realistic.

The policies that have been suggested to respond to declining competition in the domestic airline industry range from more deregulation to complete reregulation. Here is a brief summary and critique of the most probable actions, ordered from least to most interventionist

Foreign Ownership and Foreign Competition

Currently, foreign interests can hold no more than a 49 percent voting share in a U.S. airline (increased from 25 percent in 1991) and cannot otherwise control the company. Advocates of permitting greater foreign ownership argue that it would provide a quick infusion of capital to the distressed airlines.

Opposition to this proposal has rested on national defense arguments, such as the questionable view that the aircraft of foreign-controlled airlines might be unavailable for government use in times of war or other disaster. The obvious response is to require that all aircraft serving U.S. routes are subject to confiscation during national emergencies. The real weakness of this plan is that no queue of foreign investors is waiting to sink money into the crippled U.S. airlines; they are more interested in buying part of American or United than Continental or TWA. Again, the capital markets might be telling us something about these airlines.

The corollary to foreign investment is competition from foreign airlines on domestic U.S. routes. Among economists and policy-makers, this idea is seen as one whose time has come, but it will still be a long time in the implementation. The main sticking point is that the European Community and most Asian countries are not yet ready to allow U.S. airlines to fly domestic and international routes within and between their countries. U.S. negotiators are understandably hesitant to drop barriers to foreign airlines in the U.S. without gaining access to foreign markets. In fact, most foreign carriers are much less efficient than U.S. airlines, due to years of government ownership and protection, and they have comparatively little sophistication in modern airline marketing strategies. Without subsidies from their home governments, they would not be likely to offer much competition to U.S. airlines. As with foreign ownership, foreign competition is probably a good idea, but not one likely to have a dramatic effect on the domestic airline industry.

Airport Expansion, Peak-Load Pricing, and Privatization

Some critics believe that the only remaining problem in the U.S. domestic airline industry is that the government is still in the airport business. They argue that if airports were privatized, the operators would charge efficient peak/off-peak prices and would respond to market incentives for expansion. This argument ignores the fact that airports are natural monopolies, which would lead to restricted output in the absence of regulation, and that airports create large externalities, which would lead to *de facto* regulation even without an explicit regulatory body. Furthermore, without competition from other airports, an operator's profits would probably be maximized by permitting dominance of the airport by a single carrier and then extracting the carrier's rents with high facility fees.

Still, there is no doubt that current airport management fails to implement many of the market-based incentives, most notably peak-load pricing of runway and facility use, that would lessen the inefficiencies that permeate the system (Morrison, 1987). A switch to peak-load pricing— including a recognition that a general aviation plane landing or taking off creates about as much congestion as a commercial jet—would significantly improve allocation of limited airport capacity.

Rational funding of airport expansion would also greatly improve airport congestion. In a program that seems to be based more on politics than economics, the DOT currently distributes most funds for airport improvements through a program that is strongly biased towards thousands of small general aviation and commercial "reliever" airports. These airports are not operating at capacity and are not used by jet aircraft. Shifting funds towards improvements that have the highest shadow value would substantially lessen airport congestion without increased funding.

Funding is not the only constraint on airport expansion, however. Neighborhood opposition to increased air traffic is often quite strong and the incumbent dominant airlines at many airports are powerful opponents to facility expansion. Improved airport management and expansion planning would increase competition, but the impact may be disappointingly small. Even with higher capacity and peak-load pricing, airport access problems may remain. While additional capacity at an airport could facilitate new entry, the monopoly rents earned by a dominant incumbent would probably give it the incentive to outbid potential new entrants for rights to the additional capacity. Anecdotes about control of gates for the purpose of excluding competitors are commonplace.

At the four slot-controlled airports, minimum-use rules have been imposed to keep the owner of a slot from holding it for exclusionary purposes.

Limiting Loyalty–Inducing Devices for Flyers and Travel Agents

Since frequent flyer programs and travel agent commission overrides are widely thought to give a competitive advantage to the dominant airline in an area, their elimination or curtailment has been suggested. Discussion continues at DOT and in Congress about the possibility of banning frequent flyer programs or taxing them as fringe benefits. The latter approach poses practical difficulties, since the IRS would have to distinguish between awards earned from personal travel and those earned from business travel. An alternative approach would be to require that airlines allow sale and transfer of frequent flyer miles, and thus lessen the lock-in effect of these programs. The airlines have made it clear that they would respond to such a rule by cancelling their frequent flyer programs. FFPs do seem to present a barrier to entry in areas where one airline is dominant. There are clear inefficiencies from the principal-agent problem that they create, without which they would probably be abandoned by the airlines. No good data have been found on FFPs, however, so reliable estimates of the magnitudes of these effects are still lacking.

The principle argument against eliminating frequent flyer programs seems to be the generic concern that limits on the forms in which companies can do business should be enacted only in extreme situations, because the results of such rules can be unpredictable. For example, some have argued that sustainable prices may not exist for hub operations, and that the loyalty induced by frequent flyer programs could allow an airline to maintain efficient economies of density at their hubs. However, such an effect would be empirically indistinguishable from barriers to entry that enhance market power and lead to supracompetitive prices.

A minimalist proposal to address the principal-agent problem induced by travel agent commission overrides would require that agents disclose the average commission rates that they receive from each airline. If this information were posted at the travel agency and enclosed with each ticket sold, customers would be made aware that the agent receives different commission rates from different airlines and would know the direction in which the agent is likely to be biased. A more significant step would be to require that airlines pay equal commission rates to all agents. This, however, intervenes in the retailing process to a much greater extent than in other industries and possibly to a greater extent than is justified by the principal-agent problem.

Opponents of policy actions on TACOs make the arguments that the travel agent industry is very competitive and that differential commission rates are common in many industries. However, given that airlines think TACOs have an effect on the agents' choice and travel agents report in surveys that they do (*Travel Weekly*, 1988), the commission disclosure proposal seems a minimally invasive way to alert consumers to the bias.

Divestiture or New Restrictions on Computer Reservation Systems

The most frequent suggestion to correct biased treatment of carriers in listing flights and updating information on computer reservation systems is to require that airlines sell off their systems. The proposal would also eliminate differential booking fees that effectively result when one carrier owns the CRS that is charging above-cost fees. To the extent that owner-airlines use their CRSs to coordinate or enforce TACOs, divestiture will weaken the impact of commission overrides. Levine (1987) and others who are very familiar with CRSs argue that no realistic amount of rule making and enforcement will remove these advantages without divestiture.

The problem with divestiture is that it would be a very costly form of intervention. Separated from one another, the computer reservation systems and the airlines would each be worth quite a bit less, because both the "bias" advantages for the airlines and any economies of jointly operating and making innovations in these two related businesses would disappear. The litigation that would precede and follow such a move would be lengthy. The net benefits of divestiture could well be positive, but the variance of most guesses about the benefits is large both relative to the expected benefit and in actual dollar terms.CRS divestiture would not reduce concerns about tacit collusion through CRS pre-announcement of price changes.

Conclusion

The airline industry was deregulated not because economists or politicians knew what the deregulated equilibrium would look like, but because they believed that the deregulated outcome would be better than regulation. Airline executives also did not know what the new equilibrium would be. The managements of Delta and American vigorously opposed deregulation, but they have reaped the greatest benefits from it. The industry has gone through a wave of new entry and mass exit, while the survivors have reorganized to focus on hub and spoke operations. Movement towards equilibrium has been slow in part because the structure of the new equilibrium has not been clear; the players were guessing about the outcome as much as the observers, and were probably not much better informed.

The long-run equilibrium in the airline industry is still not clear. Eventually, the number of major airlines might be reduced to just a few, reinforcing calls for renewed price regulation. If so, that may be the inevitable result of network economies that may make competition unworkable. More likely, however, it would result from marketing devices that give strategic advantages to larger firms and incumbents operating hub and spoke systems.

The current task for policy-makers is to make sure that efficient production and competition, not anticompetitive marketing devices, determine the winners and losers in the airline industry as it moves towards a new equilibrium. At the least, this requires opening markets to foreign competition, improving access to and pricing of airport ground facilities, requiring that travel agents disclose their commission rates, and monitoring CRSs closely for biased and strategic uses. Of course, any future mergers among major airlines must also be examined with great skepticism. As the number of competitors has continued to decline in the last year, the arguments have been bolstered for more aggressive actions: banning frequent flyer programs, requiring airlines to pay flat and equal commission rates to all agents, and forcing divestiture of the CRSs. These moves would imply a heavier hand of government intervention, but still much less than the price and entry regulation that may otherwise result.

¥*My thanks to Bill Evans, Robert Gordon, Dan Kaplan, Nancy Rose, Carl Shapiro, Joe Stiglitz, and Timothy Taylor for helpful comments. Janet Netz provided excellent research assistance.*

References

Abramowitz, Amy D. and Stephen M. Brown, "The Effects of Hub Dominance and Barriers to Entry on Airline Competition and Fares." mimeo, U.S. General Accounting Office, Washington D.C., October 1990.

Bailey, Elizabeth E. and John C. Panzar, "The Contestability of Airline Markets During the Transition to Deregulation," *Law and Contemporary Problems*, Winter 1981, 44:1, 125-45.

Bailey, Elizabeth E., David R. Graham, and Daniel P. Kaplan, *Deregulating the Airlines*, Cambridge: MIT Press, 1985.

Banerjee, Abhijit and Lawrence Summers, "On Frequent-Flyer Programs and Other Loyalty-Inducing Economics Arrangements," Harvard Institute of Economic Research Discussion Paper # 1337, September 1987.

Berry, Steven T., "Estimating a Model of Entry in the Airline Industry." Yale University Working Paper, 1990a.

Berry, Steven T., "Airport Presence as Product Differentiation," *American Economic Review*, May 1990b, 80, 394-99.

Borenstein, Severin, "Price Discrimination in Free-Entry Markets." *Rand Journal of Economics*, Autumn 1985, 16, 380-97.

Borenstein, Severin, "Hubs and High Fares: Airport Dominance and Market Power in the U.S. Airline Industry," *Rand Journal of Economics*, Autumn 1989, 20, 344-65.

Borenstein, Severin, "Airline Mergers, Airport Dominance, and Market Power" *American Economic Review*, May 1990, 80, 400-04.

Borenstein, Severin, "The Dominant-Firm Advantage in Multi-Product Industries: Evidence from the U.S. Airlines," *Quarterly Journal of Economics*, November 1991, 106, 1237-66.

Borenstein, Severin, "Prospects for Competitive European Air Travel." In Adams, W.J., ed., *Europe After 1992*. Ann Arbor: The University of Michigan Press, forthcoming 1992.

Borenstein, Severin and Nancy L. Rose, "Competition and Price Dispersion in the U.S. Airline Industry," National Bureau of Economic Research Working Paper #3785, July 1991.

Brueckner, Jan K., Nichola J. Dyer, and Pablo T. Spiller, "Fare Determination in Airline Hub-and-Spoke Networks," University of Illinois Working Paper, June 1990.

Call, Gregory D. and Theodore E. Keeler, "Airline Deregulation, Fares, and Market Behavior: Some Empirical Evidence." In Daugherty, Andrew H., ed., *Analytic Studies in Transport Economics.* Cambridge: Cambridge University Press, 1985, 221-47.

Carlton, Dennis W., William M. Landes, and Richard A. Posner, "Benefits and Costs of Airline Mergers: A Case Study," *Bell Journal of Economics and Management Science,* Spring 1980, 11, 65-83.

Caves, Douglas W., *Air Transport and Its Regulators: An Industry Study,* Cambridge: Harvard University Press, 1962.

Caves, Douglas W., Lauritis R. Christensen, and Michael W. Tretheway, "Economies of Density Versus Economies of Scale: Why Trunk and Local Service Airline Costs Differ," *Rand Journal of Economics,* Winter 1984, 15, 471-89.

Dempsey, Paul S., *Flying Blind: The Failure of Airline Deregulation,* Washington, D.C.: Economic Policy Institute, 1990.

Douglas, George W. and James C. Miller III, *Economic Regulation of Domestic Air Transport: Theory and Policy,* Washington, D.C.: Brookings Institution, 1974.

Eads, George, Mark Nerlove, and W. Raduchel, "A Long-Run Cost Function for the Local Service Airline Industry," *Review of Economics and Statistics,* August 1969, 51:3, 258-70.

Evans, William N. and Ioannis N. Kessides, "Living by the 'Golden Rule': Multimarket Contact in the U.S. Airline Industry," University of Maryland Working Paper, January 1991.

Evans, William N. and Ioannis N. Kessies, "Localized Market Power in the U.S. Airline Industry," *Review of Economics and Statistics,* Forthcoming 1992.

Frank, Robert, "When Are Price Differentials Discriminatory?," *Journal of Policy Analysis and Management,* Winter 1983, 2:2, 238-55.

Gale, Ian and Thomas J. Holmes, "Advance-Purchase Discounts and Monopoly Allocation of Capacity," SSRI Working Paper #9005, 1990.

Gordon, Robert J., "Productivity in the Transportation Sector." In Griliches, Zvi, et al., eds., *The Measurement of Output in the Services Sector,* University of Chicago Press for NBER, forthcoming 1992.

Greenwald, Bruce C., Michael A. Salinger, and Joseph E. Stiglitz, "Imperfect Capital Markets and Productivity Growth," mimeo, Stanford University, March 1991. Paper presented at NBER Conference in Vail, Colorado, April 1991.

Holmes, Thomas J., "The Effects of Third-Degree Price Discrimination in Oligopoly," *American Economic Review*, March 1989, 79, 244-50

Hurdle, Gloria J., Richard L. Johnson, Andrew S. Joskow, Gregory J. Werden, and Michael A. Williams, "Concentration, Potential Entry, and Performance in the Airline Industry," *Journal of Industrial Economics*, December 1989, 38, 119-39.

Huston, John H. and Richard V. Butler, "The Effects of Fortress Hubs on Airline Fares and Service: The Early Returns," *Logistics and Transportation Review*, September 1988, 24, 203-15.

Jordan, William A., *Airline Regulation in America: Effects and Imperfections*, Baltimore: The Johns Hopkins University Press, 1970.

Joskow, Andrew S., Gregory J. Werden, and Richard L. Johnson, "Entry, Exit and Performance in Airline Markets," Department of Justice Discussion Paper EAG 90-10, December 1990.

Kaplan, Daniel P., "The Changing Airline Industry." In Weiss and Klass, eds., *Regulatory Reform: What Actually Happened*. Boston: Little, Brown and Company, 1986, 40-77.

Keeler, Theodore E., "Airline Regulation and Market Performance," *Bell Journal of Economics and Management Science*, Autumn 1972, 3, 399-424.

Levine, Michael E., "Is Regulation Necessary? California Air Transportation and National Regulatory Policy." *Yale Law Journal*, July 1965, 74, 1416-47

Levine, Michael E., "Airline Competition in Deregulated Markets: Theory, Firm Strategy and Public Policy," *Yale Journal on Regulation*, Spring 1987, 4, 393-494.

McGowan, Francis and Paul Seabright, "Deregulating European Airlines," *Economic Policy*, October 1989, 4, 283-344.

Morrison, Steven A., "The Efficiency and Equity of Runway Pricing," *Journal of Public Economics*, October 1987, 34, 45-60.

Morrison, Steven A. and Clifford Winston, *The Economic Effects of Airline Deregulation*. Washington D.C.: Brookings Institution, 1986.

Morrison, Steven A. and Clifford Winston, "Empirical Implications and Tests of the Contestability Hypothesis," *Journal of Law and Economics*, April 1987, 30, 53-66.

Morrison, Steven A. and Clifford Winston, "Enhancing the Performance of the Deregulated Air Transportation System," *Brookings Papers on Economic Activity: Microeconomics,* 1989, 61-112.

Morrison, Steven A. and Clifford Winston. "The Dynamics of Airline Pricing and Competition." *American Economic Review,* May 1990, 80, 389-93.

Nomani, Asra Q., "Airline May Be Using a Price-Data Network to Lessen Competition." *Wall Street Journal,* June 28, 1990, 122, A1, A6.

Reiss, Peter C. and Pablo T. Spiller, "Competition and Entry in Small Airline Markets," *Journal of Law and Economics,* October 1989, 32, S179-S202.

Salop, Steven C., "Alternative Reservation Contracts," Civil Aeronautics Board memo, 1978.

Stiglitz, Joseph E., "Technological Change, Sunk Costs, and Competition," *Brookings Papers on Economic Activity: Microeconomics,* 1987, 3, 883-937.

U.S. General Accounting Office, "Airline Competition: Fare and Service Changes at St. Louis Since the TWA-Ozark Merger," September 1988.

U.S. General Accounting Office, "Airline Competition: Higher Fares and Reduced Competition at Concentrated Airports," July 1990a.

U.S. General Accounting Office, "Airline Competition: Industry Operating and Marketing Practices Limit Market Entry," August 1990b.

U.S. Department of Transportation, *Study of Airline Computer Reservation Systems,* Washington, D.C.: U.S. Government Printing Office, 1988.

U.S. Department of Transportation, *Secretary s Task Force on Competition in the U.S. Domestic Airline Industry,* Washington, D.C.: U.S. Government Printing Office, 1990.

Werden, Gregory J., Andrew S. Joskow, and Richard L. Johnson, "The Effects of Mergers on Price and Output: Two Case Studies from the Airline Industry," *Managerial and Decision Economics,* October 1991, 12, 341-52.

Whinston, Michael D. and Scott C. Collins, "Entry and Competitive Structure in Deregulated Airline Markets: An Event Study Analysis of People Express," Harvard University Working Paper, August 1990.

"The 1988 Louis Harris Survey," *Travel Weekly,* XLVII (June 29, 1988), 9-142.

CHAPTER 22

AN APPLICATION OF THE ECONOMIC MODELLING APPROACH TO THE INVESTIGATION OF PREDATION

J.S. Dodgson*, Y. Katsoulacos** and C. R. Newton*

I. Introduction

This paper is concerned with the issue of the identification of predatory behaviour. In particular, it is concerned with a comparison of a specific application of the conventional rule-of-reason approach adopted by certain competition agencies in the United Kingdom (namely, the Office of Fair Trading (OFT) and the Monopolies and Mergers Commission (MMC)), with an Economic Modelling Approach which we have developed (Dodgson, Katsoulacos and Newton, 1992) following a proposal

* Department of Economics and Accounting, University of Liverpool.
** Department of Economics, University of Liverpool, and Athens University of Economics and Business.

This paper presents some of the results of a study on the identification of predatory behaviour in the bus industry funded jointly by the Economic and Social Research Council (grant number WD08250021) and the Department of Transport. The authors are grateful for their assistance, but neither organisation bears any responsibility for the content of this paper. The authors also thank the participants in the Inverness bus competition case for discussing the case and providing supplementary information. The views expressed in this paper are, however, the authors' own.

by Phlips (1987) on the appropriate way to identify predatory behaviour. The use of a particular case study generates data (of a sort that is normally commercially confidential) and enables us to assess both the limitations of a modelling approach and the light it casts on the more conventional rule-of-reason approach.

The case study we are concerned with is that of competition between bus operators in Inverness. This is one of the five allegations involving predatory behaviour in the British bus industry that were investigated formally by the OFT (see Office of Fair Trading, 1989a/b/c, 1990 and 1992). The OFT is concerned only with the issue of whether action is anti-competitive. If action is judged to be anti-competitive, the Director-General of Competition (the head of the OFT) has the power to refer the matter to the Monopolies and Mergers Commission. The MMC must also judge whether action is anti-competitive and, in addition, whether it operates against the public interest. Of the five formal bus industry investigations, three were judged to involve predatory/anti-competitive action, and two of these were referred to the MMC. In this paper we draw on information in the published reports of the Office of Fair Trading (1989b) and the Monopolies and Mergers Commission (1990), together with supplementary material from our own discussions with some of the participants and from additional sources of information (for example, on service levels).

The Economic Modelling Approach considers the question of whether there is a profitable entry opportunity in the market where predation is alleged. If there is, but the entrant actually makes losses, then the approach considers whether action by the incumbent might have denied the entrant its profitable entry opportunity. The Economic Modelling Approach considers the opportunities available to *both* firms and the actions they take. While the results may in some circumstances be model-specific, the paper shows how the approach can be used both to provide general insights into the process of identifying predatory behaviour and to investigate particular cases.

II. Bus Competition in Inverness: The Office of Fair Trading and Monopolies and Mergers Commission Investigations

On 21 March 1989 the Director-General of Fair Trading gave notice that his office would carry ohut an investigation under Section 3 of the 1980 Competition Act in order to establish whether Highland Scottish Omnibuses (HSO) had been or were pursuing a course of conduct which amounted to an anti-competitive practice. The matters to be investigated were:

(1) The conduct of the company in respect of its operation of local bus services in the Inverness area with particular regard to the use of additional vehicles on registered services and the reduction of fares to a level similar to those of a competitor, Inverness Traction Ltd. (ITL).

(2) Whether that conduct restricts, distorts or prevents competition in connection with the supply of local bus services in the Inverness area (Office of Fair Trading, 1989c, p. 1).

Inverness is the major town in the Scottish Highlands. The town itself has a population of some 42,600, and the surrounding district another 18,000. HSO was one of the eleven bus-operation subsidiaries of the nationalised Scottish Bus Group, itself a subsidiary of the Scottish Transport Group. HSO's network of local bus routes operating in Inverness in 1988 accounted for some 30 per cent of its total revenue from local bus services and for 21 per cent of its overall turnover.

In May 1988 a new company, Inverness Traction Ltd., commenced operations in Inverness with eight minibus routes. It was formed by 19 owner-directors, most of whom had previously worked for HSO. In August 1988 the company expanded its operations by introducing a further seven minibus routes in Inverness. Inverness Traction went into receivership in March 1989, but its operations were taken over in April by Alexanders (North East) Ltd., a bus operator set up in 1988 and based in Aberdeen. The Inverness Traction name was retained, but Alexanders themselves were to go into receivership in November 1989. ITL operations were then taken over by Magicbus (Scotland) Ltd., a

subsidiary of Stagecoach (Holdings) Ltd., the largest British bus operator. Competition in the town continued until September 1991.

Highland Scottish was privatised in August 1991. In September the
company imposed a new set of conditions on its workforce. Many of its
drivers resigned and joined Inverness Traction, and after briefly attempting to continue operation of its services in Inverness, HSO withdrew
from the town on 13 September (MacDonald, 1991).

In investigating allegations of predatory behaviour in Inverness the
OFT adopted an approach that was common with their other investigations of predation in the bus industry. They defined predatory behaviour
as follows:

> "Predatory behaviour of the sort alleged involves the deliberate acceptance
> of losses in the short run with the intention of eliminating competition, so
> that enhanced profits can be earned in the longer term by raising prices
> above the competitive level" (Office of Fair Trading, 1989c, p. 37).

The Office adopted a three-stage process in assessing whether
behaviour was predatory. The first stage considered whether predation
was *feasible* in the market under investigation. The second stage considered the *relationship between the incumbent's costs and revenue*, and in
particular whether the incumbent's actual profits were negative (that is,
$\pi_m < 0$). If the incumbent did make losses in the market where predation
was alleged, the third stage of investigation considered *evidence of
intent*.

In all its formal investigations the Office believed that predation was
a feasible strategy in the bus industry. Competition from cars and walking is limited. Asymmetries of information give existing operators an
incentive to build up a reputation for toughness in the face of competition in order to deter future entry. Firms are free to vary fares as they
wish, so that fares can be reduced once entry occurs (as happened in
Inverness on the day that ITL entered the market) rather than in antici-
pation of possible entry. In contrast, service levels have to be notified 42
days in advance, so that incumbents have prior warning of entry. Incumbents may also have greater resources to finance losses.

The OFT's Inverness report was published on 22 September 1989.

HSO's actions had clearly not prevented competition, but the Office believed that the actions had restricted competition and constituted an anti-competitive practice. The OFT judged that Highland's actions had gone beyond a legitimate competitive response and constituted a significant restriction on ITL's ability to compete. HSO had not earned enough revenue to cover total costs including overheads on their Inverness town services. The OFT (Office of Fair Trading, 1989b, p. 43) identified five features which, it believed, indicated evidence of predatory intent rather than simply the short-run consequences of competition in a previously uncontested environment. These were:

(i) the 60 per cent increase in bus-miles operated by HSO, from the pre-entry first five months of 1988 to the first five months of 1989;

(ii) the increase in HSO's costs by one third despite a fall in unit costs, as a result of the increased bus-mileage operated;

(iii) the continued operation of duplicate services on one route (route 12);

(iv) the undercutting of ITL's fares on one route;

(v) the fact that Highland's business plan indicated a willingness to accept losses over a period of time in the expectation that competition would cease.

The Office also considered that HSO's actions would be likely to restrict competition because it was better able to sustain losses than were the entrants. It should be noted that the Office did not cite the *matching* of fares (a feature of the original reference) as evidence of predatory intent.

The Office sought undertakings from Highland Scottish regarding its future behaviour, but the company was not prepared to provide acceptable undertakings. As a result on 14 December 1989 the Director-General of Fair Trading referred the case to the Monoplies and Mergers Commission under Section 5 of the 1980 Competition Act. The MMC report was published in July 1990. It covered the period of competition from 15 December 1988 to 14 December 1989, so there was some overlap with the period covered by the OFT's investigation. The MMC was required to consider: (a) whether HSO was engaging in an anti-competitive practice and, if it was, whether that practice operated, or might be expected to operated, against the public interest; (b) what adverse effects might result; and (c) what actions (if any) should be taken to remedy or prevent such adverse effects.

The MMC did find that HSO had acted in an anti-competitive manner:

> "We are clear that in providing a grossly excessive volume of services, whilst incurring substatial losses, HSO pursued a course of conduct in relation to ITL that was likely to drive it out of the market and hence to have the effect of restricting competition ... HSO's behaviour towards A (NE) [Alexanders] ... was no less anti-competitive than it was towards ITL" (Monopolies and Mergers Commission, 1990, pp. 50-51).

> HSO "went too far: its provision of new services and of duplicates was grossly excessive, incurring losses that were unjustified..." (Monopolies and Mergers Commission, 1990, p. 1)

The MMC's conclusions were based entirely on HSO's actions with regard to services operated, rather than with regard to fares. The MMC concluded that the matching of the entrant's fares was a reasonable commercial response, even though the entrant's initial fare may not have been commercially viable for the entrant. They argued that the fare undercutting on route 12 cited by the OFT as evidence of intent may not have been as significant as it first appeared. The incumbent had incorrectly anticipated that the entrant would charge its standard fare of 30p on a route extension and so lowered its own fare accordingly: the entrant then announced a fare of 50p, but in practice both operators charged 30p. Moreover, HSO continued to charge 30p for five months after the entrant had abandoned the service. On bus service levels, HSO was found to have breached the spirit of its parent Scottish Transport Group guidelines on overbussing, but *both* operators were believed to have operated extra services without regard to profitability:

> "... both HSO and ITL put on as many duplicate services as they could with no regard to the demand, and little for the cost" (Monopolies and Mergers Commission, 1990, p. 50).

The MMC believed that HSO's anti-competitive practices might have been expected to operate against the public interest, since the takeover of Inverness Traction by Alexanders had been unlikely: in the absence of competition Highland Scottish would probably have adopted lower service levels and higher fares. As it turned out, the takeover of Alexanders by Magicbus meant that Highland Scottish had not been able to do this. The MMC identified two other effects likely to be adverse to the public interest. The first was that the experience of Inverness might have a general effect in inhibiting small newcomers from challenging established operators in the bus industry. Secondly, the experience of the owner-workers of Inverness Traction in losing the capital they invested in the company might discourage workers from participating in management and employee buy-outs when the nationalised Scottish Transport Group was privatised.

Nevertheless, the MMC did not propose any remedial or preventive measures. Their argument was that the Magicbus takeover of Inverness Traction meant that there was now no need for them to constrain Highland Scottish's actions. With regard to loss of entrepreneurial confidence, the Commission thought that its best short-term remedy would be "to make it clear to the bus industry that this Commission would normally expect to recommend briskly effective remedial action in any case referred to them in which they found the public interest adversely affected by an anti-competitive practice" (Monopolies and Mergers Commission, 1990, p. 53). While the MMC has no powers to impose fines, the Commission also considered that the possibility of fines (under European Commission competition laws) might have "punitive and deterrent merits."

III. The Economic Modelling Approach

Phlips (1987) argued that predation involves the conversion of a profitable entry opportunity into an unprofitable one. Thus, proof of predation should involve a rule-of-reason approach in which evidence is provided:

"to the effect that an alleged predatory price cut turned a positive entry value into a negative one for the alleged victim. It should be shown that the present value of future profits is larger than the fixed sunk entry costs of the victim under normal competition and that the price cut made this value smaller than the fixed sunk entry cost. In simple words, this amounts to showing that without the price cut, there was room in the market for an additional firm under normal competition, that is, in a non-cooperative Nash equilibrium. And that, as a result of the price cutting, the price went below the non-cooperative Nash equilibrium price" (Phlips, 1987, pp. 67-68).

Our Economic Modelling Approach (EMA) is intended to make this proposed method operational. To do this we require a model which predicts the non-cooperative Nash equilibrium (or "normal competitive" equilibrium) in the market under investigation. We have set out such a model in Dodgson, Katsoulacos and Newton (1992).

If the model predicts that there is no positive entry value, that is, the equilibrium profits of the entrant π_e^* are negative, so that there is not room in the market for two firms, then either the entrant has entered by mistake, or alternatively the entrant is aware of the potential profitability of the market and is hoping to *displace* the existing incumbent. If, on the other hand, the model predicts that there *is* a positive entry value but the entrant actually makes losses, that is, the actual profits of the entrant π_e are negative, then predation is a possibility. However, it is necessary to be careful to distinguish predation from other possibilities that are also consistent with positive equilibrium ($\pi_e^* > 0$) and negative actual ($\pi_e < 0$) profits for the entrant. One such possibility is that the entrant chooses the *wrong* level of entry, in terms of prices and/or service level, by mistake. Another is that the entrant *deliberately* chooses a price/service level combination which is not its own best response to the incumbent's combination, in order to influence the incumbent's behaviour: in the extreme, the entrant might choose a combination which denies the incumbent any profitable response. Such deliberate responses on the entrant's part prove to be an important consideration in the competitive situation we analyse in Section 4 of this paper.

Our model of bus competition involves two firms competing on both price (fare) and service level. We measure service level in terms of the total bus-miles operated by each firm on the particular route (or in the particular town) being modelled. Bus operating costs are a function of both bus-miles and patronage, so that:

$$C_i = F_i + m_i B_i + \hat{m}_i q_i \tag{1}$$

where

C_i = total costs of firm i,
F_i = fixed costs,
B_i = bus-miles,
q_i = patronage (passenger journeys, or passenger-miles).

It is worth noting that most of the marginal costs are associated with bus-miles, so that marginal costs per journey or per passenger-mile ($\hat{m}_i$) are low in relation to marginal costs per bus-mile (m_i).

We have used both constant elasticity and non-constant elasticity formulations of demand. The constant elasticity demand function is:

$$q_i = \alpha_i \, f_i^{-\eta_i} f_j^{\hat{\eta}_i} B_i^{\varepsilon_i} B_j^{-\hat{\varepsilon}_i} \quad i,j = m,e \tag{2}$$
$$i \neq j$$

where f_i is the fare of operator i, and the elasticity parameters η_i, $\hat{\eta}_i$, ε_i and $\hat{\varepsilon}_i$ are all positive. We refer to the constant α_i as a "strength of demand" parameter.

The non-constant elasticity of demand function is:

$$q_i = \beta_i \, e^{-(\upsilon_i f_i + \hat{\upsilon}_i f_j^{-1} + \zeta_i B_i^{-1} + \hat{\zeta}_i B_j)} \tag{3}$$

where β_i, υ_i, $\hat{\upsilon}_i$, ζ_i and $\hat{\zeta}_i$ are all positive, and are related to their respective elasticities, for example,

$$\eta_i = \upsilon_i f_i \tag{4}$$

so the absolute value of fare elasticity rises with the fare.

Ideally one would wish to estimate the demand function using data on fares, service levels and patronage in a competitive situation. So far this has not proved to be possible. Generally in competitive situations firms are unwilling to release partronage data for reasons of commercial confidentiality. In the particular case study of competition in Inverness which we model in Section 4, data on patronage were published by the Monopolies and Mergers Commission for 21 four-week periods. However, we were unable to estimate demand function parameters satisfactorily for either model using these data because (a) the two competing firms charged the same prices in each period, so it was not possible to estimate the separate effect of each firm's price on their own and their rival's demand, and (b) there were insufficient data to correct for the infuence of seasonal factors on demand.

Our demand function has therfore been calibrated by using separate estimates of the own-and cross-price and service elasticities, and then solving for the parameters α_i or β_i with data on actual patronage, fares and bus miles for the particular operator on the route under consideration. We have generated demand elasticity estimates using a generalised cost-of-travel framework. Potential bus passengers are viewed as having a preferred time of departure within a Hotelling-type framework. Their decision to travel by bus then depends on the generalised cost of travel, which is a linear function of the fare, the in vehicle travel time, walking time and (if they have to choose a bus departure time which differs from their preferred time) "re-scheduling time." Potential travellers choose the bus that minimises their generalised cost of travel, and the decision as to whether to travel or not then depends on this value of generalised cost.

For any particular route it is possible to estimate generalised costs at different times of day, and hence patronage levels, using data on existing fares and the two operators' timetables, together with data from empirical studies of bus passengers' time valuations. Proportional changes in demand, and hence elasticities, can then be estimated by simulating changes in one operator's fares or his timetable and measuring the proportional effect on estimated demand. This is a second best to the actual estimation of the demand parameters, specifically because we cannot apply normal goodness-of-fit criteria to judge the demand model being used.

Nash equilibria for the constant demand elasticity version of the model are derived in Dodgson, Katsoulacos and Newton (1992), and derivations for the non-constant demand elasticity version are available from the authors on request. One advantage of the constant elasticity version over the non-constant elasticity version is that the former provides analytical, closed-form solutions for both firms' fares and both firms' bus-miles, whereas the latter provides analytical solutions for fares, but bus-miles have to be solved numerically from reaction functions. Both forms of the model permit derivation of Nash-equilibrium fares, bus-miles, patronage, revenue, costs and profits from estimates for both firms of fixed costs, the cost function parameters (m_m, $\hat{m}_m$, m_e and $\hat{m}_e$), the own-and cross-price and bus-miles elasticities, and the demand constant parameters. The resulting Nash equilibrium profits $\pi_m{}^*$ and $\pi_e{}^*$ can then be compared with actual profits π_m and π_e estimated from observed fares, patronage, fixed costs and bus-miles, and the cost function parameters.

Consider the case where the model derives a positive entry opportunity for the entrant ($\pi_e{}^*>0$) but the entrant actually makes losses ($\pi_e<0$). This situation is necessary for predation, but not sufficient, since we need to check that the entrant is actually forced by the incumbent's behaviour to make losses, rather than being in a situation where either deliberately or in error it forgoes the prospect of profitability. To do this we can use bus-miles reaction curves derived from the model. These bus-miles reaction functions show the optimal (that is, profit-maximising) bus-miles for each firm given the bus-miles (and associated optimal fare) chosen by its rival.

In Figure 1 the entrant's bus-miles are shown on the vertical axis and the incumbent's on the horizontal. The curve EE' shows the entrant's reaction function, that is, profit-maximising bus-miles for the entrant given the incumbent's bus-miles, the incumbent's optimal fare and its own optimal fare; while the curve II' shows the incumbent's reaction function. The point NE where the two reaction functions intersect is the Nash equilibrium, $B_m{}^{*'}$ $B_e{}^*$. If the incumbent produced more bus-miles than its NE value, $B_m{}^*$, then this would reduce the profits of the entrant. If positive profits could be earned by both firms at the NE ($\pi_m{}^*>0$ and

Figure 1. Bus-Miles Reaction Curves

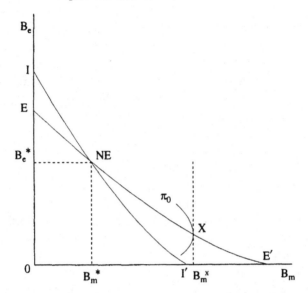

$\pi_e{}^*>0$), then an increase in the incumbent's bus-miles could eventually reduce the entrant's best-response profits to zero. This is shown in the diagram by the point X, which lies on the entrant's zero isoprofit curve π_0. Now, if the entrant actually made losses ($\pi_e<0$) but the incumbent's bus-miles lay below $B_m{}^x$, then the entrant would be able to earn profits if it changed its own bus-miles to a level which lay along its reaction curve EE'. In this latter case, the incumbent's actions have not therefore denied the entrant a profitable entry opportunity and the entrant could survive in the market. Therefore, the incumbent's actions have not *prevented* competition, though by reducing the profitability of entry in this market the incumbent may have slowed down or deterred entry into subsequent markets.

The entrant may also choose a level of bus-miles so high that the incumbent is denied a profitable opportunity, but we defer discussion of this possibility until our analysis of the case study evidence from Inverness.

IV. Modelling Bus Competition in Inverness

1. Data used in the modelling exercise

The MMC report on Inverness contains patronage data for both Highland Scottish Omnibuses (the incumbent) and Inverness Traction (the entrant) for the 21 four-week periods from May 1988 when entry occurred. The report also contains bus-mileage data for HSO for the same period, and average fare data for both operators combined. Annual cost data for HSO's Inverness town services (with a breakdown into different categories of cost) are also reported for the years 1987, 1988 and 1989. We also had data on the entrant's bus-miles over the same 21 four-week periods. We constructed cost data for ITL from unit cost data published in the OFT and MMC reports and in a national study of minibus costs (Turner and White, 1990).

Table 1 summarises key data for both incumbent and entrant in the first full period after entry and in the last period modelled, a full year after entry. Competition was modelled separately for each of the twelve four-week periods starting on 20 June 1988, three weeks after entry, and finishing on 21 May 1989.

In order to derive elasticity values for the calibration of the demand functions, service timetables for all the different routes in the town for the two operators were combined in order to simulate a "representative" timetable to capture the structure of the timeabling on a "typical" route on a "typical" day in the periods modelled. This was done by calculating the total number of departures on all the operator's routes for each four-week period and dividing by the number of routes operated and the number of days in that period. Having obtained the average number of departures per day on an average route for both operators, the "representative" timetable for each period was created by presuming that the departures for each of the two operators were timed evenly throughout the day. We regard our use of a representative route in this fashion as justified since Highland Scottish was challenged by Inverness Traction on all its urban routes, and competition and frequency levels were high throughout the network.

Unit values of in-vehicle time and walking time were taken from estimates of time values for British urban bus travellers in MVA Consultancy *et al.* (1987), adjusted by means of an index of average earnings to May 1988 prices. The same source was used to proxy schedule delay time by using estimates of the values of bus passengers' waiting time. We estimated average waiting time for bus passengers in Inverness at six minutes and average in-bus time (calculated from route length and bus speed data) at seven minutes. Together with average bus-fare values, these estimates provided us with levels of generalised costs per bus trip on our representtive route.

Generalised cost elasticity can be estimated as equal to the overall bus-fare elasticity (which we took to be -0.3) multiplied by the inverse of fare as a proportion of overall generalised cost. We then used the resulting generalised cost elasticity, together with the constant-elasticity-of-generalised-cost-of-travel demand function proposed by Goodwin (1984) to simulate the effects of a proportionate change of either fare or bus-miles on both firms in order to derive firm-specific elasticities.

The resulting own-fare elasticity values present a problem for the constant elasticity demand model because they are less than one in absolute terms, and thus inconsistent with a (profit-maximising) Nash equilibrium. To deal with this difficult problem we had to use a separate entry condition (see Klepper, 1989) to derive the own-fare elasticities.

Table 1. Competition in the Inverness BusMarkets: Key Data for Competitors

	One month after entry[a]		One year after entry[b]	
	Incumbent HSO	Entrant ITL	Incumbent HSO	Entrant ITL
Fare per passenger journey (pence)[c]	25.5	25.5	27.7	27.7
Bus-miles operated	71,700	48,400	102,300	71,900
Patronage (number of journeys)	198,700	82,300	227,300	113,000
Cost per bus-mile (pence)[c]	90.0	77.5	72.9	72.0
Profit/loss (£)[c]	-29,700	-20,400	-26,200	-24,400

[a] The period one month after entry is the four weeks 20 June-17 July 1988.
[b] The period one year after entry is the four weeks 24 April-21 Maay 1989.
[c] All financial figures have been converted to constant (May 1988) prices.

Our entry condition presumes that an entrant could break even if it operated only one single bus journey, and from this the implied own-fare elasticity is derived.

In our empirical work we have found it convenient to average elasticities across operators. To give time-invariant parameters, all the elasticities were also averaged across the sample period. The resulting (constant) elasticities used in Inverness are:

Own-fare	(η_i)	-1.02
Cross-fare	$(\hat{\eta}_i)$	+0.13
Own-service	(ε_i)	+0.43
Cross-service	$(\hat{\varepsilon}_i)$	-0.21

These elasticity parameters, along with observed values of fares, bus-miles and patronage, were then used to solve for the constants in the demand equations for each period. These were not averaged across operators, in order to allow for the possibility of different strengths of demand for different operators, but they were averaged over time. The value of this constant parameter for the incumbent was 67 per cent greater than that for the entrant in both models, indicating that with equal fares and bus-miles the incumbent would capture 62.5 per cent of the market and the entrant 37.5 per cent. This clearly gives a considerable competitive advantage to the incumbent. One possible explanation for this phenomenon, which we also found in our other detailed case study of competition between an entrant and an incumbent (see Dodgson, Katsoulacos and Newton, 1992), is that there is a "loyalty" effect among passengers acting in the incumbent's favour. This might result from the existence of pre-paid travel passes, reliability or quality of services, or from the inertia of existing passengers who choose not to try a new operator. A second possibility is that, although competition occurred on all the major corridors within the town, the entrant's particular route configuration was inferior to that of the incumbent's in terms of coverage, perhaps because the entrant's managers had less experience in designing optimal networks to meet passenger demand.

2. Modelling results

Figure 2 shows our estimated Nash equilibrium and actual profits for the constant elasticity demand model in the first period modelled (20 June-17 July 1988), while Figure 3 shows the situation in the last period modelled (24 April-21 May 1989). The Figures show that both operators made losses, but that there was a profitable Nash equilibrium for both firms. As competition proceeded, the asymmetry in the Nash equilibrium became more pronounced as the incumbent's comparative disadvantage (in unit cost levels) was reduced by cost-cutting measures while its comparative advantage (in terms of the strength of the demand for its services) remained. Both Figures, and the results for all the intervening periods, suggest a situation consistent with predation, and not inconsistent with the OFT's and MMC's findings.

However, as indicated in Section 3 above, we need to consider whether the combatants' actual losses were avoidable. This is exactly what the EMA allows us to do. Figure 4 shows the firms' bus-miles reaction functions in the first period modelled and Figure 5 in the last. To convert the profitable entry opportunity for the entrant identified in Figure 2 into an unprofitable one, the incumbent would have had to operate bus-miles to the right of CC′. Since the actual bus-mile combination is shown by point A, the entrant could have earned profits by reducing (considerably) its own bus-miles. Such an option was not open to the incumbent in the short run, since in the initial period point A lies above the line BB′. Thus no reduction in bus-mileage could restore the incumbent to profitability given the service levels operated by the entrant. However, as competition proceeded and the incumbent reduced its costs, so the line BB′ shifted upwards and the incumbent would be able to break even at higher and higher levels of service produced by its rival.

By the later stages of competition, as Figure 5 shows for the final period modelled, *both* firms had the opportunity to eliminate their own losses by moving onto their reaction functions, but chose not to do so. One explanation of such behaviour is that both operators made mistakes, but this becomes less likely as time goes by and the firms learn from experience. Another possibility is that they were engaging in Stackel-

Figure 2. *Actual and Nash Equilibrium Profits in Inverness One Month After Entry*

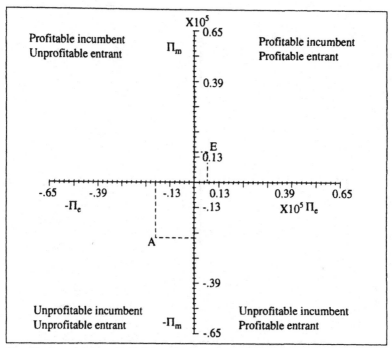

Key: Π_m: Incumbent's profit; Π_e: Entrant's profit; A: Actual; E: Estimated

Data

	Actual Outcome (A)		Nash Equilibrium (E)	
	Incumbent HSO	Entrant ITL	Incumbent HSO	Entrant ITL
Fare (pence)	25.5	25.5	50.9	50.9
Bus-miles	72,000	48,000	25,000	7,000
Patronage	199,000	82,000	104,000	23,000
Profit/loss (£)	-30,000	-20,000	+16,000	+4,000

Figure 3. Actual and Nash Equilibrium Profits in Inverness One Year After Entry

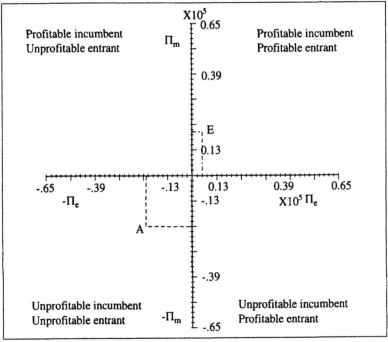

Key: Π_m: Incumbent's profit; Π_e: Entrant's profit; A: Actual; E: Estimated

Data

	Actual Outcome (A)		Nash Equilibrium (E)	
	Incumbent HSO	Entrant ITL	Incumbent HSO	Entrant ITL
Fare (pence)	27.7	27.7	47.3	47.3
Bus-miles	102,000	72,000	38,000	10,000
Patronage	227,000	113,000	137,000	38,000
Profit/loss (£)	-26,000	-24,000	+24,000	+7,000

Figure 4. Bus-miles Reaction Curves in Inverness One Month After Entry

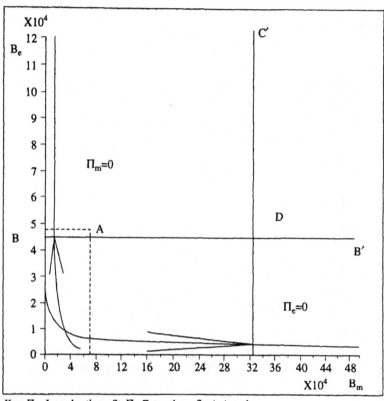

Key: Π_m: Incumbent's profit; Π_e: Entrant's profit; A: Actual;
B_m: Incumbent's bus-miles; B_e: Entrant's bus-miles

berg warfare, with both firms attempting to obtain dominance in the market by expanding bus-miles in order to secure a more favourable market position in the future (see Katsoulacos, 1991). The incumbent was producing more output than in a competitive equilibrium and in doing so was forgoing some of its profits. The main plank of the OFT and MMC cases against HSO was that the company expanded output in the face of competitive entry, and so some of its losses were avoidable. However, the other side of the coin, which is revealed by the EMA's

Figure 5. Bus-miles Reaction Curves in Inverness One Year After Entry

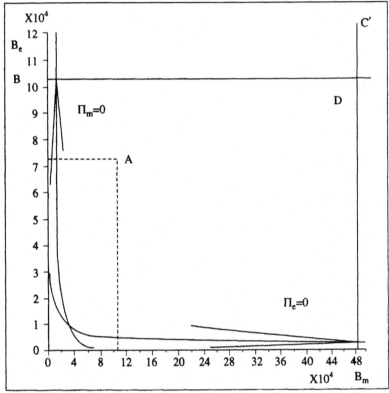

Key: Π_m: Incumbent's profit; Π_e: Entrant's profit; A: Actual;
B_m: Incumbent's bus-miles; B_e: Entrant's bus-miles

emphasis on the actions of *both* firms, is that the entrant entered with a level of ouput which was also above the competitive level (and in the initial phase of the competition so high as to deny the incumbent the possibility of a profitable response in the short run). It seems unreasonable to penalise only one of the combatants in this competitive battle, that is, to expect an incumbent to acquiesce when faced by very aggressive entry and not to fight back with a similarly aggressive response. This conclusion is strengthened by the fact that, as again the EMA reveals, the entrant could have *avoided* losses by a different response to the incumbent's post-entry bus-mile choice.

In the event, the incumbent did have an advantage in the form of a longer purse. The entrant did not respond by retreating to the much lower, but profitable, output level which our model has identified, but instead continued its Stackelberg-type warfare until it went bankrupt.

So far the analysis of the model indicates that the incumbent was not preying in the sense of seeking to eliminate competition. This is consistent with the OFT/MMC conclusion, in the sense that the OFT/MMC found that competition had not been eliminated in Inverness simply as a matter of fact. HSO's actions might deter future entry because they had made life very difficult for entrants, and HSO had forgone some of its own short-run profits in order to reduce the entrant's profits. In apportioning blame to HSO's actions we believe that due allowance should be made for the fact that the entrant was also behaving in a similarly aggressive manner and that the entrant *could* have avoided its losses by alternative responses to the incumbent's actions. Further, account must be taken of the fact that, throughout this period of warfare, consumers have benefited from better services than would otherwise have been provided.

However, one problem with the Economic Modelling Approach is that results may be specific to the particular form of model chosen. In the Inverness case the results differ between the constat elasticity and non-constant elasticity variants. While both models suggest that both firms could have performed better in Nash equilibrium than they did in practice, the non-constant elasticity version denies the possibility of a profitable entry opportunity (and hence of predation).

Although this raises the possibility that there was not a profitable entry opportunity after all, we think that the balance of evidence supports the counter view. In choosing between the models a powerful argument in favour of the constant elasticity model in this case is the fact that entry did continue in Inverness, with ITL replaced first by Alexanders and then by Magicbus/Stagecoach (itself a sophisticated operator likely to be able to assess profitability prospects). Two operators served the town from May 1988 to September 1991, a period of over three years. In its evidence to the OFT the Highland Regional Council also believed there was room for two operators in Inverness

(Office of Fair Trading, 1989b), as did the Manging Director of Magicbus in his evidence to the MMC (Monopolies and Mergers Commission, 1990).

If, on the other hand, there had been no profitable entry opportunity, the entrant must have entered by mistake *unless* it expected to displace the incumbent completely. HSO certainly claimed in its evidence both to the OFT and to the MMC that this is what it believed ITL's objective to be (Office of Fair Trading, 1989b; Monopolies and Mergers Commission, 1990). Faced with an entrant in such circumstances an incumbent which was informed about market profitablility might reasonably be expected to defend its position staunchly, especially in the period when it was reducing its costs.

V. Conclusions

This paper has compared the Economic Modelling Approach to the identification of predatory behaviour with a more conventional rule-of-reason approach. The major problem with the EMA is in choosing the particular form of model to use in order to model competition in a particular market, and in deriving the parameter estimates to be used in practice with this model. There is always the problem that results may be model-specific. The EMA involves a particular view of what constitutes "normal" competitive equilibrium, and it requires specific forms for the demand and cost functions. In our present study we have not been able to estimate the parameters of these functions statistically, though we have derived empirical values through an alternative process. Consequently we have not been able to distinguish between alternative forms of the model statistically, though this could be done in the future if suitable data became available.

The usefulness of the EMA can be viewed in two main ways. First, it provides general insights into the process of identifying predatory behaviour. Secondly, it provides a more complete picture of the various alternatives open to the competing firms in the investigation of particular cases. The early OFT/MMC investigations were primarily concerned with the incumbent's profits, and whether they were positive or (avoid-ably) negative. The EMA shifts the focus of attention to the entrant's profits, and whether they could be positive in the circumstances under investigation. The conventional approach seems to overlook the possibility that there may not have been a profitable entry opportunity in the first place. If this were so, then an incumbent might be falsely accused of predatory behaviour when it had no choice but to make losses if it wished to stay in this (natural monopoly) market. The EMA also focuses attention on the actions of *both* firms in the market. Incumbents may be accused of aggressive behaviour, but the behaviour of the entrant is also relevant: it is possible that aggressive behaviour by the incumbent may be a response to aggressive entry, and both firms may be trying to eliminate or discipline the other. (Later OFT investigations did concentrate on the actions of the entrant. See Office of Fair Trading, 1992.) The "rationality" of the entrant is also relevant: an inexperienced entrant who makes mistakes could impose losses on the incumbent (and on itself), and might be particularly difficult to counter since the incumbent cannot be sure that the entrant will respond in a profitable manner to changes in the incumbent's fares and service levels.

Finally we must consider the practicality of the EMA as a means of identifying predation in particular circumstances. Developing models to analyse competition in specific markets is a complex process. However, for the bus industry, we have developed software which has enabled the EMA to be applied to particular investigations. The model can be used to test the sensitivity of the results to changes in the form of the model or the parameter estimates. Hence, elasticity values or cost parameters, or both, can be varied to see how far this affects the results in a particular competitive situation. Where results are not particularly sensitive to changes in model specification or parameter estimates, the regulator can be reasonably confident about the results of the model, and the EMA is then a very valuable adjunct to the more conventional approach. In the Inverness case we conclude that the actions of the incumbent did, as the OFT and MMC believed, reduce the profit potential of the entrant, but we also conclude that the incumbent faced a very serious competitive threat from an entrant which was also forgoing profit in order to eliminate its rival.

References

Dodgson, J. S., and Y. Katsoulacos (1988): "Models of Competition and the Effect of Bus Service Deregulation." In J. S. Dodgson and N. Topham (eds.) *Bus Deregulation and Privatisation: an International Perspective.* Avebury, Aldershot.

Dodgson, J. S., Y. Katsoulacos and C. R. Newton (1992): "A Modelling Framework for the Empirical Analysis of Predatory Behaviour in the Bus Services Industry." *Regional Science and Urban Economics,* vol. 22, pp. 51-70.

Goodwin, P. (1984): "Choice of Form of Aggregate Demand Function." *Public Transport Demand Elasticities: Background Papers.* SU 246, Transport Studies Unit, Oxford University.

Katsoulacos, Y. (1991): *Privatisation: Government Strategy, Competition, and Social Welfare.* Mimeo, Department of Economics and Accounting, University of Liverpool.

Klepper, G. (1989): "Industrial Policy in the Transport Aircraft Industry." CEPR/NBER Workshop on Strategic Trade Policy, Cambridge, Mass. (October).

MacDonald, S. (1991): "Scottish Column." *Buses,* vol. 43, pp. 517-20.

Monopolies and Mergers Commission (1990): *Highland Scottish Omnibuses Ltd.* HMSO.

MVA Consultancy, Institute of Transport Studies University of Leeds, Transport Studies Unit University of Oxford (1987): *The Value of Travel Time Savings.* Policy Journals, Newbury.

Office of Fair Trading (1989a): *West Yorkshire Road Car Company Limited: Fares Policy on Certain Routes Between Bradford and Skipton.* OFT, London.

Office of Fair Trading (1989b): *Highland Scottish Omnibuses Ltd.: Local Bus Services in Inverness.* OFT, London.

Office of Fair Trading (1989c): *South Yorkshire Transport Ltd.: Registration and Operation of Service 74 Between High Green and Sheffield.* OFT, London.

Office of Fair Trading (1990): *Kingston upon Hull City Transport Ltd.: Local Bus Services in Kingston upon Hull.* OFT, London.

Office of Fair Trading (1992): *Southdown Motor Services Ltd.: The Registration and Operation of Services 262 and 242 in Bognor Regis.* OFT, London.

Phlips, L. (1987): *Predatory Pricing.* Commission of the European Communities, Luxembourg.

Transport and Road Research Laboratory (1980): *The Demand for Public Transport.* TRRL, Crowthorne.

Turner, R., and P. R. White (1980): *A Financial Analysis of Minibus Operation.* TRRL Contractor Report 182, Crowthorne.

CHAPTER 23

COMPETITION IN RAIL TRANSPORT: A NEW OPPORTUNITY FOR RAILWAYS?*

*Chris Nash & John Preston***

I. Introduction

In July 1992, the British government published a White Paper (Cm 2012, 1992) outlining its proposals for the privatization of and introduction of competition into British Rail. Since then, a string of consultation documents on specific aspects of the proposals have been produced by the Department of Transport (commencing in October 1992) and draft legislation ('the Railway Bill') was presented in January 1993. Ministerial statements have also served to make the intentions a great deal clearer whilst a detailed report by the House of Commons' Transport Committee (HC 246, 1993) has provided a wealth of background information. This paper aims to provide a critique of these proposals. The next section provides some background on the situation of rail transport in Western Europe, before the proposals themselves are explained. The following five sections consider in turn issues surrounding the separa-

* Submitted to the Rail Deregulation and Competition Workshop at the Third International Conference on Competition and Ownership in Surface Passenger Transport, Mississauga, Ontario, Canada. September 26 to 29, 1993.

** The authors are Professor of Transport Economics and British Rail Lecturer in Transport Ecomomics, University of Leeds respectively.

tion of infrastructure from operations, competition versus integration in the planning of rail services, whether the incentive to invest will be adequate, the problem of institutional complexity and transaction costs, and lack of competitive bidding, before we reach our conclusions. This paper updates earlier work we have presented to the European Conference of Ministers of Transport (ECMT, 1993). It is intended to complement the more quantitative work we have presented in a companion paper (Preston and Nash, 1993). For a critique from a different perspective see Glaister and Travers (1993).

II. Background

In Europe, as elsewhere, railways have suffered a continued loss of market share in a buoyant transport market in recent decades (Tables 1 and 2). Whilst this may be partly explained by external circumstances (increased car ownership, changing industrial structure from heavy industry towards high value manufactured goods and services) the failure of rail companies even to perform well in those sectors in which they have a comparative advantage, such as long distance international passenger and freight traffic, and the perpetual complaints about the price, quality of service and inflexibility of rail transport leads to doubts as to whether railways are currently running efficiently. For instance, the rail share of international intra-community freight fell from 14% in 1975 to less than 10% in 1987 (COM (89) 564 FINAL paragraph b)).

Table 1. Rail Passenger Traffic Share (% of pass km) (excluding metros)

	1980	1990
Great Britain	6.4	5.0
Belgium	9.0[1]	7.1[1]
Denmark	8.6	7.3
FR Germany	7.1	6.4
France	10.0	9.2
Italy	8.9	7.3
Netherlands	7.4	7.0
Spain	8.5	7.6

1. excludes taxis
Source: Transport Statistics Great Britain (1992)

Table 2. Rail Freight Traffic Share
(% of tonne km by rail, road, water and pipeline)

	1980	1990
Great Britain	10.6	7.1
Belgium	23.5	18.1
Denmark	9.5	12.1
FR Germany	27.3	27.7
France	30.6[2]	26.1[2]
Italy	10.2	9.5
Netherlands[1]	5.9	4.7
Spain	7.8	6.3

1. excludes pipeline
2. excludes sea-going freight
Source: Transport Statistics Great Britain (1992)

Although rail now only carries less than 10% of passenger and 20% of freight within the Community as a whole, it remains very important in certain markets. For commuting in large congested urban areas there is no realistic alternative (for instance over 70% of the million daily commuters into Central London arrive by rail). For inter city business trips over distances of 200-300 km rail remains dominant, and with higher speeds the ability to compete with air over longer distances is growing. Rail is also important in the long distance leisure travel market. For freight, its ability to carry large volumes of traffic quickly and economically between the private sidings of major customers means that it has a major role in bulk traffics except where the even cheaper option of water transport (sea or canal) is available. For traffic in unit loads, the traditional approach of handling these in individual wagons requiring marshalling en route is looking less and less able to provide the cost or quality of service available from road haulage. However, growth of intermodal systems able to reduce the cost and delay problems of transferring goods between modes is making rail more able to compete for general merchandise over longer distances.

With growing concern about congestion and the environment, rail is widely seen as having an increasingly important role in the future in these sectors. Indeed, rail investment is now running at enormous levels. A recent study concluded that the railways of Western Europe plan to spend a total of some £120-150b including £20b on urban rapid transit

Table 3. Investment Prospects to 2000 (£m, 1989)

	National Rail Total 1989-2000	Rapid Transport Total 1989-2000
Austria	3430-4410	340-440
Belgium	4350	660-990
Denmark	1530-1650	180-270
Finland	2025	
France	18390	4090-5100
Germany	20700	3450
Greece	330+	44+
Ireland	46-230	
Italy	34400-49150	4950-7370
Luxembourg	140	
Netherlands	2600	150-460
Norway	1140-1615	170
Portugal	1460	90-130
Spain	9730	830-1110
Sweden	2730-2940	100-200
Switzerland	6260-6650	780-1180
UK	8250-11000	3850-4950
Total	118000-137000	19700-25900

Source: Kennedy Henderson (1990)

by the turn of the century (Table 3). In the case of Britain, it has been estimated that investment of the order of £1b per annum is required through the 1990's even without major new projects such as a high speed line to the Channel Tunnel or new tunnels under London. Given both the opportunities and the level of investment now taking place in rail transport, it has become more important than ever to ensure that the arrangements for regulation and control of the sector are conducive to efficient marketing and operation.

Throughout Europe, rail has generally been seen as a natural monopoly, requiring both regulation and subsidy. Monopoly power was deemed to require regulation of prices charged for rail services, and 'common carrier' obligations to carry whatever traffic was offered at that price. Withdrawal of passenger services required government approval, which was frequently withheld, requiring cross-subsidy of loss making services by profitable ones. Competition was also regulated, with protection of rail traffic being a major factor in the regulation of the bus and road haulage industries. Nevertheless, railways throughout the Community fell into deficit during the course of the 1960's and 1970's. At the same time, railways typically had social obligations towards staff in the form of pension rights inherited from the days of a much greater railway workforce, no redundancy agreements and so forth. To the extent that in some countries they were required to fund the deficit by borrowing, this simply led to the further accumulation of financial difficulties until in some cases (notably the Federal Republic of Germany) the accounts of the railway company lost all contact with reality (for details see CER. 1993)

Reactions to this emerging crisis varied. In some cases, protection from other modes of transport continued and subsidy was stepped up. In Britain, the mechanism of regulation of both rail and road transport has been largely dismantled. Rail is free to practice price discrimination and charge what the market will bear in both passenger and freight markets. Subsidy is given as a lump sum, the amount of which is strictly controlled, and management has been reformed to put commercial considerations foremost.

In 1982, five sectors (covering respectively Inter City, London Commuter and Regional passenger services, freight and parcels) were established, with responsibility for the costs and revenues of their own services. The sectors were defined to be relatively homogeneous both in the types of traffic they carry (and the objectives with respect to which they carry it) and in the equipment they used. As far as possible without wasteful duplication, staff and assets were made specific to a particular sector (or subsector), which had control over how they were used. However, the sectors themselves did not operate the railway. This was done under contract to them by the operating department, which still had a traditional organization into regions and areas.

The main advantages of sector management have been twofold. In the first place, it has been possible to develop much clearer lines of managerial control, with identified sector and subsector managers responsible for each passenger service or flow of freight traffic, no matter where it goes in terms of regional boundaries. In the second place, these managers have had much tighter control over assets as a result of increased specificity of assets to sectors and subsectors and of the development of systems of costing and budgeting that make managers directly accountable for the costs they incur and the revenue they earn. The marketing advantages of being able to put a single manager in charge of an entire flow of traffic have been particularly pronounced in the case of freight traffic, which tended to flow across regional boundaries as the latter were set up with the more important flows of passenger traffic in mind.

Operation of the railway was governed by a host of contractual arrangements made between subsector managers and operating areas as to the required level and quality of service, and the price to be paid. In these relationships, the operator was of course an internal monopoly supplier who accounted for the majority of the business manager's costs. Such an arrangement now appears to be becoming the norm within European Railways. For instance, in the Netherlands, business managers buy services from supply sectors under a form of contract very similar to the RPI-x form of regulation widely used in Britain; unit prices are stipulated for, for instance, supplying a train kilometre or maintaining a passenger car, and these prices reduce by 2% per annum in real terms. However, in Britain, discontent with the extent to which the business manager was able to control the costs and quality of the operations led to a decision to internalize these relationships by fully disaggregating the operating departments to the sectors. Thus each sector became an integrated marketing and operating organization for a particular market segment.

The need for complicated internal contracts did not go away however. With the disaggregation of operations to the sectors came numerous cases where it was obviously sensible for one sector to provide services for another. This applied particularly in the case of infrastructure where for instance the East Coast Main Line might 'belong' to Inter City, but Regional Railways, Freight and Network Southeast would all want to use stretches of it. They would obviously want some form of contract specifying what they were to receive in terms of services at what price, and given the monopoly power enjoyed by the owner of the track this contract would be subject to regulation by the Board.

The operations of British Rail are now clearly divided into Commercial (Freight, Parcels and Inter City Passenger—European Passenger traffic will also form a commercial business) and subsidized (Network SouthEast, which operates commuter, inter urban and local services throughout the South East, and Regional Railways, which provides local and cross country services throughout the rest of the country). One reason for sectorization was to create a transparent distinction between these sectors in which it was more difficult for subsidy to leak from subsidized to commercial sectors. Prior to the current recession, it had been intended that by 1992/93, Network SouthEast would operate without subsidy, and to move progressively to full commercial viability. This aim has now been abandoned, whilst it has always been accepted that Regional Railways will need ongoing subsidies. In the case of the commercial sectors, the aim has been to move towards earning a fully commercial rate of return (now defined as 8% in real terms), on all assets, including property, employed in the business although less demanding interim targets have been set. In the case of the subsidized sectors, the aim in recent years has been to reduce the amount of subsidy necessary, whilst broadly maintaining the quality of service. Again, demanding targets have been set, whilst at the same time, quality of service standards have been more clearly defined. Fare increases in real terms have been permitted, although the rate of increase in the case of commuter services into London has clearly been a politically sensitive issue. Thus there has been a move towards a contractual relationship between British Rail and Central Government for a given set of services, although since 1974 subsidy has always been given as a global sum.

How successful has this approach been? Table 4 gives some key indicators to help answer this question. Figures are shown for five years. The first is 1979, which is both the start of the recession which reduced the volume of rail traffic and severely hit BR's financial performance and the year in which the Conservative Party took office. 1983 is shown,

Table 4. BR Performance 1979-1992/3 (1991/92 prices)

	1979	1983	1989/90	1991/2	1991/92
Total Grant (£m)	1237	1430	705	1035	1243
Passenger route-miles	8955	8932	8897	8880	8896
Passenger miles (m)	19000	18350	20908	19920	19709
Fare per passenger mile (p)	9.14	9.69	10.81	10.51	10.43
Passenger stations	2365	2363	2483	2473	2482
Passenger train miles (m)	196	203	225	231	228
Train miles per member of staff	1421	1686	2043	1996	2075

Source: British Railways Board, Annual Reports and Accounts
Note: Total grant includes exceptional items and excludes capital renewal provision made in 1991/2.
Number of passenger stations affected by transfers to Tyne and Wear Metro (25) and Manchester Metrolink (16).

which was the worst year in terms of financial performance (other than those affected by strikes in the railway industry or its customers) and also the first year in which clear targets for the reduction in subsidy were set by the Minister. We also show 1989/90, the final year before recession again really began to bite, and the two most recent years 1991/2 and 1992/3. In the first place, it will be seen that from their peak, total grants paid to the railway were reduced by some 50% before starting to grow again in the current recession. They are now at the same level, in real terms, as they were in 1979 but still below the levels of the early 1980s. This was accompanied by a very small pruning of the passenger network, but a substantial increase in both the volume of traffic and the amount of passenger train miles provided, although there has been some retrenchment in recent years. There has also been an increase in the number of railway stations, mainly due to local authority initiatives to open new local rail stations. Fares have risen in real terms, but the other main factor leading to improved performance is clearly the rapid rise in labour productivity, measured here as train miles per member of staff, although there was a small decrease in labour productivity in the late 1980s/early 1990s.

Table 5 shows the financial performance of the sectors in 1991/2 and 1992/3. A word is necessary on the way in which costs and revenues are measured in these figures. Costs are measured on a prime user basis, under which all the joint costs associated with any particular asset— such as a stretch of track or a station — are borne by the sector for

Table 5. British Rail   Operating Businesses
Financial Results   1991/92(£m)

	Revenue	Surplus
Inter City	896.7	2.0
Network South East	1044.3	(181.9)
Regional	312.9	(583.6)
Trainload Freight	505.3	67.5
Railfreight Distribution	174.9	(118.7)
Parcels	101.5	(34.7)
Total	3035.6	(849.4)
Grant	766.9	(82.5)

Source: BRB Annual Report and Accounts 1991/92

British Rail Operating Businesses Financial Results 1992/93 (£m)

	Revenue	Surplus	
		1992/3	1991/2 Restated
Inter City	889.0	65.1	90.6
Network South East	1069.4	(46.1)	(7.0)
Regional	349.2	(503.2)	(483.2)
Trainload Freight	490.4	103.1	102.8
Railfreight Distribution	172.3	(90.1)	(107.5)
Parcels	88.7	(22.9)	(32.3)
Total	3115.7	(494.1)	(436.6)
Grant	555.0	60.9	55.0

Source: BRB Annual Report and Accounts 1992/93
Note: Grant in 1991/ includes PSO grant to Regional Railways and Network SouthEast only.
It includes a capital renewal provision but excludes exceptional items.
Grant in 1992/3 (and restated for 1991/2) includes PSO revenue grant and Section 20 grant only

which it is considered to be primarily provided. Other sectors only pay for any additional facilities they need, and for additional maintenance or renewal expenses on facilities they share. Freight and parcels are never deemed to be prime users of facilities they share with a passenger sector. In the case of revenue from through journeys involving more than one sector, revenue is allocated pro rata to the individual fares for the different segments of the journey. In addition, it should be noted that we have some difficulties in determining the amount of grant that has gone to each business. This has been exacerbated by capital renewal provisions made in 1991/2 and the adoption of a new accounting system in 1992/3 which distinguished between revenue grants and capital grants and moved from an expenditure to a balance sheet depreciation treatment of infrastructure investment and track renewal costs. The figures for 1992/3 only include revenue grant. Capital grant for this year is likely to be £553.9 million (with the bulk, £473.9 million, going to Network South East) and grant for exceptional items £96.4 million. These figures still have to be agreed with Government.

It will be seen that InterCity and Trainload Freight are both in surplus, although neither is yet earning a fully commercial rate of return, although the change in accounting procedures has helped improve their finances. Despite restructuring, both Railfreight and Parcels have suffered substantial losses due to road competition and recession in recent years. Network SouthEast requires a modest degree of operating subsidy, and given the relative inelasticity of much of its traffic could undoubtedly return to profitability quickly by means of fares increases if this were seen as a desirable policy. However, it is doubtful whether major investment in infrastructure could be provided commercially. Only Regional Railways is in a position in which making it profitable on anything like the current basis in terms of network of services and cost allocation conventions is clearly unthinkable, although even here, a further reduction in subsidy (to £411 million in 1993/4) is intended.

Overall it may be thought that the performance of British Rail in the 1980's was commendable, even if achieved in the context of favourable external circumstances. However, the re-emergence of increasing deficits, the slow down in labour productivity improvements in the last few years and concerns about future investment may have contributed to a determination by Government to find another way forward which would increase the amount of competition in the rail market.

III. Privatization Proposals

Several European countries are now looking at proposals for rail privatization as are a number of countries in the rest of the world (most notably Argentina, Japan and New Zealand). In Europe, these proposals involve three elements:

- Separation of infrastructure from operations, as proposed in Britain, Germany, the Netherlands, and already taken place in Sweden.
- Privatization of rail operators, and possibly eventually also the infrastructure. This is being discussed in many European countries, but only Britain so far has concrete proposals and a timetable to achieve it.
- 'Open access' arrangements for other private operators to enter the market and compete with the existing operator. This is the intention in both Britain and Sweden. Furthermore, in a policy statement issued in 1989, the EEC outlined details of a Communi-

ty rail policy which includes proposals to separate infrastructure from operations and to allow access to the infrastructure to competing operators (Nash, 1991). The latter issue is now the subject of an EC Directive (91/440). Legal rights of access to railway infrastructure in EC countries have already been established for: international groupings of railway undertakings — defined as two or more operations from different countries wishing to run international services between the Member States where the undertakings are based any railway undertaking wishing to run international combined transport good services between any Member States.

When alternatives for privatization in Britain were considered, there was—as is commonly the case—a major conflict between minimizing disruption through structural change and maximizing the degree of competition (see, for example, Redwood, 1988). Any approach which maintained integration of infrastructure and operations—whether on a regional or a sectoral basis—would lead to little competition, because the infrastructure itself represents a natural monopoly. Whilst it would be possible to promote competition by granting rights of access to the infrastructure to competing operators, it is always difficult to police such arrangements to ensure that the integrated operator is not using its monopoly power in the infrastructure market to gain advantage in operations.

Thus the government has decided to adopt an arrangement which replaces BR by an infrastructure company (Railtrack) and a set of operating companies. However, passenger operations will be franchised out to private companies in around 25 groups of services, basically at what is currently profit centre or subsector level, so that the franchise will cover a group of services such as the East Coast Main Line, the South Western services of Network SouthEast or the ScotRail services of Regional Railways. In the case of some InterCity services, franchisees will be expected to pay for the right to run the services, whereas in most other cases they will be bidding on the basis of the subsidy they require. Minimum standards may be set in terms of frequencies, reliability and overcrowding, and maximum fares stipulated. A new Franchising Authority will be set up to undertake the process; franchisees will be able to lease existing BR rolling stock and take over BR staff. Where no acceptable offer is made, BR will continue to operate the service, but BR will not be allowed to bid for franchises or to continue to operate on a route that has been franchised out. It is stated that the government wants to maintain the maximum flexibility to respond to whatever sort of arrangements the private sector proposes in terms of the details of the franchises, but the expectation is that the typical length of franchises will be around seven years.

Regarding the infrastructure, Railtrack will undertake the timetabling of all services across the network; it will allocate paths and levy charges to cover costs and make a normal rate of return on its assets, although it will be eligible for grant-aid where projects show external benefits. A new regulatory authority will be set up to ensure that Railtrack provides open access to all operators on fair terms and conditions. Railtrack will be required to subcontract activities such as track maintenance to the private sector wherever it is economic to do so. Stations may be sold to private sector developers, who would not necessarily be rail operators. It should be noted that this is a more extreme separation than that in Sweden, where the state owned operator owns the stations and most maintenance depots and also controls timetabling, signal operation and real time control.

It is intended to sell the Freight and Parcels sectors in their entirety, as a number of separate companies. Traninload Freight and the contract services of Railfreight Distribution have been combined and will be sold as three regional companies. The remaining business of Railfreight Distribution will remain in public ownership for the foreseeable future but ways of increasing private sector involvement, for example through joint venture companies, will be explored. The parcels business will be split into two; Red Star (parcels services) and Rail Express Systems (postal services). Again access to the network will be available for other operators who wish to enter the market. These sectors are not discussed in much of what follows, which concentrates on the passenger business.

It must be said at the outset that the proposals are ingenious. They separate out the aspect of rail operations, the infrastructure, which is clearly a natural monopoly with heavy sunk costs, in order to try to achieve competition in operations, where economies of scale are less great, and where — even if operations by a single company turn out to be the norm — sunk costs are less severe, so there may at least be a reasonable degree of contestability (a proposition usually associated with Starkie, 1984). Where subsidies are to continue, they achieve competition for the franchise. By making it possible for a new operator to lease existing rolling stock and — in the case of the franchisee — take over existing staff, they greatly reduce the barriers to entry posed by heavy capital requirements and the need for specialized staff. They offer the prospect of competing management teams trying to come up with new ways of operating and marketing services to reduce costs and increase revenue, and of private sector investment to meet at least some of the enormous investment needs outlined in the previous section.

However, there remain great concerns at many aspects of the proposals. We shall consider these concerns under five headings:

- the relationship between infrastructure and operations
- competition versus integration in rail operations
- investment
- institutional complexity and transactions costs
- lack of competitive bidding

This list is not intended to be exhaustive. We have more general concerns about the lack of a transport policy framework within which the proposals fit whilst we have more specific concerns regarding a range of matters such as safety, research and development and the impact on the rail manufacturing industry. Nonetheless, we believe that in the next five sections we shall address the main economic issues that emerge from these proposals.

IV. The Relationship between Infrastructure and Operations

As stated above, the proposal is to create a new company called Railtrack, which will own, maintain and operate the infrastructure. It will be responsible for planning the working timetable, and for signalling and real time control. It will essentially sell paths under a variety of contracts of different lengths to open access passenger and freight operators for the highest price it can achieve, subject to their at least covering avoidable cost. It will also enter into a contract with passenger franchisees for the provision of paths. One may assume that something like the existing 'prime user' cost conventions will remain, with the passenger franchisee being required to cover any prime user costs which cannot be covered by surpluses on other contracts. The reason for not adopting a simple published tariff as in Sweden (Table 6) is that, where-

Table 6. Structure of Charges for Use of Rail Infrastructure in Sweden
Variable fees for infrastructure use, ore/gross ton kilometre

	Track Standard*	
	I	II
Locomotive trains		
Locomotives, train speed<105km/h	0.47	1.20
Locomotives, train speed 105-135km/h	0.57	1.42
	0.66	–
Locomotives, train speed>135km/h	0.68	–
Freight wagons on "Malmbanan"(iron ore)		
Loaded	0.29	–
Empty	0.03	–
Other freight wagons		
Loaded	0.20	0.48
Empty	0.04	0.13
Passenger cars		
With radial steered bogies	0.19	0.32
Without radial steered bogies	0.27	0.68
Rail cars		
<10 ton/axle	0.06	0.16
>10 ton/axle	0.21	0.52
High speed trains (>160 km/h)	0.31	–
Addendum for vehicle in electrically powered trains	0.02	0.02

* Track standard I is better than track standard II
Source: L. Hansson and J.E. Nilsson (1989) A New Swedish Railroad Policy: Separation of
Infrastructure and Traffic Production (Fifth World Conference on Transport
Research, Yokohama)

as in Sweden the infrastructure company is heavily subsidized, so that
charges can be based on marginal social cost, in Britain it is intended
that Railtrack will be largely unsubsidized and required to make a commercial return on its assets (although the possibility of grants towards
the costs of socially desirable but unprofitable projects has already been
mentioned, and in some cases freight customers will have their track
costs paid by a new government grant, where this offers sufficient environmental advantages by diverting traffic from road). Without the ability to price discriminate, and in the presence of strong economies of
scale, a single published tariff would be very inefficient, although in its

absence the task of the regulator in making sure that Railtrack behaves fairly to all operators appears a difficult one.

The first obvious objection to this organization is that Railtrack is in a position in which it is always negotiating at one remove from the market, be it the commercial market or the Government in the form of the franchising authority. It appears to have relatively little incentive to act efficiently since it can always pass on any cost increases it incurs to the franchisee; the only limit on this is the size of the franchising authorities' budget and the consequent threat of service closures. No doubt the contracts will stipulate performance criteria to be achieved by Railtrack in terms of delays due to work on the infrastructure; nevertheless this has been the source of considerable concern in Sweden, where the chairman of Swedish Railways believes the problem has become far more acute since the separation of infrastructure from operations (Larsson, 1993). It is also the case that Railtrack will be a very small organization, contracting out most of the actual construction and maintenance work to the private sector on the basis of competitive tendering. Nevertheless, as a consequence of this organization, many potential franchisees have stated that they would be unwilling to bid on the basis of the current proposals; the prospect of Railtrack controlling some 50% of their costs and heavily determining the quality of service they could provide (for example by being responsible for up to two-thirds of all delays) is not one that appeals to them.

A second objection concerns longer term planning. Many of the advances in terms of speed and cost effectiveness in rail transport in recent years come from a careful matching of rolling stock and infrastructure. For instance, track speeds, maintenance schedules and capacity requirements are intimately linked to the number of trains, schedules and types of rolling stock passing over it. It will be absolutely essential that a close planning relationship exists between Railtrack and the principal train service operators using any particular piece of infrastructure.

It has been widely suggested that the best solution to these problems would be for the principal operator, the franchisee, actually to lease the infrastructure. Railtrack would remain responsible for ownership, and would oversee investment decisions. But the day-to-day operations and maintenance would be under the management of the franchisee. Obviously the big disadvantage of this approach would be that open access operators would have to deal with a variety of franchisees if they wished to run passenger or freight services which crossed franchise boundaries, and in the case of passenger services these might include outright competitors. We return to this issue in the light of what we say about open access in the next section.

V. Competition Versus Integration in Rail Operations

The government has been concerned throughout to maintain the possibility of new entry by competing passenger operators. This is obviously most likely to occur in the case of profitable inter city operations, but may happen in almost any subsector, since most will have some services which could be commercially attractive, particularly if track only had to be paid for on an avoidable cost basis. In the first round of franchises, the franchising authority will be guaranteed the paths necessary to run the existing service, and this will obviously greatly limit the scope for competitive entry on busy parts of the network. However, in subsequent rounds, Railtrack is required to sell these paths to competing operators if they put in a higher bid than the franchisee, thus permitting a gradual switch of operations away from franchisees towards open access operators. This could have two outcomes.

In the first, the franchisee would develop an entry deterrence strategy whereby it would attempt to purchase a set of paths from Railtrack as an open access operator in such a way that it would be ideally placed to win the remaining paths through the franchise process. This strategy may also lead to greater net subsidy than in the first round and illustrates the danger of regulatory capture, particularly if there is political pressure to maintain services. Bus operators have often designed their commercial networks in this way in order to exploit the tendering process (Preston, 1991).

In the second outcome, entry deterrence fails and on-the-track competition of some form occurs. This raises two further issues. The first is whether it is actually economically efficient to split the operation of a particular set of rail passenger services between a variety of operators. There are two arguments here. One is that there is a potential loss of economies of scale and scope. For instance splitting services between a number of operators could mean poorer utilization of staff and assets, as the likelihood of their being able to move straight from one working to the next without idle time reduces. Each operator would need to make arrangements for access to facilities for cleaning, fuelling and maintenance of rolling stock. Secondly there is an argument that the service will be less attractive to the customer than an integrated planned system (for instance because of the failure to achieve even headways, because of a lack of interchangeable ticketing or of through tickets and the lack of an information and seat reservation system covering all operators). It might be argued that these issues could always be settled by sensible commercial arrangements between the companies, or if this failed (as it has, by and large, in the deregulated bus and coach sector in Britain—see Tyson, 1989), by a requirement to cooperate in such matters imposed by the Regulator.

The second issue is in some ways a more fundamental objection. Many potential franchisees have indicated that they would not be interested in bidding unless they received exclusive rights to run the service in question. It is easy to see why this is. When a franchisee bids, they undertake to provide certain services for a period of many years ahead, in return for receiving (or paying) a fixed sum of money. If they do not know what competition may arise during this period, and are greatly limited by the terms of the franchise regarding how they can react to such competition, that naturally greatly raises the degree of risk involved in their bid. Thus open access is bound to raise the cost to the franchising authority of securing the train services it wishes, and may even make it difficult to secure any bids at all for some subsectors.

In response to this situation the government has indicated its willingness to make many of the franchises exclusive, at least for the first round of franchising. It may be sensible to continue this practice. This in turn would make the objections to the franchisee leasing the infrastructure very much less significant.

VI. Investment

We indicated earlier in the paper that there are enormous requirements for investment just to keep the British Rail system operating at its current level, even without undertaking the many investments thought necessary for it to play its full part in meeting the severe transport problems facing the country. One key measure of the success of the governments proposals, then, will be the extent to which they succeed in attracting private investment into rail transport. On the infrastructure side, Railtrack will, for the foreseeable future remain a publicly owned company, although it will be able to enter into joint arrangements with the private sector for the provision of new infrastructure. It is in the rolling stock area that the new arrangements offer more potential for private investment.

As Jones et al. (1993) have pointed out contract length is likely to be a critical issue. If the typical length of a franchise is only seven years, when railway rolling stock has a life of at least 30, it is difficult to see that providing much incentive for an operator to purchase new rolling stock, or for third parties to build it and lease it to the operator, unless there is some guarantee that the rolling stock will find a further use at the end of the franchise. There appear to be two ways of dealing with this problem. One is to greatly lengthen the typical franchise, to cover 15 years or more, or to provide for automatic renewal provided that performance was deemed satisfactory. That of course has the disadvantage of greatly reducing the competitive pressures on franchisees, although it does give the franchisee a greater interest in building up the long term potential of the service. The other alternative is to intervene more directly in the rolling stock market, either by the public sector building stock for lease or by it at least offering guarantees regarding the future deployment of suitable privately built stock. This seems to be the alternative favoured by Government who have proposed BR's rolling stock should be divided between three rolling stock leasing companies.

VII. Institutional Complexity and Transaction Costs

We have so far examined a number of objections to the proposals, and found ways of resolving them, albeit in general at the price of restrictions on the commercial freedom of rail operators and on the degree of competitive pressures they bear. This section raises a rather more fundamental objection to the proposals. This is the argument that, in order to bring about a degree of competition in rail transport the government has had to postulate such a complex institutional arrangement that each organization will be involved in negotiating and monitoring a huge number of contracts, with the result that transactions costs will be prohibitive.

Consider the position of a new franchisee. The most important contracts for negotiation are of course with the Director of Franchising and with Railtrack, covering the terms of the franchise—what services are to be operated, what quality standards are required, and at what price in terms of payments from the Franchising Director to the Franchisee and from the Franchisee to Railtrack. Clearly all these conditions will need to be subject to variation in agreed circumstances given the length of the contract; circumstances may change requiring more or less services to be run at a higher or lower price per train. At the same time Railtrack will negotiate with the (possibly many different) owners of stations to secure access rights. Any disputes in this area will presumably require the franchisee to take them up with Railtrack who will in turn deal with the station owner.

The franchisee may also need to make a number of other contractual arrangements, for instance with other operators via the proposed Joint Industry Board regarding any through ticketing or revenue sharing agreements, with leasing companies regarding the provision of rolling stock, with maintenance companies regarding fuelling, cleaning and maintenance. It will need a licence from the Regulator, who will in turn examine whether it has fulfilled the safety standards laid down by the Health and Safety Executive, and whether it is acting in such a way as to unreasonably impede competition.

Suppose an incident occurs, as happens every day, whereby a problem occurs with a train of another operator, affecting this operator's services. It will presumably need to monitor whether this gives cause for a complaint to Railtrack, who will have to take the issue up with the other operator if in turn it was failing to abide by the terms of its contract with Railtrack.

Will such a network of contractual arrangements prove more effective than what went before? It must be said that even within a unified British Rail there has been a marked tendency to put relationships between different parts of the organization on to a quasi contractual basis in recent years. But there is a marked difference between that and what is proposed. In the past, the various sectors have been part of the same organization, and the Chief Executive of BR has been well placed to obtain information and to resolve any disputes as to whether the terms of the contracts were fair, and whether they were being adhered to. In the new situation, any such disputes will be conducted through an external body, the Rail Regulator, who will find it much less easy to obtain reliable data on the costs and benefits of alternative courses of action, or very probably through courts of law. One clear indicator of the success of the reforms will be the extent to which operators are able to settle disputes amongst themselves on an amicable basis, as opposed to feeling the need to resort to litigation.

Again there would be ways to proceed with franchising without the degree of institutional complexity of the current proposals. For instance, suppose that a body called British Rail continued to exist, and fulfilled the role of both Railtrack and of the Franchising Authority Suppose also that the franchisee leased from British Rail the infrastructure, rolling stock and stations on the services it operated. If franchises were exclusive, its relationship with other operators would be simplified, although there would still be many cases where other franchisees or freight operators needed the use of its tracks. Again this approach appears to offer a more workable alternative (and variants of it have been proposed by others eg Jones et al., 1993 and Steer Davies Gleave, 1993A), but at the cost of reducing the degree of competition; it also has the significant advantage of reducing the degree of disruption in the transition from existing institutional arrangements.

VIII. Lack of Competitive Bidding

So far there appear to be a number of organizations interested in taking on the role of franchisee for railway passenger services:

a) New companies formed by existing rail management:
   These obviously have the experience of running railways, which is in short supply, big advantages regarding information about the economics of existing operations and a strong incentive in terms of their interest in keeping their jobs. What is less clear is whether they will be able to raise the amount of capital required. Whilst the ability to lease assets and take over existing staff substantially reduces capital requirements, there are still substantial legal costs and costs of preparing a safety plan which have to be incurred before a bid can be considered. Thus it may be that railway man-

agers will most often bid as part of a consortium with other interested parties rather than as a separate company.

b) Bus operators:

A number of bus operators have shown an interest. Obviously they have relevant experience, and in a number of cases they have former railway managers on their staff. One of the attractions to them is the prospect of offering an integrated bus and rail public transport service throughout their area, although it currently appears unlikely that this will be permitted, in the interests of preserving competition between bus and rail.

c) Firms from other parts of the travel business, including a shipping company and an airline.

d) Manufacturers of railway equipment and civil engineering companies might be expected to be interested where major new investment it needed. Such consortia have been formed to design, build, operate and maintain light rapid transit systems in Manchester and Birmingham, whilst a consortium of Balfour Beatty, GEC and Trafalgar House has recently been formed with the West Cost Main Line in mind.

Overall it must be said that the degree of serious interest appears limited, and that many of those expressing an interest have reservations about the precise way in which franchising is to take place. We have suggested above measures to make the business more attractive to potential franchisees, in the interest of stimulating more competition and gaining more competitive prices. There is clearly a risk that the number of competitors may be so low that bids are not competitively priced or that collusion takes place, whilst an incumbent franchisee might feel that it faced relatively little threat to its future. In particular, it may be difficult for a rival firm to mount a bid without being detected by the incumbent. In such cases experience from the recent ITV franchises suggests that bids will be positively correlated with the amount of competition, suggesting a degree of non-contestability.

From the above description of the proposals we may conjecture that the franchising system will be based on near complete contracts (ie. contracts that are specified in great detail by the franchiser), administered on a net subsidy basis. There will obviously have to be agreed circumstances in which both the level of service and the payment might vary over the—relatively long—life of the contract. The franchise will be essentially an operating contract in which the franchisee supplies the management and takes over the labour. The threat of franchises being won by new operators with a totally new set of staff, which was an important factor in achieving cost reductions in the bus industry, is not a realistic possibility here. The main areas where private sector managers will have the possibility of making improvement is in marketing the product and reducing labour costs. However, labour productivity on BR is relatively high compared to other Western European railways and the scope for improvement may be modest. Unit cost reductions may be achieved by the reduction in real wages, especially outside London, that is likely to result from the break-up of the national pay bargaining system, but we would expect it to be difficult to achieve the 20-30% reductions achieved in the contracting out of other services (see, for example, Domberger et al., 1986). Privatization will introduce a bankruptcy constraint which should act as a spur to efficiency but this will be blunted by the scope for contract re-negotiation in view of the difficulties that would by posed by the need to hand over quickly to another operator in the event that bankruptcy of a franchisee really did occur. Asset handover has been a problem in other industries that have been franchised (see Williamson, 1976) and arose as an issue when the franchise for the urban rail system is Boston changed hands. A recent study by consultants (Steer Davies Gleave, 1993B) estimated that potential cost savings as a result of productivity gains may be only around the 5% mark and these could be more than offset by transaction costs and the profit requirements of intermediate bodies such a Railtrack, the rolling stock leasing companies and station owners.

IX. Conclusion

We have seen how the combination of a continued decline in the market share of rail transport with a perception of a major role for rail in the future has led governments all over Europe to start examining new ways of providing rail services, on a more competitive basis and with more private sector involvement. We then examined in depth the proposals of the British government to separate rail operations from infrastructure and to make rail operations entirely a competitive private sector activity, with competitive bidding for franchises in the case of passenger services.

We consider that there are clear advantages of these proposals in terms of increasing the incentives to efficiency and innovation, and attracting private sector capital into the rail industry. However, we also see major problems. These concern the efficient planning and provision of the infrastructure, preservation of a well integrated network of services able to full exploit the potential for economies of scale, provision of adequate incentives for private operators to invest in new rolling stock and avoidance of a heavy burden of transaction costs. In particular, we feel that head-on on-the-track competition is undesirable particularly as many of the benefits could be obtained by off-the-track competition, through franchising, as well as some peripheral competition on parallel routes and competition by emulation.

None of this argument appears particularly important in the freight sector, which is generally a minority user of the infrastructure in British conditions and where most services are operated on a contractual basis for a single customer. Indeed in the freight sector there appear to be a number of potential operators wishing to enter the market and many freight customers eager to try them out. We thus support the opening of access to the infrastructure for new freight operators. But the problems do appear to warrant significant changes to the proposals in the case of passenger services. In particular, it would seem more appropriate for British Rail (or a successor organization) to continue in the role of the provider of the infrastructure and the planner of services, but to progressively subcontract out more of their operations, including maintenance of infrastructure and the operation of signalling and real time control. In this way competitive private concerns could play a major part in rail transport without the problems of disintegration of the network into a host of small, competing operations ultimately envisaged by the current proposals. This would, in our view, allow a more optimal degree of both horizontal and vertical integration.

References

CM 2012 (1992) "New Opportunities for the Railways. The Privatization of British Rail." HMSO, London.

COM (89) 564 FINAL (1990). "Communication on a Community Railway Policy." CEC, Brussels.

COMMUNITY OF EUROPEAN RAILWAYS (1993) "The Financial Burdens Placed on CER Railways." CER, Brussels.

DOMBERGER, S., MEADOWCROFT, S.A. and THOMPSON, D.J. (1986) "Competition, Tendering and Efficiency: The Case of Refuse Collection." Fiscal Studies, 7, 69-84.

EUPOPEAN CONFERENCE OF MINISTERS OF TRANSPORT (1993). "Privatization of Railways." Round Table 90. ECMT, Paris, 1993.

GLAISTER, S. and TRAVERS, T. (1993), "New Directions for British Railways." Current Controversies 5. IEA, London.

JONES, I., MARKS, P. and WILLIS, C. (1993) "Franchising Passenger Railways." Topics 11. NERA, London.

LARSSON, S (1993). "The Case of Swedish Railways." In ECMT (1993) Ibid.

NASH, C.A. (1991) "Rail Policy in the European Community." Working Paper 324. Institute for Transport Studies, University of Leeds.

PRESTON,J. (1991) "Explaining Competitive Practices in the Bus Industry: The British Experience." Transportation Planning and Technology. 15, 277-294.

PRESTON, J. and NASH, C. (1993) "European Railway Comparisons: Lessons for Policy." Third International Conference on Competition and Ownership in Surface Passenger Transport, Mississauga, Ontario.

REDWOOD,J. (1988) 'Signals from a Railway Conference." Centre for Policy Studies, London.

STARKIE D (1984). "BR—Privatization without Tears." Economic Affairs.

STEER DAVIES AND GLEAVE (1993A). 'Rail Privatization: A Way Forward." Railway Industry Association and Transport 2000, London.

STEER DAVIES AND GLEAVE (1993B). "The Costs of Rail Privatisation." Transport 2000, London.

TYSON, W.J. (1989) "A Review of the Second Year of Bus Deregulation." AMA and PTEG, London.

WILLIAMSON, O.E. (1976) "Franchise Bidding for Natural Monopolies—in general and with respect to CATV." Bell Journal of Economics, 7.

CHAPTER 24
NORTH AMERICAN TRUCKING POLICY

Garland Chow*

I. Introduction

Transportation is a key component of the free trade infrastructure in North America. The *North American Free Trade Act of 1994* (NAFTA) between Canada, Mexico and the United States sought to reduce trade barriers in order to encourage the rationalization of production, sourcing and distribution within North America. Efficient transport systems must exist within each country and between trading partners in order to facilitate such rationalization.

Government transport policy has an important impact on the ability of the transport industry to meet the needs of industry in this new environment. This is particularly true for the trucking sector which has a long history of economic regulation in all three countries. All three countries have moved along the path of economic deregulation but at different velocities. All three countries are working together to harmonize regulatory requirements that might create invisible barriers between the countries. This paper traces the regulatory reforms that affected the domestic and transborder trucking industries within and between the three countries. The paper is a case study of how regulatory policies in adjacent

---

* Associate Professor, Faculty of Commerce and Business Administration, The University of British Columbia. The author gratefully acknowledges the assistance of Joan Caravan in preparing this paper.

and interdependent market economies are linked by market effects and influenced by broader economic concerns such as trade policy. North America is the largest and most integrated market in the world, thus the North American experience in truck transport policy is a window on the future for other countries or regions where economic barriers still exist.

II. Economic Characteristics of North American Trucking

Trade and Trucking in North America

NAFTA links three countries with a combined population exceeding 360 million, a gross national product of $6.8 trillion, and about $253 billion of trade between them.[1] Canada and the U.S. are each other's major trading partners and Mexico is rapidly supplanting Japan as the second most important trading partner of the U.S. (see Table 1).

Trucking is a critical transport segment within all three countries. Trucking accounts for about 21 to 22 percent of total intercity revenue ton-miles in the U.S. and Canada respectively.[2] In contrast, trucks transported an estimated 73 percent of total ton-miles in Mexico in 1993.[3] Trucking's role is even more important for trade between the three countries. Trucks carried over 60 percent of the goods moved between the U.S. and Canada and between Canada and Mexico, and 87 percent of Mexico-U.S. trade, as measured by freight revenues in 1992.[4]

---

1. All figures in U.S. dollars unless otherwise indicated. The average monthly exchange rates between the three countries were 1.1457 $C/$US and 3.0184 Pesos/$US in 1991; 1.2087 $C/$US and 3.0949 Pesos/$US in 1992; and 1.2901 $C/$US and 3.1156 Pesos/$US in 1993. Exchange rate data taken from International Monetary Fund (1995).
2. The U.S. estimate of 21 percent is calculated for 1991 from U.S. Department of Transportation (1993) and excludes local truck ton-miles. The Canadian estimate of 22 percent is calculated for 1990 for-hire trucking and 1988 private trucking (the last year comparable figures were available) and includes only truck and rail tonne-kilometers in the estimate of total tonne-kilometers for 1990. Canadian data from Transport Canada (1992) and Statistics Canada (1993).
3. Ton-mile statistics compiled by Felipe Ochoa y Asoicados, S.C., Mexico D.F. from public data supplied by Secretariat de Comunicaciones y Transportes and provided by the American Trucking Associations, Inc. (1995). The U.S. Department of Transportation (1993) estimated a higher modal share by truck.
4. Freight revenues generally parallel ton-miles. Estimates from U.S. Department of Transportation (1993).

Table 1. *U.S.-Canada-Mexico Comparisons: 1992*

Characteristic	U.S.	CANADA	MEXICO	TOTAL
Population (Mil)	256.0	28.8	89.5	364.3
GNP ($ Bil)	$5,956.8	$569.6	$330.9	$6,857.6
Trade from ($ Bil):				
U.S. to	–	$79.8	$40.3	$120.1
Canada to	$98.0	–	$0.66	$98.7
Mexico to	$32.3	$2.3	–	$34.6
Total Imports ($ Bil)	$130.3	$82.1	$41.0	$253.4
Major Centres (>500,000 population)	>50	6-8	8	–

Source: Fagan (1993).

Characteristics of the North American Trucking Industry

The intercity trucking market in North America is an industry of approximately $190 billion in revenues. As shown in Tables 2, 3 and 4, 1991 intercity revenues exceeded $167 billion in the U.S., $10 billion in Canada, and were estimated to be $16 billion in Mexico in 1994 for the for-hire sector only. Only a portion of this market is directly regulated in Canada or the U.S. Private carriers are not subject to any economic controls as long as the shipper moves its own freight. Certain goods such as agricultural products are exempt from federal regulation in the U.S. and similar exemptions exist in Canada at the provincial level. Intrastate revenues are approximately 2.25 percent of Interstate Commerce Commission (ICC) regulated interstate revenues so total regulated revenues were about $80.1 billion or slightly less than one-half of all intercity revenues in the U.S.[5] For-hire revenues in Canada represent freight of carriers subject to regulatory controls at both the provincial and federal levels. The regulated intercity trucking industry in North America is thus approximately $106 billion.

---

5. This estimate is taken from the Motor Carrier Ratemaking Study Commission (1983) which estimates that the ratios of interstate to intrastate revenues and ton-miles are, respectively, 44 to 1 and 42 to 1.

Table 2. Characteristics of the U.S. Intercity Trucking Industry: 1991

Characteristic	Intercity Segment		
	ICC[1] Authorized	Non-ICC[2] Authorized	Total Intercity
Revenues ($ Mil)	$78,300	$89,100	$167,400
Ton-miles (Mil)	318,724[3]	438,276[3]	758,000
Number of Carriers	45,791[4]	N/A	N/A

Notes: 1. Interstate Commerce Commission.
2. Non-ICC authorized carriers include private, intrastate and ICC-exempt interstate movements such as agricultural products.
3. Breakdown between ICC and non-ICC authorized carriers is based on 1989 proportions.
4. Figure is for 1990.
Source: U.S. Department of Transportation (1993).

Table 3. Characteristics of the Canadian Intercity Trucking Industry: 1991

Characteristic	Intercity Segment				
	Private	For-Hire			Total Intercity
		Large[1]	Small[2]	Total	
Revenues($ Mil)	$1,458[3]	$7,362	$1,363	$8,725	$10,183
Tonne-km (Mil)	N/A	69.847	N/A	N/A	N/A
Number of Carriers	521[4]	1,427	6,556	7,983	8,504

Notes: 1. Annual revenues of at least C$1.0 million.
2. Annual revenues less than C$1.0 million and greater than C$100,000.
3. Expense figure for 1989.
4. Figure is for 1989 and includes only private carriers with operating expenses of at least C$500,000.
Source: Statistics Canada (1993).

The regulated motor carrier sectors in Canada and the U.S. are composed of over 45,000 firms in the U.S. (excluding solely intrastate carriers) and over 8,000 companies in Canada (see Tables 2 and 3). With an economy and population around ten times the size of Canada, it is no surprise that the U.S. trucking industry is nearly six times the size of the

Table 4. Characteristics of the Mexican For-Hire Intercity Trucking Industry

Characteristic	Total Intercity
Revenues (1994)[1]	$ 16.0 billion
Ton-miles (Mil) (1989)[2]	105.830
Number of Carriers (1992):[3]	
General Cargo	3,880
Specialized	685
Total	4,565

Sources: 1. American Trucking Associations (1995).
2. Lyndon B. Johnson School of Public Affairs (1991).
3. American Trucking Associations (1995).

industry in Canada. In contrast, Mexico's registered trucking industry is relatively small given its population but not its level of economic activity. There are an estimated additional 100,000 to 150,000 owner-operators (called brokers in Canada) and 40,000 to 50,000 private motor carriers in the U.S. (American Trucking Associations, 1988). Owner-operators and private carriers exist in similar proportions in Canada and Mexico. All of these carriers compete in a variety of markets defined by the product and service provided, geography and regulatory jurisdiction. Important market boundary distinctions include:

- general freight (GF) versus special commodity movement;
- less than truckload (LTL) versus truckload (TL) movement;
- long haul versus short haul movement;
- intraprovincial (Canada) and intrastate (U.S.) movement versus interprovincial (Canada) and interstate (U.S.) movement; and
- domestic versus international (transborder) movement.

From an international perspective, the last of these distinctions is particularly important. Canada and the U.S. share the longest unguarded border in the world, over 3,000 miles, and the Mexican-U.S. border is over 1,500 miles long. As noted above, a significant amount of trade between the three countries is carried by truck.

The intraprovincial versus interprovincial distinction in Canada has much more significance than the intrastate versus interstate distinction in the U.S. In the U.S., regulated interstate trucking revenues are 44 times greater than intrastate trucking revenues. The dominance of interstate traffic is due in part to the longer distances of interstate shipments. In contrast, Canadian intraprovincial for-hire truck revenues are almost 40 percent higher than interprovincial truck revenues. This difference is due in large part to the larger size of the provinces in Canada compared to the size of the states in the U.S. The population distribution of Canada also results in a linear interprovincial traffic flow pattern which is both proximate to and parallel to the U.S.-Canadian border. More balanced population patterns in the U.S. result in significant traffic flows originating from and destined to practically every region of that country.

The absolute size of the truck market and the diverse pattern of freight flows have led to the emergence of a number of large carriers, especially in the U.S. The largest carriers operate extensive terminal networks in which scale and route utilization economies exist. These carriers include United Parcel Service, which earned nearly $20 billion in revenues in 1993, and the largest long distance LTL general freight carriers, each with over $3 billion in annual revenues in 1993. Over 100 U.S. motor carriers earned more than $100 million in 1993. The largest Canadian carriers earned no more than C$1 billion in 1993 with only 49 carriers earning more than C$25 million. Only eight of the 3,880 registered trucking firms in Mexico operated more than 500 trucks (American Trucking Associations, Inc., 1995). The majority of the trucking firms in all three countries are very small and compete primarily in the TL sector.

The nature of the trucking industry is evolving in all three countries. Traditionally, lower traffic densities in Canada encouraged carriers to carry a mix of TL and LTL freight. This was also the case prior to deregulation in the U.S. However, after deregulation in 1980, truckers in the U.S. rapidly specialized in one sector or the other, or created wholly separate divisions to compete in these two separate markets. This specialization is only now occurring in Canada. In contrast, Mexico has practically no LTL trucking industry or infrastructure. As international trade increases, the demand for such service will increase.

III. The Evolution and Dynamics of Trucking Deregulation in North America

Introduction

Canada, Mexico and the United States moved in opposite directions with respect to economic regulation of the intercity trucking industry in 1977. In that year the U.S. Interstate Commerce Commission began relaxing entry and rate controls while most of the Canadian provinces and Mexico maintained strict entry regulations and a mixture of rate controls. A decade later, the economic regulations governing the trucking industries in Canada and the U.S. again began to converge as Canada removed many of its entry controls over the trucking industry. Mexico also deregulated its domestic trucking industry in 1989 but maintained its policy of strict entry control of foreign trucking until 1992 when it agreed to begin the relaxation of such controls by 1995 as part of NAFTA. Deregulation in the U.S. initiated a deregulation process in North America that continues today. Moreover, NAFTA required deregulation of transborder movement. What has occurred from 1977 to 1995 is a lesson in market dynamics and political economy. U.S. deregulation and North American trade policy had both direct and indirect effects on Canadian and Mexican transportation markets and inevitably on the regulatory systems in both countries.

Trucking Regulation in North America[6]

The U.S. trucking industry was regulated at the federal level under the *Motor Carrier Act of 1935*. The Act established a system of tight entry control through the requirement of applicants to satisfy a public need criterion in order to obtain a license to operate, and the power to set maximum, minimum and actual rates. The Act specifically excluded any control over intrastate movement, even if transported by a carrier engaged in interstate movement. Economic regulation of trucking in Canada developed under the auspices of the provinces as there were no explicit provisions in any legislation for federal control over highway

---

6. See Chow and Button (1983) for a description of the early development of economic regulation of trucking in the U.S. and Canada.

carriers. The role of the provinces was made official by the *Motor Vehicle Transport Act of 1954*. That Act recognized the jurisdiction of the Federal government but left the regulation of all forms of motor transport in the hands of the provinces by means of a delegation of federal responsibility to existing provincial agencies.

By and large, the regulation of entry into the interstate and interprovincial trucking industries of the two countries followed the same paths. One year after the enactment of the *Motor Carrier Act of 1935* in the U.S., the ICC ruled that the onus was on the applicant for new operating authority to prove that the public interest was served by a showing that the proposed service '...is or will be required by the present or future public convenience and necessity' (Pan-American Bus Lines Operation, 1936). Similar tests and burdens of proof were applied by provincial regulatory boards in Canada. In contrast, rate regulation differed substantially between the two countries. *The Motor Carrier Act of 1935* in the U.S. required interstate rates to be filed with the ICC thirty days before they became effective. Each rate proposal was subject to protests and the ICC frequently suspended the rates pending an investigation of their legality. In effect, this gave the ICC ultimate control over the minimum, maximum and actual rates charged. In addition, shortly after the *Motor Carrier Act of 1935*, motor carriers started to form rate bureaus, patterned after established railroad rate bureaus, where carriers would collectively discuss and agree upon rate proposals. The legality of such organizations was continually investigated and challenged by antitrust authorities, resulting in carriers in both industries pressing Congress to enact a statutory exemption for collective ratemaking. The carriers were finally successful in 1948 when the *Reed-Bullwinkle Act* was enacted.

The decentralized approach to regulation in Canada resulted in a diverse pattern of interprovincial rate regulation that ranged from no regulation to rate filing to rate filing and approval. The minimum rate control over interprovincial traffic exerted by most of the provinces was inevitable, given the lack of coordination existing between provincial regulatory authorities. As in the U.S., collective ratemaking was practised by motor carriers through their participation in tariff bureaus. The legal status of collective ratemaking had always been in a vacuum because 'competition' legislation was a federal responsibility while 'highway transportation' was a provincial and 'regulated' concern.

In Mexico, legislation passed in 1940 provided the legal foundation for regulating the motor carrier industry.[7] Mexican law viewed transportation as a public service which was to be operated only with a concession awarded by the state government. State regulations restricted transportation markets via regulatory barriers governing the granting of concessions, restrictions on increasing route capacity, and regulated tariff structures. The Secretaria de Comunicaciones y Transportes (SCT) enforced transportation regulations.

The regulations established restrictive market entry via exclusive concessions for a limited number of route corridors. The concessions were available only to Mexican nationals and carried ceilings on the number of tons per kilometer that could be transported on any route. New entry was extremely difficult since the established carriers were consulted as well as given preference when new route or volume concessions were needed. If a shipment had to be transported across corridors, it had to be unloaded and reloaded onto another truck, or an arrangement had to be made with neighboring concessionaires to allow passage. SCT approval was required for all such arrangements. As an exception to the general rule, specialized cargo was not subject to route restrictions. Notably, private trucking was prohibited.

Cargo centres (centrales de carga), associations formed by concessionaires on a route, coordinated the demand for services and allocated cargo across carriers. The absence of direct contact between shippers and transporters precluded any negotiation of discounts. Users allege that the cargo centres contributed to the decline in service quality because the user was obliged to accept the assigned carrier even if the vehicle was inappropriate for the shipment. Finally, the SCT set and adjusted official tariffs according to an approximate cost formula. There were five rate classes; each had the same fixed component and a differing variable component. The classification of products relied to a limited extent on the risk, the fragility, and the difficulty of handling.

---

7. The Law of General means of Communication and the Regulation to the Chapter of Exploitation of Highways of the Law of General Means of Communication. This summary is taken from Lyndon B. Johnson School of Public Affairs (1991).

Regulatory Reform in the U.S.[8]

The demand for deregulation of the U.S. trucking industry and the evidence supporting this change is well documented. The ICC relaxed certain regulations administratively in 1977 but the most significant change occurred with the *Motor Carrier Act of 1980* (MCA). The MCA substantially relaxed controls on entry into interstate trucking by shifting the burden of proof from the applicant to the protestor (i.e., reverse onus). Formerly the applicant had to prove that the new operating authority was required by 'the present or future public convenience and necessity'; under the new legislation, the protesting carrier was required to show that the applicant's operations were inconsistent with public convenience and necessity. In practice, applications for new routes have been rarely denied by the ICC since the MCA. The MCA also reduced geographic and commodity operating restrictions on current carrier authorities and eliminated similar restrictions on private and contract carriers. In short, regulatory barriers to new or existing carriers to freely enter any interstate truck markets have been generally eliminated.

The MCA also sought to encourage competitive pricing by creating a zone of reasonableness and limiting the scope of collective ratemaking. The zone of reasonableness allowed carriers to adjust rates within certain limits without ICC approval. In practice, this zone of ratemaking freedom was broad enough to impose few limitations on independently filed rate changes. The ICC rarely rejected independently filed rate decreases so protests of such pricing conduct were seldom successful. The MCA did preserve collective ratemaking but it narrowed the scope of the collective ratemaking exemption to joint line and general rate adjustments only, and imposed a number of procedural restrictions to encourage competitive pricing. In particular, the rate or tariff bureau itself could no longer protest independently filed rate proposals.

Significant changes in the performance, conduct and structure of the U.S. trucking industry occurred in the years following the passage of the MCA. The changes can be summarized as follows:[9]

---

8. See Chow (1991) for a more detailed description of regulatory reform in the U.S. and Canada.

9. Numerous analyses and evaluations of the general impact of trucking deregulation in the U.S. may be found in literature. Glaskowsky (1987) and Owen (1988) provide contrasting interpretations of many of the early studies and evidence.

- Significant new entry occurred in most product and geographic markets from the expansion of existing firms and from wholly new firms. The major exception was the long haul LTL general freight market where concentration increased. Most new entry was in the truckload segment of the industry.
- Some carriers sought niches or reduced the scope of their operations. For example, LTL carriers generally got out of the TL market or if they chose to compete in this market, would do so with TL subsidiaries which were operationally distinct from the LTL operations.
- Interlining was reduced significantly as carriers were no longer restricted geographically.
- A significant increase in competitive conduct was observed. Carriers began to offer a wider range of price and service offerings. Service was not reduced with price reductions.
- Many cost reductions were at the expense of labour rates, in particular the substitution of non-union labour for union labour from the growth or entry of non-union carriers. This was particularly true in the TL sector.
- Rate competition in the form of independent action, contracts, and discounting became prevalent.

"The magnitude of the price decline directly attributable to deregulation is difficult to determine because deregulation coincided with a general economic recession" (Owen, 1988). The movement of truck prices of Class I, LTL, ICC- authorized carriers is shown in Table 5. The revenue per ton-mile of these carriers appears to have grown with general price increases in the economy from 1980 to 1991. But in the 10 year period from 1970 to 1980, truck rates increased less than general inflation (112 percent versus 126 percent) and in the 10 year period from 1960 to 1970, truck rates increased by 35 percent as opposed to an 18 percent increase in the producer price index (PPI). These prices do not reflect changes in the mix and quality of transportation services and are therefore not conclusive. However, these LTL carriers lost much of their truckload freight business after deregulation, thus the average revenue per ton- mile would be expected to increase. In contrast, the average revenue for specialized truckload freight only increased by 12 percent. Any average of the TL and LTL freight revenue indices would result in lower growth rates of truck rates versus general inflation.

All of these effects were predicted by the proponents of regulatory reform but at the same time, the predictions made by the opponents of regulatory reform were not all wrong. Concentration has increased significantly in the largest segment of trucking, the long haul LTL market. Destructive competition was reflected by a higher number of bankruptcies which continued to climb until 1987 at which time trucking bankruptcies were ten times the number recorded in 1978 (American Trucking Associations, Inc., 1988). There is little question that the distribution of the benefits of regulatory reform (e.g., rate discounts) is uneven among shippers and shipping groups. Boyer (1993) suggests that

Table 5. U.S. Average Freight Revenue Trend (Cents per Ton-mile)

Year	Class I Intercity Motor Carriers of Property -LTL[1] Average	Index:1980=100	Specialized Common Carriers Average	Index:1980=100	Producer Price Index Average	Index:1980=100
1960	6.31	35			33	38
1970	8.50	47			39	45
1976	12.00	67			61	69
1977	12.70	71			65	74
1978	13.40	74			70	79
1979	15.20	84			78	88
1980	18.00	100	8.64	100	88	100
1981	20.00	111	9.12	106	96	109
1982	20.77	115	9.32	108	100	114
1983	21.23	118	9.06	105	102	115
1984	21.54	120	9.55	111	104	118
1985	22.90	127	9.87	114	105	119
1986	21.63	120	9.85	114	103	117
1987	22.48	125	9.86	114	105	120
1988	23.17	129	9.84	114	108	123
1989	23.91	133	9.64	112	114	130
1990	24.38	135			119	135
1991	24.86	138			122	139

Note: 1. Represents Class I Instruction 27 general freight common carriers.
Sources: Revenue per ton-mile figures from U.S. Department of Transportation (1994), specialized carrier revenue per ton-mile figures from Eno Foundation for Transportation, Inc. (1990) and producer price index figures from Survey of Current Business, various years.

income distribution was the main impact of trucking deregulation.

The MCA was perceived to have resulted in improvements in performance and benefits to the overall shipping public.[10] As a result, deregulation was expanded in 1994. The *Transportation Industry Regulation Reform Act of 1994* (TIRRA) abolished ICC supervision of most truck ratemaking activities as of August 1993. Tariff filing requirements for individually set rates were eliminated but rate bureaus were permitted to continue to set rates collectively for interline service and other selected areas. After thirteen years of experience, both the majority of the carriers and the shippers agreed that the administrative burden of rate filing hindered rather than promoted time sensitive competitive responses.

Prior to the passing of the MCA, most states had some form of economic regulation but regulatory structures varied considerably among the states (Chow, 1980). Some states such as Arizona practised the concept of regulated monopoly along with regulated competition. In California, entry was relatively free, but minimum rate regulation was enforced. New Jersey and Delaware chose to regulate very little or none of the intrastate trucking industry. Following the implementation of the MCA, deregulation of trucking occurred in several states while deregulation proposals in other states were turned down.

Uniformity of regulation of trucking could never occur as long as each state had the right to decide how trucking would be regulated within its borders. There are 50 states with varying truck regulatory apparatus, economic environments, social policies and political structures. Uniformity of economic regulation, much less complete deregulation, would be difficult to achieve as each jurisdiction exerts its rights to regulate commerce within its geographic boundaries according to the perceived wishes of its constituents. State policymaking may also be more susceptible to political influence (Teske, Best and Mintrom, 1994). But economic arguments justifying the deregulation of interstate trucking were just as applicable to intrastate regulation (Taylor, 1994). Apart from State versus Federal government issues, the major question marks regarding the performance of trucking under deregulation have been safety and service to small and rural communities, areas of great concern to state governments. However, substantial evidence has been com-

---

10. There is still controversy over the overall social impact of deregulation. See for example Dempsey (1992), Davis and Cunningham (1993) and Waring (1993).

piled in both of these areas to support the view that highway safety has not been reduced by increased competition among interstate motor carriers and service to small communities has not suffered.

As in the case of interstate deregulation, large shipper interests, antitrust authorities, and the Department of Transportation have all been leading forces in the move to deregulate state trucking regulation. Federal preemption of state authority by legislative means was sought in Congress. A series of court challenges and administrative rulings resulted in the ironic situation where Federal Express, officially an air carrier, was allowed to freely operate in a state while its major competitors, which were officially motor carriers, could not. This ruling resulted in motor carrier support for state deregulation. The *Airline Improvement Act of 1994* was thus passed with the support of a coalition of major transport establishments, the American Trucking Associations, shippers, and public officials. Also called the *Federal Aviation Administration Authorization Act*, this legislation abolished state economic regulation of trucking, effective January 1, 1995. Under this preemption of state authority, states will continue to regulate safety and insurance. It is anticipated that the application of new rules will be uneven among the states. The legislation also lifts the antitrust exemption for intrastate rate bureaus as they are no longer subject to antitrust jurisdiction.

Deregulation has thus been a continuous process in the U.S. The Federal government has for decades been philosophically supportive of allowing the market to control the behaviour of industry. However, the complete and rapid removal of controls was not possible with the doubts, fears and adjustments that any deregulation process brings. After almost 20 years (i.e., since 1977), the removal of economic controls of the trucking industry by government is nearly complete. Plans are being made to abolish the ICC and transfer its remaining responsibilities to the U.S. Department of Transportation.

The regulation of trucking in all three countries created invisible barriers between them. "Not only did a carrier have to obtain operating authority from both U.S. and Canadian authorities, but in evaluating public necessity, each regulatory authority generally viewed its jurisdiction to end at the international boundary" (Chow, 1984). Mexico's border was even more restrictive since foreign carriers were prohibited from Mexican highways. The result was substantial interlining of LTL freight or equipment interchange of TL freight at the borders rather than single line movement and little incentive from the market to behave competitively.

With the passing of the *Motor Carrier Act of 1980*, Canadian entry applications into the U.S. trucking market increased substantially. Canadian carriers who already possessed authority in Canada could easily obtain complementary operating authority in the U.S. and provide single line service between the two countries. Entry into Canada for U.S. carriers with existing authority in the U.S. was no different than before, creating a non-symmetrical treatment of potential competitors from different sides of the border. Similarly, the Mexican constitution explicitly banned '...the transit of articles, products, and goods' by foreign carriers in the interest of economic protection of Mexican carriers. Only companies controlled by Mexican nationals could be licensed to operate within the country, and then only utilizing Mexican-built equipment and Mexican drivers. In the wake of the MCA which allowed both Canadian and Mexican carriers to enter freely into the U.S., the U.S. trucking industry called for reciprocal measures and the results were amendments to the *Motor Carrier Safety Act of 1984*. These amendments provided for a ban on entry by both Mexican and Canadian carriers, but the ban was lifted on Canadian entry after both countries exchanged letters of understanding which set up administrative and philosophical guidelines for jointly resolving the transborder trucking problem. The ban remained on Mexican trucking, preventing Mexican carriers from entering any interstate transportation market not exempt from ICC jurisdiction. Although the constraints imposed on Mexican truckers introduced a measure of equity in the transborder market, it did not necessarily result in an efficient transportation system between the two countries.

Until 1988, most Canadian provinces were reluctant to permit new entry which would significantly affect the existing market structure. The large number of Canadian applications for U.S. licences indicates that prior restrictive entry policies of both countries erected what has been termed 'an invisible barrier' at the international border. However, actual expansion into the U.S. by Canadian carriers since 1980 has been cautious and incremental. By 1984, several Canadian carriers were offering direct service to major population centres nearest to the international border. However, this service usually did not result in an increase in real competition since it merely substituted single line service for existing joint line service.

Rate competition increased in transborder markets due to the initiatives of U.S.-based competitors. In markets where major U.S. carriers already had single line authority (e.g., U.S.-Vancouver, B.C.), U.S. carriers made available to transborder shippers the same discount programmes used in their domestic markets. In the U.S.-Ontario/Québec transborder market, Canadian and U.S. members of the Niagara Frontier Tariff Bureau (NFTB) dominated the LTL segment and held substantial shares of the TL market. Rate competition in the U.S.-Ontario market was limited until a U.S. carrier offered discounts of 30 percent on its recently acquired authority. Canadian and other U.S.-based competitors were promptly forced to follow. Another incentive came from the availability of low cost U.S. domestic service originating at the border. It was often cheaper for small businesses to rent trucks and move their goods to the border privately than it was to use Canadian carriers (Skorochod and Bergervin, 1984). At the border, the shippers could interline with U.S. carriers at rates as much as 65 percent cheaper than those of Canadian carriers. Members of the NFTB discounted rates by 30 to 40 percent in order to remain competitive with these alternatives.

Expansion by Canadian carriers has obviously increased the availability of single line service in the short haul transborder market and eliminated much of the interlining formerly required. This is amply supported by the initial decline of the joint line percent of revenues of Ontario international traffic where joint line traffic accounted for 47 percent of revenues in 1980 but only 35 percent in 1982. This level of interlining still far exceeded the 8 and 18 percent level of interlining achieved by total U.S. trucking and total U.S. general freight trucking respectively in 1981. In 1986, more than 96 percent of all U.S. traffic was single line. The initial denial of the Yellow and Roadway applications by Canadian provincial authorities had kept the benefits of single line service from some shippers and receivers of long haul transborder freight. But by 1986, both of these U.S. industry giants and others had purchased their way into much of Canada. Further declines in interlining occurred after these and other long haul U.S. carriers entered the transborder market in the mid 1980s.

As noted above, the legislation placing a moratorium on Canadian entry into the U.S. side of the transborder market also placed a moratorium on Mexican applications for authority in the U.S. As the Mexican barrier to U.S. carrier entry into Mexico was part of the country's constitution, little compromise on the issue resulted. Consequently, the moratorium was never lifted until the implementation of NAFTA.

In summary, the dramatic structural and conduct changes that could readily be observed in the U.S. domestic trucking market were absent from the transborder scene — or at least slow in arriving. The benefits of market competition in the U.S. domestic market could be observed in the form of domestic rates that were significantly lower than those charged for comparable transborder movements, and in the much lower rate of interlining in the U.S. Expansion was one-sided and cautious, and U.S. carriers were largely prevented from expanding their direct coverage into Canada by provincial denials of applications for authority. Price competition seemed to be more intense wherever U.S. domiciled carriers could directly or indirectly provide service. Comparable competition in the transborder market did not result from the expansion of Canadian carriers alone. It was the deep pockets of the larger U.S. carriers (so mistrusted by antitrust officials as a source of sustained predatory pricing) that enabled them to purchase Canadian (or U.S.) carriers and their valued operating authority. This was the route eventually taken by Yellow and Roadway as well as several large regional carriers in order to obtain international authority to and from Canada. These moves brought discounting practices, new single line services, and a generally more competitive environment to the long haul LTL transborder market.

Regulatory Reform in Canada

The driving force behind motor carrier regulatory reform in Canada was the concern and/or belief that trucking controls had resulted in economic costs far outweighing any benefits. As in the U.S., there was a substantial body of evidence supporting this change. However, U.S. trucking deregulation and the general trend towards free trade were additional factors, perhaps the crucial factors, which finally caused the reform of trucking policy in Canada.[11]

The change in the U.S. policy on trucking regulation influenced the direction of Canadian policy in three ways. First, the U.S. experience was seen as a normative model that would help Canada predict the out-

---

11. See Chow (1983) and (1991) for a complete discussion of trucking deregulation in Canada.

comes of policy choices. Second, deregulated U.S. and regulated Canadian carriers competed indirectly with each other in the world market for goods of which domestic transportation was an input. Finally, Canadian and U.S. carriers competed directly against each other on transborder traffic lanes connecting the two countries.

Supporters of deregulation in Canada expected to see benefits comparable to the U.S. experience. However, the cautious recognized that Canada could not expect the same level of performance improvement for several reasons: Canadian provinces had never regulated rates, Canadian carriers had never utilized tariff bureaus to the degree found in the U.S., and there was a lack of enforcement in Canada. The prospect of improved price and service levels for Canadian shippers was viewed as crucial to Canadian producers competing in world markets and in particular competing against U.S. competitors. A major supporter of deregulation in Canada was the Canadian Manufacturers Association (CMA), many of whose members were in precisely that situation. Many CMA members purchased transportation in both countries or had affiliated companies in the U.S. so internal comparisons could be made about the relative performance of trucking in the two countries.

Nowhere was the impact of U.S. trucking deregulation felt more directly in Canada than in the transborder trucking market. Ironically, it was entry by Canadian carriers into the U.S. that had increased competition and encouraged entry into Canada by U.S. carriers. In addition, the transborder trucking controversy also caused most of the provinces individually or as part of the Canadian Conference of Motor Transport Administrators (CCMTA) to reexamine their international operating rights policies since a letter of agreement committed Canada to jointly negotiate with the U.S. on the matter.

Reform of transportation began in 1984 when the federal transportation ministry obtained agreement from its provincial counterparts to allow action to be taken on regulatory reform of interprovincial (including transborder) trucking. In February 1985, the Council of Ministers Responsible for Transportation and Highway Safety signed a memorandum of understanding to undertake action on the implementation of reforms to the regulation of interprovincial trucking. In July 1985, the Council released *Freedom To Move*, a plan to deregulate most of the transportation industries. Both the *National Transportation Policy Act* and the *Motor Vehicle Transport Act of 1987* (MVTA) became effective on January 1, 1988. Major components of the MVTA were:

- The establishment of a uniform nationwide entry test for inter-provincial trucking operators based on fitness.
- A fit, willing and able license test to be based on safety and insurance requirements.
- For a five year transition period, new service applications to be subject to a public interest test, with the onus placed on objectors to prove that the public interest would not be served by any new operator. The public interest test was not defined explicitly.
- All key elements of the National Safety Code to be in place well before the move from reverse onus to fit, willing and able in 1993.
- Rate regulations to be eliminated and other license conditions, such as route and commodity restrictions, to be removed at the end of the transition period.
- The federal authority be required to take appropriate action when any foreign government engages in unfair practices against Canadian motor carriers.
- A comprehensive review of reverse onus to be completed after four years with the option to extend the reverse onus test if warranted.

The MVTA continued to delegate administrative control of interprovincial trucking to the provincial regulatory boards. The legislative proposal was far reaching as it required the provincial boards to apply a reverse onus test in considering entry applications, it specified the criteria to be considered in applying the reverse onus test, and, at the end of a set period, it required that the reverse onus test sunset and a fitness test become the sole criterion for entry. The National Transportation Act Review Commission did indeed recommend that reverse onus be sunsetted and in January 1993, provinces began regulating interprovincial entry based on a fitness test only.

A delayed but more concerted trend towards less intraprovincial truck regulation occurred in Canada. In 1980, all provinces except Alberta required the applicant to prove public convenience and necessity (PCN) in order to obtain intraprovincial licenses. By 1989, five provinces and the two territories had moved to a reverse onus test. In particular, Ontario, Canada's most populated and industrially important province, passed legislation which effectively deregulated the provinces motor carrier industry. The *Truck Transport Act* eliminated the PCN test and substituted a fitness test as the primary entry control criterion. However, the regulatory board retains the discretionary power to decide whether a hearing requires that a public interest test be applied. Under all circumstances the onus is on the protesting carriers to prove that the applicant carrier is either not fit or the proposed service is not in the public interest. Even in other provinces where the statutory requirements for entry have not changed, the decisions of the provincial regulators have been decidedly pro competitive. Moreover, the *Interprovincial Trade Agreement*, signed by all the provinces and territories in July 1994, called for the deregulation of all intraprovincial trucking by 1998. By 1995, Québec, New Brunswick, Prince Edward Island, Newfoundland, the Yukon, and the Northwest Territories had joined Alberta and Ontario in changing their entry criteria to fitness only. Manitoba, Saskatchewan and Nova Scotia still maintain some regulatory barriers while British Columbia is the only province to continue the widespread use of the PCN test. The minimal control exerted over intraprovincial rates has remained more or less the same.

The MVTA of 1987 created a national agency, the National Transportation Agency (NTA), to monitor the effects of the Act. Their evaluation and other research on the Canadian interprovincial trucking experience (National Transportation Agency, 1993; Western Advisory Council, 1993) indicates that:

- Interprovincial regulation of Canadian trucking has never been as stringent as regulation in the U.S. Thus, the large performance gains observed in the U.S. were not observed in Canada.
- The overall number of competitors has increased. However, most new competition arose from the entry of existing carriers in new commodity or geographic markets.
- License applications were initially large but declined from 13,767 in 1988 to 5,634 in 1992.
- U.S. carriers have freely entered the market accounting for 28.5 percent of the license applications in 1992.
- The LTL sector continues to consolidate resulting in fewer but larger LTL carriers.
- Owner-operators represent a significant part of truck capacity. Indications are that this sector may have borne the burden of deregulation and is in financial distress.

• Rates have declined or not increased for many shippers since the MVTA. Intense rate competition is reported for all types of truck shipments. However, it is not apparent whether this is part of a trend, a function of the depressed economy during the early 1990s, or a direct affect of the Act.

• The majority of shippers have not observed significant improvements in service but the majority of shippers have been satisfied with the service levels provided by trucking firms.

These findings indicate that the impact of the MVTA of 1987 has not resulted in a significant departure from the trends that have occurred since deregulation of the industry began in the transborder markets in 1980 and the domestic interprovincial markets in the mid 1980s. Service did not appear to significantly improve after the MVTA but shippers are highly satisfied with motor carrier service. Rates appear to be competitive but there is evidence that this was the case prior to 1988. Table 6 displays the truck price index for the Canadian trucking industry defined in several ways. Observe first that the national truck price index closely tracked the PPI until 1986. Since 1986, the truck price index has fallen relative to the general price increases. From 1987 onward, roughly coinciding with deregulation initiatives, interprovincial rate increases were significantly less than intraprovincial rate increases. Finally, LTL rates rose significantly more than TL rates from 1981 to 1992. This result is consistent with the entry trends as well as the U.S. experience.

Two concerns have arisen from the MVTA of 1987. The decentralized implementation of Canadian interprovincial regulatory reform has led to disparate opportunities for carriers domiciled in one province to compete in other provinces. In circumstances similar to those leading to the 'transborder trucking war,' some provinces were slower than others to open entry restrictions. This situation has allowed carriers domiciled in these lagging provinces to enjoy the ability to start up operations in other provinces before carriers in those provinces can reciprocate.

The federal delegation of authority to the provinces in the MVTA of 1987 was based in part on the expectation that a National Safety Code would be agreed upon and implemented. The following recommendation was made in March 1993 by the National Transportation Act Review Commission: "...if resolution of the inconsistencies in extra-provincial safety regulation including the National Safety Code, interpretation and enforcement is not achieved by March 1994, the Federal Government should withdraw the delegation of extra-provincial trucking regulation and/or withhold Federal contributions to highway infrastructure for provinces not complying" (Western Advisory Council, 1993).

Table 6. Canadian Average Freight Revenue Indices

Year	Intraprovincial	Interprovincial	LTL	TL	National	Industrial Product Price Index
1981	100.00	100.00	100.00	100.00	100.00	100.00
1982	105.88	109.88	109.86	106.15	107.68	106.7
1983	106.89	106.44	109.12	105.05	106.72	110.4
1984	111.70	109.28	113.22	108.91	110.68	115.4
1985	118.46	121.42	128.06	114.49	119.85	118.6
1986	117.57	118.85	129.96	110.76	118.20	119.6
1987	114.57	111.44	125.11	105.76	113.21	122.8
1988	115.66	108.99	125.83	104.57	112.68	127.9
1989	128.61	115.16	131.68	116.51	122.53	131.0
1990	125.27	110.91	136.32	108.34	118.73	132.2
1991	130.88	113.88	137.42	114.27	123.04	129.9
1992	127.67	118.24	141.96	112.70	123.68	130.5

Sources: Freight revenue indices from Transport Canada (1994) and industrial product price index from Statistics Canada (1983-95)

Regulatory Reform in Mexico

Deregulation of domestic trucking in Mexico was part of the country's overall restructuring plan. The oil price crash in 1982 forced Mexico to abandon import substitution as a national industrialization policy and adopt new policies that would restructure the economy. One area of attention was to create conditions favorable for domestic private investment to become the main monetary source for domestic production. In July 1989, as part of the economic program to produce low inflation, stimulate growth and restore public confidence in the economy, the domestic motor carrier industry was deregulated.[12] The legal framework

---

12. See Landero (1989) for a complete discussion of the economic environment and government policies that led to deregulation in Mexico.

was modified so that domestic prices could be negotiated at any level below the maximum regulated rate. All Mexican firms were allowed to operate anywhere in the market and only the SCT has the authority to allow new entrants. The cargo centres were restructured in order to provide essential services to operators.

Private carriers can now function as for-hire carriers as well. Maquiladora operations are allowed to maintain their own fleets and haul products in both directions.[13] They may also apply to haul freight for third parties. The significant difference between deregulation in the U.S. and deregulation in Mexico is the overall lack of filing of published rates. In essence, rate negotiation and implementation is on a "contract" type arrangement rather than a tariff filing. This arrangement is intended to promote healthy transportation competition within Mexico (Consolidated Freighters, Inc., 1992). Foreign ownership of Mexican carriers continues to be restricted but this will be gradually changed under NAFTA.

Trucking deregulation in 1989 introduced significant competition in Mexico, lowered tariffs and helped encourage expansion of short haul intercity routes as well as long haul service between Mexico City and the border. Evidence is anecdotal but consistent. Rates "...are 29 percent lower than they were before deregulation" (Strah, 1995a). The Mexican motor carrier vehicle fleet increased by 85 percent from 1989 to 1992 (APL Stacktrain Services, 1994).

IV. Free Trade and Transborder Trucking Policy

North American Free Trade

During the 1980s, there was growing recognition that North American countries could not exist as islands of economic activity. The *Free Trade Act of 1988* (FTA) between Canada and the U.S. ultimately excluded transportation but it was apparent that opportunities for truly integrating the Canadian and U.S. markets were closely linked to transportation reliability, choice and effectiveness. At the very least, the FTA

---

13. Maquiladora plants process and assemble goods imported free of duties from the U.S. The finished products are exported back to the U.S. with U.S. import duties levied only on the "value added" in Mexico.

would accentuate the growth of north-south traffic flows making this transborder market relatively more important over time.

Unlike the FTA, the *North American Free Trade Act of 1994* explicitly included transport. NAFTA took effect January 1, 1994 with the following features pertaining to trucking:

- As of December 17, 1995 states on both sides of U.S.-Mexican border will be open to competition. Foreign carriers may service the Mexican border states directly. Mexican carriers can enter into four U.S. border states. Up to 49 percent of the ownership of a Mexican trucking carrier providing *international* service can be controlled by U.S. or Canadian investors.
- Full cross-border trucking access will be permitted as of January 1, 2000.
- As of January 1, 2001, U.S. investors can own a controlling interest (i. e., 51 percent) of a Mexican fleet that handles *international* traffic.
- As of January 1, 2004, 100 percent foreign ownership of Mexican motor carriers involved in *international* transport is allowed. Mexican investors will have the same rights in the U.S.
- Foreign operation of transportation in *domestic* trucking is prohibited although modifications to the prohibition may be considered.
- The U.S. has enacted reciprocal restrictions on Mexican carriers operating in the U.S. while Canada has no restrictions on either U.S. or Mexican carriers.

Prior to and after NAFTA, Mexican carriers were not prohibited from operating on the U.S. portion of commercial zones that extend across the U.S.-Mexican border. But the temporary ban (to December 1995) on transborder truck movement by U.S. and Canadian carriers into Mexico led to inefficiencies. Since neither U.S. nor Canadian carriers could transport onto Mexican soil, an unnecessary interchange of equipment occurs. Typically, the U.S. or Canadian carrier dropped its trailer on the U.S. side of the border and a Mexican drayage carrier moved the trailer to the Mexican side of the border where it went through Mexican customs and was transferred to a Mexican carrier. The need for staging areas added to the infrastructure congestion at the border towns. The act of interchange not only added non-value producing activity but it made additional requirements for coordination between carriers making transfers. Most importantly, it forced carriers to interchange at a location that does not maximize breakbulk and consolidation efficiencies. For example, many partnerships between U.S. and Canadian LTL carriers would place the transfer of freight at one of the partners natural breakbulk centres rather than artificially at the border.

This situation also led to problems for Canadian motor carriers who transported to Mexico. If the freight had to change hands on the U.S. side of the border, there was considerable concern that freight picked up by a Canadian carrier from a U.S. origin enroute to Mexico would become a domestic movement when it stopped at the U.S. side of the border for interchange. A memorandum of understanding was signed in March 1994 permitting Canadian carriers access to Mexican border states within a 12 mile zone along the border.[14] The U.S., seeking parity with the Canadians, signed a similar memorandum in April 1994 but after one year, no action by SCT has occurred (Hall, 1995b). In fact, representatives of the Mexican trucking industry have openly asked for a delay of open entry or the renegotiation of NAFTA provisions affecting their businesses (Strah, 1995a).[15]

The Level Playing Field Problem

Entry by large, well-financed and efficient U.S.-based truckers posed a competitive threat to the existing domestic trucking industries of Canada and Mexico. Canadian trucking interests claimed that trucking deregulation would leave Canada without a transborder trucking industry of its own. They asserted that either U.S.-based carriers would drive Canadian based carriers out of the transborder market, or Canadian carriers would migrate to the south in order to compete. Consequences were then extrapolated to the possibility of American domination of the domestic Canadian trucking industry.

---

14. Canadian carriers are restricted to direct trailer handoff in a border zone with a specified Mexican partner and must have an interchange agreement on file with the SCT.

15. The Mexican government, apparently under pressure from its trucking industry, has also delayed revisions to its size and weight limits which would permit the use of 53 foot trailers with cab-over configurations and twin trailers. Both of these configurations are commonly used by U.S. carriers and the result is to force U.S. and Canadian carriers to use multiple fleet configurations of to use Mexican subcontractors (Hall, 1995a).

The issue as to whether U.S. domiciled carriers possess competitive advantages over the Canadian competition is relevant if the source of that advantage is created by government policy. Chow and McRae (1989) examined nine non-tariff barriers (NTBs) and found them to be legitimate, non-discriminatory measures in force in each country. The overall economic significance of these NTBs was found to be minimal.[16] Only the long haul TL market would appear to have any significant disadvantages to operating as a Canadian-based carrier, due to driver and equipment restrictions (cabotage) on domestic movements, combined with an unfavorable spatial pattern of industry in the two countries.

Chow and McRae also observed that any disadvantages of operating as a Canadian domiciled carrier appear to be more than offset by lower input costs for Canadian carriers in the range of 10 to 14 percent less than U.S. domiciled carriers.[17] The so called "level playing field" issue was also extensively studied by the Minister of Transports Task Force on Trucking Issues. The studies conducted showed a marginal tax advantage and a significant operating cost advantage for the U.S. firms. However, this observation was again dependent on the exchange rate which dropped from over 0.85 $US/$C when the studies were being completed to 0.72 $US/$C in 1994-95. Recalculating the cost figures from the Task Force study at the lower exchange rates actually makes Canadian input costs 8 percent lower than U.S. costs on average.[18] Nevertheless, the Canadian trucking industry received concessions from the government in the form of a one time fuel tax rebate, assistance to owner operators and accelerated depreciation schedules.

The regulatory issues in the Mexico-U.S. transborder truck market are similar to those faced in the Canada-U.S. market. Mexican trucking interests view U.S. entry as "unequal competition" (Strah, 1995a) much as the Canadian trucking industry claimed an "unlevel playing field."[19]

---

16. The recent deregulation of state economic regulation in the U.S. eliminated one of these obstacles to Canadian productivity.
17. Such cost comparisons are conditional upon the currency exchange rate between the two countries.
18. See Chow (1992) for a complete discussion.
19. Mexican trucking interests refers to the Mexican trucking association, CANACAR, which is the official representative of the Mexican trucking industry in all NAFTA-related negotiations. Of course, not all Mexican carriers have the identical position of CANACAR.

When complete access to the Mexican border states occurs, U.S. carriers may discard their partnerships with Mexican carriers as U.S. carriers seek to provide single line service rather than interline with Mexican carriers for final delivery in the border states. Mexican carriers without U.S. partners may find it difficult to participate at all in the transborder market. Mexican carriers fear well-financed and efficient U.S. carriers. For example, the average age of Mexican trucks is over 10 years old versus 3 years old for U.S. carriers (Toll, 1994). The Mexican fleet averages only 0.5 trailers per tractor unit versus 1.5 to 2.0 for the typical U.S carrier and most of the Mexican equipment fleet is composed of trailers less than the standard 53 foot units possessed by U.S. carriers (Valdes and Crum, 1994). Faced with new competition in domestic markets, established Mexican carriers claim they are not able to replace their existing fleet to effectively compete with potential U.S. competition. Finally, certain sectors of the Mexican economy were depressed by the peso's devaluation which decreased the demand for trucking transport as imported goods became more costly. Combined with domestic deregulation, established Mexican carriers were faced with depressed rates and overcapacity. The Canadian trucking industry also faced a recession a few years after its deregulation with identical impacts.

The result has been various delays to promised changes in Mexican regulations that would improve transborder flows. As noted above, no action had been taken with respect to accelerating U.S. carrier access to Mexican border states which is scheduled for December 1995. The Mexican government reversed published changes that would have allowed longer combination vehicles and kept changes that would make the use of 53 foot trailers pulled by conventional tractors with a sleeper unit illegal. Both of these actions have the effect of preventing the use of vehicle configurations commonly used by U.S. carriers from being used in Mexico legally. A commitment to allow United Parcel Service (UPS) to operate the same size vehicles as its Mexican competitors has not been implemented.[20]

---

20. UPS was prevented from using any vehicle exceeding 500 cubic feet in capacity to transport parcels between cities. Competing Mexican parcel carriers are not limited and the only option for UPS is to use Mexican carriers for intercity linehauls. As of May 1, 1995, Mexican officials were in the process of drafting new size and weight restrictions which would place a limit on the size of shipments that non-Mexican parcel carriers could carry, the number of packages that could be delivered to one consignee in a single day, and maximum delivery time.

Finally, the Mexican trucking industry has asked for tax relief, lower highway tolls, guaranteed diesel fuel prices and a relaxation of new vehicle requirements to assist its members (Strah, 1995b). If given no relief, the industry argues that a delay of open entry under NAFTA or the renegotiation of the trucking provisions would give their members time to acquire the equipment and technology necessary to compete with U.S. and Canadian carriers.

V. The Future of North American Trucking Regulation

For all practical purposes, the U.S. and Canadian interstate and interprovincial trucking industries are completely deregulated. There was evidence that the remaining fitness and administrative requirements (such as rate filing) administered by the ICC remained substantial barriers to entry which caused underutilization of capacity (Wilson and Dooley, 1993). However, 1994 legislation eliminated the last elements of rate filing and further reduced ICC administrative requirements. Although some critics maintain that fitness requirements can be made so stringent so as to become economic barriers to entry, the majority view is that fitness is appropriately a form of safety regulation. This viewpoint supports the current proposal to eliminate the ICC and transfer its remaining duties to the U.S. Department of Transportation.

Although state regulation is now preempted in the U.S., the enforcement of safety regulations and the evaluation of fitness is still a state responsibility. The lack of uniformity in the administration of these requirements may lead to administrative difficulties and varying degrees of inefficiency for multistage motor carriers. Intraprovincial truck regulation in Canada remains a provincial prerogative in Canada. While most provinces have emulated the federal model, some provinces maintain substantial barriers to entry. "Provincial regulatory boards are more responsive to provincial interests and in most cases can be overruled by Cabinet order" (Chow, 1991). Unlike the U.S., the balance of government power is more evenly distributed between the provincial and federal levels, making preemption of existing provincial prerogatives unlikely. However, the consequences for truck markets that continue to be regulated, as in the case of Canadian provinces and Mexico, are inevitable. Pressure to reduce economic regulation will come because no political jurisdiction or economy can be protected from its own economic inefficiencies in the long run. The level and uniformity of economic regulation and other forms of government control over trucking are driven by this economic principle.

Although Mexico's *domestic* trucking market is open, it is open only to Mexican owners. This restriction constrains the competitiveness of foreign trucking companies since they cannot avail themselves of domestic traffic for freight complementary to their international traffic. However, unlike the Canada-U.S. transborder experience, the entry of U.S. carriers is unlikely to enhance this very competitive domestic market. The Mexican government has promised to investigate the potential opening of the domestic market to foreign-owned competitors but the prospects of prompt relief, if any relief is forthcoming, is unlikely given the political sensitivity of the issue and the fact that no principles of NAFTA are being violated. The ban on foreign involvement will have the effect of preventing capital from entering the country for such purposes as equipment replacement and terminal investment and maintain inefficiencies for foreign truckers who cannot merge international and domestic traffic.

The NAFTA articles provide a clear, albeit slow, direction for economic deregulation of transborder trucking. This path will be followed as long as Mexico remains committed to free trade as a macroeconomic policy which appears to be the case. Unfortunately, access to the transborder market to and from Mexico can be constrained by other means such as regulations concerning size and weights of vehicles and the degree of enforcement.

VI. Conclusions

The *Motor Carrier Act of 1980* was a major turning point in the philosophy of trucking industry regulation in North America. The Act not only officially reduced regulation of the American interstate motor carrier industry but it also influenced regulatory changes in U.S. intrastate markets, the U.S.-Canada transborder trucking market, the Canadian trucking market, and the Mexican trucking market. These consequences were inevitable, considering that such markets are interrelated economically and highly visible to shippers across the three countries. Carriers and shippers in the U.S. participate in both interstate and intrastate markets, and, in the wider context, interstate movements compete with intrastate movements. In a sense, federal interstate regulation was a model for intrastate regulation. Thus, pressure to deregulate intrastate markets resulted. Interstate deregulation in the U.S. created disparities between U.S. and Canadian domiciled carriers competing in the transborder market which could only be rectified by similar relaxation of entry control on the Canadian side once deregulation in the U.S. was a *fait accompli*. Canadian shippers compete with U.S. shippers in the North American and global markets, and through the principles of derived demand and geographic market competition, so do domestic carriers of both countries. Canadian shippers viewed deregulation of domestic trucking as a source of competitive advantage, and thus welcomed its implementation. Many Canadian and U.S. shippers are part of North American conglomerates with transportation movements in intrastate, interstate, intraprovincial, and interprovincial markets. As a consequence, the effects of U.S. reform could be readily observed.

The division of regulatory policymaking concerning trucking within states, within provinces and between countries demonstrates how economic efficiency objectives become but one of the factors in the calculations of policymakers representing competing interests. Here the result has been to hold back economic efficiency in the trucking industry and consequently for its customers as well. However, at the same time, market forces do promote an evolution in policy because of efficiency penalties. This was the case in all three countries.

Resistance to regulatory change typically came from the existing trucking industry. The Canadian experience showed that most industry claims were overstated or simply not true. The primary factors that caused distress to Canadian carriers two years after the 1988 deregulation were the depressed economy and the exchange rate. Both factors substantially improved by 1992 and so did the financial condition of the Canadian trucking industry. Nevertheless, the pleadings of the Canadian trucking industry resulted in government assistance in the form of tax concessions and direct financial assistance. That lesson was not lost on Mexican carriers who are now making similar pleas after the peso's devaluation reduced traffic demand and increased the cost of imported equipment and supplies.

Even if Canadian or Mexican motor carriers are supplanted by foreign-owned carriers, the domicile of the drivers and the equipment will likely remain the same. This is true to a great degree for the LTL sector where effectively servicing customers requires local terminal and pickup and delivery capability. It is also particularly true for Mexico in both the LTL and TL sectors since its domestic trucking industry is more evenly distributed far within its borders.

But what if the evidence is wrong and both Canadian and Mexican motor carriers lose substantial revenues to foreign carriers in both the transborder and domestic markets? If the market is left to govern conduct in the trucking industry, Canadian and Mexican carriers will become more efficient and will successfully obtain inputs at a lower cost in order to survive. Some carriers will specialize, develop unique services, and otherwise find unique market niches to serve. Some carriers will reconfigure the location of their operations. Other carriers will, unfortunately, go out of business as their traffic is taken over by more efficient competitors who may be owned or based in any country. From the shipping public's point of view, the North American trucking industry would be rationalizing itself just as the industries that these shippers represent are doing.

The effects of deregulation are still important issues for research and will continue to be debated as long as pockets of economic regulation in North America remain in several Canadian provinces and Mexico's domestic market. The benefits of accelerating the transborder entry provisions of NAFTA is also an issue. The trend is towards more uniform and less regulation in all jurisdictions but how fast and how far Mexico and the provinces will go depends on the perceived economic benefits conditioned by the social goals and political climate in each jurisdiction.

As economic regulation disappears in most North American trucking markets, public policy will refocus on safety and technical regulations governing such areas as vehicle size and weights, user charges, driver and safety certification, and hours of service. Uniformity will be the issue of most concern as administrative and operational difficulties created by non-uniform laws or their enforcement will create inefficiencies or unfair advantages. In addition, the issue of cabotage remains an issue that reduces the ability of carriers operating internationally to utilize their equipment fleet and labour force optimally.

The same transborder and domestic regulatory issues will arise around the world as different political jurisdictions become more economically interdependent. This is the case in Europe as the Economic

Community continues its economic integration. The lesson from North America is that inconsistent regulatory policies between countries, states and provinces create economic inefficiencies and disparate opportunities. When these jurisdictions are neighboring economies with significant trade between them, forces are generated to seek regulatory uniformity. The trend in North America has been to reduce trucking regulation to the lowest common denominator in order to achieve such uniformity.

References

APL Stacktrain Services (1994) *Entering the Mexico Market: A Transportation Assessment*, (Oakland, CA).

American·Trucking Associations, Inc. (1995) *North American Trucking Profile*, International Office, (Alexandria, VA).

American Trucking Associations, Inc. (1988) *American Trucking Trends: 1987*, (Alexandria, VA).

Boyer, K.D. (1993) "Deregulation of the Trucking Sector: Specialization, Concentration, Entry, and Financial Distress," *Southern Economic Journal*, 59(3), January, 481-495.

Chow, G. (1980) "Studies of Intrastate Trucking Regulation - A Critique," *Transportation Journal*, Summer, 23-32.

Chow, G. (1983) "How Much Longer Can We Live with Regulation of Canada's Trucking Industry?," *The Canadian Business Review*, 10(1), Spring, 45-52.

Chow, G. (1984) "Prospective Changes in the U.S.-Canada Transborder Trucking Industry," *Logistics: Change and Synthesis*, P. Gallagher, ed., (Leaseway Transportation Corp.), 261-272.

Chow, G. (1991) "U.S. and Canadian Trucking Policy," *Transport Deregulation: An International Movement*, K. Button and D. Pitfield, eds., (London: Macmillan), 141-176.

Chow, G. (1992) "Competition Between Canadian and U.S. Motor Carrier Transportation," *National Transportation Policy*, Richard Lande, principal author, (Toronto: Butterworth), 191-212.

Chow, G. and K. Button (1983) "Road Haulage Regulation: A Comparison of the Canadian, British and American Approaches," *Transport Reviews*, 3(3), July- Sept, 237-264.

Chow, G. and J.J. McRae (1989) "Non-Tariff Barriers and the Structure of the U.S.-Canadian (Transborder) Trucking Industry," *Transportation Journal*, 30(2), Spring, 4-21.

Contract Freighters, Inc. (1993) "Logistics to Mexico and Beyond...," special presentation for the Transportation Research Forum, New York City, NY, October 14.

Davis, G.M. and W.A. Cunningham (1993) "Public Policy Implications of Motor Carrier Restructuring: A Decade of Experience," *Transportation Practitioners Journal*, 60(3), Spring, 286-305.

Dempsey, P:S. (1992) "Interstate Trucking: The Collision of Textbook Theory and Empirical Reality," *Transportation Law Journal*, 20(2), 185-254.

Eno Foundation for Transportation, Inc. (1990) *Transportation in America*, Eighth Edition, May, (Westport, CT: ENO Foundation for Transportation Inc.).

Fagan, D. (1993) "Nuts and bolts of NAFTA," *Globe and Mail*, November 17, A10.

Glaskowsky, N. (1987) *Effects of Deregulation on Motor Carriers*, (Westport, CT: ENO Foundation for Transportation Inc.).

Hall, K. G. (1995a) "Mexico Reverses Trailer Size Rules, Angering US Truckers," *The Journal of Commerce*, May 11, 1A.

Hall, K. G. (1995b) "U.S. Considers Second Complaint Over Border Openings to Truckers," *The Journal of Commerce*, May 11, 8A.

International Monetary Fund (1995) *International Financial Statistics Yearbook*, (Washington, D.C.: International Monetary Fund), February.

Landero, A.D. (1989) "Economic Appraisal of the Deregulation Process in the Mexican Load Transport Market," paper presented at the Transportation Research Forum Annual Conference, Williamsburg, VA, October, 1-15.

Lyndon B. Johnson School of Public Affairs (1991) *Regulatory and Infrastructure Obstacles to Free Trade*, Texas-Mexico Transportation System Policy Research Report Number 98, University of Texas.

Motor Carrier Ratemaking Study Commission (1983) *Collective Ratemaking in the Trucking Industry*, (Washington, D.C.).

National Transportation Agency (1993, 1994) *Annual Review*, (Ottawa: Ministry of Supply and Services).

Owen, D.S. (1988) *Deregulation in the Trucking Industry*, (Washington, D.C.: Federal Trade Commission), May.

Pan-American Bus Lines Operation (1936) *1 MCC 190,202.*

Skorochod, P. and R.P. Bergervin (1984) "Issues in Transportation/Distribution for the Small/New Exporter," *Canadian Transportation Research Forum*, 19th Annual Meeting, May, 831-853.

Statistics Canada (1983-95) *Industry Price Indexes,* Catalogue 62-011, (Ottawa: Ministry of Supply and Services).

Statistics Canada (1993) *Trucking in Canada 1991*, Catalogue 53-222, (Ottawa: Ministry of Supply and Services).

Strah, T.M. (1995a) "Mexican Truckers Set Off Alarms," *Transport Topics*, March 13, 7.

Strah, T.M. (1995b) "UPS Says Mexico Reneged on Nafta," *Transport Topics*, May 1, 5.

Taylor, J.C. (1993) "Regulation of Trucking by the States," *Regulation*, Number 2, 37-47.

Teske, P., S. Best and M. Mintrom (1994) "The economic theory of regulation and trucking deregulation: Shifting to the state level," *Public Choice*, 79, June, 247-256.

Toll, E.E. (1994) "Mexican Transport Needs Work," *Journal of Commerce*, March 10, 7A.

Transport Canada (1992) *Transportation in Canada*, TP 10451-E, Economic Analysis, (Ottawa, ON).

Transport Canada (1994) *Trucking Price Indices: 1981-1992*, TP 10785-E, Economic Analysis, (Ottawa, ON).

U.S. Department of Transportation (1993) *National Transportation Statistics: Historical Compendium, 1960-1992*, Bureau of Transportation Statistics, (Washington, D.C.).

U.S Department of Transportation (1994) *North American Transportation: Statistics on Canadian, Mexican and United States Transportation*, Bureau of Transportation Statistics, (Washington, D.C.).

Valdes, R.J. and Crum, M.R. (1994) "U.S. Motor Carrier Perspectives on Trucking to Mexico," *Transportation Journal*, Summer, 5-20.

Waring, D.T., Jr. (1993) "The Downside of Motor Carrier Deregulation," *Transportation Law Journal*, 21(2), 409-431.

Westac Transportation Advisory Council (1993) "Canada's Trucking Industry: Developments and Issues Since 1986," *Westac Monitor*, 19(1), May.

Wilson, W.W. and F.J. Dooley (1993) "An Empirical Examination of Market Access," *Southern Journal of Economics*, 60(1), July, 49-62.

PART VI

PROJECT EVALUATION

CHAPTER 25

COST-BENEFIT ANALYSIS OF
TRANSPORT PROJECTS*

*Christopher A. Nash***

I. Introduction

Transport was amongst the first fields in which cost-benefit analysis (CBA) came into regular application as a part of decision taking. For instance, in Britain two of the classic seminal applications of the technique were the studies of the M1 motorway (Beesley, Coburn and Reynolds, 1960) and of the Victoria Line–an underground railway line in London (Beesley and Foster, 1963). Following these studies, techniques were developed for the routine appraisal of road schemes and of public transport schemes where these have a social intent.

It is interesting to speculate as to why transport has proved such a fruitful area for application of the technique. Perhaps it is partly the fact that there are many fairly similar schemes to rank, so that a formalized appraisal system is more attractive than relying on the use of judgement. Perhaps it is that the major benefit of transport projects—time savings— is readily measured, and does not arouse the same hostility to monetary

* Reprinted from *Efficiency in the Public Sector: The Theory and Practice of Cost-Benefit Analysis*, (Edited by Alan Williams and Emilio Giardina), Edward Elgar, Aldershot, 1993, pp. 83-105.
** Professor of Transport Economics, Institute for Transport Studies, Leeds University, England.

valuation as do the benefits of more sensitive schemes such as health projects. Whatever the reasons, the long history of transport project appraisal makes this application a good test of the value of the technique. If it is not helpful in this sector, it is unlikely to be anywhere!

In this chapter we first describe the basic methods of CBA of transport projects, illustrating them from current British Department of Transport practice, together with comment on the degree to which this approach differs from that commonly found elsewhere (these comments rest heavily on a recent survey by Sanderson, 1989), We then address some of the criticisms of the technique as commonly used. These concern the forecasting of traffic levels, the treatment of environmental, land use and development effects, the question of income distribution, the issue of comparability of appraisal methods between modes and the relationship between project appraisal and strategic choice. Following this, we turn briefly to alternative approaches to appraisal, including objectives-based and multicriteria techniques. Finally, we present our conclusions on the value of cost-benefit analysis of transport projects.

II. Methodology of Transport Appraisal

Let us consider the appraisal of a typical road scheme (Table 1). Like any other project, it will involve capital, maintenance and operating cost. Unlike many other projects, the bulk of the operating costs will be incurred by people other than the agency undertaking the project— namely motorists, bus companies and road hauliers. Moreover, to the extent that in the absence of the scheme they would have used poorer quality, more congested roads, operating cost savings appear as a benefit of the scheme; it is only in respect of any traffic generated by the road itself that they appear as a cost. In common with normal Department of Transport practice, the example in Table 1 assumes that the scheme itself generates no additional traffic that would not have existed without the scheme, so that operating costs appear solely as a benefit for existing traffic (This controversial assumption is considered further in section 8). There may also be some maintenance cost savings on existing roads as a result of the reduced level of traffic using them.

So far, the CBA appears very straightforward. All the above items are readily measured in money terms. However two categories of benefit

Table 1., Costs and benefits of a road scheme
(present values, £000, in 1979 prices, discounted at 7%)

| | Traffic growth (alternative assumptions) | |
	High	Low
Costs		
Construction	2,491	2,491
Maintenance	72	72
Delays during	32	32
construction		
Total	2,595	2,595
Benefits		
Time and operating		
cost savings	4,218	2,658
Accident savings	417	304
Total	4,635	2,962
Net present value	2,040	367

Source: Institute for Transport Studies, University of Leeds: Economic Evaluation Short
    Course, course notes.

that are usually much more significant than operating cost savings are time savings and reductions in accidents. Obviously these benefits are not normally traded in any market, therefore we are faced with the problems of imputing values to them.

In the case of time savings, there is a distinction to be made between time spent travelling during working hours (which includes bus and lorry drivers as well as business travellers) and time spent travelling during one's own time. In the former case. it is usual to value the time at the wage rate of the employee concerned plus a mark-up to allow for overhead costs of employing labour (such as social insurance charges). This assumes that the time saved can be gainfully employed and that the gross wage represents the value of the marginal product of labour in its alternative use. Doubts may be raised on a number of grounds. Is the time saving large enough to be of use, or will it simply be wasted as idle time (individual transport projects often yield savings of less than a minute, although these may be aggregated with savings from other schemes to form more useful amounts of time)? Will the labour released find alternative work, or add to unemployment? If it does find alternative employment, does the gross wage really reflect the value of its marginal product in the new use (Marks, Fowkes and Nash, 1986)?

For non-working time, the problem of valuation is greater. The approach here has been to try to discover what people are willing to pay to save time, either by 'revealed preference' or by 'stated preference' methods. Revealed preference methods rely on studying people's behaviour in situations in which they reveal an implicit value of time. The most popular case is that of the choice of travel mode, where people may have a choice between two modes, one of which is faster and more expensive than the other. If a model is estimated which forecasts the probability that someone chooses one mode rather than the other as a function of journey time, money cost and any other relevant quality differences, then the relative weight attached to time and money can be used to estimate their 'value of time.'

This approach was used for many years, but it suffered from some problems. One had to find cases where such trade-offs really exist and are perceived by a representative cross section of the population. To estimate the value of time to a reasonable degree of accuracy, samples running into thousands are needed, and the data usually have to be collected specifically for this purpose by means of a questionnaire survey. If 'stated preference' methods are used, then respondents to the survey are asked what they would choose, given hypothetical alternatives (an example is given in Table 2). This enables the individual trade-offs to be designed to reveal the maximum information about the value of time; moreover each respondent can be asked about a number of different choices. This allows great economies in sample size. After piloting and testing to ensure that the results were similar to those produced by revealed preference methods, this approach was used extensively in the studies (MVA consultants; Institute for Transport Studies, University of Leed; Transport Studies Unit, University of Oxford, 1987) that determined the values of leisure time currently used in British Department of Transport applications (Table 3).

Turning to accidents, the costs may be divided into those that are readily valued in money terms and those that are not. The former include damage to property and vehicles, health service, ambulance and police cost. With slightly more hesitation they may be said to include

Table 2. Example of a stated preference question

Please compare the following alternative combinations of train fare and service level.

A

London, dep.	2.50	3.20	3.50	4.20	4.50
Stockport.	5.10	5.40	6.10	6.40	7.10
Manchester, arr.	5.20	5.50	6.20	6.50	7.20

Fares: one-way £12, return £24
Scheduled journey time: 2hrs 30 mins
Reliability: up to *10* mins late

B

London, dep.	2.50	•	3.50	•	4.50
Stockport	5.40	•	6.40	•	7.40
Manchester, arr	5.50	•	6.50	•	7.50

Fares: one-way £10, return £20
schedule journey time: 3hrs
Reliability: up to *30* mins late

Do you:
definitely prefer A? probably prefer A? Like A and B equally? probably prefer B? definitely prefer B?

Source: Institute for Transport Studies, University of Leeds, questionnaire.

loss of production due to victims being unable to work (this again is typically valued at the gross wage). What is more difficult is to place a money value on the pain, grief and suffering caused by death or injury in an accident. For many years, in Britain, this value was determined by the political process rather than by the preferences of those directly involved. However it is possible to apply both revealed preference and stated preference techniques to this issue as well. The way to do this is to recognize that transport improvements do not save the lives of specific known individuals; rather they lead to a reduced probability of involvement in an accident for all users. Thus real or hypothetical trade-offs between safety and cost may be used to derive the 'value of a life.' Such a stated preference study (Jones-Lee, 1987) is indeed the basis of the value currently used by the British Department of Transport (Table 4), although there may be doubts as to how well people are able to

Table 3. Resource values of time per person(pence per hour)

	Average 1986 prices and values
(a) Working time	
Car driver	757.6
Car passenger	605.8
Bus passenger	502.8
Rail passenger	811.4
Underground passenger	737.0
Bus driver	510.0
Bus conductor	498.6
Light goods vehicle occupant	476.1
Other goods vehicle occupant	552.8
All workers	724.8
(b) Non-working time in vehicle	
Standard appraisal value	161.2
People of working age	190.0
Retired people	127.4
All adults	185.0
Children(under 16)	47.6
(c) Walking, waiting and cycling Double the in-vehicle values	

Soure: Department of Transport, COBA Monual, May 1987.

Table 4 Average cost per casualty, by severity(£1985 prices)

	Pre-revision	Post-1987 revision	Post-1988 revision
Fatal	180 330	252 500	500 000*
Serious	8 280	13 500	13 500
Slight	200	280	280

* 1987 price
Source: Department of Transport, Valuation of Road Accidents(1988).

respond to questions involving changes in very small probabilities.

   The British Department of Transport utilizes a computer program (COBA) to calculate the net present value of its trunk road projects. This programme includes the money values of all the items so far discussed, as indeed do the methods used in all the major countries of Western Europe. But it does not value any of the other effects of road schemes, of which by far the most important and controversial are the environmental effects of such schemes. The way in which these 'intangible' effects of transport projects are typically handled is treated in section 4, but first we discuss another controversial issue in transport appraisal—the problem of forecasting traffic levels and consequently the levels of all the above benefits in physical terms.

III. Forecasting

It will be clear from the above discussion that forecasting the volume of traffic that will use a proposed transport facility is a key input into the appraisal process. Given that transport projects frequently take ten years to plan, design and build, and are extremely long-lived, it is necessary to forecast a long way into the future. Road projects in Britain are usually appraised over a 30-year life, which requires forecasting for 40 years from the date on which the planning starts. The benefits from a scheme usually rise more than proportionately with the traffic volume, as increased volume leads to worse congestion. Thus the forecast rate of increase in traffic is very important, as well as being subject to great uncertainty. Possible approaches to forecasting range from simple time series models based on aggregate growth in population, incomes and petrol prices to more detailed modelling of trips by purpose and destination (Kanafani, 1983). The approach used by the British Department of Transport combines a car ownership model (based on incomes and driving licence holding) and a car use model (in which the kilometres run per car vary in accordance with incomes and petrol prices). For freight traffic, tonne kilometres are assumed to be proportional to gross domestic product, whilst bus and coach traffic is assumed constant over time. High and low forecasts are produced on the basis of alternative assumptions about petrol prices and economic growth (Department of Transport, 1989).

Given a traffic forecast, it is necessary to estimate the resulting travel times. The interaction between traffic volumes and speeds is usually estimated by the use of speed-flow relationships, which vary according to the characteristics of the road (lane width, number of lanes and so on). In urban areas, queuing at junctions is a much greater cause of delay, and relationships between delay at junctions and traffic volumes play a more important role.

Regarding accidents, it is usual simply to use a rate per vehicle kilometre for each type of road. Thus, when traffic is diverted from a single carriage-way to a dual carriageway or a motorway, a reduction in accidents is forecast simply because the new road is of a type which has a lower accident rate per vehicle kilometre.

IV. Environmental Effects

Road schemes have many important environmental effects, both at local and global level. At the local level, they lead to property demolition, noise nuisance, visual intrusion and air pollution. At the same time, by taking traffic off other, perhaps more environmentally sensitive roads, projects may offer environmental benefits. More globally, road schemes require inputs, such as limestone; to the extent that they generate additional traffic they also require oil production and produce pollutants with more than purely local effects, such as nitrogen oxides (implicated in acid rain) and carbon dioxide (a greenhouse gas).

It is conceivable that ways could be found to value all of these items in money terms. For instance, the effects of property demolition could be studied by means of a contingent valuation survey, asking people the minimum compensation they would need to willingly sell their existing house (this was undertaken as part of the studies of the proposed third London airport in the early 1970s (Dasgupta and Pearce, 1972, ch. 9)). Noise, visual amenity and local air pollution have all been valued by means of studies of house price differentials, which are one way in which people indirectly reveal their willingness to pay for a superior environmental quality (Pearce and Markandya, 1989). It has also been suggested that these factors could be amenable to 'stated preference' surveys, perhaps also using house prices as the payment instrument (Nash, 1990).

For global pollutants there is greater difficulty in valuation. Much of this springs from enormous uncertainty as to the physical causation and effects. For instance, what contribution does an extra tonne of nitrogen oxides make to the incidence of acid rain, and what damage does that rain do to plants, wildlife and buildings? Valuing the social cost of carbon dioxide emissions appears even more complex, although attempts have been made to do it. Two such attempts are cited by Pearce (1990).

In the current British methodology, no attempt is made to value environmental effects of road schemes. Rather the environmental effects are set out in a matrix known as the Leitch framework, after the chairman of the committee which devised it (Leitch, 1978). A summary of the elements included in this matrix is shown in Table 5. From this it will be seen that there is a wide variety of measures, all in different units—physical measures, numbers of houses, rankings, verbal descriptions. At the same time, no measures are included of non-local environmental effects of schemes. This is because, with traffic assumed constant regardless of what road schemes are built, the level of these pollutants hardly varies.

Table 5. Cost and benefits of road schemes: the Leitch framework

Incidence group	Nature of effect	No of measure	
		Financial	Other units
Road users	Accidents	1	3
	Comfort/convenience	6	
	Operating costs	5	
	Amenity		2
Non-road users directly affected	Demolition disamenity (houses, shops office, factories schools, churches public open space)		37
Land take, severance, disamenity to farmers			7
Those concerned	Landscape, scientific, historical value, land use, other transport operators		9 (+ verbal description)
Financing authority	Cost and benefits in money terms	7	
Total		19	59

Source: Leitch(1978).

By contrast, a number of other countries, including Germany and Sweden, do explicitly value certain local environmental effects in their appraisal of transport projects. For instance both of these countries value noise and local air pollution. It must be said, however, that the values used are based on somewhat shaky evidence, and are derived from estimates of the alternative costs of achieving environmental standards by alternative means (such as double glazing, or fitting catalytic convertors to vehicles). This approach presupposes that the standard is appropriate in the first place.

In the British approach, no formal method is used for trading off these various measures against each other and against the 'economic' costs and benefits. At the local level, the Leitch framework is used to reach a judgement as to which of a number of local variants of the scheme is the best overall. Even here there is a suspicion in many quarters that those elements counted as 'economic,' which include leisure time savings, are given more weight than those that are not. But it is in setting national priorities between schemes for funding that this suspicion is strongest. How could one possibly use the Leitch framework approach to rank schemes on a national level, for instance to set priorities between bypasses, motorway upgarding, new urban roads and development roads in remote areas? It appears that, to the extent that such comparisons are made at all, they are made largely on the basis of the net present value. This belief is fuelled by the frequency with which figures on the overall returns from the trunk road programme are quoted, even though these exclude all environmental effects, as well as being misleading in other respects (see section 6).

Again one may contrast this with the position in most European countries where the economic costs and benefits are included in what is more obviously a multicriterion framework used for rating schemes and setting priorities. However it is rare for formal multicriterion techniques to be used in doing this, the principal exception being the Netherlands, where a microcomputer-based decision support system is used.

V. Land Use and Development Effects

In many countries, a main motivation behind transport projects is the encouragement of economic development and the promotion of particular patterns of land use. Thus, for instance, better roads to remote areas may be built to reduce their disadvantage in terms of transport cost; improved public transport to a city centre may be used to try to reduce decentralization of jobs. It is clear from the foregoing that the approach in Britain has generally been to concentrate on the direct transport benefits of projects, on the assumption that these are overwhelmingly the most important factors. Part of the reason for this is that, in a small country with an already well developed transport system, even a major transport project will only have a small effect on the total costs of production and distribution of most industries in a particular location. Typically, in Britain, transport costs amount to some 8 per cent of total production and distribution costs, and even major projects will change total cost by less than 1 per cent (Dodgson, 1973). Moreover, even if one can reduce the disadvantage of remote areas, they will still not be favoured unless they have some advantages which outweigh the fact that their transport cost will still be higher than those in more accessible locations.

Nevertheless there clearly are cases where transport improvements do affect land use and economic development. A major estuary crossing, for example, may enable firms to concentrate their distribution facilities (or even production) on one side of the estuary, with consequent exploitation of economies of scale (Mackie and Simon, 1986). A major motorway development close to a major conurbation will tend to attract distribution and retailing activities, particularly at junctions with other motorways (McKinnon, 1988). Improved rail services to the city centre may well trigger house building for commuter purchase (Harman, 1980). It should be noted that these developments are not always beneficial. In the case of the M25 motorway around London, much new development has been attracted to a green belt area, at considerable environmental cost. Improved roads to remote parts of Scotland may promote tourist travel, but they also enable firms to serve those areas from major centres, leading to the closure of local facilities such as bakers and distribution depots. Improved rail services may lead to the growth of long distance commuting and urban sprawl.

Whilst models do exist to try to predict these sorts of repercussions of transport projects, they are complex to use and they are not yet at the stage that they can be relied on to give more than general guidance on likely effects (Webster, Bly and Paully, 1988). Thus weighing up of these factors still has to be mainly a matter of judgement. Nevertheless it appears that many European countries pay more attention to regional and land use factors when reaching a view on the overall desirability of a scheme than does Britain.

VI. Income Distribution

It is common concern that CBA does not take into account the distribution of the benefits and costs of the project concerned. Moreover, by valuing benefits at what people are willing to pay for them, and costs at the compensation people require, it is systematically biased towards the better off, who, other things being equal, will be willing to pay more, and require more compensation. In other words, cost-benefit analysis places more weight on people's preferences the better off they are (Nash, Pearce and Stanley, 1975).

If this aspect of CBA is not liked, then it is necessary to allow decision makers to place more weight on costs and benefits incurred by poorer groups, either by some explicit weighting system, or by providing the information in such a way that they can reach a judgement on this issue too. In other words, cost and benefits need to be presented by incidence group, and information is needed on the incomes of those groups.

The Leitch framework goes some way towards doing this, by dividing costs and benefits into those falling on road users, occupiers of property, those interested in the historical or scientific value of the site and so on. But there are some strange inconsistencies surrounding the treatment of public authorities. There is no clear separation of the cash flow to and from public authorities from the benefits to users–for some reason, both are treated as benefits to the financing authority. This certainly reinforces the view that the financing authority is interested in time saving for users but not in environmental costs and benefits. Amongst other groups for whom benefits are not clearly isolated are companies (involved in freight and business travel), public transport operators, cyclists and pedestrians.

A more consistent approach to the specification and measurement of effects on incidence groups has been developed by Lichfield, initially as the Planning Balance Sheet (Lichfield, Kettle and Whitbread, 1975) and later extended and renamed to form Community Impact Evaluation

(Lichfield, 1988). This approach clearly specifies all the relevant groups and consistently identifies costs and benefits to them, either in whatever the natural units of measurement of the effect in question are, or in money units where valuations are deemed to be sufficiently reliable to be of value (Table 6). Transfer payments are explicitly included (in contrast to a conventional CBA where they are excluded), but of course they are included both on the cost side and on the benefit side. Thus, for instance, a tax payment appears as a cost to the group of road users paying it and as a benefit to the public authority receiving it.

Two final points may be made on the distributional issue. Firstly, when evaluating methods of valuing time and accident savings, there is—not surprisingly—clear evidence that these are related to ability to pay. Thus, if one were CBA purely as an efficiency test, one would need to disaggregate benefits by income group and apply higher values of these benefits to the better off. This would systematically bias decisions towards improving roads used more by the affluent, for instance those in wealthier parts of the country.

Table 6 . Brigg Inner Relief Road, impact groups

PRODUCERS
On site
  Landowners and occupiers displaced
  County council as Highway Authcrity
  Borough Council as Highway Authority

Off site
  Landowners and occupiers not displaced
  Landowners–developable sites
  Borough Council as authority levying local taxation
  Brigg as economic entity
  Regional cultural heritage

CONSUMERS
  Occupiers of buildings displaced
  Vehicular traffic
  Occupiers of buildings not displaced
  New occupiers in developable sites
  Brigg local taxpayers
  Brigg residents and visitors

Source: Lichfield(1987)

In practice this has never been seen as politically acceptable. Thus it is usual simply to apply average values to all road users. This in itself could introduce some curious biases to decisions, however. For instance, it may lead authorities to spend money on securing time savings for travellers in poor areas on the basis of the average value of time, when in fact those travellers value the time savings at less than the cost of the scheme, and would rather have received the cash as a tax reduction. This illustrates the problem that effectively uprating *one* item of benefit for the poor whilst not applying similar weights to all others distorts their relative values of different types of cost and benefit. It is more consistent to value all costs and benefits at people's own willingness to pay or to accept compensation, and then to weight the sum total of costs and benefits.

A second and massive problem with distributional analysis arises regarding the incidence of the benefits. It is in the nature of the market system that the final incidence of costs and benefits tends to differ from the initial one. Thus for instance, environmental and accessibility benefits tend to become capitalized into property values, and thus ultimately to benefit property owners rather than occupiers. Where property is rented rather than owned outright this obviously changes the final incidence of benefits. Similarly benefits to firms may well be passed on through the market. For instance, given the highly competitive nature of both the road haulage and the retail industries, one might reasonably assume that benefits to road hauliers are passed on to retailers in the form of lower freight charges, and ultimately to consumers in the form of lower prices. A reasonable assumption therefore would be that these effects should be shown as benefits to consumers, in proportion to their level of consumption, rather than to firms.

When these factors are taken into account, a full analysis of the distributional effects of schemes is very much more complex than appears at first sight. It is far easier to undertake an efficiency analysis in which transfers—and therefore redistribution of costs and benefit—are ignored.

VII. Comparability between Modes

So far our discussion has focused on road projects as the typical transport application of CBA. However the technique can be readily applied to rail infrastructure projects, air and seaports, and so on. It can also be used to appraise pricing policies and levels of service on public transport. When applied to public transport, broadly the same list of issues arises as considered above in the case of roads. However it should be noted that, given the absence of appropriate pricing to cover the external costs of congestion, accidents and environmental effects on roads, benefits often arise from public transport projects in terms of relieving these problems by diverting traffic from car or lorry.

There is one major difference. In the case of public transport, usually a fare is charged for the journey, and often the fares and service decisions are left to the operator, acting on a commercial basis. This is only possible in the case of road schemes if a toll is charged and this is the exception rather than the rule. Whilst a number of countries (France, Italy and Spain) do have tolls on motorways, this is not yet the case in Britain, with the exception of estuarial crossings. Urban road pricing schemes, although under consideration in the Netherlands, Sweden and Britain, have yet to be implemented anywhere in Europe, with the exception of tolls for crossing the cordons surrounding a number of Norwegian cities. Thus it can usually be assumed that, with the exception of marginal payments of fuel tax, road use is free at the point of use.

At one level, all the presence of commercial public transport operators does is to add a further complication to the analysis. If, for instance, one was examining provision of a facility such as a bus priority system, and the agency undertaking the project had no control over the service decisions of the bus operator, it would simply be necessary to predict the reactions of the operator, just as one needs to predict the behaviour of road users in any road scheme.

However, the question arises as to whether it is desirable to change that behaviour, either by provision of grants or subsidies or by direct ownership and control. Consider, for instance, the case of a rail project, where the rail operator is usually an integrated provider of track and services. If the operator is simply set commercial objectives, it will obviously appraise investment in rail infrastructure solely on financial terms. Many of the items included in the above appraisal-user benefits (except inasmuch as they may be recouped as fare revenue), benefits of relief of road congestion, accidents and environmental degradation, and other environmental effects–will be left out of the appraisal.

Thus the use of CBA for public transport projects inevitably involves some sort of replacement of purely financial objectives with social ones, and usually some sort of grant or subsidy. For governments which believe in leaving decisions to the market wherever possible, perhaps because of a belief that grants of subsidies automatically lead to inefficiency, this is an unwelcome message. This has been the case in Britain in recent times. It has been asserted that in most cases CBA and financial appraisal yield broadly the same conclusions for public transport projects, and thus that one can directly compare cost-benefit rates of return on road schemes and financial rates of return on public transport schemes. The evidence for this assertion came from a study of a rail project which is reproduced in Table 7 (Department of Transport, 1984). It is seen that, in the case of this project, which is an electrification project, the bulk of the benefits take the form of cost reductions, which do indeed figure in both financial and cost–benefit rates of return. However, to the extent that the scheme leads to a service improvement, the extra revenue earned by the rail operator only recoups a small part of the total benefits of the improvement to rail users and remaining road users.

Table 7. Birmingham—London/Basingstoke electrification
(NPV £ m in 1979 prices at 7%)

Low-growth scenario		
Increase in passenger revenue	+	6.490
Reduction in operating costs	+	27.955
Reduction in capital and maintenance cost	–	40.095
Financial NPV	–	5.650
Consumer surplus to rail users (existing and new)	+	2.857
Consumer surplus to remaining road users	+	1.485
Saving in road accident costs	+	0.440
Tax adjustment	–	1.243
Change in London Transport revenue	–	0.063
Social NPV	–	2.175

Notes:
1. This appraisal covered inter-city passenger services only. Local and suburban services were assumed to remain diesel-operated.
2. Consumer surplus to remaining road users is shown as 1845 in the original, but comparison with figures elsewhere in the report makes it clear that this is an error.
Source: Department of Transport(1984)

Where it is accepted that public transport improvements yield social benefits (for instance in urban areas) grants towards their costs are still available. However, for the purpose of the grant, benefits to users of the system are disallowed; only benefits to third parties are included. This may drastically reduce the allowable benefits of the scheme (Nash and Preston, 1991) and lead to projects failing to go ahead when they are beneficial in straight social cost–benefit terms (see Table 8 for an example).

It should be stressed that this particular approach to public transport is a peculiarly British one; most European countries routinely conduct cost benefit analyses of public transport investments and allow grant aid to public transport on the basis of the total benefits it produces. But it does

Table 8. Comparison of net present values of two rail investment programmes (30-year project life, 7% interest rate, £000s, 1986 prices)

	West Yorkshire, 6 new stations on existing services	Leicester–Burton, new service serving 14 new stations
Gain in public transport revenue from new users	99	8 897
Loss in public transport revenue due to increased journey time	−166	–
Recurrent costs	−147	−9 154
Capital costs	−656	−5 806
Financial NPV	28	−6 063
Time savings to new rail users	515	4 582
Time savings to existing rail users	−472	–
Time saving to road users	133	3 304
Accident savings	277	2 612
Tax adjustment	−282	−2 326
Social NPV	179	2 109
Social NPV Excluding user benefits	136	−2 473

Source: Nash and Preston(1991)..

illustrate a more general problem, which is that of reconciling social and commercial aims in the transport sector. It is common for certain forms of publicly provided transport service (long-distance rail and bus services; rail freight services) to be provided on a purely commercial basis, but this gives immediate rise to a comparability problem, since a commercial operator will automatically take decisions on a financial rather than a cost-benefit basis. Sometimes it is argued that the solution is to provide the road system on a commercial basis, in the form of toll roads as well. However comparability has little value if it consists of following the wrong criteria on all modes. To the extent that transport is a sector in which externality problems abound, it seems appropriate to use CBA throughout the sector. Provided that grants are only given to public transport operators for specific purposes, and that their use is strictly monitored, any resulting problems of loss of incentives to operate efficiently can be minimized.

VIII. Strategic Considerations and the Context of Appraisal

Transport projects are typically not free-standing investments but are part of a network. As such there may be strong interdependencies both between investment projects and between investment and other policies such as traffic restraint, pricing changes, land use changes and so on. This greatly complicates the task of the appraiser. It becomes necessary to consider individual projects by themselves, given an assumed strategy and assumptions as to what other projects will be implemented and groups of projects, given an overall strategy and strategies as a whole. Three British examples will be used to demonstrate that point.

The first is again trunk road appraisal in Great Britain. The techniques described above are typically applied to small stretches of trunk road, assuming that a given level of traffic growth will be accommodated (currently 83-142 per cent by 2025) and that other proposed schemes to accommodate this growth will go ahead. Now this is a necessary tactical exercise to appraise the contribution of the particular stretch of road to the overall strategy. But discovering whether accommodating a doubling of traffic is best achieved on the existing road or on a new road is a very weak test of the investment. It is necessary to look at groups of road projects together where, for instance, they upgrade a particular route as a whole, so that the traffic on one section of road is dependent on the other investments going ahead. It is also necessary to look at alternative strategies such as traffic restraint, increased petrol prices and improved public transport, which may together alter the rate of growth of traffic. In any event, even if one individual scheme has little effect on traffic growth (and this is disputed—for instance see Beardwood and Elliot, 1985) it is surely the case that the overall level of investment does affect traffic growth. For instance, it is already observed that traffic growth is very slow in the most congested areas where there is little spare capacity, and surely this phenomenon would spread in the absence of major investment.

It is therefore quite misleading to aggregate returns on individual small schemes and regard this as the rate of return on the roads programme as a whole. Strategic studies are required to show what is the value of alternative aggregate levels of road building in the light of strategic policy alternatives involving different rates of traffic growth.

The second example relates to cities such as London. Both road and rail transport in London are extremely congested and one way of relieving the congestion is to build new underground railways across the centre, at enormous cost (Department of Transport/British Railways Board/ London Regional Transport, 1989). One might appraise these projects on the basis of existing policies, in which there is continuing severe congestion on the road. But suppose a different package of policies were to be implemented, involving, for instance, charging a supplementary fee for bringing a car into Central London or other methods of traffic restraint. This might directly increase the demand for rail travel still further. At the same time, it could free buses from road congestion and enable them to play a much more effective part in short-distance public transport. Whether the net effect is to improve or to worsen the case for the new rail tunnels is not clear, but it could hardly be expected to leave it unchanged. In congested urban areas, where modes of transport are particularly strongly interdependent, the need to see investment appraisal as part of an integrated transport planning process is particularly strong.

The third example is internal to the rail system. Rail transport, even more than road, forms a closely integrated network where infrastructure, rolling stock type and the services to be run are particularly closely linked. The case for reconstructing a particular junction or stretch of route to a certain capacity depends on the volume of traffic of each type expected to pass through or over it. That in turn depends on pricing, service level and rolling stock investment plans for all those services, which may include express passenger, local passenger and freight. Similarly it is pointless to resignal a route to allow for higher speeds unless investment is simultaneously made in track and rolling stock to permit those speeds, or to plan for freight wagons and locomotives with heavier axle loads without upgrading track and structures to take them. Since rolling stock may be switched from one part of the system to another as part of an investment strategy, railway appraisals often need to look far and wide, and may need to consider the network as a whole. (See, for instance, the financial appraisals of the case for main line railway electrification published in Department of Transport/British Railways Board, 1981)

The point of this section is to stress, then, that in all modes of transport there is a need to look not just at individual projects but also at alternative packages of projects and at projects as a whole in the light of feasible alternative strategies. This has been the practice in a number of recent British urban transport studies, such as those in Birmingham and Edinburgh (May, 1991). But again this is an area where many continental countries appear to have organized themselves better than Britain. Several countries (such as Germany and Sweden) explicitly consider the allocation of national transport infrastructure funds across all modes as part of a coordinated programme using comparable investment criteria. The Netherlands has gone a stage further in seeking to make this procedure part of an overall plan to influence transport demand and supply to achieve specific accessibility and environmental targets. Whilst the various elements of the plan may not be as internally consistent as appears at first sight, this represents one of the few attempts to relate project appraisal to strategic plans at the national level within Europe.

IX. Alternative Approaches to Appraisal

So far, the examples of transport appraisals used in this chapter have been based largely on methods devised by the British Department of Transport for central government use. Local authorities have tended to take a somewhat different approach. Perhaps because they are more concerned with planning and environmental issues than with narrow transport benefits, they have been much more ready to adopt objectives achievement or other multicriteria appraisal methods. We have also already commented on the fact that appraisals in many other European countries are more explicitly multicriteria in orientation, with economic efficiency seen as one of a number of objectives.

Multicriteria approaches are considered in detail in Munda, Nijkamp and Rietveld (1993) and this section will confine itself to some comments on how they are typically used in the transport sector. These approaches require three stages: firstly, definition of a set of objectives, which may for instance relate to accessibility, the environment, safety, economy and equity; next, measurement of the extent to which each project contributes towards the desired objective; finally, weighting of the measures in order to aggregate them and produce a ranking of projects (Mackie *et al.*, 1990).

As it stands, this method would be quite consistent with the principles of cost–benefit analysis if the following conditions held: (1) all the objectives related to factors that affect the welfare of the population concerned, and (2) the measures of achievement and weighting of them are based on the preferences of the people affected by the projects, subject possibly to some form of equity weighting. In practice, the first condition probably generally holds but the second does not. Measurement of the degree of contribution to objectives is often based not on detailed measurement but on the judgement of the professional staff planning the projects. This may be defensible where the schemes are small enough to make detailed study too costly, but other-wise it is not. Relative weighting of the measures of achievement is likewise usually based on the value judgement of the decision taker rather than the preferences of the people directly affected by the scheme. All too often, too, these relative weights are obtained with too little consideration of the differing units of measurement of the performance measures regarding the different objectives.

Whether these weightings are expressed in money terms or not, they are essentially performing the same function as money values in expressing relative valuations. Moreover, to the extent that at least one of the performance measures—cost or economy—is expressed in money terms, they can readily be transformed into money values. There is therefore less difference between this approach and traditional CBA than might at first sight be supposed.

What clearly is a major difference is the use of decision takers' preferences. Now it is clear that a CBA rests on certain value judgements; namely that decisions should be based on the preferences of those affected by the projects, and that these preferences should be weighted in a certain way (according to income if unweighted willingness to pay type measures are used). If the decision taker for some reason rejects those value judgements, he or she will clearly wish to impose their own preferences or weights. Nor would the present author wish to deny the right of the decision taker to do this, as long as they are in some way democratically accountable for their actions.

It appears then that, as currently practiced, multicriteria decision-making techniques are essentially concerned with aiding and ensuring consistency in this latter stage of weighting by the decision taker. This is a separate role from that played by the CBA, and should be seen as complementary rather than competing. To the extent that the information provided by a CBA is seen as relevant to the decision taker, it still needs to be provided. But what is clear is that it must be provided in a sufficiently disaggregated form for the decision taker to apply, explicitly or implicitly, his or her own weights. This again argues for the Planning Balance Sheet or Community Impact Evaluation form of presentation as outlined briefly in section 6 above.

X. Conclusion

We have found many criticisms of the application of CBA to transport projects as generally practiced. Foremost amongst the perceived faults are the failure to conduct appraisals at a strategic level, so that a full range of options is not properly considered, and a failure to look beyond the direct effects (construction, maintenance and operating costs, time and accident savings) to quantify and value a full range of relevant effects. Whilst examples can be found of countries where current practice is ahead of that in Britain (for example the role of strategic planning in the Netherlands and the efforts to quantify environmental costs in money terms in Germany and Sweden), in no cases can it be said that the treatment of these crucial issues is wholly satisfactory.

This sounds a fairly damning indictment of CBA as it is currently used, but it is important to realize that a simple switch to an alternative approach, based on objectives satisfaction or multicriteria methods, will not of itself solve this problem. Indeed, inasmuch as the current approach inevitably ends up with a list of effects which cannot be valued in money terms, it is already, at least in an informal sense, a multicriteria approach. What we would advocate is that a thorough attempt should always be made to identify all relevant effects of projects and to trace these back to appropriate incidence groups. For this purpose, we strongly commend the Planning Balance Sheet or Community Impact Evaluation approach. At this stage, where reliable monetary valuations of externalities can be shown they provide useful information on the preferences of those affected regarding how much it is worth spending to secure those particular benefits or to remove those particular costs.

The final task of the decision taker is to weigh up these costs and benefits one with another, taking account of who gains and who loses. Where repeated similar decisions have to be made it may be worth using some formal weighting system at this stage, and computerized systems which enable the decision taker to explore the sensitivity of decision to the weights used have great value. Thus a sensible approach will almost certainly combine elements of CBA and multicriteria decision-taking systems. It is as foolish to consider that decisions can be reduced to the simple calculation of a net present value as to believe that monetary valuation has no role in decision taking.

Bibliography

Beardwood, J. and Elliot, J.(1985), 'Roads Generate Traffic,' Planning and Transportation Research and Computation Summer Annual Meeting, University of Sussex.

Beesley, M.E. and Foster, C.D. (1963), 'Estimating the social benefits of constructing an underground railway in London,' *Journal of the Royal Statistical Society*, Series A, 126, (1).

Beesley, M.E., Coburn, T.M. and Reynolds, D.J. (1960), *The London-Birmingham Motorway-Traffic and Economics*, Road Research Laboratory Technical Paper 46, Crowthorne, Berks.

Dasgupta, A.K. and Pearce, D.W. (1972), *Cost Benefit Analysis: Theory and Practice*, London: Macmillan.

Department of Transport(1984), *Economic Evaluation Comparability*

Study - Final Report, London: Department of Transport.

Department of Transport(1989), *National Road Traffic Forecasts*, London: Department of Transport.

Department of Transport/British Railways Board(1981), *Review of Main Line Electrification. Final Report*, London: HMSO.

Department of Transport/British Railways Board/London Regional Transport(1989), *Central London Rail Study*, London: Department of Transport.

Dodgson, J.S. (1973), 'External Effects in Road Investment,' *Journal of Transport Economics and Policy*, 7.

Harman, R. (1980), *Great Northern Electrics in Hertfordshire*, Hertford: Hertfordshire County Council.

Jones-Lee, M. (1987), 'The Value of Transport Safety,' *Policy Journals*, Newbury, Berks.

Kanafani, A. (1983), *Transportation Demand Analysis*, New York: McGraw-Hill.

Leitch, Sir George, Chairman (1978), *Report of the Advisory Committee on Trunk Road Appraisal*, London: HMSO.

Lichfield, N. (1987), 'Brigg Economic Regeneration Study: Evaluation of Inner Relief Road,' unpublished report, Nathaniel Lichfield and Partners Ltd., London.

Lichfield, N. (1988). *Economics in Urban Conservation*, Cambridge: Cambridge University Press.

Lichfield, N., Kettle, P. and Whitbread, M. (1975), *Evaluation in the Planning Process*, Oxford: Pergamon Press.

Mackie, P.J. and Simon, D. (1986), 'Do Road Projects Benefit Industry? A Case Study of the Humber Bridge,' *Journal of Transport Economics and Policy*, 20, (3).

Mackie, P.J., May, A.D., Pearman, A.D. and Simon, D. (1990), *Computer-Aided Assessment for Transportation Policies*, New York: Greenwood Press.

Marks, P., Fowkes, A.S. and Nash, C.A. (1986), 'Valuing Long Distance Business Travel Time Savings for Evaluation; A Methodological Review and Application,' Planning and Transportation Research and Computation Summer Annual Meeting, Seminar on Transportation Planning Methods, University of Sussex.

May, A.D. (1991), 'Integrated transport strategies: a new approach to urban transport policy in the U.K.,' *Transport Reviews*, 11, (3) pp.

223-47.

McKinnon, A.C. (1988), 'Recent Trends in Warehouse Location,' in Cooper, James (ed.), *Logistics and Distribution Planning Strategies for Management*, London: Kogan Page.

Munda, G., Nijkamp, P. and Rietveld, P. (1993) Information Precision and Multicriteria Evaluation Methods in Williams, A and Giardina, E, Eds, Efficiency in the Public Sector, Aldershot Edward Elgar.

MVA Consultants; Institute for Transport Studies, University of Leeds; Transport Studies Unit, University of Oxford (1987), 'The Value of Travel Time Savings.' *Policy Journals*, Newbury, Berks.

Nash, C.A., (ed.) (1990), *Appraising the Environmental Effects of Road Schemes: A Response to the Standing Advisory Committee on Trunk Road Assessment*, Institute for Transport Studies Working Paper 293, University of Leeds.

Nash, C.A., and Preston, J. (1991), 'Appraisal of Rail Investment Projects: Recent British Experience,' *Transport Reviews*, 11, (4).

Nash, C.A., Pearce, D.W. and Stanley, J.K. (1975), 'An Evaluation of Cost-Benefit Analysis Criteria,' *Scottish Journal of Political Economy*, June.

Pearce, D.W. (1990), 'The Valuation of Transport-Induced Environmental Costs and Benefits,' paper presented at the Seminar on Longer Term Issues, Department of Transport, London.

Pearce, D.W. and Markandya, A. (1989), *Environmental Policy Benefits: Monetary Valuation*, Paris: OECD.

Sanderson, I. (1989), 'Road Investment Appraisal Techniques in Europe: Some International Comparisons,' Institute for Transport Studies, University of Leeds, unpublished.

Webster, F.V., Bly, P.H. and Paulley, N.J. (1988), *Urban Land-use and Transport Interaction. Policies and Models*, Aldershot: Avebury.

CHAPTER 26

BEHAVIOURAL AND RESOURCE VALUES OF TRAVEL TIME SAVINGS: A BICENTENNIAL UPDATE*

*D.A. Hensher***

I. Background

It is well recognized that a most important parameter in the economic evaluation of transportation projects is the value of travel time savings (VTTS). This parameter represents an average measure of the amount of money a representative individual is willing to outlay in order to save a unit of travel time, *ceteris paribus. Ceter is paribus* (or 'all other things being equal') is usually assumed to mean that the level of utility from the trip and the traveller's personal income remain unchanged.

Values of travel time savings in Australia were first placed on a formal economic foundation by the Commonwealth Bureau of Roads (CBR), utilizing the empirical research of the author. Since 1972, a large number of values of time savings have been applied in a wide range of transportation contexts. For example, the Australian Road Research Board currently advises NAASRA in the development of VTTS for road transport, by updating values used in previous years.

* Reprinted from *Australian Road Research*, 19 (3), 1989, 223-229.
** Transport Research Center. School of Economic and Financial Studies, Macquarie University, NSW, 2109, Australia

While the practice of updating *per se* is reasonable, the base used to undertake the update in the context of non-work travel time has become highly questionable. There has been an historical loss of control over the adjustment around a base value, which has resulted in a substantial lowering of the VTTS as a percentage of the gross wage rate. The VTTS for car commuter travel is a particular example (see the NAASRA values as reported by Thoresen and Evans (1986)).

In 1987, the concern about the VTTS was placed in the public domain with the Sydney Harbour Tunnel controversy. The updated CBR values were originally used by the New South Wales Roads and Traffic Authority (RTA) to evaluate the Tunnel Project. The resulting benefit-cost ratio was extremely low. Following a clash of views on the merits of the Harbour Tunnel between two NSW Government Departments, efforts were made to improve on certain aspects of the evaluation in order to improve the benefit-cost ratio of the Harbour Tunnel proposal. One item which had a major impact on the upward adjustment of the benefit-cost ratio was the VTTS for car commuter travel. Drawing on recent empirical evidence by the author (Hensher 1984), a substantially higher VTTS was used, resulting in a 70 percent increase in time savings' benefits.

Given that the recently derived values may not be widely known, this paper summarizes the values, citing the appropriate references containing the supporting details. The need for this statement is even more important when it is recognized that the majority of the recommended values are updates of base values derived in the early 1970s by the author. The evidence provided in this paper has, since it was first drafted, been used as the basis for the NAASRA recommended values for 1989.

In considering the recommended values outlined below, it must be emphasized that not only are values of time savings controversial, but also other supporting items. Particular items include the following.

(1) Differences are evident in the assumed number of annual hours used to convert annual gross personal income to the average gross hourly wage rate. The gross hourly wage rate is used as the yardstick for updating VTTS. This updating assumes that the VTTS is a constant proportion of income. To be correct, the gross wage rate used initially should be calculated from data on income and hours worked, obtained from the sample used to derive the empirical value of time savings.

Then in updating, definitions consistent with the initial calculations should be maintained. Often a population-wide average is used instead, both in the initial calculations and in the updating. It is particularly difficult to establish an appropriate amount of *normal* hours worked for salaried persons. The often used hours of between 1950 and 2200 per year (based on an average working week of 37.5 to 42 hours) are assumed to supply a meaningful measure of the opportunity cost of the labour resource.

(2) The distinction between *paid* and *effectively* worked hours seems important if the relationship between the two categories is likely to change over time. In practice it does not matter which definition is used once the empirical values are derived, provided all updates use the same definition and that the relationship between the two definitions is constant over time. If the latter is not true, then the opportunity cost of the labour resource should be based on the effectively worked (i.e. productive) hours, because any savings in travel time become a resource benefit in relation to the actual use of time.

(3) The occupancy rate of cars has an important influence on the vehicle-level VTTS. The mean estimates of car occupancy have not been seriously reviewed for some years. The current NAASRA recommendation is 1.6 adults for private urban travel, and 2 adults for private rural travel. The equivalent figures for business trips are respectively 1.4 and 1.6. The currency of these occupancy rates is questioned. We offer updated estimates for urban travel (reported in *Table 2*).

(4) In obtaining a value *(as distinct from a price) for time savings, it has to be recognized that there is both an opportunity cost and a marginal (relative) disutility associated with a unit of travel time.* The opportunity cost for an existing resource is equal to the market value of the resource, which can be equated to the gross wage rate plus an allowance for a marginal wage increment to cover overheads. The marginal disutility component is a measure of the individual's preference for spending an equivalent amount of time in one activity (e.g. leisure) rather than another activity (e.g. travel).

(5) Values of time savings are increasingly being derived from stated-response data (Hensher *et al.* 1988*b*; Fowkes and Wardman 1988). When the value for business travel time savings is derived from stated-choice data, and not from the productivity (or direct) approach, we get a behavioural value. Depending on how the stated preference experiment

is worded, we would get either the employer's or only the employee's
time-cost trade-off.

(6) The productivity approach for deriving a business value of time
savings is (Hensher 1977):

$$VTTS = (1-r-pg)*MP+(1-r)*vw+r*vl+MPF$$

where r =   proportion of travel time saved
which is used for leisure;

p =   proportion of travel time saved at
the expense of work done while
travelling;

q =   relative productivity of work done
while travelling compared with the
equivalent time in the office;

MP =   the marginal product of labour;

vl =   the monetary value to the
employee of leisure relative to travel time;

vw =   the monetary value to the
employee of work time while in
the office relative to travel time;
and

MPF =   the value of extra output generated
due to reduced fatigue.

II. Values of Urban Travel Time Savings

Two substantial empirical studies were undertaken in the Sydney
Metropolitan Area, one in 1981-82 and the other in 1987 (Hensher 1984
and 1986; Hensher *et al.* 1987; Hensher, Barnard and Truong 1988*a*).

The first study, in 1981-82, was specialized to the commuter trip, and
covered all available modes of transportation. A series of multinominal
logit and nested-logit models were estimated, and time values derived
for invehicle and out-of-vehicle time for car (drive, passenger) and public transport (train, bus). The values are based on a sample of 1455 commuter trips. The values from this study are summarized in *Table 1*.

The second study, completed in 1987, concentrated on VTTS for private modes using the Sydney road system. A route choice model was

Table 1. *Behavioural Values of Urban Commuter Time Savings ($1982)*

Mode	In-vehicle Time (invt)	Walk Time (wkt)	Wait Time (wt)	Ratio of wkt/invt	Values wt/invt
Car Driver	4.30	13.40	7.90	3.1	1.8
	(46)	(144)	(84)		
Car Passenger	3.25	16.90	7.90	5.2	2.4
	(35)	(181)	(85)		
Train	1.80	6.95	13.00	3.9	7.2
	(19)	(74)	(139)		
Bus	3.00	3.20	8.75	1.1	2.9
	(32)	(34)	(94)		
All Modes	2.60	7.60	12.25	2.9	4.7
	(28)	(81)	(131)		

Unit: $ per person hour
VTTS as % of average gross wage rate in ( ).

estimated using a multinomial logit model. Four trip purposes were studied in the context of drivers of automobiles:

(1) private commuter trips   (707 observations)
(2) business commuter trips   (210 observations)
(3) Travel as part of work   (616 observations)
(4) Social/recreational trips   (546 observations)

A private commuter is someone who uses a privately-registered vehicle for the work trip, in contrast to a business commuter who uses a company car. The study was motivated by an interest in the financing of major road investments by the private sector (with the possibility of a toll). However, the data were collected for a sample of travellers in the entire Sydney Metropolitan area.

The values of time savings are summarized in *Table 2*. Findings on the occupancy rates for each trip purpose are included. The private commuter, business commuter, and social/recreation values are behavioural values of travel time savings. The 'travel as part of work' value is a behavioural value. The justification for the values follows.

The absolute and relative magnitudes of the values are very plausible. The distinction between the private commuter and the business commuter is clearly justified. It confirms the view that business commuters place a higher value on time savings because they can, on average, use

*Table 2. Behavioural Values of Urban In-Vehicle Travel Time Savings
for Automobile Trips*

Purpose	In-Vhicle	Occupany		Annual Hours Worked
		Adults	Children	
Private Commuter	4.65 (34.0)	1.12	0.15	1950
Business Commuter	7.87 (44.0)	1.20	0.00	2200
Travel as Part of Work	10.10 (68.0)	1.44	0.11	2200
Social/Recreational	2.90 (—)	1.97	0.94	n.a.

Units: $ per person hour ($1987) VTTS as % of average gross wage rate in ( )
(except for social/recreational travel since personal income is not a meaningful
benchmark for the non-working travellers).

the saved time in an activity which has a higher marginal productivity
than that associated with private commuters. Given the annual average
salary of $38,400, and an average number of annual hours worked of
2200, the value of business commuter time savings as a percentage of
their wage rate is 44 percent, compared to 34 percent for the private
commuter. Previous studies have failed to make this distinction, which
is empirically important, given that the business commuter value is 65
percent higher than the private commuter value.

The traditional category of business car travel is contained in the category of 'travel as part of work.' However, this definition also includes
travel by business people in such activities as driving to the airport or a
client's office. Since a high percentage of the travel time associated with
the latter activity occurs outside of normal working hours (i.e. the person would not be travelling at this time during the normal period of
work expected by the employer), there is a leisure time trade-off being
made. The value of time of $10.10 per person hour is equal to 68 per-
cent of the gross average wage rate for this sub-population. This value,
lower than the average gross wage rate, reflects the mix of both employer time and non-work time.

At the margin it would be expected that productivity of an employee
equals his/her full wage rate. In this context the term 'full' wage rate is

used to refer to the gross wage plus on-costs. The value to the *community* of an employee spending less time travelling and more time in productive work is, therefore, approximately equal to the full wage rate. The employer, however, has to pay 50 percent of the gain in productivity in company tax. Consequently, the value *to the employer* of an employee spending less time travelling and more time in productive work is approximately equal to 50 percent of the full wage rate. With on-costs representing on average 34 percent of the pre-tax wages in Australia, it would be expected that the value of business travel time savings to an employer to be approximately 50 percent of 134 percent, i.e. 67 percent of the gross wage rate. There is an outstanding correspondence between this figure, calculated from theory, and the figure of 68 percent obtained from the response to the stated-choice design, from which our values are derived. The evidence herein suggests that the value to the employer of saving an hour of travelling time is 68 percent of the full wage rate.

The time value for non-work-related travel is plausible, with such travel mainly occurring during non-work hours when the trade-off is typically between leisure and travel.

III. Non-Urban Time Values

Very little empirical research into time valuation has been undertaken in the context of non-urban travel. The currently recommended values for *road transport* are classified under the single heading of *rural* travel (Thoresen and Evans 1986). In considering adjustments to the current non-urban values, a number of broader issues that are in need of attention are suggested.

(1) Long distance interurban travel should be given a separate categorization, distinguishing it from local rural (small town) traffic. Our preferred categories of travel are urban, long distance and local non-urban. A long-distance trip is defined as all travel except that occurring within metropolitan areas and within non-urban small-town areas.

(2) The majority of values of travel time savings recommended for rural contexts have been based on urban studies. The same values have been assumed per person hour, with differences at the car level explained by vehicle occupancy.

(3) while the local-rural values may closely align with urban values, it is questionable that long distance values would be the same. This concern has important implications for the priorities in investment between urban and major national highways. In the absence of any substantive evidence, it is hypothesized that, for non-business passenger traffic, the long distance values have been too low, but they should be higher than the recommended urban values reported earlier.

(4) Based upon new data collected as part of an inter-regional pre-feasibility study of passenger trips, associated with the Very Fast Train Project, multinomial logit mode-choice models have been used to derive long-distance (interurban) mode choice models (Hensher and Horowitz 1987). The behavioural values of non-business travel time savings ($1987) is $6.52 per person hour, equivalent to 68 percent of the samples average gross wage rate. The method of derivation was very similar to that used in the second urban study reported above.

The value is quite different from the currently recommended person value of approximately $1.50, i.e. the resource value for private car with indirect tax added in (see below). the equivalent urban behavioural value (the categories in *Table 2* of private commuter) is $4.65 per person hour. This equivalencing for non-business travel is, however, somewhat misleading because the long distance *private* car travel is substantially non-commuter and hence more aligned to the social/recreation purpose.

The business behavioural VTTS (based predominantly on plane and car travel), derived from the prefeasibility study, was $25.00 per person hour, equivalent to 156 percent of the samples average gross wage rate. This value is specialized to movements between Sydney, Canberra and Melbourne, tending to provide an above-average estimate for all long-distance travel. There is a strong air-mode effect for these city pairs for business travel. In the absence of other long-distance business evidence, it is suggested that a mean VTTS lies in the range $12.50 to $25.00.

It is quite common for the car to be used for travel between Sydney and Canberra for business meetings, given the average door-to-door travel time of 3.5 hours. The mean for travel by plane is nearly 3 hours, with the associated interchange inconvenience. In 1987, 29 percent of all inter-regional passenger travel by car in the Sydney-Canberra-Melbourne corridor was on business, and 71 percent on non-business.

Long distance business travel includes a high percentage of time outlayed outside of normal working hours.

(5) The local rural values can be aligned with the urban trip purposes, with slightly lower behavioural values for private commuter, business commuter and social/recreation purposes to reflect lower average incomes.

IV. Linking Behavioural, Resource and Equity Values

The values of travel time savings documented in this paper are appropriate values for assessing the effect on demand of changes in travel time, as expressed as a generalized cost. The behavioural value tells us what role travel time plays in the individual's decision to travel under particular circumstances. Thus it is appropriate for demand prediction.

When the application of time savings values is concerned with the change in the level of economic resources, a willingness-to-pay measure does not always represent the resource implications of the savings or loss of travel time. Alternative approaches to correcting for the resource effect have been suggested in the past, and although all proposals can be questioned on theoretical and empirical grounds, the desire for practical guidelines has resulted in some simple rules for adjustment.

For *non-working time*, the willingness-to-trade time for money approach assumes that the traded money would have been spent on goods which carry indirect taxation. The resources associated with the time trade are thus equal to the expenditure less the indirect taxation. Therefore non-working time savings should be valued at the behavioural value adjusted by the inverse of (1 + the average rate of indirect taxation). The taxation adjustment is normally applied to an equity value of time savings, i.e. a behavioural value which treats everyone as if they had the same mean income.

For *working time*, a marginal productivity argument is normally invoked, in which it is assumed that valuation is based on gross income. In resource cost terms, the value of output to the employer equals its return net of any *indirect* tax. If the resource cost of labour is its price in employment before the removal of income tax, then it is traditionally valued before indirect taxation is added. This would be 134 percent of the average gross wage rate. The behavioural value for travel as part of work should be based on the rationale used to justify the empirical evidence in *Table 2*. A controversial issue comes in when work-related travel time, such as a business traveller going to the airport or to a client's location, occurs during a period commonly thought of as leisure time. The correct way of handling this situation is to use a weighted average of the appropriate work and non-work values. The weights represent the proportions of time in and out of *normal* working hours. In the past, all such time has been assumed to occur during normal working hours.

Deriving the working-time values from a stated-choice approach administered to the employee implies that the employee behaves as if he is representing the employer. The results in *Table 2* are derived with the employee (the traveller) being asked to answer the time-cost trade-off experiment on the assumption that the employer is covering all the costs including the relative marginal disutility of travel compared to the disutility of the equivalent time at work not travelling. The latter item is normally assumed to be reflected in the received salary.

There is a view that for non-working time the behavioural value of time savings should be the same for all modes and trip purposes. The resulting *equity value* is inconsistent with the position that the scarce investment dollar should not be directed towards projects which are more likely to benefit individual travellers with a higher willingness to pay simply because they have a greater ability to pay. This argument rests on the proposition that the value of travel time savings is a function of personal income. Although the empirical evidence on the relationship between VTTS and personal income is ambiguous, despite its theoretical appeal, equity 'behavioural' values of travel time savings can be derived from the behavioural values reported in *Tables 1* and *2* for non-working time. If equity values are used, then the resource value of non-working time should be derived from this equity value.

V. Conclusion: Recommended Values

Table 3 summarizes our recommended values, in 1987 dollars. The effective average rate of indirect tax is 14 percent. It is calculated from the ratio of indirect taxes less subsidies to gross domestic product at market prices. The Table summarizes four sets of travel time values. Users seeking to update the working-time estimates post-May 1988 will need to adjust the values for changes in company taxes.

Updates of the time values are based on kilometre-weighted average

Table 3. Values of Travel Time Savings per Person: A Summary ($1987)

	Behavioural		Resource	
	In Vehicle	Out of Vehicle	In Vehicle	Out of Vehicle
1. Non-work				
Urban/Local non-urban:				
Commuter by private car	4.65	12.50	4.08	10.96
Commuter by company car	7.87	21.20*	6.90	18.60*
Social/Recreation as driver or passenger	2.90	7.80*	2.54	6.84*
Commuter by private car as passenger	3.25	9.40	2.85	8.25
Communter train	2.43**	12.98**	2.13**	11.39**
Commuter bus	4.00**	7.97**	3.51**	6.99**
Long Distance:				
Non-business	6.52	14.00*	5.72	12.28*

2. Work (i.e. trips made in the course of work)

	Employer Behavioural Value		Resource Value	
Urban (car) travel as part of work	10.10	—	20.20	—
long distance (air, car)	12.50-25.00	—	21.40-25.00	—

3. Non-Work Equity Values†

(Assuming average annual gross income of $25,640, with 100 annual hours worked.)

In-vehicle time:	$4.18
Out-of-vehicle time:	$11.98

Notes:
* indicates that the value was not derived from an empirical model, but from other purposes which are assumed to reflect the relative utility of alternative components of time.
** is an update of the 1982 values in Table 1. Income has increased by a factor of 1.35 since 1982.
†† indicates that relating this trip purpose value to income is problematic because a large number of trips are by individuals who do not go to work. One could use the mean income of the employed sub-group.
† The reported equity values are simple averages of the six non-work values. This approach assumes that each individual has one market vote of equal power so that no one group is given market power by their ability to pay.

gross personal income for the relevant trip purposes and modes. For working time, the marginal wage increment has to be updated to allow for changes in the cost of employment-related 'add-ons.' If the pattern of trip-lengths for different income groups is likely to change through time; for example, the low income trips become longer and the high income trips become shorter, then *it is possible that the real vale of time savings could decline.* This appropriate updating procedure is an added burden because of the general absence of reliable data on kilometres travelled, particularly when it has to be income-related.

In concluding, it is important to note that the values of time savings in *Table 3* are base values in particular situations. If, for example, a time value is required for travel in the peak and off-peak periods, it is necessary to identify the composition of traffic in terms of trip purpose and to calculate an appropriately weighted time value. The common practice of applying a commuter value to all times of day is not correct practice, leading in general to an overestimate of the value of travel time savings at all times of the day.

References

Fowkes, T. and Wardman, M. (1988). Design of stated preference travel choice experiments with special reference to inter-personal taste variations. *J. Transp. Econ. Policy* XXII(1), January, pp. 27-44.

Hensher, D.A. (1977). *Value of Business Travel Time.* (Pergamon Press: Oxford.)

_____. (1984). Full information maximum likelihood estimation of a nested logit mode choice model. Working Paper No. 13, Transport Research Centre, School of Economic and Financial Studies, Macquarie Univ. 32 pp.

_____. (1986). Sequential and full information maximum likelihood estimation of a nested logit model. Rev. econ. Stat. LXVIII(4), November, pp. 657-67.

_____ and Horowitz, J.L. (1987). A bounded-size likelihood ratio test for non-nested probabilistic discrete-choice models estimated from choice-based samples. Transport Research Centre, School of Economic and Financial Studies, Macquarie Univ. (draft).

Hensher, D.A., Baranrd, P.O., Smith, N.C. and Milthorpe, F.W. (1987). The F5 Freeway Study. Report prepared for the State Bank of NSW, Sydney, May, 110 pp.

Hensher, D.A., Barnard, P.O., Milthorpe, F.W. and Smith, N.C. (1988*a*). Urban tolled roads and the value of travel time savings. Working Paper No. 41, Transport Research Centre, School of Economic and Financial Studies, Macquarie Univ., 21 pp. Econ. Rec. (forthcoming, 1990).

Hensher, D.A., Barnard, P.O. and Truong, T.P. (1988*b*). The role of stated preference methods in studies of travel choice. *J. Transp. Econ. Policy* XXII(1), January, pp. 45-58.

Thoresen, T. and Evans, S. (1986). Updating economic parameter values for use in the Nimpac Road Planning Model: unit values as at 31 March 1984 and 1985. Australian Road Research Board. Internal Report, AIR 384-1A.

CHAPTER 27

THE ECONOMIC BENEFITS OF
THE CHANNEL TUNNEL*

*John Kay, Alan Manning & Stefan Szymanski***

I. Introduction

Since the early 19th century both public and private sectors in the UK
and France have contemplated the construction of a fixed link between
the UK and the continent. Whilst the technology of the project has never
been particularly challenging, all earlier projects had failed to convince
investors that the revenue stream would meet the substantial sunk cost.
In 1987 however, Eurotunnel, a private company possessing a monopoly
franchise awarded by the UK and French governments, raised over £1bn
of equity and £5bn of loan finance to build and operate a rail only tunnel
between Dover and Calais.

The Channel Tunnel presents a radically different technology from
existing ferry services. The major part of its costs are literally sunk and
its marginal costs are negligible. This compares to existing ferry services which have relatively low fixed and sunk costs and relatively high
marginal costs. In this paper we attempt to measure the contribution of
the Tunnel to economic welfare. To do so we measure the increase in
consumer and producer surplus generated by the existence of the Tunnel. In principle, four outcomes are possible from the welfare point of

* Reprinted from *Economic Policy* (1989), pp. 212-234.
** The authors are at London Business School and Birkbeck College respectively.

Table 1. *Private and social profitability*

		Is the Tunnel privately profitable?	
		YES	NO
Is the Tunnel	YES	allow private financing	finance with public funds
socially profitable?	NO	do not allow scheme to go ahead	do nothing

view. These are presented in Table 1.

The two most interesting cases are the ones where social and private profitability differ. The case where the project may be socially profitable but privately unprofitable is the familiar one where the introduction of a low-cost technology leads to a fall in prices so part of the benefits accrues to the consumers. Rather more interesting is the possibility that the tunnel may be privately profitable yet socially undesirable. There are two reasons why this might occur: first, if one sees the existing ferry companies as very competitive, then given that there are some sunk costs to entry in the ferry market, the opening of the tunnel may see the replacement of a competitive industry by a monopoly leading to higher prices; second, if one sees the existing ferry companies as not very competitive, the building of the tunnel may simply be a way for Eurotunnel to capture the existing rents of the ferry companies. This may be a privately profitable exercise, but it is socially useless. So, in the absence of regulation, it is quite conceivable that the building of the tunnel is socially undesirable, yet it will make a healthy return for its investors. This type of argument is one that seems to lie behind a series of reports produced by flexilink, a lobbying organization funded by the existing cross-channel ferry companies and the main port authorities.

The result of our analysis is that under our central assumptions, the Tunnel is both privately and socially profitable. However, the benefits in consumer welfare are enormous, whilst the private financing benefits can disappear under some adverse scenarios, suggesting that there were some grounds for public provision of finance. The situation of private profitability and no gain in consumer surplus is plausible, if the ferry companies are driven from the market, which seems to be a very strong possibility on existing Dover routes, but less likely for services operating outside of Dover. In addition to these welfare results, we are also able to calculate the dates at which the digging of the Tunnel became socially and privately profitable. This question is interesting in the light of public policy in the post-war era. Between the 1950s and 1979, the Tunnel was always considered as a public investment (and always post-poned) but in the 1980s the Thatcher government decided that it should be treated as a private sector project. In fact we find that, on the basis of historic and forecast traffic volumes, it was socially optimal to open it in 1980 and privately profitable in 1981.

The rest of the paper is divided up as follows. In Section 2 we present some background to the decision to build the Channel Tunnel. In Section 3 we present our model of pre- and post-entry cross-channel competition and in Section 4 we look at the market segments in more detail. Section 5 contains our welfare analysis and Section 6 our conclusions.

II. Background

1. Recent History

Since its earliest conception, the idea of building a Channel tunnel has passed back and forth between the private sector and the State. In 1802 the first known plans for connecting the UK to the continent were presented to Napoleon. In the 1970s there were several attempts both in the UK and France to construct a tunnel, all of which raised substantial sums of money and in some cases actually made it some way out to sea (one of these companies is still quoted on the UK stock market, although it has recently become loss-making). However, interest waned after the Victorian era and did not revive until after the Second World War. In the 1950s and 1960s several studies were made by the UK and French governments for what was now seen as a state backed project. Plans proceeded some way until the Labour government withdrew in 1975, not wanting to commit large sums of Treasury money after their experience with Concorde.

Plans for a privately funded link were revived by the British and French governments in 1980, starting a process which culminated in the granting of a franchise to what is now known as Eurotunnel, an Anglo-French company founded originally by a consortium of construction companies and banks and now a publicly quoted company incorporated in the UK and France. The other competitors for the franchise included a plastic bridge and single bore road/rail tunnel (it was planned that cars would use the tunnel most of the time, but every half hour or so it would be cleared to allow a train to run through!) The most serious competitor, however, was a combination of bridge and tunnel which would have provided a road link. This project (Euroroute) would have been 45% more expensive and appears to have been rejected at least partly for this reason. It turns out that our analysis supports the decision to award the franchise to Eurotunnel rather than Euroroute.

2. The Eurotunnel Scheme

Eurotunnel has commissioned the construction of a 31 mile twin bore rail only tunnel between Dover and Calais to be opened in May 1993. The company will offer two services. First, foot passengers and rail freight will be able to travel through the Tunnel on scheduled services offered by BR and SNCF (the UK and French national rail companies) at prices negotiated between ET and the rail companies (through rail services). Second, ET will offer a shuttle service between Dover and Calais for carrying cars, lorries and coaches (shuttle services). In both cases the journey time from end to end is expected to be 33 minutes with 15 minutes allowed at each end for loading, payment of tolls, and frontier formalities. The capacity of the system will be huge. Initially, it will be "20 standard paths' per hour (half in each direction) i.e. 20 shuttles and/or trains per hour travelling at normal speed, with 30 standard paths representing maximum capacity. It is intended that this will be split roughly equally between through rail and shuttle services. Each car/coach shuttle will be capable of carrying up to 200 cars (or 100 cars and 24 coaches) whilst lorry shuttles will be able to carry 25 lorries.

The number of through passengers and freight which the system can accommodate will depend on the number of wagons per train, so the exact capacity of the system is difficult to specify. But as an example, cross-Channel analysts often measure capacity in terms of pcu (passenger car units). For example, 1 lorry is equal to 6 pcu. In 1987 total cross Channel crossings from all ports amounted to some 19.6m pcu (mainly container freight). By 1994 using ETs forecast growth rates this will amount to some 26.4m pcu. ET capacity in 1994 will amount to 35m pcu. Theoretically, at least, ET will have more than enough capacity to carry the entire freight and passenger vehicle traffic between the UK and Europe. Given the rates of growth forecast by ET the maximum market size would be equivalent to 95% of ET capacity. It is conceivable that growth could exceed this level sufficiently to surpass ET capacity. If this were to happen then there might even be scope for building another tunnel (a view which is being encouraged by the British and French governments). However, at the moment, this seems somewhat speculative.

The project has been financed by £1bn of equity capital raised primarily in London and Paris and £5bn of syndicated loans provided by a consortium of 60 international banks. The expected cost of the project is some £4.9bn, allowing for inflation and financing costs thus providing a significant contingency reserve in case of cost overruns. The ET franchise will last for 50 years, i.e. until 2042, at which point ownership reverts to the two governments.

Since the aim of this paper is to consider the likely competition in the cross-channel market after the entry of the tunnel, we do not consider in detail the issues surrounding the construction of the Tunnel. Recent reports of delays and missed deadlines confirms a natural skepticism about the reliability of forecast completion dates. We have assumed in our forecasts that the Tunnel will open within budget, but with seven months delay, in January 1994. The effect of further delays would be to reduce the value of producer surplus and possibly to generate negative returns to shareholders. Any delay to the Tunnel causes the loss of some consumer surplus. However, even substantial delay is unlikely to cause the project to become socially unprofitable. These observations also apply to variations in market growth rates.

III. The Market

1. The Pre-entry Cross-Channel Market

The most noticeable stylized fact about the market is the huge level of excess capacity on most ferry routes. According to the Dover Harbour Board, capacity utilization on all Dover routes averaged only 45.5% for 1979, although this load improved somewhat to 51.7% in 1984. Even on peak days of the year it is often possible to sail on a ferry without prior booking. On non-Dover routes, capacity utilization tends to be higher,but it is still only necessary to book on limited number of peak days. This raises some strange questions about the nature of pre-entry competition.

Two companies currently dominate the market for cross-channel traffic, P&O European ferries and Sealink. The latter is a pooled service operated by the nationalized Sealink companies of Belgium, France and the Netherlands, as well as the privatized Sealink UK. These two have roughly equal market share of around 40%. In addition, there are a number of peripheral companies operating either specialist services (e.g. Olau, Brittany Ferries) or cut-price fringe routes (e.g. Sally Line).

In the UK the Office of Fair Trading (OFT) has frequently expressed concern that the major cross-channel companies have been colluding. In 1979, the OFT extracted an undertaking from European Ferries and Sealink not to agree joint-pricing or pooling arrangements. The latter requested this restriction be withdrawn in 1987 and although they were refused, they are confident of receiving permission in 1993. Following the OFT agreement a major price war occurred. For example, average annual car tariffs fell by 17% in real terms in two years. Since then average prices have risen back to the levels of 1979 (in real terms), so it would appear that the OFT agreement has had little long-term effect.

The Port Authorities regulate competition by fixing the timing and allocation of slots (to avoid ferries sailing at identical times) but the ferry companies compete by providing round the clock services, even if nearly empty. this observation seems to call into question the policy of the ferry companies in increasing the average capacity of their ships— the latest generation of ferries has four times the capacity of the average ferry 20 years ago (Source: Flexilink). Whilst it is clear that some ferries are full on the very busiest crossings (Bank Holiday weekends, etc) it would appear that the ferry companies could more profitably use smaller ships.

Whilst we argue that there is potential for collusion on pricing on car or foot passengers (apart from some off-peak competitive discounting) the freight market appears much more competitive. One freight company suggested to us that prices had fallen by 50% in real terms between 1979 and 1988. The reason for this is not hard to see. First, collusive agreements are much easier to maintain when there are published tariffs by which everyone abides. This is true of passenger traffic where even special deals are widely publicized. In freight, however, prices are often negotiated directly between hauliers and ferry companies who offer a variety of discounts. It has been suggested that average freight prices are more than 50% below published tariffs. Second, entry in the freight market is much easier since there are lower marketing costs.

In general, the limit on prices appears to be set by the tariffs charged by the competitive fringe which offers cut price services which tend to be less attractive than Dover routes. For example, Sally Line operates out of Ramsgate just along the coast with fewer sailings at prices some 10% lower on average. Industry analysts however argue that this service is not profitable. More profitable are the fringe routes offering a premium service such as Brittany Ferries (Plymouth-Roscoff and Portsmouth-Saint Malo).

2. The Post-entry Cross-Channel Market: A Theoretical Model

We focus on three factors determining prices after the opening of the Tunnel: first, the superiority or inferiority of the Tunnel service; second the substitutability of demand between the Tunnel and the ferries; third the extent of competition among the two main ferry operators.

First, suppose that the ferries and the Tunnel set the same price. If the market share of the Tunnel was then greater than 50%, this would imply that the Tunnel was seen as a superior service by most consumers. The higher the market share of the Tunnel, the more consumers see it as superior. we use the parameter s to denote the market share of the Tunnel at equal prices.

Now suppose that the Tunnel cuts prices in order to gain market share. The responsiveness of market share to relative prices will be important in determining the profitability of this strategy. We measure this parameter by p which must be between zero and one. The higher is p, the more sensitive is market share to relative prices. In the extreme case, $p=1$, a tunnel and a ferry crossing will be seen as identical products and all consumers will corss using the least cost alternative. Finally, the extent to which the ferries compete among themselves will also influence the level of prices. We denote the extent of this competition by n: $n=1$ corresponds to the case where the ferries collude in setting prices while a higher n denotes more competition. $n=\infty$ corresponds to the case of perfect competition.

One other important feature of competition in this market is that whereas the ferries can discriminate by charging a different price for Dover and non-Dover crossings, the tunnel cannot do this and must charge the same price for all crossings, irrespective of whether the passengers would otherwise have crossed via Dover or not. This puts the Tunnel at something of a disadvantage. The way in which this is incorporated into price-setting is described in Appendix A.

IV. Market Segmentation

The cross-Channel markets include services both by air and by sea in three main categories: freight, foot passengers, and car passengers, each of which will be analyzed in turn. We will concentrate on the sea crossing market which will be by far the most important competitor for Eurotunnel. Current ferry routes primarily link the South Eastern coastline of the UK with Germany, the Netherlands, Belgium, and France. The two major UK ports are Felixstowe on the East coast, linking mainly with Holland and Belgium, and Dover, connecting to Calais in France along the narrowest stretch of the English Channel as well as to Belgium. The former tends to dominate the freight trade and has much longer crossing times (up to six hours) whilst the latter dominates the passenger trade. Peripheral ports such as Southampton and the Port of London have tended to decline relative to the two main ports in recent years due to more efficient labour practices and economies of scale. We now present some stylized facts about each of the relevant cross-channel markets. In calculating the size of the markets in 1994 we have adopted ET growth figures and applied them to a set of disaggregated traffic figures drawn from British Port Statistics and the CAA.

1. The Freight Market

Freight traffic comes in three forms: in bulk form, a cheap traffic of minor importance in this market, and in containers, either load on-load off (lo-lo) or attached to lorries (roll on-roll off (ro-ro)). Lo-lo traffic dominates at Felixstowe which is also a major port for goods coming from the US and the Far East. Whilst this traffic is not currently 'cross-channel' it may well become so when the Tunnel opens, since the deep-sea shipping companies may well choose to tranship from, say, Rotterdam and so reduce the number of ports of call.

By contrast, all traffic at Dover is ro-ro and crosses either to France or Belgium. The price per container unit we use (£147 per container unit) is the estimate published in the Eurotunnel prospectus and is an approximation at best. Published tariffs are little guide in a market where discounting is endemic. The price tends to vary according to the required delivery time and the quality of the service including documentation handling. The market is extremely fragmented on the demand side, with a few major users such as the freight forwarding and large haulage groups, but a large number of small haulage companies. One sizeable freight handler suggested to us that £147 per standard container unit represented a bargain basement price and that average prices are perhaps 15% higher than this. This was contrasted to an average price of £200 in 1979, a fall in real terms of 50%. This factor may reflect the difficulty in colluding in a market where secret discounting is possible, compared to the car and passenger markets where tariffs are easy to find out. We have treated the freight market as highly competitive ($n=2$) and also with a high elasticity of substitution between ferries and the Tunnel. In addition we have assumed that the Tunnel offers an equal service to that offered by the ferries on Dover routes ($s=0.5$), but an inferior service on non-Dover ($s=0.25$).

Growth in freight traffic has been extremely rapid in recent years. In the decade to 1987 the total volume of freight has risen by nearly 102%, an average annual growth rate of 8%. Eurotunnel forecast market growth for this traffic at 4.3% p.a.. from 1985 until 1993, and 3.8% p.a. to 2003 and saturation thereafter. On this basis total potential cross-Channel traffic in 1994 will amount to some 3.8m container units compared to around 2.8m currently.

2. The Car and Passenger Market

Dover is by far and away the market leader in car passenger services offering the shortest crossing at the lowest price. The higher prices charged on other routes reflect the higher costs involved with longer crossings and the relatively specialist nature of these markets. Overall this market has grown less spectacularly than the freight market over the last decade, but has still risen by 56% or about 4.5% p.a. Eurotunnel forecast that this market will grow by around 4.2% p.a. until 1993, 3.4% p.a. to 2003 and 2.4% to 2013, followed by saturation. This gives a total market size of 3.7m cars in 1994 compared to 2.8m in 1987.

Prices in the car market have on average remained stable in real terms

over recent years, but there has been a tendency for peak prices to rise
and off-peak prices to fall, reflecting the attempts of the ferry companies
to improve load factors. In fact, Dover Habour board claim that average
annual load factors on all Dover routes have risen from 45.5% in 1979
to 51.7% in 1984. The ferry companies in Dover offer a range of four
tariffs depending on the time of day. Average peak prices have risen by
around 10% since 1979 and average off-peak prices have fallen by a
similar amount (all this in real terms).

On this basis we treat the existing car passenger market as considerably less competitive than the freight market ($n=1$). We also allow for a
relatively low elasticity of substitution between ferries and the Tunnel,
particularly on non-Dover routes, since substitution may imply a considerable diversion. We assume that the tunnel provides an equivalent service for travellers via Dover ($s=0.5$), but an inferior service for car passengers who would otherwise select a non-Dover route ($s=0.3$).

3. The Foot Passenger Market

This is the most difficult market to analyze since it is made up of a
number of different categories: air passengers, passengers currently
using rail/ferry services, scheduled coach service passengers, excursionists—day trip coach passengers, almost exclusively from the UK to
France to take advantage of duty free shopping,

For the purposes of their forecasts, ET included the entire 28m or so
air passengers between the UK and continental Europe. More realistically they quote a figure of six million passengers travelling to France, Belgium and the Netherlands. According to Flexilink, this traffic has grown
by round 3% p.a. over the last ten years. A significant percentage of this
traffic is businessmen paying premium rates. Rail/ferry users constitute
a relatively small percentage of traffic (now 1.8m according to Flexilink). This type of service has declined rapidly in recent years and is
likely to be withdrawn by the railways in 1994 to make way for Tunnel
services.

According to Flexilink, 5.6m passengers travel by coach services, an
increase of 270% over the decade, an annual growth rate of 14%. This is
largely a result of the development of privatized bus services in the UK
and the redevelopment of package tours by coach, reflecting the
improved quality of the coaches themselves. Excursionists totalled some

3.4m passengers in 1987 having grown by about 3% p.a. over the previous decade. This market was created out of nothing by the ferry companies in the 1970s, although its prospects for survival may be somewhat limited by the proposed abolition of the duty free concession by 1992 (These figures are taken from Flexilink, 1987).

Combining these with 7.4 million passengers travelling in cars and around 0.8m lorry drivers, gives a total passenger market of 25m which ET forecast to grow at the same rate as the car passenger market 4.2% p.a. to 1993, 3.4% p.a. to 2003, 2.4% p.a. to 2013 and thereafter stagnation. This will give a passenger market of around 21.6m sea/foot passengers in 1994 and 8m air/foot passengers in 1994. Given that the Tunnel will provide a high speed link between city centers, we have assumed that the Tunnel is a superior service on passenger routes. Competitiveness and substitutability are treated as the same as for the car passenger market.

We have simply assumed that there are two market segments, air and sea foot passengers. For air/foot we have made some simple assumptions of the cost structure of the airlines. In addition we have assumed that the Tunnel provides a superior service to air transport as well as to Dover foot passengers. Only non-Dover ferry services are assumed to provide an equivalent service.

Our assumptions about the nature of the different market segments are presented in Table 2.

Table 2. Assumptions about the nature of the market

	Tunnel market share at equal price, s		Elasticity of substitution, p		Extent of ferry competition, n
	Dover	Non-Dover	Dover	Non-Dover	
Freight	50%	25%	0.9	0.8	2
Cars	50%	30%	0.9	0.67	1
Foot passengers	90%	50%	0.9	0.67	1
Air-diverted Passengers	50%		0.9		

4. The Railway Agreement

Eurotunnel has negotiated with BR and SNCF a payment scheme consisting of a fixed fee, plus a fee per passenger and unit of through rail freight, together with a minimum payment of (1987) £108.5m p.a. indexed to the RPI for the first 12 years. Whilst the precise details of this contract are not public knowledge, it is widely believed that the average fee per passenger will be around (1987) £8 per passenger. The form of this contract may seem surprising as the railways are certain to price discriminate by class and time of travel, yet there seems to be no such price discrimination by the Tunnel. However, we can understand this in terms of the 'chain of monopolies' problem. If the Tunnel price discriminated, then with the railways' mark-up as well, price would be too high from the point of the view of the Tunnel. Both railways and Tunnel could be made better off by negotiating a contract where the price charged by the Tunnel is reduced and there is a lump sum payment from the railways to the Tunnel. The actual contract seems to be of this form. The first-best contract with risk-neutrality, would involve the Tunnel charging a marginal price equal only to marginal cost. Hence there would be no price discrimination by the Tunnel in this case. The actual contract appears to have a marginal price above marginal cost: this can probably be explained as a mechanism to share risk, as is the guaranteed minimum payment.

5. Duty Free Concessions

Duty free concessions within Europe are to be abolished by 1992 in line with the completion of the internal market. Nonetheless, the ferry companies and others have argued that duty free is unlikely to be abolished on time due to political unpopularity within the UK. This we consider a rather sanguine viewpoint. Duty free sales between the UK and the rest of Europe is the only such concession within the EC. Even if complete fiscal harmonization is not achieved by 1992, it is likely that the other member countries will demand the removal of what is essentially a British perk. It has already been decided that there will be no duty free sales available to through rail passengers on ET.

V. Welfare Analysis

1. The Simulations

We divide the market into seven segments: freight, cars and foot passengers for both Dover and non-Dover, and air-diverted passengers. For all segments of the market we used the framework described in Section 3.2, and formally in Appendix A to calculate prices, market shares and net revenues in a single year. The estimates of marginal costs and market size are described in Appendix B. The model predicts that prices will be approximately a small mark-up over ferry marginal cost with the bulk of the market going to the low-cost Tunnel. These estimates and estimates of the market growth rate (also described in Appendix B) were then used to calculate the future value of the Tunnel project to consumers, ferry operators, the Tunnel, the airlines and the railways. This was then compared with estimates of what would have happened without the Tunnel to derive the net private and social benefit of the Tunnel.

Table 3. Prices and Market share

Prices(1994)(£)	Post-Tunnel			
	Pre-Tunnel	Dover ferry	non-Dover ferry	Tunnel
Foot passengers	10.87	8.23	13.11	7.65
Cars	115.42	50.72	85.16	41.44
Freight	214.16	177.04	196.19	128.79
Air diverted passengers	75.54	–	–	46.00

Market share		
	Dover ferry	non-Dover ferry
Foot Passengers	0.13	0.17
Cars	0.12	0.21
Freight	0.04	0.27
Air diverted passengers	–	–

2. Results

Table 3 presents predictions with our base assumptions for the characteristics of the sub-markets and marginal costs after the opening of the Tunnel. The most important feature is the predicted reduction in prices. of the order of 64% for cars crossing through the Tunnel or Dover. It is also noticeable that the predicted market share of the ferries is very low, especially on the Dover routes. Indeed, it is hardly surprising in the light of these results that the ferry companies campaigned so vigorously to try and prevent the Tunnel from being built. What is perhaps more surprising in the light of the expected loss of market share of the airlines is that they have not expressed any particular concern about the Tunnel. In general we believe that this is because much of the diversion will be tourist traffic which is barely profitable. Indeed, the prospect of increasing deregulation in the European airline market will tend further to diminish profitability on popular routes. Furthermore, the London-Paris/Brussels/Amsterdam routes contribute only a small proportion of total traffic for the major airlines such as BA or Air France.

Table 4 presents the results of using our base case results to calculate the private and social returns from the opening of the Tunnel. For these calculations we have used Eurotunnel forecasts of market growth and a real interest rate of 5%. The private return to Eurotunnel is less than the social return to the Tunnel operator, as Eurotunnel's lease expires in 2042. From Table 4, it would appear that we are in a situation where the Tunnel is both socially and privately profitable. However, the social benefit is much larger than the private benefit, because the main benefit

Table 4. Welfare Analysis: Base Case(1994)(£m)

	Net social benefit	Private benefit to Eurotunnel
Consumers	31,039	–
Ferry operators	-1.577	–
Tunnel operators	18,336	15,942
Air/rail operators	-4,143	–
Cost of building Tunnel	-11,839	-11,839
Total	31,816	4,103

of the Tunnel is to lower prices which benefits the consumers. Another way of expressing the same point is to calculate the social and private internal rates of return. The social rate of return is slightly above 11%, but the private (pre-tax) rate of return is about 6.5%.

So the private sector could be relied upon to make the socially optimal decision to open a tunnel in 1994. But if the private sector had been free to build the Tunnel at any date in the post-war period, would it have done so at the socially optimal date? There are two opposing factors at work here. First, because the private return to building the Tunnel is below the social return this will tend to make the private sector build the Tunnel after the socially optimal date. The second opposing factor is that the private sector will choose to build the Tunnel at the first date at which it became privately profitable as different potential operators compete to get the franchise. However, the socially optimal time to build the Tunnel is the date which maximizes the social net present value, which will be after the date at which the social return first becomes positive (see Gilbert and Newbery, 1982, for more details). Our calculations suggest that these two effects just about cancelled out. The socially optimal date to open the Tunnel was 1980, although social net present value is very flat about this date so this estimate is probably subject to quite a large error. The first date at which the private sector would open the Tunnel was, on our calculations, 1981. So by chance the private sector might have built the Tunnel at the correct date.

How sensitive are our results to the assumptions underlying our base case? From this sensitivity analysis our main conclusion is that it is relatively easy to make the Tunnel privately unprofitable but very hard to make it socially unprofitable. First, consider the case of a less optimistic growth forecast. In the extreme case where demand remains constant at 1994 levels, the net private profitability of the Tunnel falls to (1994)— £2bn, but the social profitability is still large at (1994) £15bn. Second, we considered the consequences of assuming that the ferries' pricing policy was more competitive. This has very little effect as, in our scenario, ferry prices are only slightly above ferry marginal costs. Even if ferry companies were perfectly competitive, ferry prices would only fall to ferry marginal costs. Third, we considered the consequences of assuming that there is some overall price elasticity of demand in the market. Such a possibility only makes the Tunnel look even more desirable. If total market demand is sensitive to price, this increases the incentive to cut prices which benefits the low-cost Tunnel. If the price elasticity of demand was even slightly above one (which is not very plausible) then the price that the Tunnel would like to set as an unconstrained monopolist would be below ferry marginal cost: in this case the ferries would disappear.

We also considered the case of a reduction in ferry marginal cost. This is quite likely given the introduction of more efficient ships and the reduction in manning and/or wage levels following the 1988 strike at P&O. Our calculations suggest that a 20% reduction in ferry marginal cost is enough to reduce the private profitability of the tunnel at 5% real interest rate to zero. A 40% ferry marginal cost reduction leads to a Eurotunnel loss of (1994) £4bn. However, these ferry cost reductions have virtually no effect on the social profitability of the Tunnel because all prices are a mark-up on ferry marginal costs. So reductions in these costs lead to substantial increases in consumer surplus, while reducing the increase in producer surpluses; the net effect is close to zero.

This raises the possibility that the Tunnel is socially profitable not because the reduction in marginal costs outweighs the costs of construction, but because of the desirable effects that the Tunnel has on competition. To see whether this was the case, we looked at the social profitability of the Tunnel in the case where prices, both before and after opening, are set at marginal cost and where ferry excess capacity costs do not exist. For our base case, the net social benefit of the Tunnel is reduced to (1994) £21bn. Even with a 40% reduction in ferry marginal costs, the social profitability of the Tunnel is still (1994) £7bn. If a marginal cost pricing policy was pursued, operating the tunnel would require a much larger public subsidy as more of its costs are fixed. This might be undesirable if it is costly to raise revenue for the government. However, the social desirability of the Tunnel remains even if each £1 put into the project by the government led to a fall of £1.75 in the income of the private sector. This suggests that the Tunnel is profitable not only because of its effects on competition, but also because it reduces marginal costs. However, there would appear to be substantial benefits available from increasing competition in this market even if the Tunnel was not built.

The picture that emerges so far is that the Tunnel is likely to be socially profitable in any plausible scenario but that, under reasonable assumptions, it may not be privately profitable. Given this it appears that although leaving the decision to build the Tunnel to the private sector produced the right decision, it also left it unnecessarily to chance. Indeed, Eurotunnel did have trouble in raising the necessary capital. On the one hand, the London equity market proved extremely reluctant to provide its share of the capital and it did appear at one point that private finance would private impossible. On the other, raising £5bn of bank loans required ET to issue debt at extremely favourable rates and to sign a loan agreement on terms which appear to grant the lending banks extraordinary powers. For instance, in the Share Prospectus, it states that an event of default under the loan agreement consists of failing to meet various debt service ratios specified. These are essentially ratios of debt to forecast revenues. The forecasts are to be determined by negotiation between the banks and ET, but in the event of dispute, will be determined by the banks. Hence the banks can, in principle, declare ET in default at any time (simply by reducing the forecasts!), which would permit them, *inter alia*, to enforce their security and 'take over the concession.' Clearly, a loan agreement of this kind was not negotiated by a borrower with a strong bargaining position.

One possible explanation for the apparent stringency of the loan agreements which has been explored in an earlier paper (Manning and Szymanski, 1988) is that the loan agreements could act as some kind of commitment device should the ferries be in a position to compete effectively with Eurotunnel. For example, the ET shareholders might not want to push prices too low in the early years of operation (for cash flow reasons) and the threat of bankruptcy followed by an immediately more aggressive owner of the Tunnel might act as a credible deterrent to the ferry companies.

Are there any circumstances in which the Tunnel might be privately profitably yet socially unprofitable? The analysis above has assumed that the Tunnel and the ferries compete in price-setting. What happens if they collude or the Tunnel forces the ferries from the market? This might be a plausible outcome, as Dover might not remain viable (Table 3). Indeed, the ferries may want to shut down Dover for strategic reasons, as, because it is a close substitute for the Tunnel, competition with Dover ferries keeps Tunnel prices low, which forces non-Dover ferry prices to be low as well. Without Dover, Tunnel and non-Dover prices can both be higher. In fact, our calculations suggest that if Dover ferries were to disappear, the constraint on prices would no longer be competition between the ferries and the Tunnel, but the threat of the competitive fringe suppliers. In these circumstances, prices might not fall at all following the opening of the Tunnel.

To consider what happens in this case, we assumed that the ferries quit the market leaving the Tunnel as a monopolist. Prices remain the same as before, so consumer surplus is unchanged. Now building the Tunnel is simply a way of capturing the monopoly profits of the ferries and so may be privately profitable even if it is socially useless. Our calculations suggest that even in this very pessimistic case, the increase in the producer surplus of the Tunnel will outweigh the loss of the ferries and the airlines. The main reason for this is that the excess of revenues over marginal costs for the ferries is mostly dissipated in excess capacity costs, so the producer surplus of the ferries is currently very small. But, even if we assume a 40% reduction in ferry marginal cost and the elimination of excess capacity costs, the Tunnel producer surplus still exceeds that of the ferries, simply because it has lower marginal costs and the cost savings exceed the cost of construction.

Finally, we have looked at the consequences of imperfect competition in the cross-Channel market but we implicitly assumed that all other markets are competitive (the prices in these markets reflect true social opportunity cost). This is obviously unreasonable. One of the factors taken into account in previous studies of the impact of the tunnel is the loss of jobs. The *Kent Impact Study*, 1987, estimated that 13,000 jobs in Kent depended on the ferries with, perhaps, similar numbers in France and Belgium. These jobs would be at risk with the opening of the Tunnel. But even if we look at a very pessimistic scenario, the permanent loss of 10,000 jobs paying the 1987 UK average wage of (1994) £14,500 the discounted employment cost of the Tunnel opening is (1994) £3.15bn. This is small relative to our estimate of the total benefit of £31bn.

One other remaining issue of some interest is whether the rail-only tunnel option was the most desirable one, The most likely alternative was the road half tunnel/half bridge option proposed by Euroroute. This would have cost substantially more to build so could only be socially preferred if it had lower marginal costs or it offered a superior service. Marginal costs are unlikely to have been much below Eurotunnel's as the road option would have had substantially higher maintenance costs. And journey times are unlikely to have been much lower than with the Eurotunnel option so it is likely that the best option was for a rail only tunnel.

There are several other factors which it would be relevant to include in a complete cost-benefit analysis. First, the building of the Tunnel is likely to increase substantially the level of road congestion in the Kent and Pas de Calais regions, particularly in the area of Folkestone and Boulogne. In fact both governments have already undertaken construction of additional roads. Second, both through the construction itself and the additional road traffic, the Tunnel will add to noise and atmospheric pollution as a result of less air traffic. Third, it has been argued that the Tunnel will promote trade and growth by allowing goods to move more easily between the UK and the continent. However, we are skeptical about the likely size of any wider benefits generated by the Tunnel, for the simple reason that crossing the Channel and the associated costs form quite a small part of the process of importing and exporting. (For a further discussion of these issues, see Manning and Szymanski, 1989). Whilst these and possibly other factors might have been relevant, we do not believe that any value attached to them could reasonably be large enough to overturn the central result that the Tunnel is socially profitable.

VI. Conclusions

We have analysed the benefits of building the Channel Tunnel from both a social and a private point of view. Our main conclusion is that the Tunnel is likely to provide a huge social benefit through substantially lower prices for consumers. This reflects the fact that the Tunnel will have almost unlimited capacity and negligible marginal costs. However, so long as there remains any competition for the Tunnel from either the airlines or the ferry companies, the private profitability of the Tunnel will be relatively small. In addition, the level of profitability is very sensitive and may even go negative in some extreme cases. This suggests that leaving the private sector to finance the project was a somewhat risky decision on the part of the UK and French governments, witness the difficulties which accompanied the raising of private finance (particularly in the UK). However, there is an important caveat to this story of unmitigated social benefit. If the Tunnel were ever to successfully drive its competitors, particularly the ferry companies, from the market, and thus obtain a monopoly, there would be a very strong case for regulation. Indeed, it has been argued that the most efficient solution would be for the governments to repurchase the franchise once the Tunnel has been built and run the operation at marginal cost. Although such a decision seems unlikely in the present political climate, it is plausible that a government may emerge to carry out this plan at some point in the next 50 years.

Appendix A. The Model Used in the Simulations

1. Preferences and demand

The indirect utility function of consumers of Channel crossings in year t is assumed to be given by:

$$U_t(P_{Ft}, P_{Tt}, Y_t) = -\sum_{i=1}^{6} \alpha_{it} [P_{Fit}^{1/\beta_i} + (P_{Tit}/A_i)^{1/\beta_i}]^{-\beta_i} + 1/\alpha_{0t} Y_t^{\alpha_{0t}} \quad (A1)$$

where (P_{Fit}, P_{Tit}) are the prices of ferry and tunnel respectively in market segment i in year t and Y_t is the level of GDP in year t.

Applying Roy's Identity, the demands in each each segment are given by:

$$X_{Fit} = \alpha_{it} Y_t^{(1-\alpha_{0t})} \left(\frac{Q_{it}}{P_{Fit}} \right)^{1/(1-p_i)} \quad (A2)$$

$$X_{Tit} = \alpha_{it} Y_t^{(1-\alpha_{0t})} \left(\frac{Q_{it}A_i}{P_{Tit}} \right)^{1/(1-p_i)} \quad (A3)$$

where

$$Q_{it} = [P_{Fit}^{1/\beta_i} + (P_{Tit}/A_i)^{1/\beta_i}]^{-\beta_i} \text{ and } p_i = \frac{1}{1+\beta_i} \quad (A4)$$

The parameter A_i is related to the market share of the Tunnel by the formula

$$A_i = \left(\frac{s}{(1-s_i)} \right)^{1-p_i}$$

2. Price setting

Total ferry profits are given by $\sum_{i=1} (P_{Fit} - C_{Fit}) X_{Fit}$. In order to have a general framework we assume that competition is of the Cournot type with linear conjectural variations. Using (A2) and (A4) it can be shown that this leads to a ferry reaction function:

$$P_{Fit} = \frac{n_i P_{Fit}^{1/\beta_i}}{(n_i + p_i - 1) P_{Fit}^{1/\beta_i} - (1-p_i) P_{Tit}^{1/\beta_i}} C_{Fit} \quad (A5)$$

In (A5) n_i is a measure of the extent of competition in market segment
i. $n_i=1$ corresponds to the case of collusion while $n_i=\infty$ corresponds to
perfect competition which leads to $P_{Fit} = C_{Fit}$.

Now consider the pricing decision of the tunnel. This is slightly more
complicated as when the tunnel sets a price in a Dover segment of the
market it must also set the same price for the non-Dover segment. Suppose that segment 1 represents a Dover market and segment 2 a non-
Dover market. Then the tunnel will want to set a price P_T in both mar-
kets to maximize $X_{T1t}\,(P_T\text{-}C_T)+X_{T2t}\,(P_T\text{-}C_T)$. Using (A3) and (A4) this
leads to a tunnel reaction function:

$$\alpha_1\left(\frac{Q_1 A_1}{P_T}\right)^{1/(1-p_1)}\left[\frac{1}{1-p_1}\,\frac{P_T\text{-}C_T}{P_T}\left(\left(\frac{Q_1 A_1}{P_T}\right)^{1/\beta_1}-1\right)+1\right]$$

$$+\alpha_2\left(\frac{Q_2 A_2}{P_T}\right)^{1/(1-p_2)}\left[\frac{1}{1-p_2}\,\frac{P_T\text{-}C_T}{P_T}\left(\left(\frac{Q_2 A_2}{P_T}\right)^{1/\beta_2}-1\right)+1\right]=0 \quad (A6)$$

Our model of pricing involves solving (A5) and (A6) from ferry and
tunnel prices.

3. Welfare Analysis

1. Tunnel Producer Surplus.

If the Tunnel were not built, Eurotunnel would make zero profits. So
the producer surplus of the Tunnel is simply the level of tunnel profits
after opening. From the solution to the pricing problem described above,
we can calculate the level of Tunnel net revenues in each period Π_{Ti}.
From this we deduct the fixed costs of operating the Tunnel FC_T to
derive the producer surplus for the Tunnel in year t, $(\Pi_{Tt}\text{-}FC_T)$. This is
then discounted using the market discount factor.

2. Ferry Producer Surplus.

For the ferries we can calculate the net revenues if the Tunnel did not
exist Π^1_{Ft} and the net revenues after the Tunnel opens Π^2_{Ft}. From these
we also need to deduct the capital costs of the ferries.

Our model of capacity determination is the following. Suppose the net
revenues of the ferries is Π. Assume that the market share of the first

ferry company is $k_1^\varepsilon/(k_1^\varepsilon+k_2^\varepsilon)$ where k_1 is its capacity and k_2 the capacity of its rival. Then if the cost of capacity is c, k_1 will be chosen to maximize

$$\Pi k_1^\varepsilon/(k_1^\varepsilon+k_2^\varepsilon) - ck_1 \tag{A7}$$

Taking first-order condition for (A7) and imposing the symmetry condition $k_1 = k_2$ yields the following:

$$k_1 = k_2 = \frac{\varepsilon\Pi}{4c} \tag{A8}$$

This shows that capacity will be related not to the level of demand but to the level of profitability. Suppose that we have an estimate of total capacity costs without the Tunnel C_1. Then capacity costs after the Tunnel has opened will be: $(\pi_2/\pi_1)C_1$ so the increase in capacity costs is $(1/\pi_1)(\pi_2-\pi_1)C_1$.

So the total change in ferry producer surplus in year t is:

$$(\pi_{Ft}^2-\pi_{Ft}^1) \left(1 - \frac{C_{1t}}{\pi_{Ft}^1} \right) \tag{A9}$$

3. Consumers.

Looking at (A1) denote the term involving prices as u_t^1 without the Tunnel and u_t^2 With the Tunnel. We want to calculate the amount of income the consumers would be prepared to pay to have the Tunnel open. This is given by Y_t.

$$u_{1t} + \frac{1}{\alpha_{0t}}Y_t^{\alpha_\alpha} = u_{2t} + \frac{1}{\alpha_{0t}}(Y_t - \Delta Y_t)^{\alpha_\alpha} \tag{A10}$$

Rearranging yields:

$$Y_t = Y_t - [Y_t^{\alpha_\alpha} - \alpha_{0t}(u_{1t}-u_{2t})]^{1/\alpha_\alpha} \tag{A11}$$

This is used as our measure of consumer surplus in year t. It is discounted using the market discount factor. There are some small errors in this procedure as we are not using the fact that the utility function should explain the distribution of income over time. These errors will, however, be small for α_{0t} close to 1.

Appendix B. The Data

This appendix explains the sources used to estimate current ferry and airline prices, ferry, tunnel and airline costs, and market growth rates and market size.

1. Current Ferry and Airline Prices

The 1987 Eurotunnel Share prospectus was an important source of information: p32 of the prospectus gives estimates of current freight and air tariffs. Our prices for car and foot passengers are based on current P&O and Sealink brochure prices.

2. Market Size

The Eurotunnel prospectus does not break the passenger market between foot and car passengers. It includes all European air traffic (instead of just London to Paris, Brussels and Amsterdam) and uses 1985 figures. We have chosen to use 1987 CAA and British Port Statistics' figures which break down traffic by the categories we have used.

3. Ferry, Tunnel and Airline Costs

Very limited data is available of ferry and airline costs. We have therefore assumed that current prices reflect a percentage markup on total cost. Costs on the ferries were then divided between fixed and variable costs and variable costs (crew, fuel and port dues on which some data is available) were then taken as a proxy for marginal cost. Tunnel marginal costs were based on the same assumptions and the prospectus (p.54) quotes Tunnel variable costs.

4. Market Growth Rates

These figures were taken from the prospectus (pp 30-31).

Reference

Channel Tunnel Joint Consultative Committee (1987). Kent Impact
  Study.
Civil Aviation Authority, UK Airports, Annual Statements of Move-
  ments: Passengers and Cargo
Department of Transport, Port Statistics.
Eurotunnel (1987). Share Prospectus.
Flexilink (1985). Campaign for Cross Channel Choice.
_____ (1987). The Channel Tunnel: Some Weaknesses of the Financial
  Case.
Gilbert, R. J. and E. M. G. Newbery (1982) 'Preemptive Patenting and
  the Persistence of Monopoly, American Economic Review.
Manning, A. and S. Szymanski (1988). "Price Increasing Entry: Who's
  Afraid of the Channel Tunnel?,' Birkbeck College Discussion
  Paper No 88/3.
_____ (1989). "The Impact of the Channel Tunnel on 1992,' Centre for
  Business Strategy, London Business School.
P&O European Ferries (1988). Car Ferry Guide.

Printed in the United States
by Baker & Taylor Publisher Services